Cornell University Library

BOUGHT WITH THE INCOME
FROM THE
SAGE ENDOWMENT FUND
THE GIFT OF
Henry W. Sage
1891

Olin
PA
4500
Z42
1891

THE FRAGMENTS

OF

ZENO AND CLEANTHES.

London: C. J. CLAY AND SONS,
CAMBRIDGE UNIVERSITY PRESS WAREHOUSE,
AVE MARIA LANE.

Cambridge: DEIGHTON, BELL, AND CO.
Leipzig: F. A. BROCKHAUS.
New York: MACMILLAN AND CO.

THE FRAGMENTS

OF

ZENO AND CLEANTHES

WITH INTRODUCTION AND EXPLANATORY
NOTES.

AN ESSAY WHICH OBTAINED THE HARE PRIZE

IN THE YEAR 1889.

BY

A. C. PEARSON, M.A.

LATE SCHOLAR OF CHRIST'S COLLEGE, CAMBRIDGE.

LONDON:
C. J. CLAY AND SONS,
CAMBRIDGE UNIVERSITY PRESS WAREHOUSE.
1891

[*All Rights reserved.*]

Cambridge:
PRINTED BY C. J. CLAY, M.A. AND SONS,
AT THE UNIVERSITY PRESS.

PREFACE.

THIS dissertation is published in accordance with the conditions attached to the Hare Prize, and appears nearly in its original form. For many reasons, however, I should have desired to subject the work to a more searching revision than has been practicable under the circumstances. Indeed, error is especially difficult to avoid in dealing with a large body of scattered authorities, the majority of which can only be consulted in a public library.

The obligations, which require to be acknowledged for the present collection of the fragments of Zeno and Cleanthes, are both special and general. The former are soon disposed of. In the *Neue Jahrbücher für Philologie* for 1873, p. 435 foll., Wellmann published an article on Zeno of Citium, which was the first serious attempt to discriminate the teaching of Zeno from that of the Stoa in general. The omissions of Wellmann were supplied and the first complete collection of the fragments of Cleanthes was made by Wachsmuth in two Gottingen programs published in 1874—1875 (*Commentationes I et II de Zenone Citiensi et Cleanthe Assio*). Mullach's collection of the fragments of Cleanthes in vol. I of the *Fragmenta Philosophorum Graecorum* is so inadequate as hardly to deserve mention.

Among the general aids the first place is claimed by Zeller's *Philosophie der Griechen,* which has been constantly consulted. The edition referred to is the Second edition of the English Translation of the part dealing with the Stoics, Epicureans, and Sceptics, which appeared in 1880. In a few cases the fourth German edition has also been quoted. Reference is also made to the English Translations of the other parts of Zeller's book, wherever available. Except incidentally, Zeller gives up the attempt to trace the development of the Stoa in the hands of its successive leaders, and this deficiency is to some extent supplied by the ingenious work of Hirzel, *die Entwicklung der Stoischen Philosophie,* forming the second volume of his *Untersuchungen zu Cicero's Philosophischen Schriften.* To Hirzel belongs the credit of having vindicated the originality of Cleanthes against ancient and modern detractors, although in working out his views he often argues on somewhat shadowy foundations, and has unduly depreciated the importance of the contributions made by Zeno. Lastly, Stein's two books *die Psychologie der Stoa* (1886), and *die Erkenntnistheorie der Stoa* (1888), have been of great service, and his views, where he disagrees with Hirzel, have been generally adopted. Many other books have of course been consulted and will be found cited from time to time, among which Krische's *die theologischen Lehren der Griechischen Denker,* and Diels' *Doxographi Graeci,* deserve special mention. Although the results arrived at have been checked by the aid of modern writers, the ancient authorities and especially Diogenes Laertius, Plutarch, Sextus Empiricus, Stobaeus (*Eclogae*), and Cicero have been throughout treated as the primary source of information. The references to Stobaeus are accommodated to Wachsmuth's edition (Berlin, 1884). Susemihl's article on the birth-year of Zeno in the *Neue Jahrbücher für Philologie* for 1889 appeared too late to be utilised for the introduction.

A word must be said with reference to the plan of the present collection. No attempt has been made to disentangle in every case the words of the writer from the body of the citation in which they appear. Although this is practicable in some cases, in others it is mere guess-work, and a uniform system has therefore been adopted. For similar reasons the fragments have been arranged as far as possible in natural sequence, without regard to the comparatively few cases in which we know the names of the books from which they were derived. However, the arrangement has been a matter of much perplexity, especially in those cases where the authorities overlap each other, and several modifications in the order would have been introduced as the result of a larger experience, were it not that each alteration throws all the references into confusion. The collection was made and put together practically in its present form before an opportunity offered of consulting Wachsmuth's pamphlets, and it was satisfactory to find that only a few of his passages had been missed. On the other hand, the additional matter which will be found here for the first time is not large. It may, therefore, be reasonably concluded that we now possess the greater portion of the material, which is available for reconstructing the history of the earlier Stoa. For the sake of completeness I have included even those notices, whose authenticity is open to suspicion, as well as a collection of the so-called *Apophthegmata*, though it is often impossible to draw a strict line between written and oral tradition.

I desire to thank Mr R. D. Hicks, Fellow of Trinity College, for many valuable suggestions and criticisms.

CORRIGENDA.

p. 37, l. 13, for "he was only able" read "he alone was able".
p. 53, l. 23, add "see however on Cleanth. frag. 114."

INTRODUCTION.

§ 1. *Life of Zeno.*

THE chronology of Zeno's life[1], formerly a subject of much dispute, has been almost entirely cleared up by an important passage discovered in one of the papyrus rolls found at Herculaneum, which contains a history of the Stoic philosophers and was first edited by Comparetti in 1875[2]. From this we learn that Cleanthes was born in 331 B.C., and, as we know from other sources[3] that he lived to the age of 99, he must have died in B.C. 232 in the archonship of Jason[4]. But, according to the papyrus (col. 29), at the time of his death he had presided over the School for 32 years[5], which fixes the death of Zeno as having taken place in B.C. 264, thus confirming the authority of Jerome, who says under the year Ol. 129, 1 = B.C. 264, 3[6] "Zeno Stoicus moritur post quem Cleanthes philosophus agnoscitur." Now, in Diog. Laert. VII. 28 we have two distinct

---

[1] See Rohde in Rhein. Mus. 33, p. 622. Gomperz ib. 34, p. 154. Susemihl's article in Fleckeisen's Jahrb. for 1882, vol. 125, pp. 737—746, does not add anything to our knowledge of the chronology of Zeno's life.

[2] Col. 28, 29. Comparetti believes this book to be the work of Philodemus.

[3] Lucian Macrob. 19. Val. Max. VIII. 7, Ext. 11.

[4] So too the papyrus col. 28 (ἀ)πηλλάγ(η ἐπ' ἄρχοντος Ἰ)άσονος.

[5] Such at least is the restoration of Gomperz: Comparetti reads τριάκοντα καὶ ὀκτώ, but admits that δύο is possible. The word after καὶ is illegible.

[6] So Rohde states, but in Migne's ed. of Eusebius I. p. 498 the statement appears to belong to Ol. 128.

accounts of his age at the time of his death, the one, that of Persaeus, in his ἠθικαὶ σχολαί, who makes him 72, and the other apparently derived from Apollonius Tyrius[1], declaring that he lived to be 98 years old. Apart from internal considerations, the authority of Persaeus is unquestionably the higher, and reckoning backwards we are thus enabled to place the birth of Zeno in the year 336 B.C.[2] Rohde suggests that the other computation may have been deduced by Apollonius Tyrius from the letter to Antigonus, now on other grounds shown to be spurious, but which Diogenes unquestionably extracted from Apollonius' book on Zeno[3]. In this Zeno is represented as speaking of himself as an octogenarian, so that on the assumption that the letter was written in B.C. 282, shortly after Antigonus first became king of Macedonia, and, calculating to the true date of Zeno's death (B.C. 264), he would have been 98 years of age in the latter year[4].

Zeno, the son of Mnaseas[5], was born at Citium, a Greek city in the south-east of Cyprus, whose population had been increased by Phoenician immigrants[6]. Whether he was of pure Greek blood or not we cannot tell[7], but we can readily believe that his birthplace, while it in no degree influenced his philosophical genius, which was truly Hellenic, yet gave an

---

[1] A Stoic philosopher (floruit in the earlier half of the 1st century B.C.). For his work on Zeno's life see Diog. L. VII. 1. 2. 24. 28. Strabo XVI. 2. 24.

[2] Gomperz l. c. undertook to prove that Zeno died in the month Scirophorion (Ol. 128, 4) = June 264 B.C., offering to produce the proofs in a later article, but this promise does not seem to have been fulfilled.

[3] Diog. L. VII. 7. 8.

[4] The weakness of this hypothesis lies in the fact that Antigonus Gonatas did not become King of Macedon until 278—277 B.C., although no doubt he was struggling for the crown from the time of the death of his father Demetrius in B.C. 283. This is met to some extent by Rohde l. c. p. 624 n. 1.

[5] Diog. L. VII. 1 mentions Demeas as another name given to his father but elsewhere he is always Ζήνων Μνασέου.

[6] Cimon died while besieging this place (Thuc. I. 112).

[7] Stein, Psychologie der Stoa n. 3 sums up, without deciding, in favour of a Phoenician origin. So also Ogereau p. 4 whereas Heinze thinks that everything points the other way (Bursian's Jahresbericht vol. 50, p. 53).

Oriental complexion to his tone of mind, and affected the character of his literary style, so that the epithet "Phoenician," afterwards scornfully cast in his teeth by his opponents[1], is in any case not altogether unwarranted.

Again following the authority of Persaeus (Diog. L. l.c.)[2], we may conclude that he arrived at Athens at the age of 22, but as to the cause which brought him thither we are differently informed, and it is uncertain whether he came for the express purpose of studying philosophy[3], or in furtherance of some mercantile enterprise[4]. There is however a consensus of testimony to the effect that he suffered shipwreck on his voyage to Athens, a misfortune which he afterwards learnt to bless as it had driven him to philosophy[5]. The story of his first meeting with Crates is characteristic[6]: Zeno, who had recently arrived at Athens, one day sat down by a bookseller's stall and became engrossed in listening to the perusal of the second book of Xenophon's Memorabilia. Suddenly he enquired of the bookseller where such men as Socrates were to be found. At that moment Crates happened to pass down the street, and Zeno, acting on a hint from the bookseller, from that time attached himself to the Cynic teacher.

It is impossible to reconcile the dates, which we have taken as correct, with the remaining indications of time, which are scattered through the pages of Diogenes. Thus we are told that Zeno was a pupil of Stilpo and Xenocrates for ten years, that the whole time spent under the tuition of Crates, Stilpo, Xenocrates and Polemo was twenty years, and that Zeno presided over the School, which he himself founded, for fifty-eight years[7]. This last is the statement of Apollonius,

---

[1] So φοινικίδιον Crates ap. Diog. L. vii. 3. Cf. Cic. de Fin. iv. 56 et saep.
[2] Another account gives his age as thirty (Diog. L. vii. 2).
[3] Diog. L. vii. 32.
[4] Diog. L. vii. 3.
[5] See Zeno apoph. 3, and the notes.
[6] Diog. L. vii. 3.
[7] Diog. L. vii. 2. 4. 28. The other tradition is traced by Rohde to Apollodorus known as ὁ τοὺς χρόνους ἀναγράψας. Evidence of his having dealt with Zeno's chronology will be found in Philod. περὶ φιλοσόφων

and must be taken in connection with his opinion that Zeno lived till he was ·98 years of age. Probably, Apollonius adopted the tradition that Zeno came to Athens at the age of thirty, and allowed ten years for the period of tuition. He must have assigned B.C. 322 as the date of the foundation of the Stoa, which is obviously far too early. According to the chronology adopted above, Zeno came to Athens about B.C. 314, and, if so, he cannot have been a pupil of Xenocrates, who died in that year. All that can be said with any approach to certainty is that after a somewhat extended period of study under Crates, Stilpo, and Polemo, Zeno at length, probably soon after 300 B.C.[1], began to take pupils on his own account, without attaching himself to any of the then existing philosophical schools. These pupils were at first called Zenonians, but when their master held his lectures in the Stoa Poikile, they adopted the name of Stoics which they afterwards retained[2].

Though not yet rivalling the Peripatetic school in respect of the number of its followers[3], the Stoic philosophy steadily won its way into general esteem no less by the personal influence of its founder than through the fervour of its adherents. So great, indeed, was the respect which the character of Zeno inspired at Athens, that shortly before his death[4] a decree

col. XI. (Herc. vol. coll. prior vol. VIII.) For Zeno's teachers cf. Numenius ap. Euseb. P. E. XIV. 5, p. 729 Πολέμωνος δὲ ἐγένοντο γνώριμοι Ἀρκεσίλαος καὶ Ζήνων...Ζήνωνα μὲν οὖν μέμνημαι εἰπὼν Ξενοκράτει εἶτα δὲ Πολέμωνι φοιτῆσαι, αὖθις δὲ παρὰ Κράτητι κυνίσαι. νυνὶ δὲ αὐτῷ λελογίσθω, ὅτι καὶ Στίλπωνός τε μετέσχε, καὶ τῶν λόγων τῶν Ἡρακλειτείων. ἐπεὶ γὰρ συμφοιτῶντες παρὰ Πολέμωνι ἐφιλοτιμήθησαν ἀλλήλοις συμπαρέλαβον εἰς τὴν πρὸς ἀλλήλους μάχην, ὁ μὲν Ἡράκλειτος καὶ Στίλπωνα ἅμα καὶ Κράτητα, ὧν ὑπὸ μὲν Στίλπωνος ἐγένετο μαχητής, ὑπὸ δὲ Ἡρακλείτου αὐστηρός, κυνικὸς δὲ ὑπὸ Κράτητος.

[1] According to Sext. Emp. adv. Math. VII. 321, Zeno was a πρεσβύτης when he προσεμαρτύρησεν ἑαυτῷ τὴν εὕρεσιν τῆς ἀληθείας. This refers to the publication of his writings, but this must have shortly followed the opening of the school. Jerome on Euseb. Chron. (I. p. 498 Migne) says opposite Ol. 126 "Zeno Stoicus philosophus agnoscitur."

[2] Diog. L. VII. 5.

[3] Zeno apoph. 6.

[4] The decree was carried in the archonship of Arrhenides, i.e. Nov. 265 B.C., if Arrhenides was archon 265—264 as seems to be Gomperz's opinion, vid. supr. p. 2, n. 2.

was passed by the assembly awarding him a golden crown and entitling him to a public funeral in the Ceramicus on his decease. The grounds mentioned in the body of the decree, which is preserved by Diog. L. VII. 10, for conferring this special honour on Zeno were the high moral tone of his teaching and the example which he set to his pupils in the blamelessness of his private life. Greatly however as he was honoured by the Athenians, he steadily refused the offer of their citizenship[1], and on one occasion, when holding an official position, insisted on being described as a citizen of Citium[2]. This devotion to his native town, whether a genuine sentiment of the heart or assumed in order to avow his conviction of the worthlessness of all civic distinctions, seems to have been appreciated by his countrymen, who erected his statue[3] in their market-place, where it was afterwards seen by the elder Pliny[4].

In the later years of his life, Zeno's fame extended beyond the limits of Athenian territory; there is ample record of his intimacy with Antigonus Gonatas[5], the son of Demetrius Poliorcetes and king of Macedon, and from one anecdote we learn that he had attracted the attention of Ptolemy Philadelphus[6]. Now that Athens had completely lost her freedom, she became a hotbed of political intrigue in the interests of the various successive pretenders to the Macedonian throne; some beguiled her with the promise of liberty[7], but by far the most potent instrument to gain her favour was gold. Thus, while the internal politics of Athens had become of purely municipal interest, the greatest services to which Demochares, the nephew of Demosthenes, could lay claim as meriting the gratitude of the Athenians were the substantial money presents

---

[1] Plut. Sto. Rep. 4, 1.
[2] Diog. L. VII. 12.
[3] Diog. L. VII. 6.
[4] H. N. XXXIV. 19. 32.
[5] See Zeno apoph. 25 and 26.
[6] See note on apoph. 25.
[7] So Demetrius Poliorcetes: Grote vol. XII. p. 196.

which he had obtained for the treasury from Lysimachus, Ptolemy, and Antipater[1]. We cannot be surprised that, in such a period as this, Ptolemy and Antigonus, hoping to gain him over by personal condescension and munificent liberality, should have eagerly courted the adherence of one, whose influence like that of Zeno extended over a wide circle among the youth of Athens. It seems clear however that, in general, Zeno avoided politics altogether[2]; and, although it may be doubtful whether his friendship for Antigonus may not have induced Zeno to espouse his political cause, we can at least be sure that the presents of the king were not accepted as bribes by the Stoic philosopher. If Zeno died in B.C. 264, he cannot have lived to see the conclusion of the so-called Chremonidean war, when Athens was besieged by Antigonus and defended by the joint efforts of Ptolemy and the Spartans, and it is impossible to say on which side his sympathies were enlisted, although he is said to have been a lover of Chremonides[3].

In voluntarily hastening his own end, Zeno only illustrated the teaching of his school. One day, on leaving the Stoa, he stumbled and fell, breaking one of his fingers in his fall. Regarding this as a warning of Providence, which it was folly to neglect, and convinced that the right course for a wise man is willingly to assist in carrying out the decrees of destiny, he returned home and at once committed suicide[4].

His personal appearance was evidently not attractive. Timotheus[5], in his work περὶ βίων, described him as wrynecked, while Apollonius called him lean, rather tall, and of a dark complexion[6], with thick calves, flabby flesh, and a weak

---

[1] See Grote vol. XII. p. 214.
[2] Cf. Seneca de Tranq. An. I. 7 Zenonem Cleanthem Chrysippum, quorum nemo ad rempublicam accessit.
[3] Zeno apoph. 44.
[4] Zeno apoph. 56.
[5] Nothing seems to be known of the date of this writer: see Dict. Biog. These authorities are quoted by Diog. L. VII. 1.
[6] An uncomplimentary epithet, cf. Theocr. x. 26 Βομβύκα χαρίεσσα Σύραν καλέοντί τυ πάντες, ἰσχνὰν ἁλιόκαυστον, ἐγὼ δὲ μόνος μελίχλωρον. id. iii. 35 ἁ μελανόχρως.

digestion. The last-named defect is said to have been the cause of his frugal diet[1], but this was no doubt also recommended to him by his philosophical views. In spite of his habitual abstinence, he enjoyed the company of his friends at a convivial banquet, where his severity relaxed with the wine he drank, just as (to use his own comparison) beans are improved by soaking[2]. For the rest, he seems to have been a man of few words, but quick at repartee, disliking all display and effeminacy, and generally of a somewhat stern and reserved cast of mind, though not without consideration for the wants of others.

§ 2. *Stoicism as established by Zeno.*

It will be convenient at this point to summarise those leading doctrines which the evidence here collected establishes as having been introduced by Zeno into the Stoic school, without paying regard to isolated expressions or to views of minor philosophical importance.

Zeno divided philosophy into three parts, logic, physics and ethics, and we may take them in the order named, as being that which he recommended.

To the formal side of logic Zeno paid but little attention, regarding it as useful only for the detection of error, rather than as a means towards the establishment of truth. The doctrine of the four categories, and the elaborate treatment of ἀξιώματα and syllogisms, belong almost entirely to Chrysippus, and, when we remember that out of 750 books which he is said to have written no fewer than 311 were devoted to logical studies, it is not improbable that he owed much of his reputation to his performances in this branch. In Zeno's eyes the most important division of logic was the question of the standard of knowledge, although strictly speaking this should rather be considered as belonging to psychology. He

---

[1] εἷς ἄρτος, ὄψον ἰσχάς, ἐπιπιεῖν ὕδωρ. Philemon ap. Diog. L. vii. 27.
[2] See Zeno apoph. 27.

held that, though the senses themselves are unerring, the impressions they convey are often erroneous, and that only such impressions are to be trusted as are in themselves perspicuous. The ultimate test of truth resides in the strength of tension in the impression, as it strikes the sense-organ. If satisfied in this way that the impression is such that it must proceed from a real object, the mind in the exercise of its ever present activity grasps the impression, and assents to it. This is the meaning which Zeno expressed by saying that φαντασία καταληπτική is the criterion of truth[1]. Diogenes Laertius, however, mentions certain ἀρχαιότεροι τῶν Στωικῶν as teaching that ὀρθὸς λόγος is the standard of truth. This passage has been treated by Hirzel (in whose judgment other authorities have concurred) as proving that Zeno and Cleanthes were the philosophers indicated, and that Chrysippus was the first to introduce the definition of the φαντασία καταληπτική. The only other evidence, by which he connects Zeno with ὀρθὸς λόγος, is Philo quis virtuti studet p. 880 appearing in our collection as frag. 157. To this might have been added Arr. Epict. diss. IV. 8. 12 (frag. 4) and Philodem. περὶ εὐσεβ. col. 8 (frag. 117). It is submitted, however, that these passages by no means prove the point in question, as against the positive testimony which attributes to Zeno the φαντασία καταληπτική. In Philo there is no question of a logical criterion at all, but Zeno is

---

[1] As the matter is one of considerable importance, in order to relieve the notes, it is desirable to quote Stein's remarks (Erkenntnistheorie, p. 174):—"Mit Zeller muss man annehmen, dass das καταληπτικόν ursprünglich einen aktiven Sinn halte, da der Tonus desselben Zweifelsohne auf die διάνοια einwirkt. Andererseits muss man Hirzel wieder darin Recht geben, dass die διάνοια sich unmöglich rein leidend verhalten kann, dass vielmehr das καταληπτικόν auch einen passiven Beigeschmack hat. Und doch lassen sich beide, sich scheinbar ausschliessende Standpunkte vereinigen, wenn man in das καταληπτικόν den von uns vermuteten Doppelsinn hineinlegt, den Zeno wohl absichtlich andeuten wollte. Danach wären die φαντασία und διάνοια bei der κατάληψις gleicherweise teils aktiv, teils passiv, woraus sich die schwankende Anwendung dieses Ausdrucks sehr wohl erklärt." For the connection of τόνος with κατάληψις, which is not however proved to be Zenonian, cf. Sext. Emp. adv. Math. VII. 408 ἀλλὰ γὰρ αὕτη μὲν ἡ ἀπαραλλαξία τῶν τε καταληπτικῶν καὶ τῶν ἀκαταλήπτων φαντασιῶν κατὰ τὸ ἐναργὲς καὶ ἔντονον ἰδίωμα παρίσταται.

speaking of the state of mind of the wise man, whose soul is in perfect conformity with the law of reason, and who has mastered all his impulses and passions. This is still more plain in the extract from Philodemus, where ὀρθοὺς λόγους are coupled with σπουδαίας διαθέσεις[1]. The weight of evidence the other way must remain to be stated hereafter, but it may be remarked that, even if Cicero's testimony is discredited, the fact of the controversy between Zeno and Arcesilas is not thereby disproved[2]. Again, if Zeno defined φαντασία as a τύπωσις, and discriminated between the truth of various φαντασίαι, he must have pursued the subject still farther; and, if art and memory are defined with reference to κατάληψις and opinion is distinguished therefrom, it follows of necessity that he must have defined κατάληψις itself. Still, even admitting to the full the ethical significance of ὀρθὸς λόγος[3], the passage in Diogenes is not thereby disposed of, for if Zeno and Cleanthes are not indicated by the words οἱ ἀρχαιότεροι τῶν Στωικῶν to whom does this expression refer? Must we, then, suppose that Zeno put forward two criteria of knowledge, rational thought (ὀρθὸς λόγος) as well as the experience of sense (κατάληψις)? Such a conclusion would be inconsistent with the clearness and directness of Zeno's teaching. The only way out of the difficulty is to adopt the theory of Stein, who regards the doctrine of ὀρθὸς λόγος as a concession to rationalism. ὀρθὸς λόγος becomes, in this view, a subsidiary and secondary criterion[5], so that the results of thought must be confirmed by experience. In other words, the potential notions inspired in us by the divine λόγος require to be completed and corrected on the side

[1] For Epict. l. c. see note on Zeno frag. 4.
[2] It is satisfactory to find that Stein, Erkenntnistheorie n. 341, claims for Zeno the φαντασία καταληπτικὴ on precisely similar grounds to those stated in the notes to frag. 11.
[3] For this see Stein, Erkenntnistheorie pp. 259—264.
[4] It should be mentioned that Corssen de Posidonio Rhodio (1878) pp. 17—19 proposed to eliminate Στωικῶν as a blunder of Diogenes or his authority, assuming that Posidonius was speaking of Empedocles, the Pythagoreans, and Plato.
[5] The meaning of the word ἀπολείπουσιν should in this case be pressed. Stein, Erkenntnistheorie p. 259.

of sensible experience before they can attain to objective actuality[1].

From this point of view, then, it is not unreasonable to credit Zeno with the substance of the teaching recorded in Cic. Acad. I. 41, 42. If so much be admitted, it is most unlikely that he should have refrained from enquiring into the nature of knowledge and ignorance, which carry with them the doctrine of assent. On the other hand, it is most probable that he only touched lightly the doctrine of ἔννοιαι and not at all that of προλήψεις[2].

The remainder of the logical fragments are not of much importance as regards the positive teaching of the school. They include a nominalistic criticism of the Platonic theory of ideas, a curious statement of the nature of causation, a few scraps dealing with various rhetorical terms, a definition of geometry, some discussion as to the meaning of the word σόλοικος, and a symbolical explanation, recorded by Cicero, of the different degrees of knowledge.

Zeno's contributions to Physics have been unduly depreciated by some authorities but, while it is true that the development of this branch is largely due to Cleanthes, still a fair estimate of the fragments here collected will lead us to the conclusion that the essential groundwork of the Stoic physical teaching was laid by the founder of the school[3]. Zeno started from the proposition that nothing exists but the material, inasmuch as body alone is capable of acting and being acted upon. All body is thus either active or passive and the material world is itself the result produced from the

---

[1] Stein, Erkenntnistheorie p. 314, 315.

[2] Stein holds that πρόληψις was substituted by Chrysippus for Zeno's ὀρθὸς λόγος, in so far as the latter is concerned with epistemology (Erkenntnistheorie p. 269, 270).

[3] See Stein, Psychologie p. 56 and n. 77, whose reference to the number of fragments in Wachsmuth's collection is however misleading. As regards Zeno, Wachsmuth's fragments are only intended to be supplementary to Wellmann's article in Fleckeisen's Jahrb. for 1873, so that no inference can be drawn from the fact that there are more physical than ethical fragments. It will be seen from the present collection that the numbers are very nearly equal.

operation of these two principles. The active principle is God, and the passive is matter. God is more closely defined as the fiery aether[1], which permeates the whole of the universe, even as honey passes through the honeycomb. He is at once the embodiment of reason and of law, and the power which binds in one the various portions of the universe, who, though his essence is constant, appears in different forms in everything that exists. Nature, forethought and fate are thus only different names for the same being; as nature he creates the world, and creates it in entire harmony with the law of fate. Matter, on the other hand, is formless and indeterminate, though limited in extent, and can exist only in conjunction with some active quality; although it is itself eternal, its parts are subject to change. The creation of the world is brought about by the action of God upon matter, whereby the creative fire through an intermediate watery stage passes into the four elements fire, air, water and earth out of which everything else is formed. To explain the production of the individual thing by the intermingling of its elements, Zeno broached the celebrated theory of $\kappa\rho\hat{a}\sigma\iota\varsigma$ $\delta\iota'$ $\ddot{o}\lambda ov$, which is in effect a denial of the axiom that two bodies cannot occupy the same space.

The world, however, will not last for ever, nor are we left without indications of its destructibility. In the inequality of the earth's surface, in the retrocession of the sea, in the mortality of every substance with which we are acquainted, and lastly in the fact that the human race and all living creatures can be shown to have had a beginning in time Zeno saw clear proofs that the universe itself is destined to pass away. There will come a time when by the unceasing law of fate the world and all that it contains will again be merged in the primeval fire, only to be created anew, as the embryo is formed from the seed. For the process is unvarying no less than never-ending; a new Heracles will free a young world from its plagues, and a new Socrates will plead his cause against the same accusers.

---

[1] Stein, Psychologie p. 58, remarks that there is no evidence of Zeno having used the term $\pi\nu\epsilon\hat{v}\mu a$ in this connection.

The individual and the cosmos are thus partakers in the same decree of fate, but their likeness does not stop here. Not only is the world a unity, but also a living unity; it is moreover sentient, rational, intelligent, and wise.

Two characteristics are especially prominent in Zeno's system, first, his metaphysical contrast between God and matter, and, secondly, his materialism. He seems to have been animated by a desire to combine the results of later thought with the simplicity and directness of the early Ionian physicists. All is to be evolved out of fire: but fire is clothed with divine attributes, and sharply contrasted with the passive material on which it works. But Zeno did not observe that the combination is in reality self-destructive, and that with a materialistic system metaphysics are superseded. It remained for his successors to eradicate the dualism which is here involved, and, while thrusting into the background the points borrowed from Aristotle, to take their stand upon pantheism pure and simple.

Passing from the account of the cosmogony to the description of the different component parts of the universe, we find that the circumference of the sphere is occupied by a revolving belt of aether, in which are the sun, moon and stars, divine beings formed of creative fire. No void exists within the world, but outside it there is unlimited void; at the same time the world is kept together and preserved from dissolution into space by the attraction of its parts to the centre, in which the earth is placed. Zeno also explains certain natural phenomena such as eclipses, lightning, thunderbolts and comets, and defines time and colour.

We proceed to his anthropology, in which the account of the soul is most important. Although he apparently omitted to describe God, who is the soul of the universe, as fiery breath, yet the soul, which is the moving principle of the body, is defined as a warm breath, or (after Heraclitus) as a sentient exhalation. For the soul is fed by exhalation from the blood, just as the heavenly bodies are by particles from the lower elements. Moreover, it is corporeal and grows up with the body, gradually expanding under the influence of external impressions, so that the perfect power of reason is only developed at the age of puberty. Though it is a simple essence, its faculties are diverse, and being extended from the ἡγεμονικὸν which is situated in the heart to the various organs of sense, it is said to have eight parts, namely, the ἡγεμονικὸν itself, the five senses, and the capacities of speech and generation. The soul entirely permeates the body, and at its departure the composite structure of soul and body is destroyed. The soul itself endures for a time after its separation from the body but is not immortal, and its condition after death is determined by the grade of purity to which it has attained. Such, at least, seems to be a fair inference from a passage of Lactantius in which Zeno speaks of the separation of the unholy from the holy and contrasts the misery of the former with the blessedness of the latter. On his discussion of the voice, sleep, vision, and the seed we need not dwell.

It remains to consider Zeno's attitude towards the popular religion. Although, in the strict sense, he teaches that there is but one God, yet he admits that there is a certain amount of truth in polytheism, as implying a recognition of the ubiquity of the divine presence. The manifestation of God in the powers of nature is symbolised by Zeus, Here and Poseidon, who represent the aether, the air, and the water respectively. In his interpretation of Hesiod's Theogony he gives the reins to his etymological fancy, so as to bring the cosmogony of the poet into accordance with Stoic views. Lastly the existence of divination is inferred from the forethought, which characterises the divine government.

Ethics, which are the crowning point of the Stoic system, come next in order. The aim and object of life is to live in agreement with nature, which is, in other words, to live according to virtue: for this is the goal to which nature conducts us. It would seem that Zeno did not accurately explain what he meant by nature, since Chrysippus and

Cleanthes took divergent views of its character, but, recognising the manner in which the different branches of the Stoic system are interlaced with one another[1], we may reasonably conclude that by the prominence given to nature Zeno desired to connect his moral teaching with the divine creative aether, which permeates the universe[2]. Our first impulses, however, tend not to virtue but to self-preservation, and virtue is impossible in the child or the brute, since neither of them possesses the informing power of reason. These natural impulses require the guidance of reason, and in their proper subordination to it is to be found the condition of happiness, which may be described as the unruffled flow of life. For happiness nothing is required but virtue, and no external circumstances, nothing but what is morally evil, can diminish the satisfaction belonging to the virtuous. In this way we are led to discriminate between ἀγαθά and κακά: only virtue and vice or their accessories can be classed as good and evil; everything else, even life and death, is morally indifferent. But this classification does not exhaust the capacities of τὰ κατὰ φύσιν. The value of virtue is absolute and for all time: but, just as the supremacy of the monarch does not imply the absolute equality of his subjects, so the ἀδιάφορα are ranged between virtue and vice in a graduated scale of negative and positive value (ἀπαξία and ἀξία), the middle place being occupied by τὰ καθάπαξ ἀδιάφορα, i.e. such matters as having an even or odd number of hairs in one's head. Everything possessing ἀξία is κατὰ φύσιν, and everything possessing ἀπαξία is παρὰ φύσιν. At the same time ἀξία is not a permanent attribute of any ἀδιάφορον, for that which is at one time κατὰ

---

[1] Cf. Stein, Psychologie p. 13.
[2] Hirzel, Untersuchungen II. p. 108, thinks otherwise and the point is certainly a doubtful one. If Zeno spoke only of human nature, Cleanthes may have here, as elsewhere, shown the connection of ethical with physical doctrine by explaining φύσις as κοινὴ φύσις. Then Chrysippus would have united both views. If this was the real development, there would be some pretext for Stobaeus' assertion that Cleanthes added τῇ φύσει to the definition, while the authority of Diogenes Laertius would remain unimpaired. See however Stein, Erkenntnistheorie p. 260.

φύσιν might, under certain circumstances, become παρὰ φύσιν. Herein lies the vital distinction between ἀδιάφορα and ἀγαθά, for the latter are unaffected by any possible change of circumstances: a virtuous action can never be contrary to nature. Still, although there is not an absolute, there is yet a practical permanence in the value of certain things, which in the absence of some paramount objection (= κατὰ προηγούμενον λόγον or ἄνευ περιστάσεως) we shall always choose in preference to their contraries. These then are the προηγμένα. Corresponding with this classification of objects, we have a scale of actions ranging from κατόρθωμα (virtuous action) to ἁμάρτημα (sinful action), wherein καθῆκον answers to the class of ἀδιάφορα. Every καθῆκον is thus directed to the choice of τὰ κατὰ φύσιν and the avoidance of τὰ παρὰ φύσιν. The doctrines of καθῆκον and προηγμένον are not to be regarded as an excrescence foisted on to the Stoic system in consequence of the pressure of the arguments of opponents, but are an integral and necessary portion of the original structure as established by Zeno. The apparent inconsistency, which the application of these doctrines sometimes produces e.g. in the remarks on marriage, often disappears when we remember that the πολιτεία proposed to establish a socialistic constitution under which the importance of ἀδιάφορα would be reduced to a minimum.

Zeno held further that virtue is one and indivisible, springing from the ἡγεμονικόν, of which it is a fixed and permanent condition. Consistently with this, he maintains that all sinful actions are equally wrong, since all alike imply an aberration from a standard, which excludes increase or diminution. None the less, however, can we distinguish between different manifestations of virtue or separate virtues: virtue itself is identical with wisdom (φρόνησις), and justice, courage, and temperance are the particular applications of wisdom in diverse spheres. Whether Zeno also distinguished between two different kinds of φρόνησις, one as the groundwork, and the other as a particular species of virtue, must remain doubtful. Hirzel (l.c. p. 99) infers that he did, but Plutarch's words do not necessarily lead to such a conclusion, and we ought to hesitate to attribute such an inconsistency to Zeno without direct evidence. No doubt the Stoic school generally put forward four cardinal virtues φρόνησις, δικαιοσύνη, ἀνδρεία and σωφροσύνη, but inasmuch as Zeno's position was admittedly modified by his successors we are left to judge of his views entirely from the two passages in Plutarch, in which he is mentioned by name.

The theory of the emotions, which was introduced by Zeno, constitutes one of the most distinctive features of Stoic ethics. Whereas Plato and Aristotle agreed in admitting the legitimacy of certain emotions, Zeno declared all alike to be sinful, as being due to an irrational and unnatural movement in the soul, or an excess of impulse. The four chief emotions are pleasure, grief, fear and desire, and Zeno in describing their nature dwelt, if we may trust Galen's statements, rather on the psychological effects of the irrational impulse upon the soul than on the mental conditions which produce them. The special difficulties surrounding this subject will be discussed in the notes to the fragments themselves.

The whole of mankind was divided by Zeno into two classes, entirely distinct from one another, that of the wise and that of the foolish. Every action of the wise man is prompted by virtue and every action of the fool by vice. Hence it is generally true that the wise man performs every action well, and the fool fails in everything. Friendship, freedom, piety, riches, beauty, the arts of kingship and generalship, even success in culinary operations belong to the wise man alone: he is never mistaken, never regrets what he has done, feels no compassion, and is absolutely free from every form of emotion. At the same time, it is clear that Zeno contemplates a progress from the state of folly to that of wisdom as practicable; this advance is characterised by the purgation of the soul from emotional and delusive affections under the influence of reason. Even though he ultimately emerges from the conflict with success, the wise man still feels the scars from the wounds he has received during its course, and is often reminded of his former evil impulses after he has completely suppressed them. Finally, since death belongs to the class ἀδιάφορα, suicide is justifiable in the wise man, if circumstances prescribe such a course.

It is obvious that a teacher, whose ethical views were of the nature, which we have just indicated, could not rest satisfied with the existing constitution of civic life in Greece. Equally unsatisfactory to him was the aristocratical community of Plato, with the sharply drawn dividing line between the guardians and the rest of the citizens. For this reason Eros, the god of friendship and concord, is taken as the presiding deity of Zeno's ideal state, a state which in no way corresponds to the Greek πόλις, but comprises the whole of mankind living together like a herd of cattle[1]. In this state there will be no temples, law-courts, or gymnasia; no work of human craftsmen is worthy of divine acceptance; the state must be adorned not with costly offerings, but by the virtues of its inhabitants. Zeno likewise advocates an abolition of coinage, a community of wives, and a thorough revolution of the current system of education.

The remaining fragments, dealing mainly with particular καθήκοντα, do not require to be summarised here.

§ 3. *Zeno's relation to previous philosophers.*

The opponents of the Stoic school were fond of accusing its members of plagiarism and want of originality. Zeno is the keen Phoenician trader, pilfering other men's wares, and passing them off as his own[2]: if all that belongs to others were withdrawn from the voluminous writings of Chrysippus, we should have a blank page[3]. Antiochus, in Cicero[4], represents

[1] Cf. Newman, Politics of Aristotle, vol. I. p. 88.
[2] Cf. Diog. L. VII. 25.
[3] Diog. L. VII. 181.
[4] Acad. I. 43. The same argument is put forward by Cicero himself against Cato in the 4th book of the de Finibus.

the views of Zeno as merely immaterial changes in minor points of the genuine Academic doctrine, while Juvenal only repeats current opinion in speaking of the Stoic dogmas as "a Cynicis tunica distantia"[1]. Even a slight acquaintance with the Stoic system is sufficient to refute these gross charges: indeed, its originality is abundantly vindicated when we point to the influence it exercised for several centuries on the intellectual life of Greece and Rome[2]. At the same time it must be admitted that Zeno was largely indebted to his predecessors—especially to Antisthenes and Heraclitus—for the bricks and mortar with which he constructed so splendid an edifice. Of Cynicism in particular he appropriated the kernel, while discarding the husk. It is, however, when we look at Stoicism as a whole that we are able to appreciate the skill with which its incongruous elements were fused, and the unity of thought which pervades a variety of detail. The Stoic wise man is as far removed from Diogenes in his tub, as is the all permeating aether from the fiery element of Heraclitus. We proceed to discuss in detail the various points in which Zeno's obligation to previous thinkers is most strongly marked.

A. *To Antisthenes and the Cynics.*

The resemblances between Zeno and the Cynics are naturally to be found chiefly in their ethical doctrines. Physics were almost entirely neglected by the Cynics, and their nominalistic logic was not of great importance for Stoicism, although we may observe in passing that both schools maintained in similar terms[3] that Plato's ideas were a mere fiction of the brain and had no objective existence. The Stoic doctrine of life in accordance with nature finds its historical origin in the

---

[1] XIII. 121.
[2] "Die Stoa war vielmehr die weitaus selbständigste Schule der nacharistotelischen Philosophie," Stein, Psychologie p. 10.
[3] Antisthenes ap. Simpl. in Cat. p. 54 b ὦ Πλάτων, ἵππον μὲν ὁρῶ ἱππότητα δὲ οὐχ ὁρῶ. Cf. Zeno frag. 23.

teaching as well as in the life of Diogenes[1]. Like Zeno, Antisthenes teaches that virtue is in itself sufficient to secure happiness[2], that nothing is a Good but virtue, nothing an Evil but vice, and that everything else is indifferent[3]. Accordingly Diogenes held that death, since it involves no disgrace, cannot be an Evil[4]. Hence it is not surprising to learn that many of the Cynics put an end to their lives by suicide, though we have sayings both of Antisthenes and Diogenes on record denying the legitimacy of such a course[5]. Virtue itself is described, after Socrates, as consisting in wisdom and prudence: "prudence," says Antisthenes, "is the safest wall; it cannot be undermined or betrayed"[6]. At the same time the futility of the ordinary course of Greek education is strongly insisted on[7]. The distinction between virtue and vice draws with it that between the wise and the foolish; the philosopher's wallet preserves a chosen few from a condition bordering on madness[8].

We are told, on the authority of Diogenes Laertius[9], that Zeno adopted the Cynic form of life. This is probably to be taken with some limitation, as the incidents recorded of his life only partially agree with it. It is certain, however, that his life was one of abstinence and simplicity[10], and for this reason he became the butt of the comic poets, who thus unconsciously testified to his merit. Apollodorus Ephillus, a later Stoic writer, declared that the wise man would cynicise, and that Cynicism was a short cut to virtue[11]. It should, however, always be borne in mind that the Stoic ideal was

---

[1] Diog. L. vi. 71 δέον οὖν ἀντὶ τῶν ἀχρήστων πόνων τοὺς κατὰ φύσιν ἑλομένους ζῆν εὐδαιμόνως. Zeno frag. 120.
[2] Diog. L. vi. 11. Zeno frag. 125.
[3] Diog. L. vi. 105. Zeno frag. 128.
[4] Arr. Epict. Diss. i. 24. 6. Zeno frag. 129.
[5] Zeller Socrates, etc. Eng. Tr. p. 319, n. 5. Cf. Zeno frag. 161.
[6] Diog. L. vi. 13. Zeno frag. 134.
[7] Diog. L. vi. 103. Zeno frag. 167.
[8] Diog. L. vi. 33, 35. Zeno frag. 148.
[9] Diog. L. vi. 104.
[10] Diog. L. vii. 26, 27.
[11] Diog. vi. 104. vii. 121.

humanised and elevated to an extent entirely incompatible with Cynicism, mainly owing to the attention which was bestowed on mental culture[1].

Turning to the views of the two schools in applied moral science, we find a curious agreement as to the relations of the sexes: Zeno and Diogenes both held that, in the ideal state, there should be a community of wives, and neither saw anything revolting in marriage between the nearest relations[2]. At the same time marriage and the begetting of children are recommended for the wise man both by Zeno and Antisthenes, and apparently we must regard this as intended to apply to the existing condition of life, in which marriage was a civil institution[3]. Both teachers allow to the wise man the passion of love, as he alone will be able to select a suitable object[4]: both maintain that the virtuous alone are capable of genuine friendship[5].

Lastly, Zeno copied Antisthenes in his treatment of the Homeric poems, and particularly in explaining certain apparent contradictions as due to the fact that the poet speaks at one time κατὰ δόξαν and at another κατ' ἀλήθειαν[6]. The allegorising method of interpretation is common to both, and was afterwards developed to an excessive degree by Cleanthes and Chrysippus[7].

Though we have thus seen that Zeno's ethical teaching is largely founded on Cynicism, we must not forget the many points of divergence. Thus, for example, we find the Cynics treating honour and wealth as absolute evils[8]; these things,

---

[1] The difference of spirit in the two schools is well put by Sir A. Grant (Ar. Eth. vol. I. p. 317 ed. 3).
[2] Diog. L. VI. 72. Dio. Chrys. x. 29. Cf. Zeno frags. 176 and 179. These passages are from the πολιτεία of Zeno, which is supposed to have been written while he was still an exponent of orthodox Cynicism. Chrysippus, however, is reported to have also held this repulsive doctrine.
[3] Diog. L. VI. 11. Zeno frag. 171.
[4] Diog. L. VI. 11. Zeno frag. 172.
[5] Diog. L. VI. 12. Zeno frag. 149.
[6] Dio. Chrys. 53, 4. Zeno frag. 195.
[7] See Cic. N. D. II. 63 foll.
[8] See the passages collected by Zeller Socrates, etc. E. T. p. 304.

according to Zeno, belonged to the class of προηγμένα. Again, to take their attitude towards the popular religion, we know that Zeno expressly countenanced divination, while the existence of prophets made Diogenes think man the most foolish of animals[1].

B. *To Heraclitus.*

There can be no doubt that Zeno borrowed some important principles in his physical teaching from the writings of Heraclitus, and particularly from his account of the cosmogony. There is, however, a difficulty in comparing the doctrines of the two schools minutely, owing to the obscurity in which our knowledge of the Heraclitean theories is involved, and which is often increased by the doubt as to whether some particular doctrine belonged equally to the Stoics and the philosopher of Ephesus, or whether some later development, introduced by the former, has not been wrongly ascribed to the latter by our authorities. For instance, it was at one time stoutly maintained that the conflagration of the world was not taught by Heraclitus but that it was first propounded by Zeno, although the contrary opinion seems now to prevail[2]. Again, it is not entirely clear whether we are to class Heraclitus, as Aristotle does[3], with the early Ionian physicists, starting from his dogma that all things are fire, or whether we are to regard this principle as a metaphysical abstraction, metaphorically shadowing forth the eternal flux of all things, a view which is more in accordance with Plato's criticism in the Theaetetus[4]. However this may be, Heraclitus is essentially a hylozoist, who, following Anaximenes, chooses fire as being the rarest element, and insists on the continuity of change in order to escape from the mechanical theories of Anaxagoras and Em-

[1] Diog. vi. 24 and contrast Zeno frag. 118.
[2] See the elaborate discussion in Zeller, Pre-Socr. Phil. Eng. Tr. ii. pp. 62—77. See however Bywater, Journ. Phil. i. 42.
[3] Met. i. 3. 8. This is the view of Ueberweg p. 40 and is also held by Dr Jackson.
[4] Zeller's position (p. 20 foll.) combines the two views.

pedocles on the one hand, and the Parmenidean immobility on the other. The λόγος ξυνός is with him the expression of the truth that nothing can be known but the law of mutability, the harmony in difference, which he likens to the stretching of a bowstring[1]. This law he calls γνώμη, δίκη, εἱμαρμένη, τὸ περιέχον ἡμᾶς λογικόν τε ὂν καὶ φρενῆρες, and ὁ Ζεύς[2], but these terms are mere metaphors and we should be wrong in straining their philosophic import: they represent, in fact, the law of change and nothing more. Still, there can be no doubt that the use which Heraclitus made of his formula λόγος was one of the chief points in his system which attracted the attention of Zeno. As a disciple of Cynicism he was familiar with λόγος as a dialectical and an ethical principle: neither of these aspects of λόγος was discarded by him in broaching his own system. Yet, through the help of the Heraclitean λόγος, he was enabled to take one step further. Just as Plato gave to the Socratic ὑπόθεσις or general conception a metaphysical existence in the form of the idea, so did Zeno elevate the λόγος of Antisthenes from its position as a criterion for thought and duty to that of the physical cause of being and movement[3]. The Stoic deity is, like the Heraclitean λόγος, provided with many names, such as God, Mind, the all pervading Aether, Fate, Forethought, and Zeus, but on the other hand it belongs to an essentially later period of thought. We have here set forth the teleological view of Nature, which is regarded as creating all things out of itself for a good purpose[4]. The Stoics, at least after Cleanthes, are also pantheists in so far as they acknowledge that God and the world are identical. Even where Zeno followed Heraclitus most closely there are essential differences in treatment. The fire of Heraclitus becomes

[1] Heraclitus frag. 56 ed. Bywater. Hirzel finds here the origin of the Stoic τόνος, but this is very questionable.
[2] For a detailed statement see Krische, Forschungen p. 368 foll.
[3] The comparison is suggested by Hirzel II. p. 42. But Hirzel very much underestimates the influence of Heraclitus on Zeno, as Heinze has pointed out. It is quite contrary to the evidence to attribute the Heraclitean tendencies of the Stoa solely, or even mainly, to Cleanthes.
[4] Cic. N. D. II. 58.

aether or πῦρ τεχνικόν—for this distinction is unknown to the Ephesian—and is thereby spiritualised and rarefied. Instead of three elements the Stoics have four, according to the universal practice of post-Aristotelian writers. Cleanthes, at least, regarded these four elements merely as graduations of τόνος, a notion entirely alien to Heraclitus. The doctrine of πάντα ῥεῖ is replaced by that of μεταβολή, and ἀλλοίωσις gives way to the characteristic theory of the mixture of substances, known as κρᾶσις δι' ὅλων. In stating the differences between the two schools we have indicated how the Stoic physics were built upon Heraclitus. The remaining resemblances are comparatively unimportant. It was a natural corollary to both systems to maintain the unity of the cosmos[1]. Zeno seems to have adopted Heraclitus' definition of the soul as an ἀναθυμίασος, but, instead of regarding this exhalation as imbibed from the outer air (τὸ περιέχον), he taught that the soul was fed by emanation from the warm blood. Where Heraclitus regarded dryness as an essential characteristic of the wise soul[2], the Stoics rather looked for warmth or εὐκρασία. Lastly, we may observe that Heraclitus attributed immortality to the soul, and that in Ethics he counselled submission to the common law and the regulation of speech and thought in accordance with the demands of nature[3].

C. *To Plato and Aristotle.*

It has often been observed as a remarkable fact that the influence exercised both by Plato and Aristotle on their immediate successors was comparatively small. Zeno and Epicurus sought the groundwork of their ethics in the systems of Antisthenes and Aristippus, and followed in their physics, with surprising closeness, the pre-Socratic philosophers Heraclitus and Democritus. Indeed, the Peripatetic school itself showed no great vitality after Theophrastus, the new Academy

[1] Stob. Ecl. I. 22. 3 b p. 199, 10.
[2] Heracl. frag. 74, Bywater.
[3] Stob. Floril. III. 84.

of Arcesilas and Carneades bore no resemblance to that founded by Plato, and Antiochus owed more to the Stoa than to the old Academy which he professed to resuscitate. In the post-Aristotelian philosophy, taken as a whole, we find a universal tendency to materialistic views, a striking decline of interest in purely intellectual research, as an end in itself, and a general agreement in confining the area of speculation to the two questions of the standard of ethics and the logical criterion. However we are to explain this phenomenon, and even if we consider inadequate the explanation of Zeller, who attributes this result to the loss of political freedom and the consequent concentration of thought on the needs of the individual, we are more concerned with the fact itself than with its possible causes[1]. It is enough to say that the system founded by Zeno was in no sense the offspring of those of Plato and Aristotle, although in many points it presupposes their existence.

In the case of Chrysippus we may go further, for there is no doubt that his logic was largely a development, and that not a very happy one, of the Aristotelian doctrine of the syllogism. Zeno, however, although the titles of several of his logical treatises have come down to us, was not considered to have paid great attention to this branch of philosophy. The principal contribution made by Zeno to the theory of knowledge is the establishment of the φαντασία καταληπτική as the criterion: in this, the essential point, whereby the convincing power of the impression is made the test of its reality, is due entirely to Zeno, but he was obviously influenced by the Aristotelian treatment of φαντασία, in which it appears as "decaying sense,"[2] and is more accurately defined as "the movement resulting from the actual operation of the sense faculty"[3]. Again, in the Zenonian definitions of memory and art there will be found a familiarity with the progressive stages in the growth of knowledge, as enunciated by

[1] This question is discussed in Benn's Greek Philosophers (Preface).
[2] Rhet. I. 11. 1370 a 28.
[3] de An. III. 3. 429 a 1.

Aristotle[1], and his terminology, at any rate, is recognisable in a logical fragment preserved by Stobaeus[2].

Diogenes Laertius introduces his discussion of the Stoic physics by stating that the two ἀρχαί posited by the school were God and Indeterminate Matter: here we have not only the well-known Aristotelian distinction between the formal and the material cause, but also his description of matter as that which is entirely formless and contingent[3]. The aether, the so called quinta essentia of Aristotle, of which the heavenly bodies were composed, has its representative under the system of Zeno, who held that the circumference of the world was surrounded by a moving belt of aether.

Cicero puts into the mouth of professed Antiocheans, and, when speaking in the character of Antiochus, himself makes the charge that Zeno's Ethics are identical with those of the Academy, and that the only change is one of terminology. This is developed at length in the fourth book of the de Finibus, where Cicero points out the inconsistency of denying that external goods contribute to happiness, while admitting that they have a certain positive value. There is considerable force in the objection in so far as it lays bare a weak point in the Stoic stronghold, but, if it is meant for a charge of plagiarism, it is grossly unfair. In fact, as has been remarked, Antiochus, who himself stole the clothes of Zeno, was always anxious to prove that they never belonged to Zeno at all. As we know, however, that Zeno was a pupil of Polemo, it is not unnatural to find that he was to some extent influenced by his teaching. Thus, life according to nature was one of Polemo's leading tenets, and Clement of Alexandria has preserved the title of one of his books which deals with this subject[4]. Zeller well

[1] Met. I. 1. Anal. Post. II. 19.
[2] Zeno frag. 24.
[3] Metaph. VI. 3. 1029 a 20 λέγω δ' ὕλην ᾗ καθ' αὑτὴν μήτε τι μήτε ποσὸν μήτε ἄλλο μηδὲν λέγεται οἷς ὥρισται τὸ ὄν.
[4] Cic. Fin. IV. 6. 14. Clem. Alex. Strom. VIII. p. 304 Sylb. Polemo himself is represented as saying to Zeno:—οὐ λανθάνεις, ὦ Ζήνων, ταῖς κηπαίαις παρεισρέων θύραις, καὶ τὰ δόγματα κλέπτων φοινικικῶς μεταμφιεννύς (Diog. L. VII. 25). One of the doctrines, which were in this way appro-

sums up the extent of Academic influence when he says[1] that "such points in Platonism as the Socratic building of virtue on knowledge, the comparative depreciation of external goods, the retreat from sensuality, the elevation and the purity of moral idealism, and, in the older Academy, the demand for life according to nature, the doctrine of the self-sufficiency of virtue and the growing tendency to confine philosophy to practical issues—all these were questions for a Stoic full of interest." Amongst the particular points, in which Zeno seems to have felt the influence of Plato, may be mentioned the doctrines of the cardinal virtues (frag. 134) and the πάθη (frag. 142) and the explanation of the world as ζῷον ἔμψυχον (frag. 62).

We have endeavoured briefly to indicate certain leading points of doctrine in which Zeno was influenced by his predecessors, leaving minor resemblances to be pointed out in the notes.

§ 4. *The writings of Zeno.*

A list of the titles of Zeno's works is preserved in Diog. L. VII. 4, but is admittedly incomplete, as the same writer himself makes additions to it in his exposition of the philosophical views of the Stoic school. This list was probably derived by Diogenes from two distinct sources, as it is divisible into two separate portions. The first or main division gives the names of 13 (or 14) works, of which 6 deal with ethical, 4 with physical, and 3 (or 4) with logical and miscellaneous subjects; then follows a kind of appendix giving 4 (or 3) additional titles. Apollonius Tyrius has been with much probability suggested as the authority to whom the main division is due[2],

---

priated by the Stoa, appears to be the third definition of ἔρως preserved by Andronicus περὶ παθῶν c. 4 as ὑπηρεσία θεῶν εἰς νέων κατακόσμησιν καὶ καλῶν: cf. Plut. ad prin. iner. 780 D Πολέμων ἔλεγε τὸν ἔρωτα εἶναι θεῶν ὑπηρεσίαν εἰς νέων ἐπιμέλειαν (Kreuttner, Andronicus p. 49).

[1] Stoics etc. p. 399.
[2] See Wilamowitz-Moellendorf, Antigonos p. 107: Zeller and Wachsmuth adopt Nietzsche's hypothesis (Rhein. Mus. XXIV. 185) that all the lists in Diog. are, with certain exceptions, derived from Demetrius of

for not only does Diogenes in several places cite him by name (e.g. § 2) but also Strabo (XVI. 2. 24, p. 757) expressly mentions a work of his with the title πίναξ τῶν ἀπὸ Ζήνωνος φιλοσόφων καὶ τῶν βιβλίων; who supplied Diogenes with the appendix has not been determined.

The works, of which any record has survived to us, may be divided into four classes :—

I. Logical.

(1) περὶ λόγου. From this work, not mentioned in the general catalogue, Diog. L. (VII. 39. 40) cites the triple division of philosophy and the order of arrangement for its study, which Zeno recommended. According to Susemihl, this book contained Zeno's epistemology, but, being superseded by the writings of Chrysippus, lost its place in the canon.

(2) καθολικά. Nothing is known of this work but the title (Diog. 4)[1]: Wachsmuth thinks that καθολικὰ περὶ λέξεων is the title of a single work.

(3) περὶ λέξεων (Diog. 4). In Stoic terminology λέξις is defined as φωνὴ ἐγγράμματος as opposed to λόγος which is φωνὴ σημαντικὴ ἀπὸ διανοίας ἐκπεμπομένη (Diog. VII. 56). It is probable, therefore, that this work dealt specially with the definition of terms, and to it may perhaps belong the fragments in which Zeno explains the proper meaning of σολοικίζειν (frags. 30 and 31). Wellmann (Neue Jahrb. für Philol. 107, p. 478) suggests that this treatise gave rise to the oft-repeated accusation made by Cicero that Zeno's innovations in philosophy were solely of a verbal character, and that Chrysippus had defended his master from a similar charge in the work περὶ τοῦ κυρίως κεχρῆσθαι Ζήνωνα τοῖς ὀνόμασιν.

(4) τέχνη (Diog. 4). This is identified by Zeller and

Magnesia, who is specified by name with reference to Xenophon's works (Diog. L. II. 57). Susemihl (Jahrbücher für Philol. 125, p. 741) thinks that the Diogenes catalogue comprises only those writings of Zeno which were included in the Stoic canon, and that the πολιτεία, the τέχνη ἐρωτική, and the διατριβαί were treated as apocryphal while their genuineness was admitted.

[1] See however on frag. 23.

Wellmann with the ἐρωτικὴ τέχνη of § 34, while Wachsmuth writes τέχνη καὶ λύσεις καὶ ἔλεγχοι β' as one title. The third course, which at first sight seems the most natural inasmuch as τέχνη bears this special meaning from Corax and Tisias downwards, is to regard it as an art of rhetoric. The objection to this view is that it is inferred from Cicero de Fin. IV. 7 that no work of Zeno bearing this title was known to Cicero or his authority, but too much reliance need not be placed on this, as it is clear that Zeno's logical treatises had been cast into the shade by the more elaborate performances of Chrysippus. On the other hand, there is a fair amount of evidence to show that Zeno did to some extent busy himself with rhetoric (frags. 25, 26, 27, 32), and though Zeller suggests that the definitions of διήγησις and παράδειγμα may belong to some other Zeno, this does not apply to the passages in Sextus and Quintilian.

(5) λύσεις καὶ ἔλεγχοι β' (Diog. 4). Possibly owing to the influence of Stilpo the Megarian, Zeno may have devoted some attention to this branch of logic, which in general he regards as of less importance[1]: see frag. 6.

II. Physical.

(6) περὶ τοῦ ὅλου (Diog. 4) seems to have been the most important of Zeno's physical writings. Diogenes refers to it as containing Zeno's views about the elements (VII. 136) and the creation and destruction of the world (ib. 142), and quotes from it the statement that there is only one world (ib. 143). It also contained an account of the eclipses of the sun and moon (ib. 145), and explanations of the phenomena of thunder and lightning (ib. 153).

(7) περὶ φύσεως cited by Stobaeus Ecl. I. 5. 15. p. 78, 18. for Zeno's views on the subject of εἱμαρμένη: Krische (p. 367) would identify it with the last named treatise.

---

[1] This is the only work which deals with the formal side of logic, so that Stein's argument in Erkenntnistheorie n. 689 might have been put more strongly. He follows the old reading and speaks of two treatises, τεχνικαὶ λύσεις and ἔλεγχοι β'.

(8) περὶ οὐσίας unnecessarily identified by Wellmann (l.c. p. 442) and Susemihl with περὶ ὅλου and περὶ φύσεως is quoted by Diog. (134) for Zeno's definition of the two first principles, God and Matter.

(9) περὶ σημείων: a treatise on divination (Diog. 4). Thus μαντικὴ is defined in Stob. Ecl. II. 122, 238 as ἐπιστήμη θεωρητικὴ σημείων τῶν ἀπὸ θεῶν ἢ δαιμόνων πρὸς ἀνθρώπινον βίον συντεινόντων. This is no doubt the work referred to by Cic. de Div. I. 3, 6 sed cum Stoici omnia fere illa diffunderent quod et Zeno in suis commentariis quasi semina quaedam sparsisset. Its position in the catalogue makes against Prantl's hypothesis[1], who classes it as a logical work.

(10) περὶ ὄψεως only known by its title (Diog. 4) is regarded as logical by Stein.

(11) Πυθαγορικά (Diog. 4) classed by Wachsmuth as a physical book owing to its position in the catalogue, but nothing else is known concerning it.

III. Ethical.

(12) περὶ τοῦ καθήκοντος (Diog. 4). Here must belong Zeno's definition of duty (frag. 145), from the terms of which Wellmann conjectures without much probability that we should identify this treatise with the following.

(13) περὶ τοῦ κατὰ φύσιν βίου (Diog. 4).

(14) περὶ ὁρμῆς ἢ περὶ ἀνθρώπου φύσεως (Diog. 4). Diogenes quotes the Zenonian definition of the summum bonum from this book (VII. 87); Fabricius (Bibl. Gr. III. 580) proposed to separate this title reading η′ = octo, and Weygoldt adopting this further identified περὶ ἀνθρώπου φύσεως with περὶ φύσεως, but the latter is not an anthropological work.

(15) περὶ παθῶν (Diog. 4) containing the general definition of emotion and the discussion of its several subdivisions, pain, fear, desire and pleasure (ib. 110).

(16) πολιτεία. This seems to have been the most generally known, as it is certainly the most often quoted, of Zeno's writings; it was also one of the earliest in point of

---
[1] I. p. 458. So also Stein, Erkenntnistheorie n. 689.

time, having been written while its author was still under the influence of Cynicism (Diog. 4). Plutarch informs us that it was written as a controversial answer to Plato's Republic. The allusions to it are too numerous to be specified here in detail[1].

(17) περὶ νόμου (Diog. 4). From its position in the catalogue this work must have belonged to the political side of ethics, and Krische's supposition (p. 368) that it treated of the divine law of nature is therefore rebutted. Themist. Or. XXIII. p. 287 A speaks of the νόμοι of Zeno but appears to be referring generally to his philosophical precepts.

(18) περὶ τῆς Ἑλληνικῆς παιδείας (Diog. 4): cf. frag. 167, which however is stated to belong to the πολιτεία.

(19) ἐρωτικὴ τέχνη (Diog. 34). To this book probably belongs the interesting fragment (174) preserved by Clem. Alex. relating to the behaviour suitable to young men.

(20) διατριβαί (Diog. 34): a similar work, as we are told by Diog. whose statement is confirmed by the passages (frags. 179, 180) quoted from it by Sextus. As we are told by Plutarch that something of the same kind was contained in the πολιτεία, we may believe that this and the last three works were written in close connection with it, as shorter appendages dealing with special topics, and before Zeno had worked out the distinctive features of Stoicism. From the general meaning of "lectures, discussions" (for which cf. Plat. Apol. 37 D τὰς ἐμὰς διατριβὰς καὶ τοὺς λόγους) διατριβή seems to have assumed the special sense of a short ethical treatise, if we may trust the definition of Hermogenes (Rhett. Gr. ed. Waltz, t. III. p. 406) διατριβή ἐστι βραχέος διανοήματος ἠθικοῦ ἔκτασις. Zeller's identification with the χρεῖαι is improbable, and Susemihl

---

[1] A summary will be found in Wellmann l. c. p. 437 foll. As regards its Cynic tendencies Susemihl observes:—Wer den Witz machte, er sei bei ihrer Abfassung wohl schon über den Hund gekommen, aber noch nicht über den Schwanz, schrieb eben damit dies Werk einer etwas spätern Zeit, zu frühesten etwa als er von Krates zu Stilpon übergegangen war.

believes that the διατριβαί was excluded from the πίναξ as being an earlier Cynic work.

(21) ἠθικά (Diog. 4). The title is somewhat doubtful, as Wachsmuth reads ἀπομνημονεύματα Κράτητος ἠθικά as a single title, and Wellmann would emend ἢ χρεῖαι for ἠθικά: more probably however it was a collection of short ethical προβλήματα.

IV. Miscellaneous.

(22) προβλημάτων Ὁμηρικῶν ε' (Diog. 4): we learn from Dio. Chrys. 53, 4 that Zeno wrote on the Iliad, Odyssey and Margites, and that his object was to show the general consistency of Homer by explaining that a literal meaning was not to be applied throughout the poems, which ought in many instances to be interpreted allegorically. That he in some cases proposed emendations may be seen from Strabo VII. 3. 6, cf. ib. I. p. 41, XVI. p. 1131. Krische p. 392 shows that there is no foundation for the suggestion that Zeno attributed the Iliad and the Odyssey to different authors.

(23) περὶ ποιητικῆς ἀκροάσεως (Diog. 4). Stein, Erkenntnistheorie n. 689, speaks of this work, the προβλ. Ὁμηρ. and the περὶ Ἑλλην. παιδ. as an educational series, and regards them as an appendix to the πολιτεία.

(24) ἀπομνημονεύματα Κράτητος (Diog. 4) also mentioned by Athen. iv. 162 B as Ζήνωνος ἀπομνημονεύματα, from which Persaeus is said to have made extracts. There seems little doubt that this was identical with the χρεῖαι mentioned in Diog. VI. 91 in connection with Crates, or that Wachsmuth is right in referring to this book the story of Crates and the cobbler (frag. 199). Aphthonius' definition of χρεῖαι runs thus:—ἀπομνημόνευμα σύντομον εὐστόχως ἐπί τι πρόσωπον ἀναφερόμενον.

(25) ἐπιστολαί (Maxim. Floril. ed. Mai, c. 6). This reference was first pointed out by Wachsmuth, see frag. 190.

The passage in Cic. N. D. I. 36 (cum vero Hesiodi Theogoniam interpretatur) led Fabricius to insert among his list of Zeno's writings (III. p. 580) ὑπομνημόνευμα εἰς τὴν Ἡσιόδου θεογονίαν[1], and there can be no doubt from the statements in Proclus and the other Scholiasts[2] that Zeno's labours extended to Hesiod as well as to Homer. It is, however, impossible to say in what work these fragments appeared, and we do not feel much inclined to accept Krische's view (p. 367) that the allegorical explanations of Hesiod were worked into the περὶ ὅλου[3]. May they not belong to the περὶ ποιητικῆς ἀκροάσεως?

It remains to call attention to Clem. Alex. Strom. v. 9. 58 p. 245, S. p. 681, P. ἀλλὰ καὶ οἱ Στωικοὶ λέγουσι Ζήνωνι τῷ πρώτῳ γεγράφθαι τινα ἃ μὴ ῥᾳδίως ἐπιτρέπουσι τοῖς μαθηταῖς ἀναγιγνώσκειν μὴ οὐχὶ πεῖραν δεδωκόσι πρότερος εἰ γνησίως φιλοσοφοῖεν, but similar suggestions of esotericism are made against all the post-Aristotelian schools, and especially against the New Academy. (Mayor on Cic. N. D. I. 11.)

§ 5. *Zeno's style.*

The fragments which survive of Zeno's writings are not sufficient to enable us to form any satisfactory opinion of his style, and it would be unsafe to generalise from such scanty data. We shall therefore only attempt to point out those characteristics about which there can be no doubt.

The later Greek philosophers troubled themselves but little with the graces of literary ornament. Philosophy had now become scientific in its treatment and ceased to be artistic in form. Zeno was no exception to this rule, and was satisfied if he presented his arguments to his readers with directness and perspicacity. In this respect, he has been successful in avoiding obscurity[4], though he lays himself open to the charge of

---

[1] See Flach, Glossen und Scholien zur Hesiodischen Theogonie, p. 29 foll.
[2] Cf. also Diog. L. VIII. 48, Minuc. Felix Octav. XIX. 10 Chrysippus Zenonem interpretatione physiologiae in Hesiodi Homeri Orpheique carminibus imitatur.
[3] Zeller who formerly supported this view (Stoics p. 40) now thinks otherwise (Ph. d. Gr. III.⁴ 1. 32).
[4] Fronto ad Verum Imperat. I. p. 114 ad docendum planissimus Zenon. Cf. Diog. L. VII. 38 ἔστι μὲν οὖν αὐτοῦ καὶ τὰ προσγεγραμμένα βιβλία

abruptness and want of finish. To this tendency was due his custom of couching his arguments in syllogistic formulae, which often served to cloak a somewhat obvious fallacy[1]. This formally logical style subsequently grew so habitual with the Stoics that they earned for themselves the title of διαλεκτικοί. Cicero (N. D. III. 22) especially observes on Zeno's fondness for certain "breues et acutulas conclusiones," and several examples of these are to be found in his remaining fragments. "That which is reasonable is better than that which is unreasonable: but nothing is better than the world: therefore the world is reasonable." "That thing at whose departure the living organism dies is corporeal: but the living organism dies when the breath that has been united with it departs: therefore this breath is corporeal: but this breath is the soul; therefore the soul is corporeal." "That is altogether destructible all whose parts are destructible: but all the parts of the world are destructible; therefore the world is itself destructible," cf. also frags. 59, 60, 61, 129, 130.

Passing to quite a different characteristic, we remark in Zeno's style a certain picturesqueness and love of simile, which perhaps may be regarded as traceable to the Oriental influence of his birth-place[2]. Particularly striking is his observation that those who are in a state of προκοπή may from their dreams discover whether they are making progress, if then the imaginative and emotional part of the soul is clearly seen dispersed and ordered by the power of reason, as in the transparent depth of a waveless calm (frag. 160). Zeno, says Cicero (N. D. II. 22), "similitudine, ut saepe solet, rationem concludit hoc modo." "If tuneful flutes were produced from an olive should not we regard some knowledge of

πολλά, ἐν οἷς ἐλάλησεν ὡς οὐδεὶς τῶν Στωικῶν in which passage Stein, Psychologie n. 2, finds evidence of "die Klarheit und Gediegenheit der Schriften Zenos."

[1] In Cic. N. D. II. 20 the Stoic claims that such arguments "apertiora sunt ad reprehendendum." Elsewhere Cicero calls them "contortulis quibusdam et minutis conclusiunculis nec ad sensum permanentibus." Tusc. II. 42.

[2] Cf. Wellmann l. c. p. 445.

flute-playing as inherent in the olive?" (frag. 63). In like manner he uses the simile of the minister in a royal court to explain his doctrine of the προηγμένον (frag. 131), and likens his ideal commonwealth to a herd grazing on a common pasture (frag. 162).

Not only in elaborate comparisons but also in single expressions may the same picturesque touch be seen. Thus character is said to be the fountain of life (frag. 146), emotion a fluttering of the soul (frag. 137), and happiness the unruffled flow of life (frag. 124).

It will be remembered that Cicero, or his authority, constantly taunts Zeno with being the inventor of new words, and new words only[1]. When scrutinised, this appears to mean not so much that he was a coiner of new expressions, as that for the purposes of his system he appropriated words already in existence as part of his special terminology. Putting aside προηγμένον and ἀποπροηγμένον, which stand on rather a different footing, we may instance προκοπή, ἐνάργεια, συγκατάθεσις, κατόρθωμα, κατάληψις, καθῆκον, ἔννοια(?), and τύπωσις: πρόληψις is certainly not due to Zeno. Yet, although none of these words are new coinages, κατάληψις and καθῆκον are instances specially selected by Cicero in support of his statement.

Diog. Laert. x. 27 speaking of Chrysippus observes:—καὶ τὰ μαρτύρια τοσαῦτα ἐστίν, ὡς ἐκείνων μόνων γέμειν τὰ βιβλία, καθάπερ καὶ παρὰ Ζήνωνί ἐστιν εὑρεῖν καὶ παρὰ Ἀριστοτέλει. The existing fragments however do not justify this assertion.

Finally, although doubtless the circumstances under which the fragments have been preserved render this tendency more noticeable than it otherwise would be, we shall not be wrong in attributing to Zeno a love of precise definition. The school afterwards became famous for their definitions (cf. Sext. Pyrrh. II. 205—212), and it is not unreasonable to suppose that the habit originated with the founder. Instances of this

---

[1] Cic. Fin. III. 5. 15. Tusc. v. 32. 34. Legg. I. 38, etc. Cf. Galen de diff. puls. VIII. 642 ed Kühn Ζήνων δὲ ὁ Κιτιεὺς ἔτι πρότερον ἐτόλμησε καινοτομεῖν τε καὶ ὑπερβαίνειν τὸ τῶν Ἑλλήνων ἔθος ἐν τοῖς ὀνόμασιν.

will occur passim. In fact, his writings in their general character were dogmatic and terse rather than discursive and polemical. The longest extract in the following pages is of dubious authenticity, and therefore for a specimen of the style of our author we would refer to the description of youthful modesty in frag. 174.

§ 6. *Cleanthes.*

In discussing the dates of Zeno's life we have seen that there is good reason to believe that Cleanthes was born in the year B.C. 331, and if so he was only five years younger than Zeno. We also saw that he lived to the age of 99 and presided over the Stoa for 32 years from B.C. 264 till his death in B.C. 232. Against this computation there is to be taken into account the fact that Diogenes (VII. 176) states that he lived to the age of 80 and was a pupil of Zeno for nineteen years. Unless we are prepared to reject the authority of the papyrus altogether, we have in Diogenes' account either a different tradition or a stupid blunder[1]. In any case, Cleanthes was well advanced in life when he became head of the Stoic School.

He was born at Assos, a town in the Troad, but at what age he came to Athens or under what circumstances he became a pupil of Zeno we have no information. His circumstances were those of extreme poverty: he is said to have been a boxer before he embraced philosophy, and the story is well known how he earned his living by drawing water at night, in order to devote his daytime to study[2]. Hence the nickname of Φρεάντλης was given to him by his opponents, while his friends in admiration of his laborious activity called him a "second Heracles." The man's mind is shadowed forth in these anecdotes: the same earnestness and thoroughness which

---

[1] Rohde l. c. p. 622 n. 1 suggests that Diogenes subtracted the 19 years passed under Zeno's tuition from the years of his life, but this is hardly credible.

[2] Diog. L. VII. 168.

characterised his life are no less apparent in his teaching. Whatever he did was marked by energy and completeness and was grounded on deeply-rooted conviction. Philosophy with him was not merely an intellectual exercise, but far more a religious enthusiasm. This religious fervour led him to regard the theological side of philosophy as of the highest importance, and, feeling that the praise of the divine majesty should be set forth in something higher than sober prose, his genius expressed itself in poetical compositions of the greatest merit. It is easy to believe that a man of this character may have proved an unsuccessful teacher, and there is some evidence that under his presidency the Stoic school was in danger of losing ground, cf. Diog. L. VII. 182 οὗτος (Chrysippus) ὀνειδισθεὶς ὑπό τινος ὅτι οὐχὶ παρὰ Ἀρίστωνι μετὰ πολλῶν σχολάζοι, εἰ τοῖς πολλοῖς, εἶπε, προσεῖχον, οὐκ ἂν ἐφιλοσόφησα. His apparent want of success possibly stimulated the unfavourable estimate with which his written works were received by antiquity[1]. The Stoa was now fiercely assailed by various opponents—its ethics by the Epicureans, and its logical theories by Arcesilas. Skill in controversy was more than ever needed, if the position won by Zeno's efforts was to be maintained. Herein lay the special strength of Chrysippus, who was very probably employed in defending Stoicism during his predecessor's life[2], and who surpassed Cleanthes in fineness and subtlety, even if he was inferior to him in depth[3]. Most suggestive, in this view, becomes the passage in Diog. L. VII. 179 διηνέχθη (Chrysippus)...πρὸς Κλεάνθην ᾧ καὶ πολλάκις ἔλεγε μόνης τῆς τῶν δογμάτων διδασκαλίας χρῄζειν, τὰς

[1] There is no direct evidence for this, but the whole of Diogenes' account implies it.
[2] Cf. Diog. L. VII. 182 πρὸς δὲ τὸν κατεξανιστάμενον Κλεάνθους διαλεκτικόν, καὶ προτείνοντα αὐτῷ σοφίσματα, πέπαυσο, εἶπε, παρέλκων τὸν πρεσβύτερον ἀπὸ τῶν πραγματικωτέρων, ἡμῖν δὲ τοῖς νέοις ταῦτα προτίθει.
[3] So Hirzel II. p. 180 "Kleanthes war keine die Begriffe zergliedernde, sondern eine anschauende Natur, er war wohl minder rührig aber vielleicht tiefer angelegt als sein Schüler," and Stein, Psychologie p. 171 "Kleanthes erscheint als der rauhschaalige, mühsam stammelnde, aber tiefe Denker, Chrysipp dagegen als der feinere, leichtbewegliche, elegant vermittelnde Schönredner."

δὲ ἀποδείξεις αὐτὸν εὑρήσειν. The anecdote leads us to infer that Chrysippus was conscious of a want of originality in himself, and a want of combative force in his master.

The position of Cleanthes among the early leaders of the Stoic school has quite recently been subject to a considerable modification in current opinion. He has been generally regarded as merely the exponent of his master's teaching, and as having contributed no new views of his own to the development of the system. This opinion is not without justification in the ancient authorities. Diogenes Laertius expressly asserts that Cleanthes adhered to the same tenets as his predecessor (VII. 168), and that he did not object to be called an ass, declaring that he was only able to bear Zeno's burden (ib. 170). This estimate of his powers was for some time acquiesced in by modern investigators, so that even Zeller says of him (p. 41):—"Cleanthes was in every way adapted to uphold his master's teaching, and to recommend it by the moral weight of his own character, but he was incapable of expanding it more completely, or of establishing it on a wider basis" (see also Krische, Forschungen, pp. 417 and 418). Now however a reaction in his favour has set in, and from a closer scrutiny of the notices concerning him the opinion has been formed that "his contributions were more distinctive and original than those of any other Stoic" (Encycl. Brit. Art. Stoics)[1]. In a question of such importance it is singularly unfortunate that the hand of time has dealt so hardly with him, not only in the actual amount of the fragments which have been preserved to us, but also in their relative importance for his philosophic system. For one fragment of supreme value such as frag. 24 we have six or seven trifling etymologies of the names of the gods,

---

[1] Hirzel has carried this view to an extreme, which the facts do not warrant. At II. p. 137 he curiously says:—"Da wir aber nichts unversucht lassen dürfen, um eine eigentümliche Lehre des Kleanthes herauszubringen." On the other hand, Windelband, writing as late as 1888, says of Cleanthes:—"als Philosoph ist er unbedeutend gewesen" (Müller's Handbuch, v. 292).

of so extravagant a character that it is hard to credit their seriousness. The happy chance that has preserved to us the Hymn to Zeus is counterbalanced by the consideration that we only know of his theory of tension through two or three passages.

Cleanthes divides philosophy into six branches, but in reality this is only the triple division of Zeno, logic being subdivided into dialectic and rhetoric, physics into physics and theology, and ethics into ethics and politics.

In his estimate of logic he resembles Zeno: at least it seems to have played only a subsidiary part in his system, judging both from the number of his recorded works on this subject (about 10 out of a total of 56) and from the insignificance of the fragments which remain. Four only are of any importance, and one of these, his criticism of the Platonic idea, is involved in such obscurity that it will be convenient to defer its consideration for the notes. As it is clear throughout all his teaching that Cleanthes was the most advanced materialist in the Stoic school, so we find that his epistemology rests on a still stronger empirical basis than that of his predecessor Zeno or his successor Chrysippus. Zeno had not defined φαντασία further than by describing it as an impression on the soul. Cleanthes explained this as an actual material concavity impressed by the object, an explanation which found no favour with Chrysippus. There is also high probability in the view which ascribes to Cleanthes the authorship of the "tabula rasa" theory, a theory made celebrated in modern philosophy owing to its adoption by Locke, namely, that when a man is born his mind is like a blank sheet of parchment ready to receive a copy. At least we know of no other Stoic philosopher to whom the introduction of this extreme result of sensualistic views so properly belongs. Since Chrysippus, in express opposition to Cleanthes, defined φαντασία as ἑτεροίωσις ἡγεμονικοῦ, it is less likely that he should have propounded a theory which in its very terms carries out the more materialistic doctrine of his opponent.

We have therefore, in accordance with Stein's view, included the passage of Plutarch, which attributes the doctrine to the Stoics in general, among the fragments of Cleanthes. Stein, however, goes further[1]. Zeno had conceded this much to rationalism, that we derive directly from God the capacity for abstract thought, and that certain notions are the product of this potentiality when actualised by experience. In an ingenious and closely-reasoned argument, whose force it is difficult to reproduce within short limits, Stein contends that this position was thrown over by Cleanthes. According to the latter, the capacity given us by nature is solely that for moral and not for intellectual activity[2]. The belief in God himself does not, as with Zeno, arise from a "certa animi ratio" but rather from induction founded on empirical observation[3]. The conclusion is that Cleanthes is a thoroughgoing advocate of empiricism. But a divergence from the rest of the school in a matter of such importance ought not to be assumed on mere inference resting on ambiguous statements, although were this doctrine explicitly ascribed to Cleanthes in a single passage we should not hesitate to accept it, as being in entire consonance with his general bent of mind. What then is the evidence which Stein produces apart from the passage of Cicero just referred to, which is by no means conclusive? In the first place he appeals to two passages which prove that moral impulses are transmitted to us from our parents and implanted in us by nature[2], and lays stress on the fact that intellectual powers are not included. This, however, is only negative evidence, and for positive proof we are referred to frags. 106 and 100; in the first of these we read that the uneducated differ from the brutes only in shape, and in the second that the undiscerning opinion of the many should be totally discarded. Surely these grounds are insufficient to support the conclusion:

[1] Erkenntnistheorie, pp. 322—328.
[2] Cleanth. frags. 82 and 36.
[3] Cleanth. frag. 52. (Cic. N. D. II. 13.)

Plato himself might have greeted these sentiments with approbation. But a more serious stumbling-block remains in the oft quoted passage from Diog. L. vii. 54. If, as Stein himself admits, Chrysippus substituted πρόληψις for the Zenonian ὀρθὸς λόγος, Cleanthes must of necessity be included in the term ἀρχαιότεροι τῶν Στωικῶν, for there is no one else to whom the words could apply[1]. Were further positive evidence of Cleanthes' "concession to rationalism" required, it would surely be as reasonable to supply it from frag. 21 ψυχήν...ἧς μέρος μετέχοντας ἡμᾶς ἐμψυχοῦσθαι as to deduce the contrary from frags. 100 and 106. For these reasons we feel bound to withhold assent to Stein's hypothesis, until some weightier proof is put forward to support it.

Cleanthes was also involved in a controversy with reference to the sophism known as ὁ κυριεύων and first propounded by the Megarian Diodorus. This sophism was concerned with the nature of the possible; and Cleanthes tries to escape from the dilemma in which Diodorus would have involved him by denying that every past truth is necessary, or, in other words, by asserting that since that which is possible can never become impossible, it is possible for the past to have been otherwise, in the same way that it is possible for a future event to occur even though that event will never take place. Besides this we learn that he introduced the term λεκτὸν in the sense of κατηγόρημα[2], that he left definitions of art and rhetoric, and that he explained the names given to a certain kind of slippers and a drinking-cup.

The first five of the physical fragments need not detain us here, containing, as they do, with one exception, merely a restatement of positions already taken up by Zeno. The exception referred to is the introduction of πνεῦμα as the

---

[1] Stein himself supplies the materials for his own refutation. At p. 267 in dealing with a similar question he says:—"Ohne Not sollte Niemand unter ἀρχαιότεροι andere Stoiker als Zeno Kleanthes und Chrysipp verstehen." Chrysippus is here excluded by the nature of the case: the inference need not be stated.

[2] See Stein, Erkenntnistheorie p. 327.

truest description of the divine permeating essence, which Zeno had characterised as aether. With frag. 17 however we are on a different footing. Cleanthes teaches, according to Cicero's account, that the world is God, and it is significant that, although the same doctrine is attributed by him to Chrysippus (N. D. I. 39), no such statement is found with regard to Zeno (ib. 36). Zeno had indeed declared that God permeates every part of the universe: would he have gone so far as to identify the universe with God? It is true that we find among his fragments (frag. 66) οὐσίαν δὲ θεοῦ τὸν ὅλον κόσμον καὶ τὸν οὐρανόν, but this is not conclusive. Not only the general cast of the expression, but also the addition of the words καὶ τὸν οὐρανόν, make us hesitate to ascribe to these words their full pantheistic sense. However, even if Cleanthes was not following in his master's footsteps, he was only carrying Zeno's teaching to its logical conclusion. The dualism of God and Matter was inconsistent in a materialistic system. But Cleanthes went further. Teaching that God creates the world through the medium of the four elements[1], and teaching that these elements themselves do not remain stable but are in a restless and continual mutation, he was led to search for the cause of this ceaseless movement. The question may be put in another form, why did God create the world? The answer was found in a comparison of the structure of individual things. Every creature is produced at the proper time by means of certain proportions of the soul's parts, which are found in the seed. The soul, however, is material and is braced up by that tension which is elsewhere described as "a stroke of fire." This tension is ever varying and is the cause of movement in the human frame. Now, since the individual is a pattern of the universe[2], the cause of movement in the cosmos must be the tension which permeates all its parts.

[1] Not three in spite of Hirzel's Excursus II. 737—755. See Stein, Psychologie n. 113.
[2] This is probably the meaning of l. 4 in the Hymn to Zeus, where see note. For the doctrine of the macrocosm and the microcosm in general see Stein's Appendix to Psych. pp. 205—214.

Thus the phenomenal world is created and again destroyed by the successive phases in the ever varying tension of the fiery breath, which is at once identified with God and with the universe[1].

As the ἡγεμονικὸν of the human soul is placed in the breast, so did Cleanthes teach that the ruling part of the world is in the sun, to which is due day and night and the seasons of the year. He was led to this opinion by his investigations in natural science. Observing that nothing can exist without warmth, he inferred that warmth constitutes the essence of things. Since however warmth is given to the whole world and to each individual thing from the sun, the sun must be the ἡγεμονικὸν of the world. In the sun is the fiery breath found in its purest form, and at the conflagration, when the world is destroyed, the sun will assimilate to itself moon and stars and all the heavenly bodies. If Aristarchus therefore taught that the earth revolves round the sun, he was guilty of impiety for displacing the earth, which is the hearth of the world. The sun is fed by exhalations from the sea, and moves in an oblique course through the zodiac. The stars are formed of the same fiery substance as the sun, and, as the sun is the cause of life to everything, its essence must be akin not to the earthly fire, which is destructive, but to the creative. As the sun strikes the world with his rays, he is called a plectrum. Sun, moon, and stars are alike conical in shape.

Cleanthes proved that the soul is material by two syllogistic arguments, founded on the mental resemblance between parents and children and the sympathy of the soul with the body. So far indeed did his materialism extend that he even maintained that the act of walking was the extension of πνεῦμα from the ἡγεμονικὸν to the feet. In other respects he seems to have concurred in Zeno's psychology, teaching that the

---

[1] For the tension-theory in general see Stein, Psychologie, pp. 73 and 74, nn. 109 and 110. The notion of τόνος is not entirely unknown to Zeno: cf. Zeno frags. 56, 67, 103.

reasoning powers are developed by external impressions, and that all souls exist after death till the time of the general conflagration. His views on zoology comprise a statement that the pig was provided with a soul to keep him fresh for sacrifice and a curious anecdote proving the intelligence of ants.

To the theological branch of physics Cleanthes devoted considerable attention[1], but in practice no sharp dividing line can be drawn between physics and religion, since in the Stoic system they necessarily overlap. It is hardly necessary to analyse the Hymn to Zeus, but it may be observed that Cleanthes refuses to admit that evil is due to the divine agency, a remark which must be taken in connection with the statement of Chalcidius that, while Chrysippus identified fate with forethought, Cleanthes distinguished them. Five distinct reasons are given for the existence of God:—(1) the ascending series of organisms from plants to man, which shows that there must be some being who is best of all, and this cannot be man with all his imperfections and frailties, (2) the foreknowledge of coming events, (3) the fruitfulness of the earth and other natural blessings, (4) the occurrence of portents outside the ordinary course of nature, and (5) the regular movements of the heavenly bodies. Zeus i.e. $πῦρ$ $ἀείζῳον$ is the only eternal god; the rest are perishable and will be destroyed at the $ἐκπύρωσις$. The popular religion is a representation of truth, but requires interpretation if we would understand its real significance. Thus, the Eleusinian mysteries are an allegory; Homer, if properly understood, is a witness to truth; the very names given to Zeus, Persephone, Dionysus, Apollo, and Aphrodite are indications of the hidden meaning which is veiled but not perverted by the current belief, and the same is true of the myths of Heracles and Atlas. It is difficult now-a-days to enter into the spirit with which the Stoic school pursued these etymological fancies. At times it is hard not to acquiesce in Plutarch's opinion (see

---

[1] Cic. N. D. II. 63, III. 63.

frag. 55), who attributes them to παιδιά and εἰρωνεία. But, if this is so, it is impossible to account for the extreme diligence, which was expended upon them. Rather, having once taken up the position that the popular belief can only be explained by Stoic methods, they were often driven to defend it by arguments which they must themselves have perceived to be of questionable validity. For example, Cleanthes may not have been satisfied with the derivation of Dionysus from διανύσαι, but his explanation could not be disproved, and he was bound to explain the name somehow, since, so long as it remained unexplained, it was a standing objection to his method[1].

The number of ethical works attributed to Cleanthes, 32 out of a total of 56, shows that he paid considerable attention to this branch of philosophy. Yet, in the main, he seems to have accepted the principles laid down by Zeno, except in those cases where his physical innovations demanded a separate treatment, and many of the fragments which have come down to us deal rather with the practical than with the theoretical side of morals. This agrees with what we are told as to the titles of his books (see infra, p. 52). Defining the aim of life and happiness in the same manner as Zeno, Cleanthes laid special stress on the agreement with the general law of nature, while Chrysippus is said to have emphasised the necessity for agreement with human nature no less than with nature in general. This view is thoroughly in consonance with the general bias of Cleanthes' teaching. One of the most striking and important of his doctrines is the parallelism between the macrocosm of the world and the microcosm of the individual. The more, therefore, that man brings himself into harmony with the spirit which breathes throughout the universe, the more does he fulfil the rôle to which he is destined. The same spirit may be traced in the

[1] The etymologies of Plato in the Cratylus are quite as bad as any of these, but they are professedly in part at least playful. The most recent exposition of this dialogue is by Mr Heath in the Journal of Philology XVII. 192.

lines in which the subordination of the individual to the decrees of Zeus and of destiny is so forcibly advocated. Cleanthes is perhaps the author of a distinction which subsequently became of some importance whereby happiness is described as σκοπός, and the attainment of happiness as τέλος[1].

The doctrine of τόνος was applied by Cleanthes, with important results, to two branches of his master's ethical system, namely, the nature of virtue and the emotions. Zeno had identified virtue with φρόνησις, but Cleanthes, while retaining the intellectual basis which Zeno made the groundwork of virtue, sought to explain its character more precisely. Again he had recourse to his physical theories. Every body contains within it a material air-current with ever-varying tension. When this tension is strong enough to perform its fitting duties it is regarded as strength and power, and this strength and power as applied to different spheres of activity gives rise to the four virtues ἐγκράτεια, ἀνδρεία, δικαιοσύνη, and σωφροσύνη. It will be observed that ἐγκράτεια here occupies the position which by Chrysippus and his followers is assigned to φρόνησις. Thus Cleanthes fortifies his main position, that strength of tension is the necessary starting-point of virtue, by a tacit appeal to the authority of Socrates, who had pointed to ἐγκράτεια as κρηπὶς ἀρετῆς. A recurrence to the same teacher may also be recognised in the approbation with which his identification of τὸ συμφέρον with τὸ δίκαιον is cited. To return to τόνος; when the tension is relaxed, a weakness of soul follows, and in this weakness is to be found the explanation of the πάθη. Thus the essence of virtue and emotion, which Zeno had left unexplained on the physical side, is traced to a single source, and this source is the same power which is the origin of all movement and life.

The application of τόνος to the πάθη leads us to the consideration of another question, not indeed directly raised by the fragments of Zeno and Cleanthes, but having an important

[1] See however Hirzel II. p. 557.

bearing on our general view of their ethical doctrines. What position do the πάθη occupy in the classification of goods? Zeno classified ἡδονή and therefore presumably the other πάθη among the ἀδιάφορα, and the reason is not far to seek. He regarded πάθη as distinct from vice, because they have nothing to do with ignorance (Plut. Virt. Mor. 10 τὰς ἐπιτάσεις τῶν παθῶν καὶ τὰς σφοδρότητας οὔ φασι γίγνεσθαι κατὰ τὴν κρίσιν ἐν ᾗ τὸ ἁμαρτητικόν). Only κακία or τὸ μέτεχον κακίας is κακόν, according to Zeno, and πάθος is neither, but rather an ἐπιγέννημα. (Cf. τὰ ἐπιγιγνόμενα κρίσεσιν Zeno frag. 139 and for the distinction between ἐπιγεννήματα and μετέχοντα cf. Diog. L. VII. 95.) That this applies to all the πάθη and not merely to ἡδονή is made clear by the following considerations. In frag. 169 Zeno recommends the rational use of wealth ὅπως ἀδεῆ καὶ ἀθαύμαστον πρὸς τἆλλα τὴν διάθεσιν τῆς ψυχῆς ἔχοντες ὅσα μήτε καλά ἐστι μήτε αἰσχρὰ τοῖς μὲν κατὰ φύσιν ὡς ἐπὶ πολὺ χρῶνται τῶν δ' ἐναντίων μηδὲν δεδοικότες λόγῳ καὶ μὴ φόβῳ τούτων ἀπέχωνται. This shows that the ἀδιάφορα are the field of φόβος, and for λύπη we may refer to Cic. Tusc. III. 77 nihil enim esse malum quod turpe non sit si *lugenti* persuaseris...et tamen non satis mihi videtur vidisse hoc Cleanthes, suscipi aliquando *aegritudinem* posse ex eo ipso, quod esse summum malum Cleanthes ipse fateatur. It is noteworthy, moreover, that Cleanthes, who is allowed to have been the severest opponent of pleasure[1], declares ἡδονὴν μήτε κατὰ φύσιν εἶναι μήτε ἀξίαν ἔχειν ἐν τῷ βίῳ (frag. 88) but does not venture to class it as κακόν. The result of this discussion is that Zeno and Cleanthes did not class λύπη and φόβος with κακά, and therefore Wachsmuth cannot be right in attributing to Zeno a passage in Stobaeus[2] where this classification is implied.

---

[1] Zeller, Stoics p. 237. The remarks in the text are intended to obviate the difficulty as to the classification of ἡδονή suggested by Heinze, de Stoicorum affectibus p. 37.

[2] See Wachsmuth's Stobaeus vol. II. p. 58. That this question was much debated appears from Cic. Tusc. IV. 29. Some appear to have held that πάθος was κακὸν but not κακία (Stob. l. c.), because πάθος is κίνησις but κακία is διάθεσις (Cic. l. c. 30).

That this view did not continue to be the orthodox view of the school after their time is possible, but to pursue the subject further would be foreign to our purpose.

The uncorrupted impulses given by nature tend towards virtue, and, when they are suitably developed, wisdom founded on firm apprehension, so that it can never be lost, follows in due course. Secure in the possession of virtue, the wise man partakes of the same excellence as God.

In the treatise περὶ ἡδονῆς Cleanthes seems to have engaged in a spirited controversy with the Epicureans, and to have attacked their moral teaching, just as he perhaps assailed their physics in the work περὶ ἀτόμων. Pleasure is a mere useless ornament: it possesses no value whatever, nay, it is absolutely contrary to nature. If, as we are told, pleasure is the ultimate goal of life, it was an evil spirit which gave to mankind the faculty of wisdom. He sarcastically likened his opponents' position to an imaginary picture in which Pleasure, seated on a throne in gaudy apparel, is ministered to by the virtues, who form her willing slaves, declaring that this service is the sole reason of their existence.

Passing to those fragments, which seem more strictly to belong to the παραινετικὸς or ὑποθετικὸς τόπος (i.e. the region of applied morals), we notice that Cleanthes frequently refers his precepts to the general principle, which is a leading characteristic of Stoic morals, namely, that virtuous conduct depends not on the nature of the deed but on the disposition of the agent. The same action may be either vicious or virtuous, according to the motive which prompts its performance. To many of the subjects which fall under this branch separate treatises were devoted, among which are the books περὶ εὐβουλίας, περὶ χάριτος, περὶ φθονερίας, περὶ τιμῆς, περὶ δόξης, περὶ φιλίας, περὶ συμποσίου κ.τ.λ. To the book περὶ χάριτος we may assign three of the extant fragments (frags. 97, 98, 99) all of which are preserved by Seneca in the de Beneficiis. The theory of consolation (frags. 93 and 94) may belong either to the περὶ ἀρωγῆς or the περὶ φιλίας. Frags. 100—103 all in verse and one in hexameter metre ought to be referred to the περὶ δόξης.

One solitary fragment attests the political studies of Cleanthes, to which at least four of the works in the catalogue must be referred.

The result of our investigation has been to show conclusively that all those doctrines which are most characteristic of the true essence of Stoicism were contributed by Zeno and Cleanthes. To Zeno belong the establishment of the logical criterion, the adaptation of Heraclitean physics, and the introduction of all the leading ethical tenets. Cleanthes revolutionised the study of physics by the theory of tension, and the development of pantheism, and by applying his materialistic views to logic and ethics brought into strong light the mutual interdependence of the three branches. The task of Chrysippus was to preserve rather than to originate, to reconcile inconsistencies, to remove superfluous outgrowths, and to maintain an unbroken line of defence against his adversaries. Although it might seem to many that this less ambitious rôle requires less brilliant capacities in its performer, yet Chrysippus was commonly regarded as the second founder of the Stoa, and the general opinion of his contemporaries is aptly summed up in the line εἰ μὴ γὰρ ἦν Χρύσιππος οὐκ ἂν ἦν Στοά (Diog. L. VII. 183). The reason of this has been already indicated. The extraordinary fertility of the writer commanded admiration even where it failed to win assent, nor was his dialectical skill (Diog. L. VII. 180) a matter of small moment. Though logic was only the propaedeutic of philosophy, it was the battleground of the fiercest controversy. Vitally opposed in other respects, Epicureans and Stoics here at least were allied in maintaining the possibility of knowledge against the universal scepticism of the New Academy. It is not surprising, therefore, that the foremost champion of dogmatism should have taken the highest place in the Stoic triad.

§ 7. *The writings of Cleanthes.*

The relation of the poetical to the prose writings of Cleanthes has not been accurately determined, and the evidence does not enable us to decide whether the former were published separately from, or in conjunction with the latter. The only indication we possess is in frag. 49, in which Cleanthes describes poetry as being peculiarly adapted to theological subjects. Yet the only book in the catalogue with a distinctively theological title is the work περὶ θεῶν, and there is direct evidence that this contained etymological explanations of the names of the gods, and that part of it, at any rate, was written in prose. Krische p. 422 supposes that the Hymn to Zeus was a poetical supplement incorporated with this treatise, but such treatment would surely have produced highly incongruous results. It is possible that we ought to separate Cleanthes the philosopher from Cleanthes the poet, and to infer that works published by him in the latter capacity were not included in the list of his philosophical treatises. At the same time we should remember that Chrysippus (Galen. plac. Hipp. et Plat. p. 315) and Posidonius (ib. p. 399 ῥήσεις τε ποιητικὰς παρατίθεται καὶ ἱστορίας παλαιῶν πράξεων μαρτυρούσας οἷς λέγει) were accustomed to freely interpolate poetical quotations in their prose writings, and Cleanthes may have composed his own florilegia, just as Cicero translated from the Greek where the Latin poets failed him (Tusc. D. II. 26). A catalogue of the titles known to us is subjoined; where not otherwise indicated, the source of reference is Diog. L. VII. 174, 175.

I. Logical.

(1) περὶ ἰδίων. For ἴδια cf. Ar. Top. i. 5, p. 102 a 17: the essential attributes of a thing are its ἴδια: thus γραμματικῆς δεκτικός is an ἴδιον of man.

(2) περὶ τῶν ἀπόρων.

(3) περὶ διαλεκτικῆς.

(4) περὶ τρόπων. Probably this is logical rather than rhetorical.

(5) περὶ κατηγορημάτων.. To this book may be referred frag. 7.

(6) περὶ μεταλήψεως (Athen. XI. 467 d, 471 b).

(7) περὶ τοῦ κυριεύοντος (Arr. Epict. II. 19. 9). Krische p. 427 n. gives to this work the title περὶ δυνατῶν, but Epict. distinctly contrasts Chrysippus' work bearing the general title with a treatise by Cleanthes on the particular fallacy (Κλεάνθης δ' ἰδίᾳ γέγραφε περὶ τούτου), Wachsmuth, Comm. I. p. 18.

(8) περὶ τέχνης may be the same work as the ars rhetorica mentioned in Cic. Fin. IV. 3, but if so it is out of its place in the catalogue, where it appears between nos. 4 and 5 of the physical books.

(9) περὶ τοῦ λόγου γ'. This and the following book appear in the catalogue among the ethical works.

(10) περὶ ἐπιστήμης.

Stein, Erkenntnistheorie n. 722, counts among the logical works the books περὶ χρόνου περὶ αἰσθήσεως and περὶ δόξης, but omits, probably by an oversight, the book περὶ τρόπων. He also observes that from the number of books treating of the theory of knowledge Cleanthes must have displayed more activity in treating of the subject than the remaining fragments would lead us to suppose.

II. Physical.

(1) περὶ χρόνου.

(2) περὶ τῆς Ζήνωνος φυσιολογίας β'.

(3) τῶν Ἡρακλείτου ἐξηγήσεων δ'. Cf. Diog. L. IX. 15 πλεῖστοί τε εἰσὶν ὅσοι ἐξήγηνται αὐτοῦ τὸ σύγγραμμα. καὶ γὰρ Ἀντισθένης καὶ Ἡρακλείδης ὁ Ποντικὸς Κλεάνθης τε καὶ Σφαῖρος ὁ Στωικός. The influence of Heraclitus on Cleanthes has been variously estimated. Hirzel is the chief advocate in favour of it, holding e.g. that Cleanthes agreed with him in his hypo-

thesis of three elements, and that τόνος is traceable to παλίντονος (or παλίντροπος) ἁρμονίη. Stein's more moderate estimate appears to us truer.

(4) περὶ αἰσθήσεως.

(5) πρὸς Δημόκριτον, perhaps the same as περὶ τῶν ἀτόμων (Diog. L. vii. 134) so Krische p. 430.

(6) πρὸς Ἀρίσταρχον, see on frag. 27. Some have erroneously supposed that the Aristarchus here referred to was the Homeric critic, whose date is a century later than Cleanthes; cf. Krische p. 394 and Wilamowitz-Moellendorf in Hermes xx. 631.

(7) ὑπομνήματα φυσικά (Plut. Sto. Rep. c. 8).

The books next in order treat of θεολογικόν.

(8) ἀρχαιολογία has been identified with μυθικά (Athen. xiii. 572 e, Porphyr. vit. Pyth. c. 1), but the genuineness of the latter work is seriously questioned. Müller frag. hist. Gr. ii. p. 5. 9. 11 thinks that the τὰ κατὰ πόλιν μυθικὰ of Neanthes of Cyzicus (cf. Plut. quaest. syrup. i. 10) is referred to in both passages and Zeller Pre-Socr. i. p. 308 says:—The Cleanthes of Porphyry is certainly not the Stoic but most likely a misspelling for Neanthes of Cyzicus.

(9) περὶ θεῶν, cf. Plut. de vit. aer. alien. c. 7. To this work Wachsmuth refers frags. 47. 54. 56. 57. 58. 59. 60. 61. 62. 63. Krische (p. 418, 422) also the statements in Cic. N. D. i. 37 (frags. 14—17) and the hymn to Zeus (frag. 48). See also Osann Praef. Cornut. p. ix.

(10) περὶ γιγάντων.

(11) περὶ Ὑμεναίου. This is a curious title. Perhaps it should rather be classed as ethical. Cf. Persaeus' book περὶ γάμου (Diog. L. vii. 36).

(12) περὶ τοῦ ποιητοῦ. This book treated of the interpretation of Homer, and Wachsmuth accordingly refers to it frags. 55. 65. 66. 67. To these should be added frag. 63 and perhaps frag. 54.

(13) θεομαχία (ps.-Plut. de Fluv. v. 3. 4) was identified by Krische with the book περὶ γιγάντων supra (p. 434) but this

and the next book are rightly described by Wachsmuth as "ficta ab impostore ps.-Plutarcho," see note on frag. 69.

(14) περὶ ὁρῶν, ib. v. 17. 4.

Fabricius Bibl. Gr. III. p. 552 infers from Simplic. in Epict. Man. c. 78 that one of Cleanthes' works bore the title Ἰαμβεῖα, but the words simply mean "in his well known Iambic lines."

III. Ethical.

(1) πρὸς Ἥριλλον. For Herillus see Zeller p. 42.
(2) περὶ ὁρμῆς β'.
(3) περὶ τοῦ καθήκοντος γ'.
(4) περὶ εὐβουλίας.
(5) περὶ χάριτος.
(6) προτρεπτικός. Cf. Diog. L. VII. 91.
(7) περὶ ἀρετῶν.
(8) περὶ εὐφυΐας.
(9) περὶ Γοργίππου "num πρὸς Γόργιππον qui idem fuerit atque Γοργιππίδης ad quem complura scripta Chrysippus misit?" Wachsm. Mohnike p. 100 wishes to read Γοργιππίδου.
(10) περὶ φθονερίας.
(11) περὶ ἔρωτος. Here belongs perhaps frag. 108.
(12) περὶ ἐλευθερίας.
(13) ἐρωτικὴ τέχνη.
(14) περὶ τιμῆς.
(15) περὶ δόξης.
(16) πολιτικός. Here belongs frag. 104, cf. Plut. Sto. Rep. c. 2.
(17) περὶ βουλῆς.
(18) περὶ νόμων.
(19) περὶ τοῦ δικάζειν.
(20) περὶ ἀρωγῆς.
(21) περὶ τέλους.
(22) περὶ καλῶν.
(23) περὶ πράξεων.
(24) περὶ βασιλείας.

(25) περὶ φιλίας.

(26) περὶ συμποσίου. Persaeus wrote συμποτικὰ ὑπομνήματα or διάλογοι (Athen. IV. 162 b, XIII. 607 a).

(27) περὶ τοῦ ὅτι ἡ αὐτὴ ἀρετὴ ἀνδρὸς καὶ γυναικός. So Antisthenes also taught (Diog. L. VI. 12) and cf. Socrates in Xen. Symp. II. 9. Otherwise Aristotle, Pol. I. 13. 1260 a 21. Eth. VIII. 14. 1162 a 26.

(28) περὶ τοῦ τὸν σοφὸν σοφιστεύειν.

(29) περὶ χρειῶν.

(30) διατριβῶν β'.

(31) περὶ ἡδονῆς. For this book see Krische p. 430 foll.

(32) περὶ χαλκοῦ (Diog. L. VII. 14). The title of this book has been much discussed. It was altered to περὶ χάριτος by Casaubon, to περὶ χρόνου by Menagius, Fabricius and Mohnike, and to περὶ χρειῶν by Wachsmuth. It is possible that χαλκοῦ is due to the scribe's eye catching the word χαλκὸν which closely precedes in the citation, and, if so, we have no clue to the true title.

(33) περὶ στοᾶς. This book is supposed to have existed from a mutilated passage of Philodemus περὶ φιλοσόφων in vol. Herc. VIII. col. 13 v. 18 ὡς αἵ τ' ἀναγραφαὶ τῶν π(ι)νάκων (αἵ)τε βιβλιοθῆκαι σημαίνουσιν, (παρὰ Κλ)εάνθῃ ἐν τῷ περὶ στ(οᾶς ἐ)σ(τιν) Διογένους αὕτη ἡ μνήμη.

THE FRAGMENTS OF ZENO.

1. Diog. L. VII. 39, τριμερῆ φασὶν εἶναι τὸν κατὰ φιλοσοφίαν λόγον. εἶναι γὰρ αὐτοῦ τὸ μέν τι φυσικόν· τὸ δὲ ἠθικόν· τὸ δὲ λογικόν. οὕτω δὲ πρῶτος διεῖλε Ζήνων ὁ Κιτιεὺς ἐν τῷ περὶ λόγου.

The triple division of philosophy was first brought into prominence by Zeno and the Stoics, though it seems to have been adopted before them by Xenocrates and the Peripatetics, cf. Sext. Emp. adv. Math. VII. 16 ἐντελέστερον δὲ...οἱ εἰπόντες τῆς φιλοσοφίας τὸ μέν τι εἶναι φυσικὸν τὸ δὲ ἠθικὸν τὸ δὲ λογικόν· ὧν δυνάμει μὲν Πλάτων ἐστὶν ἀρχηγός, περὶ πολλῶν μὲν φυσικῶν πολλῶν δὲ ἠθικῶν οὐκ ὀλίγων δὲ λογικῶν διαλεχθείς· ῥητότατα δὲ οἱ περὶ τὸν Ξενοκράτην καὶ οἱ ἀπὸ τοῦ περιπάτου ἔτι δὲ οἱ ἀπὸ τῆς στοᾶς ἔχονται τῆσδε τῆς διαιρέσεως. Ar. Top. I. p. 105 b 19 ἔστι δ' ὡς τύπῳ περιλαβεῖν τῶν προτάσεων καὶ τῶν προβλημάτων μέρη τρία· αἱ μὲν γὰρ ἠθικαὶ προτάσεις εἰσίν, αἱ δὲ φυσικαί, αἱ δὲ λογικαὶ must not be taken as indicating that Aristotle had in view the triple division (see Waitz *in loc.*). Cicero speaking of Speusippus, Aristotle, Xenocrates, Polemo, and Theophrastus says (de Fin. IV. 4):—totam philosophiam tres in partes diviserunt, quam partitionem a Zenone esse retentam videmus. In Acad. I. 19 he wrongly attributes the division to Plato (fuit ergo jam accepta a Platone philosophandi ratio triplex): Diog. L. III. 56 only says that Plato introduced the διαλεκτικὸς τόπος, not that he recognised the triple division. With the Stoics it became so fundamental that they did not hesitate to refer to it the three heads of Cerberus and Athene's name Τριτογένεια (Zeller, pp. 363, 364). Hirzel (de logica Stoicorum in Sauppe's Satura Philologa, p. 71) thinks that Zeno was the inventor of the term λογική in place of Xenocrates' διαλεκτική.

2. Diog. L. VII. 40, ἄλλοι δὲ πρῶτον μὲν τὸ λογικὸν τάττουσι· δεύτερον δὲ τὸ φυσικόν· καὶ τρίτον τὸ ἠθικόν. ὧν ἐστι Ζήνων ἐν τῷ περὶ λόγου.

As logic is obviously the least important to the Stoics of the three divisions, Zeno regarded Ethics, not Physics, as the kernel of his system. The authorities are however very confusing on this point, for of Chrysippus, who is coupled with Zeno in Diog., Plut. Sto. Rep. 9, 1 says:— τούτων (μερῶν) δεῖν τάττεσθαι πρῶτον μὲν τὰ λογικά, δεύτερα δὲ τὰ ἠθικά, τρίτα δὲ τὰ φυσικά—and yet in the same passage we find attributed to Chrysippus the statement οὐδ' ἄλλου τινὸς ἕνεκεν τῆς φυσικῆς θεωρίας παραληπτῆς οὔσης ἢ πρὸς τὴν περὶ ἀγαθῶν ἢ κακῶν διάστασιν, which shows that he must have regarded ethics as containing the consummation of philosophy. Again, the Stoics compared the three parts of philosophy to a fruit garden surrounded by a wall and also to an egg, but whereas according to Diog. (VII. 40) physics are likened to the fruit of the garden and the yolk of the egg, in Sextus (adv. Math. VII. 17—19) they are compared to the trees in the garden and the white of the egg, having changed places with ethics. But both alike in recording the comparison, which Posidonius thought more apt, yield the place of honour to ethics, which are compared to the soul of man. It is not improbable, as Wellmann and Stein (Erkenntnistheorie, p. 302) think, that the two former of these similes may be due to Zeno, on whòse fondness for such similes we have remarked in the Introd. p. 33, but there is no evidence to decide. The confusion about the whole matter seems to have arisen from the distinction made by the Stoics between the order of relative importance and the order of teaching (cf. Sext. l. c. 22, 23). At any rate, as regards Zeno, it is most natural to suppose that the pupil of Crates and the admirer of Socrates placed ethics in the forefront of his system. [Ritter and Preller, § 390 n. and Ueberweg, p. 192 apparently regard as the earlier view that which gave physics the most important position, but see Stein, Psychologie n. 7.]

LOGICA.

3. Arr. Epict. diss. IV. 8, 12, θεωρήματα τοῦ φιλοσόφου...ἃ Ζήνων λέγει γνῶναι τὰ τοῦ λόγου στοιχεῖα, ποῖόν τι ἕκαστον αὐτῶν ἐστι καὶ πῶς ἁρμόττεται πρὸς ἄλληλα καὶ ὅσα τούτοις ἀκόλουθά ἐστι.

It is difficult, in the absence of Zeno's context, to decide the exact meaning of τὰ τοῦ λόγου στοιχεῖα. There is no doubt that the Stoics used this phrase in the sense of "parts of speech" (Diog. VII. 58 ῥῆμα δέ ἐστι... στοιχεῖον λόγου ἄπτωτον), but this meaning is not general enough and is certainly excluded by the words immediately preceding in Epictetus τί τέλος; μή τι φορεῖν τρίβωνα; οὔ, ἀλλὰ τὸ ὀρθὸν ἔχειν τὸν λόγον. It is suggested, therefore, that Zeno is here expressing, possibly in an earlier work, the nominalism of Antisthenes and that λόγου στοιχεῖα = the (indefinable) elements of definition. It is now generally admitted (see e.g. Dr Jackson in Journ. Phil. XIII. 262) that the opinion stated at some length by Socrates in Theaet. p. 201 E—202 C is that of Antisthenes, and the words στοιχεῖον and λόγος in this sense must have belonged to his terminology (see the whole passage and especially τὰ μὲν πρῶτα οἰονπερεὶ στοιχεῖα...λόγον οὐκ ἔχει 201 E, οὕτω δὴ τὰ μὲν στοιχεῖα ἄλογα καὶ ἄγνωτα εἶναι, αἰσθητὰ δέ, cf. 206 E τὸ ἐρωτηθέντα τί ἕκαστον δυνατὸν εἶναι τὴν ἀπόκρισιν διὰ τῶν στοιχείων ἀποδοῦναι τῷ ἐρομένῳ): with this should be compared the passages in Ar. Metaph. VIII. 3. 1043 b 23, XIV. 3. 1091 a 7 ὥστ' οὐσίας ἔστι μὲν ἧς ἐνδέχεται εἶναι ὅρον καὶ λόγον οἷον τῆς συνθέτου ἐάν τε αἰσθητὴ ἐάν τε νοητὴ ᾖ· ἐξ ὧν δ' αὕτη πρώτων οὐκ ἔστιν. It is not a necessary inference from this passage that Zeno treated ὀρθὸς λόγος as κριτήριον ἀληθείας, or that he and Cleanthes are the ἄλλοι τινες τῶν ἀρχαιοτέρων Στωικῶν whom Diogenes (VII. 54) mentions as holding this opinion, although Hirzel thinks this established, comparing frag. 157 (Untersuchungen, II. pp. 14 f. 23). Indeed it is difficult to understand how, except on the hypothesis of a change of opinion, this is reconcilable with the fact that Zeno introduced the φαντασία καταληπτική, as will appear hereafter. Hirzel further remarks:—"Unter den τῶν ἀπὸ τῆς Στοᾶς τινες des Alexand. Aphrod. zur Topik (schol. Arist. p. 256 b 14) welche den λόγος durch τί ἦν definirten könnte Zenon gemeint sein." The latter part of this note requires some modification if Stein's view referred to in the Introd. p. 9 be accepted. The same writer (Erkenntnistheorie, p. 90, 91) explains γνῶναι τὰ τοῦ λόγου στοιχεῖα as "die Erkenntnis der Elemente des Denkens d. h. wie das Denken beschaffen sei und worin die gegenseitige Verbindung der Gedanken bestehe und welche Konsequenzen sich aus dieser Gedankenverbindung ergeben."

4. Arr. Epict. diss. I. 17. 10, 11, καὶ τὰ λογικὰ ἄκαρπά ἐστι...καὶ περὶ τούτου μὲν ὀψόμεθα, εἰ δ' οὖν καὶ τοῦτο δοίη τις, ἐκεῖνα ἀπαρκεῖ, ὅτι τῶν ἄλλων ἐστι διακριτικὰ καὶ ἐπισκεπτικὰ καὶ ὡς ἄν τις εἴποι μετρητικὰ καὶ στατικά· τίς λέγει ταῦτα; μόνος Χρύσιππος καὶ Ζήνων καὶ Κλεάνθης;

This and the two following fragments show us the view which Zeno took of the value of logical studies, which were recommended not so much on account of the value of the results obtained, as because they enable us to test the theories and expose the fallacies of others and to clear the ground for further enquiries, cf. Ar. Top. I. 104 b 1 τοῦτο δ' ἴδιον ἢ μάλιστα οἰκεῖον τῆς διαλεκτικῆς ἐστιν· ἐξεταστικὴ γὰρ οὖσα πρὸς τὰς ἁπασῶν τῶν μεθόδων ἀρχὰς ὁδὸν ἔχει, cf. also the title ὄργανον given to Aristotle's logical treatises (Waitz II. 294) and the name κανονικὴ adopted by the Epicureans. For the distinction between the Peripatetic and Stoic views of logic see Stein, Erkenntnistheorie n. 207. Hirzel's remarks about Zeno (de log. Stoic. p. 72) do not take into account this evidence.

στατικά, "weighing." The word is used by Plato, cf. Phileb. 55 E οἷον πασῶν που τεχνῶν ἄν τις ἀριθμητικὴν χωρίζῃ καὶ μετρητικὴν καὶ στατικήν, ὡς ἔπος εἰπεῖν. Charmid. 166 B.

5. Stob. Ecl. II. 2. 12 p. 22, 12 Wachsm. [vulgo Floril. LXXXII. 5], Ζήνων τὰς τῶν διαλεκτικῶν τέχνας εἴκαζε τοῖς δικαίοις μέτροις οὐ πυρὸν οὐδ' ἄλλο τι τῶν σπουδαίων μετροῦσιν ἀλλ' ἄχυρα καὶ κόπρια.

At first sight this and the next fragm. appear contradictory, but probably this is directed against some particular opponents. The Megarians, the Eristics of this period, are most likely to be meant, and we know that they were often called διαλεκτικοί, as the Stoics themselves are by Sextus (Zeller, Socrates etc. p. 250 n. 3). Moreover Alexinus was a determined opponent of Zeno

(Diog. II. 109 διεφέρετο δὲ μάλιστα πρὸς Ζήνωνα) and Sextus tells us how he controverted Zeno's proof that the world is λογικός (Math. IX. 107). Stein thinks that the inconsistency is to be explained by the importance attributed by Zeno to the question of the criterion (Erkenntnistheorie, p. 303), but surely διαλεκτικῶν in frag. 5 and διαλεκτικὴν in frag. 6 must refer to the same branch of logic. The explanation is however perfectly valid to explain the difference of statement between Cic. Fin. IV. 9 and id. Acad. I. 40. τέχνας = treatises.

δικαίοις: so the three best MSS AM and S: εἰκαίοις adopted by Mein. from MS B (late and untrustworthy) is virtually a conjecture. Wachsm. suggests χυδαίοις but, on the interpretation given above, δικαίοις is more forcible: the methods are good enough (cf. μετρητικά frag. 4) but they are put to base uses, i.e. to mere quibbling. After μέτροις Gaisf. add. οἷς.

If the fragment be interpreted quite generally as a depreciation of logical studies, we have here an approximation to the position of Aristo (Stob. Ecl. II. 2. 14, 18, 22 = Floril. LXXXII. 7, 11, 18) in one of the points on which he severed himself from the Stoic school.

6. Plut. Sto. Rep. VIII. 2, ἔλυε δὲ (scil. Zeno) σοφίσματα καὶ τὴν διαλεκτικὴν ὡς τοῦτο ποιεῖν δυναμένην ἐκέλευε παραλαμβάνειν τοὺς μαθητάς. Hence Schol. ad Arist. 22 b 29 ed. Brandis speaking of Zeno of Elea says that he was called ἀμφοτερόγλωσσος οὐχ ὅτι διαλεκτικὸς ἦν ὡς ὁ Κιτιεύς.

σοφίσματα, cf. the anecdote related by Diog. VII. 25. A logician showed Zeno seven διαλεκτικαὶ ἰδέαι in the Reaper fallacy, and received 200 drachmas, although his fee was only half that amount, ib. VII. 47 οὐκ ἄνευ δὲ τῆς διαλεκτικῆς θεωρίας τὸν σοφὸν ἄπτωτον ἔνεσθαι ἐν λόγῳ...τό τε ἀμφιβόλως λεγόμενον διευκρινεῖσθαι.

τὴν διαλεκτικήν. Strictly speaking, λογικὴ is a wider term than διαλεκτική, cf. Diog. VII. 41 τὸ δὲ λογικὸν μέρος φασὶν ἔνιοι εἰς δύο διαιρεῖσθαι ἐπιστήμας, εἰς ῥητορικὴν καὶ εἰς διαλεκτικήν, Sen. Ep. 89, 16.

7. φαντασία ἐστὶ τύπωσις ἐν ψυχῇ. Sext. Emp. Math. VII. 228, 236 distinctly attributes this definition to Zeno. Diog. VII. 45 τὴν δὲ φαντασίαν εἶναι τύπωσιν ἐν ψυχῇ, τοῦ ὀνόματος οἰκείως μετενηνεγμένου ἀπὸ τῶν τύπων ἐν τῷ κηρῷ ὑπὸ τοῦ δακτυλίου γιγνομένων, ib. 50 quoting Chrysippus' gloss ἀλλοίωσις : cf. Plut. Comm. Not. 47.

For the use of τύπωσις see Introd. p. 34. That Zeno did not define his meaning further than by the bare statement is evident from the controversy which afterwards arose between Cleanthes and Chrysippus as to the exact meaning of τύπωσις: for which see on Cleanth. frag. 3. It would seem however from the expressions "effictum" and "impressum" in Zeno's definition of φαντασία καταληπτικὴ (frag. 11) that Cleanthes is a truer exponent of his master's teaching in this matter than Chrysippus. Zeno must have been influenced by Aristotle's treatment of φαντασία (de An. III. 3): see Introd. p. 24. See further Stein, Erkenntnistheorie, p. 157.

8. τὰς μὲν αἰσθήσεις ἀληθεῖς τῶν δὲ φαντασιῶν τὰς μὲν ἀληθεῖς τὰς δὲ ψευδεῖς. This is attributed to the Stoics generally by Stob. Ecl. I. 50. 21, Plut. plac. IV. 8. 9, but must belong to Zeno having regard to Sext. Emp. adv. Math. VIII. 355, Δημόκριτος μὲν πᾶσαν αἰσθητὴν ὕπαρξιν κεκίνηκεν, Ἐπίκουρος δὲ πᾶν αἰσθητὸν ἔλεξε βέβαιον εἶναι ὁ δὲ Στωικὸς Ζήνων διαιρέσει ἐχρῆτο; Cic.

N. D. I. 70 urgebat Arcesilas Zenonem, cum ipse falsa omnia diceret quae sensibus viderentur; Zeno autem nonnulla visa esse falsa, non omnia; Cic. Acad. I. 41 visis non omnibus adjungebat fidem.

Zeno is not entirely a sensualist: Stein, Erkenntnistheorie, p. 307. For the general doctrine see ib. p. 142— 151. Zeno is here again following the lead of Aristotle, cf. de An. III. 3. 7 εἶτα αἱ μὲν (scil. αἰσθήσεις) ἀληθεῖς ἀεί, αἱ δὲ φαντασίαι γίνονται αἱ πλείους ψευδεῖς. On the other hand Epicurus held πάσας τὰς φαντασίας ἀληθεῖς εἶναι (Sext. Math. VII. 204).

9. Cic. Acad. I. 41, (Zeno) adjungebat fidem...iis (visis) solum, quae propriam quamdam haberent declarationem earum rerum, quae viderentur.

Cicero is here speaking of the Greek ἐνάργεια, for which he elsewhere suggests as translations perspicuitas or evidentia (ib. II. 17). Every sense impression is ἐναργὲς according to the Epicureans (Zeller, p. 428), but with Zeno ἐνάργεια is simply introduced as an attribute of καταληπτικὴ φαντασία: cf. Sext. Math. VII. 257 speaking of the κ. φ. αὕτη γὰρ ἐναργὴς οὖσα καὶ πληκτικὴ μόνον οὐχὶ τῶν τριχῶν λαμβάνεται κατασπῶσα ἡμᾶς εἰς συγκατάθεσιν καὶ ἄλλου μηδενὸς δεομένη εἰς τὸ τοιαύτη προσπίπτειν ἢ εἰς τὸ τὴν πρὸς τὰς ἄλλας διαφορὰν ὑποβάλλειν. Hirzel (Untersuchungen, II. pp. 3, 6) attributes ἐνάργεια to the Cynics but his authorities merely show that Diogenes proved the possibility of motion by walking about (Diog. VI. 39), which Sextus (Math. X. 68) calls a proof δι' αὐτῆς τῆς ἐναργείας.

10. Sext. Math. VII. 253, ἀλλὰ γὰρ οἱ μὲν ἀρχαιότεροι τῶν Στωικῶν κριτήριόν φασιν εἶναι τῆς ἀληθείας τὴν καταληπτικὴν φαντασίαν. ib. 227 κριτήριον ἀληθείας εἶναι τὴν καταληπτικὴν φαντασίαν. This is to be at-

tributed to Zeno partly as an inference from the word ἀρχαιότεροι, partly as a necessary corollary from the next fragment, and partly in accordance with the testimony of Cic. Acad. I. 42 sed inter scientiam et inscientiam comprehensionem illam (κατάληψιν) quam dixi collocabat eamque neque in rectis neque in pravis numerabat sed soli credendum esse dicebat. Diog. L. VII. 46 refers the citation to the school generally and in 54 quotes it from Chrysippus ἐν τῇ δυωδεκάτῃ τῶν φυσικῶν.

For the doctrine of the καταληπτικὴ φαντασία see Zeller, pp. 87—89. Stein, Erkenntnistheorie, p. 167 foll. Four different explanations of the meaning of the term have been given (1) καταλ. active. The irresistible character of the impression compels assent, Zeller. (2) καταλ. passive: the perception is grasped by the mind, Hirzel. (3) The object of representation (τὸ ὑπάρχον) and not the perception is grasped by the mind, Ueberweg, p. 192 (now given up by Heinze). (4) καταλ. both active and passive, Stein, thus reconciling the apparent contradiction between Cic. Acad. I. 41, and Sext. Math. VII. 257. For the exact meaning of κατάληψις)(καταληπτικὴ φαντασία cf. Sext. Emp. Math. XI. 182 κατάληψίς ἐστι καταληπτικῆς φαντασίας συγκατάθεσις: a distinction, possibly due to Zeno, which tends to disappear in practice. See also Stein, Erkenntnistheorie, p. 182. κατάληψις καταληπτικὴ, etc. were new terminology invented by Zeno, according to Cic. Acad. I. 41 comprehensionem appellabat similem iis rebus, quae manu prehenderentur: ex quo etiam nomen hoc dixerat cum eo verbo antea nemo tali in re usus est, ib. II. 145, but the verb καταλαμβάνειν had been used by Plato in the sense " to grasp with the mind," Phaedr. 250 D περὶ δὲ κάλλους, ὥσπερ εἴπομεν, μετ᾽ ἐκείνων τε ἔλαμπεν ὄν, δεῦρό τε ἐλθόντες κατειλήφαμεν αὐτὸ διὰ τῆς ἐναργεστάτης αἰσθήσεως τῶν ἡμετέρων στίλβον ἐναργέστατα. Zeno, therefore, only specialised the meaning of the word, see Introd. p. 34 and generally Introd. p. 9.

11. Sext. Math. VII. 248, φαντασία καταληπτική ἐστιν ἡ ἀπὸ τοῦ ὑπάρχοντος καὶ κατ' αὐτὸ τὸ ὑπάρχον ἐναπομεμαγμένη καὶ ἐναπεσφραγισμένη ὁποία οὐκ ἂν γένοιτο ἀπὸ μὴ ὑπάρχοντος, ib. 426, Pyrrh. II. 4. Diogenes gives the definition in substantially the same words in § 50 adding however καὶ ἐναποτετυπωμένη after ἐναπομεμαγμένη: in § 46 he omits ὁποία—ὑπάρχοντος but adds:—ἀκατάληπτον δὲ τὴν μὴ ἀπὸ ὑπάρχοντος, ἢ ἀπὸ ὑπάρχοντος μέν, μὴ κατ' αὐτὸ δὲ τὸ ὑπάρχον τὴν μὴ τρανῆ μηδὲ ἔκτυπον, which very possibly belongs also to Zeno. The evidence attaching the definition to Zeno is as follows:—Cic. Acad. II. 18 si illud esset, sicut Zeno definiret, tale visum impressum effictumque ex eo unde esset quale esse non posset ex eo unde non esset, id nos a Zenone definitum rectissime dicimus; ib. 113, ib. I. 41 id autem visum cum ipsum per se cerneretur comprehendibile (of Zeno) ib. II. 77. Speaking of the controversy between Arcesilas and Zeno, Cic. states that the last words of the definition were added by Zeno because of the pressure put upon him by Arcesilas. Numenius ap. Euseb. P. E. XIV. 6, p. 733 τὸ δὲ δόγμα τοῦτο αὐτοῦ (scil. Ζήνωνος) πρώτου εὑρομένου καὐτὸ τὸ ὄνομα βλέπων εὐδοκιμοῦν ἐν ταῖς Ἀθήναις τὴν καταληπτικὴν φαντασίαν πάσῃ μηχανῇ ἐχρῆτο ἐπ' αὐτήν (of Arcesilas). August. c. Acad. III. 9, 18 sed videamus quid ait Zeno. Tale scilicet visum comprehendi et percipi posse, quale cum falso non haberet signa communia.

The controversy between Arcesilas and Zeno is a historical fact about which there can be no doubt, and, apart from direct evidence, the chronology proves that our definition can hardly be due to Chrysippus, who only succeeded to the headship of the Stoa eight years after the death of Arcesilas (cf. Plut. Com. Not. c. 1). This question of the criterion was the chief battle-ground of the Stoics and the New Academy, and in later times Carneades maintained ἀκατάληπτα πάντα εἶναι οὐ πάντα δὲ ἄδηλα (Zeller, p. 555). In the second book of Cicero's Academica the question is discussed at length. Sext. Math. VII. 248— 252 shows in detail the reason for the insertion of each member of the definition: the impression must be from the object to exclude the visions of madmen, and with reference to the object to exclude a case like that of Orestes, who mistook his sister for a Fury. It must be imprinted and stamped on the mind to ensure that the percipient shall have noticed all the characteristics of the object. Lastly, the addition ὁποία οὐκ ἂν γένοιτο ἀπὸ μὴ ὑπάρχοντος was inserted to meet the Academic objection that two impressions, one true and the other false, might be so entirely alike (ἀπαράλλακτον) as to be incapable of distinction, which of course the Stoics did not admit. For ἐναπομεμαγμένη cf. Ar. Ran. 1040 ὅθεν ἡμὴ φρὴν ἀπομαξαμένη πολλὰς ἀρετὰς ἐποίησεν.

12. Olympiodorus in Plat. Gorg. pp. 53, 54 (ed. Jahn ap. Neue Jahrb. für Philol. supplement bd. XIV. 1848 p. 239, 240) Ζήνων δέ φησιν ὅτι τέχνη ἐστὶ σύστημα ἐκ καταλήψεων συγγεγυμνασμένον (? -ων) πρός τι τέλος εὔχρηστον τῶν ἐν τῷ βίῳ.

Cf. Lucian Paras. c. 4 τέχνη ἐστίν, ὡς ἐγὼ διαμνημονεύω σοφοῦ τινος ἀκούσας, σύστημα ἐκ καταλήψεων συγγεγυμνασμένων πρός τι τέλος εὔχρηστον τῶν ἐν τῷ βίῳ. Schol. ad. Ar. Nub. 317 οὕτω γὰρ ὁριζόμεθα τὴν τέχνην οἷον σύστημα ἐκ καταλήψεων ἐγγεγυμνασμένων καὶ τὰ ἐφεξῆς. Sext. Emp. Math. II. 10 πᾶσα τοίνυν τέχνη σύστημά εστίν εκ καταλήψεων συγγεγυμνασμένων και επί τέλος εύχρηστον τω βίω λαμβανόντων την αναφοράν. The same definition partially in id. Pyrrh. III. 188, 241, 251, Math. I. 75, VII. 109, 373, 182. Wachsm. also quotes (Comm. I. p. 12), Schol. Dionys. Thrac. p. 649, 31, ib. p. 721, 25 οἱ Στωικοὶ οὕτως ὁρίζονται τὴν τέχνην· τέχνη εστι σύστημα περὶ ψυχὴν γενόμενον ἐγκαταλήψεων ἐγγεγυμνασμένων κ.τ.λ. Cf. also Quintil. II. 17, 41 Nam sive, ut Cleanthes voluit, ars est potestas via, id est, ordine efficiens: esse certe viam atque ordinem in benedicendo nemo dubitaverit; sive ille ab omnibus fere probatus finis observatur artem constare ex praeceptionibus consentientibus et coexercitatis ad finem vitae utilem. Cic. frag. ap. Diomed 414 ed. Putsch ars est perceptionum exercitarum constructio ad unum exitum utilem vitae pertinentium. Cic. Acad. II. 22 ars vero quae potest esse nisi quae non ex una aut duabus sed ex multis animi perceptionibus constat. Fin. III. 18 artes...constent ex cognitionibus et contineat quiddam in se ratione constitutum et via (illustrating also the next frag.). N. D. II. 148 ex quibus (perceptis) collatis inter se et comparatis artes quoque efficimus partim ad usum vitae...necessarias.

It is worth while to compare with Zeno's definition of art those to be found in Aristotle: both philosophers alike recognise its practical character (cf. Eth. VI. 4. 6 ἡ μὲν οὖν τέχνη ἕξις τις μετὰ λόγου ἀληθοῦς ποιητική ἐστιν) and that it proceeds by means of regulated principles (cf. Met. I. 1. 5 γίνεται δὲ τέχνη ὅταν ἐκ πολλῶν τῆς ἐμπειρίας ἐννοημάτων μία καθόλου γένηται περὶ τῶν ὁμοίων ὑπόληψις). Aristotle's distinction that τέχνη is concerned with γένεσις while ἐπιστήμη deals with ὄν (Anal. Post. II. 19. 4) is of course foreign to Zeno's system.

Zeller's note on p. 266, 2 (Eng. Tr.) is inaccurate but appears correctly in the 4th German ed. (III. 1. 247).

13. Schol. ad Dionys. Thracis Gramm. ap. Bekk. Anecd. p. 663, 16, ὡς δηλοῖ καὶ ὁ Ζήνων λέγων τέχνη ἐστὶν ἕξις ὁδοποιητική, τουτέστι, δι' ὁδοῦ καὶ μεθόδου ποιοῦσά τι.

The authenticity of this fragment is rendered doubtful (1) by the fact that Zeno had defined τέχνη differently, as we have seen, (2) because Cleanthes defined τέχνη as ἕξις ὁδῷ πάντα ἀνύουσα (frag. 5). It is of course possible that Zeno left two alternative definitions as in the case of πάθος (frags. 136 and 137), and that Cleanthes adopted one of these with verbal alterations, but it seems most probable that the Schol. has made a mistake, and certainly ὁδοποιητικὴ has a suspicious look. Stein however, Erkenntnistheorie, p. 312, accepts the definition.

14. μνήμη θησαυρισμός ἐστι φαντασιῶν.

These words are shown to belong to Zeno by the following considerations. Sext. Emp. Math. VII. 372 foll. is describing the controversy between Cleanthes and Chrysippus as to the meaning of Zeno's τύπωσις and introduces one of Chrysippus' arguments εἰ γὰρ κηροῦ τρόπον τυποῦται ἡ ψυχὴ φανταστικῶς πάσχουσα ἀεὶ τὸ ἔσχατον κίνημα ἐπισκοτήσει τῇ προτέρᾳ φαντασίᾳ, ὥσπερ καὶ ἡ τῆς δευτέρας σφραγῖδος τύπος ἐξαλειπτικός ἐστι τοῦ προτέρου. ἀλλ' εἰ τοῦτο, ἀναιρεῖται μὲν μνήμη, θησαυρισμὸς οὖσα φαντασιῶν, ἀναιρεῖται δὲ πᾶσα τέχνη· σύστημα γὰρ ἦν καὶ ἄθροισμα καταλήψεων κ.τ.λ. Now one might suspect from internal evidence alone that Chrysippus is appealing to the school definitions of Memory and Art as established by Zeno in support of his argument against Zeno's pupil, but the inference becomes irresistible when we find that the definition of Art is certainly Zeno's, as has already been shown. Cf. Cic. Acad. II. 22 quid quisquam meminit quod non animo comprehendit et tenet? ib. 106 memoria perceptarum comprehensarumque rerum est. Plut. plac. IV. 11. 2. Aristotle discusses the relation between μνήμη and φαντασία in the tract de Memoria (see Grote's Aristotle, pp. 475, 476). μνήμη = μονὴ τοῦ αἰσθήματος, An. Post. II. 19. 99 b 36.

15. Sext. Emp. adv. Math. VII. 151, δόξαν εἶναι τὴν ἀσθενῆ καὶ ψευδῆ συγκατάθεσιν attributed to Zeno by Cic. Acad. I. 41 ex qua (inscientia) exsisteret etiam opinio, quae esset imbecilla et cum falso incognitoque communis, cf. ib. Tusc. IV. 15 opinationem autem...volunt esse imbecillam assensionem. Stobaeus speaks of two Stoic definitions of δόξα Ecl. II. 7. 11^m, p. 112, 2 [= II. 231] διττὰς γὰρ εἶναι δόξας τὴν μὲν ἀκαταλήπτῳ συγκαταθέσιν, τὴν δ' ὑπόληψιν ἀσθενῆ, cf. ib. II. 7. 10. p. 89, 1[= II. 169] παραλαμβάνεσθαι τὴν δόξαν ἀντὶ τῆς ἀσθενοῦς ὑπολήψεως. It is possible from a consideration of the next frag. that Zeno's word was οἴησις. Thus, as with Plato, δόξα and ἄγνοια are ultimately identical. See further Stein, Erkenntnistheorie pp. 204, 205.

16. Diog. L. VII. 23, ἔλεγε δὲ μηδὲν εἶναι τῆς οἰήσεως ἀλλοτριώτερον πρὸς κατάληψιν τῶν ἐπιστημῶν.

τῶν ἐπιστημῶν. The plural is used because ἐπιστήμη in the narrower sense in which Zeno used the word is a single κατάληψις. The Stoics also defined ἐπιστήμη as a σύστημα (cf. Stob. Ecl. II. 7. 5^1 p. 73, 21 = II. 129) of such perceptions. At the same time we must beware of supposing that ἐπιστήμη is according to Zeno identical with κατάληψις. ἐπιστήμη is the conscious knowledge of the wise man, whereas κατάληψις may be possessed by the φαῦλος. The latter may occasionally and accidentally assent to the καταληπτικὴ φαντασία, but the former's assent is regular and unerring. Cf. Sext. Math. VII. 152 ὧν τὴν μὲν ἐπιστήμην ἐν μόνοις ὑφίστασθαι λέγουσι τοῖς σοφοῖς, τὴν δὲ δόξαν ἐν μόνοις τοῖς φαύλοις τὴν δὲ κατάληψιν κοινὴν ἀμφοτέρων εἶναι. We have here, in fact, the Platonic distinction between δόξα ἀληθὴς and ἐπιστήμη in another form.

17. Cic. Acad. I. 41, si ita erat comprehensum ut convelli ratione non posset scientiam sin aliter inscientiam nominabat (Zeno).

The Greek sources for this will be found in Stob. Ecl. II. 7, 5¹ p. 73, 19 = II. 129 εἶναι τὴν ἐπιστήμην κατάληψιν ἀσφαλῆ καὶ ἀμετάπτωτον ὑπὸ λόγου, ib. 11ᵐ p. 111, 20 = II. 231, τὴν ἄγνοιαν μεταπτωτικὴν εἶναι συγκατάθεσιν καὶ ἀσθενῆ, cf. Sext. Emp. Math. VII. 151, ἐπιστήμην εἶναι τὴν ἀσφαλῆ καὶ βεβαίαν καὶ ἀμετάθετον ὑπὸ λόγου κατάληψιν, see also Stein, p. 311 and n. 711, who concludes that these definitions are Zenonian. Diog. L. VII. 47, αὐτήν τε τὴν ἐπιστήμην φασὶν ἢ κατάληψιν ἀσφαλῆ, ἢ ἕξιν ἐν φαντασιῶν προσδέξει, ἀμετάπτωτον ὑπὸ λόγου. The definition of ἐπιστήμη as ἕξις κ.τ.λ. is due to Herillus, cf. ib. VII. 165, but I am unable to see why on that ground Zeller, p. 82, n. 1, and Wellmann, p. 480, should also infer that it was introduced by Zeno. It is far more natural to suppose that the simplest form of the definition was first put forward by the founder of the school, and that it was subsequently modified by his successors in accordance with their different positions: thus Herillus' definition is undoubtedly modelled on Zeno's, but is adapted to his conception of ἐπιστήμη as the ethical τέλος.

18. Cic. Acad. I. 42, inter scientiam et inscientiam comprehensionem collocabat, eamque neque in rectis neque in pravis numerabat.

Cf. Sext. Math. VII. 151, ἐπιστήμην καὶ δόξαν καὶ τὴν ἐν μεθορίᾳ τούτων τεταγμένην κατάληψιν...κατάληψιν δὲ τὴν μεταξὺ τούτων: ib. 153, ὁ Ἀρκεσίλαος...δεικνὺς ὅτι οὐδέν ἐστι μεταξὺ ἐπιστήμης καὶ δόξης κριτήριον ἡ κατάληψις. (It will be observed that where Cicero speaks of inscientia Sextus mentions δόξα, but, as has been shown, they are practically identical.) Wellmann, p. 484, thinks that either there is some mistake in the text or that Cicero has misunderstood his authorities, but the passage in Sextus l.c. 151—153 makes the meaning perfectly clear: see the note on frag. 16. The latter part of Cicero's statement may be either an inference by his authority ex silentio, or a record of an express statement by Zeno. In any case, it derives its force here simply from the antithesis to scientia and inscientia: thus the Stoics classed certain virtues (goods) as ἐπιστῆμαι and certain vices (evils) as ἄγνοιαι, cf. Stob. Ecl. II. 7. 5[b], p. 58, 5—59, 3 = II. 92—94.

19. Cic. Acad. I. 41, Zeno ad haec quae visa sunt et quasi accepta sensibus assensionem adiungit animorum: quam esse vult in nobis positam et voluntariam.

In this case it is impossible to recover Zeno's actual words, nor can we tell how much of the Stoic doctrine handed down by Sext. Math. VIII. 397, belonged to Zeno; cf. especially συγκατάθεσις ἥτις διπλοῦν ἔοικεν εἶναι πρᾶγμα καὶ τὸ μέν τι ἔχειν ἀκούσιον τὸ δὲ ἑκούσιον καὶ ἐπὶ τῇ ἡμετέρᾳ κρίσει κείμενον. A full list of authorities is given by Zeller, Stoics, p. 88, n. 1. The free power of assent must be understood only in the limited sense in which free will is possible in consequence of the Stoic doctrine of εἱμαρμένη: see Wellmann, l. c. pp. 482, 483. It is moreover only the wise man who can distinguish accurately the relative strength of divers impressions, and he alone will consistently refuse assent to mere φαντάσματα.

20. Cic. Acad. I. 41, Quod autem erat sensu comprehensum, id ipsum sensum appellabat.

For the different meanings of αἴσθησις in the Stoic school, see Diog. L. VII. 52 αἴσθησις δὲ λέγεται κατὰ τοὺς Στωικοὺς τό τε ἀφ᾽ ἡγεμονικοῦ πνεῦμα καὶ ἐπὶ τὰς αἰσθήσεις διῆκον, καὶ ἡ δι᾽ αὐτῶν κατάληψις, καὶ ἡ περὶ τὰ αἰσθητήρια κατασκευή, καθ᾽ ἥν τινες πηροὶ γίνονται: the second of these definitions is thus attributed by Cicero to Zeno. So Dr Reid: it is however possible that sensum is past part. pass. of sentio and is a translation of αἰσθητὸν or αἰσθητικὸν rather than of αἴσθησις, in which case cf. Diog. L. VII. 51 τῶν δὲ φαντασιῶν κατ᾽ αὐτοὺς αἱ μέν εἰσιν αἰσθητικαὶ αἱ δ᾽ οὔ. αἰσθητικαὶ μὲν αἱ δι᾽ αἰσθητήριον ἢ αἰσθητηρίων λαμβανόμεναι κ.τ.λ.

21. Cic. Acad. I. 42, Zeno sensibus etiam fidem tribuebat quod comprehensio facta sensibus et vera illi et fidelis videbatur, non quod omnia quae essent in re comprehenderet sed quia nihil quod cadere in eam posset relinqueret quodque natura quasi normam scientiae et principium sui dedisset, unde postea notiones rerum in animis imprimerentur, e quibus non principia solum sed latiores quaedam ad rationem inveniendam viae reperiuntur.

For the general sense see Zeller, p. 80, n. 1.

non quod omnia: Dr Reid cites Sext. Pyrrh. I. 92 ἕκαστον τῶν φαινομένων ἡμῖν αἰσθητῶν ποικίλον ὑποπίπτειν δοκεῖ οἷον τὸ μῆλον λεῖον εὐῶδες γλυκὺ ξανθόν. ἄδηλον οὖν πότερόν ποτε ταύτας μόνας ὄντως ἔχει τὰς ποιότητας ἢ μονοποιὸν μέν ἐστι παρὰ δὲ τὴν διάφορον κατασκευὴν τῶν αἰσθητηρίων διάφορον φαίνεται ἢ καὶ πλείονας μὲν τῶν φαινομένων ἔχει ποιότητας, ἡμῖν δὲ οὐχ ὑποπίπτουσί τινες αὐτῶν, ib. 97. These passages however do not refer to Stoic teaching but are used in furtherance of the Sceptical argument.

notiones: a translation of ἔννοιαι. It seems certain that the distinction between προλήψεις and ἔννοιαι (for which see R. and P. § 393 and note c. and Stein, Erkenntnistheorie, p. 237) is not at least in terms Zenonian, though he may have spoken of κοιναὶ ἔννοιαι. Reid (on Acad. II. 30) suggests that the word πρόληψις was introduced by Zeno, but cf. Cic. N. D. I. 44 ut Epicurus ipse πρόληψις appellavit, quam antea nemo eo verbo nominarat, so that it is more probable that Chrysippus borrowed it from the rival school; but see Stein, l. c. p. 248—250. ἔννοια, on the other hand, used by Plato (Phaed. 73 C) in quite a general sense, and defined by the Peripatetics as ὁ ἀθροισμὸς τῶν τοῦ νοῦ φαντασμάτων καὶ ἡ συγκεφαλαίωσις τῶν ἐπὶ μέρους εἰς τὸ καθόλου (Sext. Emp. Math. VII. 224) must have received its special Stoic sense from Zeno.

principia: it is difficult to determine whether this is a translation of a Stoic technical term, cf. Acad. II. 21.

22. Cic. Acad. I. 42, Errorem autem et temeritatem et ignorantiam et opinationem et suspicionem et uno nomine omnia quae essent aliena firmae et constantis adsensionis a virtute sapientiaque removebat.

With this may be compared the Stoic definitions of ἀπροπτωσία, ἀνεικαιότης, ἀνελεγξία, and ἀματαιότης quoted by Diog. L. VII. 46, 47. Temeritas is probably a translation of προπέτεια, a favourite word with Sextus when speaking of the dogmatists (e.g. Pyrrh. I. 20) but also used by the Stoics (Diog. VII. 48). Reid also quotes (on Ac. II. 66) Epict. d. III. 22. 104 προπετὴς συγκατάθεσις.

23. Stob. Ecl. I. 12. 3, p. 136, 21, Ζήνωνος <καὶ τῶν ἀπ' αὐτοῦ>. τὰ ἐννοήματά φασι μήτε τινὰ εἶναι μήτε ποιά, ὡσανεὶ δέ τινα καὶ ὡσανεὶ ποιὰ φαντάσματα ψυχῆς·

ταῦτα δὲ ὑπὸ τῶν ἀρχαίων ἰδέας προσαγορεύεσθαι. τῶν γὰρ κατὰ τὰ ἐννοήματα ὑποπιπτόντων εἶναι τὰς ἰδέας, οἷον ἀνθρώπων, ἵππων, κοινότερον εἰπεῖν πάντων τῶν ζῴων καὶ τῶν ἄλλων ὁπόσων λέγουσιν ἰδέας εἶναι. [ταύτας δὲ οἱ Στωικοὶ φιλόσοφοί φασιν ἀνυπάρκτους εἶναι καὶ τῶν μὲν ἐννοημάτων μετέχειν ἡμᾶς, τῶν δὲ πτώσεων, ἃς δὴ προσηγορίας καλοῦσι, τυγχάνειν].

Cf. Euseb. P. E. xv. 45, οἱ ἀπὸ Ζήνωνος Στωικοὶ ἐννοήματα ἡμέτερα τὰς ἰδέας. Plut. Plac. I. 10, 4, οἱ ἀπὸ Ζήνωνος Στωικοὶ ἐννοήματα ἡμέτερα τὰς ἰδέας ἔφασαν.

Wellmann, p. 484, (followed by Stein, Erkenntnistheorie, n. 689) suggests that this may have come from the book entitled καθολικά. Possibly this criticism of the ideas formed part of the attack upon Plato mentioned by Numenius, ap. Euseb. P. E. XIV. 6, p. 733, ὁ δ' (Ζήνων) ἐν τῷ ἀσθενεστέρῳ ὢν ἡσυχίαν ἄγων οὐ δυνάμενος ἀδικεῖσθαι Ἀρκεσιλάου μὲν ἀφίετο, πολλὰ ἂν εἰπεῖν ἔχων, ἀλλ' οὐκ ἤθελε, τάχα δὲ μᾶλλον ἄλλως, πρὸς δὲ τὸν οὐκέτι ἐν ζῶσιν ὄντα Πλάτωνα ἐσκιαμάχει, καὶ τὴν ἀπὸ ἁμάξης πομπείαν πᾶσαν κατεθορύβει, λέγων ὡς οὔτ' ἂν τοῦ Πλάτωνος ἀμυννομένου, ὑπερδικεῖν τε αὐτοῦ ἄλλῳ οὐδένι μέλον· εἴτε μελήσειεν Ἀρκεσιλάῳ, αὐτός γε κερδανεῖν ᾤετο ἀποτρεψάμενος ἀφ' ἑαυτοῦ τὸν Ἀρκεσίλαον. τοῦτο δὲ ἤδη καὶ Ἀγαθοκλέα τὸν Συρακόσιον ποιήσαντα τὸ σόφισμα ἐπὶ τοὺς Καρχηδονίους. At any rate, both the circumstances and the chronology indicate that the reference is not to the Πολιτεία (Introd. p. 29).

ἐννοήματα. For the definition cf. Plut. Plac. IV. 11 ἔστι δὲ νόημα φάντασμα διανοίας λογικοῦ ζῴου, i.e., as he goes on to explain, ἐννόημα stands to φάντασμα in the relation of εἶδος to γένος: φαντάσματα are shared with us by all other animals whereas ἐννοήματα belong to the gods and mankind alone. Diog. VII. 61, ἐννόημα δέ ἐστι φάντασμα διανοίας, οὔτε τι ὂν οὔτε ποιόν, ὡσανεὶ δέ τι

74 THE FRAGMENTS OF ZENO.

ὂν καὶ ὡσανεὶ ποιόν, οἷον γίνεται ἀνατύπωμα ἵππου καὶ μὴ παρόντος.

τινα...ποιά, i.e. they have no existence or definiteness. For the Stoic conception of τι and ποιόν, see Zeller, pp. 98 f. and 102 f. It has been inferred from this passage that the doctrine of the four categories does not belong entirely to Chrysippus (Petersen, Chrys. phil. fundam. p. 18).

ἰδέας. The meaning is that the Platonic ideas are identical with ἐννοήματα, inasmuch as they possess no objective existence, but are mere figments of the mind. Plato himself deals with this very point, Parm. 132 B ἀλλὰ...μὴ τῶν εἰδῶν ἕκαστον ᾖ τούτων νόημα, καὶ οὐδαμοῦ αὐτῷ προσήκῃ ἐγγίγνεσθαι ἄλλοθι ἢ ἐν ψυχαῖς. Antisthenes had already criticised the theory of ideas from this point of view: see Introd. p. 18.

ὑποπιπτόντων: the regular word for the presentation of external impressions to the organs of sense (e. g. Sext. Pyrrh. I. 40 οὐχ αἱ αὐταί...ὑποπίπτουσι φαντασίαι).

ὁπόσων, κ.τ.λ. So far as it goes this passage is in agreement with Aristotle's statement that Plato recognised ideas of ὁπόσα φύσει only (Metaph. Λ. 3. 1070 a 18): see Dr Jackson in Journ. Phil. x. 255, etc.

ταύτας—τυγχάνειν. These words are not expressly attributed to Zeno: hence Diels followed by Wachsm. adds to the lemma Ζήνωνος the words καὶ τῶν ἀπ' αὐτοῦ.

τῶν δὲ πτώσεων, κ.τ.λ. This passage is extremely difficult and is supposed to be corrupt by Zeller, III⁴. 2. 79 and Wachsmuth. The latter suggests τὰς δὲ ποιότητας ἐπωνυμιῶν, κ.τ.λ. or if πτώσεων is corrupt for ἐπωνυμιῶν "in fine talia fere interciderint τὰς κοινὰς ποιότητας, cf. Diog. VII. 58," the former (coll. Sext. Math. VII. 11) would read τὰ τυγχάνοντα in place of τυγχάνειν (die Gedanken seien in uns, die Bezeichnungen gehen auf die Dinge). The text, as it stands, has been interpreted in three ways: (1) notitiae rerum rationi nostrae insitae sunt, nomina fortuito obveniunt, Diels. (2) πτώσεις = omnes singulae res cuiuscumque qualitatis)(γενικὰ ποιά, i.e. ἰδέαι. These impress themselves on the mind of man (τυγχάνειν), Petersen, l. c. p. 82, foll.: but this interpretation of πτῶσις is unwarranted and is founded on a misconception of Diog. L. VII. 58. (3) Prantl's interpretation (I. p. 421, n. 63) is a combination of these two views. That the text is sound in the main is, I think, proved by Simplic. Cat. p. 54 (quoted by Petersen) οἱ δὲ ἀπὸ τῆς 'Ακαδημίας ἐκάλουν τὰ μεθεκτὰ ἀπὸ τοῦ μετέχεσθαι καὶ τὰς πτώσεις τευκτὰς ἀπὸ τοῦ τυγχάνεσθαι, and Clem. Alex. VIII. 9. 26: after saying that the πτῶσις for the κατηγόρημα "τέμνεται" is "τὸ τέμνεσθαι," and for ναῦς γίγνεται "τὸ ναῦν γίνεσθαι" and explaining that Aristotle called the πτῶσις προσηγορία he proceeds ἡ πτῶσις δὲ ἀσώματος εἶναι ὁμολογεῖται· διὸ καὶ τὸ σόφισμα ἐκεῖνο λύεται, ὃ λέγεις διέρχεται σοῦ διὰ τοῦ στόματος, ὅπερ ἀληθές, οἰκίαν δὲ λέγεις, οἰκία ἄρα διὰ τοῦ στόματος σοῦ διέρχεται ὅπερ ψεῦδος· οὐδὲ γὰρ τὴν οἰκίαν λέγομεν σῶμα οὖσαν, ἀλλὰ τὴν πτῶσιν ἀσώματον οὖσαν, ἧς οἰκία τυγχάνει. A consideration of the latter passage, which it is surprising that no one has cited, warrants the suggestion that τὰ ὑπάρχοντα or some such words have fallen out after τυγχάνειν. All would then be plain: πτῶσις = name)(ἐννόημα = thought. πτῶσις was also) (κατηγόρημα as noun to verb (Plut. qu. Plat. x. 1, 2). For the present use of πτῶσις, cf. also Sext. Math. XI. 29, VI. 42, for πτῶσις in Aristotle see Waitz, Organon, vol. I. p. 328, 329. προσηγορία is a common noun, such as "man" "horse" (Diog. VII. 58, Sext. Pyrrh. III. 14) tending in practice to become identical with πτῶσις, though theoretically narrower.

24. Stob. Ecl. I. 13, 1ᶜ, p. 138, 14 (Ar. Did. 457, Diels), αἴτιον δ' ὁ Ζήνων φησὶν εἶναι δι' ὅ· οὗ δὲ αἴτιον συμβεβηκός· καὶ τὸ μὲν αἴτιον σῶμα, οὗ δὲ αἴτιον κατηγόρημα· ἀδύνατον δ' εἶναι τὸ μὲν αἴτιον παρεῖναι οὗ δέ ἐστιν αἴτιον μὴ ὑπάρχειν. τὸ δὲ λεγόμενον τοιαύτην ἔχει δύναμιν· αἴτιόν ἐστι δι' ὃ γίγνεταί τι, οἷον διὰ τὴν φρόνησιν γίνεται τὸ φρονεῖν καὶ διὰ τὴν ψυχὴν γίνεται τὸ ζῆν καὶ διὰ τὴν σωφροσύνην γίνεται τὸ σωφρονεῖν. ἀδύνατον γὰρ εἶναι σωφροσύνης περί τινα οὔσης μὴ σωφρονεῖν ἢ ψυχῆς μὴ ζῆν ἢ φρονήσεως μὴ φρονεῖν.

It is difficult to understand why Zeller, Stoics, p. 95, n. 2, regards the main point of this fragment as a grammatical distinction between noun and verb: it appears rather that Zeno is discussing the nature of αἴτιον from a logical standpoint, and that κατηγόρημα is introduced to explain αἴτιον and not vice versa. The fragments of Chrysippus and Posidonius which follow our passage in Stobaeus should be compared with it. Zeno did not adopt the four Aristotelian causes because his materialistic views led him to regard the efficient as the only true cause.

συμβεβηκός = "result" or "inseparable consequence," cf. Stob. Ecl. I. 13 ad init. αἴτιόν ἐστι δι' ὃ τὸ ἀποτέλεσμα ἢ δι' ὃ συμβαίνει τι. This meaning of συμβεβηκός is also to be found in Aristotle, who uses the word in two distinct senses: see an elaborate note of Trendelenburg on de An. I. 1 p. 402 a 8 who quotes amongst other passages Metaph. Δ 30 1025 a 30 λέγεται δὲ καὶ ἄλλως συμβεβηκὸς οἷον ὅσα ὑπάρχει ἑκάστῳ καθ' αὑτὸ μὴ ἐν τῇ οὐσίᾳ ὄντα οἷον τῷ τριγώνῳ τὸ δύο ὀρθὰς ἔχειν. That συμβεβηκός must be used in this sense here and not in its more common Aristotelian sense of "accident" seems indubitable, when we read infra that the αἴτιον can never be present unless accompanied by the οὗ αἴτιον.

σῶμα: the materialism of the Stoics is well known: to what lengths it was pushed may be seen from Zeller, Stoics pp. 127—132, with the examples given in the notes.

κατηγόρημα: the οὗ αἴτιον was therefore something incorporeal, and Chrys. and Posid. accordingly speak of it as non-existent. Probably this inference did not present itself to Zeno's mind, as the question of the ὕπαρξις of λεκτά only arose later: see further on Cleanth. frag. 7. The present passage is illustrated by Sext. Pyrrh. III. 14 οἱ μὲν οὖν σῶμα, οἱ δ' ἀσώματον τὸ αἴτιον εἶναί φασιν. δόξαι δ' ἂν αἴτιον εἶναι κοινότερον κατ' αὐτοὺς δι' ὃ ἐνεργοῦν γίνεται τὸ ἀποτέλεσμα, οἷον ὡς ὁ ἥλιος ἢ ἡ τοῦ ἡλίου θερμότης τοῦ χεῖσθαι τὸν κηρὸν ἢ τῆς χύσεως τοῦ κηροῦ. καὶ γὰρ ἐν τούτῳ διαπεφωνήκασιν, οἱ μὲν προσηγοριῶν αἴτιον εἶναι τὸ αἴτιον φάσκοντες, οἷον τῆς χύσεως, οἱ δὲ κατηγορημάτων, οἷον τοῦ χεῖσθαι. ib. Math. IX. 211 Στωικοὶ μὲν πᾶν αἴτιον σῶμά φασι σώματι ἀσωμάτου τινὸς αἴτιον γενέσθαι, οἷον σῶμα μὲν τὸ σμιλίον, σώματι δὲ τῇ σαρκί, ἀσωμάτου δὲ τοῦ τέμνεσθαι κατηγορήματος, καὶ πάλιν σῶμα μὲν τὸ πῦρ, σώματι δὲ τῷ ξύλῳ, ἀσωμάτου δὲ τοῦ καίεσθαι κατηγορήματος.

φρόνησιν κ.τ.λ. A parallel to this will be found at Stob. Ecl. II. 7 11[f] p. 98, 3 τὴν γὰρ φρόνησιν αἱρούμεθα ἔχειν καὶ τὴν σωφροσύνην, οὐ μὰ Δία τὸ φρονεῖν καὶ σωφρονεῖν, ἀσώματα ὄντα καὶ κατηγορήματα. Stein, Erkenntnistheorie p. 307, infers from this passage that, according to Zeno, not a single moment in life passes without thought, but that the ἡγεμονικόν always thinks.

25. Anonymi τέχνη ap. Spengel Rhet. Gr. I. 434, 23, Ζήνων δὲ οὕτω φησί· διήγησίς ἐστι τῶν ἐν τῇ ὑποθέσει πραγμάτων ἔκθεσις εἰς τὸ ὑπὲρ τοῦ λέγοντος πρόσωπον ῥέουσα.

Perhaps this frag. comes from the τέχνη of Zeno: see Introd. p. 27. Zeller is inclined to doubt whether the words do not belong to some other Zeno, but inasmuch as this anonymous writer also quotes Chrysippus (p. 454, 4), the presumption is that he refers to Zeno of Citium, and there is no a priori reason to discredit his authorship.

διήγησις: the narrative portion of a speech containing the statement of facts, cf. Diog. L. VII. 43 τὸν δὲ ῥητορικὸν λόγον εἴς τε τὸ προοίμιον καὶ εἰς τὴν διήγησιν καὶ τὰ πρὸς τοὺς ἀντιδίκους καὶ τὸν ἐπίλογον. Dion. Hal. Ant. Rhet. x. 12 ἔστι δὲ τὰ τῆς ὑποθέσεως στοιχεῖα τέσσαρα, προοίμιον, διήγησις, πίστεις, ἐπίλογοι. Lysias especially excelled in his treatment of this branch of his art. Dion. H. Lys. c. 18 ἐν δὲ τῷ διηγεῖσθαι τὰ πράγματα, ὅπερ, οἶμαι, μέρος πλείστης δεῖται φροντίδος καὶ φυλακῆς, ἀναμφιβόλως ἡγοῦμαι κράτιστον αὐτὸν εἶναι πάντων ῥητόρων κ.τ.λ.

ὑποθέσει: cf. Sext. Emp. Math. III. 4 ὑπόθεσις προσαγορεύεται ἐν ῥητορικῇ ἡ τῶν ἐπὶ μέρους ζήτησις.

εἰς τὸ κ.τ.λ. "adapted to the character maintained on behalf of the speaker." πρόσωπον is technical)(πρᾶγμα. τὸ δὲ κεφάλαιον τοῦ προοιμίου δόξα προσώπων τε καὶ πραγμάτων Dion. H. Ant. Rhet. x. 13, cf. the Latin persona. Cic. pro Mil. § 32 itaque illud Cassianum cui bono fuerit in his personis valeat, pro Cluent. § 78 huius Staleni persona ab nulla turpi suspicione abhorrebat. For ῥέουσα cf. Plat. Rep. 485 D ὅτῳ γε εἰς ἕν τι αἱ ἐπιθυμίαι σφόδρα ῥέουσιν...ᾧ δὴ πρὸς τὰ μαθήματα καὶ πᾶν τὸ τοιοῦτον ἐρρυήκασιν.

26. Anonymi τέχνη ap. Spengel Rhet. Gr. I. 447, 11 ὡς δὲ Ζήνων· παράδειγμά ἐστι γενομένου πράγματος ἀπομνημόνευσις εἰς ὁμοίωσιν τοῦ νῦν ζητουμένου. Maxi-

mus Planudes ap. Walz. Rhet. Gr. v. 396 παράδειγμα δέ έστιν, ώς Ζήνων φησίν, γενομένου πράγματος άπομνημόνευσις εις όμοίωσιν του νυν ζητουμένου.

This frag. must stand or fall with frag. 25.

παράδειγμα: a technical term in rhetoric. Aristotle regards the example of the orator as an imperfect representation of the Induction of the philosopher: cf. Anal. Post. I. 1, 71 a 9 ώς δ' αύτως και οί ρητορικοί συμπείθουσιν· ή γάρ διά παραδειγμάτων, ό έστιν έπαγωγή, ή δι' ένθυμημάτων, όπερ έστι συλλογισμός.

27. Quintil. Inst. Or. IV. 2. 117 hic expressa (verba) et ut vult Zeno sensu tincta esse debebunt.

It has been supposed by some that these words are a reference to apoph. 13, but inasmuch as sensu is a very inappropriate translation of εις νοῦν, and Quintilian is speaking of the narrative portion of a speech, the meaning is rather "coloured by the actual impressions of sense" i.e. giving a vivid and clear representation of the actual facts.

28. Anonymi variae collectiones mathematicae in Hultschiana Heronis geometricorum et stereometricorum editione p. 275, Ταύρου Σιδονίου έστιν υπόμνημα εις Πολιτείαν Πλάτωνος έν ῷ έστι ταῦτα· ώρίσατο ὁ Πλάτων τήν γεωμετρίαν...'Αριστοτέλης δ'...Ζήνων δέ έξιν έν προσδέξει φαντασιών άμετάπτωτον υπό λόγου.

This frag. is due to Wachsmuth (Comm. I. p. 12) who emends as above for the meaningless έξιν πρός δείξιν φαντασιών άμεταπτώτως υποδίκου, coll. Diog. L. VII. 45. It is barely credible that Zeno can have defined geometry in the same words by which Herillus certainly and he himself possibly defined knowledge. There is doubtless some mistake in the tradition: possibly μαθηματικών has dropped out. I cannot find any evidence to illustrate Stoic views on mathematics.

29. Plut. Sto. Rep. 8, 1, πρὸς τὸν εἰπόντα μηδὲ δίκην δικάσῃς πρὶν (qu. add ἂν) ἀμφοῖν μῦθον ἀκούσῃς

ἀντέλεγεν ὁ Ζήνων, τοιούτῳ τινὶ λόγῳ χρώμενος· εἴτ' ἀπέδειξεν ὁ πρότερος εἰπὼν οὐκ ἀκουστέον τοῦ δευτέρου λέγοντος· πέρας γὰρ ἔχει τὸ ζητούμενον· εἴτ' οὐκ ἀπέδειξεν· ὅμοιον γὰρ ὡς εἰ μηδὲ ὑπήκουσε κληθεὶς ἢ ὑπακούσας ἐτερέτισεν· ἤτοι δ' ἀπέδειξεν ἢ οὐκ ἀπέδειξεν· οὐκ ἀκουστέον ἄρα τοῦ δευτέρου λέγοντος. The same is preserved by Schol. ad Lucian. Cal. 8 with unimportant variations.

μηδὲ κ.τ.λ. A verse of uncertain authorship commonly referred to Phocylides on the authority of the Schol. ad Lucian. l.c. but called by Cicero Ψευδησιόδειον (Att. VII. 18), see Bergk Poet. Lyr. Gk. p. 464: cf. Ar. Vesp. 725 ἦ που σοφὸς ἦν ὅστις ἔφασκεν, πρὶν ἂν ἀμφοῖν μῦθον ἀκούσῃς οὐκ ἂν δικάσαις. Eur. Heracl. 179 τίς ἂν δίκην κρίνειεν ἢ γνοίη λόγον πρὶν ἂν παρ' ἀμφοῖν μῦθον ἐκμάθῃ σαφῶς;

λόγῳ. The argument is couched in the syllogistic form which Zeno especially affected: see Introd. p. 33. Whether the first speaker proves his case or not, the argument of the second speaker is immaterial; but he must have either proved his case or failed to do so: therefore the second speaker should not be heard.

ὑπήκουσε: appeared in court when the case was called on—answered to his name: cf. Dem. F. L. p. 423 § 257 ἠτίμωσεν ὑπακούσαντά τιν' αὐτοῦ κατήγορον "procured the disfranchisement of a man who had actually appeared as his accuser." The word was used indifferently of plaintiff and defendant, ib. p. 434 § 290 οὐδ' ὑπακοῦσαι καλούμενος ἤθελεν. Meid. p. 580, 581 καλούμενος ὀνομαστί ...διὰ ταῦτ' οὐχ ὑπήκουσε. Andoc. Myst. § 112 κἂθ' ὁ κῆρυξ ἐκήρυττε τίς τὴν ἱκετηρίαν καταθείη, καὶ οὐδεὶς ὑπήκουσεν. Isae. p. 49, 25 = 84 R. ἀπογραφεὶς εἰς τὴν βουλὴν κακουργῶν ὑποχωρῶν ᾤχετο καὶ οὐχ ὑπήκουσεν.

κληθείς: either (1) by the presiding magistrate, cf. Dem. Olymp. p. 1174 ἐπειδὴ δ' ἐκάλει ὁ ἄρχων εἰς τὸ δικαστήριον ἅπαντας τοὺς ἀμφισβητοῦντας κατὰ τὸν νόμον. Ar. Vesp. 1441 ὕβριζ' ἕως ἂν τὴν δίκην ἄρχων καλῇ, or (2) by the officer of the court solemnly calling him by name. We know that this procedure (κλήτευσις) was adopted in the case of a defaulting witness, and it may also have been applied if one of the parties failed to put in an appearance.

30. Diog. L. VII. 18, ἔφασκε δὲ τοὺς μὲν τῶν ἀσολοίκων λόγους καὶ ἀπηρτισμένους ὁμοίους εἶναι τῷ ἀργυρίῳ τῷ Ἀλεξανδρείῳ· εὐοφθάλμους μὲν καὶ περιγεγραμμένους, καθὰ καὶ τὸ νόμισμα, οὐδὲν δὲ διὰ ταῦτα βελτίονας. τοὺς δὲ τοὐναντίον ἀφωμοίου τοῖς Ἀττικοῖς τετραδράχμοις εἰκῆ μὲν κεκομμένους καὶ σολοίκως, καθέλκειν μέντοι πολλάκις τὰς κεκαλλιγραφημένας λέξεις.

λόγους. For the comparison of words to coins cf. Hor. A. P. 59 licuit semperque licebit signatum praesente nota producere nomen. Juv. VII. 54 qui communi feriat carmen triviale Moneta and Prof. Mayor's note. Possibly this and the following frag. came from the work περὶ λέξεων.

Ἀλεξανδρείῳ: in this phrase which recurs at VIII. 85 I have followed Köhler (Rhein. Mus. XXXIX. 297) in reading Ἀλεξανδρείῳ for Ἀλεξανδρίνῳ. It appears that Alexandria had struck no coinage in the reign of the Ptolemies (Head, Historia Numorum p. 718); on the other hand the tetradrachm of Alexander was part of the current coinage all over Greece (ib. p. 198 foll. and see Hultsch, Gr. and Rom. Metrologie pp. 243—245).

κεκομμένους...σολοίκως. MSS. κεκομμένοις. Bywater (Journ. Phil. XVII. 76) reads κεκομμένους καὶ σολοίκους and the former certainly seems necessary to restore the balance of the sentence.

καθέλκειν: this meaning of καθέλκω is omitted by L. and S. s. v.

λέξεις bracketed by v. Wilamowitz and Köhler is rightly retained by Bywater.

31. Zonarae Lex. s.v. σολοικίζειν col. 1662, σολοικίζειν οὐ μόνον τὸ κατὰ φωνὴν καὶ λόγον χωρικεύεσθαι ἀλλὰ καὶ ἐπὶ ἐνδυμάτων ὅταν τις χωρικῶς ἐνδιδύσκηται ἢ ἀτάκτως ἐσθίῃ ἢ ἀκόσμως περιπατῇ ὥς φησι Ζήνων. Wachsmuth, Comm. I. p. 12, cites Cyrilli, Lex. cod. Bodl. ant. T. II. 11. ap. Cramer anec. Paris IV. p. 190 V. σολοικισμός· ὅτε τις ἀτέχνως διαλέγεται· σολοικίζειν οὐ μόνον τὸ κατὰ λέξιν καὶ φωνὴν ἰδιωτεύειν, ἀλλὰ καὶ ἐπὶ φορημάτων, ὅταν τις χωρικῶς ἐνδέδυται ἢ ἀτάκτως ἐσθίει ἢ ἀκόσμως περιπατεῖ ἅς φησι Ζήνων ὁ Κιτιεύς.

σολοικίζειν. Zeno is not alone in using the word in this extended sense, cf. Xen. Cyr. VIII. 3. 21 Δαϊφέρνης δέ τις ἦν σολοικότερος ἄνθρωπος τῷ τρόπῳ.

ἐπὶ ἐνδυμάτων. The Athenians attached great importance to κοσμιότης in dress as in other matters of personal behaviour. The cloak was required to be of a certain length, cf. Theophr. Char. 24 (Jebb) of the Penurious Man:—φοροῦντας ἐλάττω τῶν μηρῶν τὰ ἱμάτια; and to wear it in the fashionable style (ἐπὶ δεξιὰ ἀναβάλλεσθαι) was a mark of sobriety. Cf. Ar. Av. 1567 οὗτος τί δρᾷς; ἐπ' ἀριστέρ' οὕτως ἀμπέχει; οὐ μεταβαλεῖς θοἰμάτιον ὧδ' ἐπὶ δεξιάν;

ἀτάκτως ἐσθίῃ. How carefully children were trained

in this respect may be seen from three passages of Plutarch cited by Becker, Charicles, E. T. pp. 236, 237. Cf. e.g. de Educ. Puer. 7 τῇ μὲν δεξιᾷ συνεθίζειν τὰ παιδία δέχεσθαι τὰς τροφάς, κἂν προτείνειε τὴν ἀριστεράν, ἐπιτιμᾶν.

ἀκόσμως περιπατῇ. Fast walking in the streets was so severely criticised that it was a circumstance which might be used to damage an opponent before a jury; cf. Dem. Pantaen. p. 981 § 52 Νικόβουλος δ' ἐπίφθονός ἐστι, καὶ ταχέως βαδίζει καὶ μέγα φθέγγεται, καὶ βακτηρίαν φορεῖ and see Sandys on id. Steph. I. §§ 68, 77. Lysias protests against such matters being considered of any importance in a law court, Or. XVI. § 19 πολλοὶ μὲν γὰρ μικρὸν διαλεγόμενοι καὶ κοσμίως ἀμπεχόμενοι μεγάλων κακῶν αἴτιοι γεγόνασιν, ἕτεροι δὲ τῶν τοιούτων ἀμελοῦντες πολλὰ κἀγαθὰ ὑμᾶς εἰσιν εἰργασμένοι.

32. Sext. Emp. Math. II. 7, ἔνθεν γοῦν καὶ Ζήνων ὁ Κιτιεὺς ἐρωτηθεὶς ὅτῳ διαφέρει διαλεκτικὴ ῥητορικῆς συστρέψας τὴν χεῖρα καὶ πάλιν ἐξαπλώσας ἔφη " τούτῳ" κατὰ μὲν τὴν συστροφὴν τὸ στρογγύλον καὶ βραχὺ τῆς διαλεκτικῆς τάττων ἰδίωμα διὰ δὲ τῆς ἐξαπλώσεως καὶ ἐκτάσεως τῶν δακτύλων τὸ πλατὺ τῆς ῥητορικῆς δυνάμεως αἰνιττόμενος. Cic. Fin. II. 17 Zenonis est inquam hoc Stoici omnem vim loquendi, ut jam ante Aristoteles, in duas tributam esse partes, rhetoricae palmam, dialecticam pugni similem esse dicebat, quod latius loquerentur rhetores, dialectici autem compressius. Orat. 32, 113 Zeno quidem ille, a quo disciplina Stoicorum est, manu demonstrare solebat quid inter has artes interesset, nam cum compresserat digitos pugnumque fecerat, dialecticam aiebat eiusmodi esse; cum autem diduxerat et manum dilataverat, palmae illius similem eloquentiam esse dicebat. Quint. Inst. Or. II. 20 Itaque cum duo sint genera orationis, altera perpetua, quae rhetorice dicitur, altera

6—2

concisa, quae dialectice; quas quidem Zeno adeo coniunxit ut hanc compressae in pugnum manus, illam explicitae, diceret similem.

Although this extract and the next purport to be merely spoken remarks of Zeno, it has been thought better to insert them at this place, as distinctly belonging to λογική. Very probably in their original form they came from some written work.

τὸ στρογγύλον is used of a terse and compact as opposed to a florid and elaborate style: thus Dion. Halic. in contrasting the styles of Lysias and Isocrates says:— ἐν τῷ συστρέφειν τὰ νοήματα καὶ στρογγύλως ἐκφέρειν ὡς πρὸς ἀληθινοὺς ἀγῶνας ἐπιτήδειον Λυσίαν ἀπεδεχόμην (Isocr. 11). The translation "well rounded" while seeming to preserve the metaphor conveys a false impression.

33. Cic. Acad. II. 145, At scire negatis quemquam rem ullam nisi sapientem. Et hoc quidem Zeno gestu conficiebat. Nam, cum extensis digitis adversam manum ostenderat, "visum" inquiebat "huiusmodi est." Deinde, cum paullum digitos contraxerat, "adsensus huiusmodi." Tum cum plane compresserat pugnumque fecerat, comprehensionem illam esse dicebat: qua ex similitudine nomen ei rei quod antea non fuerat κατάληψιν imposuit. Cum autem laevam manum adverterat et illum pugnum arte vehementerque compresserat scientiam talem esse dicebat, cuius compotem nisi sapientem esse neminem.

Stein, Erkenntnistheorie p. 181, 313, finds in this passage an indication of the tension theory, but surely this is somewhat far-fetched, for although it is no doubt true that the Stoic theory of knowledge is often made to depend on τόνος, yet probably the introduction of τόνος is later than Zeno. He suggests with more reason p. 126 that the activity of the ἡγεμονικὸν in the process of reasoning may be inferred from this, i.e. the ἡγεμονικόν is not merely receptive (κατὰ πεῖσιν) but also productive (κατ' ἐνέργειαν).

scire: we have already seen that ἐπιστήμη is peculiar to the wise man, while κατάληψις is also shared by the φαῦλος: see note on frag. 16. Sextus speaking of the inconsistency of the Stoics, who would not admit that even Zeno, Cleanthes, and Chrysippus had attained to perfect wisdom, cites as a Stoic dogma πάντα ἀγνοεῖ ὁ φαῦλος (Math. VII. 434). Reid quotes Sext. Pyrrh. II. 83 διόπερ τὴν μὲν ἀλήθειαν ἐν μόνῳ σπουδαίῳ φασὶν εἶναι, τὸ δὲ ἀληθὲς καὶ ἐν φαύλῳ· ἐνδέχεται γὰρ τὸν φαῦλον ἀληθές τι εἰπεῖν.

visum = φαντασία frag. 7. *adsensus* = συγκατάθεσις frag. 19. *comprehensionem* = κατάληψιν, see on frag. 10. *scientiam*, frag. 17.

PHYSICA.

34. Cic. Acad. I. 39, (Zeno) nullo modo arbitrabatur quicquam effici posse ab ea (scil. natura) quae expers esset corporis nec vero aut quod efficeret aliquid aut quod efficeretur posse esse non corpus.

Zeno adopted the Platonic dogma that everything which exists is capable either of acting or being acted upon, cf. Soph. 247 D λέγω δὴ τὸ καὶ ὁποιανοῦν κεκτημένον δύναμιν, εἴτ' εἰς τὸ ποιεῖν ἕτερον ὁτιοῦν πεφυκός, εἴτ' εἰς τὸ παθεῖν καὶ σμικρότατον ὑπὸ τοῦ φαυλοτάτου, κἂν εἰ μόνον εἰσάπαξ, πᾶν τοῦτο ὄντως εἶναι: he differed, however, widely from Plato in limiting these things to material objects. For Stoic materialism cf. Plut. plac. IV. 20 πᾶν γὰρ τὸ δρώμενον ἢ καὶ ποιοῦν σῶμα (quoted by Zeller, Stoics p. 126) and further references ap. Stein, Psychologie n. 21. For the application of this doctrine to theories of sensation and thought see the authorities collected in Dr Reid's note.

35. Diog. L. VII. 134, δοκεῖ δ' αὐτοῖς ἀρχὰς εἶναι τῶν ὅλων δύο τὸ ποιοῦν καὶ τὸ πάσχον. τὸ μὲν οὖν πάσχον εἶναι τὴν ἄποιον οὐσίαν τὴν ὕλην· τὸ δὲ ποιοῦν τὸν ἐν αὐτῇ λόγον τὸν θεόν. τοῦτον γὰρ ὄντα ἀΐδιον διὰ πάσης ὕλης δημιουργεῖν ἕκαστα. τίθησι δὲ τὸ δόγμα τοῦτο Ζήνων ὁ Κιτιεὺς ἐν τῷ περὶ οὐσίας. Plut. plac. I. 3. 39 Ζήνων Μνασέου Κιτιεὺς ἀρχὰς μὲν τὸν θεὸν καὶ τὴν ὕλην, ὧν ὁ μέν ἐστι τοῦ ποιεῖν αἴτιος ἡ δὲ τοῦ πάσχειν, στοιχεῖα δὲ τέτταρα. Stob. Ecl. I. 10. 14 f. 126, 17 Ζήνων Μνασέου Κιτιεὺς ἀρχὰς τὸν θεὸν καὶ τὴν ὕλην στοιχεῖα δὲ τέτταρα. Diels, p. 289, adds the following passages:—Achill. Tat. p. 124 E Ζήνων ὁ Κιτιεὺς ἀρχὰς εἶναι λέγει τῶν ὅλων θεὸν καὶ ὕλην, θεὸν μὲν τὸ ποιοῦν, ὕλην δὲ τὸ ποιούμενον, ἀφ' ὧν τὰ τέσσαρα στοιχεῖα γεγονέναι. Philo, de Provid. I. 22 Zeno Mnaseae filius aerem deum materiam et elementa quatuor [aerem is a blunder arising from ἀρχάς (Diels), which seems better than Stein's suggestion (Psych. n. 31) to substitute aethera]. Theodoret, Gr. cur. aff. IV. 12 Ζήνων δὲ ὁ Κιτιεύς, ὁ Μνασέου, ὁ Κράτητος φοιτητὴς ὁ τῆς Στωικῆς ἄρξας αἱρέσεως τὸν θεὸν καὶ τὴν ὕλην ἀρχὰς ἔφησεν εἶναι.

Cf. Sext. Math. IX. 11: further authorities for the Stoic school in general are given by Zeller, p. 141.

In distinguishing between God as the active efficient cause of the universe and formless indeterminate matter as its underlying substratum Zeno is following on the lines laid down by Plato in the Timaeus and by Aristotle, cf. Theophr. frag. 48 Wimmer (speaking of Plato) δύο τὰς ἀρχὰς βούλεται ποιεῖν τὸ μὲν ὑποκείμενον ὡς ὕλην, ὃ προσαγορεύει πανδεχές, τὸ δ' ὡς αἴτιον καὶ κινοῦν, ὃ περιάπτει τῇ τοῦ θεοῦ καὶ τῇ τἀγαθοῦ δυνάμει: see Introd. p. 25. When we remember that God is by the

Stoics identified with fiery breath, the purest and rarest of all substances, while on the other hand the world itself is merely a temporal manifestation of the primary fire, it becomes apparent that the Stoic dualism is ultimately reducible to a monism and that the system is essentially hylozoistic, like those of the early Ionians (Zeller, Stoics, p. 155, 6. Stein, Psychologie n. 25, collects the passages which prove this). How far this was worked out by Zeno may be doubted: indeed there is no evidence to show that he ever passed beyond the stage of regarding the dual origin of the world as fundamental, and the opinion is now prevalent that Cleanthes by his principle of τόνος was the first to consciously teach the pantheistic doctrines, which subsequently became characteristic of Stoicism.

δημιουργεῖν: a favourite Platonic word, recalling the δημιουργὸς of the Timaeus. For the distinction between ἀρχαὶ and στοιχεῖα cf. Diog. L. VII. 134 διαφέρειν δὲ φασὶν ἀρχὰς καὶ στοιχεῖα· τὰς μὲν γὰρ εἶναι ἀγεννήτους καὶ ἀφθάρτους· τὰ δὲ στοιχεῖα κατὰ τὴν ἐκπύρωσιν φθείρεσθαι.

36. Hippolyt. Philosoph. 21, 1. p. 571 Diels Χρύσιππος καὶ Ζήνων οἳ ὑπέθεντο καὶ αὐτοὶ ἀρχὴν μὲν θεὸν τῶν πάντων σῶμα ὄντα τὸ καθαρώτατον διὰ πάντων δὲ διήκειν τὴν πρόνοιαν αὐτοῦ. Galen. Hist. Philos. 16. p. 241. Diels p. 608 Πλάτων μὲν οὖν καὶ Ζήνων ὁ Στωικὸς περὶ τῆς οὐσίας τοῦ θεοῦ διεληλυθότες οὐχ ὁμοίως περὶ ταύτης διενοήθησαν, ἀλλ' ὁ μὲν Πλάτων θεὸν ἀσώματον, Ζήνων δὲ σῶμα περὶ τῆς μορφῆς μηδὲν εἰρηκότες [if we may rely on Diels' text here, some modification will be required in Stein, Psychologie n. 88, where Kühn's reading οὐ κόσμον ἀλλὰ παρὰ ταῦτα...τι ἄλλο is adopted].

Cf. generally Tatian ad Graec. c. 25 p. 162 c (speaking of the Stoics) σῶμά τις εἶναι λέγει θεόν, ἐγὼ δὲ ἀσώματον. August. adv. Acad. III. 17. 38 (quoted below).

τὸ καθαρώτατον. "God is spoken of as being Fire, Aether, Air, most commonly as being πνεῦμα or Atmospheric Current, pervading everything without exception, what is most base and ugly as well as what is most beautiful," Zeller, Stoics p. 148, who gives the authorities in the notes. καθαρώτατον is used with special reference to διήκειν, cf. Sext. Emp. VII. 375 οὐδὲ τὸ πνεῦμα φύσιν ἔχει πρὸς τοῦτο [τύπωσιν] ἐπιτήδειον, λεπτομερέστατον καὶ εὔρουν παρὰ τὰ τοιαῦτα τῶν σωμάτων ὑπάρχον. Ar. Metaph. I. 8. 3, 4 (speaking of those of his predecessors who had explained generation by σύγκρισις and διάκρισις) τῇ μὲν γὰρ ἂν δόξειε στοιχειωδέστατον εἶναι πάντων ἐξ οὗ γίγνονται συγκρίσει πρῶτον, τοιοῦτον δὲ τὸ μικρομερέστατον καὶ λεπτότατον ἂν εἴη τῶν σωμάτων. διόπερ ὅσοι πῦρ ἀρχὴν τιθέασι μάλιστα ὁμολογουμένως ἂν τῷ λόγῳ τούτῳ λέγοιεν. Krische, Forschungen p. 382.

πρόνοιαν like rationem in the next frag. brings into prominence the spiritual side of the Stoic conception of God, which is everywhere strangely blended with the material.

37. Cic. N. D. I. 36, rationem quandam per omnem rerum naturam pertinentem vi divina esse affectam putat. Cf. Epiphan. adv. Haeres. III. 2. 9 (III. 36) Diels. p. 592 ἔλεγε δὲ πάντα διήκειν τὸ θεῖον.

rationem: the Heraclitean λόγος, Introd. p. 22.

38. Tertullian, ad Nat. II. 4, ecce enim Zeno quoque materiam mundialem a deo separat et eum per illam tamquam mel per favos transisse dicit. Cf. id. adv. Hermog. 44 Stoici enim volunt deum sic per materiam decucurrisse quomodo mel per favos (quoted by Stein, Psychologie, p. 35, n. 43).

favos: κηρία. Zeno's fondness for simile has been

observed upon in the Introd. p. 33. Virgil's lines are well known, Georg. IV. 219 sqq. His quidam signis atque haec exempla secuti Esse apibus partem divinae mentis et haustus Aetherios dixere; deum namque ire per omnes Terrasque tractusque maris caelumque profundum. It is curious that bees should have suggested themselves to both writers, though in a different way, in connection with the same thought, cf. Cic. Acad. II. 120 cuius (divinae sollertiae) vos majestatem deducitis usque ad apium formicarumque perfectionem ut etiam inter deos Myrmecides aliquis minutorum opusculorum fabricator fuisse videatur.

separat: if this is pressed, we must conclude that Zeno never identified God with matter: see n. on frag. 35.

39. Cic. N. D. I. 36, Zeno naturalem legem divinam esse censet eamque vim obtinere recta imperantem prohibentemque contraria. Lactant. Inst. I. 5 Item Zeno (deum nuncupat) divinam naturalemque legem. Minuc. Felic. Octav. 19. 10 Zeno naturalem legem atque divinam... omnium esse principium.

Cf. Diog. L. VII. 88, ὡς ἀπαγορεύειν εἴωθεν ὁ νόμος ὁ κοινὸς ὅπερ ἐστὶν ὁ ὀρθὸς λόγος διὰ πάντων ἐρχόμενος ὁ αὐτὸς ὢν τῷ Διὶ καθηγεμόνι τούτῳ τῆς τῶν ὄντων διοικήσεως ὄντι. Schol. on Lucan II. 9 hoc secundum Stoicos dicit, qui adfirmant mundum prudentia ac lege firmatum, ipsumque deum esse sibi legem. Law regarded in its moral rather than its physical aspect is defined in similar terms in Stob. Ecl. II. 7. 11^d p. 96, 10 = Floril. 46, 12 τόν τε νόμον σπουδαῖον εἶναί φασι λόγον ὀρθὸν ὄντα προστακτικὸν μὲν ὧν ποιητέον, ἀπαγορευτικὸν δὲ ὧν οὐ ποιητέον repeated at II. 7. 11^1, p. 102, 4.

Gods and men are influenced by the same law "quae est recti praeceptio pravique depulsio" Cic. N.D. II. 78.

Law is the human counterpart of the "ratio summa insita in natura" id. Leg. I. 18. The origin of law is simultaneous with that of the divine mind: quamobrem lex vera atque princeps apta ad jubendum et ad vetandum ratio est recta summi Iovis, id. ib. II. 10. For Zeno Right exists φύσει and not merely θέσει, cf. Krische p. 371. Stein, Erkenntnistheorie n. 708.

40. Philodemus περὶ εὐσεβ. c. 8, δεῖ τὴν <δ>ύναμιν οὖσαν συνα<π>τικὴν οἰκε<ί>ως τῶν μερῶ<ν> πρὸ<ς ἄ>λληλα καὶ ἐκ...ων τὴν δ᾽ ἀνα<τολὴ>ν ἡ<λί>ου καὶ κύ<κλησιν> ἢ περίοδον.

The position of these words with reference to their context corresponding to Cic. N.D. I. 36 points to Zeno's authorship. "Stoica frustula dubitanter ad Zenonem refero" Diels p. 542.

τὴν δύναμιν. This is evidently a Stoic description of God as the power which binds the parts of the world together and keeps them in union.

συναπτικήν. We should expect συνεκτικήν, which is the more natural word in this connection. Sext. Math. IX. 84 ἀνάγκη ἄρα ὑπὸ τῆς ἀρίστης αὐτὸν (τὸν κόσμον) φύσεως συνέχεσθαι ἐπεὶ καὶ περιέχει τὰς πάντων φύσεις ...τοιαύτη δὲ τυγχάνουσα θεός ἐστιν. On the other hand συνάπτω συναφή and the like are technically applied to the structure of manufactured articles, which are said to be ἐκ συναπτομένων) (ἡνωμένα: ib. 78 ἐκ συναπτομένων δὲ τὰ ἔκ τε παρακειμένων καὶ πρὸς ἕν τι κεφάλαιον νευόντων συνεστῶτα ὡς ἁλύσεις καὶ πυργίσκοι καὶ νῆες.

41. Cic. N.D. I. 36, aethera deum dicit (Zeno). Tertullian adv. Marcion I. 13 deos pronuntiaverunt...ut Zeno aerem et aetherem. Minuc. Fel. 19. 10 aethera interdiu omnium esse principium. Cic. Acad. II. 126 Zenoni et reliquis fere Stoicis aether videtur summus deus [if fere is pressed here, it points to the exception of Cleanthes, but see on Cleanth. fr. 15].

aethera not to be confounded with ἀήρ, which is one of the four elements and subject to destruction; aerem in Tertull. is probably a blunder, unless with Stein, Psych. n. 80, aut should be read for et. The aether here in question is an equivalent of πνεῦμα or of πῦρ τεχνικόν, i.e. it is merely one of the labels convenient to express the material essence of God. Neither πῦρ nor αἰθήρ is regarded in itself as a complete description. For the distinction between the Stoic αἰθήρ and the Heraclitean πῦρ see Stein, Psychologie p. 26 and n. 31. The Stoic deity is at once corporeal and rational: but how far it may be said to have been personified cannot be determined: in fact, as has been remarked, the ancients seem to have grasped the notion of personification with much less distinctness than modern thinkers.

42. Stob. Ecl. I. 1. 29^b p. 35, 9, Ζήνων ὁ Στωικὸς νοῦν κόσμου πύρινον (scil. θεὸν ἀπεφήνατο). August. adv. Acad. III. 17. 38 nam et deum ipsum ignem putavit (Zeno).

Cf. Stob. Ecl. I. 1. 29^b p. 38, 2 ἀνωτάτω πάντων νοῦν ἐναιθέριον εἶναι θεόν.

For the Stoic conception of the World-Soul see Stein, Psychologie p. 41, who distinguishes the world soul from the Aether God, the former being an offshoot from the latter. "Die Weltseele ist nur ein Absenker jenes Urpneumarestes der als Gott Aether unser Weltganzes umspannt; sie ist als Ausfluss der Gottheit jenes künstlerische göttliche Feuer (πῦρ τεχνικὸν) das die Keimkräfte (σπερματικοὺς λόγους) der Weltbildung im allgemeinen und der Einzelbildungen insbesondere in sich enthält." In regarding νοῦς as an indwelling material essence Zeno revived the position formerly taken up by Diogenes of

Apollonia in opposition to Anaxagoras: see the fragment quoted by Zeller, Pre-Socraties, E. T. I. p. 287 n. 7.

The MSS κόσμον was corrected to κόσμου by Krische p. 378, who supplies θεὸν ἀπεφήνατο. Hirzel II. p. 220, 2 prefers to put a comma after κόσμου: otherwise καὶ πύρινον is necessary.

43. Themist. de An. 72 b [ed. Speng. II. p. 64, 25] τάχα δὲ καὶ τοῖς ἀπὸ Ζήνωνος σύμφωνος ἡ δόξα διὰ πάσης οὐσίας πεφοιτηκέναι τὸν θεὸν τιθεμένοις καὶ ποῦ μὲν εἶναι νοῦν ποῦ δὲ ψυχὴν ποῦ δὲ φύσιν ποῦ δὲ ἕξιν.

This same force, appearing in different substances, is called ἕξις as the bond of union for inorganic matter, φύσις in the case of plants, ψυχή in the case of animals, and νοῦς as belonging to rational beings. Diog. L. VII. 139 δι' ὧν μὲν γὰρ ὡς ἕξις κεχώρηκεν ὡς διὰ τῶν ὀστῶν καὶ τῶν νεύρων δι' ὧν δὲ ὡς νοῦς ὡς διὰ τοῦ ἡγεμονικοῦ, cf. Cleanth. Frag. 51. Some Stoics seem however to have denied this distinction between ψυχή and νοῦς. Nemes. Nat. Hom. c. 1 (quoted by Stein, Psych. pp. 92, 3) τινὲς δὲ οὐ διέστειλαν ἀπὸ τῆς ψυχῆς τὸν νοῦν· ἀλλὰ τῆς οὐσίας αὐτῆς ἡγεμονικὸν εἶναι τὸ νοερὸν ἡγοῦνται. Stein however is not justified in holding that the living principle of animals occupies a position midway between φύσις and ψυχή, as will be shown on Cleanth. frag. 44. That the passage is good evidence that the distinction between ἕξις, φύσις and ψυχή is Zenonian may be inferred from the words σύμφωνος ἡ δόξα.

44. Lactant. de Vera Sap. c. 9, Zeno rerum naturae dispositorem atque artificem universitatis λόγον praedicat quem et fatum et necessitatem rerum et deum et animum Iovis nuncupat. Tertull. Apol. 21 Apud vestros quoque sapientes λόγον id est sermonem atque rationem constat artificem videri universitatis. Hunc enim Zeno determinat factitatorem qui cuncta in dispositione formaverit eundem et fatum vocari et deum et animum Iovis et necessitatem omnium rerum. Minuc. Fel. 19. 10 rationem deum vocat Zeno. Lact. Inst. IV. 9 siquidem Zeno rerum naturae dispositorem atque opificem universitatis λόγον praedicat quem et fatum et necessitatem rerum et deum et animum Iovis nuncupat: ea scilicet consuetudine qua solent Iovem pro deo accipere.

45. Stob. Ecl. I. 5. 15. p. 78, 18, Ζήνων ὁ Στωικὸς ἐν τῷ περὶ φύσεως (τὴν εἱμαρμένην) δύναμιν κινητικὴν τῆς ὕλης κατὰ ταὐτὰ καὶ ὡσαύτως ἥντινα μὴ διαφέρειν πρόνοιαν καὶ φύσιν καλεῖν. Theodoret, Graec. Aff. Cur. VI. 14. p. 87, 26 Ζήνων δὲ ὁ Κιτεὺς δύναμιν κέκληκε τὴν εἱμαρμένην κινητικὴν τῆς ὕλης τὴν δὲ αὐτὴν καὶ πρόνοιαν καὶ φύσιν ὠνόμασεν.

μὴ διαφέρειν. God receives different names, while his essence is constant, owing to the various phases of his union with matter (τὰς προσηγορίας μεταλαμβάνειν δι' ὅλης τῆς ὕλης δι' ἧς κεχώρηκε παράλλαξαν Stob. Ecl. I. 1. 29b p. 37, 23, according to Diels and Wachsmuth a mistake for διὰ τὰς τῆς ὕλης δι' ἧς κεχώρηκε παραλλάξεις). Thus he is Fate as acting in accordance with a constant law, Forethought as working to an end, and Nature as creator of the word. Cf. Athenag. Supplic. c. 6. p. 7 B οἱ δὲ ἀπὸ τῆς στοᾶς κἂν ταῖς προσηγορίαις κατὰ τὰς παραλλάξεις τῆς ὕλης, δι' ἧς φασι τὸ πνεῦμα χωρεῖν τοῦ θεοῦ, πληθύνωσι τὸ θεῖον τοῖς ὀνόμασι, τῷ γοῦν ἔργῳ ἕνα νομίζουσι τὸν θεόν· εἰ γὰρ ὁ μὲν θεὸς πῦρ τεχνικὸν ὁδῷ βαδίζον ἐπὶ γενέσεις κόσμου ἐμπεριειληφὸς ἅπαντας τοὺς σπερματικοὺς λόγους καθ' οὓς ἕκαστα καθ' εἱμαρμένην γίνεται, τὸ δὲ πνεῦμα αὐτοῦ διήκει δι' ὅλου τοῦ κόσμου, ὁ θεὸς εἷς κατ' αὐτοὺς Ζεὺς μὲν κατὰ τὸ ζέον τῆς ὕλης ὀνομαζόμενος Ἥρα δὲ κατὰ τὸν ἀέρα καὶ τὰ λοιπὰ καθ' ἕκαστον τῆς ὕλης μέρος δι' ἧς κεχώρηκεν καλούμενος. In this connection it may be observed that Gercke (Chrysippea, p. 697) is mistaken in speaking of a fragment of Zeno as preserved by Aristocles ap. Euseb. P. E. xv. 14. The reference there is to the Stoics generally and not to Zeno in particular.

45 A. Diog. L. VII. 149, καθ' εἱμαρμένην δέ φασι τὰ πάντα γίγνεσθαι Χρύσιππος...καὶ Ποσειδώνιος...καὶ Ζήνων Βοηθὸς δέ.

Since εἱμαρμένη is identical with πρόνοια, it follows that everything is produced κατὰ πρόνοιαν. Cleanthes, however, demurred to this (frag. 18).

46. Cic. N.D. II. 57, Zeno igitur ita naturam definit ut eam dicat ignem esse artificiosum ad gignendum progredientem via. Censet enim artis maxime proprium esse creare et gignere, quodque in operibus nostrarum artium manus efficiat, id multo artificiosius naturam efficere, id est, ut dixi, ignem artificiosum magistrum artium reliquarum. Cic. Acad. I. 39 Zeno statuebat ignem esse ipsam naturam. N.D. III. 27 naturae artificiose ambulantis, ut ait Zeno. Wachsmuth (Comm. I. p. 9) adds Tertull. ad. Nat. II. 2 cuius (ignis) instar vult esse naturam Zeno.

The Greek of the definition is ἡ φύσις ἐστι πῦρ τεχνικὸν ὁδῷ βαδίζον εἰς γένεσιν, Diog. L. VII. 156. Clem. Alex. Strom. v. p. 597. φύσις is only another name for God viewed in his creative capacity. Hence Stob. Ecl. I. 1. 29[b] p. 37, 20 οἱ Στωικοὶ νοερὸν θεὸν ἀποφαίνονται πῦρ τεχνικὸν ὁδῷ βαδίζον ἐπὶ γενέσει κόσμου, ἐμπεριειληφὸς πάντας τοὺς σπερματικοὺς λόγους καθ' οὓς ἅπαντα καθ' εἱμαρμένην γίνεται: Athenag. l. c. Wellmann, p. 472 and Weygoldt p. 35 think that λόγος σπερματικὸς is a Zenonian expression. So Stein, Psych. p. 49 and n. 87.

47. Tatian ad Graec. c. 3, p. 143 c, καὶ ὁ θεὸς ἀποδειχθήσεται κακῶν κατ' αὐτὸν (scil. Ζήνωνα) ποιητής, ἐν ἀμάραις τε καὶ σκώληξι καὶ ἀρρητουργοῖς καταγινόμενος.

Cf. Clem. Alex. Protrept. 5 § 66 οὐδὲ μὴν τοὺς ἀπὸ τῆς Στοᾶς παρελεύσομαι διὰ πάσης ὕλης καὶ διὰ τῆς ἀτιμοτάτης τὸ θεῖον διήκειν λέγοντας· οἳ καταισχύνουσιν ἀτεχνῶς τὴν φιλοσοφίαν: Sext. Pyrrh. III. 218 Στωικοὶ δὲ πνεῦμα διῆκον καὶ διὰ τῶν εἰδεχθῶν: Cic. Acad. II. 120 cur deus omnia nostra causa cum faceret—sic enim voltis—tantam vim natricum viperarumque fecerit? cur mortifera tam multa et perniciosa terra marique disperserit? We have no information as to what answer Zeno made to this objection, but the later Stoics said that physical evils ultimately served a good purpose: so Chrysippus ap. Plut. Sto. Rep. 21, 4 quoted by Zeller, p. 189. As to the existence of moral evil see on Cleanth. fr. 48, l. 17 and Wellmann's discussion at p. 472.

48. Cic. N. D. II. 58, Ipsius vero mundi qui omnia complexu suo coercet et continet natura non artificiosa solum sed plane artifex ab eodem Zenone dicitur consultrix et provida utilitatum opportunitatumque omnium.

An ingenious explanation of this difficult passage is given by Stein, Psychologie, pp. 42, 43 in accordance with his view of the distinction between World-Soul and Aether-God. "Die natura artificiosa ist unseres Erachtens die Weltseele, während die natura plane artifex sich auf den Gott Aether oder das ἡγεμονικὸν der Welt bezieht." The πνεῦμα which permeates the universe is ignis artificiosus and only secondarily represents God, since it is an efflux from him. It cannot be described as plane artifex, a term which is applied to God (σῶμα τὸ καθαρώτατον), whereas the world-soul is less καθαρὸν from its combination with matter.

artifex: probably a translation of τεχνίτης Diog. L. VII. 86, but Hirzel II. p. 220 represents it by δημιουργός, in which case cf. Diog. L. VII. 137.

49. Chalcid. in Tim. c. 290, Plerique tamen silvam separant ab essentia, ut Zeno et Chrysippus. Silvam quippe dicunt esse id quod subest his omnibus quae habent qualitates, essentiam vero primam rerum omnium silvam vel antiquissimum fundamentum earum, suapte natura sine vultu et informe: ut puta aes, aurum, ferrum, et caetera huius modi silva est eorum, quae ex iisdem fabrefiunt, non tamen essentia. At vero quod tam his quam ceteris ut sint causa est, ipsum esse substantiam.

This passage shows that Zeno distinguished between οὐσία and ὕλη—the former the indeterminate and formless matter underlying the universe, and the latter the stuff out of which a particular thing is made. ὕλη is thus from one point of view the more general term, since οὐσία = πρώτη ὕλη (frag. 51). Cf. Dexipp. ad Cat. Schol. Arist. Brandis 45 a 21 ἐστὶ τὸ ὑποκειμένον διττὸν καὶ κατὰ τοὺς ἀπὸ τῆς στοᾶς καὶ κατὰ τοὺς πρεσβυτέρους ἓν μὲν τὸ λεγόμενον πρῶτον ὑποκείμενον ὡς ἡ ἄποιος ὕλη ἣν δυνάμει σῶμα ὁ Ἀριστοτέλης φησὶν δεύτερον δὲ ὑποκείμενον τὸ ποιὸν ὃ κοινῶς ἢ ἰδίως ὑφίστατο κ.τ.λ. Similarly Arist. Metaph. VII. 4. 1044 a 15 distinguishes πρώτη and οἰκεία ὕλη and ib. IV. 24. 1023 a 27 says that material origin may be specified in two ways ἢ κατὰ τὸ πρῶτον γένος ἢ κατὰ τὸ ὕστατον εἶδος οἷον ἔστι μὲν ὡς ἅπαντα τὰ τηκτὰ ἐξ ὕδατος (i.e. brass as being fusible comes from water) ἔστι δ' ὡς ἐκ χαλκοῦ ὁ ἀνδριάς. The point of view of Posidonius is different: he holds διαφέρειν τὴν οὐσίαν τῆς ὕλης τὴν <αὐτὴν> οὖσαν κατὰ τὴν ὑπόστασιν, ἐπινοίᾳ μόνον. Stob. Ecl. I. 11. 5ᶜ, p. 133, 22. Wellmann (Neue Jahrb. vol. 115, p. 808) denies that it is a necessary inference from this passage that Zeno taught the doctrine of the four Stoic categories. Stein, Psych. n. 73, explaining the passage generally as above, apparently identifies οὐσία with κοινῶς ποιόν, and ὕλη with ἰδίως ποιόν, but this distinction is a subordinate one, for οὐσία is entirely distinct from ποιόν, whether κοινῶς or ἰδίως, as Dexipp. l.c. shows.

50. Chalcid. in Tim. c. 292. Deinde Zeno hanc ipsam essentiam finitam esse dicit unamque eam communem omnium quae sunt esse substantiam, dividuam quoque et usque quaque mutabilem: partes quippe eius verti, sed non interire, ita ut de existentibus consumantur in nihilum. Sed ut innumerabilium diversarum, etiam cerearum figurarum, sic neque formam neque figuram nec ullam omnino qualitatem propriam fore censet fundamenti rerum omnium silvae, coniunctam tamen esse semper et inseparabiliter cohaerere alicui qualitati. Cumque tam sine ortu sit quam sine interitu, quia neque de non existente subsistit neque consumetur in nihilum, non deesse ei spiritum ac vigorem ex aeternitate, qui moveat eam rationabiliter totam interdum, nonnumquam pro portione, quae causa sit tam crebrae tamque vehementis universae rei conversionis; spiritum porro motivum illum fore non naturam, sed animam et quidem rationabilem, quae vivificans sensilem mundum exornaverit eum ad hanc, qua nunc inlustratur, venustatem. Quem quidem beatum animal et deum adpellant.

finitam. This is in strong contrast with Epicurean teaching: it follows from the Stoic doctrine of the unity of the world, and is connected with that of the infinity of space, cf. Chrysippus ap. Stob. Ecl. I. 18. 4^d p. 161, 19 τὸν δὲ τόπον (i.e. full space) πεπερασμένον διὰ τὸ μηδὲν σῶμα ἄπειρον εἶναι. καθάπερ δὲ τὸ σωματικὸν πεπερασμένον είναι ούτως τὸ ἀσώματον ἄπειρον, Diog. VII. 150 σῶμα δέ ἐστι κατ' αὐτοὺς ἡ οὐσία καὶ πεπερασμένη. The Stoic view is refuted by Lucr. I. 1008—1051, who concludes thus:— infinita opus est vis undique materiai. Similarly Diog. L. x. 41 εἴτε γὰρ ἦν τὸ κενὸν ἄπειρον τὰ δὲ σώματα ὡρισμένα, οὐδαμοῦ ἂν ἔμενε τὰ σώματα, ἀλλ' ἐφέρετο κατὰ τὸ ἄπειρον κενὸν διεσπαρμένα, οὐκ ἔχοντα τὰ ὑπερείδοντα καὶ στέλλοντα κατὰ τὰς ἀντικοπάς.

unamque eam etc. See on frag. 51.

cerearum: wax is chosen as being one of the most pliable substances. Cf. Sext. Math. VII. 375 ὁ μαλακώτατος κηρός...τυποῦται μὲν ὑπό τινος ἅμα νοήματι διὰ τὴν ὑγρότητα οὐ συνέχει δὲ τὸν τύπον. A very close parallel will be found in Ov. Met. XV. 169: (of Pythagoras)

utque novis facilis signatur cera figuris,
nec manet ut fuerat, nec formas servat easdem,
sed tamen ipsa eadem est; animam sic semper eandem
esse, sed in varias doceo migrare figuras.

neque formam etc. Cf. Posid. ap. Stob. Ecl. I. 11. 5[c] p. 133, 18 τὴν τῶν ὅλων οὐσίαν καὶ ὕλην ἄποιον καὶ ἄμορφον εἶναι καθ' ὅσον οὐδὲν ἀποτεταγμένον ἴδιον ἔχει σχῆμα οὐδὲ ποιότητα καθ' αὐτὴν ἀεὶ δ' ἔν τινι σχήματι καὶ ποιότητι εἶναι. In this respect the Stoics simply adopted Aristotle's conception of ὕλη, cf. Metaph. Z. 3. 1029 a 20 λέγω δ' ὕλην ἢ καθ' αὐτὴν μήτε τι μήτε ποσὸν μήτε ἄλλο μηδὲν λέγεται οἷς ὥρισται τὸ ὄν. Arist. ap. Stob. Ecl. I. 11. 4, p. 132 foll. concluding thus:—δεῖν γὰρ ἀμφοῖν (i.e. ὕλης καὶ εἴδους) τῆς συνόδου πρὸς τὴν τοῦ σώματος ὑπόστασιν. The distinction between the two schools is that, whereas the Stoics defined ὕλη as σῶμα (Stob. Ecl. I. 11. 5[b] p. 133, 16), Aristotle declared it to be σωματική merely, but this distinction is more apparent than real.

sine ortu: ἀίδιος, σύγχρονος τῷ θεῷ, infra frag. 51.

neque de non existente: the denial of ἁπλῶς γένεσις ἐκ μὴ ὄντος is common to all ancient philosophy. See Tyndall, fragments of Science p. 91 (quoted by Munro on Lucr. I. 150), "One fundamental thought pervades all these statements, there is one taproot from which they all spring: this is the ancient notion that out of nothing nothing comes, that neither in the organic world, nor in the inorganic, is power produced without the expenditure of other power." Cf. Posidonius ap. Stob. Ecl. I. 20. 7, p. 178, 2, τὴν μὲν γὰρ ἐκ τῶν οὐκ ὄντων καὶ τὴν εἰς οὐκ ὄντα (φθορὰν καὶ γένεσιν)...ἀπέγνωσαν ἀνύπαρκτον οὖσαν. M. Aurel. IV. 4.

moveat, κινητικὴν τῆς ὕλης, frag. 45.

non naturam: in apparent contradiction to frag. 46, but we shall probably explain: the πνεῦμα is not merely φύσις, it is also ψυχή, nay more it is ψυχὴ λόγον ἔχουσα, i.e. νοῦς.

animal, frag. 62. *deum:* observe that this is attributed to the school in general and not to Zeno in particular, cf. frag. 66.

51. Stob. Ecl. I. 11. 5[a], p. 132, 26. Ζήνωνος· οὐσίαν δὲ εἶναι τὴν τῶν ὄντων πάντων πρώτην ὕλην, ταύτην δὲ πᾶσαν ἀίδιον καὶ οὔτε πλείω γιγνομένην οὔτε ἐλάττω· τὰ δὲ μέρη ταύτης οὐκ ἀεὶ ταὐτὰ διαμένειν ἀλλὰ διαιρεῖσθαι καὶ συγχεῖσθαι. διὰ ταύτης δὲ διαθεῖν τὸν τοῦ παντὸς λόγον, ὃν ἔνιοι εἱμαρμένην καλοῦσιν, οἷόνπερ ἐν τῇ γονῇ τὸ σπέρμα. Epiphan. Haeres. I. 5, Diels, p. 558, φάσκει οὖν καὶ οὗτος (Ζήνων) τὴν ὕλην σύγχρονον καλῶν τῷ θεῷ ἴσα ταῖς ἄλλαις αἱρέσεσιν, εἱμαρμένην τε εἶναι καὶ γένεσιν ἐξ ἧς τὰ πάντα διοικεῖται καὶ πάσχει. Diog. L. VII. 150, οὐσίαν δέ φασι τῶν ὄντων ἁπάντων τὴν πρώτην ὕλην ὥς...Ζήνων...καλεῖται δὲ διχῶς οὐσία τε καὶ ὕλη ἥ τε τῶν πάντων καὶ ἡ τῶν ἐπὶ μέρους. ἡ μὲν οὖν τῶν ὅλων οὔτε πλείων οὔτε ἐλάττων γίνεται· ἡ δὲ τῶν ἐπὶ μέρους καὶ πλείων καὶ ἐλάττων. Tertull. de Praes. Cup. c. 7, et ubi materia cum deo exaequatur Zenonis disciplina est.

Cf. Chalcid. in Tim. c. 294, Stoici deum scilicet hoc esse quod silva sit vel etiam qualitatem inseparabilem deum silvae, eundemque per silvam meare, velut semen per membra genitalia.

οὔτε πλείω. The ἄποιος ὕλη is, as we have seen, ὡρισμένη and πεπερασμένη: being also ἀΐδιος it is incapable of increase or diminution. Its parts however (i.e. matter as seen in the ἰδίως ποιὸν or individually determined thing) are subject to destruction and change. See the further authorities cited by Zeller, Stoics, p. 101, n. 2.

διαιρεῖσθαι καὶ συγχεῖσθαι. Strictly speaking both these terms are to be distinguished from the theory of intermingling which was characteristic of Stoicism (κρᾶσις δι' ὅλων, and see infra). Thus διαίρεσις is the separation of substances which have been combined by παράθεσις, e.g. a heap of barley, wheat or beans, while σύγχυσις is the chemical fusion of two distinct substances which lose their essential properties in consequence of the process (Chrysipp. ap. Stob. Ecl. I. 17. 4, p. 154, 10—155, 14). The Stoic κρᾶσις or μῖξις is distinguished from the former by its implication of entire permeation, and from the latter owing to the retention of their properties by the ingredients.

52. Stob. Ecl. I. 17. 3, p. 152, 19. Ζήνωνα δὲ οὕτως ἀποφαίνεσθαι διαρρήδην· τοιαύτην δὲ δεήσει εἶναι ἐν περιόδῳ τὴν τοῦ ὅλου διακόσμησιν ἐκ τῆς οὐσίας, ὅταν ἐκ πυρὸς τροπὴ εἰς ὕδωρ δι' ἀέρος γένηται, τὸ μέν τι ὑφίστασθαι καὶ γῆν συνίστασθαι [καὶ] ἐκ τοῦ λοιποῦ δὲ τὸ μὲν διαμένειν ὕδωρ, ἐκ δὲ τοῦ ἀτμιζομένου ἀέρα γίνεσθαι λεπτυνομένου δὲ τοῦ ἀέρος πῦρ ἐξάπτεσθαι, τὴν δὲ μῖξιν <καὶ> κρᾶσιν γίνεσθαι τῇ εἰς ἄλληλα τῶν στοιχείων μεταβολῇ σώματος ὅλου δι' ὅλου τινὸς ἑτέρου διερχομένου. Diog. L. VII. 135, 136, ἕν τε εἶναι θεὸν καὶ νοῦν καὶ εἱμαρμένην καὶ Δία πολλαῖς τε ἑτέραις ὀνομασίαις προσονομάζεσθαι. κατ' ἀρχὰς μὲν οὖν καθ' αὑτὸν ὄντα τρέπειν τὴν πᾶσαν οὐσίαν δι' ἀέρος εἰς ὕδωρ· καὶ ὥσπερ ἐν τῇ γονῇ τὸ σπέρμα περιέχεται οὕτω καὶ τοῦτον σπερματικὸν λόγον ὄντα τοῦ κόσμου, τοιόνδε ὑπολείπεσθαι ἐν τῷ ὑγρῷ εὐεργὸν αὑτῷ ποιοῦντα τὴν ὕλην πρὸς τὴν τῶν ἑξῆς γένεσιν· εἶτα ἀπογεννᾶν πρῶτον τὰ τέσσαρα στοιχεῖα πῦρ, ὕδωρ, ἀέρα, γῆν. λέγει δὲ περὶ αὐτῶν Ζήνων ἐν τῷ περὶ τοῦ ὅλου. Diog. L. VII. 142, γίνεσθαι δὲ τὸν κόσμον ὅταν ἐκ πυρὸς ἡ οὐσία τραπῇ δι' ἀέρος εἰς ὑγρότητα, εἶτα τὸ παχυμερὲς αὐτοῦ συστὰν ἀποτελεσθῇ γῆ τὸ δὲ λεπτομερὲς ἐξαερωθῇ, καὶ τοῦτ' ἐπὶ πλέον λεπτυνθὲν πῦρ ἀπογεννήσῃ· εἶτα κατὰ μῖξιν ἐκ τούτων φυτά τε καὶ ζῷα καὶ τὰ ἄλλα γένη. περὶ δὴ οὖν τῆς γενέσεως καὶ τῆς φθορᾶς τοῦ κόσμου φησὶ Ζήνων μὲν ἐν τῷ περὶ ὅλου, κ.τ.λ. Probus ad Verg. p. 10, 33 K. ex his (quatuor elementis) omnia esse postea effigiata Stoici tradunt Zenon Citieus et Chrysippus Solaeus et Cleanthes Assius.

ἐν περιόδῳ: these words seem to refer to the periodic renewal of the world after each ἐκπύρωσις and to a constantly recurring cycle in the course of the universe, rather than to the mutual interchange of the four elements which goes on during the actual existence of the world, cf. Marc. Aurel. x. 7, ὥστε καὶ ταῦτα ἀναληφθῆναι εἰς τὸν τοῦ ὅλου λόγον, εἴτε κατὰ περίοδον ἐκπυρουμένου εἴτε κ.τ.λ. Numenius ap. Euseb. P. E. xv. 18. 1, ἀρέσκει δὲ τοῖς πρεσβυτάτοις τῶν ἀπὸ τῆς αἱρέσεως ταύτης ἐξυγροῦσθαι πάντα κατὰ περιόδους τινὰς τὰς μεγίστας εἰς πῦρ αἰθερῶδες ἀναλυομένων πάντων.

ὅταν ἐκ πυρὸς τροπή κ.τ.λ. The evolution of ὕδωρ from the πῦρ τεχνικὸν is first described and then the subsequent generation of the four elements from τὸ ὑγρόν. This appears more clearly in the first extract from Diogenes than in the actual words of Zeno as reported by Stobaeus. Zeno is here following very closely in the footsteps of Heraclitus (πυρὸς τροπαὶ πρῶτον θάλασσα· θαλάσσης δὲ τὸ μὲν ἥμισυ γῆ τὸ δὲ ἥμισυ πρηστήρ, R. and P. § 30) but differs from him in adopting the theory of the four elements, and to this fact is due the introduction of the words δι' ἀέρος. Cf. also the account of Anaximenes, ap. Simpl. Phys. p. 6 a, Ἀναξιμένης ἀραιούμενον μὲν τὸν ἀέρα πῦρ γίγνεσθαί φησι, πυκνούμενον δὲ ἄνεμον, εἶτα νέφος, εἶτα ἔτι μᾶλλον ὕδωρ, εἶτα γῆν, εἶτα λίθους τὰ δὲ ἄλλα ἐκ τούτων. The ἄνω κάτω ὁδὸς appears clearly in the passage in Stobaeus, cf. Cleanth. frag. 21. There are certain difficulties in this account of the διακόσμησις, which, although not discussed in the authorities, it is right to state even if no satisfactory solution of them can be given. (1) Is the ἐξύγρωσις entirely distinct from and anterior to the formation of the four elements? If Diog.'s account is based upon Zeno, this question must be answered in the affirmative, but in Stobaeus it appears rather as an ordinary stage in the κάτω ὁδός. That an entire resolution of the πῦρ τεχνικὸν into ὑγρόν (except as regards τὸ ἔσχατον τοῦ πυρός) was taught by the Stoa is also clear from Cornut. c. 17, p. 85, Osann. ἔστι δὲ Χάος μὲν τὸ πρὸ τῆς διακοσμήσεως γενόμενον ὑγρόν, ἀπὸ τῆς χύσεως οὕτως ὠνομασμένον, ἢ τὸ πῦρ, ὅ ἐστιν οἱονεὶ κάος...ἦν δέ ποτε, ὦ παῖ, πῦρ τὸ πᾶν καὶ γενήσεται πάλιν ἐν περιόδῳ· σβεσθέντος δ' εἰς ἀέρα αὐτοῦ μεταβολὴ ἀθρόα γίνεται εἰς ὕδωρ· ὃ δὴ λαμβάνει τοῦ μὲν ὑφισταμένου μέρους τῆς οὐσίας κατὰ πύκνωσιν τοῦ δὲ λεπτυνομένου κατὰ ἀραίωσιν.

(2) Is the ἐξύγρωσις merely a step in the creative process or is it to be regarded, as it apparently was by Cleanthes, as the antithesis of the ἐκπύρωσις? Perhaps it is safest to regard Zeno as an exponent of the simple ὁδὸς ἄνω κάτω and to treat the complications in connection with the τόνος theory of Cleanthes (frag. 24).

τροπῆ, codd. corr. Heeren. τραπῆ, Mein. (del. γένηται) coll. D. L. VII. 142.

λεπτυνομένου, κ.τ.λ. is the corr. of Wachsm. for the MSS. ἔκ τινος δὲ τοῦ ἀέρος, coll. Chrysipp. ap. Plut. Sto. Rep. 41, 3.

μῖξιν. The mixture of dry substances)(κρᾶσιν the fusion of moist. For a full discussion of the peculiar Stoic doctrine, see Zeller, Stoics, p. 136 foll. It carries with it practically a negation of the physical truth that two bodies cannot occupy the same space. Chrysippus, who devoted much attention both to the positive exposition and controversial defence of this doctrine, illustrated it by several practical examples, one of which, from its obscurity, deserves consideration: καὶ γὰρ εἰς πέλαγος ὀλίγος οἶνος βληθεὶς ἐπὶ πόσον ἀντιπαρεκταθήσεται συμφθαρήσεται (Diog. L. VII. 151), i.e. the disappearance of the wine particles can only be explained on the hypothesis of their equable distribution. Stein observes (Psych. nn. 29,35) that the Ionian ἀλλοίωσις is not found in the Stoa before Marcus Aurelius, but this is inaccurate. Thus Posidonius, ap. Stob. Ecl. I. 25, p. 178, 7, after explaining that there are four kinds of μεταβολή, (1) κατὰ διαίρεσιν, (2) κατ' ἀλλοίωσιν, (3) κατὰ σύγχυσιν, (4) ἐξ ὅλων or κατ' ἀνάλυσιν, proceeds:—τούτων δὲ τὴν κατ' ἀλλοίωσιν περὶ τὴν οὐσίαν γίνεσθαι τὰς δ' ἄλλας τρεῖς περὶ τοὺς ποιοὺς λεγομένους τοὺς ἐπὶ τῆς οὐσίας γινομένους.

53. Galen, εἰς τὸ Ἱπποκράτου ὑπόμνημα περὶ χυμῶν I. (XVI. 32 K.) Ζήνων τε ὁ Κιτιεὸς [ὃς] τὰς ποιότητας οὕτω

καὶ τὰς οὐσίας δι' ὅλου κεράννυσθαι ἐνόμιζεν, id. de nat. facult. I. 2, εἰ δ' ὥσπερ τὰς ποιότητας καὶ τὰς οὐσίας δι' ὅλων κεράννυσθαι χρὴ νομίζειν, ὡς ὕστερον ἀπεφήνατο Ζήνων ὁ Κιτιεός. (Galen says that this theory was ultimately due to Hippocrates, from whom Aristotle took it.)

The best commentary on this frag. is to be found in Sext. Pyrrh. III. 57—62, which contains a statement and refutation of the doctrine here referred to. The following short summary will make the meaning clear:—Things which are subject to the influence of κρᾶσις are themselves a combination of οὐσία and ποιότητες: when mixture takes place, we must either say that the οὐσίαι are mixed or that the ποιότητες are mixed, or that both or neither are mixed. The last alternative is obviously absurd, and the same may be shown to be the case with either of the two first, λείπεται λέγειν ὅτι καὶ αἱ ποιότητες τῶν κιρναμένων καὶ αἱ οὐσίαι χωροῦσι δι' ἀλλήλων καὶ μιγνύμεναι τὴν κρᾶσιν ἀποτελοῦσιν (§ 59). But this is still more absurd. Mix one spoonful of hemlock juice with ten of water: if both entirely permeate each other, they must occupy the same space and be equal to each other. The result of the mixture ought therefore to give us either 20 spoonfuls or 2. The whole discussion is one which strikes a modern reader as particularly barren and pedantic, but it should never be forgotten that to the Stoics ποιότης was material no less than οὐσία. "Aristotle's εἶδος becomes a current of air or gas (πνεῦμα), the essential reason of the thing is itself material, standing to it in the relation of a gaseous to a solid body." (Encycl. Brit. Art. Stoics.)

54. Stob. Ecl. I. 20. 1ᵉ, p. 171, 2. Ζήνωνι καὶ Κλεάνθει καὶ Χρυσίππῳ ἀρέσκει τὴν οὐσίαν μεταβάλλειν οἷον εἰς σπέρμα τὸ πῦρ, καὶ πάλιν ἐκ τούτου τοιαύτην ἀποτελεῖσθαι τὴν διακόσμησιν οἵα πρότερον ἦν. Euseb. P. E. xv. 18. 3, ἀρέσκει γὰρ τοῖς Στωικοῖς φιλοσόφοις τὴν ὅλην οὐσίαν μεταβάλλειν εἰς πῦρ οἷον εἰς σπέρμα καὶ πάλιν ἐκ τούτου αὐτὴν ἀποτελεῖσθαι τὴν διακόσμησιν οἵα τὸ πρότερον ἦν καὶ τοῦτο τὸ δόγμα τῶν ἀπὸ τῆς αἱρέσεως οἱ πρῶτοι καὶ πρεσβύτατοι προσήκαντο Ζήνων τε καὶ Κλεάνθης καὶ Χρύσιππος. Arnob. ad Nat. II. 9, qui ignem minatur mundo et venerit cum tempus arsurum, non Panaetio, Chrysippo, Zenoni (credit)?

The Stoic authorities for the doctrine of ἐκπύρωσις will be found collected in Zeller, p. 164 n. 2. On this point they were opposed to the Peripatetics who held the ἀφθαρσία of the κόσμος, and even some of the later Stoics, notably Panaetius and Boethus, diverged from the teaching of their predecessors. It is doubtful whether Zeno derived the ἐκπύρωσις from Heraclitus (see Introd. p. 21): it may however be observed that it was far more in accordance with his historical position to maintain the destructibility of the world, at any rate, so long as we concede any materiality to his primal fire; if fire is a mere metaphor to express πάντα ῥεῖ, the case is of course very different. Cf. Marc. Aurel. III. 3. The Christian writers often allude to the ἐκπύρωσις, which serves at once as a parallel and a contrast to their own doctrine, e.g. Tatian, adv. Graec. c. 25, p. 162 C, ἐκπύρωσιν (λέγει τις) ἀποβαίνειν κατὰ χρόνους ἐγὼ δὲ εἰσάπαξ. Justin Martyr, Apol. I. 20. 20, p. 66 D.

τὸ πῦρ, add. εἰς Heeren whom Heinze, Logos, p. 111, follows, but the alteration is needless. For σπέρμα cf. M. Aurel. IV. 36.

55. Tatian, adv. Graec. c. 5, τὸν Ζήνωνα διὰ τῆς ἐκπυρώσεως ἀποφαινόμενον ἀνίστασθαι πάλιν τοὺς αὐτοὺς ἐπὶ τοῖς αὐτοῖς, λέγω δὲ Ἄνυτον καὶ Μέλητον ἐπὶ τῷ κατη-

γορεῖν Βούσιριν δὲ ἐπὶ τῷ ξενοκτονεῖν καὶ Ἡρακλέα πάλιν ἐπὶ τῷ ἀθλεῖν παραιτητέον.

Cf. Nemes. Nat. Hom. c. 38, ἔσεσθαι γὰρ πάλιν Σωκράτη καὶ Πλάτωνα καὶ ἕκαστον τῶν ἀνθρώπων σὺν τοῖς αὐτοῖς καὶ φίλοις καὶ πολίταις καὶ τὰ αὐτὰ πείσεσθαι καὶ τοῖς αὐτοῖς συντεύξεσθαι καὶ τὰ αὐτὰ μεταχειριεῖσθαι καὶ πᾶσαν πόλιν καὶ κώμην καὶ ἀγρὸν ὁμοίως ἀποκαθίστασθαι. The exact repetition in some future cycle of the world's course of the events that have already happened was maintained also by the Pythagoreans, cf. Simpl. Phys. 173 a, εἰ δέ τις πιστεύσειε τοῖς Πυθαγορείοις, ὡς πάλιν τὰ αὐτὰ ἀριθμῷ, κἀγὼ μυθολογεύσω τὸ ῥαβδίον ἔχων ὑμῖν καθημένοις οὕτω, καὶ τὰ ἄλλα πάντα ὁμοίως ἕξει καὶ τὸν χρόνον εὔλογόν ἐστι τὸν αὐτὸν εἶναι (quoted by Zeller, Pre-Socratics I. p. 474, n. 2). The Stoics were the more inclined to adopt such a view in consequence of their belief in the unswerving operation of the decrees of destiny. Somewhat analogous are the consequences which flowed from the Epicurean theory of an infinite number of worlds: cf. Cic. Acad. II. 125, et ut nos nunc simus ad Baulos Puteolosque videamus, sic innumerabilis paribus in locis isdem esse nominibus, honoribus, rebus gestis, ingeniis, formis, aetatibus isdem de rebus disputantis? The subject is well treated by Ogereau, Essai, p. 70.

παραιτητέον: Tatian's objection to the Stoic theory is based on the ground that there is no progress towards perfection, the bad will be again more numerous than the just: Socrates and Heracles belong to a very small minority.

56. [Philo.] περὶ ἀφθαρσίας κόσμου, cc. 23, 24, p. 510, 11, foll. Mang. p. 264, 3 Bern. p. 486, Diels. Θεόφραστος μέντοι φησὶ τοὺς γένεσιν καὶ φθορὰν τοῦ κόσμου κατηγοροῦντας ὑπὸ τεττάρων ἀπατηθῆναι τῶν μεγίστων, γῆς

ἀνωμαλίας, θαλάττης ἀναχωρήσεως, ἑκάστου τῶν τοῦ ὅλου
μερῶν διαλύσεως, χερσαίων φθορᾶς κατὰ γένη ζῴων. κατασκευάζειν δὲ τὸ μὲν πρῶτον οὕτως· 'εἰ μὴ γενέσεως ἀρχὴν
ἔλαβεν ἡ γῆ, μέρος ὑπανεστὸς οὐδὲν ἂν ἔτι αὐτῆς ἑωρᾶτο,
χθαμαλὰ δ' ἤδη τὰ ὄρη πάντ' ἐγεγένητο, καὶ οἱ γεώλοφοι
πάντες ἰσόπεδοι τῇ πεδιάδι· τοσούτων γὰρ καθ' ἕκαστον
ἐνιαυτὸν ὄμβρων ἐξ ἀϊδίου φερομένων εἰκὸς ἦν τῶν διηρμένων 10
πρὸς ὕψος τὰ μὲν χειμάρροις ἀπερρῆχθαι, τὰ δ' ὑπονοστή-
σαντα κεχαλάσθαι, πάντα δὲ διὰ πάντων ἤδη λελειάνθαι·
νυνὶ δὲ συνεχῶς ἀνωμαλίαι καὶ παμπόλλων ὀρῶν αἱ πρὸς
αἰθέριον ὕψος ὑπερβολαὶ μηνύματ' ἐστὶ τοῦ τὴν γῆν μὴ
ἀΐδιον εἶναι· πάλαι γάρ, ὡς ἔφην, ἐν ἀπείρῳ χρόνῳ ταῖς 15
ἐπομβρίαις ἀπὸ περάτων ἐπὶ πέρατα πᾶσ' ἂν λεωφόρος
ἐγεγένητο. πέφυκε γὰρ ἡ ὕδατος φύσις καὶ μάλιστα ἀφ'
ὑψηλοτάτων καταράττουσα τὰ μὲν ἔξωθεν τῇ βίᾳ, τὰ δὲ
τῷ συνεχεῖ τῶν ψεκάδων κολάπτουσα κοιλαίνειν ὑπερ-
γάζεσθαί τε τὴν σκληρογέων καὶ λιθωδεστάτην ὀρυκτήρων 20
οὐκ ἔλαττον.' 'καὶ μὴν ἥ γε θάλασσα,' φασίν, 'ἤδη
μεμείωται· μάρτυρες δ' αἱ νήσων εὐδοκιμώταται Ῥόδος
τε καὶ Δῆλος· αὗται γὰρ τὸ μὲν παλαιὸν ἠφανισμέναι
κατὰ τῆς θαλάττης ἐδεδύκεσαν ἐπικλυζόμεναι, χρόνῳ δ'
ὕστερον ἐλαττουμένης ἠρέμα κατ' ὀλίγον ἀνίσχουσαι, ὡς 25
αἱ περὶ αὐτῶν ἀναγραφεῖσαι μηνύουσιν ἱστορίαι· [τὴν δὲ
Δῆλον καὶ Ἀναφὴν ὠνόμασαν δι' ἀμφοτέρων ὀνομάτων
πιστούμενοι τὸ λεγόμενον, ἐπειδὴ γὰρ δήλη ἀναφανεῖσα
ἐγένετο ἀδηλουμένη καὶ ἀφανὴς οὖσα τὸ πάλαι] πρὸς δὲ
τούτοις μεγάλων πελαγῶν μεγάλους κόλπους καὶ βαθεῖς 30
ἀναξηρανθέντας ἠπειρῶσθαι καὶ γεγενῆσθαι τῆς παρακει-
μένης χώρας μοῖραν οὐ λυπρὰν σπειρομένους καὶ φυτευο-
μένους, οἷς σημεῖ' ἄττα τῆς παλαιᾶς ἐναπολελεῖφθαι
θαλαττώσεως ψηφῖδάς τε καὶ κόγχας καὶ ὅσα ὁμοιότροπα
πρὸς αἰγιαλοὺς εἴωθεν ἀποβράττεσθαι. [διὸ καὶ Πίνδαρος 35
ἐπὶ τῆς Δήλου φησί·

Χαίρ', ὦ θεοδμάτα, λιπαροπλοκάμου

παίδεσσι Λατοῦς ἱμεροέστατον ἔρνος
Πόντου θύγατερ, χθονὸς εὐρείας ἀκίνητον τέρας· ἄν τε βροτοὶ
40 Δᾶλον κικλήσκουσιν, μάκαρες δ' ἐν Ὀλύμπῳ τηλέφαντον κυανέας χθονὸς ἄστρον.
θυγατέρα γὰρ Πόντου τὴν Δῆλον εἴρηκε τὸ λεχθὲν αἰνιττόμενος]. εἰ δὴ μειοῦται ἡ θάλαττα, μειωθήσεται μὲν ἡ γῆ, μακραῖς δ' ἐνιαυτῶν περιόδοις καὶ εἰς ἅπαν ἑκάτερον στοιχεῖον ἀναλωθήσεται, δαπανωθήσεται <δὲ> καὶ ὁ
45 σύμπας ἀὴρ ἐκ τοῦ κατ' ὀλίγον ἐλαττούμενος, ἀποκριθήσεται δὲ πάντ' εἰς μίαν οὐσίαν τὴν πυρός.'

πρὸς δὲ τὴν τοῦ τρίτου κεφαλαίου κατασκευὴν χρῶνται λόγῳ τοιῷδε· 'φθείρεται πάντως ἐκεῖνο, οὗ πάντα τὰ μέρη φθαρτά ἐστι, τοῦ δὲ κόσμου πάντα τὰ μέρη φθαρτά ἐστι,
50 φθαρτὸς ἄρα ὁ κόσμος ἐστίν.' ὃ δ' ὑπερεθέμεθα νῦν ἐπισκεπτέον. ποῖον μέρος τῆς γῆς, ἵν' ἀπὸ ταύτης ἀρξώμεθα, μεῖζον ἢ ἔλαττον, οὐ χρόνῳ διαλυθήσεται; λίθων οἱ κραταιότατοι ἆρ' οὐ μυδῶσι καὶ σήπονται κατὰ τὴν ἕξεως ἀσθένειαν—[ἡ δ' ἐστι πνευματικὸς τόνος, δεσμὸς οὐκ
55 ἄρρηκτος, ἀλλὰ μόνον δυσδιάλυτος]—θρυπτόμενοι καὶ ῥέοντες εἰς λεπτὴν τὸ πρῶτον ἀναλύονται κόνιν; [εἶθ' ὕστερον δαπανηθέντες ἐξαναλύονται] τί δέ; εἰ μὴ πρὸς ἀνέμων ῥιπίζοιτο τὸ ὕδωρ, ἀκίνητον ἐαθὲν οὐχ ὑφ' ἡσυχίας νεκροῦται; μεταβάλλει γοῦν καὶ δυσωδέστατον γίγνεται
60 οἷα ψυχὴν ἀφῃρημένον ζῷον. αἵ γε μὴν ἀέρος φθοραὶ παντί τῳ δῆλαι· νοσεῖν γὰρ καὶ φθίνειν καὶ τρόπον τιν' ἀποθνῄσκειν πέφυκεν. ἐπεὶ τί ἄν τις, μὴ στοχαζόμενος ὀνομάτων εὐπρεπείας ἀλλὰ τἀληθοῦς, εἴποι λοιμὸν εἶναι πλὴν ἀέρος θάνατον τὸ οἰκεῖον πάθος ἀναχέοντος ἐπὶ
65 φθορᾷ πάντων ὅσα ψυχῆς μεμοίραται; τί χρὴ μακρηγορεῖν περὶ πυρός; ἀτροφῆσαν γὰρ αὐτίκα σβέννυται χωλόν, ᾗ φασιν οἱ ποιηταί, γεγονὸς ἐξ ἑαυτοῦ. διὸ σκηριπτόμενον ὀρθοῦται κατὰ τὴν τῆς ἀναφθείσης ὕλης νομήν, ἐξαναλωθείσης δ' ἀφανίζεται. [τὸ παραπλήσιον μέντοι

καὶ τοὺς κατὰ τὴν Ἰνδικὴν δράκοντάς φασι πάσχειν. 70 ἀνέρποντας γὰρ ἐπὶ τὰ μέγιστα τῶν ζῴων ἐλέφαντας περὶ νῶτα καὶ νηδὺν ἅπασαν εἰλεῖσθαι, φλέβα δ' ἣν ἂν τύχῃ διελόντας ἐμπίνειν τοῦ αἵματος, ἀπλήστως ἐπισπωμένους βιαίῳ πνεύματι καὶ συντόνῳ ῥοίζῳ. μέχρι μὲν οὖν τινος ἐξαναλουμένους ἐκείνους ἀντέχειν ὑπ' ἀμηχανίας 75 ἀνασκιρτῶντας καὶ τῇ προνομαίᾳ τὴν πλευρὰν τύπτοντας ὡς καθιξομένους τῶν δρακόντων, εἶτ' ἀεὶ κενουμένου τοῦ ζωτικοῦ πηδᾶν μὲν μηκέτι δύνασθαι, κραδαινομένους δ' ἑστάναι, μικρὸν δ' ὕστερον καὶ τῶν σκελῶν ἐξασθενησάντων κατασεισθέντας ὑπὸ λιφαιμίας ἀποψύχειν· πεσόντας 80 δὲ τοὺς αἰτίους τοῦ θανάτου συναπολλύναι τρόπῳ τοιῷδε· μηκέτ' ἔχοντες τροφὴν οἱ δράκοντες, ὃν περιέθεσαν δεσμὸν ἐπιχειροῦσιν ἐκλύειν ἀπαλλαγὴν ἤδη ποθοῦντες, ὑπὸ δὲ τοῦ βάρους τῶν ἐλεφάντων θλιβόμενοι πιεζοῦνται καὶ πολὺ μᾶλλον ἐπειδὰν τύχῃ στέριφον <ὂν> καὶ λιθῶδες 85 τὸ ἔδαφος· ἰλυσπώμενοι γὰρ καὶ πάντα ποιοῦντες εἰς διάλυσιν ὑπὸ τῆς τοῦ πιέσαντος βίας πεδηθέντες ἑαυτοὺς πολυτρόπως ἐν ἀμηχάνοις καὶ ἀπόροις γυμνάσαντες ἐξασθενοῦσι <καὶ> καθάπερ οἱ καταλευσθέντες ἢ τείχους αἰφνίδιον ἐπενεχθέντες προκαταληφθέντες, οὐδ' ὅσον ἀνα- 90 κῦψαι δυνάμενοι πνιγῇ τελευτῶσιν.] εἰ δὴ τῶν μερῶν ἕκαστον τοῦ κόσμου φθορὰν ὑπομένει, δηλονότι καὶ ὁ ἐξ αὐτῶν παγεὶς κόσμος ἄφθαρτος οὐκ ἔσται.' τὸν δὲ τέταρτον καὶ λοιπὸν λόγον ἀκριβωτέον ὧδέ φασιν. ' εἰ δ' ὁ κόσμος ἀΐδιος ἦν, ἦν ἂν καὶ τὰ ζῷα ἀΐδια καὶ πολύ γε μᾶλλον τὸ 95 τῶν ἀνθρώπων γένος ὅσῳ καὶ τῶν ἄλλων ἄμεινον. ἀλλὰ καὶ ὀψίγονον φανῆναι τοῖς βουλομένοις ἐρευνᾶν τὰ φύσεως. εἰκὸς γὰρ μᾶλλον δ' ἀναγκαῖον ἀνθρώποις συνυπάρξαι τὰς τέχνας ὡς ἂν ἰσηλίκας οὐ μόνον ὅτι λογικῇ τὸ ἐμμέθοδον οἰκεῖον ἀλλὰ καὶ ὅτι ζῆν ἄνευ τούτων οὐκ ἔστιν· 100 ἴδωμεν τοὺς ἑκάστων χρόνους ἀλογήσαντες τῶν ἐπιτραγῳδουμένων θεοῖς μύθων * * * εἰ μὴ ἀΐδιος ἄνθρωπος, οὐδ' ἄλλο τι ζῷον, ὥστ' οὐδ' αἱ δεδεγμέναι ταῦτα χῶραι γῆ καὶ ὕδωρ καὶ ἀήρ. ἐξ ὧν τὸ φθαρτὸν εἶναι τὸν κόσμον δῆλόν ἐστιν.'

It will be seen that the writer attributes to Theophrastus the statement and criticism of certain views as to the creation and destruction of the world, which were opposed to the Peripatetic doctrine of its eternity. After the above extract this hostile view is refuted by arguments obviously derived, in part at least, from Peripatetic sources[1], although the name of Theophrastus is not again introduced. The question arises, assuming the good faith of the extract, to whom do these criticised views belong? This point was first raised by Zeller in Hermes XI. 422—429 and by an ingenious process of reasoning he concluded that Zeno is the philosopher who is here attacked. First, the four arguments, by which the proposition that the world is mortal is supported, belong to the Stoic school. They cannot belong to a pre-Aristotelian philosopher, for the doctrine of the eternity of the world and of mankind, against which they are directed, had not been broached before Aristotle (see de Caelo I. 10. 279^{b}12); of the post-Aristotelians they obviously alone suit the Stoics, who were alone in holding the periodical destruction of the world. The second argument, built on the retrocession of the sea, finds a parallel in the views of a world-flood attributed to the Stoa by Alexander Aphrod. Meteor. 90^a m.; and the dialectical form in which the third and fourth arguments are couched suggests the same origin. Again, the authority of Diog. L. VII. 141 is conclusive as to the third argument, and the terminology of ἕξις, τόνος, πνεῦμα, and πνευματικὴ δύναμις, to which may be added οὐσία, ἀναφθείσης ὕλης, and φύσει οἰκεῖον, is undoubtedly Stoic. Next, it being proved that these arguments belong to the Stoic school, Zeno is the only Stoic whom Theo-

[1] This point is proved in detail by Zeller, l. c. p. 424, 5.

phrastus could have criticised, for the latter died in Ol. 123, that is between 288 and 284 B.C., at a time when Zeno's school had been founded for about 15 years. For the avoidance of a direct mention of Zeno, if such was really the case in the Theophrastean original, Zeller quotes the parallel cases in which Aristotle combats the views of Xenocrates and Speusippus without referring to them by name. As an additional circumstance pointing to Zeno's authorship, we may refer to the form in which the syllogism introducing the third argument is cast. This is undoubtedly one of those breves et acutulae conclusiones, so often mentioned by Cicero as characteristic of the style of the founder of Stoicism and of which examples (in addition to those in Cicero) have been preserved by Sextus Empiricus and Seneca: see the collection in Introd. p. 33. This is perhaps the right place to observe that a supposed frag. of Zeno, extracted by Wachsmuth (Comm. I. p. 8) from Philo de Provid. I. 12, and to the same effect as the third argument here, can no longer be regarded as belonging to Zeno on the authority of that passage after the explanation of Diels, Doxogr. Gr. proleg. p. 3.

These views of Zeller have however been vigorously criticised by Diels (Doxogr. Gr. pp. 106—108). His main contention is that the authority of the compiler of the pseudo-Philonian treatise is too weak to support so important a discovery as the alleged controversy between Theophrastus and Zeno, of which no trace has come down to us from other sources. He does not believe that this "nebulo" had ever read Theophrastus, and suggests that, finding the name of Theophrastus attached to the first two arguments in some work of Critolaus, he left his readers to assume that the elder Peripatetic was really responsible for those passages in which Critolaus himself attacks what is undoubtedly Stoic doctrine. The result is that Diels, though he prints cc. 23—27 in the body of his work, does not believe that they contain (even after allowing for later accretions) a genuine excerpt from the φυσικαὶ δόξαι of the Eresian philosopher. Now it is obvious that we are only concerned with the question of the fontes of the Philonian treatise and its general credibility, in so far as its solution enables us to authenticate these fragments as belonging to Zeno. Thus, altogether apart from its appearance in this passage, the Zenonian authorship of the syllogism in ll. 48—50 is extremely probable not only from internal indications, but also because of the evidence of Diogenes Laertius VII. 141, 142 (observe especially the words περὶ δὴ οὖν τῆς γενέσεως καὶ τῆς φθορᾶς τοῦ κόσμου φησὶ Ζήνων ἐν τῷ περὶ ὅλου). But, as to the general body of the fragment, the case is different: if we cannot trust the good faith of the writer, as giving us a genuine statement of the refutation by Theophrastus of his opponents' doctrine, it may well be that the two earlier arguments represent early Ionian, possibly Heraclitean, views (with Stoic additions), and that in the later portions we have the work of one of Zeno's successors as set out by a later Peripatetic. On the other hand, if Theophrastus is responsible for the exposition of all four arguments, they certainly belong to a single teacher or a single school, and that teacher, as has been shown above, must be Zeno. It is therefore necessary for us to consider the tenor of Zeller's rejoinder in Hermes XV. 137—146, which, briefly stated, resolves itself into a theory as to the origin of the pseudo-Philonian treatise. He fully admits the many absurdities with which the text is strewn, but argues that they can all be eliminated without interfering with the nexus of the arguments; nay more, that the original writing, though not of great value, was at least a clear and trustworthy exposition of the views of the Peripatetic school, to which the writer belonged, but that the sequence of its thought has been distorted and its whole character changed by the blundering additions of a later hand. We are able to recognise in this treatise the work of two distinct authors, the first probably an Alexandrian philosopher of the latter half of the first century before Christ, and a contemporary of Arius Didymus and Boethus, and the second an Alexandrian Jew of the first or second century of the Christian era. The references of the original writer to Greek philosophy are found to be correct in all cases where his statements can be scrutinised by the light of other evidence: why then should we mistrust his citation of Theophrastus? To test this theory in detail would require a thorough examination of the treatise in question with reference to the suggested additions, an examination which would be out of place here. But we can gauge the character of the proposed explanation by the three passages which Zeller expels from our extract, and which may be fairly said to be typical of the accretions in the general body of the work. All three are certainly futile and purposeless, but that which is especially remarkable is the manner in which the course of the argument is improved by their removal. In particular, the long digression about the serpents and the Indian elephants prevents the conclusion founded on the destructibility of the several elements from following in natural sequence the last of the arguments by which this destructibility is proved of each element in detail. The latest treatment of this question is to be found in von Arnim's Quellen Studien zu Philo von Alexandria (Berlin 1888) p. 41 foll. He believes that the compiler of the treatise only had later Peripatetic writings—especially those of Critolaus—before him, and that the main portion of our passage was derived from one of them. All that belongs really to Theophrastus is the statement of the headings of the four arguments (ll. 1—5) and these headings, if taken alone, might refer to pre-Aristotelians. Yet, holding in agreement with Zeller and against Diels that the arguments by which the headings are supported are undeniably Stoic, he concludes that a younger Peripatetic adopted the Theophrastean scheme, originally a doxographical statement of pre-Aristotelian doctrines, as a groundwork for his polemic against the Stoics, who on their side had adopted these four arguments, perhaps from Heraclitus and Empedocles. Finally he suggests, on very inadequate grounds (p. 47), that Antipater of Tarsus was the particular Stoic whose views are summarised. If this theory is correct, it is certainly an extraordinary coincidence that Theophrastus should have selected from the older philosophy four particular statements, which go to prove the destructibility of the world, and that the Stoics should have unconsciously taken up identically the same ground in support of their own theory. Zeller's opinion still appears to me more reasonable: see also Stein, Psych. n. 86, who has anticipated the argument used above from the syllogism in ll. 33—35.

8. τὰ ὄρη cf. Cornut. c. 17. p. 85 Osann, τὰ δ' ὄρη (γέγονε) κατὰ ἐξοστρακισμὸν τῆς γῆς. Schol. Hes. Theog. p. 238, τὰ ὄρη περὶ τὸ ἀνώμαλον τῆς συνιζήσεως ἔλαβε τὰς ἐξοχὰς καὶ κατὰ ἐξοστρακισμὸν αὐτῆς.

ἐγεγένητο)(ἐγένετο indicates that the process would have been already complete at the time specified i.e. long ago. In the case of verbs denoting an action the distinction between plup. and aor. with ἄν is less apparent, though always present: cf. e.g. Dem. Timocr. p. 746 § 146, if imprisonment were contrary to the Ath. constitution οὔθ' ὅσων ἔνδειξίς ἐστιν ἡ ἀπαγωγή, προσεγέγραπτο ἂν ἐν τοῖς νόμοις κ.τ.λ. "There would *not have been found a clause enacted* in the laws" etc.

16. ἀπὸ περάτων κ.τ.λ. "The whole earth would have become a highway from end to end." πᾶσ' ἄν: so Bücheler and Diels for πᾶσα.

19. τῇ συνεχεῖ, MS. Med. whence Bücheler reads τῇ συνεχείᾳ, recalling the line κοιλαίνει πέτρην ῥανὶς ὕδατος ἐνδελεχείᾳ.

26. τήν—πάλαι expelled by Zeller, Herm. xv. p. 140.

28. γάρ: the sentence would run more smoothly if this word were omitted.

33. οἷς σημεῖ' ἄττα κ.τ.λ. The observation of similar facts induced in Xenophanes the belief that the earth was originally in a fluid state: cf. Hippolyt. I. 14 (quoted by Zeller, pre-Socrat. I. p. 570), ὁ δὲ Ξενοφάνης μῖξιν τῆς γῆς πρὸς τὴν θάλασσαν γενέσθαι δοκεῖ καὶ τῷ χρόνῳ ἀπὸ τοῦ ὑγροῦ λύεσθαι φάσκων τοιαύτας ἔχειν ἀποδείξεις, ὅτι ἐν μέσῃ γῇ καὶ ὄρεσιν εὑρίσκοντο κόγχαι καὶ ἐν Συρακούσαις δὲ ἐν ταῖς λατομίαις λέγει εὑρῆσθαι τύπον ἰχθύος καὶ φωκῶν, ἐν δὲ Πάρῳ τύπον ἀφύης ἐν τῷ βαθεῖ τοῦ λίθου, ἐν δὲ Μελίτῃ πλάκας συμπάντων θαλασσίων.

35. διό—αἰνιττόμενος expelled by Zeller l. c. and also by Bücheler.

37. Pindar, frag. 64[87] Bergk.

43. περιόδοις: see on frag. 52.

45. ἀποκριθήσεται "will be merged," cf. Thuc. I. 3, "Ελληνας...εἰς ἓν ὄνομα ἀποκεκρίσθαι, Diog. L. VII. 148, φύσις...τοιαῦτα δρῶσα ἀφ' οἵων ἀπεκρίθη.

48—50. Cf. Diog. L. VII 141. Philo, de provid. I. 12.

53. ἕξεως: lit. hold, an undoubtedly Stoic term. The ἕξις of inorganic matter answers to the φύσις of plants, and the ψυχή of animals: supra frag. 43. Cf. Sext. Math.

IX. 81, τῶν ἡνωμένων σωμάτων τὰ μὲν ὑπὸ ψιλῆς ἕξεως συνέχεται...καὶ ἕξεως μέν, ὡς λίθοι καὶ ξύλα (Zeller, p. 208).

54. πνευματικὸς τόνος: the favourite doctrine of Cleanthes: if this passage belongs to Zeno, we have an indication here that the master prepared the way for the pupil, cf. Cleanth. frag. 24. The words however may in any case be a later addition, and under the circumstances they have been bracketed.

56. ῥέοντες "passing away" in the Heraclitean sense; yet even Plato has εἰ γὰρ ῥέοι τὸ σῶμα...(Phaed. 87 D). λεπτὴν κόνιν, cf. Soph. Ant. 256.

εἶθ'—ἔξαναλ. Om. Med. MS. cf. Bücheler Rhein. Mus. 32. 442.

58. ἀνέμων: the illustration is suggestive in connection with the doctrine of πνεῦμα. For ῥιπίζοιτο cf. frag. 106 κινούμενον καὶ ἀναριπιζόμενον ὑπ' ἐκείνου.

60. ψυχὴν appears to be attributed to animals in general and not exclusively to man, see on frag. 43.

63. εὐπρεπείας. Cf. Plat. Euthyd. 305 E, καὶ γὰρ ἔχει ὄντως ὦ Κρίτων εὐπρέπειαν μᾶλλον ἢ ἀλήθειαν. It is possible that there is a reference to some contemporary school here, which had explained λοιμὸς after the manner of Prodicus. For the definition cf. M. Aurel. IX. 2.

69—91 ejected by Zeller, l. c.

85. ὃν add. Diels. 89. καὶ add. Bernays.

99. ὡς ἂν not merely equivalent to ὥσπερ but elliptical. The full phrase would be ὡς εἰκὸς ἦν ἂν εἰ ἰσήλικες ἦσαν. Xen. Mem. II. 6. 38, ἢ εἴ σοι πείσαιμι κοινῇ τὴν πόλιν ψευδόμενος ὡς ἂν στρατηγικῷ καὶ πολιτικῷ ἑαυτὴν ἐπιτρέψαι, where see Kühner. In this way is to be explained Thuc. I. 33. 1.

102. "Deesse quibus εὑρημάτων tempora explicaverant vidit Mangey," Usener.

57. Philargyrius ad Verg. Georg. II. 336, Zenon ex hoc mundo quamvis aliqua intereant tamen ipsum perpetuo manere quia inhaereant ei elementa e quibus generantur materiae: ut dixit crescere quidem, sed ad interitum non pervenire manentibus elementis a quibus revalescat.

If taken literally, the doctrine here referred to would be inconsistent with the destructibility of the κόσμος, which, as we have seen, was held by Zeno: again, elementa can hardly be a translation of στοιχεῖα, which undoubtedly perished. We must suppose therefore that Zeno is speaking not of the visible world, but of the universe, and that elementa = ἀρχαί. According to Diog. L. VII. 137 κόσμος is used by the Stoics in three senses: the first of these is αὐτὸν τὸν θεὸν τὸν ἐκ τῆς ἁπάσης οὐσίας ἰδίως ποιὸν ὃς δὴ ἄφθαρτός ἐστι καὶ ἀγέννητος, and this is the sense which mundus must bear here. If this explanation be thought impossible, we can only suppose that there is a confusion with Zeno of Tarsus who is said to have withheld assent to the doctrine of the ἐκπύρωσις, Zeller, p. 168 n. 1. Stein, Psych. p. 64 and n. 92, thinks that Zeno held that at the ἐκπύρωσις the various manifestations of God—world-soul, λόγος σπερματικὸς etc.—lose themselves in the divine unity, but that the indeterminate matter (ἄποιος ὕλη) remains, cf. ib. p. 34, n. 42.

58. Diog. Laert. VII. 143, ὅτι τε εἷς ἐστιν (ὁ κόσμος) Ζήνων φησὶν ἐν τῷ περὶ τοῦ ὅλου. Stob. Ecl. I. 22. 3^b p. 199, 10, Ζήνων ἕνα εἶναι τὸν κόσμον.

This was one of the points which distinguished the Stoics from the Epicureans, who held that there are an infinite number of worlds. See further Zeller, p. 183 and the notes: the characteristic and important view of συμπάθεια μερῶν or συντονία is one of the developments introduced by Cleanthes.

59. Sext. Math. ΙΧ. 101, Ζήνων δὲ ὁ Κιτιεύς, ἀπὸ Ξενοφῶντος τὴν ἀφορμὴν λαβών, οὑτωσὶ συνερωτᾷ· τὸ προϊέμενον σπέρμα λογικοῦ καὶ αὐτὸ λογικόν ἐστιν· ὁ δὲ κόσμος προΐεται σπέρμα λογικοῦ· λογικὸν ἄρ' ἐστὶν ὁ κόσμος. ᾧ συνεισάγεται καὶ ἡ τούτου ὕπαρξις. Cic. N. D. II. 22, nihil quod animi quodque rationis est expers, id generare ex se potest animantem compotemque rationis. Mundus autem generat animantes compotesque rationis. Animans est igitur mundus composque rationis.

We need not infer from this passage that Zeno expressed himself to be adopting Socrates' argument, for in the preceding paragraphs in Sext. l. c. 92 f. the passage referred to (Xen. Mem. I. 4 §§ 2—5. 8) is set out and discussed. The parallel passage is § 8 καὶ ταῦτα εἰδὼς ὅτι γῆς τε μικρὸν μέρος ἐν τῷ σώματι πολλῆς οὔσης ἔχεις κ.τ.λ. ...νοῦν δὲ μόνον ἄρα οὐδαμοῦ ὄντα σε εὐτυχῶς πως δοκεῖς συναρπάσαι, καὶ τάδε τὰ ὑπερμεγέθη καὶ πλῆθος ἄπειρα δι' ἀφροσύνην τινά, ὡς οἴει, εὐτάκτως ἔχειν; cf. Sext. Math. IX. 77, M. Aurel. IV. 4 and see Stein, Psych. n. 53.

τούτου. Bekker with some plausibility suggests τοῦ θεοῦ. The Stoics argued from the existence of God that the world must be reasonable and vice versa. For the relation of God to the world see infra, frag. 66.

60. Cic. N. D. II. 22, Idemque (Zeno) hoc modo: "Nullius sensu carentis pars aliqua potest esse sentiens. Mundi autem partes sentientes sunt: non igitur caret sensu mundus."

Cf. Sext. Math. IX. 85, ἀλλὰ καὶ ἡ τὰς λογικὰς περιέχουσα φύσεις πάντως ἐστὶ λογική· οὐ γὰρ οἷόν τε τὸ ὅλον τοῦ μέρους χεῖρον εἶναι· ἀλλ' εἰ ἀρίστη ἐστὶ φύσις ἡ τὸν κόσμον διοικοῦσα νοερά τε ἔσται καὶ σπουδαία καὶ ἀθάνατος.

THE FRAGMENTS OF ZENO. 119

61. Sext. Math. IX. 104, καὶ πάλιν ὁ Ζήνων φησὶν "[εἰ] τὸ λογικὸν τοῦ μὴ λογικοῦ κρεῖττόν ἐστιν· οὐδὲν δέ γε κόσμου κρεῖττόν ἐστιν· λογικὸν ἄρα ὁ κόσμος. καὶ ὡσαύτως ἐπὶ τοῦ νοεροῦ καὶ ἐμψυχίας μετέχοντος. τὸ γὰρ νοερὸν τοῦ μὴ νοεροῦ καὶ τὸ ἔμψυχον τοῦ μὴ ἐμψύχου κρεῖττόν ἐστιν· οὐδὲν δέ γε κόσμου κρεῖττον· νοερὸς ἄρα καὶ ἔμψυχός ἐστιν ὁ κόσμος." Cic. N. D. II. 21, quod ratione utitur id melius est quam id quod ratione non utitur. Nihil autem mundo melius: ratione igitur mundus utitur. Cf. ib. III. 22, 23.

Alexinus the Megarian attacked Zeno's position with the remark that in the same way the world might be proved to be poetical and possessed of grammatical knowledge. The Stoics retorted that it is not true that in the abstract τὸ ποιητικὸν is better than τὸ μὴ ποιητικὸν or τὸ γραμματικὸν than τὸ μὴ γραμματικόν: otherwise Archilochus would be better than Socrates, Aristarchus than Plato (Sext. l. c. 108—110). For the fact cf. Diog. VII. 139, οὕτω δὴ καὶ τὸν ὅλον κόσμον ζῷον ὄντα καὶ ἔμψυχον καὶ λογικὸν κ.τ.λ. Stein adds Philo, de incorr. m. p. 506 M, ὁ κόσμος καὶ φύσις λογική, οὐ μόνον ἔμψυχος ὤν, ἀλλὰ καὶ νοερὸς πρὸς δὲ καὶ φρόνιμος. Siebeck refers to Arist. de Gen. An. II. 1. 731[b] 25, τὸ ἔμψυχον τοῦ ἀψύχου βέλτιον.

62. Sext. Math. IX. 107, δυνάμει δὲ τὸν αὐτὸν τῷ Ζήνωνι λόγον ἐξέθετο (scil. Plato) καὶ γὰρ οὗτος τὸ πᾶν κάλλιστον εἶναί φησιν κατὰ φύσιν ἀπειργασμένον ἔργον καὶ κατὰ τὸν εἰκότα λόγον, ζῷον ἔμψυχον νοερόν τε καὶ λογικόν.

Hirzel's theory, II. p. 217, 218, that Zeno called the world ἔμψυχον and λογικὸν only but not ζῷον is controverted by Stein, Psych. n. 82 from this passage. The passage in Plato, part of which is quoted by Sextus, is

Timaeus, p. 29 foll.; and see esp. 30 A, B which illustrates this and the last frag., cf. M. Aurel. IV. 40.

63. Cic. N. D. II. 22, Idemque similitudine, ut saepe solet, rationem conclusit hoc modo: 'si ex oliva modulate canentes tibiae nascerentur, num dubitares quin inesset in oliva tibicinii quaedam scientia? quid? si platani fidiculas ferrent numerose sonantes, idem scilicet censeres in platanis inesse musicam. Cur igitur mundus non animans sapiensque judicetur, quum ex se procreet animantes atque sapientes?'

This recalls the anecdote about Amoebeus: apoph. 19.

64. Stob. Ecl. I. 23. 1, p. 200, 21, Ζήνων πύρινον εἶναι τὸν οὐρανόν.

Stobaeus couples Zeno with Parmenides, Heraclitus and Strato. For the Stoic authorities see Zeller, p. 201.

65. Achill. Tat., Isag. in Arat. 5. p. 129 e, Ζήνων ὁ Κιτιεὺς οὕτως αὐτὸν ὡρίσατο· 'οὐρανός ἐστιν αἰθέρος τὸ ἔσχατον· ἐξ οὗ καὶ ἐν ᾧ ἐστι πάντα ἐμφανῶς· περιέχει γὰρ πάντα πλὴν αὑτοῦ· οὐδὲν γὰρ ἑαυτὸ περιέχει· ἀλλ' ἑτέρου ἐστὶ περιεκτικόν.

αἰθέρος τὸ ἔσχατον: cf. Diog. L. VII. 138 quoted below. The genitive is partitive: "the extreme part of the aether." This becomes clear when we remember that Zeno is closely following Aristotle here, cf. Phys. IV. 5 καὶ διὰ τοῦτο ἡ μὲν γῆ ἐν τῷ ὕδατι, τοῦτο δ' ἐν τῷ ἀέρι, οὗτος δ' ἐν τῷ αἰθέρι, ὁ δ' αἰθὴρ ἐν τῷ οὐρανῷ, ὁ δ' οὐρανὸς οὐκέτι ἐν ἄλλῳ. Just before he had said: ἐν τῷ οὐρανῷ πάντα· ὁ γὰρ οὐρανὸς τὸ πᾶν ἴσως.

περιέχει. A direct parallel to this may be found in the teaching of the Pythagoreans (Zeller, pre-Socratics, I. p. 465), but there is possibly also a reminiscence of Plato, Timaeus 31 A, where οὐρανὸς is spoken of as τὸ περιέχον πάντα ὁπόσα νοητὰ ζῷα: cf. also the περιέχον φρενῆρες of Heraclitus (Sext. Math. VII. 127 foll.). M. Aurel. VIII. 54.

66. Diog. L. VII. 148, οὐσίαν δὲ θεοῦ Ζήνων φησὶ τὸν ὅλον κόσμον καὶ τὸν οὐρανόν.

Cf. Stob. Ecl. I. 1. 29, p. 38, 1. The Stoics held θεοὺς... τὸν κόσμον καὶ τοὺς ἀστέρας καὶ τὴν γῆν. In so far as God is manifested in the world, the world is God. Many more references are given in Zeller, p. 157. The words καὶ τὸν οὐρανὸν are added because in it the material essence of divinity exists in its purest form. Diog. L. VII. 138, οὐρανὸς δέ ἐστιν ἡ ἐσχάτη περιφέρεια, ἐν ᾗ πᾶν ἴδρυται τὸ θεῖον. Hence Chrysippus and Posidonius spoke of the οὐρανὸς as τὸ ἡγεμονικὸν τοῦ κόσμου (ib. 139). Certainly, if these words are pressed, pantheism, involving the identification of God and matter, is distinctly attributed to Zeno. Wellmann, p. 469, suggests that Zeno may really only have said that the world is formed out of the divine essence (ὁ κόσμος οὐσία θεοῦ) and that Diog. through a confusion of subject and predicate interpreted this as a definition of the essence of God. Another possibility is that κόσμος is used in the same sense as in frag. 71. See also Stein, Psychologie n. 88.

67. Stob. Ecl. I. 19. 4, p. 166, 4, Ζήνωνος. τῶν δ' ἐν τῷ κόσμῳ πάντων τῶν κατ' ἰδίαν ἕξιν συνεστώτων τὰ μέρη τὴν φορὰν ἔχειν εἰς τὸ τοῦ ὅλου μέσον, ὁμοίως δὲ καὶ αὐτοῦ τοῦ κόσμου· διόπερ ὀρθῶς λέγεσθαι πάντα τὰ μέρη τοῦ κόσμου ἐπὶ τὸ μέσον τοῦ κόσμου τὴν φορὰν ἔχειν, 5 μάλιστα δὲ τὰ βάρος ἔχοντα. ταὐτὸν δ' αἴτιον εἶναι καὶ τῆς τοῦ κόσμου μονῆς ἐν ἀπείρῳ κενῷ, καὶ τῆς γῆς παραπλησίως ἐν τῷ κόσμῳ περὶ τὸ τούτου κέντρον καθιδρυμένης ἰσοκρατῶς. οὐ πάντως δὲ σῶμα βάρος ἔχειν, ἀλλ' ἀβαρῆ εἶναι ἀέρα καὶ πῦρ· τείνεσθαι δὲ καὶ ταῦτά πως 10

ἐπὶ τὸ τῆς ὅλης σφαίρας τοῦ κόσμου μέσον, τὴν δὲ σύστασιν πρὸς τὴν περιφέρειαν αὐτοῦ ποιεῖσθαι· φύσει γὰρ ἀνώφοιτα ταῦτ' εἶναι διὰ τὸ μηδενὸς μετέχειν βάρους. παραπλησίως δὲ τούτοις οὐδ' αὐτόν φασι τὸν κόσμον
15 βάρος ἔχειν διὰ τὸ τὴν ὅλην αὐτοῦ σύστασιν ἔκ τε τῶν βάρος ἐχόντων στοιχείων εἶναι καὶ ἐκ τῶν ἀβαρῶν. τὴν δ' ὅλην γῆν καθ' ἑαυτὴν μὲν ἔχειν ἀρέσκει βάρος παρὰ δὲ τὴν θέσιν διὰ τὸ τὴν μέσην ἔχειν χώραν (πρὸς δὲ τὸ μέσον εἶναι τὴν φορὰν τοῖς τοιούτοις σώμασιν) ἐπὶ τοῦ τόπου
20 τούτου μένειν.

2. συνεστώτων. This is the most general term, elsewhere opposed to συνάπτεσθαι, συνέχεσθαι etc.

4. πάντα τὰ μέρη κ.τ.λ. This centralising tendency is called by Diogenes (VII. 140) τὴν τῶν οὐρανίων πρὸς τὰ ἐπίγεια σύμπνοιαν καὶ συντονίαν. In the Stoic doctrine of the microcosm and the macrocosm there is one discrepancy, in that while the ἡγεμονικὸν of the world is at its extreme periphery the ἡγεμονικὸν of man is in the breast. Stein, Psych. p. 211, finds in this passage an attempt to remove this inconsistency by making the earth the central point from which all motion originates and to which it returns.

9. οὐ πάντως δὲ κ.τ.λ. Cf. Stob. Ecl. I. 14. 1 f. p. 142, 9, οἱ Στωικοὶ δύο μὲν ἐκ τῶν τεσσάρων στοιχείων κοῦφα πῦρ καὶ ἀέρα· δύο δὲ βαρέα ὕδωρ καὶ γῆν. κοῦφον γὰρ ὑπάρχει φύσει, ὃ νεύει ἀπὸ τοῦ ἰδίου μέσου, βαρὺ δὲ τὸ εἰς μέσον, i.e. light is opposed to heavy not relatively, as in our use of the words, but absolutely, implying motion in an outward or upward direction. Cic. Tusc. I. 40, persuadent mathematici...eam naturam esse quattuor omnia gignentium corporum, ut, quasi partita habeant inter se ac divisa momenta, terrena et umida suopte nutu et suo pondere ad paris angulos in terram et in mare ferantur, reliquae duae partes, una ignea, una animalis,...rectis

lineis in caelestem locum subvolent, sive ipsa natura superiora adpetente, sive quod a gravioribus leviora natura repellantur. N. D. II. 116, 117. The Stoics were following Aristotle (ap. Stob. Ecl. I. 19. 1, p. 163, 9, τῆς δὲ κατὰ τόπον κινήσεως τὴν μὲν ἀπὸ τοῦ μέσου γίνεσθαι, τὴν δὲ ἐπὶ τὸ μέσον, τὴν δὲ περὶ τὸ μέσον· πυρὸς μὲν οὖν καὶ ἀέρος ἀπὸ τοῦ μέσου, γῆς καὶ ὕδατος ἐπὶ τὸ μέσον, τοῦ πέμπτου περὶ τὸ μέσον.).

10. **τείνεσθαι δέ**: So Diels for MSS. γίνεσθαι, a correction more probable for palaeographical reasons and in itself more attractive than Meineke's κινεῖσθαι. Cf. Nemes. 2. p. 29, τονικὴν εἶναι κίνησιν περὶ τὰ σώματα εἰς τὸ ἔσω ἅμα καὶ τὸ ἔξω κινουμένην. Chrysipp. ap. Plut. Sto. Rep. 44. 7. 1054 E, οὕτω δὲ τοῦ ὅλου τεινομένου εἰς ταὐτὸ καὶ κινουμένου κ.τ.λ. The explanation is as follows:—the natural motion of the elements is restrained and modified by the continual process of change (μεταβολή) by whose action the world is formed and exists. Fire and Air are perpetually being transformed into Water and Earth and thus, before their upward tendency has time to assert itself, they themselves becoming possessed of βάρος start again in the opposite direction. Thus each of the four elements is apparently stationary and remains constant: in reality its component parts are in continual motion. Cf. Chrysippus ap. Plut. Sto. Rep. 44. 6, a passage too long to quote. This explanation is supported by the statement which is attributed to the Stoics by Stobæus, that at the ἐκπύρωσις the world is resolved into the void (Ecl. I. 18. 4 b. p. 160, 11 and Euseb. P. E. xv. 40): cf. ib. I. 21. 3 b, μήτε αὔξεσθαι δὲ μήτε μειοῦσθαι τὸν κόσμον τοῖς δὲ μέρεσιν ὁτὲ μὲν παρεκτείνεσθαι πρὸς πλείονα τόπον ὁτὲ δὲ συστέλλεσθαι. This is not necessarily inconsistent with Prof. Mayor's explanation (on N. D. II. 116) that "the all-pervading aether, while it has a naturally ex-

pansive and interpenetrative force, has also a strong cohesive force and thus holds all things together round the centre." See also M. Aurel. XI. 20.

11. σφαίρας: for the Stoic doctrine of the rotundity of the world, cf. Stob. Ecl. I. 15. 6ᵇ οἱ Στωικοὶ σφαιροειδῆ τὸν κόσμον ἀπεφήναντο, Diog. VII. 140, Cic. N. D. I. 24, hence ἀντίποδες Cic. Acad. II. 123.

17. παρὰ δὲ τὴν θέσιν: in itself earth βάρος ἔχει and so tends to move πρὸς τὸ μέσον, but owing to the accident of its position in the centre of the κόσμος its natural motion has no opportunity of becoming apparent.

18. μέσην. For the position of the earth cf. Diog. L. VII. 137, 155, Cic. N. D. I. 103.

68. Stob. Ecl. I. 15. 6ᵃ p. 146, 21, Ζήνων ἔφασκε τὸ πῦρ κατ' εὐθεῖαν κινεῖσθαι.

Cf. Stob. Ecl. I. 14. 1. f. p. 142, 12, τὸ μὲν περίγειον φῶς κατ' εὐθεῖαν...κινεῖται. This is only true of πῦρ ἄτεχνον, for the aether or πῦρ τεχνικὸν has a circular motion in the same manner as the πέμπτον σῶμα of Aristotle. So Ar. de Caelo, I. 2. 9, τό τε γὰρ πῦρ ἐπ' εὐθείας ἄνω φέρεται.

69. Stob. Ecl. I. 18. 1ᵈ p. 156, 27, Ζήνων καὶ οἱ ἀπ' αὐτοῦ ἐντὸς μὲν τοῦ κόσμου μηδὲν εἶναι κενόν, ἔξω δ' αὐτοῦ ἄπειρον. διαφέρειν δὲ κενόν, τόπον, χώραν· καὶ τὸ μὲν κενὸν εἶναι ἐρημίαν σώματος, τὸν δὲ τόπον τὸ ἐπεχόμενον ὑπὸ σώματος, τὴν δὲ χώραν τὸ ἐκ μέρους ἐπεχόμενον.

Cf. Diog. VII. 140, ἔξωθεν δὲ αὐτοῦ περικεχυμένον εἶναι τὸ κενὸν ἄπειρον· ὅπερ ἀσώματον εἶναι· ἀσώματον δὲ τὸ οἷόν τε κατέχεσθαι ὑπὸ σωμάτων οὐ κατεχόμενον· ἐν δὲ τῷ κόσμῳ μηδὲν εἶναι κενόν. Plut. plac. I. 18, οἱ Στωικοὶ ἐντὸς μὲν τοῦ κόσμου οὐδὲν εἶναι κενόν, ἔξωθεν δ' αὐτοῦ ἄπειρον. M. Aurel. X. 1. Diels adds Theodoret IV. 14, ἐντὸς μὲν τοῦ παντὸς μηδὲν εἶναι κενόν, ἐκτὸς δὲ αὐτοῦ πάμπολύ τε καὶ ἄπειρον. The Epicureans held that without the existence of void within the world motion was impossible (Lucr. I. 329 foll., Reid on Acad. I. 27, II. 125). The Stoics were unaffected by this argument in consequence of their doctrine of κρᾶσις δι' ὅλων, see further on frag. 50, supra. Aristotle denied the existence of void altogether either within or without the universe.

κενόν, τόπον, χώραν. The Stoics and the Epicureans were in virtual agreement in their definitions of these terms: see Sext. Emp. adv. Math. x. 2, 3. For a fuller exposition cf. Chrysipp. ap. Stob. Ecl. I. 18. 4^d p. 161, 8, who compares κενὸν to an empty, τόπος to a full, and χώρα to a partially filled vessel, cf. the similar views of Aristotle quoted by R. and P. § 327.

70. Themist. Phys. 40^b Speng. II. 284, 10, (τὸ κενόν) κεχωρισμένον καὶ ἀθρόον εἶναι καθ' αὐτὸ περιέχον τὸν οὐρανόν, ὡς πρότερον μὲν ᾤοντο τῶν ἀρχαίων τινές, μετὰ δὲ ταῦτα οἱ περὶ Ζήνωνα τὸν Κιτιέα. Philopon. on Ar. Phys. IV. 6. p. 213 a 31, φασὶ δὲ καὶ τοὺς περὶ Ζήνωνα τὸν Κιτιέα οὕτω (scil. ἔξω τοῦ οὐρανοῦ εἶναι κενόν τι καθ' αὐτὸ) δοξάζειν.

τῶν ἀρχαίων τινὲς are probably the Pythagoreans who believed in an ἄπειρον πνεῦμα outside the universe, called κενὸν by some of the authorities (Zeller, pre-Socratics I. pp. 467, 8).

71. Stob. Ecl. I. 25. 5, p. 213, 15, Ζήνων τὸν ἥλιόν φησι καὶ τὴν σελήνην καὶ τῶν ἄλλων ἄστρων ἕκαστον εἶναι νοερὸν καὶ φρόνιμον πύρινον πυρὸς τεχνικοῦ. δύο γὰρ γένη πυρός, τὸ μὲν ἄτεχνον καὶ μετάβαλλον εἰς ἑαυτὸ τὴν τροφήν, τὸ δὲ τεχνικόν, αὐξητικόν τε καὶ τηρητικόν, οἷον ἐν τοῖς φυτοῖς ἔστι καὶ ζῴοις, ὃ δὴ φύσις ἔστι καὶ

ψυχή· τοιούτου δὴ πυρὸς εἶναι τὴν τῶν ἄστρων οὐσίαν· τὸν δ' ἥλιον καὶ τὴν σελήνην δυὸ φορὰς φέρεσθαι, τὴν μὲν ὑπὸ τοῦ κόσμου ἀπ' ἀνατολῆς εἰς ἀνατολήν, τὴν δ' ἐναντίαν τῷ κόσμῳ ζῴδιον ἐκ ζῳδίου μεταβαίνοντας. τὰς δ' ἐκλείψεις τούτων γίγνεσθαι διαφόρως, ἡλίου μὲν περὶ τὰς συνόδους, σελήνης δὲ περὶ τὰς πανσελήνους· γίγνεσθαι δ' ἐπ' ἀμφοτέρων τὰς ἐκλείψεις καὶ μείζους καὶ ἐλάττους. Stob. Ecl. I. 26. 1, p. 219, 12, Ζήνων τὴν σελήνην ἔφησεν ἄστρον νοερὸν καὶ φρόνιμον πύρινον δὲ πυρὸς τεχνικοῦ.

πύρινον: they are situated in the external periphery of aether, and are themselves composed of the same substance. The later Stoics, at any rate, held that the heavenly bodies are fed by exhalations of grosser matter, and hence their differentiation from their environment. Cf. Cleanth. frags. 29 and 30.

δύο γένη: cf. Cleanth. frag. 30.

φύσις refers to *φυτοῖς* and *ψυχὴ* to *ζῴοις*: cf. frag. 43.

φοράς. The first movement is the diurnal revolution from east to west (from one rising to another): the second is the orbit described κατὰ τὸν ζῳδιακὸν κύκλον, occupying either a year or a month, as the case may be. For the Zodiac cf. Diog. L. VII. 155, 156.

ὑπὸ τοῦ κόσμου, i.e. they move with the aether which revolves round the three lower strata of the world. These latter are themselves stationary, so that κόσμου is used as in Cleanth. frag. 48, l. 7, where see note. The whole structure of the cosmos is very clearly expounded by Chrysippus ap. Stob. Ecl. I. 21. f. p. 184, 185; and cf. especially τοῦ...κόσμου τὸ μὲν εἶναι περιφερόμενον περὶ τὸ μέσον τὸ δ' ὑπόμενον· περιφερόμενον μὲν τὸν αἰθέρα ὑπόμενον δὲ τὴν γῆν καὶ τὰ ἐπ' αὐτῆς ὑγρὰ καὶ τόν ἀέρα...τὸ δὲ περιφερόμενον αὐτῷ ἐγκυκλίως αἰθέρα εἶναι, ἐν ᾧ τὰ ἄστρα καθίδρυται τά τ' ἀπλανῆ καὶ τὰ πλανώμενα, θεῖα τὴν φύσιν ὄντα καὶ ἔμψυχα καὶ διοικούμενα κατὰ τὴν πρόνοιαν.

ζῴδιον: according to Diels, the acc. is "insolenter dictum" and requires the addition of εἰς, but it has been pointed out to me that the true explanation of the acc. is to be found in the fact that ζῴδιον is a measure of space = 30 μοῖραι, Hippol. Haer. v. 13: we should not therefore compare μεταβὰς βίοτον Eur. Hipp. 1292, which is in any case different. For the fact cf. Diog. VII. 144.

τὰς δ' ἐκλείψεις: see infra frag. 73.

μείζους καὶ ἐλάττους: " entire and partial."

72. Cic. N. D. I. 36, idem (Zeno) astris hoc idem (i.e. vim divinam) tribuit tum annis, mensibus, annorumque mutationibus.

astris. On the other hand the Epicureans taught that the stars could not possess happiness or move in consequence of design. Diog. L. x. 77, μήτε αὖ πυρώδη τινὰ συνεστραμμένα τὴν μακαριότητα κεκτημένα κατὰ βούλησιν τὰς κινήσεις ταύτας λαμβάνειν.

annis: probably Zeno did not stop to enquire whether the seasons etc. were corporeal or not: he regarded them as divine "als regelmässig erfolgende Umläufe der Sonne und des Mondes" (Krische, p. 389). Chrysippus must have been hard pressed when he delivered the extraordinary opinion quoted by Plut. Comm. Not. 45, 5 (see Zeller, Stoics p. 131). Krische appositely quotes Plat. Leg. x. p. 899 B, ἄστρων δὲ δὴ περὶ πάντων καὶ σελήνης ἐνιαυτῶν τε καὶ μηνῶν καὶ πασῶν ὡρῶν πέρι, τίνα ἄλλον λόγον ἐροῦμεν ἢ τὸν αὐτὸν τοῦτον, ὡς ἐπειδὴ ψυχὴ μὲν ἢ ψυχαὶ πάντων τούτων αἴτιαι ἐφάνησαν, ἀγαθαὶ δὲ πᾶσαν ἀρετήν, θεοὺς αὐτὰς εἶναι φήσομεν, εἴτε ἐν σώμασιν ἐνοῦσαι, ζῷα ὄντα, κοσμοῦσι πάντα οὐρανόν, εἴτε ὅπῃ τε καὶ ὅπως; In Sext. Math. IX. 184 an argument of Carneades is quoted of the Sorites type, disproving the existence of God. If the sun is a god, so are days, months and years. This the Stoics might have admitted, but he concludes thus:—σὺν τῷ ἄτοπον εἶναι τὴν μὲν ἡμέραν θεὸν εἶναι λέγειν, τὴν δὲ ἕω καὶ τὴν μεσημβρίαν καὶ τὴν δείλην μηκέτι.

73. Diog. L. VII. 145, 6, ἐκλείπειν δὲ τὸν μὲν ἥλιον ἐπιπροσθούσης αὐτῷ σελήνης κατὰ τὸ πρὸς ἡμᾶς μέρος, ὡς Ζήνων ἀναγράφει ἐν τῷ περὶ ὅλου. φαίνεται γὰρ ὑπερχομένη ταῖς συνόδοις καὶ ἀποκρύπτουσα αὐτὸν καὶ πάλιν παραλλάττουσα. γνωρίζεται δὲ τοῦτο διὰ λεκάνης ὕδωρ ἐχούσης. τὴν δὲ σελήνην ἐμπίπτουσαν εἰς τὸ τῆς γῆς σκίασμα. ὅθεν καὶ ταῖς πανσελήνοις ἐκλείπειν μόναις, καίπερ κατὰ διάμετρον ἱσταμένην κατὰ μῆνα τῷ ἡλίῳ· ὅτι κατὰ λοξοῦ ὡς πρὸς τὸν ἥλιον κινουμένη παραλλάττει τῷ πλάτει ἢ βορειοτέρα ἢ νοτιωτέρα γινομένη. ὅταν μέντοι τὸ πλάτος αὐτῆς κατὰ τὸν ἡλιακὸν καὶ τὸν διὰ μέσων γένηται εἶτα διαμετρήσῃ τὸν ἥλιον τότε ἐκλείπει.

ἐκλείπειν. The eclipse of the sun owing to the interposition of the moon between it and the earth is a doctrine attributed by Stobaeus to Thales, the Pythagoreans, and Empedocles (Ecl. I. 25. 1[i] 3[b] 3[e]): the same explanation was also given by Anaxagoras (Zeller, pre-Socratics II. p. 361). The same account is given by the Stoic in Cic. N. D. II. 103, luna...subiecta atque opposita soli radios eius et lumen obscurat, tum ipsa incidens in umbram terrae, cum est e regione solis, interpositu interiectuque terrae repente deficit.

ταῖς συνόδοις "at the period of conjunction." Cf. Cic. Rep. I. 25, Pericles...docuisse cives suos dicitur, id quod ipse ab Anaxagora, cuius auditor fuerat, exceperat, certo illud (eclipse of sun) tempore fieri et necessario, cum tota se luna sub orbem solis subiecisset: itaque, etsi non omni intermenstruo, tamen id fieri non posse nisi certo intermenstruo tempore. Thuc. II. 28.

σελήνην, cf. Stob. Ecl. I. 26. 3, p. 221, 23, Χρύσιππος ἐκλείπειν τὴν σελήνην τῆς γῆς αὐτῇ ἐπιπροσθούσης καὶ εἰς σκιὰν αὐτῆς ἐμπίπτουσαν.

πανσελήνοις: the fact was a matter of common observation: cf. Thuc. VII. 50, ἡ μήνη ἐκλείπει· ἐτύγχανε γὰρ πανσέληνος οὖσα.

κατὰ λοξοῦ: hence ἑλικοειδῆ in Diog. L. VII. 144, see Krische p. 389.

διὰ μέσων scil. ζῳδίων. There is nothing distinctively Stoic in these explanations. Zeno was simply repeating the ordinary scientific theories of his age. Epicurus gave alternative explanations, of which this is one (Diog. L. X. 96).

74. Diog. L. VII. 153, 154, ἀστραπὴν δὲ ἔξαψιν νεφῶν παρατριβομένων ἢ ῥηγνυμένων ὑπὸ πνεύματος, ὡς Ζήνων ἐν τῷ περὶ ὅλου· βροντὴν δὲ τὸν τούτων ψόφον ἐκ παρατρίψεως ἢ ῥήξεως· κεραυνὸν δὲ ἔξαψιν σφοδρὰν μετὰ πολλῆς βίας πίπτουσαν ἐπὶ γῆς νεφῶν παρατριβομένων ἢ ῥηγνυμένων.

Cf. Chrysippus ap. Stob. Ecl. I. 29. 1, p. 233, 9, ἀστραπὴν ἔξαψιν νεφῶν ἐκτριβομένων ἢ ῥηγνυμένων ὑπὸ πνεύματος, βροντὴν δ' εἶναι τὸν τούτων ψόφον...ὅταν δὲ ἡ τοῦ πνεύματος φορὰ σφοδροτέρα γένηται καὶ πυρώδης, κεραυνὸν ἀποτελεῖσθαι. ib. p. 234, 1 where the same views are attributed to οἱ Στωικοί. Here again there is nothing specially characteristic of the Stoa: Epicurus, as was his wont, gave a number of possible explanations and amongst them these: see Diog. L. X. 100—103, cf. Lucr. VI. 96 f. (thunder), 162 f. (lightning), 246 f. (thunderbolts). Lucan I. 151, qualiter expressum ventis per nubila fulmen aetheris impulsi sonitu etc. Aristoph. Nub. 404 foll.

75. Senec. Nat. Quaest. VII. 19. 1, Zenon noster in illa sententia est: congruere iudicat stellas, et radios inter se committere: hac societate luminis existere imaginem stellae longioris.

On this point the majority of the Stoic school seem to have deviated from the teaching of Zeno, considering his view unsatisfactory: thus Diog. VII. 152, κομήτας δὲ καὶ πωγωνίας καὶ λαμπαδίας πυρὰ εἶναι ὑφεστῶτα, πάχους ἀέρος εἰς τὸν αἰθερώδη τόπον ἀνενεχθέντος, cf. Stob. Ecl. I. 28. 1ᵃ p. 228, 6, Βοηθὸς ἀέρος ἀνημμένου φαντασίαν. Sen. N. Q. VII. 21, placet ergo nostris cometas...denso aere creari.

76. Stob. Ecl. I. 8. 40ᵉ p. 104, 7, Ζήνων ἔφησε χρόνον εἶναι κινήσεως διάστημα, τοῦτο δὲ καὶ μέτρον καὶ κριτήριον τάχους τε καὶ βραδύτητος ὅπως ἔχει <ἕκαστα>. κατὰ τοῦτον δὲ γίγνεσθαι τὰ γινόμενα καὶ τὰ περαινόμενα ἅπαντα καὶ τὰ ὄντα εἶναι. Simplic. ad Cat. 80 a 4, τῶν δὲ Στωικῶν Ζήνων μὲν πάσης ἁπλῶς κινήσεως διάστημα τὸν χρόνον εἶναι, who goes on to say that Chrysippus limited the definition by adding the words τοῦ κόσμου. Cf. Diog. VII. 141, ἔτι δὲ καὶ τὸν χρόνον ἀσώματον, διάστημα ὄντα τῆς τοῦ κόσμου κινήσεως. Varro L. L. VI. 3 (quoted by Prof. Mayor on Cic. N. D. I. 21.), tempus esse dicunt intervallum mundi motus. See also Zeller p. 198 and add Plotin. Ennead. III. 7. 6, Sext. Pyrrh. III. 136 f. Math. X. 170 f. Zeno held as against Chrysippus that time existed from eternity, and that it is not merely coeval with the phenomenal world. Stein, Erkenntnistheorie, pp. 223—225.

ἕκαστα is added by Wachsm. and some word is clearly wanted: Posidonius however in reproducing the clause has ὅπως ἔχει τὸ ἐπινοούμενον (Stob. Ecl. I. 8. 42, p. 105, 21). It seems better to remove the comma usually placed after βραδύτητος, as the genitives depend at least as much on ὅπως ἔχει as on μέτρον καὶ κριτήριον, cf. e.g. Thuc. II. 90. 4, ὡς εἶχε τάχους ἕκαστος.

ἅπαντα must be corrupt, as some verb is required to balance γίνεσθαι and εἶναι. Usener suggests ἀπαρτίζεσθαι, which gives the required sense, cf. ἀπαρτισμόν. Chrysipp. ap. Stob. Ecl. I. 8. 42, p. 106, 17. Diels' correction ἀπαντᾶν is less satisfactory in meaning.

77. Censorinus de die Nat. XVII. 2, quare qui annos triginta saeculum putarunt multum videntur errasse. hoc enim tempus genean vocari Heraclitus auctor est, quia orbis aetatis in eo sit spatio. orbem autem vocat aetatis dum natura ab sementi humana ad sementim revertitur. hoc quidem geneas tempus alii aliter definierunt. Herodicus annos quinque et viginti scribit, Zenon triginta.

genean: this substantially accords with the popular reckoning as recorded by Herod. II. 142, γενεαὶ γὰρ τρεῖς ἀνδρῶν ἑκατὸν ἔτεά ἐστι.

Heraclitus: for the other authorities which attribute this statement to Heraclitus see Zeller pre-Socratics II. p. 87, n. 4 and frags. 87 and 88 ed. Bywater.

sementi: saeculum is properly used with the meaning "generation" and this supports the derivation from sero, satus (Curtius G. E. I. p. 474 Eng. Tr.). For examples see the Lexx.

Herodicus: either (1) the Alexandrian grammarian, or (2) the physician of Selymbria: see D. Biog.

Zenon: according to Wachsmuth Jahn proposes to substitute Xenon, but the agreement with Heraclitus rather points to the founder of the Stoa.

78. Stob. Ecl. I. 16. 1, p. 149, 8, Ζήνων ὁ Στωικὸς τὰ χρώματα πρώτους εἶναι σχηματισμοὺς τῆς ὕλης. The

same words occur also in Plut. plac. I. 15. 5 and in Galen Hist. Phil. c. 10. XIX. 258 Kühn.

The above extracts appear to represent all that is known of the Stoic theories about colour: for the Epicurean view cf. Lucr. II. 795 foll. Stein, Erkenntnistheorie p. 310, rightly observes that the definition, implying that colour is an actual attribute of matter, indicates Zeno's reliance on sense-impressions.

79. Epiphan. adv. Haeres. III. 2. 9 (III. 36), Diels p. 592, τὰς δε αἰτίας τῶν πραγμάτων πῆ μὲν ἐφ' ἡμῖν πῆ δὲ οὐκ ἐφ' ἡμῖν, τουτέστι, τὰ μὲν τῶν πραγμάτων ἐφ' ἡμῖν τὰ δὲ οὐκ ἐφ' ἡμῖν.

We have already seen that Zeno held καθ' εἱμαρμένην τὰ πάντα γίγνεσθαι, frag. 45. How then are we to reconcile with this doctrine of necessity the fact that free will is here allowed to mankind even in a limited degree? The Stoic answer is most clearly given by the simile with which they supported their position, cf. Hippolyt. adv. Haeres. I. 18, καὶ αὐτοὶ δὲ τὸ καθ' εἱμαρμένην εἶναι πάντη διεβεβαιώσαντο παραδείγματι χρησάμενοι τοιούτῳ ὅτι ὥσπερ ὀχήματος ἐὰν ᾖ ἐξηρτημένος κύων, ἐὰν μὲν βούληται ἕπεσθαι καὶ ἕλκεται καὶ ἕπεται ἑκών, ποιῶν καὶ τὸ αὐτεξούσιον μετὰ τῆς ἀνάγκης οἷον τῆς εἱμαρμένης· ἐὰν δὲ μὴ βούληται ἕπεσθαι πάντως ἀναγκασθήσεται· τὸ αὐτὸ δή που καὶ ἐπὶ τῶν ἀνθρώπων· καὶ μὴ βουλόμενοι γὰρ ἀκολουθεῖν ἀναγκασθήσονται πάντως εἰς τὸ πεπρωμένον εἰσελθεῖν. The simile itself very possibly belongs to Cleanthes as it accords exactly with his lines in frag. 91. Chrysippus struggled vigorously with the difficulties in which he was involved in maintaining this theory: see the authorities collected by Zeller p. 177 foll. Stein, Erkenntnistheorie pp. 328—332, who ascribes to Cleanthes the introduction of the Stoic answer to the dilemma, has omitted to notice the present frag. and does an injustice to Zeno in asserting that the conflict between free will and necessity never presented itself to his mind.

80. Censorinus de die Nat. IV. 10, Zenon Citieus, Stoicae sectae conditor, principium humano generi ex novo mundo constitutum putavit, primosque homines ex solo adminiculo divini ignis, id est dei providentia, genitos.

This doctrine is connected with that of the destructibility of the world: cf. frag. 56, where however there is unfortunately a lacuna at the point where the origin of man is being discussed. ὀψίγονον in that passage must not be supposed to be at variance with this: the argument there is simply to show that the world cannot be without beginning, because facts show that mankind has not existed from eternity. Zeno is, therefore, distinctly opposed to a theory of progression; mankind was produced in the first instance, when the primary fire was in full sway, and was entirely formed out of the divine essence; the inference must be that men have degenerated through the assimilation of coarser substances, and in this connection we may perhaps point to Posidonius' belief in the popular view of a golden age, when there was a complete supremacy of wise men. Senec. Ep. 90, 5. There is a parallel to this passage in Sext. Math. IX. 28 where the arguments given by various schools for the existence of gods are being recited, τῶν δὲ νεωτέρων στωικῶν φασί τινες τοὺς πρώτους καὶ γηγενεῖς τῶν ἀνθρώπων κατὰ πολὺ τῶν νῦν συνέσει διαφέροντας γεγονέναι, ὡς πάρεστι μαθεῖν ἐκ τῆς ἡμῶν πρὸς τοὺς ἀρχαιοτέρους καὶ ἥρωας ἐκείνους, ὥσπερ τι περιττὸν αἰσθητήριον σχόντας τὴν ὀξύτητα τῆς διανοίας ἐπιβεβληκέναι τῇ θείᾳ φύσει καὶ νοῆσαί τινας δυνάμεις θεῶν. Cf. Cic. Leg. I. 24. Tusc. III. 2, nunc parvulos nobis dedit (natura) igniculos quos celeriter malis moribus opinionibusque depravati sic restinguimus, ut nusquam naturae lumen appareat. For the anthropological aspect of this passage see Stein, Psych. p. 115.

81. Varro de Re Rust. II. 1, 3, sive enim aliquod fuit principium generandi animalium, ut putavit Thales Milesius et Zeno Citieus, sive contra principium horum exstitit nullum, ut credidit Pythagoras Samius et Aristoteles Stagirites.

It is obvious that only on the hypothesis of the world in its present form being without beginning is the doctrine of the eternity of the human race or of animals possible. Aristotle, however, expressly says (de Caelo I. 10 279 b 12) that none of his predecessors had held the world to be without beginning in this sense. Unless therefore Aristotle is mistaken, the reference to Pythagoras in the present passage must be erroneous: see the discussion in Zeller pre-Socratics I. pp. 439—442 and especially p. 439 n. 2 and for the similar case of Xenophanes ib. p. 570: see also Newman on Ar. Pol. II. 8 1269 a 5. At any rate Zeno is in agreement with the great majority of those who went before him: the early philosophers held for the most part that animal life was produced by the action of the sun's rays on the primitive slime, as Anaximander, Xenophanes, Parmenides, and Archelaus (Zeller l. c. I. pp. 255, 577, 601, II. p. 392), or on the earth, as Diogenes of Apollonia (ib. I. p. 296). Somewhat similar were the views of Empedocles and Anaxagoras (ib. II. pp. 160, 365).

82. Schol. ad Plat. Alcib. I. p. 121 E δὶς ἑπτὰ ἐτῶν] τότε γὰρ ὁ τέλειος ἐν ἡμῖν ἀποφαίνεται λόγος, ὥς Ἀριστοτέλης καὶ Ζήνων καὶ Ἀλκμαίων ὁ Πυθαγόρειός φασιν.

Cf. Stob. Ecl. I. 48. 8, p. 317, 21, πάλιν τοίνυν περὶ τοῦ νοῦ καὶ πασῶν τῶν κρειττόνων δυνάμεων τῆς ψυχῆς οἱ μὲν Στωικοὶ λέγουσι μὴ εὐθὺς ἐμφύεσθαι τὸν λόγον, ὕστερον δὲ συναθροίζεσθαι ἀπὸ τῶν αἰσθήσεων καὶ φαντασιῶν περὶ δεκατέσσαρα ἔτη. Plut. plac. IV. 11, ὁ δὲ λόγος καθ᾽ ὃν προσαγορευόμεθα λογικοὶ ἐκ τῶν προλήψεων συμπληροῦσθαι λέγεται κατὰ τὴν πρώτην ἑβδομάδα. (This points to some slight divergence in the school itself as to the exact period of life at which ὁ λόγος τελειοῦται: secus Stein, Erkenntnistheorie p. 116, but how can συμπληροῦσθαι="begin"?) Diog. VII. 55, φωνή...ἀπὸ διανοίας ἐκπεμπομένη, ὡς ὁ Διογένης φησίν· ἥτις ἀπὸ δεκατεσσάρων ἐτῶν τελειοῦται. The mind at birth is a tabula rasa: reason lies in the application of προλήψεις and ἔννοιαι, which are themselves ultimately founded on external impressions, cf. Cleanth. fr. 37 θύραθεν εἰσκρίνεσθαι τὸν νοῦν. The present fragment has been generally overlooked.

Ἀλκμαίων: this statement is not referred to in Zeller's account of Alcmaeon (pre-Socr. I. pp. 521—526). For Aristotle cf. Pol. I. 13 1260 a 14.

83. Euseb. P. E. xv. 20, 2. Ar. Did. fr. phys. 39, Diels p. 470, περὶ δὲ ψυχῆς Κλεάνθης μὲν τὰ Ζήνωνος δόγματα παρατιθέμενος πρὸς σύγκρισιν τὴν πρὸς τοὺς ἄλλους φυσικοὺς φησιν, ὅτι Ζήνων τὴν ψυχὴν λέγει αἰσθητικὴν ἀναθυμίασιν, καθάπερ Ἡράκλειτος. βουλόμενος γὰρ ἐμφανίσαι ὅτι αἱ ψυχαὶ ἀναθυμιώμεναι νοεραὶ ἀεὶ γίνονται εἴκασεν αὐτὰς τοῖς ποταμοῖς λέγων οὕτως 'ποταμοῖσι τοῖσιν αὐτοῖσιν ἐμβαίνουσιν ἕτερα καὶ ἕτερα ὕδατα ἐπιρρεῖ' καὶ ψυχαὶ δὲ ἀπὸ τῶν ὑγρῶν ἀναθυμιῶνται· ἀναθυμίασιν μὲν οὖν ὁμοίως τῷ Ἡρακλείτῳ τὴν ψυχὴν ἀποφαίνει Ζήνων, αἰσθητικὴν δὲ αὐτὴν εἶναι διὰ τοῦτο λέγει, ὅτι τυποῦσθαί τε δύναται [τὸ μέγεθος] τὸ μέρος τὸ ἡγούμενον αὐτῆς ἀπὸ τῶν ὄντων καὶ ὑπαρχόντων διὰ τῶν αἰσθητηρίων καὶ παραδέχεσθαι τὰς τυπώσεις· ταῦτα γὰρ ἴδια ψυχῆς ἐστιν.

αἰσθητικήν: the MSS. have αἴσθησιν ἥ but the correction (made by Wellmann p. 475 and Zeller p. 212) is rendered certain by the parallel passage in ps-Plut. vit. hom. c. 127, τὴν ψυχὴν οἱ Στωικοὶ ὁρίζονται πνεῦμα συμφυὲς καὶ ἀναθυμίασιν αἰσθητικὴν ἀναπτομένην ἀπὸ τῶν ἐν σώματι ὑγρῶν.

ἀναθυμίασιν: cf. Ar. de Anim. I. 2. 16. 405 a 25, καὶ Ἡράκλειτος δὲ τὴν ἀρχὴν εἶναί φησι ψυχήν, εἴπερ τὴν ἀναθυμίασιν, ἐξ ἧς τἆλλα συνίστησιν, i.e. Aristotle identifies the ἀναθυμίασις ("fiery process" Wallace) with πῦρ. Zeno adopts the word as an apt description of the warm breath of which the soul is composed.

νοεραί. The soul's rational power is constantly renewed by the fiery process, because it is fed by the emanations from the περιέχον according to Heraclitus or from the moist parts of the body, i.e. the blood, according to Zeno. In this way Heraclitus explained his famous saying αὔη ψυχὴ σοφωτάτη (frag. 74 ed. Bywater), while the Stoics from their point of view regarded the excellence of the soul as consisting in a suitable admixture of heat. Stein, Psych. p. 105. Hence, as Diels observes, there is no necessity to read ἕτεραι ἀεί.

εἴκασεν αὐτάς: the principle of πάντα ῥεῖ applies no less to the soul than to the world in general: thus Arist. l.c. continues καὶ ἀσωματώτατόν τε καὶ ῥέον ἀεί· τὸ δὲ κινούμενον κινουμένῳ γιγνώσκεσθαι· ἐν κινήσει δ᾽ εἶναι τὰ ὄντα κἀκεῖνος ᾤετο καὶ οἱ πολλοί. The soul is νοερὰ because it is in flux. For ποταμοῖσι cf. Plat. Crat. 402 A, Ἡράκλειτος...ποταμοῦ ῥοῇ ἀπεικάζων τὰ ὄντα λέγει ὡς δὶς ἐς τὸν αὐτὸν ποταμὸν οὐκ ἂν ἐμβαίης. R and P § 26.

καί...ἀναθυμιῶνται. Bywater Heracl. fr. 42 ascribes these words to Zeno and not to Heraclitus: the importance of this will appear presently.

ὁμοίως: i.e. in the same sense as Heraclitus: the latter however would not have called the soul αἰσθητική, distinguishing as he did between sensation and knowledge: κακοὶ μάρτυρες ἀνθρώπων ὀφθαλμοὶ καὶ ὦτα βαρβάρους ψυχὰς ἐχόντων frag. 11 Sch. and Stein, Erkenntnistheorie, p. 12: hence Sextus infers that Heraclitus held τὴν αἴσθησιν ἄπιστον εἶναι (Math. VII. 126).

τυποῦσθαι: cf. frag. 7, and for ἀπὸ τῶν ὄντων κ.τ.λ. frag. 11.

84. Rufus Ephes. de part. hom. p. 44 ed. Clinch, θερμασίαν δὲ καὶ πνεῦμα Ζήνων τὸ αὐτὸ εἶναί φησιν.

This passage has been discovered by Stein, Psych. n. 81 to whose remarks the reader is referred.

85. Diog. L. VII. 157, Ζήνων δὲ ὁ Κιτιεύς...πνεῦμα ἔνθερμον εἶναι τὴν ψυχήν. τούτῳ γὰρ ἡμᾶς εἶναι ἐμπνόους, καὶ ὑπὸ τούτου κινεῖσθαι.

Cf. Alex. Aphr. de an. p. 26, 16 ed. Bruns, οἱ ἀπὸ τῆς Στοᾶς πνεῦμα αὐτὴν λέγοντες εἶναι συγκείμενόν πως ἔκ τε πυρὸς καὶ ἀέρος. Sext. Pyrrh. II. 70, ἐπεὶ οὖν ἡ ψυχὴ πνεῦμα καὶ τὸ ἡγεμονικὸν ἢ λεπτομερέστερόν τι πνεύματος κ.τ.λ. If any of the authorities seem to assert that Heraclitus defined the soul as πνεῦμα, this is doubtless either due to Stoic influence or is a mere gloss on ἀναθυμίασις: see the reff. in Zeller pre-Socratics II. p. 80 where however the reference to Sext. Math. IX. 363 (leg. 361) is a mistake, as the passage is dealing with τὰ τῶν ὄντων στοιχεῖα. Not dissimilar is the Epicurean definition of the soul: Diog. L. x. 63, ἡ ψυχὴ σῶμά ἐστι λεπτομερὲς παρ᾽ ὅλον τὸ ἄθροισμα παρεσπαρμένον· προσεμφερέστατον δὲ πνεύματι θερμοῦ τινα κρᾶσιν ἔχοντι. Sext. Emp. Math. IX. 71, λεπτομερεῖς γὰρ οὖσαι (αἱ ψυχαὶ) καὶ οὐχ ἧττον πυρώδεις ἢ πνευματώδεις εἰς τοὺς ἄνω μᾶλλον τόπους κουφοφοροῦσιν.

ὑπὸ τούτου κινεῖσθαι: frag. 91.

86. Cic. Acad. I. 39, (Zeno) statuebat ignem esse ipsam naturam quae quidque gigneret et mentem atque sensus. Fin. IV. 12, cum autem quaereretur res admodum difficilis, num quinta quaedam natura videretur esse ex qua ratio et intellegentia oriretur, in quo etiam de animis cuius generis essent quaereretur, Zeno id dixit esse ignem. Tusc. I. 19, Zenoni Stoico animus ignis videtur.

See also Stein, Psychologie p. 101.

87. Galen plac. Hippocr. et Plat. II. 8 (v. 283 Kühn), εἰ δέ γε ἔποιτο (Διογένης ὁ Βαβυλώνιος) Κλεάνθει καὶ Χρυσίππῳ καὶ Ζήνωνι τρέφεσθαι μὲν ἐξ αἵματος φήσασι τὴν ψυχὴν οὐσίαν δ' αὐτῆς ὑπάρχειν τὸ πνεῦμα.

It is doubtful whether the doctrine of the nourishment of the soul by the blood was held by Heraclitus and from him derived by Zeno. The only authority, besides the doubtful passage of Arius Didymus (frag. 83), from which it can be argued that such a view belonged to him is Nemes. Nat. Hom. c. 2 p. 28 (quoted by Zeller, pre-Socratics II. p. 80) Ἡράκλειτος δὲ τὴν τοῦ παντὸς ψυχὴν ἀναθυμίασιν ἐκ τῶν ὑγρῶν, who however goes on expressly to distinguish the individual soul from the world-soul and states that the former is composed ἀπὸ τῆς ἐκτὸς (ἀναθυμιάσεως). It is best therefore to regard this as a Stoic innovation: just as the stars in the fiery aether are fed by the moist particles rising from the watery zone which they enclose, so is the fiery soul fed by the moist blood: thus man is in himself an organic whole, and the microcosm of the individual is an exact parallel to the macrocosm of the universe. Further references ap. Zeller p. 212 n. 2. With regard to this passage, Wachsmuth (Comm. I. p. 10) suggests that there is here a confusion between Zeno of Citium and Zeno of Tarsus, but there is no necessity to adopt this supposition: that Zeno held the soul to be fed from the internal moisture of the body, which must be the blood, is clear from frag. 83 even if we leave out of account the frag. next following.

88. Longinus ap. Euseb. P. E. xv. 21, Ζήνωνι μὲν γὰρ καὶ Κλεάνθει νεμεσήσειέ τις ἂν δικαίως οὕτω σφόδρα ὑβριστικῶς περὶ αὐτῆς (scil. ψυχῆς) διαλεχθεῖσι καὶ ταυτὸν ἄμφω τοῦ στερεοῦ αἵματος εἶναι τὴν ψυχὴν ἀναθυμίασιν φήσασι. Theodoret, gr. aff. cur. p. 934 Migne, ἄμφω γὰρ (Ζήνων καὶ Κλεάνθης) τοῦ στερεοῦ αἵματος εἶναι τὴν ψυχὴν ἀναθυμίασιν.

In both cases the MSS. have σώματος for αἵματος, but the words are often confused and σώματος yields no satisfactory sense. The emendation is made by Stein, Psychol. p. 107, and is confirmed by the passages which he cites from Marcus Aurelius (v. 33, vi. 15). στερεοῦ αἵματος is rather an odd expression, but was probably introduced by way of contrast to ψυχή as λεπτομερέστατον πνεῦμα. For ἄμφω Viger suggested ἀμφοῖν, but the word is sometimes indeclinable.

89. Tertullian de Anima, c. 5, denique Zeno consitum spiritum definiens animam hoc modo instruit, "quo" inquit "digresso animal emoritur, corpus est: consito autem spiritu digresso animal emoritur: ergo consitus spiritus corpus est: consitus autem spiritus anima est: ergo corpus est anima." Macrob. Somn. Sc. I. 14. 19, Zenon (dixit animam) concretum corpori spiritum.

Cf. Chrysipp. ap. Nem. Nat. Hom. c. 2, p. 33, ὁ θάνατός ἐστι χωρισμὸς ψυχῆς ἀπὸ σώματος· οὐδὲν δὲ ἀσώματον ἀπὸ σώματος χωρίζεται· οὐδὲ γὰρ ἐφάπτεται σώματος ἀσώματον· ἡ δὲ ψυχὴ καὶ ἐφάπτεται καὶ χωρίζεται τοῦ σώματος. σῶμα ἄρα ἡ ψυχή. See Zeller, Stoics

p. 211, where further illustrations to this and the following frag. will be found in the notes. concretum or consitum corpori spiritum = Chrys. ap. Galen. Hipp. et Plat. III. 1 (v. 287 Kühn), ἡ ψυχὴ πνεῦμά ἐστι σύμφυτον ἡμῖν συνεχὲς παντὶ τῷ σώματι διῆκον (quoted by Zeller). For quo digresso etc. cf. Cic. Tusc. I. 18, sunt qui discessum animi a corpore putent esse mortem. Plat. Phaed. 64 C, ἆρα μὴ ἄλλο τι (ἡγούμεθα τὸν θάνατον εἶναι) ἢ τὴν τῆς ψυχῆς ἀπὸ τοῦ σώματος ἀπαλλαγήν;

90. Chalcid. in Tim. c. 220, Spiritum quippe animam esse Zenon quaerit hactenus: quo recedente a corpore moritur animal, hoc certe anima est. naturali porro spiritu recedente moritur animal: naturalis igitur spiritus anima est.

It is possible that this passage and the extract from Tertullian (fr. 89) are derived from a common original, but, as in their present form the syllogisms are directed to distinct points, it has been thought better to keep them separate.

91. Galen, Hist. Phil. 24, Diels, p. 613, τὴν δὲ οὐσίαν αὐτῆς (ψυχῆς) οἱ μὲν ἀσώματον ἔφασαν ὡς Πλάτων, οἱ δὲ σώματα κινεῖν ὡς Ζήνων καὶ οἱ ἐξ αὐτοῦ. πνεῦμα γὰρ εἶναι ταύτην ὑπενόησαν καὶ οὗτοι.

σώματα κινεῖν. So MS. A, but B has σώματα συγκινοῦν and the Latin version of Nicolaus has "corpus simul secum movens." Wachsm. conj. σῶμα σώματα ἅμα κινοῦν. Usener: σῶμα τὰ σώματα κινοῦν. Diels: σῶμα αὐτὸ κινοῦν sive ἐξ ἑαυτοῦ κινούμενον. Coll. Gal. def. Med. 30 κατὰ δὲ τοὺς Στωικοὺς σῶμα λεπτομερὲς ἐξ ἑαυτοῦ κινούμενον. Whatever may be the right reading, σῶμα certainly seems wanted as well as σώματα to point the contrast with Plato. For the doctrine of the soul regarded as the principle of movement, see the summary of the views of previous philosophers given by Arist. de An. I. 2. §§ 2—6, 403 b 27—404 b 7. That the soul was self-moving as being the principle of motion, was a distinctively Platonic dogma. Phaedr. 245 c, μὴ ἄλλο τι εἶναι τὸ αὐτὸ ἑαυτὸ κινοῦν ἢ ψυχήν. Legg. 895 A, ψυχήν ...τὴν δυναμένην αὐτὴν κινεῖν κίνησιν, where the argument is made use of to prove the immortality of the soul.

For the Stoics cf. Sext. Math. IX. 102, πάσης γὰρ φύσεως καὶ ψυχῆς ἡ καταρχὴ τῆς κινήσεως γίνεσθαι δοκεῖ ἀπὸ ἡγεμονικοῦ, and the references collected by Stein, Psych. nn. 217 and 221 to which add M. Aurel. v. 19. The theory of τόνος throws an entirely new light on this, as on many other Stoic doctrines, which were originally adopted on independent grounds.

92. Stob. Ecl. I. 49. 33, p. 367, 18, ἀλλὰ μὲν οἵ γε ἀπὸ Χρυσίππου καὶ Ζήνωνος φιλόσοφοι καὶ πάντες ὅσοι σῶμα τὴν ψυχὴν νοοῦσι τὰς μὲν δυνάμεις ὡς ἐν τῷ ὑποκειμένῳ ποιότητας συμβιβάζουσι, τὴν δὲ ψυχὴν ὡς οὐσίαν προϋποκειμένην ταῖς δυνάμεσι τιθέασιν, ἐκ δ' ἀμφοτέρων τούτων σύνθετον φύσιν ἐξ ἀνομοίων συνάγουσιν.

ποιότητας...οὐσίαν. This distinction we have already met with in frag. 53. It properly belongs to the department of logic but, in consequence of the Stoic materialism, it has also a quasi-physical application: see Zeller, Stoics, pp. 105, 127, Reid on Cic. Ac. I. 24 foll. The different activities of the soul bear the same relation to the soul as a whole, as the qualities of any particular object bear to its substance: hence Sext. Emp. Math. VII. 234, φασὶ γὰρ ψυχὴν λέγεσθαι διχῶς τό τε συνέχον τὴν ὅλην σύγκρισιν καὶ κατ' ἰδίαν τὸ ἡγεμονικόν.

προϋποκειμένην: for the significance of this expression, see Stein, Erkenntnistheorie, p. 310.

93. Nemes. de Nat. Hom. p. 96, Ζήνων δὲ ὁ Στωικὸς ὀκταμερῆ φησιν εἶναι τὴν ψυχήν, διαιρῶν αὐτὴν εἴς τε τὸ ἡγεμονικὸν καὶ εἰς τὰς πέντε αἰσθήσεις καὶ εἰς τὸ φωνητικὸν καὶ τὸ σπερματικόν. Stob. Ecl. I. 49. 34, p. 369, 6, οἱ ἀπὸ Ζήνωνος ὀκταμερῆ τὴν ψυχὴν διαδοξάζουσι περὶ <ἣν> τὰς δυνάμεις εἶναι πλείονας, ὥσπερ ἐν τῷ ἡγεμονικῷ ἐνυπαρχουσῶν φαντασίας, συγκαταθέσεως, ὁρμῆς, λόγου.

We must distinguish the μέρη ψυχῆς from the δυνάμεις, for they are not identical, as the passage in Stobæus shows. Sext. Emp. Math. VII. 237, καὶ γὰρ ἡ ὁρμὴ καὶ ἡ συγκατάθεσις καὶ ἡ κατάληψις ἑτεροιώσεις εἰσὶ τοῦ ἡγεμονικοῦ. In spite of this eightfold division of local extension (see Zeller, p. 214 n. 2) the Stoics held the unity of the soul as an essence: see especially Stein, Psych. pp. 119, 122, who suggests "soul-functions" as a more suitable expression for the Stoics than "parts of the soul".

τὸ ἡγεμονικόν. We have clear evidence here that the term ἡγεμονικὸν is Zenonian. Stein, Erkenntnistheorie nn. 219 and 693, is inconsistent on this point, in the former passage attributing its introduction to Cleanthes and in the latter to Zeno. It is very possible that Cleanthes first spoke of τὸ ἡγεμονικὸν τοῦ κόσμου, which with him was the sun, in furtherance of his view of man as a microcosm.

94. Tertullian de Anima, c. 14, dividitur autem in partes nunc in duas a Platone, nunc in tres a Zenone.

This passage is at variance with the account given by Nemesius. Wellmann, l. c. p. 476, prefers the authority of Tertullian, thinking that the three divisions in question are the ἡγεμονικόν, the φωνητικόν, and the σπερματικόν, and that the five organs of sense were regarded by Zeno as parts of the body, though the centre of sense resides in the ἡγεμονικόν. On the other hand Weygoldt, l. c. p. 36, and Heinze in Bursian's Jahresb. I. p. 191, think Nemesius more trustworthy than Tertullian, and certainly the better opinion is that Zeno taught the eightfold division (see Stein's full discussion, Psych. pp. 158—160). It is just possible that the triple division mentioned by Tertullian is (1) τὸ ἡγεμονικόν, (2) the five senses, and (3) the voice and the reproductive organism, and that, if we were in possession of the full text of Zeno, the discrepancy would explain itself. If all that we knew of Plato's psychological divisions had been contained in this passage and a statement that he divided the soul into λόγον ἔχον, θυμοειδές, and ἐπιθυμητικόν, we should have had some difficulty in reconciling the two. Hirzel, II. p. 154, 155 appears to be unaware of the passage in Nemesius: he accepts the evidence of Tertullian, but explains it as an ethical rather than a physical distinction.

95. Epiphan. adv. Haeres. III. 2. 9 (III. 36), Ζήνων ὁ Κιτιεὺς ὁ Στωικὸς ἔφη...δεῖν...ἔχειν τὸ θεῖον ἐν μόνῳ τῷ νῷ μᾶλλον δὲ θεὸν ἡγεῖσθαι τὸν νοῦν. ἔστι γὰρ ἀθάνατος......ἔλεγε δὲ καὶ μετὰ χωρισμὸν τοῦ σώματος * * * καὶ ἐκάλει τὴν ψυχὴν πολυχρόνιον πνεῦμα, οὐ μὴν δὲ ἄφθαρτον δι' ὅλου ἔλεγεν αὐτὴν εἶναι. ἐκδαπανᾶται γὰρ ὑπὸ τοῦ πολλοῦ χρόνου εἰς τὸ ἀφανές, ὥς φησι. Cf. August. contra Acad. III. 17, 38, quamobrem cum Zeno sua quadam de mundo et maxime de anima, propter quam vera philosophia vigilat, sententia delectaretur, dicens eam esse mortalem, nec quidquam esse praeter hunc sensibilem mundum, nihilque in eo agi nisi corpore ; nam et deum ipsum ignem putabat.

τὸ θεῖον: cf. Cleanth. frag. 21, Stein, Psychol. p. 97.

πολυχρόνιον: the language of this extract recalls the objection of Cebes in the Phaedo to Socrates' proof of the immortality of the soul p. 87 A—88 B, recapitulated by Socrates p. 95 B—E, cf. especially τὸ δὲ ἀποφαίνειν ὅτι ἰσχυρόν τί ἐστιν ἡ ψυχὴ καὶ θεοειδὲς καὶ ἦν ἔτι πρότερον πρὶν ἡμᾶς ἀνθρώπους γενέσθαι οὐδὲν κωλύειν φῂς πάντα ταῦτα μηνύειν ἀθανασίαν μὲν μή, ὅτι δὲ πολυχρόνιόν τέ ἐστιν ψυχή, καὶ ἦν που πρότερον ἀμήχανον ὅσον χρόνον καὶ ᾔδει τε καὶ ἔπραττεν πολλὰ ἄττα κ.τ.λ. For the limited future existence which the Stoics allowed to the soul see Zeller, p. 218 foll. and add Schol. ad Lucan. IX. 1, alii (animas) solidas quidem, postquam exierint de corpore, permanere, sed deinde tractu temporis dissipari: haec opinio Stoicorum. There was considerable variation in points of detail among the various members of the soul: see on Cleanth. frag. 41.

τοῦ σώματος: some such words as χρόνον τινὰ διαμένειν have fallen out here.

οὐ...ἄφθαρτον: this is not inconsistent with ἀθάνατος above. The soul never perishes entirely, although eventually it passes into a higher power, Diog. VII. 156. ψυχὴν μετὰ θάνατον ἐπιμένειν, φθαρτὴν δὲ εἶναι. Stein Psychol. p. 145.

96. Themist. de An. 68 a Speng. II. p. 30, 24, ἀλλ' ὅμως Ζήνωνι μὲν ὑπολείπεταί τις ἀπολογία κεκρᾶσθαι ὅλην δι' ὅλου τοῦ σώματος φάσκοντι τὴν ψυχὴν καὶ τὴν ἔξοδον αὐτῆς ἄνευ φθορᾶς τοῦ συγκρίματος μὴ ποιοῦντι.

The passage of Aristotle is de An. I. 3 § 6, p. 406 a 30—65, where he says that one of the objections to the view that the soul κινεῖ τὸ σῶμα is that in that case the soul's movements will correspond to those of the body, so that if the body moves locally, the soul may do the same and change its position with regard to the body by leaving it. εἰ δὲ τοῦτ' ἐνδέχεται, ἔποιτ' ἂν τὸ ἀνίστασθαι τὰ τεθνεῶτα τῶν ζῴων. We might therefore infer from this passage that Zeno taught that the soul moved the body (frag. 91).

Themistius says that Zeno is rescued from this dilemma by the doctrine of κρᾶσις δι' ὅλων, for which see on frag. 52. He seems to refer to the Stoic view of the soul as the bond of union for the body, so that body cannot exist qua body without the presence of soul, cf. Iambl. ap. Stob. Ecl. I. 49. 33, p. 368, 6, καθ' οὓς δὲ μία ζωὴ τῆς ψυχῆς ἐστιν ἡ τοῦ συνθέτου, συγκεκραμένης τῆς ψυχῆς τῷ σώματι. Sext. Math. IX. 72, οὐδὲ γὰρ πρότερον τὸ σῶμα διακρατητικὸν ἦν αὐτῶν (τῶν ψυχῶν) ἀλλ' αὐταὶ τῷ σώματι συμμονῆς ἦσαν αἴτιαι κ.τ.λ. The best illustration however is Sext. Math. VII. 234, φασὶ γὰρ ψυχὴν λέγεσθαι διχῶς, τό τε συνέχον τὴν ὅλην σύγκρισιν καὶ κατ' ἰδίαν τὸ ἡγεμονικόν. ὅταν γὰρ εἴπωμεν συνεστάναι τὸν ἄνθρωπον ἐκ ψυχῆς καὶ σώματος, ἢ τὸν θάνατον εἶναι χωρισμὸν ψυχῆς ἀπὸ σώματος, ἰδίως καλοῦμεν τὸ ἡγεμονικόν, the meaning of which passage seems to be that only the ἡγεμονικὸν and not the whole soul is said to depart, inasmuch as the corpse must possess συνεκτικὴ δύναμις in the form of ἕξις, for otherwise it will be altogether non-existent. (See Stein, Erkenntnistheorie, p. 105 foll.) But there is no inconsistency with the present passage, since the change of τὸ συνέχον from ψυχὴ to ἕξις is φθορὰ τοῦ συγκρίματος (for φθορά)(θάνατος see on frag. 95).

97. Lactant. Inst. VII. 7. 20, Esse inferos Zenon Stoicus docuit et sedes piorum ab impiis esse discretas: et illos quidem quietas et delectabiles incolere regiones, hos vero luere poenas in tenebrosis locis atque in caeni voraginibus horrendis.

Cf. Tertull. de anima c. 54, quos quidem miror quod imprudentes animas circa terram prosternant cum illas a sapientibus multo superioribus erudiri adfirment. ubi erit scholae regio in tanta distantia diversoriorum? qua ratione discipulae ad magistros conventabunt, tanto discrimine invicem absentes? quid autem illis postremae eruditionis usus ac fructus iam iam conflagratione perituris? reliquas animas ad inferos deiciunt. Hirzel thinks that Virgil's description of the souls of the lost in Aen. VI. is derived from Stoic sources, and therefore ultimately from Zeno, and refers to Ecl. VI. 31, Georg. IV. 220, Aen. VI. 724, for the influence of Stoicism on Virgil. The same writer correctly points out the distinction between the treatment of popular religion in this doctrine of Zeno and that which appears in those passages (to be presently considered) where the attributes of the popular deities are explained away by rationalistic allegory. He compares the spirit of the present passage with the Platonic myths, called by Grote "fanciful illustrations invented to expand and enliven general views," and suggests that it may have occurred in the πολιτεία, which Zeno, as we are told by Plutarch, directed against the Platonic school (see Hirzel, Untersuchungen II. pp. 25—31). It is certainly hardly credible that Zeno can have attached any philosophical importance to a theory stated in these terms, and it is better to regard it as a concession to popular belief in a matter which could not be formulated with scientific precision. See also Stein, Psych. p. 149 and 162, who infers that Zeno agreed with Chrysippus rather than with Cleanthes in the controversy appearing in Cleanth. frag. 41. The general view of the school was that the soul after death ascends to the upper aether and is preserved there among the stars to which it is akin: Sext. Math. IX. 73, 74, Cic. Tusc. I. 42, 43.

98. Plut. plac. IV. 21. 4, τὸ δὲ φωνᾶεν ὑπὸ τοῦ Ζήνωνος

εἰρημένον, ὃ καὶ φωνὴν καλοῦσιν, ἔστι πνεῦμα διατεῖνον ἀπὸ τοῦ ἡγεμονικοῦ μέχρι φάρυγγος καὶ γλώττης καὶ τῶν οἰκείων ὀργάνων.

Cf. on Cleanth. frag. 43.

99. Eustath. in Il. Σ 506, p. 1158, 37, ἡεροφώνους κήρυκας "Ὅμηρος κἀνταῦθα εἰπὼν τὸν κατὰ Ζήνωνα τῆς φωνῆς ὅρον προϋπέβαλεν εἰπόντα· "φωνή ἐστιν ἀὴρ πεπληγμένος."

Cf. Diog. L. VII. 55, ἔστι δὲ φωνὴ ἀὴρ πεπληγμένος. This frag. is taken from Wachsmuth, Comm. I. p. 12. Sound is produced by the breath coming in contact with the external air; in the case of an animal the air is said to be struck ὑπὸ ὁρμῆς, while the voice of man is ἔναρθρος καὶ ἀπὸ διανοίας ἐκπεμπομένη, Diog. l. c. See also the passages quoted by Stein, Psychol. n. 248.

Cf. Plato's definition, Tim. p. 67 B., ὅλως μὲν οὖν φωνὴν θῶμεν τὴν δι' ὤτων ὑπ' ἀέρος ἐγκεφάλου τε καὶ αἵματος μέχρι ψυχῆς πληγὴν διαδιδομένην. Ar. de An. II. 8 discusses ψόφος, ἀκοή, and φωνή. Sound is formed ὅταν ὑπομένῃ πληγεὶς ὁ ἀὴρ καὶ μὴ διαχυθῇ (§ 3, p. 419 b 21): voice is then defined as ψόφος τις ἐμψύχου (§ 9, p. 420 b. 5) and is minutely described.

100. Galen, Hipp. et Plat. plac. II. 5, V. p. 241, K, ὁ θαυμαζόμενος ὑπὸ τῶν στωικῶν λόγος ὁ Ζήνωνος... ἔχει γὰρ ὧδε. "φωνὴ διὰ φάρυγγος χωρεῖ. εἰ δὲ ἦν ἀπὸ τοῦ ἐγκεφάλου χωροῦσα, οὐκ ἂν διὰ φάρυγγος ἐχώρει. ὅθεν δὲ λόγος, καὶ φωνὴ ἐκεῖθεν χωρεῖ. λόγος δὲ ἀπὸ διανοίας χωρεῖ, ὥστ' οὐκ ἐν τῷ ἐγκεφάλῳ ἐστὶν ἡ διάνοια."

It is tempting to suggest that λόγος and φωνή have changed places: the argument would certainly be more transparent if the transposition were made: cf. the following passage in Galen, speaking of Diogenes Babylonius: ὅθεν ἐκπέμπεται ἡ φωνή, καὶ ἡ ἔναρθρος· οὐκοῦν καὶ ἡ σημαίνουσα ἔναρθρος φωνὴ ἐκεῖθεν· τοῦτο δὲ λόγος. καὶ λόγος ἄρα ἐκεῖθεν ἐκπέμπεται ὅθεν καὶ ἡ φωνή. Galen's comment is that Zeno has omitted some of the necessary ἀξιώματα, while Diogenes has too many. He also points out the fallacy underlying the preposition ἀπό, which is ambiguous; either ἐξ or ὑπό ought to have been used, in which case the argument could never have stood the test of daylight. The gist however of his argument against Zeno, which is given at some length, is that Zeno has been deceived by the following fallacy: ὅθεν ὁ λόγος ἐκπέμπεται, ἐκεῖ δεῖ καὶ τὸν διαλογισμὸν γίγνεσθαι, τουτέστιν, ἐν ἐκείνῳ τῷ μορίῳ. τοῦτο δὲ φήσομεν ἄντικρυς εἶναι ψεῦδος, οὐ γὰρ εἴ τι κατὰ προαίρεσιν ἔκ τινος ἐκπέμπεται κατ' ἐκεῖνο τὸ μόριον δείκνυται τὴν διάνοιαν ὑπάρχειν, καθάπερ οὐδὲ τὸ οὖρον οὐδε τὸ πτύελον οὐδὲ ἡ κόρυζα οὐδὲ τὸ ἀποπάτημα. Wachsmuth quotes further passages from Galen's argument in which Zeno's name is mentioned, but they add nothing to the words cited above. Chrysippus, and after him Diogenes of Babylon (Cic. N. D. I. 41), laboured to prove that the birth of Athene from the head of Zeus in no way conflicted with their view that the breast was the seat of reason (Zeller, p. 364). See generally Stein, Psychol. p. 137.

101. Galen, Hipp. et Plat. plac. II. 5, v. p. 247, Kühn, καὶ τοῦτο βούλεταί γε Ζήνων καὶ Χρύσιππος ἅμα τῷ σφετέρῳ χορῷ παντὶ διαδίδοσθαι τὴν ἐκ τοῦ προσπεσόντος ἔξωθεν ἐγγενομένην τῷ μορίῳ κίνησιν εἰς τὴν ἀρχὴν τῆς ψυχῆς, ἵν' αἴσθηται τὸ ζῷον.

This passage occurs in the course of the discussion as to φωνὴ and διάνοια as a parenthetical argument, and Galen objects that there is no perceptible interval of time between the impression and the sensation. Cf. Plut. plac. IV. 23. 1, impressions are made on the organ of sense but

THE FRAGMENTS OF ZENO. 149

the seat of feeling is in the ἡγεμονικόν. Philo de mund. Opif. p. 114 Pfeiff. (quoted on Cleanthes, frag. 3). See also Stein, Erkenntnistheorie, p. 306.

102. Galen, Hipp. et Plat. plac. III. 5, v. p. 322, Kühn, ὅ τε Ζήνων πρὸς τοὺς ἐπιλαμβανομένους, ὅτι πάντα τὰ ζητούμενα εἰς τὸ στόμα φέρει, ἔφησεν "ἀλλ' οὐ πάντα καταπίνεται", οὔτε τῆς καταπόσεως ἄλλως ἂν οἰκειότερον λεγομένης οὔτε τῆς καταβάσεως τῶν ῥηθέντων, εἰ μὴ περὶ τὸν θώρακα τὸ ἡγεμονικὸν ἡμῖν ἦν, εἰς ὃ ταῦτα πάντα φέρεται.

φέρει, so I. Müller for MSS. φέρειν. This obscure passage was formerly punctuated as though Zeno's words extended from ἀλλ' οὐ πάντα to φέρεται, but, if the context is read, it is at once plain that I. Müller is right in putting the inverted commas after καταπίνεται. Chrysippus, who is being quoted, is aiming to prove the location of the ἡγεμονικόν in the breast by the usage of ordinary speech: e.g. ἀναβαίνειν τὸν θυμόν—καταπίνειν τὴν χολήν—σπαράγματα καταπίνεσθαι—καταπιὼν τὸ ῥηθὲν ἀπῆλθεν: then comes this reference to Zeno, and the conclusion οὔτε—φέρεται is the inference drawn by Chrysippus from the facts stated. Still, it is by no means clear what was the force of the objection made to Zeno or of his rejoinder. Müller translates:—Et Zeno reprehendentibus, quod omnia, quae in quaestionem vocarentur, in ore gestaret, 'at,' inquit, 'non omnia a me devorantur,' apparently making Zeno the subject of φέρει, but the Latin is in other respects hardly less obscure than the Greek. Wachsmuth, who has the old punctuation, interprets πάντα τὰ ζητούμενα as "affectus" and suggests φέρεται for φέρειν, but what meaning he deduces from the passage I do not understand. In this perplexity, the following explanation is suggested. πάντα τὰ ζητούμενα is the subject of φέρει and the objectors say:—all objects of investigation are ultimately concerned with the mouth. For φέρει see L. and S. οἱ ἐπιλαμβανόμενοι are the Epicureans, who denied the existence of any intermediate σημαινόμενον (λεκτόν) between σημαῖνον (φωνή) and τυγχάνον (τὸ ἐκτὸς ὑποκείμενον), cf. Sext. Math. VIII. 11 foll. and esp. 13, οἱ δὲ περὶ τὸν Ἐπίκουρον...φαίνονται... περὶ τῇ φωνῇ τὸ ἀληθὲς καὶ ψεῦδος ἀπολείπειν. Diog. L. X. 33, πᾶν οὖν πρᾶγμα ὀνόματι τῷ πρώτως ἐπιτεταγμένῳ ἐναργές ἐστι. But this nominalism went hand in hand with the most absolute credence in every sense-perception. To the Stoic, however, not every φαντασία is ἐναργής, but only that which is καταληπτική. Hence Zeno's reply:— however this may be, we can't swallow everything. καταπίνεται is substituted for καταλαμβάνεται, just as στόμα takes the place of φωνή. Some confirmation of this guess may be found in the recurrence of τὸ ζητούμενον, ζητεῖν, etc. in Epicurean texts (Diog. X. 33, 37, 38, Sext. Math. XI. 21). If Müller's punctuation is adopted, this fragment ought rather to be numbered with the ἀποφθέγματα, but, in a matter of so much uncertainty, I have not ventured to remove it from the physical fragments, among which it is placed by Wachsmuth.

οὔτε κ.τ.λ.. It would not be correct to speak of "swallowing" or "imbibing" another's words, in any other case unless (ἄλλως εἰ μή) the dominant part of the soul were in the breast. For καταπόσεως cf. Ar. Ach. 484 (of Dicaearchus encouraging his θυμός to persevere in taking the part of the Lacedaemonians) ἕστηκας; οὐκ εἰ καταπιὼν Εὐριπίδην;

103. Cic. de Divin. II. 119, contrahi autem animum Zeno et quasi labi putat atque concidere et ipsum esse dormire.

Elsewhere sleep is said to be caused by a slackening of the tension in the πνεῦμα. Diog. L. VII. 158, τὸν δὲ ὕπνον γίνεσθαι ἐκλυομένου τοῦ αἰσθητικοῦ τόνου περὶ τὸ ἡγεμονικόν. Plut. plac. v. 23. 4, Πλάτων οἱ Στωικοὶ τὸν μὲν ὕπνον γίνεσθαι ἀνέσει τοῦ αἰσθητικοῦ πνεύματος, οὐ κατ' ἀναχαλασμόν, καθάπερ ἐπὶ τῆς γῆς, φερομένου δὲ ὡς ἐπὶ τὸ ἡγεμονικὸν μεσόφρυον. For Plato's theory of sleep cf. Tim. p. 45 D, E, and for the Stoics, Stein, Psychol. p. 141.

104. Stob. Flor. Monac. 198, ὁ αὐτὸς (Ζήνων) ἔφη τὴν μὲν ὅρασιν ἀπὸ τοῦ ἀέρος λαμβάνειν τὸ φῶς, τὴν δὲ ψυχὴν ἀπὸ τῶν μαθημάτων.

For the Stoic theory of vision see Zeller, p. 221, n. 4. Stein, Psych. n. 241. In Plut. plac. IV. 21, ὅρασις is defined as πνεῦμα διατεῖνον ἀπὸ ἡγεμονικοῦ μέχρις ὀφθαλμῶν. The views of the ancient philosophers before Aristotle will be found concisely stated in Grote's Plato, III. 265 n., and for Aristotle see Grote's Aristotle, p. 465.

105. Varro de L. L. v. 59, sive, ut Zenon Citieus, animalium semen ignis is, qui anima ac mens.

Mueller's punctuation of the passage has been followed: in Spengel's edition, Zeno's statement is made to extend farther. ignis = πνεῦμα in the next fragment. Zeller remarks: "Plutarch (Plac. v. 16, 2. 17, 1. 24, 1) draws attention to the inconsistency of saying that the animal soul, which is warmer and rarer than the vegetable soul, has been developed thereout by cooling and condensation," p. 213, n. 1. Stein's explanation of this paradox (Psych. p. 115—117) is ingenious, but he is driven to assume that φύσις is warmer than ψυχή, which seems questionable.

106. Euseb. P. E. xv. 20. 1, Ar. Did. fr. phys. 39,

Diels p. 470, τὸ δὲ σπέρμα φησὶν ὁ Ζήνων εἶναι ὃ μεθίησιν ἄνθρωπος πνεῦμα μεθ᾽ ὑγροῦ, ψυχῆς μέρος καὶ ἀπόσπασμα καὶ τοῦ σπέρματος τοῦ τῶν προγόνων κέρασμα καὶ μῖγμα τῶν τῆς ψυχῆς μερῶν συνεληλυθός· ἔχον γὰρ τοὺς λόγους τῷ ὅλῳ τοὺς αὐτοὺς τοῦτο, ὅταν ἀφεθῇ εἰς τὴν μήτραν συλληφθὲν ὑπ᾽ ἄλλου πνεύματος, μέρος ψυχῆς τῆς τοῦ θήλεος κρυφθέν τε φύει κινούμενον καὶ ἀναρριπιζόμενον ὑπ᾽ ἐκείνου προσλάμβανον ἀεὶ [εἰς] τὸ ὑγρὸν καὶ αὐξόμενον ἐξ αὐτοῦ. Theodoret freely copies Euseb. gr. aff. cur. v. 25, Ζήνων δὲ ὁ Κιτιεὺς ὁ τῆσδε τῆς αἱρέσεως ἡγησάμενος τοιάδε περὶ ψυχῆς δοξάζειν τοὺς οἰκείους ἐδίδαξε φοιτητάς· τὸν γάρ τοι ἀνθρώπινον θορὸν ὑγρὸν ὄντα καὶ μετέχοντα πνεύματος τῆς ψυχῆς ἔφησεν εἶναι μέρος τε καὶ ἀπόσπασμα καὶ τοῦ τῶν προγόνων σπέρματος κέρασμα τε καὶ μῖγμα ἐξ ἁπάντων τῶν τῆς ψυχῆς μορίων συναθροισθέν. Plut. de cohib. Ira, 15, καίτοι (καθάπερ ὁ Ζήνων ἔλεγε τὸ σπέρμα σύμμιγμα καὶ κέρασμα τῶν τῆς ψυχῆς δυναμέων ὑπάρχειν ἀπεσπασμένον) οὕτω κ.τ.λ. ib. plac. v. 4. 1, Ζήνων (τὸ σπέρμα) σῶμα· ψυχῆς γὰρ εἶναι ἀπόσπασμα. Same in Galen, hist. phil. 31. XIX. 322 K., cf. Galen, ὅροι ἰατρ. 94 (XIX. 370 K.), σπέρμα ἐστὶν ἀνθρώπου ὃ μεθίησιν ἄνθρωπος μεθ᾽ ὑγροῦ ψυχῆς μέρους ἅρπαγμα καὶ σύμμιγμα τοῦ τῶν προγόνων γένους, οἷόν τε αὐτὸ ἦν καὶ αὐτὸ συμμιχθὲν ἀπεκρίθη. Diog. VII. 158, ἀνθρώπου δὲ σπέρμα, ὃ μεθίησιν ὁ ἄνθρωπος, μεθ᾽ ὑγροῦ συγκίρνασθαι (λέγουσιν) τοῖς τῆς ψυχῆς μέρεσι κατὰ μιγμὸν τοῦ τῶν προγόνων λόγου.

See also Zeller, p. 212, 213. Stein, Psych. n. 252, collects the various points of resemblance between the Stoics and the Hippocratean school of medicine.

συλληφθέν: conceptum, cf. Sext. Math. v. 55 foll.

φύει: is productive (not intrans.). So perhaps in the well known line: Hom. Il. VI. 149, ὡς ἀνδρῶν γενεή, ἡ μὲν φύει ἡ δ᾽ ἀπολήγει. Otherwise, as τε is not required by the sense, we might suggest that τεφυει arose from φυεται, cf. Diog. L. VII. 159, τῶν εἰς τὴν γῆν καταβαλλομένων σπερμάτων ἃ παλαιωθέντα οὐκ ἔτι φύεται. Cleanth. fr. 24, ὥσπερ γὰρ ἑνός τινος τὰ μέρη πάντα φύεται κ.τ.λ. Diels suggests κερασθέν τε φύει and Usener κρύφα ἐπισχύει.

εἰς after ἀεὶ is perhaps due to dittography.

107. Plut. plac. v. 5. 2, Ζήνων (τὰς θηλείας) ὕλην μὲν ὑγρὰν προΐεσθαι, οἱονεὶ ἀπὸ τῆς συγγυμνασίας ἱδρῶτας, οὐ μὴν σπερματικόν. The same in Galen, hist. phil. c. 31, XIX. 322 K., cf. Diog. L. VII. 159, τὸ δὲ τῆς θηλείας (σπέρμα) ἄγονον ἀποφαίνονται· ἄτονόν τε γὰρ εἶναι καὶ ὀλίγον καὶ ὑδατῶδες, ὡς ὁ Σφαῖρος φησίν.

σπερματικόν. Diels, p. 418 reads σπέρμα πεπτικόν.

108. Sext. Emp. adv. Math. IX. 133, Ζήνων δὲ καὶ τοιοῦτον ἠρώτα λόγον· τοὺς θεοὺς εὐλόγως ἄν τις τιμῴη. τοὺς δὲ μὴ ὄντας οὐκ ἄν τις εὐλόγως τιμῴη· εἰσὶν ἄρα θεοί.

Sextus proceeds to describe the forced interpretation which Diogenes of Babylon and others put upon Zeno's words in order to get rid of the transparent sophistry (ib. 133—136). Theon, Progymn. 12, p. 251 (Spengel, Rhet. gr. p. 126, 16) gives proofs of the existence of the gods, among which is: ἑξῆς δὲ ὅτι καὶ τοῖς σοφοῖς δοκεῖ, οἷον Πλάτωνι, Ἀριστοτέλει, Ζήνωνι.

109. Lactant. de ira Dei c. 11, Antisthenes...unum esse naturalem Deum dixit, quamvis gentes et urbes suos habeant populares. Eadem fere Zeno cum suis Stoicis. Cf. Philod. περὶ εὐσεβ. p. 84 Gomp., πάντες οὖν οἱ ἀπὸ Ζήνωνος, εἰ καὶ ἀπέλειπον τὸ δαιμόνιον...ἕνα θεὸν λέγουσιν εἶναι.

At first sight these passages are inconsistent with frag. 108, but in reality there is no such difficulty: cf. Athenag. Suppl. c. 6, p. 73, quoted supra on frag. 45. The Stoics strongly opposed the follies of the popular belief, while at the same time they called attention to the germ of truth which it contained, being no doubt anxious to preserve it as a basis for morality. Zeller well observes, p. 347, "Holding that the name of God belongs in its full and original sense only to the one primary being, they did not hesitate to apply it in a limited and derivative sense to all those objects by means of which the divine power is especially manifested." In testing how far this admission goes, it should be observed that the Stoic in Cic. N. D. II. 45 distinctly denies that the derivative gods are human in shape, cf. Philod. περὶ εὐσεβ. p. 85 G., ἀνθρωποειδεῖς γὰρ ἐκεῖνοι οὐ νομίζουσιν ἀλλὰ ἀέρας καὶ πνεύματα καὶ αἰθέρας. For Antisthenes cf. Philod. περὶ εὐσεβ. p. 73 G., παρ' Ἀντισθένει δ' ἐν μὲν τῷ φυσικῷ λέγεται τὸ κατὰ νόμον εἶναι πολλοὺς θεούς, κατὰ δὲ φύσιν ἕνα.

110. Cic. N. D. I. 36, Cum vero Hesiodi θεογονίαν interpretatur, tollit omnino usitatas perceptasque cognitiones deorum; neque enim Iovem neque Iunonem neque Vestam neque quemquam qui ita appelletur in deorum habet numero sed rebus inanimis atque mutis per quandam significationem haec docet tributa nomina.

Hesiodi θεογονίαν: Introd. p. 31.

Iovem: see on frag. 111 and cf. Flach, Glossen u. Scholien zur Hesiodischen Theogonie, p. 66.

Iunonem = air: see infra and cf. Cic. N. D. II. 66; she is identified with air as being the wife of Iuppiter (= aether), and air is regarded as feminine, quod nihil est eo mollius. Similarly Ἥρη = air in Empedocles (R. and P. § 131). ἀήρ is also one of Plato's derivations, who says the order of the letters has been reversed, γνοίης δ' ἂν εἰ πολλάκις λέγοις τὸ τῆς "Ηρας ὄνομα, Crat. p. 404 c.

Vestam: cf. N. D. II. 67. "Wahrscheinlich leitete Zenon ihren Namen von ἑστάναι ab und brachte hiermit, anspielend auf den Altar der Hestia im Prytaneum, den Stillstand der Erde im Mittelpunkt der Welt in Verbindung." Krische, p. 401.

This is perhaps the best place to refer to a supposed fragment of Zeno contained in Philodem. περὶ θεῶν διαγωγῆς, Hercul. vol. VI. Tab. I. 1, <αὐ> δᾷ <ὁ> Ζήνων ἕκαστον <τὸν θεὸν ἄπειρα κατέχειν> δὴ τὰ εὐε <τήρια>... <οὐκ ἀ>ν συνακο<λούθει εἰ μή τι> τῶν αἰών<ων> καὶ ἀ<ξι>οῦται δια<φ>θισάμε<νος> ὡς με<τὰ τὰ>ς θεάς. It will be seen that so little of the papyrus is legible here that the sense for which it is quoted by Zeller, p. 165 n. 5, is entirely due to the imagination of the Naples editor. Prof. Scott (Fragm. Hercul. p. 181) rightly characterises this as "gibberish," and wonders that Zeller should have seriously quoted it: see also Wachsm. Comm. I. p. 9 n. If we are to follow the conjectures of the Naples editor of this work of Philodemus, there are at least three other fragments of Zeno preserved in it. In no place but this, however, does the name of Zeno occur, and, though the doctrines appear to belong to some Stoic, there is no reason whatever for supposing that they originated with Zeno. They will be found at Tab. IV. 7. c. iv. col. I. c. xi. and col. II. c. xii.

111. Minucius Felix Octav. 19. 10, Idem (Zeno) interpretando Iunonem aera Iovem caelum Neptunum mare ignem esse Vulcanum et ceteros similiter vulgi deos elementa esse monstrando publicum arguit graviter et revincit errorem.

Iovem: it is clear that Zeus was identified with the

aether or pure fiery essence, of which caelum is here an equivalent, as in Pacuvius ap. Cic. N. D. II. 91, hoc quod memoro nostri caelum Grai perhibent aethera. Cf. Chrysipp. ap. Philod. περὶ εὐσεβ. p. 79 Gomp., "Ἥφαιστον δὲ πῦρ εἶναι...Δία δὲ τὸν αἰθέρα. Diog. L. VII. 147 God is the creator of the universe, and, as it were, the father of all; his various manifestations are described by different names. Δία μὲν γάρ φασι δι' ὃν τὰ πάντα· Ζῆνα δὲ καλοῦσι παρ' ὅσον τοῦ ζῆν αἴτιός ἐστιν, ἢ διὰ τοῦ ζῆν κεχώρηκεν...... "Ἥραν δὲ κατὰ τὴν εἰς ἀέρα· καὶ "Ἥφαιστον κατὰ τὴν εἰς τὸ τεχνικὸν πῦρ· καὶ Ποσειδῶνα κατὰ τὴν εἰς τὸ ὑγρόν. The extract from Minuc. Felix lends some slight weight to Krische's theory (p. 398) that the whole of Diogenes' description is ultimately derived from Zeno. The same writer thinks that the explanation of the myths of the mutilation of Uranus and the binding of Cronos (Cic. N. D. II. 63, 64) belongs to Zeno.

ignem. Diogenes' πῦρ τεχνικὸν is, according to Krische, a blunder: Hephaestus is elsewhere identified with earthly fire (τὴν φλόγα in Plut. de Iside c. 66, for which however see on Cleanth. frag. 23). But see Zeller, p. 359, 1. These explanations were not novelties introduced by the Stoa, except in so far as they were specially adapted to Stoic dogmas. Cf. Sext. Math. IX. 18 (after citing Euhemerus and Prodicus), καὶ διὰ τοῦτο τὸν μὲν ἄρτον Δημήτραν νομισθῆναι τὸν δὲ οἶνον Διόνυσον τὸ δὲ ὕδωρ Ποσειδῶνα τὸ δὲ πῦρ "Ἥφαιστον καὶ ἤδη τῶν εὐχρηστούντων ἕκαστον.

112. Valer. Probus in Virg. Ecl. VI. 31, p. 21, 14 Keil: sunt qui singulis elementis principia adsignaverunt... Thales Milesius magister eius (Anaximenis) aquam. Hanc quidem Thaletis opinionem ab Hesiodo putant manare qui dixerit: ἤτοι μὲν πρώτιστα χάος γένετ', αὐτὰρ ἔπειτα. Nam Zenon Citieus sic interpretatur aquam χάος appellatum ἀπὸ τοῦ χέεσθαι, quamquam eandem opinionem ab Homero possumus intellegere quod ait 'Ωκεανόν τε θεῶν γένεσιν καὶ μητέρα Τηθύν. This frag. is cited by Wachsmuth Comm. I. p. 11, who adds "eadem originatio est apud Achill. Tat., Isag. in Arat. phaen. 3. 125 e. Petav."

The lines of Hesiod, Theog. 116 foll. are often quoted, e.g. by Plato, Symp. 178 B, to prove the antiquity of love, and by Ar. Met. I. 4. 1 as an indication that Hesiod recognised both the efficient and the final cause. Aristotle also refers to the passage in Phys. IV. 1 and de Caelo III. 1. 298 b. 25, and Krische suggests (p. 395) that the application which is put upon it by him in the latter place prevented Zeno from identifying χάος with his own πρώτη ὕλη as might have been expected. Cf. also the anecdote related of Epicurus in Sext. Math. x. 18, 19.

ἀπὸ τοῦ χέεσθαι. Krische l. c. remarks that this derivation is probably referred to in Plat. Cratyl. 402 B where Socrates, after saying that Heraclitus likened all things to a flowing river, and that Homer's line showed that he was of the same opinion, proceeds: οἶμαι δὲ καὶ Ἡσίοδος.

113. Schol. on Apoll. Rhod. I. 498, καὶ Ζήνων δὲ τὸ παρ' Ἡσιόδῳ χάος ὕδωρ εἶναί φησιν, οὗ συνιζάνοντος ἰλὺν γίνεσθαι, ἧς πηγνυμένης ἡ γῆ στερεμνιοῦται. τρίτον δὲ Ἔρωτα γεγονέναι καθ' Ἡσίοδον, ἵνα τὸ πῦρ παραστήσῃ· πυρωδέστερον γὰρ πάθος Ἔρως.

This passage shows clearly that Zeno must have rejected or been ignorant of ll. 118 and 119 of the Theog. see Krische, p. 396.

χάος. See on frag. 112 and add Cornut. c. 17, p. 85 Osann, ἔστι δὲ χάος μὲν τὸ πρὸ τῆς διακοσμήσεως γενόμενον ὑγρόν, ἀπὸ τῆς χύσεως οὕτως ὠνομασμένον.

ἰλύν: similar views with regard to the formation of the

earth are attributed to Xenophanes. Hippolyt. I. 14, ταῦτα δέ φησι γενέσθαι ὅτε πάντα ἐπηλώθησαν πάλαι τὸν δὲ τόπον ἐν τῷ πηλῷ ξηρανθῆναι κ.τ.λ., and to Anaxagoras (Zeller, pre-Socratics II. p. 356). Hence Zeno himself spoke of earth as ὑποστάθμη πάντων, frag. 114.

πυρωδέστερον: a familiar comparison. Pind. P. IV. 219 Medea ἐν φρασὶ καιομέναν. Virg. Aen. IV. 68, uritur infelix Dido. Georg. III. 244, in furias ignemque ruunt: amor omnibus idem. Cf. Schol. ad Hes. Theog. 120, ἠδ' ἔρος...ἔνιοι δὲ πῦρ· τὸ πυρῶδες γὰρ τῆς ἐπιθυμίας.

The authorities give two further Stoic explanations of Hesiod's Eros; (1) with a reference to λόγος σπερματικός. Cornut. c. 17, p. 86 Osann, ὁ δὲ Ἔρως σὺν αὐτοῖς γεγονέναι ἐρρήθη, ἡ ὁρμὴ ἐπὶ τὸ γεννᾶν. (2) Fire regarded as συνεκτικὴ δύναμις: Schol. ad Hes. Theog. 120, τὰ τρία στοιχεῖα εἰπὼν τὸ δ λέγει τὸ πῦρ ὅπερ δαιμονίως ἔρωτά φησι, συναρμόζειν γὰρ καὶ συνάγειν καὶ ἑνοῦν πέφυκεν. On the passage generally cf. Flach, Glossen u. Scholien, p. 37, who attributes to Zeno the words in the Schol. on l. 115, ἐκ δὲ τοῦ ὕδατος ἐγένοντο τὰ στοιχεῖα, γῆ κατὰ συνίζησιν, ἀὴρ κατὰ ἀνάδοσιν· τὸ δὲ λεπτομερὲς τοῦ ἀέρος γέγονε πῦρ, τὰ δὲ ὄρη κατὰ ἐξοστρακισμὸν τῆς γῆς, which appear also in Cornut. c. 17, p. 84 Osann. This is likely enough, but there is no direct evidence. The same remark applies to the derivation of Κρόνος from χρόνος id. p. 44 (cf. Cic. N. D. II. 64). Flach refers many other definitions to Zeno: a list of some of them will be found at p. 48 of his work, but those of his inferences which are not supported by direct evidence cannot be dealt with here.

114. Schol. on Hes. Theog. 117, Ζήνων δὲ ὁ Στωικὸς ἐκ τοῦ ὑγροῦ τὴν ὑποστάθμην γῆν γεγεννῆσθαί φησιν, τρίτον δὲ Ἔρωτα γεγονέναι, ὅθεν ὁ ἐπαγόμενος ἀθετεῖται στίχος. Cf. Diog. L. VII. 137, ὑποστάθμην δὲ πάντων τὴν γῆν, μέσην ἁπάντων οὖσαν.

Wachsmuth connects this with frag. 113. For the general sense cf. frag. 52. The word ὑποστάθμη is Platonic (Phaed. 109 c).

115. Schol. on Hes. Theog. 134 Gaisf. Gr. Poet. Min. II. 482, ὁ Ζήνων φησὶ τοὺς Τιτᾶνας διὰ παντὸς εἰρῆσθαι τὰ στοιχεῖα τοῦ κόσμου. Κοῖον γὰρ λέγει τὴν ποιότητα κατὰ τροπὴν Αἰολικὴν τοῦ π πρὸς τὸ κ, Κρεῖον δὲ τὸ βασιλικὸν καὶ ἡγεμονικόν, Ὑπερίονα δὲ τὴν ἄνω κίνησιν ἀπὸ τοῦ ὑπεράνω ἰέναι. ἐπεὶ δὲ φύσιν ἔχει πάντα τὰ βάρη ἀφιέμενα πίπτειν ἄνωθεν τὸ τοιοῦτον εἶδος Ἰάπετον ἐκάλεσε.

ποιότητα, frag. 53. πάντα τὰ βάρη, frag. 67. βάρη...ἄνωθεν... εἶδος: so Flach, p. 223 after Schoemann. The old reading was κοῦφα...ἄνω...μέρος. Osann suggested ἵπτειν for πίπτειν. Cf. Cornut. c. 17, p. 91 Osann, οὕτως ὑπὸ τῶν παλαιῶν Ἰάπετος μὲν ὠνομάσθη ὁ λόγος καθ' ὃν φωνητικὰ τὰ ζῷα ἐγένετο καὶ ὅλος ὁ ψόφος ἀπετελέσθη, ἰαφετός τις ὤν· ἰὰ γὰρ ἡ φωνή. Κοῖος δὲ καθ' ὃν ποῖά τινα τὰ ὄντα ἐστί· τῷ γὰρ κ πολλαχοῦ οἱ Ἴωνες ἀντὶ τοῦ π χρῶνται... Κρῖος δὲ καθ' ὃν τὰ μὲν ἄρχει καὶ δυναστεύει τῶν πραγμάτων τὰ δ' ὑποτέτακται καὶ δυναστεύεται· ἐντεῦθεν τάχα καὶ τοῦ ἐν τοῖς ποιμνίοις κριοῦ προσαγορευομένου. Ὑπερίων δὲ καθ' ὃν ὑπεράνω τινὰ ἑτέρων περιπορεύεται. See Flach, Glossen u. Scholien zur Hes. Th. p. 42 foll.

116. Schol. on Hes. Theog. 139, Gaisf. Gr. Poet. Min. II. 484. Κύκλωπας. Ζήνων δὲ πάλιν φυσικωτέρως τὰς ἐγκυκλίους φορὰς εἰρῆσθαί φησι· διὸ καὶ τὰ ὀνόματα τούτων ἐξέθετο Βρόντην τε καὶ Στερόπην· Ἄργην δὲ ἐπειδὴ φασι τὸν ἀργῆτα κεραυνόν· παῖδας δέ φησιν αὐτοὺς τοῦ Οὐρανοῦ ἐπειδὴ πάντα ταῦτα τὰ πάθη περὶ τὸν οὐρανόν εἰσι...[ἐν χρόνῳ γάρ τινι ἐγένοντο ἔγκυκλοι περιφοραὶ τοῦ πυρὸς ἐκ τοῦ ἀέρος].

Flach's arrangement of the text is quite different: he inserts the words ἐν χρόνῳ—ἀέρος after εἰρῆσθαί φησιν, altering φορὰς into περιφοράς. See his interpretation, p. 50.

ἐγκυκλίους φοράς. The band of aether which formed the external stratum of the world revolved in a circle round it. Stob. Ecl. I. 14. 1ʳ, p. 142, 13, τὸ αἰθέριον (φῶς) περιφερῶς κινεῖται. In the matter of the revolving aether Zeno followed Aristotle, whose quinta essentia is described by Sextus as τὸ κυκλοφορητικὸν σῶμα (Pyrrh. II. 31). Aristotle himself approves of the Platonic derivation from ἀεὶ θεῖν and censures Anaxagoras for referring it to αἴθω (de Caelo I. 2); see also Krische, p. 306 foll.

Βρόντην τε καὶ Στερόπην. Wachsmuth says:—"immo βρόντην τε καὶ στερόπην," but surely Hesiod is the subject to ἐξέθετο as to φησι below. τίθεσθαι ὄνομα is used regularly of the father: e.g. Isae. II. § 36, τῷ ἐμῷ παιδίῳ ἐθέμην τὸ ὄνομα τὸ ἐκείνου.

ἐν χρόνῳ κ.τ.λ. These words cannot belong to Zeno, unless Flach's view of the passage is adopted, as they are inconsistent with the rest of the explanation.

117. Philod. περὶ εὐσεβ. col. 8, τ<οὺ>ς δὲ ὀρθοὺς <λόγ>ους καὶ σπουδαίας διαθέσεις Διοσκούρους.

From the position of these words in the fragments of Philodemus περὶ εὐσεβείας it appears probable that they belong to Zeno: see on frag. 40. Gomperz however p. 74 puts a full stop after διαθέσεις.

ὀρθοὺς λόγους: see Introd. p. 8, and for the ethical importance of the expression Stein, Erkenntnistheorie, p. 259 foll. Cic. Tusc. IV. 34, ipsa virtus brevissime recta ratio dici potest.

διαθέσεις are opposed to ἕξεις as "permanent forms admitting neither of increase nor diminution," Zeller, p. 103. Thus intellectual goods are divided into (1) virtues = διαθέσεις, (2) σπουδαίας ἕξεις such as μαντική, and (3) ἐπαινετὰς ἐνεργείας = οὔτε ἕξεις οὔτε διαθέσεις, such as φρονίμευμα, Stob. Ecl. II. 7. 5, e and f, Diog. VII. 98, Cleanth. frag. 51, cf. Sext. Pyrrh. III. 243, αὐτὴ γὰρ ἡ φρονίμη διάθεσις ἀκατάληπτός ἐστι μήτε ἐξ αὐτῆς ἁπλῶς καὶ αὐτόθεν φαινομένη μήτε ἐκ τῶν ἔργων αὐτῆς· κοινὰ γάρ ἐστι ταῦτα καὶ τῶν ἰδιωτῶν. For the distinction between ἕξις and διάθεσις in Aristotle see Wallace on de An. II. 5. 417 b. 15.

Διοσκούρους: explained physically by Xenophanes as clouds made to shine by their movement (Stob. Ecl. I. 24. 1ⁿ p. 204, 18). See also the explanations cited by Sext. Math. IX. 37. 86: the latter passage appears to be Stoic, as recognising the belief in demons.

118. Diog. L. VII. 149, καὶ μὴν καὶ μαντικὴν ὑφεστάναι πᾶσάν φασιν, εἰ καὶ πρόνοιαν εἶναι· καὶ αὐτὴν καὶ τέχνην ἀποφαίνουσι διά τινας ἐκβάσεις, ὥς φησι Ζήνων.

μαντική. The Stoic definition was as follows: Stob. Ecl. II. 7. 5b 12, p. 67, 16, εἶναι δὲ τὴν μαντικὴν φασιν ἐπιστήμην θεωρητικὴν σημείων τῶν ἀπὸ θεῶν ἢ δαιμόνων πρὸς δὲ ἀνθρώπινον βίον συντεινόντων. Substantially the same in Sext. Math. IX. 132.

εἰ καί. Others read ᾗ καί, reversing the argument: in fact, the Stoics seem to have appealed to the truth of μαντική as a proof of the existence of God, no less than vice versa. See the references in Zeller, pp. 175, 3; 372, 2 and 3.

τέχνην. They prove that it is an art by the truth of certain results, cf. Cic. de Divin. I. 23, Quid? quaeris, Carneades, cur haec ita fiant aut qua arte perspici possint?

Nescire me fateor, evenire autem te ipsum dico videre. That its professors are sometimes deceived does not invalidate the title of divination as an art (ib. § 24), cf. N. D. II. 12.

ETHICA.

119. Diog. L. VII. 84, τὸ δὲ ἠθικὸν μέρος τῆς φιλοσοφίας διαιροῦσιν εἴς τε τὸν περὶ ὁρμῆς καὶ εἰς τὸν περὶ ἀγαθῶν καὶ κακῶν τόπον καὶ εἰς τὸν περὶ παθῶν καὶ περὶ ἀρετῆς καὶ περὶ τέλους περί τε τῆς πρώτης ἀξίας καὶ τῶν πράξεων καὶ περὶ τῶν καθηκόντων προτροπῶν τε καὶ ἀποτροπῶν· καὶ οὕτω δ᾽ ὑποδιαιροῦσιν οἱ περὶ Χρύσιππον καὶ Ἀρχέδημον καὶ Ζήνωνα τὸν Ταρσέα κ.τ.λ. ὁ μὲν γὰρ Κιτιεὺς Ζήνων καὶ ὁ Κλεάνθης ὡς ἂν ἀρχαιότεροι ἀφελέστερον περὶ τῶν πραγμάτων διέλαβον.

There is a full discussion of this passage in Zeller, p. 223, 1: its difficulties, however, do not affect Zeno or Cleanthes.

120. Diog. L. VII. 87, διόπερ πρῶτος ὁ Ζήνων ἐν τῷ περὶ ἀνθρώπου φύσεως τέλος εἶπε τὸ ὁμολογουμένως τῇ φύσει ζῆν, ὅπερ ἐστὶ κατ᾽ ἀρετὴν ζῆν· ἄγει γὰρ πρὸς ταύτην ἡμᾶς ἡ φύσις. Lactant. Inst. III. 7, Zenonis (summum bonum) cum natura congruenter vivere. id. III. 8, audiamus igitur Zenonem; nam is interdum virtutem somniat. Summum, inquit, est bonum cum natura consentanee vivere. Stob. Ecl. II. 7. 6ᵃ, p. 75, 11, τὸ δὲ τέλος ὁ μὲν Ζήνων οὕτως ἀπέδωκε 'τὸ ὁμολογουμένως ζῆν'· τοῦτο δ᾽ ἔστι καθ᾽ ἕνα λόγον καὶ σύμφωνον ζῆν, ὡς τῶν μαχομένως ζώντων κακοδαιμονούντων. Plut. Comm. Not. 23, 1, οὐχὶ καὶ Ζήνων τούτους (scil. Peripatetics) ἠκολούθησεν ὑποτιθεμένοις στοιχεῖα τῆς εὐδαιμονίας τὴν φύσιν καὶ τὸ κατὰ φύσιν. (Cf. Cic. Fin. IV. 72, videsne igitur Zenonem tuum cum Aristone verbis consistere, re dissidere; cum Aristotele et illis re consentire, verbis discrepare? ib. v. 88.) Clem. Alex. Strom. II. 21. 129, p. 496 P., 179 S., πάλιν δ' αὖ Ζήνων μὲν ὁ Στωικὸς τέλος ἡγεῖται τὸ κατ' ἀρετὴν ζῆν, cf. Cic. Fin. IV. 14, hunc ipsum Zenonis aiunt esse finem, declarantem illud, quod a te dictum est, convenienter naturae vivere (where see Madv.): ib. III. 21, summum...bonum, quod cum positum sit in eo, quod ὁμολογίαν Stoici, nos appellemus convenientiam, etc.

There is a conflict of testimony here between Diog. and Stob. as to whether Cleanthes added the words τῇ φύσει to Zeno's definition or found them there already. On the whole the fact that Diogenes quotes from a named book of Zeno's makes his authority the more trustworthy. So Wellmann, l. c. pp. 446—448, cf. Krische, p. 372, 3. Ueberweg, p. 199, adds that Diog.'s statement is all the more credible, because Speusippus, Polemo, and Heraclitus had enounced similar principles. Zeller, p. 228, 2, does not decide the point. Hirzel, II. p. 105—112, argues the question at some length and decides in favour of Stobaeus, but his arguments are always biassed by the desire to vindicate the originality of Cleanthes. See also Introd. p. 14.

121. Plut. fragm. de an. ed. Wyttenb. v². p. 899, καὶ οἰκειώσεως πάσης καὶ ἀλλοτριώσεως ἀρχὴ τὸ αἰσθάνεσθαι ...οἱ ἀπὸ Ζήνωνος.

This frag. has been taken from Stein, Erkenntnistheorie, p. 271. Although we cannot with certainty attribute to Zeno a statement, which is only expressed to belong to οἱ ἀπὸ Ζήνωνος, yet there is no reason why he should not have taught this. The soul at birth is only open to the impressions of sensation, and its first impulse is towards self-preservation. Cf. Plut. Sto. Rep. 12, 5, p. 1038 C, ἀλλ' οὔτ' αἴσθησίς ἐστιν οἷς μηδὲν αἰσθητόν, οὔτ' οἰκείωσις οἷς μηδὲν οἰκεῖον· ἡ γὰρ οἰκείωσις αἴσθησις ἔοικε τοῦ οἰκείου καὶ ἀντίληψις εἶναι.

122. Porphyr. de Abstin. III. 19, τὴν δὲ οἰκείωσιν ἀρχὴν τίθενται δικαιοσύνης οἱ ἀπὸ Ζήνωνος.

δικαιοσύνη is one of the four cardinal virtues (see infra, frag. 134) and is founded on οἰκείωσις in the same sense as ἀρετὴ generally. The natural impulse of every animal is towards self-preservation, so that it seeks after those things which are κατὰ φύσιν and shuns those which are παρὰ φύσιν. Diog. L. VII. 85; Cic. Fin. III. 16; Alex. Aphr. de an. p. 150, 28 ed. Bruns. οἱ μὲν οὖν Στωικοὶ οὐ πάντες δὲ λέγουσιν πρῶτον οἰκεῖον εἶναι τὸ ζῷον αὐτῷ· ἕκαστον γὰρ ζῷον εὐθὺς γενόμενον πρός τε αὐτὸ οἰκειοῦσθαι, καὶ δὴ καὶ τὸν ἄνθρωπον· οἱ δὲ χαριέστερον δοκοῦντες λέγειν αὐτῶν καὶ μᾶλλον διαρθροῦν περὶ τοῦδέ φασιν πρὸς τὴν σύστασιν καὶ τήρησιν ᾠκειῶσθαι εὐθὺς γενομένους ἡμᾶς τὴν ἡμῶν αὐτῶν. Stob. Ecl. II. 7. 13, p. 118, 11 (where the doctrine is attributed to the Peripatetics). For τὰ πρῶτα κατὰ φύσιν, see Madv. de Fin. Exc. IV. and especially p. 818[3], "Stoici...ita disputabant, ut, quae postea demum, orto subito rationis lumine, quod in infante nondum esset accensum, et animadversa constantia convenientiaque naturae, nasceretur *voluntas* cum natura consentiendi, in qua et virtus et perfectio rationis esset, eam omnino a prima conciliatione dirimerent, bonumque constituerent, quod expeteretur, a primis, quae appeterentur, genere seiunctum."

123. Epict. diss. I. 20. 14, καίτοι αὐτὸς μὲν ὁ προηγούμενος λόγος τῶν φιλοσόφων λίαν ἐστὶν ὀλίγος. εἰ θέλεις γνῶναι, ἀναγνῶθι τὰ Ζήνωνος, καὶ ὄψει· τί γὰρ ἔχει μακρὸν εἰπεῖν ὅτι τέλος ἐστὶ τὸ ἕπεσθαι θεοῖς, οὐσία δ' ἀγαθοῦ χρῆσις οἵα δεῖ φαντασιῶν;

προηγούμενος λόγος, "leading doctrine": not in the technical sense to be noticed on frag. 169.

ἕπεσθαι θεοῖς is only another way of expressing ὁμολογία τῇ φύσει. This passage furnishes an argument in support of the view taken in the Introd. p. 14 as to the character of Zeno's φύσις.

φαντασιῶν. Zeno went back to the Socratic doctrine that virtue is knowledge, so that it is not surprising to find that his epistemology is brought into connection with practical morality. That particular class of impressions which is directed towards the performance of some moral action gives rise to corresponding ὁρμαὶ in the soul, cf. Stob. Ecl. II. 7. 9, p. 86. 17, τὸ δὲ κινοῦν τὴν ὁρμὴν οὐδὲν ἕτερον εἶναι λέγουσιν ἀλλ' ἢ φαντασίαν ὁρμητικὴν τοῦ καθήκοντος αὐτόθεν. Virtue consists in the proper direction of these ὁρμαὶ in accordance with the dictates of ὀρθὸς λόγος: hence Diog. L. VII. 86 says of reason:—τεχνίτης γὰρ οὗτος ἐπιγίγνεται τῆς ὁρμῆς, cf. Cleanth. frag. 66. The doctrine depends on the freedom of the assent: supra, frag. 19, cf. Stob. Ecl. II. 7. 9[b], p. 88, 1, πάσας δὲ τὰς ὁρμὰς συγκαταθέσεις εἶναι, τὰς δὲ πρακτικὰς καὶ τὸ κινητικὸν περιέχειν, and see Windelband in Müller's Handbuch, v. 295. Stein, Erkenntnistheorie, pp. 166, 167, points out that the ethical application of φαντασίαι is very often mentioned by the younger Stoics, although not unknown in the earlier period, cf. Diog. VII. 48, ὥστε εἰς ἀκοσμίαν καὶ εἰκαιότητα τρέπεσθαι τοὺς ἀγυμνάστους ἔχοντας τὰς φαντασίας.

124. Stob. Ecl. II. 7. 6[e], p. 77, 20, τὴν δὲ εὐδαιμονίαν ὁ Ζήνων ὡρίσατο τὸν τρόπον τοῦτον· εὐδαιμονία δ' ἐστὶν εὔροια βίου. Sext. Math. XI. 30, εὐδαιμονία δέ ἐστιν, ὡς οἵ τε περὶ τὸν Ζήνωνα καὶ Κλεάνθην καὶ Χρύσιππον ἀπέδοσαν, εὔροια βίου. Cf. Cleanth. frag. 74, Diog. VII. 88.

M. Aurel. II. 5, v. 9, x. 6. εὐδαιμονία is not identical with τέλος, which rather consists in τὸ τυχεῖν τῆς εὐδαιμονίας.

125. Diog. VII. 127, αὐτάρκη εἶναι ἀρετὴν πρὸς εὐδαιμονίαν, καθά φησι Ζήνων. August. contra Acad. III. 7. 16, clamat Zenon et tota illa porticus tumultuatur hominem natum ad nihil esse aliud quam honestatem; ipsam suo splendore in se animos ducere, nullo prorsus commodo extrinsecus posito et quasi lenocinante mercede; voluptatemque illam Epicuri solis inter se pecoribus esse communem; in quorum societatem et hominem et sapientem tendere nefas esse. August. de trin. XIII. 5. 8, diximus ibi quosque posuisse beatam vitam quod eos maxime delectavit...ut virtus Zenonem. Cic. Fin. V. 79, a Zenone hoc magnifice tamquam ex oraculo editur: " virtus ad bene vivendum seipsa contenta est." Cf. Acad. I. 7, 35; II. 134, 135; Paradox. II. This position was borrowed from the Cynics, Introd. p. 19.

126. Cic. Fin. IV. 47, errare Zenonem, qui nulla in re nisi in virtute aut vitio propensionem ne minimi quidem momenti ad summum bonum adipiscendum esse diceret, et, cum ad beatam vitam nullum momentum cetera haberent. ad appetitionem tamen rerum esse in iis momenta diceret. ib. IV. 60, Zeno autem quod suam quod propriam speciem habeat cum appetendum sit, id solum bonum appellat, beatam autem vitam eam solam, quae cum virtute degatur.

This point constitutes the main gist of Cicero's argument against the Stoic virtue in de Fin. IV., viz. that while the πρῶτα κατὰ φύσιν are an object of desire, they have no weight in the explanation of virtue itself. Madvig points out (1) that Cicero has throughout confused the Stoic prima constitutio, which excludes virtue, with that of Antiochus which includes it, (2) that throughout the Fourth Book he attributes far more importance to the doctrine of οἰκείωσις than the Stoics themselves did (pp. 820, 821), and (3) that he fails to notice the Stoic distinction between τὸ τυγχάνειν τῶν κατὰ φύσιν and τὸ πάντα ποιεῖν ἕνεκα τοῦ τυγχάνειν αὐτῶν (Stob. Ecl. II. 7. 6ᵃ, p. 76. 13; Plut. Sto. Rep. c. 26; Cic. Fin. II. 22). On the subject in general see Zeller, p. 278 foll. For the nature of the πρῶτα κατὰ φύσιν cf. Stob. Ecl. II. 7. 3ᶜ, p. 47. 12 f.; ib. 7ᵃ, p. 80. 9; 7ᵈ, p. 82. 12. The position of Zeno will have to be considered with reference to the προηγμένα, where the same inconsistency appears.

aut vitio: these words were bracketed by some of the edd. and are, of course, logically indefensible, but see Madv.

127. Cic. Tusc. II. 29, Nihil est, inquit (Zeno), malum, nisi quod turpe atque vitiosum est...Numquam quidquam, inquit (scil. doleas necne interest), ad beate quidem vivendum, quod est in una virtute positum, sed est tamen reiciendum. Cur? Asperum est, contra naturam, difficile perpessu, triste, durum. ib. v. 27, si Stoicus Zeno diceret qui, nisi quod turpe esset, nihil malum duceret. Cf. ib. II. 15.

In Stob. Ecl. II. 7. 5ᵇ, p. 58, 14, we read ἀνάλογον δὲ τῶν κακῶν τὰ μὲν εἶναι κακίας, τὰ δ' οὔ, and the examples given of the latter class are λύπη and φόβος. This occurs in the course of a passage which Wachsmuth attributes to Zeno, but see on frag. 128. Just before this, in what is clearly Zeno's classification of ἀγαθὰ and κακά, we find ἡδονὴ classed among the ἀδιάφορα, cf. Diog. L. VII. 103, and this agrees with the statement in the present passage that dolor is an ἀποπροηγμένον. So dolor is classed in Cic. Fin. III. 51, where Zeno's name appears in the immediate context, and it is to be observed that the corresponding προηγμένον in that passage is not ἡδονὴ but "doloris vacuitas." The entire subject of the relation which the emotions bear to the classification of ἀγαθὰ and κακὰ is extremely obscure, and the ancient authorities are not only defective but, as we have seen, contradictory. See Introd. p. 46, where this passage should have been referred to. Zeller's account is not clear on this point: at p. 253 he apparently asserts that the emotions are to be classed as κακά.

128. Stob. Ecl. II. 7. 5ᵃ, p. 57, 18, ταῦτ' εἶναί φησιν ὁ Ζήνων ὅσα οὐσίας μετέχει, τῶν δ' ὄντων τὰ μὲν ἀγαθά, τὰ δὲ κακά, τὰ δὲ ἀδιάφορα. ἀγαθὰ μὲν τὰ τοιαῦτα· φρόνησιν, σωφροσύνην, δικαιοσύνην, ἀνδρείαν καὶ πᾶν ὅ ἐστιν ἀρετὴ ἢ μετέχον ἀρετῆς· κακὰ δὲ τὰ τοιαῦτα· ἀφροσύνην, ἀκολασίαν, ἀδικίαν, δειλίαν, καὶ πᾶν ὅ ἐστι κακία ἢ μετέχον κακίας· ἀδιάφορα δὲ τὰ τοιαῦτα· ζωὴν θάνατον, δόξαν ἀδοξίαν, πόνον ἡδονήν, πλοῦτον πενίαν, νόσον ὑγίειαν, καὶ τὰ τούτοις ὅμοια.

Substantially the same account appears in Diog. L. VII. 101, 102, where Hecaton, Apollodorus, and Chrysippus are referred to as authorities.

τῶν δ' ὄντων κ.τ.λ. This classification is attributed by Sext. Math. XI. 3, 4, to the Old Academy, the Peripatetics, and the Stoics in common: he quotes from Xenocrates, πᾶν τὸ ὂν ἢ ἀγαθόν ἐστιν ἢ κακόν ἐστιν ἢ οὔτε ἀγαθόν ἐστιν οὔτε κακόν ἐστιν. In the same passage he states that the name ἀδιάφορον was applied to the third class by all three schools, but probably this is a mistake, as all the other evidence points to Zeno as having been the first to use the word in this special ethical sense. On the other hand, there is not much likelihood in Hirzel's opinion (II. p. 45 n.) that Aristotle was the first to introduce the term ἀδιάφορον, and that Zeno spoke of μέσα.

φρόνησιν κ.τ.λ. cf. frag. 134.

πᾶν ὅ ἐστιν ἀρετή: cf. Sext. Math. XI. 77, ἄλλον μὲν Ζήνων, δι' οὗ τὴν ἀρετὴν ἀγαθὸν εἶναι δεδόξακεν. ib. 184, καθὸ καὶ ὁριζόμενοί τινες ἐξ αὐτῶν φασιν ἀγαθόν ἐστιν ἀρετὴ ἢ τὸ μετέχον ἀρετῆς. The meaning of μετέχον ἀρετῆς is made clear by Diog. L. VII. 94, 95, where it is explained as including actions in accordance with virtue, and good men: the converse is true of μετέχον κακίας.

ἡδονήν: cf. Aul. Gell. IX. 5, 5. Zeno censuit voluptatem esse indifferens, id est neutrum neque bonum neque malum, quod ipse Graeco vocabulo ἀδιάφορον appellavit. For the attitude of the Stoics towards the Epicurean summum bonum see Wellmann l.c. pp. 449, 450. Heinze, de Stoicorum affectibus p. 37, doubts, without sufficient ground, whether Gellius' statement is accurate, thinking that Zeno would rather have classed ἡδονή among the κακά. It will be observed that, omitting πόνον ἡδονήν, every pair of ἀδιάφορα here mentioned contains a προηγμένον and an ἀποπροηγμένον, and that, except in the case of νόσον ὑγίειαν (which Wachsm. transposes), the προηγμένον is mentioned first. We should naturally suppose the same to be the case with ἡδονή and πόνος, but which then is the προηγμένον? Wachsmuth evidently thinks ἡδονή, since he transposes the words, and at first sight Diog. L. VII. 102 is conclusive. But it should be observed that Hecaton is the main authority there cited, and there is reason to believe that this was one of the points on which the view of the School altered as time went on. With Zeno and Cleanthes, at least, it seems better to suppose that πόνος is the προηγμένον, and ἡδονή the ἀποπροηγμένον, and that ἡδονή is contrasted with πόνος rather than with λύπη, because the latter certainly belouged to the class of ἀποπροηγμένα (frag. 127). For πόνος cf. Diog. L. VII. 172, Λάκωνός τινος εἰπόντος ὅτι ὁ πόνος ἀγαθόν, διαχυθεὶς φησιν (Κλεάνθης) αἵματος εἰς ἀγαθοῖο φίλον τέκος, Zeno, frag. 187, and for ἡδονή cf. Sext. Math. XI. 73, οἱ δὲ ἀπὸ τῆς στοᾶς ἀδιάφορον (scil. ἡδονὴν εἶναί φασιν) καὶ οὐ προηγμένον. Cleanth. frag. 88.

Wachsmuth would continue to Zeno the passage following this in Stobaeus down to p. 59. 3, but the evidence is against this. The prominence given to ἰσχὺς ψυχῆς rather points to an origin subsequent in date to Cleanthes, and λύπη and φόβος are here classed as κακά, which is inconsistent with frag. 127, not to speak of ἡδονὴ in the present fragment.

129. Senec. Epist. 82, 7, Zenon noster hac collectione utitur: "Nullum malum gloriosum esse; mors autem gloriosa est; mors ergo non est malum."

In the subdivision of the ἀδιάφορα death belongs to the ἀποπροηγμένα Diog. L. VII. 106; cf. Cic. Fin. III. 29, ut enim, qui mortem in malis ponit, non potest eam non timere, sic nemo ulla in re potest id, quod malum esse decreverit, non curare idque contemnere.

130. Cic. Acad. I. 36, Cetera autem, etsi nec bona nec mala essent, tamen alia secundum naturam dicebat (Zeno), alia naturae esse contraria. His ipsis alia interiecta et media numerabat. Quae autem secundum naturam essent, ea sumenda et quadam aestimatione dignanda dicebat, contraque contraria; neutra autem in mediis relinquebat, in quibus ponebat nihil omnino esse momenti.

In this and the following §§ of Cicero it is unsafe to attribute entirely to Zeno the summary of Stoic doctrines there set forth, in the absence of other testimony pointing in the same direction. At the same time there is no reason a priori why Zeno should not have sub-divided ἀδιάφορα into (1) τὰ κατὰ φύσιν, (2) τὰ παρὰ φύσιν, and (3) τὰ καθάπαξ ἀδιάφορα = media, or have identified τὰ κατὰ φύσιν with ληπτὰ or τὰ ἀξίαν ἔχοντα, and τὰ παρὰ φύσιν with ἄληπτα or τὰ ἀπαξίαν ἔχοντα. Cf. Stob. Ecl. II. 7. 7^d, p. 82, 11; 7^f, p. 84, 3.

131. Stob. Ecl. II. 7. 7^g, p. 84, 21, τῶν δ' ἀξίαν ἐχόντων τὰ μὲν ἔχειν πολλὴν ἀξίαν τὰ δὲ βραχεῖαν. ὁμοίως δὲ καὶ τῶν ἀπαξίαν ἐχόντων ἃ μὲν ἔχειν πολλὴν ἀπαξίαν, ἃ δὲ βραχεῖαν. τὰ μὲν οὖν πολλὴν ἔχοντα ἀξίαν προηγμένα λέγεσθαι, τὰ δὲ πολλὴν ἀπαξίαν ἀποπροηγμένα, Ζήνωνος 5 ταύτας τὰς ὀνομασίας θεμένου πρώτου τοῖς πράγμασι. προηγμένον δ' εἶναι λέγουσιν, ὃ ἀδιάφορον <ὂν> ἐκλεγόμεθα κατὰ προηγούμενον λόγον. τὸν δὲ ὅμοιον λόγον ἐπὶ τῷ ἀποπροηγμένῳ εἶναι καὶ τὰ παραδείγματα κατὰ τὴν ἀναλογίαν ταὐτά. οὐδὲν δὲ τῶν ἀγαθῶν εἶναι προηγμένον 10 διὰ τὸ τὴν μεγίστην ἀξίαν αὐτὰ ἔχειν. τὸ δὲ προηγμένον, τὴν δευτέραν χώραν καὶ ἀξίαν ἔχον, συνεγγίζειν πως τῇ τῶν ἀγαθῶν φύσει· οὐδὲ γὰρ ἐν αὐλῇ τῶν προηγμένων εἶναι τὸν βασιλέα ἀλλὰ τοὺς μετ' αὐτὸν τεταγμένους. προηγμένα δὲ λέγεσθαι οὐ τῷ πρὸς εὐδαιμονίαν τινὰ συμ- 15 βάλλεσθαι συνεργεῖν τε πρὸς αὐτήν, ἀλλὰ τῷ ἀναγκαῖον εἶναι τούτων τὴν ἐκλογὴν ποιεῖσθαι παρὰ τὰ ἀποπροηγμένα. Plut. Sto. Rep. 30, 1. Some of the πρεσβύτεροι said that Zeno's προηγμένον was in as bad a way as the sour wine, which its owner could not dispose of as wine or vinegar: so the προηγμένον is neither an ἀγαθὸν nor an ἀδιάφορον.

4. πολλὴν ἔχοντα ἀξίαν. In Stob. Ecl. II. 7. 7^f, p. 83, 10 every thing which is in accordance with nature is said ἀξίαν ἔχειν. Diog. L. VII. 105 identifies προηγμένα with τὰ ἔχοντα ἀξίαν, Sext. Emp. Math. XI. 62 with τὰ ἱκανὴν ἀξίαν ἔχοντα, cf. Stob. Ecl. II. 7. 7^b, p. 80, 17. Cicero's

phrase, Acad. I. 37 (sed quae essent sumenda ex iis alia pluris esse aestimanda, alia minoris), is of doubtful import: see Reid in loc. In Fin. III. 51 we have:—quae autem aestimanda essent, eorum in aliis satis esse causae, quamobrem quibusdam anteponerentur, where Madvig remarks that none of the authorities give examples of those things which are ληπτά without being προηγμένα.

5. Ζήνωνος: apart from the evidence of Stob. and Plut. it is clear that the προηγμένα must have formed part of Zeno's system from the fact that Aristo expressly dissented from him on this point (Cic. Acad. II. 130), cf. Cic. Fin. III. 51. According to Hirzel p. 418 the word was discarded by the later Stoics, and εὔχρηστα substituted by Posidonius.

8. προηγούμενον λόγον: see on frag. 169.

τῷ ἀποπροηγμένῳ: so Wachsmuth for τὸ ἀποπροηγμένον MSS. Heeren reads τῶν—ων.

13. οὐδὲ γὰρ ἐν αὐλῇ: cf. Cic. Fin. III. 52, ut enim, inquit (Zeno), nemo dicit in regia regem ipsum quasi productum esse ad dignitatem—id est enim προηγμένον—sed eos qui in aliquo honore sunt, quorum ordo proxime accedit, ut secundus sit, ad regium principatum, sic in vita non ea, quae primario loco sunt, sed ea, quae secundum locum obtinent, προηγμένα, id est, producta nominentur.

τῶν προηγμένων: so Madv. ad de Fin. l.c. for MSS. τὸν προαγόμενον: he is followed by Wachsmuth. Hirzel II. p. 823 prefers προηγουμένων.

15. τινά: so MSS. τινὶ Davies. <μοῖράν> τινα Hense.
16. τε: Mein. τι MSS.

ἀλλὰ τῷ κ.τ.λ. On the subject of the προηγμένα in general consult Zeller, pp. 278—287. This sentence contains the gist of the Stoic position in the matter. Although sickness e.g. does not impede the happiness of the wise man, since he is secure in the possession of virtue, it is at the same time impossible ceteris paribus not to prefer health to sickness, cf. Stob. Ecl. II. 7. 7, p. 79, 12—17.

132. Diog. L. VII. 120, ἀρέσκει τε αὐτοῖς ἴσα ἡγεῖσθαι τὰ ἁμαρτήματα, καθά φησι...Ζήνων. Sext. Math. VII. 422, κἀντεῦθεν ὁρμώμενοι οἱ περὶ τὸν Ζήνωνα ἐδίδασκον ὅτι ἴσα ἐστὶ τὰ ἁμαρτήματα. Cic. Mur. § 61, omnia peccata esse paria (among the sententiae et praecepta Zenonis). Lactant. Inst. III. 23, Zenonis paria peccata quis probat?

Cf. Cic. Paradox. III. Hor. Sat. I. 3. 120 foll. Both Sextus and Diog. give as the ground for this doctrine an argument from the relation of truth to falsehood. As one true thing cannot be more true or one false thing more false than another in respect of its truth or falsity, so one sin cannot be more sinful than another. ἁμάρτημα is the correlative of κατόρθωμα and is defined as τὸ παρὰ τὸν ὀρθὸν λόγον πραττόμενον, ἢ ἐν ᾧ παραλέλειπταί τι καθῆκον ὑπὸ λογικοῦ ζῴου, Stob. Ecl. II. 7. 11[a], p. 93, 16. See further Zeller, p. 267.

133. Cic. Mur. § 61, omne delictum scelus esse nefarium, nec minus delinquere eum, qui gallum gallinaceum, cum opus non fuerit, quam eum, qui patrem suffocaverit.

This is quoted among the sententiae et praecepta Zenonis, but it is extremely unlikely that the illustration used is that of Zeno. Cicero attempts (Paradox. III. 25) to answer this objection by the remark, doubtless borrowed from some Stoic source, that whereas the wrongful killing of a slave involves a single ἁμάρτημα, many ἁμαρτήματα are committed in the act of parricide.

134. Plut. Sto. Rep. VII. 1, 2, ἀρετὰς ὁ Ζήνων ἀπολείπει πλείονας κατὰ διαφοράς, ὥσπερ ὁ Πλάτων, οἷον φρόνησιν ἀνδρείαν σωφροσύνην δικαιοσύνην, ὡς ἀχωρίστους μὲν οὔσας, ἑτέρας δὲ καὶ διαφερούσας ἀλλήλων. πάλιν δὲ ὁριζόμενος αὐτῶν ἑκάστην, τὴν μὲν ἀνδρείαν φησὶ φρόνησιν εἶναι ἐν ἐνεργητέοις· τὴν δὲ δικαιοσύνην φρόνησιν ἐν ἀπονεμητέοις· ὡς μίαν οὖσαν ἀρετὴν ταῖς δὲ πρὸς τὰ πράγματα σχέσεσι κατὰ τὰς ἐνεργείας διαφέρειν δοκοῦσαν. Plut. de Virt. Mor. 2, ἔοικε δὲ καὶ Ζήνων εἰς τοῦτό πως ὑποφέρεσθαι ὁ Κιτιεύς, ὁριζόμενος τὴν φρόνησιν ἐν μὲν ἀπονεμητέοις δικαιοσύνην· ἐν δὲ διαιρετέοις σωφροσύνην· ἐν δὲ ὑπομενετέοις ἀνδρείαν· ἀπολογούμενοι δὲ ἀξιοῦσιν ἐν τούτοις τὴν ἐπιστήμην φρόνησιν ὑπὸ τοῦ Ζήνωνος ὠνομάσθαι. Diog. L. VII. 161, ἀρετάς τε οὔτε πολλὰς εἰσήγεν (scil. Aristo) ὡς ὁ Ζήνων. Cic. Acad. I. 38, hic (Zeno) omnis (virtutes) in ratione ponebat...nec ullo modo... (seiungi) posse disserebat, nec virtutis usum modo...sed ipsum habitum per se esse praeclarum, nec tamen virtutem cuiquam adesse quin ea semper uteretur. Cf. ib. II. 31, Fin. IV. 54.

Cf. Stob. Ecl. II. 7. 5^{b2}, p. 60, 12, καὶ τὴν μὲν φρόνησιν περὶ τὰ καθήκοντα γίνεσθαι· τὴν δὲ σωφροσύνην περὶ τὰς ὁρμὰς τοῦ ἀνθρώπου· τὴν δὲ ἀνδρείαν περὶ τὰς ὑπομονάς· τὴν δὲ δικαιοσύνην περὶ τὰς ἀπονεμήσεις. Diog. VII. 126. Zeno taught that virtue is one and indivisible, but that in different spheres it is manifested in different forms. He resumed the Socratic position (for which see Zeller, Socrates E. T. p. 140 foll., and especially Xen. Mem. III. 9, Plat. Men. 88 C), that virtue is knowledge, but adopted the terminology of Aristotle by making use of the word φρόνησις instead of ἐπιστήμη, and thus indicated that moral insight is to be distinguished from intellectual research (cf. Ar. Eth. VI. 13). There is therefore high probability in Zeller's suggestion (p. 258 n.) that "perhaps Zeno had already defined φρόνησις as ἐπιστήμη ἀγαθῶν καὶ κακῶν." At the same time he must have been influenced by the Platonic doctrine of the four cardinal virtues (Rep. p. 441 foll.), but he traced the differences in virtue to the diversity of the objects with which it is concerned, while Plato treated them as arising from the distinct parts of the soul, which produce different mental states.

ἀπονεμητέοις = the rendering every man his due (ἀπονεμητικὴ τῆς ἀξίας ἑκάστῳ Stob. l.c.), cf. the definition attributed to Simonides in Plat. Rep. i. p. 331 E, ὅτι τὸ τὰ ὀφειλόμενα ἑκάστῳ ἀποδιδόναι δίκαιόν ἐστι. It is more general in meaning than Aristotle's τὸ ἐν ταῖς διανομαῖς δίκαιον (Eth. N. v. 2. 12).

διαιρετέοις: distinguishing between things with a view to choice: it deals with τὰς αἱρέσεις καὶ ἐκκλίσεις (Cleanth. frag. 76).

ὑπομενετέοις...ἐνεργητέοις. Hirzel suggests that there is a lacuna in Plut. Sto. Rep. l.c. and that we ought to read there φρόνησιν εἶναι ἐν <ὑπομενετέοις τὴν δὲ σωφροσύνην φρόνησιν ἐν> αἱρετέοις (in place of ἐνεργητέοις). For ὑπομ. cf. Ar. Eth. III. 6, 6, ὁ ἀνδρεῖος...οὐδεὶς γὰρ ὑπομενετικώτερος τῶν δεινῶν: for the general sense cf. Thuc. II. 40. 3, κράτιστοι δ' ἂν τὴν ψυχὴν δικαίως κριθεῖεν οἱ τά τε δεινὰ καὶ ἡδέα σαφέστατα γιγνώσκοντες καὶ διὰ ταῦτα μὴ ἀποτρεπόμενοι ἐκ τῶν κινδύνων.

σχέσεσι. This word has a technical meaning with the Stoics, being opposed to κίνησις on the one hand (cf. Cic. Tusc. IV. 30), and to ἕξις (non-essential)(essential) on the other (Stob. Ecl. II. 7. 5^k, p. 73, 1). The virtues themselves are διαθέσεις, for which see on frag. 117.

135. Plut. Virt. Mor. c. 3, κοινῶς δὲ ἅπαντες οὗτοι (scil. Menedemus, Aristo, Zeno, Chrysippus) τὴν ἀρετὴν τοῦ ἡγεμονικοῦ τῆς ψυχῆς διάθεσίν τινα καὶ δύναμιν γεγενη-

μένην ὑπὸ λόγου, μᾶλλον δὲ λόγον οὖσαν αὐτὴν ὁμολογούμενον καὶ βέβαιον καὶ ἀμετάπτωτον ὑποτίθενται· καὶ νομίζουσιν οὐκ εἶναι τὸ παθητικὸν καὶ ἄλογον διαφορᾷ τινι καὶ φύσει ψυχῆς τοῦ λογικοῦ διακεκριμένον, ἀλλὰ τὸ αὐτὸ τῆς ψυχῆς μέρος (ὃ δὴ καλοῦσι διάνοιαν καὶ ἡγεμονικόν), διόλου τρεπόμενον καὶ μεταβάλλον ἔν τε τοῖς πάθεσι καὶ ταῖς κατὰ ἕξιν ἢ διάθεσιν μεταβολαῖς, κακίαν τε γίνεσθαι καὶ ἀρετήν, καὶ μηδὲν ἔχειν ἄλογον ἐν ἑαυτῷ· λέγεσθαι δὲ ἄλογον, ὅταν τῷ πλεονάζοντι τῆς ὁρμῆς ἰσχυρῷ γενομένῳ καὶ κρατήσαντι πρός τι τῶν ἀτόπων παρὰ τὸν αἱροῦντα λόγον ἐκφέρηται· καὶ γὰρ τὸ πάθος εἶναι λόγον πονηρὸν καὶ ἀκόλαστον, ἐκ φαύλης καὶ διημαρτημένης κρίσεως σφοδρότητα καὶ ῥώμην προσλαβόντα.

τὴν ἀρετὴν κ.τ.λ. cf. Stob. Ecl. II. 7. 5^b7, p. 64, 18, ἀρετάς δ' εἶναι πλείους φασὶ καὶ ἀχωρίστους ἀπ' ἀλλήλων καὶ τὰς αὐτὰς τῷ ἡγεμονικῷ μέρει τῆς ψυχῆς καθ' ὑπόστασιν.

ὁμολογούμενον: frag. 120.

ἀμετάπτωτον: cf. the definition of knowledge in frag. 17. Virtue is knowledge as applied to conduct.

καὶ νομίζουσι κ.τ.λ. This is principally aimed at Plato (see e.g. Rep. 436 A), but partly also at Aristotle, although the latter denies that the soul is μεριστὴ in the Platonic sense (de An. i. 5, 24, but cf. Eth. i. 13, 10). With Zeno the local extension of the soul as a πνεῦμα throughout the body does not detract from its unity either on the physical or the moral side: πάθος and ἀρετὴ are alike affections of the ἡγεμονικόν: see on frag. 93. "The battle between virtue and vice did not resemble a war between two separate powers, as in Plato and Aristotle, but a civil war carried on in one and the same country." Reid on Acad. I. 38.

διάνοιαν καὶ ἡγεμονικόν. For the distinction between these two terms see Stein, Erkenntnistheorie, p. 132, 306.

ἕξιν ἢ διάθεσιν: see on frag. 117. The πάθη are distinguished, being neither ἕξεις nor διαθέσεις but κινήσεις, Cic. Tusc. IV. 30.

τῷ πλεονάζοντι. Zeno's view of the πάθη will be considered in the next following fragments. Cf. Stob. Ecl. II. 7. 10, p. 88, 10, εἶναι δὲ πάθη πάντα τοῦ ἡγεμονικοῦ τῆς ψυχῆς.

136. Diog. L. VII. 110, ἔστι δὲ αὐτὸ τὸ πάθος κατὰ Ζήνωνα ἡ ἄλογος καὶ παρὰ φύσιν ψυχῆς κίνησις, ἢ ὁρμὴ πλεονάζουσα. Cic. Tusc. IV. 11, est igitur Zenonis haec definitio ut perturbatio sit, quod πάθος ille dicit, aversa a recta ratione, contra naturam animi commotio. Quidam brevius, perturbationem esse appetitum vehementiorem. ib. 47, definitio perturbationis, qua recte Zenonem usum puto; ita enim definit ut perturbatio sit aversa a ratione contra naturam animi commotio, vel brevius ut perturbatio sit appetitus vehementior.

Cf. Cic. Off. I. § 136, perturbationes, id est, motus animi nimios rationi non obtemperantes. Stob. Ecl. II. 7. 2, p. 44, 4, πᾶν πάθος ὁρμὴ πλεονάζουσα. ib. 7. 10, p. 88, 8, πάθος δ᾽ εἶναί φασιν ὁρμὴν πλεονάζουσαν καὶ ἀπειθῆ τῷ αἱροῦντι λόγῳ ἢ κίνησιν ψυχῆς <ἄλογον> παρὰ φύσιν. Plut. in fragm. utr. anim. an corp. libid. et aegrit. c. VII. Andron. περὶ παθῶν c. I. The comments in Stob. l.c. 10ᵃ, p. 89, 3—90, 5, are important. They appear to belong to Chrysippus and show that, while defining the πάθη as κρίσεις, he did not give to that word the restricted interpretation which Galen (see infra, frag. 139) places upon it, and that he recognised the influence of the will in determining the nature of emotion. We may also infer that the words ἀπειθῆς τῷ αἱροῦντι λόγῳ are a gloss of Chrysippus upon Zeno's term ἄλογος. This is also clear from Galen, Hipp. et Plat. p. 368 K, 338 M, where the reason is given, namely, the desire to enforce the doctrine of the unity of the soul (frag. 135). In maintaining that every πάθος is essentially ἄλογον and παρὰ φύσιν, Zeno goes far beyond Plato and Aristotle, although he has much in common with the Platonic point of view. Thus in the Phaedo 83 B, we read ἡ τοῦ ὡς ἀληθῶς φιλοσόφου ψυχὴ οὕτως ἀπέχεται τῶν ἡδονῶν τε καὶ ἐπιθυμιῶν καὶ λυπῶν καὶ φόβων καθ' ὅσον δύναται, although elsewhere Plato admits that certain pleasures and pains are allowable (see Zeller's Plato, p. 444). Similarly Aristotle, while classing certain πάθη as ἄλογα, declares that under certain circumstances wrath and desire are legitimate (Eth. N. III. 1. 24—26).

137. Stob. Ecl. II. 7. 1, p. 39, 5, ὡς δ' ὁ Στωικὸς ὡρίσατο Ζήνων· πάθος ἐστὶν ὁρμὴ πλεονάζουσα. οὐ λέγει ' πεφυκυῖα πλεονάζειν', ἀλλ' ἤδη ἐν πλεονασμῷ οὖσα· οὐ γὰρ δυνάμει, μᾶλλον δ' ἐνεργείᾳ. ὡρίσατο δὲ κἀκείνως· πάθος ἐστὶ πτοία ψυχῆς, ἀπὸ τῆς τῶν πτηνῶν φορᾶς τὸ εὐκίνητον τοῦ παθητικοῦ παρεικάσας.

Cf. ib. II. 7. 10, p. 88, 11, διὸ καὶ πᾶσαν πτοίαν πάθος εἶναι <καὶ> πάλιν <πᾶν> πάθος πτοίαν. Wachsmuth refers to Chrysipp. ap. Galen. de Hipp. et Plat. plac. IV. 5, p. 364, 23, Müll. οἰκείως δὲ τῷ τῶν παθῶν γένει ἀποδίδοται καὶ ἡ πτοία κατὰ τὸ ἐνσεσοβημένον τοῦτο καὶ φερόμενον εἰκῇ, where the use of the word ἀποδίδοται points to Zeno's authorship. ἀπὸ τῆς—παρεικάσας seems to be merely the comment of Didymus, although it is possible that Zeno derived πτοία from πέτεσθαι, as Wachsmuth thinks.

138. Cic. Acad. I. 38, Zeno omnibus his (perturbationibus) quasi morbis voluit carere sapientem...nam et perturbationes voluntarias esse putabat opinionisque iudicio suscipi et omnium perturbationum arbitrabatur matrem esse immoderatam quandam intemperantiam.

quasi morbis: see on frag. 144. ἀπαθῆ εἶναι τὸν σοφόν, Diog. VII. 117.

opinionisque iudicio: in view of what follows this is important, and the expression aptly illustrates Galen's statement that Zeno regarded the πάθη as τὰ ἐπιγιγνόμενα κρίσεσιν.

intemperantiam. The particular virtue which is concerned with regulating the ὁρμαὶ is σωφροσύνη: see on Cleanth. frag. 76, so that excess of impulse or πάθος is said to be produced by its opposite, ἀκολασία (ἄγνοια αἱρετῶν καὶ φευκτῶν καὶ οὐδετέρων, Stob. Ecl. II. 7. 5[b1], p. 60, 2), cf. Tusc. IV. 22, Quemadmodum igitur temperantia sedat appetitiones et efficit, ut eae rectae rationi pareant, conservatque considerata iudicia mentis: sic huic inimica intemperantia omnem animi statum inflammat conturbat incitat; itaque et aegritudines et metus et reliquae perturbationes omnes gignuntur ex ea.

139. Galen. Hippocr. et Plat. plac. v. 1, v. 429 K., Ζήνων οὐ τὰς κρίσεις αὐτὰς ἀλλὰ τὰς ἐπιγιγνομένας αὐταῖς συστολὰς καὶ λύσεις ἐπάρσεις τε καὶ [τὰς] πτώσεις τῆς ψυχῆς ἐνόμιζεν εἶναι τὰ πάθη, ib. IV. 3, v. 377 K. Chrysippus contradicts himself, Zeno, and other Stoics as to this οἳ οὐ τὰς κρίσεις αὐτὰς τῆς ψυχῆς ἀλλὰ [καὶ] τὰς ἐπὶ ταύταις ἀλόγους συστολὰς καὶ ταπεινώσεις καὶ δήξεις ἐπάρσεις τε καὶ διαχύσεις ὑπολαμβάνουσιν εἶναι τὰ τῆς ψυχῆς πάθη. Wachsmuth, Comm. I. p. 7, adds ibid. IV. 2, v. p. 367 K., τοιαύτην τινὰ τὴν οὐσίαν τῶν παθῶν (i.e. ὅτι αἱ μειώσεις καὶ αἱ ἐπάρσεις καὶ αἱ συστολαὶ καὶ αἱ διαχύσεις...τῆς ἀλόγου δυνάμεώς ἐστι παθήματα ταῖς δόξαις ἐπιγιγνόμενα) Ἐπίκουρος...καὶ Ζήνων ὑπολαμβάνει. Galen distinguishes between three different views of the nature of πάθη, (1) that they have no connection at all with λογισμὸς or κρίσις, which is the view of Plato and

Posidonius, and in which Galen himself concurs. He infers that Cleanthes was of the same opinion (but see on Cleanth. frag. 84); (2) that they are κρίσεις, cf. Diog. L. VII. 111. This is the view of Chrysippus and is in Galen's opinion the worst of the three; (3) between these two extreme views that of Zeno in identifying them with ἐπιγιγνόμενα κρίσεσιν occupies a middle position. It would seem however that in this respect Galen has done Chrysippus an injustice: for it is clear from other evidence (see e.g. on frag. 136) that Chrysippus did not confine himself to the view that πάθη are solely an intellectual affection (Zeller, p. 245, 246). At the same it is probably true that he made a distinct advance upon Zeno by identifying πάθη with κρίσεις and connecting them with συγκαταθέσεις: cf. Stein, Erkenntnistheorie, p. 198, 199.

συστολάς. This refers to λύπη, which is defined as συστολὴ ἄλογος (Diog. L. VII. 111, cf. M. Aurel. II. 10) or ἀπειθὴς λόγῳ (Stob. Ecl. II. 7. 70[b], p. 90, 14): in the same way ἔπαρσις refers to ἡδονή (Diog. L. VII. 114, Stob. l. c., l. 16).

λύσεις. For this word Müller substitutes διαχύσεις, but this is perhaps questionable, cf. Cic. Tusc. III. 61, ex quo ipsam aegritudinem λύπην Chrysippus [quasi λύσιν id est] solutionem totius hominis appellatam putat.

τάς, delet Müller.

καὶ is expunged by Zeller, p. 246, and Müller, but this corr. is by no means certain: see on frag. 143, and cf. Heinze, Stoicorum de Affectibus doctrina, p. 37.

δήξεις. Zeller's correction, accepted by Müller, for δείξεις, is made almost certian by Cic. Tusc. IV. 15, ut aegritudo quasi morsum aliquem doloris efficiat, cf. Tusc. III. 83, cited on frag. 158.

διαχύσεις. In Diog. L. VII. 114 this word appears as a subdivision of ἡδονή and is defined as ἀνάλυσις ἀρετῆς.

In Suidas, col. 818, however ἡδονὴ itself is defined as ἄλογος διάχυσις, cf. deliquescat in Cic. Tusc. IV. 37. It is worthy of observation that all these words (excepting perhaps ταπεινώσεις) refer to λύπη and ἡδονή, and that ἐπιθυμία and φόβος are not so prominent. For ταπεινώσεις, cf. exanimatione humili atque fracta connected with metus in Cic. Tusc. IV. 13, and for πτώσεις demitti (of aegritudo) ib. 14, 37. In the face of the evidence already cited, Wellmann, p. 454, seems to be wrong in supposing λύσεις and πτώσεις to be equivalent to ὄρεξις and ἔκκλισις in Diog. and Stob. ll. cc.

μείωσις refers to λύπη, Chrysipp. ap. Galen, IV. 2, p. 367.

140. Themist. de An. 90 b, Spengel, II. 197, 24, καὶ οὐ κακῶς οἱ ἀπὸ Ζήνωνος τὰ πάθη τῆς ἀνθρωπίνης ψυχῆς τοῦ λόγου διαστροφὰς εἶναι τιθέμενοι καὶ λόγου κρίσεις ἡμαρτημένας.

In the face of Galen's testimony this statement is of no importance so far as Zeno is concerned and may be discarded.

141. Galen, Hipp. et Plat. plac. III. c. 5, v. p. 322 K., οὐ μόνον Χρύσιππος ἀλλὰ καὶ Κλεάνθης καὶ Ζήνων ἑτοίμως αὐτὰ τιθέασιν (τοὺς φόβους καὶ τὰς λύπας καὶ πάνθ' ὅσα τοιαῦτα πάθη κατὰ τὴν καρδίαν συνίστασθαι). This passage is taken from Wachsmuth, Comm. I. p. 7. The emotions are placed in the heart because it is the seat of the ἡγεμονικόν (frag. 100), of which the πάθη are affections (frag. 135), Zeller, p. 213, Stein, Psych. n. 258.

142. Diog. VII. 140, τῶν παθῶν τὰ ἀνωτάτω (καθά φησιν...Ζήνων ἐν τῷ περὶ παθῶν) εἶναι γένη τέτταρα, λύπην, φόβον, ἐπιθυμίαν, ἡδονήν.

Stob. Ecl. II. 7. 10, p. 88, 14, πρῶτα δ' εἶναι τῷ γένει

ταῦτα τὰ τέσσαρα, ἐπιθυμίαν, φόβον, λύπην, ἡδονήν, cf. Cic. Off. I. 69, Tusc. III. 24, IV. 11, Jerome Epist. cxxxiii. illi enim quae Graeci appellant πάθη nos perturbationes possumus dicere, aegritudinem videlicet et gaudium, spem et metum, quorum duo praesentia, duo futura sunt, asserunt extirpari posse de mentibus et nullam fibram radicemque vitiorum in homine omnino residere, meditatione et assidua exercitatione virtutum. Plato had already recognised λύπη, φόβος, ἐπιθυμία and ἡδονή as the four chief πάθη, cf. Phaed. 83 B, cited on frag. 136. From τὰ ἀνωτάτω...γένη it is obvious that Zeno classed certain εἴδη under each of the principal πάθη, but how much of the exposition in Diog. L. VII. 111—116, Stob. Ecl. II. 7, 10[b&c] is derived from him the evidence does not enable us to determine, nor can we tell whether the doctrine of the εὐπάθειαι belongs to him.

143. Cic. Tusc. III. 74, 75, Satis dictum esse arbitror aegritudinem esse opinionem mali praesentis, in qua opinione illud insit, ut aegritudinem suscipere oporteat. Additur ad hanc definitionem a Zenone recte ut illa opinio praesentis mali sit recens. Galen de Hipp. et Plat. plac. IV. 7, p. 416, 'ὁ γοῦν ὅρος οὗτος', φησίν [Posidonius], 'ὁ τῆς λύπης, ὥσπερ οὖν καὶ ἄλλοι πολλοὶ τῶν παθῶν ὑπό τε Ζήνωνος εἰρημένοι καὶ πρὸς τοῦ Χρυσίππου γεγραμμένοι σαφῶς ἐξελέγχουσι τὴν γνώμην αὐτοῦ. δόξαν γὰρ εἶναι πρόσφατον τοῦ κακὸν αὐτῷ παρεῖναί φησι (? φασι) τὴν λύπην. ἐν ᾧ καὶ συντομώτερον ἐνίοτε λέγοντες ὧδέ πως προσφέρονται· λύπη ἐστὶ δόξα πρόσφατος κακοῦ παρουσίας.' λύπης is the necessary correction of Cornarius, Bake and I. Müller for the MSS. ἄτης. The unfortunate currency, which Kühn's ἄσης has obtained, has given rise to much perplexity.

These passages, and especially that of Cicero, have been

strangely neglected by the authorities. A difficulty arises here, because it is generally inferred from frag. 139 that the treatment of the πάθη by Zeno and Chrysippus was radically different, and it is strange that, if Zeno defined λύπη, for example, as ἄλογος συστολή, he should also have defined it as δόξα πρόσφατος κακοῦ παρουσίας. (For the connection of Chrysippus with the latter definition cf. Galen, op. cit. IV. p. 336 K., 336, 9 M., ἐν τοῖς ὁρισμοῖς τῶν γενικῶν παθῶν τελέως ἀποχωρεῖ τῆς γνώμης αὐτῶν [scil. his own writings] τὴν λύπην ὁριζόμενος δόξαν πρόσφατον κακοῦ παρουσίας τὸν δὲ φόβον προσδοκίαν κακοῦ τὴν δὲ ἡδονὴν δόξαν πρόσφατον ἀγαθοῦ παρουσίας, but at the same time defines ἐπιθυμία as ἄλογος ὄρεξις.) For, in that case, how could Galen or Posidonius have treated Chrysippus as diverging from Zeno by explaining the πάθη as κρίσεις, especially as Posidonius is the ultimate authority on whom the attribution of the δόξα definition to Zeno rests?

Now the evidence of Galen establishes almost beyond a doubt that the definitions of λύπη as ἄλογος συστολὴ and of ἡδονὴ as ἄλογος ἔπαρσις (Diog. L. VII. 111, 114) were propounded by Zeno. From this it would seem to follow as a natural corollary that he also defined ἐπιθυμία as ἄλογος ὄρεξις (Diog. VII. 113), and φόβος as ἄλογος ἔκκλισις (Stob. Ecl. II. 7. 10[b], p. 90, 11, ἔκκλισιν ἀπειθῆ λόγῳ), cf. Andron. περὶ παθῶν, c. I., λύπη μὲν οὖν ἔστιν ἄλογος συστολή, φόβος δὲ ἄλογος ἔκκλισις, ἐπιθυμία δὲ ἄλογος ὄρεξις, ἡδονὴ δὲ ἄλογος ἔπαρσις; and see Kreuttner, p. 31. On other grounds it seems probable (see on frag. 136) that Chrysippus is responsible for the substitution of ἀπειθὴς λόγῳ for ἄλογος in Stob. l. c., but we cannot tell who added the words ἐπὶ φευκτῷ δοκοῦντι and ἐφ' αἱρετῷ δοκοῦντι ὑπάρχειν (Galen, Hipp. et Plat. IV. 2, p. 367), which appear also in Diog. 114. It remains therefore to decide whether the definitions of which δόξα πρόσφατος κακοῦ παρουσίας is a type were introduced by Zeno or Chrysippus. The latter alternative would be the most satisfactory solution and is generally adopted (e.g. by Wellmann, p. 454, 455, Zeller, pp. 249, 250, Siebeck, Geschichte der Psychologie, II. 232, 233 and 504), but if Posidonius' evidence is to be accepted in the one case, why is it to be discarded in the other, especially where it tells most strongly against himself? cf. Galen, p. 390 K., (Ποσειδώνιος) πειρᾶται μὴ μόνον ἑαυτὸν τοῖς Πλατωνικοῖς ἀλλὰ καὶ τὸν Κιτιέα Ζήνωνα προσάγειν. We must remember that Posidonius was anxious to pick holes in Chrysippus, in order to excuse his own heresy. Hence he charges Chrysippus not merely with divergence from his predecessors but with inconsistency (τὴν αὐτοῦ πρὸς αὐτὸν ἐναντιολογίαν τοῦ Χρυσίππου, Galen, p. 390). It would seem therefore that he is less worthy of credence as a witness, when he affirms a discrepancy between Zeno and Chrysippus than when he testifies to the identity of their doctrine. Nor ought we to neglect the fact that in Diog. L. VII. 112 φόβος is defined as κακοῦ προσδοκία, being thus differentiated from the other πάθη, and that this definition is ultimately traceable to Plato (Protag. 358 D, Lach. 198 B). If however we suppose that Zeno made use of a double set of definitions, what was the nature of the contribution made by Chrysippus? Only two answers seem possible. If Zeno in his oral lectures (εἰρημένοι), and subsequently to the publication of the work περὶ παθῶν, put forward the δόξα definitions, it would devolve on Chrysippus to reconcile as against opponents the written and the oral tradition of the school. Or again it is quite conceivable that Posidonius may have been misled by the desire of Chrysippus to represent his own developments as the natural out-growth of Zeno's system. In any case the difference was comparatively unimportant: 'hanc differentiam levissimam esse quis est quin videat, cum uterque id semper docuerit, πάθη esse voluntaria?' (Heinze, Stoicorum de Affectibus doctrina, p. 10, and see also pp. 23, 24, 36, 37).

144. Lactant. Inst. III. 23, inter vitia et morbos misericordiam ponit (Zeno). id. Epist. ad Pentad. 38, Zeno Stoicorum magister, qui virtutem laudat, misericordiam...tamquam morbum animi diiudicavit.

It is probable that Zeno spoke of the πάθη in general terms as νόσοι and that Chrysippus is responsible for the distinction between νοσήματα and ἀρρωστήματα, as the passage in Cic. Tusc. IV. 23 suggests. Cf. Zeller, p. 251, 252, and Stein, Psych. n. 267. At the same time morbus may here be simply the translation of πάθος, which Cicero rejected (Tusc. III. 7, IV. 10). For ἔλεος, a subdivision of λύπη, cf. Diog. VII. 111, Stob. Ecl. II. 7. 10ᶜ, p. 92, 12, Cic. Tusc. IV. 18.

145. Diog. VII. 107, 108, ἔτι δὲ καθῆκόν φασιν εἶναι ὃ πραχθὲν εὔλογόν τιν' ἴσχει ἀπολογισμόν· οἷον τὸ ἀκόλουθον ἐν τῇ ζωῇ, ὅπερ καὶ ἐπὶ τὰ φυτὰ καὶ ζῷα διατείνει. ὁρᾶσθαι γὰρ κἀπὶ τούτων καθήκοντα. κατωνομάσθαι δὲ ὑπὸ πρώτου Ζήνωνος τὸ καθῆκον ἀπὸ τοῦ κατά τινας ἥκειν τῆς προσωνομασίας εἰλημμένης. Cf. ib. 25, φασὶ δὲ καὶ πρῶτον καθῆκον ὠνομακέναι καὶ λόγον περὶ αὐτοῦ πεποιηκέναι (referring to the treatise περὶ τοῦ καθήκοντος, Introd. p. 29).

Stob. Ecl. II. 7. 8, p. 85, 13, ὁρίζεται δὲ τὸ καθῆκον· τὸ ἀκόλουθον ἐν ζωῇ, ὃ πραχθὲν εὔλογον ἀπολογίαν ἔχει· παρὰ τὸ καθῆκον δὲ τὸ ἐναντίως. τοῦτο διατείνει καὶ εἰς τὰ ἄλογα τῶν ζῴων, ἐνεργεῖ γάρ τι κἀκεῖνα ἀκολούθως τῇ ἑαυτῶν φύσει· ἐπὶ <δὲ> τῶν λογικῶν ζῴων οὕτως ἀποδίδοται· τὸ ἀκόλουθον ἐν βίῳ. Cic. de Fin. III. 58, est autem officium quod ita factum est ut eius facti probabilis ratio reddi possit (where see Madv.).

καθῆκον is, according to Zeno, any action for the performance of which a sufficient reason can be given and it is entirely distinct from virtuous action, which is described as κατόρθωμα. That Zeno must have treated of κατόρθωμα is a supposition which is rendered necessary by the circumstances of the case, but the evidence to connect him with it is wanting. The doctrine of καθῆκον is closely connected with that of προηγμένον (ἀκόλουθος δ' ἔστι τῷ περὶ τῶν προηγμένων ὁ περὶ τοῦ καθήκοντος τόπος, Stob. l. c.) inasmuch as in the ordinary course of life we are forced to regulate our conduct with regard to external circumstances, which are strictly speaking ἀδιάφορα. Hence we must explain κατά τινας where κατά means "over against" (die jenige Pflicht, die von aussen an uns herantritt, von der unterschieden werden soll, die in unserem eigensten Wesen, in der Vernunft selber ihren Ursprung hat), as Hirzel has shown by a comparison of Epict. Enchir. 15, μέμνησο ὅτι ὡς ἐν συμποσίῳ δεῖ σε ἀναστρέφεσθαι. περιφερόμενον γέγονέ τι κατά σε; ἐκτείνας τὴν χεῖρα κοσμίως μετάλαβε· παρέρχεται; μὴ κάτεχε. οὔπω ἥκει; μὴ ἐπίβαλλε πόρρω τὴν ὄρεξιν· ἀλλὰ περίμενε, μέχρις ἂν γένηται κατά σε. οὕτω πρὸς τέκνα, οὕτω πρὸς γυναῖκα, οὕτω πρὸς ἀρχάς, οὕτω πρὸς πλοῦτον, καὶ ἔσῃ ποτὲ ἄξιος τῶν θεῶν συμπότης. καθῆκον, therefore, in Zeno's system is not a general term of which κατορθώματα and μέσα καθήκοντα are subdivisions, but rather καθήκοντα and κατορθώματα are mutually exclusive, so that the distinctions between ἀεὶ καθήκοντα and οὐκ ἀεὶ καθήκοντα, and μέσα καθήκοντα and τέλεια καθήκοντα belong to later Stoics: see Hirzel, Untersuchungen, II. pp. 403—410. εὔλογον does not imply action in accordance with right reason, i.e. virtue, as Zeller and Ueberweg suppose, for reason in this sense cannot be attributed to φυτά and ἄλογα ζῷα, which are nevertheless capable of καθήκοντα according to the authorities. (The use of εὔλογος in this narrower sense is justified by Hirzel, II. 341, 1, from a comparison of Diog. VII. 76. Seneca, de Benef. IV. 33, sequimur qua ratio non qua virtus trahit; Diog. VII. 130, εὐλόγως ἐξάξειν ἑαυτὸν τοῦ βίου τὸν σοφόν.) If Hirzel's explanation is correct, it follows that in Sext. Math. VII. 158, where κατόρθωμα is defined as ὅπερ πραχθὲν εὔλογον ἔχει τὴν ἀπολογίαν, Arcesilas adopts the Stoic definition of καθῆκον as the true basis of κατόρθωμα. Wellmann, p. 461, believes that κατόρθωμα belongs solely to the later Stoics, but surely Zeno must have given some name to virtuous action, and it is most reasonable to assume that this was κατόρθωμα. It is unnecessary to observe that Zeno was not the first to use καθῆκον in the sense of "duty": all that is meant is that he gave the word its special technical sense, cf. κατάληψις. As to the divergence of Stobaeus from Diogenes we should note (1) that τὸ ἀκόλουθον ἐν ζωῇ is made the main point in the definition, which is probably a mistake, cf. Cic., (2) the distinction between βίος and ζωή, for which cf. Arist. ap Ammon. in Steph. Thes. βίος ἐστὶ λογικὴ ζωή (quoted by Hirzel).

146. Stob. Ecl. II. 7. 1, p. 38, 15, οἱ δὲ κατὰ Ζήνωνα τὸν Στωικὸν τροπικῶς· ἦθός ἐστι πηγὴ βίου, ἀφ' ἧς αἱ κατὰ μέρος πράξεις ῥέουσι.

The Stoics regarded not so much the act itself as the character of the agent (cf. σπουδαία διάθεσις). For πηγή cf. Plat. Leg. 808 C, who says that a young boy ἔχει πηγὴν τοῦ φρονεῖν μήπω κατηρτυμένην.

147. Diog. L. VII. 173, κατὰ Ζήνωνα καταληπτὸν εἶναι τὸ ἦθος ἐξ εἴδους.

Cf. Stob. Ecl. I. 50. 34, οἱ Στωικοὶ τὸν σοφὸν αἰσθήσει καταληπτὸν ἀπὸ τοῦ εἴδους τεκμηριωδῶς. Euripides regrets that it is impossible to distinguish men in this manner. Med. 516—520,

ὦ Ζεῦ, τί δὴ χρυσοῦ μὲν ὃς κίβδηλος ᾖ
τεκμήρι' ἀνθρώποισιν ὤπασας σαφῆ,
ἀνδρῶν δ' ὅτῳ χρὴ τὸν κακὸν διειδέναι,
οὐδεὶς χαρακτὴρ ἐμπέφυκε σώματι;

cf. Hippol. 924 foll. Cic. Lael. 62. So Shaksp. Macb. I. 4. 11, There's no art to find the mind's construction in the face.

148. Stob. Ecl. II. 7. 11^g, p. 99, 3, ἀρέσκει γὰρ τῷ τε Ζήνωνι καὶ τοῖς ἀπ' αὐτοῦ Στωικοῖς φιλοσόφοις δύο γένη τῶν ἀνθρώπων εἶναι, τὸ μὲν τῶν σπουδαίων, τὸ δὲ τῶν φαύλων· καὶ τὸ μὲν τῶν σπουδαίων διὰ παντὸς τοῦ βίου
5 χρῆσθαι ταῖς ἀρεταῖς, τὸ δὲ τῶν φαύλων ταῖς κακίαις· ὅθεν τὸ μὲν ἀεὶ κατορθοῦν ἐν ἅπασιν οἷς προστίθεται, τὸ δὲ ἁμαρτάνειν. καὶ τὸν μὲν σπουδαῖον ταῖς περὶ τὸν βίον ἐμπειρίαις χρώμενον ἐν τοῖς πραττομένοις ὑπ' αὐτοῦ πάντ' εὖ ποιεῖν, καθάπερ φρονίμως καὶ σωφρόνως καὶ
10 κατὰ τὰς ἄλλας ἀρετάς· τὸν δὲ φαῦλον κατὰ τοὐναντίον κακῶς. καὶ τὸν μὲν σπουδαῖον μέγαν καὶ ἁδρὸν καὶ ὑψηλὸν καὶ ἰσχυρόν. μέγαν μὲν ὅτι δύναται ἐφικνεῖσθαι τῶν κατὰ προαίρεσιν ὄντων αὐτῷ καὶ προκειμένων· ἁδρὸν δέ, ὅτι ἐστὶν ηὐξημένος πάντοθεν· ὑψηλὸν δ', ὅτι μετεί-
15 ληφε τοῦ ἐπιβάλλοντος ὕψους ἀνδρὶ γενναίῳ καὶ σοφῷ. καὶ ἰσχυρὸν δ', ὅτι τὴν ἐπιβάλλουσαν ἰσχὺν περιπεποίηται, ἀήττητος ὢν καὶ ἀκαταγώνιστος. παρ' ὃ καὶ οὔτε ἀναγκάζεται ὑπό τινος οὔτε ἀναγκάζει τινα, οὔτε κωλύεται οὔτε κωλύει, οὔτε βιάζεται ὑπό τινος οὔτ' αὐτὸς
20 βιάζει τινα, οὔτε δεσπόζει οὔτε δεσπόζεται, οὔτε κακοποιεῖ τινα οὔτ' αὐτὸς κακοποιεῖται, οὔτε κακοῖς περιπίπτει <οὔτ'

ἄλλον ποιεῖ κακοῖς περιπίπτειν>, οὔτε ἐξαπατᾶται οὔτε ἐξαπατᾷ ἄλλον, οὔτε διαψεύδεται οὔτε ἀγνοεῖ οὔτε λανθάνει ἑαυτόν, οὔτε καθόλου ψεῦδος ὑπολαμβάνει· εὐδαίμων δέ ἐστιν μάλιστα καὶ εὐτυχὴς καὶ μακάριος καὶ ὄλβιος καὶ 25 εὐσεβὴς καὶ θεοφιλὴς καὶ ἀξιωματικός, βασιλικός τε καὶ στρατηγικὸς καὶ πολιτικὸς καὶ οἰκονομικὸς καὶ χρηματιστικός. τοὺς δὲ φαύλους ἅπαντα τούτοις ἐναντία ἔχειν.

It is a matter of doubt how much of this extract can be reasonably regarded as derived from Zeno, but if the whole of it is to be traced to a single source, that source may be Zeno, as there is some evidence for connecting him with the statements appearing at the end of the passage. On the doctrine of the wise man in general see Zeller, p. 268 foll., Cic. Fin. III. 75, 76.

9. πάντ' εὖ ποιεῖν: cf. infra frag. 156. Ambrosius, de Abraham II. 7. 328, 37, cites Gen. XIII. 14 and 15 and continues, hinc tamquam a fonte hauserunt Stoici philosophi dogmatis sui sententiam: omnia sapientis esse... unde et Salomon in Proverbiis ait: eius qui fidelis sit totus mundus divitiarum (Prov. XVII. 6). Quanto prior Salomon quam Zenon Stoicorum magister atque auctor sectae ipsius.

12. μέγαν. Physical excellence can only be predicated of the wise man, even if in the popular sense of the term he does not possess it, for no kind of excellence can be attributed to the φαῦλος. Further, inasmuch as the only good is ἀρετή or τὸ μετέχον ἀρετῆς, physical advantages only have value when found in conjunction with virtue.

17. ἀήττητος. Cf. frag. 157, the parallelism of which is perhaps a circumstance of some weight in favour of Zeno's authorship here.

19. βιάζεται: for this verb, see Shilleto on Thuc. I. 2. 1.

20. δεσπόζει: cf. Diog. L. VII. 122, ᾗ (δουλείᾳ) ἀντι-

τίθεται ἡ δεσποτεία φαύλη οὖσα καὶ αὕτη. Stob. Ecl. II. 7. 11^k, p. 104, 5.

23. διαψεύδεται: because falsehood consists not merely in stating something contrary to fact but in doing so advisedly in order to deceive others (Stob. Ecl. II. 7. 11^m, p. 111, 10; Sext. Math. VII. 44, 45). So, on the other hand the φαῦλος may speak ἀληθές τι but is devoid of ἀλήθεια.

26. εὐσεβὴς καὶ θεοφ. Similar assertions in an amplified form occur in Diog. L. VII. 119.

ἀξιωματικός: this appears to mean "high in rank," see Plut. Mor. 617 D, and cf. the use of ἀξίωμα in Thuc. as applied to Pericles. It can hardly mean "speaking axioms" as when used of Arcesilas in Diog. IV. 31.

βασιλικός. Among the sententiae et praecepta Zenonis cited by Cic. Mur. § 61 occurs solos sapientes esse si servitutem serviant reges. It is extremely probable that this paradox was asserted by Zeno from Diog. L. VII. 122, ἀλλὰ καὶ βασιλέας (εἶναι τοὺς σοφούς) τῆς βασιλείας οὔσης ἀρχῆς ἀνυπευθύνου, ἥτις περὶ μόνους ἂν τοὺς σοφοὺς σταίη, καθά φησι Χρύσιππος ἐν τῷ περὶ τοῦ κυρίως κεχρῆσθαι Ζήνωνα τοῖς ὀνόμασιν. Cf. Hor. Sat. I. 3. 125, Stob. Ecl. II. 7. 11^m, p. 108, 26.

27. στρατηγικός. Plut., vit. Arat. 23, 3, quotes μόνον στρατηγὸν εἶναι τὸν σοφόν as a δόγμα Ζήνωνος.

149. Diog. VII. 33, πάλιν ἐν τῇ πολιτείᾳ παρίσταντα (Ζήνωνα) πολίτας καὶ φίλους καὶ οἰκείους καὶ ἐλευθέρους τοὺς σπουδαίους μόνον. Clem. Alex. Strom. v. 14. 95, p. 703 P, 253 S, Ζήνων τε ὁ Στωικὸς παρὰ Πλάτωνος λαβών, ὁ δὲ ἀπὸ τῆς βαρβάρου φιλοσοφίας, τοὺς ἀγαθοὺς πάντας ἀλλήλων εἶναι φίλους λέγει. The same in Euseb. P. E. XIII. 13, p. 671.

πολιτείᾳ. Introd. p. 29.

πολίτας: the question naturally arises, how is this statement to be connected with the cosmopolitanism which Zeno in the same treatise advocated (see frag. 162, ἵνα... πάντας ἀνθρώπους ἡγώμεθα δημότας καὶ πολίτας)? Zeno's ideal state is not a community of the wise alone, but of all mankind. He seems to be arguing here against the ordinary civic distinctions, which are utterly valueless as compared with the broad line drawn between σοφοὶ and φαῦλοι. Presumably in the ideal state everyone would be so trained in Stoic precepts as to become thereby σπουδαῖος.

φίλους: cf. Diog. L. VII. 124, Stob. Ecl. II. 7. 11^m, p. 138, 15, where friendship is based upon ὁμόνοια which can only be found among the wise. Cic. Off. I. 56, N. D. I. 121. A full discussion of the subject is given by Zeller, p. 317 foll. This is one of the doctrines borrowed by Zeno from the Cynics, see Introd. p. 19; it had already been taught by Socrates (Xen. Mem. II. 6. 14 foll.). The view is rejected as inadequate by Plato in the Lysis (p. 214), but no doubt Clement is thinking rather of the Phaedrus and Symposium: he adds his usual comment that Plato's views are borrowed from the Jews.

ἐλευθέρους. Stob. Ecl. II. 7. 11^1, p. 101, 18, Diog. L. VII. 121, Cic. Parad. v. This again is derived from the Cynics: see Zeller, Socrates, p. 322.

150. Cic. Mur. § 61, solos sapientes esse, si distortissimi, formosos. This occurs among the "Sententiae et praecepta Zenonis" cited by Cicero in his banter against Cato, so that the evidence is not very trustworthy, a remark which also applies to frags. 152, 153 and 155. The wise man is beautiful because virtue alone is beautiful and attractive: Zeller, p. 270 and n. 4, to whose references add Cic. Fin. III. 75, recte etiam pulcher appellabitur: animi enim lineamenta sunt pulcriora quam corporis.

151. Cic. Fin. v. 84, Zeno sapientem non beatum modo sed etiam divitem dicere ausus est. Cic. Mur. § 61, solos sapientes esse, si mendicissimi, divites.

For the sense cf. Cic. Paradox. VI., Stob. Ecl. II. 7. 11[1], p. 101, 18, and further references ap. Zeller p. 270, nn. 5 and 6.

152. Cic. Mur. § 61, sapientiam gratia nunquam moveri, numquam cuiusquam delicto ignoscere; neminem misericordem esse nisi stultum et levem; viri non esse neque exorari neque placari.

The reasons for this opinion are given by Diog. VII. 123, ἐλεήμονάς τε μὴ εἶναι, συγγνώμην τε ἔχειν μηδενί· μὴ γὰρ παριέναι τὰς ἐκ τοῦ νόμου ἐπιβαλλούσας κολάσεις· ἐπεὶ τό γε εἴκειν καὶ ὁ ἔλεος αὐτή τε ἡ ἐπιείκεια οὐδένειά ἐστι ψυχῆς πρὸς κολάσεις προσποιουμένης χρηστότητα μηδὲ οἴεσθαι σκληροτέρας αὐτὰς εἶναι. The same at greater length in Stob. Ecl. II. 7. 11[d], p. 95, 25—96, 9; see also Zeller, p. 254. It should be remembered that ἔλεος is a subdivision of λύπη (ἐπὶ τῷ δοκοῦντι ἀναξίως κακοπαθεῖν Stob. Ecl. II. 7. 10[c], p. 92, 12) and therefore one of the πάθη: possibly this is all that is meant by Lactant. Inst. III. 23 (frag. 144).

153. Cic. Mur. § 61, sapientem nihil opinari, nullius rei poenitere, nulla in re falli, sententiam mutare numquam. Lact. Inst. III. 4, ergo si neque sciri quidquam potest, ut Socrates docuit, nec opinari oportet, ut Zeno, tota philosophia sublata est. Cic. Acad. II. 113, sapientem nihil opinari...horum neutrum ante Zenonem magno opere defensum est. August. contra Acad. II. 11, cum ab eodem Zenone accepissent nihil esse turpius quam opinari.

The Greek authorities for this fall partly under frag. 148, l. 22, οὔτε ἐξαπατᾶται οὔτε ἐξαπατᾷ ἄλλον, οὔτε διαψεύδεται οὔτε ἀγνοεῖ οὔτε λανθάνει ἑαυτὸν οὔτε καθόλου ψεῦδος ὑπολαμβάνει, and the rest may be supplied from Stob. Ecl. II. 7. 11^m, p. 112, 1, μηδὲν δ᾽ ὑπολαμβάνειν ἀσθενῶς ἀλλὰ μᾶλλον ἀσφαλῶς καὶ βεβαίως διὸ καὶ μηδὲ δοξάζειν τὸν σοφόν... p. 113, 5, οὐδὲ μετανοεῖν δ᾽ ὑπολαμβάνουσι τὸν νοῦν ἔχοντα...οὐδὲ μεταβάλλεσθαι δὲ κατ᾽ οὐδένα τρόπον οὐδὲ μετατίθεσθαι οὐδὲ σφάλλεσθαι. Diog. VII. 121, ἔτι τε μὴ δοξάσειν τὸν σοφόν. For Zeno's definition of δόξα see on frag. 15.

154. Diog. VII. 32, ἐχθροὺς καὶ πολεμίους καὶ δούλους καὶ ἀλλοτρίους λέγειν αὐτὸν (Ζήνωνα) ἀλλήλων εἶναι πάντας τοὺς μὴ σπουδαίους καὶ γονεῖς τέκνων καὶ ἀδελφοὺς ἀδελφῶν, οἰκείους οἰκείων.

This is the natural antithesis of frag. 149. Even parents are enemies to their children, if φαῦλοι, because natural relationship and parental love are absolutely ἀδιάφορα as compared with ἀρετή. On the subject of these paradoxes in general consult Ritter and Preller § 420 with the notes.

155. Cic. Mur. § 61, nos autem, qui sapientes non sumus, fugitivos, exules, hostes, insanos denique esse.

But for the sake of uniformity this might have been omitted, as we can feel very little confidence that we have here the actual words of Zeno. For exules cf. Stob. Ecl. II. 7. 11^1, p. 103, 9, λέγουσι δὲ καὶ φυγάδα πάντα φαῦλον εἶναι, καθ᾽ ὅσον στέρεται νόμου καὶ πολιτείας κατὰ φύσιν ἐπιβαλλούσης.

156. Athen. IV. 158 B, Στωικὸν δὲ δόγμα ἐστίν· ὅτι

τε πάντα εὖ ποιήσει ὁ σοφὸς καὶ φακῆν φρονίμως ἀρτύσει· διὸ καὶ Τίμων ὁ Φλιάσιος ἔφη

καὶ [Ζηνώνειόν] γε φακῆν ἑψεῖν ὃς μὴ φρονίμως μεμάθηκεν

ὡς οὐκ ἄλλως δυναμένης ἑψηθῆναι φακῆς εἰ μὴ κατὰ τὴν Ζηνώνειον ὑφήγησιν ὃς ἔφη

εἰς δὲ φακῆν ἔμβαλλε δυωδέκατον κοριάννου.

ὅτι τε κτ.λ. This follows from the doctrine that all virtue is wisdom (φρόνησις): since φρόνησις is required in the preparation of a φακῆ, the wise man can alone prepare it properly. This applies even if the wise man has no experience in the particular practical task under consideration, because he alone possesses the necessary capacity, cf. frag. 148, l. 9. Diog. L. VII. 125, πάντα τε εὖ ποιεῖν τὸν σοφόν, ὡς καὶ πάντα φαμὲν τὰ αὐλήματα εὖ αὐλεῖν τὸν Ἰσμηνίαν, which furnishes a close parallel to Hor. Sat. 1. 3. 126 foll., 'non nosti quid pater,' inquit, 'Chrysippus dicat:' 'sapiens crepidas sibi numquam nec soleas fecit, sutor tamen est sapiens.' qui? 'ut quamvis tacet Hermogenes, cantor tamen atque optimus est modulator etc.' Cf. also Stob. Ecl. II. 7. 5[b 10], p. 66, 14 foll.

157. Philo, liber quis virtuti studet, p. 880, ἄξιον τὸ Ζηνώνειον ἐπιφωνῆσαι ὅτι θᾶττον ἂν ἀσκὸν βαπτίσαις πλήρη πνεύματος ἢ βιάσαιο τὸν σπουδαῖον ὁντινοῦν ἄκοντα δρᾶσαί τι τῶν ἀβουλήτων· ἀνένδοτος γὰρ καὶ ἀήσσητος ψυχὴ ἣν ὀρθὸς λόγος δόγμασι παγίοις ἐνεύρωσε.

βαπτίσαις... βιάσαιο. So Mangey, followed by Wachsmuth, for the MSS. βαπτίσαι...βιάσαιτο. The same editor suggests the alternative of inserting τις, which is less probable.

βιάσαιο: for the freedom of the wise man's will cf. Cic. Tusc. IV. 12, eiusmodi appetitionem Stoici βούλησιν appellant, nos appellamus voluntatem. Eam illi putant in solo esse sapiente ; quam sic definiunt: voluntas est, quae quid cum ratione desiderat, and see Stein, Erkenntnistheorie, p. 196.

ἀνένδοτος : cf. supra frag. 148, ἰσχυρὸν δ' (τὸν σοφόν) ὅτι τὴν ἐπιβάλλουσαν ἰσχὺν περιπεποίηται ἀήττητος ὢν καὶ ἀκαταγώνιστος. M. Aurel. I. 16 fin.

ὀρθὸς λόγος : see Introd. pp. 8, 9.

158. Seneca, de Ira, I. 16, 7, Nam, ut dixit Zeno, in sapientis quoque animo etiam quum vulnus sanatum sit cicatrix manet. Sentiet itaque suspiciones quasdam et umbras affectuum, ipsis quidem carebit.

This is a concession to popular feeling, although at the same time the absolute ἀπάθεια (Diog. L. VII. 117, Cic. Acad. I. 38) of the wise man is maintained. It would be a mistake to infer from this passage that Zeno is responsible for the doctrine of εὐπάθειαι. Further references are given by Zeller, p. 291. Cf. Diog. VII. 118, προσπεσεῖσθαι μέντοι ποτὲ αὐτῷ φαντασίας ἀλλοκότους, διὰ μελαγχολίαν ἢ λήρησιν κ.τ.λ., where however the point is rather different. Remembering that Zeno described the effect of grief as δήξεις, we may compare Socrates' description of the result of violent love in Xen. Symp. IV. 28, ὥσπερ ὑπὸ θηρίου τινὸς δεδηγμένος τόν τε ὦμον πλεῖον ἢ πέντε ἡμέρας ὤδαξον καὶ ἐν τῇ καρδίᾳ ὥσπερ κνῆσμά τι ἐδόκουν ἔχειν. Cic. Tusc. III. 83, hoc detracto, quod totum est voluntarium, aegritudo erit sublata illa maerens, morsus tamen et contractiuncula quaedam animi relinquetur. The best account of the sensibility of the wise man to pain is given by Heinze, Stoicorum de aff. doctr. pp. 14, 15. The wise man cannot resist the impact of the φαντασία, but will refuse συγκατάθεσις. See further on Cleanth. frag. 94.

159. Seneca, Epist. 83. 8, Ebrio secretum sermonem nemo committit: viro autem bono committit: ergo vir bonus ebrius non erit.

Seneca finds no difficulty in refuting this fallacy, in spite of the defence which he quotes from Posidonius. For the syllogistic form of the argument see Introd. p. 33. Von Arnim, Quellen Studien p. 104, has pointed out the original in Philo de Plantatione Noë p. 350, εἰ τῷ μεθύοντι οὐκ ἄν τις εὐλόγως λόγον ἀπόρρητον παρακατάθοιτο <τῷ δὲ σοφῷ παρακατατίθενται> οὐκ ἄρα μεθύει ὁ ἀστεῖος.

ebrius non erit: cf. Diog. L. VII. 118, καὶ οἰνωθήσεσθαι μέν (τὸν σοφόν), οὐ μεθυσθήσεσθαι δέ. Stob. Ecl. II. 7, 11^m, p. 109, 5, οὐχ οἷον δὲ μεθυσθήσεσθαι τὸν νοῦν ἔχοντα· τὴν γὰρ μέθην ἁμαρτητικὸν περιέχειν, λήρησιν εἶναι <γὰρ> παρὰ τὸν οἶνον, ἐν μηδενὶ δὲ τὸν σπουδαῖον ἁμαρτάνειν κ.τ.λ. Similarly Socrates in Xen. Symp. II. 26. The Peripatetics held, on the contrary, according to Stobaeus, that the wise man μεθυσθήσεσθαι κατὰ συμπεριφοράς, κἂν εἰ μὴ προηγουμένως (Ecl. II. 7. 24, p. 144, 10).

160. Plut. de prof. in virt. 12, ὅρα δὴ καὶ τὸ τοῦ Ζήνωνος ὁποῖόν ἐστιν· ἠξίου γὰρ ἀπὸ τῶν ὀνείρων ἕκαστον ἑαυτοῦ συναισθάνεσθαι προκόπτοντος, εἰ μήτε ἡδόμενον αἰσχρῷ τινι ἑαυτὸν μήτε τι προσιέμενον ἢ πράττοντα τῶν δεινῶν καὶ ἀδίκων ὁρᾷ κατὰ τοὺς ὕπνους ἀλλ' οἷον ἐν βυθῷ γαλήνης ἀκλύστῳ καταφανεῖ διαλάμπει τῆς ψυχῆς τὸ φανταστικὸν καὶ παθητικὸν ὑπὸ τοῦ λόγου διακεχυμένον.

ἀπὸ τῶν ὀνείρων: it was a popular Greek notion that the vision of the mind's eye is clearer in sleep. Aesch. Eum. 104. Pind. frag. 108 [96], Fennell.

προκόπτοντος: Wellmann p. 462 argues that Zeno, while

maintaining to the full the possibility of acquiring virtue, did not admit the practical non-existence of wise men or the consequent distinction between οἱ προκόπτοντες and οἱ σπουδαῖοι: these latter views, he thinks, may have originated with Chrysippus. On προκοπή in general see Zeller, p. 293 foll.

προσιέμενον, "approving" (cf. Dem. Timocr. § 156). The words αἰσχρῷ δεινῶν ἀδίκων point to the acquisition of the three leading virtues σωφροσύνη ἀνδρεία and δικαιοσύνη.

ἀλλ' οἷον κ.τ.λ. The emotions are dispersed by reason in the mind of the προκόπτων, which remains clear and unsullied, like the transparent ocean on a calm day when shingle and sand settle down to the bottom: cf. Cleanth. frag. 66.

φανταστικόν, has no objective reality but is merely διάκενος ἑλκυσμός, πάθος ἐν τῇ ψυχῇ ἀπ' οὐδενὸς φανταστοῦ γινόμενον (Plut. plac. IV. 12). Observe that it is described as a πάθος. Stein, Erkenntnistheorie, p. 156, n. 309.

161. Seneca, Epist. 104. 21, quod si convivere etiam Graecis juvat [cum Socrate, cum Zenone versare: alter te docebit mori, si necesse erit: alter, antequam necesse erit.

antequam necesse erit. Suicide (ἐξαγωγή) is justifiable under certain circumstances. It is important to remember that life and death belong to the class of the ἀδιάφορα, and suicide therefore has no connection with ἀρετή, but is merely to be regarded as a matter of καθῆκον (τοῖς δὲ καθήκουσι καὶ τοῖς παρὰ τὸ καθῆκον <παρα>μετρεῖσθαι τήν τε ζωὴν καὶ τὸν θάνατον Stob. Ecl. II. 7. 11^m p. 110, 13 and see on frag. 145). This point is emphasised by Zeller p. 338.

162. Plut. Alex. virt. 6, καὶ μὴν ἡ πολὺ θαυμαζομένη πολιτεία τοῦ τὴν Στωικῶν αἵρεσιν καταβαλομένου Ζήνωνος εἰς ἓν τοῦτο συντείνει κεφάλαιον ἵνα μὴ κατὰ πόλεις μηδὲ κατὰ δήμους οἰκῶμεν, ἰδίοις ἕκαστοι διωρισμένοι δικαίοις, ἀλλὰ πάντας ἀνθρώπους ἡγώμεθα δημότας καὶ πολίτας, εἷς δὲ βίος ᾖ καὶ κόσμος, ὥσπερ ἀγέλης συννόμου νομῷ κοινῷ συντρεφομένης. τοῦτο Ζήνων μὲν ἔγραψεν ὥσπερ ὄναρ ἢ εἴδωλον εὐνομίας φιλοσόφου καὶ πολιτείας ἀνατυπωσάμενος: id. de Sto. Rep. II. 1, ἐπεὶ τοίνυν πολλὰ μέν, ὡς ἐν λόγοις αὐτῷ Ζήνωνι...γεγραμμένα τυγχάνει περὶ πολιτείας καὶ τοῦ ἄρχεσθαι καὶ ἄρχειν καὶ δικάζειν καὶ ῥητορεύειν. Chrysost. Hom. I. in Matth. 4, οὐ γὰρ καθάπερ Πλάτων ὁ τὴν καταγέλαστον ἐκείνην πολιτείαν συνθεὶς καὶ Ζήνων καὶ εἴ τις ἕτερος πολιτείαν ἔγραψεν ἢ νόμους συνέθηκεν.

πάντας ἀνθρώπους: see on frag. 149. The idea of cosmopolitanism was largely developed by the later Stoics, especially Seneca and Marcus Aurelius. Zeno's disregard of the fundamental distinction between Greeks and barbarians may partly be due to the influence of his birthplace, as Zeller remarks, but at the same time he only carries out Cynic teaching (Diog. L. VI. 72, μόνην τε ὀρθὴν πολιτείαν εἶναι τὴν ἐν κόσμῳ). As to Socrates, see Zeller's Socrates p. 167 n. 8, R. and P. § 219[c].

ὥσπερ ἀγέλης συννόμου. As Zeno is generally admitted to have written the πολιτεία when he was still under the influence of the Cynic school, Zeller (Socrates p. 325) treats this passage as being typical of Cynicism, and suggests that Plato, in the Politicus (267 D, οὐκοῦν τῶν νομευτικῶν ἡμῖν πολλῶν φανεισῶν ἄρτι τεχνῶν μία τις ἦν ἡ πολιτικὴ καὶ μιᾶς τινὸς ἀγέλης ἐπιμέλεια; κ.τ.λ.) and in his description of the ὑῶν πόλις in Rep. 372 A. foll. is referring to Antisthenes. The reference is however extremely doubtful (see Ueberweg p. 93), and it is worth noticing that the comparison of the ruler of a state to a herdsman was a favourite one with Socrates. Xen. Mem. I. 2, 32, εἰπέ που ὁ Σωκράτης ὅτι θαυμαστόν οἱ δοκοίη εἶναι, εἴτις γενόμενος βοῶν ἀγέλης νομεὺς καὶ τὰς βοῦς ἐλάττους τε καὶ χείρους ποιῶν μὴ ὁμολογοίη κακὸς βουκόλος εἶναι· ἔτι δὲ θαυμαστότερον εἴ τις προστάτης γενόμενος πόλεως κ.τ.λ., with which cf. Plat. Gorg. 516 A. See also Newman, Politics of Aristotle, vol. I. p. 30.

163. Athen. XIII. 561 C, Ποντιανὸς δὲ Ζήνωνα ἔφη τὸν Κιτιέα ὑπολαμβάνειν τὸν Ἔρωτα θεὸν εἶναι φιλίας καὶ ἐλευθερίας ἔτι δὲ καὶ ὁμονοίας παρασκευαστικόν, ἄλλου δ' οὐδενός. διὸ καὶ ἐν τῇ πολιτείᾳ ἔφη "τὸν Ἔρωτα θεὸν εἶναι, συνεργὸν ὑπάρχοντα πρὸς τὴν τῆς πόλεως σωτηρίαν." Plut. vit. Lycurg. 31. Lycurgus' object was not to leave Sparta with a large empire, ἀλλ' ὥσπερ ἑνὸς ἀνδρὸς βίῳ καὶ πόλεως ὅλης νομίζων εὐδαιμονίαν ἀπ' ἀρετῆς ἐγγίνεσθαι καὶ ὁμονοίας τῆς πρὸς αὐτήν, πρὸς τοῦτο συνέταξε καὶ συνήρμοσεν, ὅπως ἐλευθέριοι καὶ αὐτάρκεις γενόμενοι καὶ σωφρονοῦντες ἐπὶ πλεῖστον χρόνον διατελῶσι. ταύτην καὶ Πλάτων ἔλαβε τῆς Πολιτείας ὑπόθεσιν καὶ Διογένης καὶ Ζήνων κ.τ.λ.

τὸν Ἔρωτα. Love is in Hesiod to be regarded as an allegorical presentment of fire, frag. 113. In the ideal state Love is taken as a presiding deity, because all discord and party strife are to be banished from it, and the wise men, who are its citizens, are to be united by friendship and concord. Cf. Stob. Ecl. II. 7. 11[m], p. 108, 15, ἐν μόνοις τε τοῖς σοφοῖς ἀπολείπουσι φιλίαν, ἐπεὶ ἐν μόνοις τούτοις ὁμόνοια γίνεται περὶ τῶν κατὰ τὸν βίον, τὴν δ' ὁμόνοιαν εἶναι κοινῶν ἀγαθῶν ἐπιστήμην. Chrysipp. ap. Philod. περὶ εὐσεβ. col. 12, p. 79, Gomp., καὶ τὴν αὐτὴν εἶναι καὶ Εὐνομίαν καὶ Δίκην καὶ Ὁμόνοιαν καὶ Εἰρήνην καὶ Ἀφροδίτην καὶ τὸ παραπλήσιον πᾶν. It is probable that

Zeno took the same objection, that of want of unity, to Plato's Republic as is taken by Aristotle Pol. II. 5, p. 1264 a 24, ἐν μιᾷ γὰρ πόλει δύο πόλεις ἀναγκαῖον εἶναι, καὶ ταύτας ὑπεναντίας ἀλλήλαις. Cf. also ib. II. 4 1262 b 7, Xen. Mem. IV. 4. 16, and contrast Ar. Pol. II. 2. 1261 b 10. Hirzel, II. p. 36, finds here a divergence from Antisthenes, comparing Clem. Alex. Strom. II. 485 P., but he apparently forgets Diog. L. VI. 12, which shows that the inconsistency, if it exists, is with Antisthenes himself.

164. Clem. Alex. Strom. v. 12, 76, p. 691 P. 249 S., λέγει δὲ καὶ Ζήνων, ὁ τῆς Στωικῆς κτίστης αἱρέσεως, ἐν τῷ τῆς πολιτείας βιβλίῳ μήτε ναοὺς δεῖν ποιεῖν μήτε ἀγάλματα· μηδὲν γὰρ εἶναι τῶν θεῶν ἄξιον κατασκεύασμα, καὶ γράφειν οὐ δέδιεν αὐταῖς λέξεσι τάδε· ἱερά τε οἰκοδομεῖν οὐδὲν δεήσει· ἱερὸν γὰρ μὴ πολλοῦ ἄξιον, καὶ ἅγιον οὐδὲν χρὴ νομίζειν, οὐδὲν δὲ πολλοῦ ἄξιον καὶ ἅγιον οἰκοδόμων ἔργον καὶ βαναύσων. The same in Orig. c. Cels. I. 5, p. 324. Plut. Sto. Rep. VI. 1, ἔτι δόγμα Ζήνωνος ἔστιν· ἱερὰ θεῶν μὴ οἰκοδομεῖν· ἱερὸν γὰρ μὴ πολλοῦ ἄξιον καὶ ἅγιον οὐκ ἔστιν· οἰκοδόμων δ' ἔργον καὶ βαναύσων οὐδέν ἐστι πολλοῦ ἄξιον. Theodoret, Gr. Aff. Cur. III. p. 780 = p. 49, 45, ταῦτα συνορῶν καὶ Ζήνων ὁ Κιτιεὺς ἐν τῷ τῆς Πολιτείας ἀπαγορεύει βιβλίῳ καὶ ναοὺς οἰκοδομεῖν καὶ ἀγάλματα τεκταίνειν· οὐδὲν γὰρ εἶναι τούτων φησὶν θεῶν ἄξιον κατασκεύασμα. Epiphan. Haeres. III. 36, Ζήνων ὁ Κιτιεὺς ὁ Στωικὸς ἔφη μὴ δεῖν θεοῖς οἰκοδομεῖν ἱερά.

The Cynics also deny the sanctity of temples: Diog. L. VI. 73, μηδέν τε ἄτοπον εἶναι ἐξ ἱεροῦ τι λαβεῖν. Zeno's language in some particulars recalls St Paul's address to the Athenians, Acts XVII. 24, ὁ Θεὸς ὁ ποιήσας τὸν κόσμον καὶ πάντα τὰ ἐν αὐτῷ, οὗτος οὐρανοῦ καὶ γῆς Κύριος ὑπάρχων οὐκ ἐν χειροποιήτοις ναοῖς κατοικεῖ.

165. Stob. Floril. 43, 88, Ζήνων ἔφη δεῖν τὰς πόλεις κοσμεῖν οὐκ ἀναθήμασιν ἀλλὰ ταῖς τῶν οἰκούντων ἀρεταῖς.

In a similar spirit Crates promised to honour Hermes and the Muses οὐ δαπάναις τρυφεραῖς ἀλλ᾽ ἀρεταῖς ὁσίαις (Julian Or. VI. 200 A, quoted by Zeller, Socrates p. 329 n. 1).

166. Diog. L. VII. 33, καὶ κατὰ τοὺς διακοσίους στίχους μήθ᾽ ἱερὰ μήτε δικαστήρια μήτε γυμνάσια ἐν ταῖς πόλεσιν οἰκοδομεῖσθαι.

κατά...στίχους. Prose writings were cited according to the number of lines, cf. Diog. L. VII. 187, (Chrysippus) ἐν τῷ περὶ τῶν ἀρχαίων φυσιολόγων συγγράμματι λέγων κατὰ τοὺς ἑξακοσίους στίχους. Dion. Hal. de Thuc. hist. jud. c. 19, προοίμιον τῆς ἱστορίας μέχρι πεντακοσίων ἐκμηκύνει στίχων.

δικαστήρια: "wozu Gerichtshöfe, wo überall Gerechtigkeit waltet? wozu Gymnasien, wenn Korperkraft und Gewandtheit ohne Wert sind?" Wellmann p. 438. The reference to γυμνάσια confirms the statement of Plutarch (Sto. Rep. 8, 2) that Zeno wrote against Plato's Republic: with Plato γυμναστική forms an important element in the training of the φύλακες (Rep. III. p. 410—411).

167. Diog. VII. 32, ἔνιοι μέντοι...ἐν πολλοῖς κατηγοροῦντες τοῦ Ζήνωνος τὴν ἐγκύκλιον παιδείαν ἄχρηστον ἀποφαίνειν λέγουσιν ἐν ἀρχῇ τῆς πολιτείας.

ἐγκύκλιος παιδεία. The ordinary course of Greek education comprised the three branches of γράμματα, μουσική, and γυμναστική (Becker's Charicles E. T. p. 231 foll.). Zeno intended to imply, probably again in opposition to Plato, that, as compared with the acquisition of virtue or true wisdom, the wisdom which education proposes to supply is worthless (cf. Wellmann p. 437, 8). Such at least seems to be the ground on which the Cynics put forward a similar opinion, Diog. L. VI. 11, τήν τε ἀρετὴν τῶν ἔργων εἶναι, μήτε λόγων πλειόνων δεομένην, μήτε μαθημάτων. 73, μουσικῆς τε καὶ γεωμετρικῆς καὶ ἀστρολογίας καὶ τῶν τοιούτων ἀμελεῖν ὡς ἀχρήστων καὶ οὐκ ἀναγκαίων. 103, παραιτοῦνται δὲ καὶ τὰ ἐγκύκλια μαθήματα. γράμματα γοῦν μὴ μανθάνειν ἔφασκεν ὁ Ἀντισθένης τοὺς σώφρονας γενομένους, ἵνα μὴ διαστρέφοιντο τοῖς ἀλλοτρίοις. Epicurus agreed with Zeno on this point (see Prof. Mayor on Cic. N. D. I. 72), while Aristotle considered that τὰ ἐγκύκλια μαθήματα are useful for the acquisition of virtue (Diog. L. v. 31). It is important to observe that Chrysippus held εὐχρηστεῖν τὰ ἐγκύκλια μαθήματα (Diog. L. VII. 129, cf. Stob. Ecl. II. 7, 5[b11], p. 67, 5), and it is possible that Zeno may at a later period of his life have modified his conclusion on this point, just as he diverged from the Cynics in recommending Dialectic and Physics as well as Ethics, Zeller p. 63, 3, Hirzel II. p. 523, 4, cf. Cleanth frag. 106.

168. Diog. VII. 33, περί τε νομίσματος οὕτως γράφειν (Ζήνωνα), νόμισμα δ᾽ οὔτ᾽ ἀλλαγῆς ἕνεκεν οἴεσθαι δεῖν κατασκευάζειν οὔτ᾽ ἀποδημίας ἕνεκεν.

νόμισμα. "Diogenes in the πολιτεία proposed a coinage of bones or stones (ἀστράγαλοι) instead of gold and silver, Athen. IV. 159 E." Zeller, Socrates, p. 325 n.

ἀλλαγῆς ἕνεκεν. This again is pointed at Plato Rep. II. 371 B, ἀγορὰ δὴ ἡμῖν καὶ νόμισμα ξύμβολον τῆς ἀλλαγῆς ἕνεκα γενήσεται ἐκ τούτου. Aristotle's statement is more exact, explaining that money is a security with a view to future exchange: ὑπὲρ τῆς μελλούσης ἀλλαγῆς, εἰ νῦν μηδὲν δεῖται, ὅτι ἔσται ἐὰν δεηθῇ, τὸ νόμισμα οἷον ἐγγυητής ἐσθ᾽ ἡμῖν. Eth. v. 5. 14. Cf. especially Ar. Pol. I. 9. 1257 a 32 foll. and Newman on ib. 1257 b 11.

169. Athen. VI. 233 B, C, Ζήνων δὲ ὁ ἀπὸ τῆς

Στοᾶς πάντα τἆλλα πλὴν τοῦ νομίμως αὑτοῖς (i.e. gold and silver) καὶ καλῶς χρῆσθαι νομίσας ἀδιάφορα, τὴν μὲν αἵρεσιν αὐτῶν καὶ φυγὴν ἀπειπών, τὴν χρῆσιν δὲ τῶν λιτῶν καὶ ἀπερίττων προηγουμένως ποιεῖσθαι προστάσσων· ὅπως ἀδεῆ καὶ ἀθαύμαστον πρὸς τἆλλα τὴν διάθεσιν τῆς ψυχῆς ἔχοντες οἱ ἄνθρωποι, ὅσα μήτε καλά ἐστι μήτε αἰσχρά, τοῖς μὲν κατὰ φύσιν ὡς ἐπὶ πολὺ χρῶνται, τῶν δ' ἐναντίων μηδὲν ὅλως δεδοικότες λόγῳ καὶ μὴ φόβῳ τούτων ἀπέχωνται.

The opinions professed with regard to money bear the same relation to the last frag. as frag. 171 bears to frag. 176. This passage affords another good illustration of the doctrine of the καθήκοντα as applied to those things which are morally indifferent. The σπουδαῖος, who is unaffected either by fear or desire (ἀπαθής), and whose ὁρμαί are properly directed by right reason, will know how to discriminate between τὰ κατὰ φύσιν and τὰ παρὰ φύσιν, so as to cling to the former and avoid the latter. Thus πλοῦτος is a προηγμένον (Diog. L. VII. 106), and possesses value as being of advantage for life in accordance with nature (ib. 105), while ἡ ὀρθὴ χρῆσις πλούτου which is characteristic of the σπουδαῖος is sharply distinguished from the φιλοπλουτία (Stob. Ecl. II. 7. 10[1], p. 91, 18) of the φαῦλος.

αἵρεσιν: suggested by Schweighäuser and adopted by Kaibel for the MSS. ἀρχήν. After τὴν χρῆσιν δὲ Schweig. thought some words had fallen out such as τὴν μὲν ὀρθὴν εἴα.

λιτῶν. Cf. M. Aurel. I. 3, τὸ λιτὸν κατὰ τὴν δίαιταν.

ἀπερίττων. So Casaubon in place of MSS περιττῶν. Contrast M. Aurel. v. 5 with id. IX. 32.

προηγουμένως. This word is difficult. In Sext. Emp., with whom it occurs at least eight times, it always means "principally" or "in the first place," being often opposed to ἀκολούθως. cf. προηγούμενος λόγος frag. 123 = leading doctrine. Here however it seems to have the special Stoic sense = in the absence of overriding circumstances)(κατὰ περίστασιν, cf. Epict. diss. III. 14. 7, Stob. Ecl. II. 7. 24. p. 144, 19, frag. 131. In this connection we may compare Diog.'s division of καθήκοντα into τὰ ἄνευ περιστάσεως, such as ὑγιείας ἐπιμελεῖσθαί (or καλῶς χρῆσθαι πλούτῳ as here), and τὰ κατὰ περίστασιν, such as τὴν κτῆσιν διαρρίπτειν (VII. 109). Hirzel, p. 825, denies that προηγουμένως belongs to the elder Stoics, thinking that it was taken over subsequently from the Academics and Peripatetics. He would substitute here ὡς προηγμένων.

ἀδεῆ points to the purging of the soul from the influence of the πάθη: δέος is a subdivision of φόβος not very explicitly defined ap. Stob. Ecl. II. 7. 10^c p. 92, 5.

ἀθαύμαστον. Cf. Hor. Epist. I. 6. 1, 2, nil admirari prope res est una Numici solaque quae possit facere et servare beatum; where see Orelli, who properly observes that τὸ θαυμάζειν, which Plato and Aristotle speak of as the starting point of philosophy, is something quite different. Cf. Marc. Aurel. I. 15, Cic. Tusc. III. 30. Hence Arr. Epict. Diss. I. 18, 11, μὴ θαύμαζε τὸ κάλλος τῆς γυναικὸς καὶ τῷ μοιχῷ οὐ χαλεπανεῖς. For διάθεσιν see on frag. 117.

170. Seneca de Otio 30, 2, Zenon ait: accedet ad rempublicam (sapiens), nisi si quid impedierit. id. Tranq. An. I. 7, Promptus compositusque sequor Zenonem, Cleanthem, Chrysippum; quorum tamen nemo ad rempublicam accessit, nemo non misit.

The same doctrine is attributed to Chrysippus in Diog. L. VII. 121, πολιτεύεσθαι φασὶ τὸν σοφόν, ἂν μή τι κωλύῃ, ὥς φησι Χρύσιππος ἐν πρώτῳ περὶ βίων: cf. Cic. Fin. III. 68, Schol. on Lucan II. 380, Stoicorum sapiens erit civilis, hoc est, in administratione rei publicae.

τὸ πολιτεύεσθαι is another instance of καθῆκον which is to be undertaken κατὰ τὸν προηγούμενον λόγον (Stob. Ecl. II. 7. 11^m, p. 111, 5) = προηγουμένως (see on last frag.). We may say then that, while τὸ πολιτεύεσθαι is καθῆκον προηγουμένως or ἄνευ περιστάσεως, τὸ μὴ πολιτεύεσθαι is καθῆκον κατὰ περίστασιν, just as a careful use of wealth is contrasted with the condition of the spendthrift.

171. Diog. VII. 121, καὶ γαμήσειν, ὡς ὁ Ζήνων φησὶν ἐν πολιτείᾳ, (τὸν σοφόν) καὶ παιδοποιήσεσθαι.

Cf. Stob. Ecl. II. 7. 11^m, p. 109, 16, Cic. Fin. III. 68. The statement refers to the duty of a wise man under existing circumstances, and while living in an ordinary civil community. It has no reference to the ideal state in which wives are to be held in common (frag. 176): γάμος clearly belongs to the ἀδιάφορα and γαμεῖν is a καθῆκον. This seems better that Wellmann's view p. 439, who strains the meaning of γάμος to bring this passage into conformity with frag. 176, and is strongly supported by the analogous case of the duty of the wise man to enter public life. The latter clearly refers to existing political institutions, cf. Stob. Ecl. II. 7. 11^b, p. 94, 9, πολιτεύεσθαι τὸν σοφὸν καὶ μάλιστα ἐν ταῖς τοιαύταις πολιτείαις ταῖς ἐμφαινούσαις τινὰ προκοπὴν πρὸς τὰς τελείας πολιτείας. The same explanation will account for the two passages in Diog. VI. 11 and 72, where similar views are attributed to the Cynics, without supposing (with Zeller, Socrates p. 320) a divergence of opinion between Antisthenes and Diogenes.

172. Diog. L. VII. 129, καὶ ἐρασθήσεσθαι δὲ τὸν σοφὸν τῶν νέων τῶν ἐμφαινόντων διὰ τοῦ εἴδους τὴν πρὸς ἀρετὴν εὐφυΐαν, ὥς φησι Ζήνων ἐν τῇ πολιτείᾳ.

For the Cynics see Introd. p. 20. This passage is no

doubt inspired by the influence of the Phaedrus and Symposium. Speaking of the ἔρως of Socrates Dr Thompson remarks (Phaedrus App. I. p. 152):—"It was not the beauty of Alcibiades, but his splendid mental endowments, his great capacity for good or for evil, which excited the admiration and the solicitude of Socrates." Cf. Symp. 208 B foll. and for εὐφυΐαν ib. 209 B, ψυχῇ καλῇ καὶ γενναίᾳ καὶ εὐφυεῖ, cf. frag. 147, καταληπτὸν εἶναι τὸ ἦθος ἐξ εἴδους. We must distinguish between the ἔρως of the σπουδαῖος and the φαῦλος. τὸ ἐρᾶν itself belongs to the class of ἀδιάφορα, and implies, therefore, a corresponding καθῆκον, the duty, that is, τοῦ καλῶς ἐρᾶν, Stob. Ecl. II. 7. 5^{b9}, p. 66, 3—10. If then the objection is raised that the σπουδαῖος should avoid ἔρως, if he is to retain his ἀπάθεια, since ἔρως is a subdivision of ἐπιθυμία and a πάθος, the answer is that this is untrue of that particular form of ἔρως which is defined as ἐπιβολὴ φιλοποιΐας διὰ κάλλος ἐμφαινόμενον (Stob. l. c. l. 12, ib. 10^c p. 91, 15, 11^s p. 115, 1, Diog. L. VII. 113, 120, Sext. Emp. Math. VII. 239), and which is not an ἐπιθυμία. Under ἐπιθυμία are to be classed ἔρωτες σφοδροὶ only, and in Diog. VII. 113 the distinction between the two classes of ἔρως is clearly indicated. Cic., Fin. III. 68, speaks of amores sanctos.

173. Athen. XIII. 563 E, καὶ τοῦτο μὲν ἐζηλωκότες τὸν ἀρχηγὸν ὑμῶν τῆς σοφίας Ζήνωνα τὸν Φοίνικα, ὃς οὐδεπώποτε γυναικὶ ἐχρήσατο παιδικοῖς δ' ἀεί· ὡς Ἀντίγονος ὁ Καρύστιος ἱστορεῖ ἐν τῷ περὶ τοῦ βίου αὐτοῦ· θρυλλεῖτε γὰρ ὅτι "δεῖ μὴ τῶν σωμάτων ἀλλὰ τῆς ψυχῆς ἐρᾶν."

δεῖ μὴ κ.τ.λ. It is most natural to suppose that these are Zeno's words from the position of his name in the context. For the sense see on frag. 172.

174. Clem. Alex. Paedag. III. 11. 74, p. 296 P. 109 S., ὑπογράφειν ὁ Κιτιεὺς ἔοικε Ζήνων εἰκόνα νεανίου καὶ οὕτως αὐτὸν ἀνδριαντουργεῖ· ἔστω, φησί, καθαρὸν τὸ πρόσωπον, ὀφρὺς μὴ καθειμένη, μηδ' ὄμμα ἀναπεπταμένον, μηδὲ διακεκλασμένον, μὴ ὕπτιος ὁ τράχηλος, μηδ' ἀνιέμενα τὰ τοῦ σώματος μέλη, ἀλλὰ [τὰ] μετέωρα ἐντόνοις ὅμοια· ὀρθὸς νοῦς πρὸς τὸν λόγον, ὀξύτης καὶ κατοκωχὴ τῶν ὀρθῶς εἰρημένων, καὶ σχηματισμοὶ καὶ κινήσεις μηδὲν ἐνδιδοῦσαι τοῖς ἀκολάστοις ἐλπίδος. αἰδὼς μὲν ἐπανθείτω καὶ ἀρρενωπία· ἀπέστω δὲ καὶ ὁ ἀπὸ τῶν μυροπωλίων καὶ χρυσοχοείων καὶ ἐριοπωλίων ἅλυς καὶ ὁ ἀπὸ τῶν ἄλλων ἐργαστηρίων, ἔνθα καὶ ἑταιρικῶς κεκοσμημένοι, ὥσπερ ἐπὶ τέγους καθεζόμενοι, διημερεύουσιν.

This remarkable fragment was first restored by Cobet in Mnemos. O. S. VI. p. 339, who saw that the writer was necessarily speaking of young men and not of young women, as the word ἀρρενωπία of itself shows. It seems probable, as Wachsmuth suggests, that this frag. comes from the ἐρωτικὴ τέχνη (Introd. p. 30).

νεανίου. So Cobet l.c. for νεανίδα. Dind. with two MSS. reads νεανία.

καθαρόν. Cf. Plut. de Audiendo 13, p. 45 C, προσώπῳ κατάστασις καθαρὰ καὶ ἀνέμφατος.

ἀναπεπταμένον: barefaced, impudent, cf. Xen. Mem. II. 1. 22, τὰ δὲ ὄμματα ἔχειν ἀναπεπταμένα, of the woman representing Vice in Prodicus' fable. See Aesch. Suppl. 198, 9 and the comm. μηδὲ διακεκλασμένον is an emendation of Cobet's (Mnemos. XI. 387) for the MSS. μηδ' ἀνακεκλασμένον, the meaning of which is not clear. With the alteration ἀναπ. est hominis protervi et petulantis, διακ. mollis et impudici.

τά is rejected by Wachsm. with great improvement to the sense.

ὀρθὸς νοῦς, so Wachsm. for vulg. ὀρθόνου· πρὸς κ.τ.λ.

Perhaps it would be better to place a comma after νοῦς, and connect πρὸς τὸν λόγον with ὀξύτης. Dind. brackets ὀξύτης.

κίνησις...ἐνδιδοῦσα Dind. with some MSS.

μυροπωλίων: these shops are mentioned as the lounges frequented by young men. Ar. Eq. 1375, τὰ μειράκια ταυτὶ λέγω, τἀν τῷ μύρῳ. Lys. Or. 24 § 20, ἕκαστος γὰρ ὑμῶν εἴθισται προσφοιτᾶν ὁ μὲν πρὸς μυροπωλεῖον, ὁ δὲ πρὸς κουρεῖον, ὁ δὲ πρὸς σκυτοτομεῖον, ὁ δ' ὅποι ἂν τύχῃ: id. Or. 23. § 3, Isoc. Or. 7. § 48, οὐκ ἐν τοῖς σκιραφείοις οἱ νεώτεροι διέτριβον οὐδ' ἐν ταῖς αὐλητρίσιν οὐδ' ἐν τοῖς τοιούτοις συλλόγοις ἀλλ' ἐν τοῖς ἐπιτηδεύμασιν ἔμενον ἐν οἷς ἐτάχθησαν. In Homer's time the smith's shop was used for this purpose: Od. XVIII. 38, Hes. Op. 491: later the barber's shop is most frequently mentioned: see the comm. on Hor. Sat. I. 7. 3. Other authorities are collected by Becker, Charicles E. T. p. 272.

κεκοσμημένοι...καθεζόμενοι. So Cobet for κεκοσμημέναι... καθεζόμεναι. For the former word cf. Xen. Mem. III. 11. 4 where Theodota is spoken of as πολυτελῶς κεκοσμημένην, and Lucian, Ver. Hist. II. 46, γυναῖκας πάνυ ἑταιρικῶς κεκοσμημέναι (quoted by Becker, Charicles E. T. p. 249); and for the latter Aeschin. Timarch. § 74 τοὺς ἐπὶ τῶν οἰκημάτων καθεζομένους (referred to by Wachsm.), and Catull. XXXVII. 8, 14.

175. Diog. L. VII. 22, δεῖν τε ἔλεγε τοὺς νέους πάσῃ κοσμιότητι χρῆσθαι καὶ πορείᾳ καὶ σχήματι καὶ περιβολῇ.

Possibly this is only a reference to the preceding frag. For πορείᾳ see on frag. 31. περιβολῇ = clothing.

176. Diog. L. VII. 131, ἀρέσκει δὲ αὐτοῖς καὶ κοινὰς εἶναι τὰς γυναῖκας δεῖν παρὰ τοῖς σοφοῖς ὥστε τὸν ἐντυχόντα τῇ ἐντυχούσῃ χρῆσθαι, καθά φησι Ζήνων ἐν τῇ πολιτεία. ib. 33, κοινάς τε τὰς γυναῖκας δογματίζειν ὁμοίως Πλάτωνι ἐν τῇ πολιτείᾳ.

For the Cynics see Introd. p. 20. Observe, however, that Chrysippus concurred in this opinion, which must not therefore be treated as merely Cynical.

177. Diog. L. VII. 33, καὶ ἐσθῆτι δὲ τῇ αὐτῇ κελεύει (Ζήνων) χρῆσθαι ἄνδρας καὶ γυναῖκας καὶ μηδὲν μόριον ἀποκεκρύφθαι.

The same view seems to have been advocated by the Cynics. Hence the point of Menander's lines quoted by Diog. L. VI. 93, συμπεριπατήσεις γὰρ τρίβων' ἔχουσ' ἐμοί, ὥσπερ Κράτητι τῷ Κυνικῷ ποθ' ἡ γυνή. Socrates in Xen. Symp. II. 3 says:—ἐσθὴς ἄλλη μὲν γυναικὶ ἄλλη δὲ ἀνδρὶ καλή. With regard to the words μηδὲν μόριον ἀποκ. Zeller, p. 308 n. 2, remarks:—"The latter act is only conditional and allowed in certain cases, such as for purposes of gymnastics." But the limitation is Plato's (Rep. V. 452 A, 457 A) and we have already seen that Zeno proposed to abolish γυμνάσια: it may well be that Zeno, like the Cynics, disclaimed the theoretical propriety of the ordinary rules of modesty in dress. There is no question here of the καθήκοντα of ordinary life, and Zeno's departure from the Cynical point of view is largely to be found in this direction.

178. Origen c. Celsum, VII. 63, p. 739, ἐκκλίνουσι τὸ μοιχεύειν οἱ τὰ τοῦ Κιτιέως Ζήνωνος φιλοσοφοῦντες... διὰ τὸ κοινωνικὸν καὶ παρὰ φύσιν εἶναι τῷ λογικῷ ζώῳ νοθεύειν τὴν ὑπὸ τῶν νόμων ἑτέρῳ προκαταληφθεῖσαν γυναῖκα καὶ φθείρειν τὸν ἄλλου ἀνθρώπου οἶκον.

Since strictly speaking marriage is an ἀδιάφορον, τὸ μοιχεύειν cannot be contrary to virtue, and such an offence would be impossible in the ideal state. Still, with society constituted as it is, μὴ μοιχεύειν is καθῆκον ἄνευ περιστάσεως and therefore κατὰ φύσιν. The wise man will recognise the laws of the state in which he lives in the same spirit in which he takes part in its public affairs (Stob. Ecl. II. 7. 11ᵇ 94, 8 foll.). In Sext. Pyrrh. III. 209 we find τούς γε μὴν μοιχοὺς κολάζει παρ' ἡμῖν νόμος, παρὰ δέ τισιν ἀδιάφορόν ἐστι ταῖς τῶν ἑτέρων γυναιξὶ μίγνυσθαι· καὶ φιλοσόφων δέ τινές φασιν ἀδιάφορον εἶναι τὸ ἀλλοτρίᾳ γυναικὶ μίγνυσθαι. The Stoics are probably indicated, and the passage is in no way inconsistent with the present, cf. Theoph. ad Autol. III. 3 p. 118 D, οὐχὶ καὶ περὶ σεμνότητος πειρώμενοι γράφειν ἀσελγείας καὶ πορνείας καὶ μοιχείας ἐδίδαξαν ἐπιτελεῖσθαι, ἔτι μὴν καὶ τὰς στυγητὰς ἀρρητοποιΐας εἰσηγήσαντο;

179. Sext. Emp. Pyrrh. III. 245, οἷον γοῦν ὁ αἱρεσιάρχης αὐτῶν Ζήνων ἐν ταῖς διατριβαῖς φησι περὶ παίδων ἀγωγῆς ἄλλα τε ὅμοια καὶ τάδε· " διαμηρίζειν μηδὲν μᾶλλον μηδὲ ἧσσον παιδικὰ ἢ μὴ παιδικὰ μηδὲ θηλέα ἢ ἄρρενα· οὐ γάρ [ἐστι] παιδικοῖς ἄλλα ἢ μὴ παιδικοῖς οὐδὲ θηλείαις ἢ ἄρρεσιν, ἀλλὰ ταὐτὰ πρέπει τε καὶ πρέποντα ἐστίν." The same fragment is preserved by Sext. Emp. adv. Math. XI. 190, introduced by the words καὶ μὴν περὶ μὲν παίδων ἀγωγῆς ἐν ταῖς διατριβαῖς ὁ αἱρεσιάρχης Ζήνων τοιαῦτά τινα διέξεισιν, and with the variant ἄλλα παιδικοῖς for ἐστὶ παιδικοῖς ἄλλα.

ἐν ταῖς διατριβαῖς. For this book see Introd. p. 30. The true aspect from which to regard this and the four next following fragments is very clearly set forth in a passage of Origen, c. Cels. IV. 45 (quoted by Zeller, p. 310, n. 1). "The Stoics made good and evil depend alone on the intention, and declared external actions, independent of intentions, to be indifferent: εἶπον οὖν ἐν τῷ περὶ ἀδιαφόρων τόπῳ ὅτι τῷ ἰδίῳ λόγῳ (the action taken by itself) θυγατράσι μίγνυσθαι ἀδιάφορον ἐστίν, εἰ καὶ μὴ χρὴ ἐν ταῖς καθεστώσαις πολιτείαις τὸ τοιοῦτον ποιεῖν, καὶ ὑποθέσεως χάριν...παρειλήφασι τὸν σοφὸν μετὰ τῆς θυγατρὸς μόνης καταλελειμμένον παντὸς τοῦ τῶν ἀνθρώπων γένους διεφθαρμένου, καὶ ζητοῦσιν εἰ καθηκόντως ὁ πατὴρ συνελεύσεται τῇ θυγατρὶ ὑπὲρ τοῦ μὴ ἀπολέσθαι...τὸ πᾶν τῶν ἀνθρώπων γένος." This also illustrates frag. 178.

180. Sext. Emp. Pyrrh. III. 246, περὶ δὲ τῆς εἰς τοὺς γονεῖς ὁσιότητος ὁ αὐτὸς ἀνήρ (Ζήνων) φησιν εἰς τὰ περὶ τὴν Ἰοκάστην καὶ τὸν Οἰδίποδα ὅτι οὐκ ἦν δεινὸν τρίβειν τὴν μητέρα καὶ εἰ μὲν ἀσθενοῦσαν ἕτερόν τι μέρος τοῦ σώματος τρίψας ταῖς χερσὶν ὠφέλει οὐδὲν αἰσχρόν· εἰ δὲ ἕτερα μέρη τρίψας εὔφραινεν, ὀδυνωμένην παύσας, καὶ παῖδας ἐκ τῆς μητρὸς γενναίους ἐποίησεν, αἰσχρόν. Sext. Emp. Math. XI. 191, καί γε ὁ μὲν Ζήνων τὰ περὶ τῆς Ἰοκάστης καὶ Οἰδίποδος ἱστορούμενά φησιν ὅτι οὐκ ἦν δεινὸν τρῖψαι τὴν μητέρα. καὶ εἰ μὲν ἀσθενοῦσαν τὸ σῶμα ταῖς χερσὶ τρίψας ὠφέλει, οὐδὲν αἰσχρόν· εἰ δὲ ἑτέρῳ μέρει τρίψας ἐφ' ᾧ εὗρεν ὀδυνωμένην παύσας καὶ παῖδας ἐκ τῆς μητρὸς γενναίους ποιήσας τί ἦν αἰσχρόν; ib. Pyrrh. III. 205, ἀλλὰ καὶ ὁ Κιτιεὺς Ζήνων φησὶ μὴ ἄτοπον εἶναι τὸ μόριον τῆς μητρὸς τῷ ἑαυτοῦ μορίῳ τρῖψαι καθάπερ οὐδὲ ἄλλο τι μέρος τοῦ σώματος αὐτῆς τῇ χειρὶ τρῖψαι φαῦλον ἂν εἴποι τις εἶναι. Plut. Quaest. Conv. III. 6. 1, § 6, ὡς ἔγωγε νὴ τὸν κύνα καὶ τοῦ Ζήνωνος ἂν ἐβουλόμην ἔφη διαμηρισμοὺς ἐν συμποσίῳ τινὶ καὶ παιδιᾷ μᾶλλον ἢ σπουδῆς τοσαύτης ἐχομένῳ συγγράμματι τῇ πολιτείᾳ κατατετάχθαι.

It should be observed that Sextus does not state that this extract as well as the last comes from the διατριβαί, so that we may perhaps refer Plutarch's words to this passage: Wellmann however, p. 440, thinks that both the

Sextus passages come from the διατριβαί, in which case Plutarch's statement should form a separate fragment. Cf. Chrysipp. ap. Sext. Pyrrh. III. 246, id. ap. Epiphanius adv. Haeres. III. 2. 9 (III. 39), Diels, p. 593, ἔλεγε γὰρ δεῖν μίγνυσθαι ταῖς μητράσι τοὺς παῖδας τοῖς δὲ πατράσι τὰς θυγατέρας. Diog. L. VII. 188, Theoph. ad Autol. III. 6, 120 D.

181. Sext. Emp. adv. Math. XI. 190, καὶ πάλιν (ὁ Ζήνων) "διαμεμήρικας τὸν ἐρώμενον; οὐκ ἔγωγε. πότερον οὐκ ἐπεθύμησας αὐτὸν διαμηρίσαι; καὶ μάλα. ἀλλ' ἐπεθύμησας παρασχεῖν σοι αὐτὸν ἢ ἐφοβήθης κελεῦσαι; μὰ Δί'. ἀλλ' ἐκέλευσας; καὶ μάλα. εἶτ' οὐκ ὑπηρέτησέ σοι; οὐ γάρ."

The line taken here is that the intention is all important, and not the act in itself: hence virtue belongs only to σπουδαία διάθεσις, cf. Cleanth. frag. 95,

ὅστις ἐπιθυμῶν ἀνέχετ' αἰσχροῦ πράγματος
οὗτος ποιήσει τοῦτ' ἐὰν καιρὸν λάβῃ.

Bekker suggests ἀλλ' ἐπιθυμήσας...εἶτ' ἐφοβήθης.

182. Sext. Emp. Pyrrh. III. 200, καὶ τί θαυμαστόν, ὅπου γε καὶ οἱ ἀπὸ τῆς κυνικῆς φιλοσοφίας καὶ οἱ περὶ τὸν Κιτιέα Ζήνωνα καὶ Κλεάνθην καὶ Χρύσιππον ἀδιάφορον τοῦτο (i.e. ἀρρενομιξίαν) εἶναί φασιν;

183. Sext. Emp. Pyrrh. III. 206, τό τε αἰσχρουργεῖν ἐπάρατον ὂν παρ' ἡμῖν ὁ Ζήνων οὐκ ἀποδοκιμάζει.

184. Theoph. ad Autol. III. 5, p. 119 C, τί σοι ἔδοξε τὰ Ζήνωνος ἢ τὰ Διογένους καὶ Κλεάνθους, ὁπόσα περιέχουσιν αἱ βίβλοι αὐτῶν διδάσκουσαι ἀνθρωποβορίας, πατέρας μὲν ὑπὸ ἰδίων τέκνων ἔψεσθαι καὶ βιβρώσκεσθαι

καί, εἴ τις οὐ βούλοιτο ἢ μέρος τι τῆς μυσερᾶς τροφῆς ἀπορρίψειεν, αὐτὸν κατεσθίεσθαι τὸν μὴ φαγόντα;

Cf. Diog. L. VII. 121, γεύσεσθαί τε καὶ ἀνθρωπίνων σαρκῶν κατὰ περίστασιν, ib. 188 (Chrysippus) ἐν δὲ τῷ γ' περὶ δικαίου κατὰ τοὺς χιλίους στίχους, καὶ τοὺς ἀποθανόντας κατεσθίειν κελεύων. Sext. Pyrrh. III. 207, 247 foll., Math. XI. 192—194, Mayor on Juv. XV. 107. Cannibalism was also recommended by the Cynics, Diog. VI. 73, μηδ' ἀνόσιον εἶναι τὸ καὶ ἀνθρωπείων κρεῶν ἅψασθαι, ὡς δῆλον ἐκ τῶν ἀλλοτρίων ἐθῶν, with which cf. an amusing summary of the various modes of disposing of the dead prevalent in different countries, ap. Sext. Pyrrh. III. 226—229. It should be observed however that the Stoics only enjoined this practice κατὰ περίστασιν.

185. Epiphan. Haeres. III. 36, τοὺς δὲ τελευτῶντας ζῴοις παραβάλλειν χρῆναι ἢ πυρί. καὶ τοῖς παιδικοῖς χρῆσθαι ἀκωλύτως.

Chrysippus, ap. Sext. Emp. Pyrrh. III. 248, Math. XI. 194, recommends that the flesh of deceased relations should be eaten if suitable for food, but, if useless for that purpose, ἢ κατορύξαντες τὸ μνῆμα ἐποίσουσιν ἢ κατακαύσαντες τὴν τέφραν ἀφήσουσιν. The meaning of these obscure words of Epiphanius appears to be similar, and παραβάλλειν is certainly commonly used in this sense (see L. and S.). Others however have explained the words very differently. Thus Stein, Psychol. p. 161, n. 314, finds some allusion in them to the doctrine of metempsychosis. In the same spirit Diogenes ordered his body to be cast forth unburied (Diog. L. VI. 79, Cic. Tusc. I. 104). Chrysippus proved the absolute unimportance of any particular form of burial from a comparison of the varying practice of different nations (Cic. Tusc. I. 108, Sext. Pyrrh. III. 226—9).

186. Cic. Ep. Fam. IX. 22. 1, Atqui hoc (libertas loquendi) Zenoni placuit...sed ut dico placet Stoicis suo quamque rem nomine appellare.

Cf. Cic. Off. I. 128, nec vero audiendi sunt Cynici, aut ei qui fuerunt Stoici poene Cynici, qui reprehendunt et invident, quod ea quae re turpia non sunt nominibus ac verbis flagitiosa ducamus: and see Zeller, Socrates, p. 326.

187. Clem. Alex. Strom. II. 20. 125 P. p. 494, S. p. 178, καλῶς ὁ Ζήνων ἐπὶ τῶν Ἰνδῶν ἔλεγεν ἕνα Ἰνδὸν παροπτώμενον ἐθέλειν <ἂν> ἰδεῖν ἢ πάσας τὰς περὶ πόνου ἀποδείξεις μαθεῖν.

The allusion to the Indians is explained by the words the Indian philosophers are said to have used to Alexander: σώματα μὲν μετάξεις ἐκ τόπου εἰς τόπον, ψυχὰς δ' ἡμετέρας οὐκ ἀναγκάσεις ποιεῖν ἃ μὴ βουλόμεθα. πῦρ ἀνθρώποις μέγιστον κολαστήριον, τούτου ἡμεῖς καταφρονοῦμεν. Clem. Alex. Strom. IV. 7. 50. Similarly Philo, in telling the same story: quod omnis probus sit liber, p. 879, πῦρ μεγίστους τοῖς ζῶσι σώμασι πόνους καὶ φθορὰν ἐργάζεται, τούτου ὑπεράνω ἡμεῖς γινόμεθα, ζῶντες καιόμεθα. The historians attest the custom of burning themselves alive said to have been practised by the Brahmans. Strabo, XV. 1. 65, αἴσχιστον δ' αὐτοῖς νομίζεσθαι νόσον σωματικήν· τὸν δ' ὑπονοήσαντα καθ' αὑτοῦ τοῦτο ἐξάγειν ἑαυτὸν διὰ πυρὸς νήσαντα πυράν, ὑπαλειψάμενον δὲ καὶ καθίσαντα ἐπὶ τὴν πυρὰν ὑφάψαι κελεύειν, ἀκίνητον δὲ καίεσθαι. Curt. VIII. 9. 32, apud hos occupare fati diem pulcrum, et vivos se cremari iubent, quibus aut segnis aetas aut incommoda valitudo est:...inquinari putant ignem nisi qui spirantes recipit. Cic. Tusc. II. 40, (Mueller) uri se patiuntur Indi. The case of Calanus is particularly recorded, Cic. Tusc. II. 52 etc.

ἄν, added by Cobet, Ἑρμῆς λόγιος, I. p. 487.

τάς...ἀποδείξεις. There is no doubt some particular reference in this, the point of which it is difficult now to ascertain. May it refer to Antisthenes? In Diog. L. VI. 2, we read of him: ὅτι ὁ πόνος ἀγαθὸν συνέστησε διὰ τοῦ μεγάλου Ἡρακλέους καὶ τοῦ Κύρου, and in the list of his works preserved by the same writer (VI. 15—18) we find three with the title Ἡρακλῆς, two of which bear the alternative title ἢ περὶ ἰσχύος.

188. Galen de cogn. animi morbis, v. 13, οὕτω γοῦν καὶ Ζήνων ἠξίου πάντα πράττειν ἡμᾶς ἀσφαλῶς, ὡς ἀπολογησομένους ὀλίγον ὕστερον παιδαγωγοῖς· ὠνόμαζε γὰρ οὕτως ἐκεῖνος ὁ ἀνὴρ τοὺς πολλοὺς τῶν ἀνθρώπων ἑτοίμους ὄντας τοῖς πέλας ἐπιτιμᾶν κἂν μηδεὶς αὐτοὺς παρακαλῇ.

παιδαγωγοῖς: for their duties see Becker, Charicles, E. T. p. 226.

189. Stob. Flor. 14, 4 = Anton. Meliss. I. 52,

ἔλεγχε σαυτόν, ὅστις εἶ, μὴ πρὸς χάριν
ἄκου᾽, ἀφαιροῦ δὲ κολάκων παρρησίαν.

ἔλεγχε σαυτόν recalls γνῶθι σεαυτόν, for which see the authorities ap. Mayor on Juv. XI. 27.

πρὸς χάριν ἄκου᾽ = do not listen to flatterers, is the passive form of πρὸς ἡδονήν τι λέγειν (Thuc. II. 65), πρὸς ἡδονὴν δημηγορεῖν (Dem. Phil. I. § 38), πρὸς χάριν ἐρεῖς (Soph. O. T. 1152). The best illustration however is Stob. Ecl. II. 7. 11ᵍ, p. 114, 23, the wise man οὔτε προσφέρει τινὶ οὔτε προσίεται τὸν πρὸς χάριν λόγον, Diog. L. VII. 117.

Meineke would also ascribe to Zeno the couplet quoted by Stob. Flor. II. 12, where the lemma in the MSS. is Ζηνοδότου.

190. Maxim. Floril. c. 6, ed. Mai, ὁ μὲν γεωργὸς ἀφ' ὧν ἂν πολὺν καὶ καλὸν θέλοι καρπὸν λαβεῖν ὠφέλιμον ἑαυτὸν ἐκείνοις παρέχεται καὶ πάντα τρόπον ἐπιμελεῖται καὶ θεραπεύει· πολὺ δὲ μᾶλλον ἄνθρωποι τοῖς ὠφελίμοις πεφύκασι χαρίζεσθαι καὶ περὶ τοὺς τοιούτους μάλιστα σπουδάζειν· καὶ θαυμαστὸν οὐδέν. καὶ γὰρ καὶ τῶν μερῶν τοῦ σώματος ἐκείνων ἐπιμελούμεθα μᾶλλον ἅπερ ὠφελιμώτερα ἑαυτοῖς πρὸς τὴν ὑπηρεσίαν νομίζομεν εἶναι, ὅθεν ὁμοίως ὑφ' ὧν εὖ πάσχειν ἀξιοῦμεν, ὠφελίμους αὐτοῖς ἔργοις, ἀλλὰ μὴ τοῖς λόγοις εἶναι δεῖ. οὐδὲ γὰρ ἡ ἐλαία τῷ θεραπεύοντι αὐτὴν ἐπαγάλλεται, ἀλλ' ἐκφέρουσα πολλούς τε καὶ καλοὺς καρποὺς ἔπεισεν ἑαυτῆς ἐπιμελεῖσθαι μᾶλλον.

This fragment is taken from Wachsmuth (Comm. i. p. 6): see Introd. p. 31.

θέλοι: unless θέλῃ be read, ἄν belongs to the verb. Cf. Dem. de Cor. § 246, ἀλλὰ μὴν ὧν γ' ἂν ὁ ῥήτωρ ὑπεύθυνος εἴη, πᾶσαν ἐξέτασιν λάμβανε. But it is often difficult to determine whether the optative is really potential. See Fennell on Pind. Nem. iv. 8, Goodwin § 557, Madvig § 137.

ὠφέλιμον, cf. Cleanth. frags. 75 and 77.

ἄνθρωποι, "οἱ addendum?" Wachsm.

ἑαυτοῖς: Jelf § 654 b.

191. Athen. XIII. 565 D, ὁ δὲ σοφὸς ἐκεῖνος Ζήνων, ὥς φησιν Ἀντίγονος ὁ Καρύστιος, προμαντευόμενος ὑμῶν ὡς τὸ εἰκὸς περὶ τοῦ βίου καὶ τῆς προσποιήτου ἐπιτηδεύσεως, ἔφη ὡς οἱ παρακούσαντες αὐτοῦ τῶν λόγων καὶ μὴ συνέντες ἔσονται ῥυπαροὶ καὶ ἀνελεύθεροι· καθάπερ οἱ τῆς Ἀριστίππου παρενεχθέντες αἱρέσεως ἄσωτοι καὶ θρασεῖς.

Cic., N. D. III. 77, attributes this remark to Aristo: si verum est quod Aristo Chius dicere solebat, nocere audientibus philosophos iis, qui bene dicta male interpretarentur: posse enim asotos ex Aristippi, acerbos e Zenonis schola exire. It should be observed, however, that Athenaeus specifies Antigonus of Carystus as the source of his information, so that he is at least as much entitled to credit as Cicero.

192. Stob. Floril. 6. 62, εὖ γὰρ εἴρηται, ἔφη, τὸ τοῦ Ζήνωνος ὅτι τούτου ἕνεκα καρτέον οὗ καὶ κομητέον, τοῦ κατὰ φύσιν, ἵνα μὴ βαρούμενός τις ὑπὸ τῆς κόμης μηδ' ἐνοχλούμενος ᾖ πρὸς μηδεμίαν ἐνέργειαν.

τοῦ κατὰ φύσιν. Conformity to nature, i.e. external environment, is taken as the basis of all those actions, which, although unconnected with virtue, yet constitute the objects of καθήκοντα, Diog. L. VII. 108, ἐνέργημα δὲ αὐτὸ (καθῆκον) εἶναι, ταῖς κατὰ φύσιν κατασκευαῖς οἰκεῖον, Stob. Ecl. II. 7. 8ᵃ, p. 86, 13; Diog. L. VII. 105.

193. Diog. L. VIII. 48, ἀλλὰ μὴν καὶ τὸν οὐρανὸν πρῶτον (i.e. Pythagoras) ὀνομάσαι κόσμον καὶ τὴν γῆν στρογγύλην· ὡς δὲ Θεόφραστος Παρμενίδην· ὡς δὲ Ζήνων Ἡσίοδον.

The lines of Hesiod supposed to be referred to are Theog. 126—128, Γαῖα δέ τοι πρῶτον μὲν ἐγείνατο ἶσον ἑαυτῇ οὐρανὸν ἀστερόενθ' ἵνα μιν περὶ πάντα καλύπτοι ὄφρ' εἴη μακάρεσσι θεοῖς ἕδος ἀσφαλὲς αἰεί, which are a very poor basis for the two assertions. For the limited sense in which κόσμος is used, cf. Diog. VII. 138, καὶ αὐτὴν δὲ τὴν διακόσμησιν τῶν ἀστέρων κόσμον εἶναι λέγουσιν, Krische, p. 396, 397.

194. Diog. L. VI. 91, Ζήνων δ' αὖθ' ὁ Κιτιεὺς ἐν ταῖς χρείαις καὶ κῴδιον αὐτὸν (Crates) φησί ποτε προσράψαι τῷ τρίβωνι ἀνεπιτρεπτοῦντα.

ἐν ταῖς χρείαις. Introd. p. 31.

τῷ τρίβωνι. The Cynics adopted this as their characteristic dress, following Socrates (Zeller, Socrates p. 316. Becker, Charicles, E. T. p. 419). Zeno himself wore the τρίβων (cf. apoph. 3).

ἀνεπιτρεπτοῦντα i.e. "nec curavisse deformitatem." The word is omitted in L. and S. and also in Steph. Th.

195. Dio. Chrysost. LIII. 4, γέγραφε δὲ καὶ Ζήνων ὁ φιλόσοφος εἴς τε τὴν Ἰλιάδα καὶ τὴν Ὀδυσσείαν καὶ περὶ τοῦ Μαργίτου δέ· δοκεῖ γὰρ καὶ τοῦτο τὸ ποίημα ὑπὸ Ὁμήρου γεγονέναι νεωτέρου καὶ ἀποπειρωμένου τῆς αὑτοῦ φυσέως πρὸς ποίησιν. ὁ δὲ Ζήνων οὐδὲν τῶν τοῦ Ὁμήρου ψέγει ἅμα διηγούμενος καὶ διδάσκων ὅτι τὰ μὲν κατὰ δόξαν τὰ δὲ κατὰ ἀλήθειαν γέγραφεν, ὅπως μὴ φαίνηται αὐτὸς αὑτῷ μαχόμενος ἔν τισι δοκοῦσιν ἐναντίως εἰρῆσθαι. ὁ δὲ λόγος οὗτος Ἀντισθένους ἐστὶ πρότερον ὅτι τὰ μὲν δόξῃ τὰ δὲ ἀληθείᾳ εἴρηται τῷ ποιητῇ· ἀλλ' ὁ μὲν οὐκ ἐξειργάσατο αὐτόν, ὁ δὲ καθ' ἕκαστον τῶν ἐπὶ μέρους ἐδήλωσεν.

For the object of Zeno's Homeric studies cf. Krische p. 393, 394, who points out that, although Zeno may have incidentally controverted some of the Chorizontes of his time, yet his main object was to fortify Stoic precepts by appealing to Homer's authority. For Antisthenes see Zeller, Socrates p. 330.

Μαργίτου. This work seems to have resisted the disintegrating process, which from early times was applied to Homer's works, better than any other of the poems ascribed to him, except the Iliad and Odyssey. Aristotle (Poet. IV. 10) does not question Homer's authorship.

196. Plut. comm. Hesiod. IX., Ζήνων ὁ Στωικὸς ἐνήλλαττε τοὺς στίχους λέγων

κεῖνος μὲν πανάριστος ὃς εὖ εἰπόντι πίθηται·
ἐσθλὸς δ' αὖ κἀκεῖνος ὃς αὐτὸς πάντα νοήσῃ,

τῇ εὐπειθείᾳ τὰ πρωτεῖα διδούς, τῇ φρονήσει δὲ τὰ δευτερεῖα. The same in Proclus on Hesiod, Op. 291, Gaisf. Poet. Gr. Min. II. p. 200, cf. Diog. L. VII. 25, 26, whose comment on the change of place in the lines is as follows:—κρείττονα γὰρ εἶναι τὸν ἀκοῦσαι καλῶς δυνάμενον τὸ λεγόμενον καὶ χρῆσθαι αὐτῷ, τοῦ δι' αὑτοῦ τὸ πᾶν συννοήσαντος. τῷ μὲν γὰρ εἶναι μόνον τὸ συνεῖναι. τῷ δ' εὖ πεισθέντι προσεῖναι καὶ τὴν πρᾶξιν. Themist. Or. VIII. 108 C, ἐμοὶ δὲ καὶ Ζήνων ὁ Κιτιεὺς λίαν ἀρεστὸς τὴν εὐπείθειαν ἀποφηνάμενος τῆς ἀγχινοίας ἀρετὴν εἶναι βασιλικωτέραν καὶ τὴν τάξιν τὴν Ἡσιόδου μεταθεὶς κ.τ.λ. id. Or. XIII. 171 D, ὀρθῶς γὰρ ὑπελάμβανε Ζήνων ὁ Κιτιεὺς βασιλικωτέραν εἶναι τῆς ἀγχινοίας τὴν εὐπείθειαν.

The lines of Hesiod (Op. 291) are often quoted or imitated: cf. Ar. Eth. I. 4, 7, Liv. XXII. 29, 8, Soph. Ant. 720 φήμ' ἔγωγε πρεσβεύειν πολὺ φῦναι τὸν ἄνδρα πάντ' ἐπιστήμης πλέων· εἰ δ' οὖν...καὶ τῶν λεγόντων εὖ καλὸν τὸ μανθάνειν.

197. Plut. de aud. poet. p. 33 E, καὶ ὁ Ζήνων ἐπανορθούμενος τὸ τοῦ Σοφοκλέους,

ὅστις δὲ πρὸς τύραννον ἐμπορεύεται
κείνου 'στι δοῦλος κἂν ἐλεύθερος μόλῃ,

μετέγραφεν

οὐκ ἔστι δοῦλος ἂν (? ἢν) ἐλεύθερος μόλῃ,

τῷ ἐλευθέρῳ νῦν συνεκφαίνων τὸν ἀδεῆ καὶ μεγαλόφρονα καὶ ἀταπείνωτον.

The fragm. is no. 711 (Dind.). This was also given to Aristippus or Plato by other authorities: see Diog. L. II. 82. For ἐλεύθερος cf. frag. 149.

198. Strabo VII. 3. 6, Homer never mentions Arabia εἰ μὴ Ζήνωνι τῷ φιλοσόφῳ προσεκτέον γράφοντι·

Αἰθίοπας δ' ἱκόμην καὶ Σιδονίους Ἀραβάς τε.

Hom. Od. IV. 83 where the edd. now adopt καὶ Ἐρεμβοὺς the reading of Posidonius: Crates of Mallus preferred Ἐρεμνούς (Krische p. 393).

199. Stob. Floril. 95. 21, Ζήνων ἔφη Κράτητα ἀναγιγνώσκειν ἐν σκυτείῳ καθήμενον τὸν Ἀριστοτέλους προτρεπτικὸν ὃν ἔγραψε πρὸς Θεμίσωνα τῶν Κυπρίων βασιλέα λέγων ὅτι οὐδενὶ πλείω ἀγαθὰ ὑπάρχει πρὸς τὸ φιλοσοφῆσαι, πλοῦτόν τε γὰρ πλεῖστον αὐτὸν ἔχειν ὥστε δαπανᾶν εἰς ταῦτα ἔτι δὲ δόξαν ὑπάρχειν αὐτῷ. ἀναγιγνώσκοντος δὲ αὐτοῦ τὸν σκυτέα ἔφη προσέχειν ἅμα ῥάπτοντα, καὶ τὸν Κράτητα εἰπεῖν ἐγώ μοι δοκῶ, ὦ Φιλίσκε, γράψειν πρὸς σὲ προτρεπτικόν· πλείω γὰρ ὁρῶ σοι ὑπάρχοντα πρὸς τὸ φιλοσοφῆσαι ὧν ἔγραψεν Ἀριστοτέλης.

This passage belongs to the work entitled Κράτητος ἀπομνημονεύματα: Introd. p. 31.

200. Stob. Floril. 36. 26, Ζήνων τῶν μαθητῶν ἔφασκε τοὺς μὲν φιλολόγους εἶναι τοὺς δὲ λογοφίλους.

The meaning is made clear by Stob. Ecl. II. 7. 11[k] p. 105, 4, where it is said of the φαῦλος:—μηδὲ εἶναι φιλόλογον, λογόφιλον δὲ μᾶλλον, μέχρι λαλιᾶς ἐπιπολαίου προβαίνοντα, μηκέτι δὲ καὶ τοῖς ἔργοις ἐκβεβαιούμενον τὸν τῆς ἀρετῆς λόγον.

201. Stob. Floril. 6. 34, ὁ Ζήνων ᾐτιᾶτο τοὺς πλείστους λέγων, ἐξὸν ἀπὸ τῶν πόνων τὰς ἡδονὰς φέρειν, ἀπὸ τῶν μαγειρείων λαμβάνοντας.

πόνων. This passage should have been quoted in the note on frag. 128.

202. Stob. Floril. 4. 107, Ζήνων δὲ ἔφη γελοῖον ἑκάστους μὲν τοῖς πράγμασιν ὡς δεῖ ζῆν μὴ προσέχειν ὡς οὐκ εἰδότων, τὸν δὲ παρὰ πάντων ἔπαινον θαυμάζειν ὡς ἐχόμενον κρίσεως. πράγμασιν is clearly corrupt and Wachsmuth reads παραγγείλασιν, but Mr R. D. Hicks suggests τοῖς παρὰ τῶν σοφῶν παραγγέλμασιν which restores the balance of the sentence.

For the sense cf. Cleanth. frag. 100.

APOPHTHEGMATA OF ZENO.

1. Diog. L. VII. 2, χρηστηριαζομένου αὐτοῦ (Ζήνωνος) τί πράττων ἄριστα βιώσεται, ἀποκρίνασθαι τὸν θεὸν εἰ συγχρωτίζοιτο τοῖς νεκροῖς. ὅθεν ξυνέντα, τὰ τῶν ἀρχαίων ἀναγιγνώσκειν. The same in Suid. s. v. συγχρωτίζεσθαι col. 938.

2. Diog. L. VII. 3, πορφύραν ἐμπεπορευμένος ἀπὸ τῆς Φοινίκης πρὸς τῷ Πειραιεῖ ἐναυάγησεν. ἀνελθὼν δὲ εἰς τὰς Ἀθήνας ἤδη τριακοντούτης, ἐκάθισε παρά τινα βιβλιοπώλην, ἀναγιγνώσκοντος δὲ ἐκείνου τὸ δεύτερον τῶν Ξενοφῶντος ἀπομνημονευμάτων ἡσθεὶς ἐπύθετο ποῦ διατρίβοιεν οἱ τοιοῦτοι ἄνδρες. εὐκαίρως δὲ παριόντος Κράτητος, ὁ βιβλιοπώλης δείξας αὐτόν φησι, τούτῳ παρακολούθησον. Cf. Themist. Or. XXIII. 295 D, τὰ δὲ ἀμφὶ Ζήνωνος ἀρίδηλά τε ἐστι καὶ ᾀδόμενα ὑπὸ πολλῶν ὅτι αὐτὸν ἡ Σωκράτους ἀπολογία ἐκ Φοινίκης εἰς τὴν Ποικίλην ἤγαγεν.

3. Plut. de Inimic. Util. 2, Ζήνων δέ, τῆς ναυκληρίας αὐτῷ συντριβείσης, πυθόμενος εἶπεν, εὖ γε, ὦ τύχη, ποιεῖς εἰς τὸν τρίβωνα συνελαύνουσα ἡμᾶς. Plut. de Tranq. An. 6, Ζήνωνι τῷ Κιτιεῖ μία ναῦς περιῆν φορτηγός· πυθόμενος δὲ ταύτην αὐτόφορτον ἀπολωλέναι συγκλυσθεῖσαν, εὖ γε, εἶπεν κ.τ.λ. with καὶ τὴν στοὰν added after τρίβωνα. Substantially the same account in Plut. de Exilio 11, with

καὶ βίον φιλόσοφον in place of καὶ τὴν στοάν. Suidas col. 1023 s. v. νῦν εὐπλόηκα ὅτε νεναυάγηκα. ἐπὶ τῶν παρ' ἐλπίδα εὐτυχησάντων. Ζήνων γὰρ ὁ Κιτιεὺς καταλιπὼν τοὺς πρὶν διδασκάλους καὶ Κράτητος τοῦ φιλοσόφου φοιτητὴς γενόμενος τοῦτο εἴρηκε, ναυαγίῳ περιπεσὼν καὶ εἰπών, εὖ γε ποεῖ ἡ τύχη προσελαύνουσα ἡμᾶς φιλοσοφίᾳ * * * οὕτω τραπῆναι πρὸς φιλοσοφίαν. That the story was given in various forms appears from the account in Diog. L. VII. 4, 5. Senec. de Tranq. An. 14, 2, Nuntiato naufragio Zeno noster, quum omnia sua audiret submersa, "Iubet" inquit "me fortuna expeditius philosophari."

4. Diog. L. VII. 19, πρὸς δὲ τὸν φάσκοντα ὡς τὰ πολλὰ αὐτῷ Ἀντισθένης οὐκ ἀρέσκει, χρείαν Σοφοκλέους προενεγκάμενος, ἠρώτησεν εἴ τινα καὶ καλὰ ἔχειν αὐτῷ δοκεῖ. τοῦ δ' οὐκ εἰδέναι φήσαντος, εἶτ' οὐκ αἰσχύνῃ, ἔφη, εἰ μέν τι κακὸν ἦν εἰρημένον ὑπ' Ἀντισθένους τοῦτ' ἐκλεγόμενος καὶ μνημονεύων, εἰ δέ τι καλόν, οὐδ' ἐπιβαλλόμενος κατέχειν;

5. Diog. L. VII. 20, λέγοντος δέ τινος αὐτῷ περὶ Πολέμωνος, ὡς ἄλλα προθέμενος ἄλλα λέγει σκυθρωπάσας, ἔφη, πόσου γὰρ ἠγάπας τὰ διδόμενα;

The explanation is thus given by Aldobrand: videbatur ergo cupiditatis Polemonem accusare, ac si illa ita docere consuevisset, quomodo a discipulis tractaretur.

6. Plut. de prof. in virt. c. 6, ὁ δὲ Ζήνων ὁρῶν τὸν Θεόφραστον ἐπὶ τῷ πολλοὺς ἔχειν μαθητὰς θαυμαζόμενον, ὁ ἐκείνου μὲν χορός, ἔφη, μείζων, οὑμὸς δὲ συμφωνότερος. Plut. de seips. citra inv. laud. c. 17, οὕτω γὰρ ὁ Ζήνων πρὸς τὸ πλῆθος τῶν Θεοφράστου μαθητῶν, ὁ ἐκείνου χορός, ἔφη, μείζων, ὁ ἐμὸς δὲ συμφωνότερος.

7. Diog. L. VII. 24, φησὶ δ' Ἀπολλώνιος ὁ Τύριος ἕλκοντος αὐτὸν Κράτητος τοῦ ἱματίου ἀπὸ Στίλπωνος εἰπεῖν, ὦ Κράτης, λαβὴ φιλοσόφων ἐστὶν ἐπιδέξιος ἡ διὰ τῶν ὤτων· πείσας οὖν ἕλκε τοῦτον. εἰ δέ με βιάζῃ, τὸ μὲν σῶμα παρά σοι ἔσται, ἡ δὲ ψυχὴ παρὰ Στίλπωνι.

Cf. Cleanth., frag. 108, and for the concluding words of the anecdote Arist. Ach. 398, ὁ νοῦς μὲν ἔξω ξυλλέγων ἐπύλλια οὐκ ἔνδον αὐτὸς δ' ἔνδον κ.τ.λ. Plaut. Aulul. 179, nunc domum properare propero: nam egomet sum hic, animus domist. Pseudol. 32, nam istic meus animus nunc est non in pectore, and Lorenz ad loc.

8. Diog. L. VII. 21, ἔλεγε δὲ καὶ τῶν φιλοσόφων τοὺς πλείστους, τὰ μὲν πολλὰ ἀσόφους εἶναι, τὰ δὲ μικρὰ καὶ τυχηρὰ ἀμαθεῖς.

Wilamowitz (Antigonos p. 117) says:—" die Philosophen sind in den meisten Dingen ungeschickt, von den gewöhnlichen begreifen sie nichts: sie wissen nur das eine was Not tut," but probably we should read εὐμαθεῖς, with Meric Casaubon.

9. Diog. L. VII. 20, εἰπόντος δέ τινος ὅτι μικρὰ αὐτῷ δοκεῖ τὰ λογάρια τῶν φιλοσόφων, λέγεις, εἶπε, τἀληθῆ. δεῖ μέντοι καὶ τὰς συλλαβὰς αὐτῶν βραχείας εἶναι, εἰ δυνατόν.

10. Diog. L. VII. 25, καὶ πρὸς τὸν δείξαντα δὲ αὐτῷ διαλεκτικὸν ἐν τῷ θερίζοντι λόγῳ ἑπτὰ διαλεκτικὰς ἰδέας πυθέσθαι πόσας εἰσπράττεται μισθοῦ· ἀκούσαντα δὲ ἑκατὸν διακοσίας αὐτῷ δοῦναι.

The fallacy known as θερίζων was concerned with the nature of the possible. "According to Ammon. de Inter. 106 a [§ 3 p. 160 ed. Or.], Lucian, Vit. Auct. 22 the θερίζων was as follows:—Either you will reap or you will not reap:

it is therefore incorrect to say, *perhaps* you will reap." Zeller, p. 182.

11. Suidas col. 1202 s.v. δέλτος = Diog. L. VII. 37, Κλεάνθης, ὃν καὶ ἀφωμοίου τοῖς σκληροκήροις δέλτοις, αἳ μόλις μὲν γράφονται, διατηροῦσι δὲ τὰ γραφέντα. Cf. Plut. de Audiendo c. 18, ὥσπερ ὁ Κλεάνθης καὶ Ξενοκράτης, βραδύτεροι δοκοῦντες εἶναι τῶν συσχολαστῶν, οὐκ ἀπεδίδρασκον ἐκ τοῦ μανθάνειν οὐδὲ ἀπέκαμνον, ἀλλὰ φθάνοντες εἰς ἑαυτοὺς ἔπαιζον, ἀγγείοις τε βραχυστόμοις καὶ πινακίσι χαλκαῖς ἀπεικάζοντες, ὡς μόλις μὲν παραδεχόμενοι τοὺς λόγους ἀσφαλῶς δὲ καὶ βεβαίως τηροῦντες. For πίνακες see Becker, Charicles, Eng. Tr. p. 162.

12. Diog. L. VII. 18, Ἀρίστωνος δὲ τοῦ μαθητοῦ πολλὰ διαλεγομένου οὐκ εὐφυῶς, ἔνια δὲ καὶ προπετῶς καὶ θρασέως, ἀδύνατον, εἶπεν, εἰ μή σε ὁ πατὴρ μεθύων ἐγέννησεν. ὅθεν αὐτὸν καὶ λάλον ἀπεκάλει, βραχυλόγος ὤν. Attributed to Diogenes by Plut. de Educ. Puer. 3.

13. Stob. Floril. 36, 23, τῶν τις ἐν Ἀκαδημείᾳ νεανίσκων περὶ ἐπιτηδευμάτων διελέγετο ἀφρόνως· ὁ δὲ Ζήνων ἐὰν μὴ τὴν γλῶτταν, ἔφη, εἰς νοῦν ἀποβρέξας διαλέγῃ, πολὺ πλείω ἔτι καὶ ἐν τοῖς λόγοις πλημμελήσεις. Plut. Phoc. v. 2, Ζήνων ἔλεγεν ὅτι δεῖ τὸν φιλόσοφον εἰς νοῦν ἀποβάπτοντα προφέρεσθαι τὴν λέξιν. Cf. Suidas I. p. 328 (of Aristotle), τῆς φύσεως γραμματεὺς ἦν τὸν κάλαμον ἀποβρέχων εἰς νοῦν. Some have regarded these words as the original of Quintilian's sensu tincta (frag. 27, where see note). Cf. M. Aurel. v. 16.

14. Diog. L. VII. 20, δεῖν δὲ ἔφη τὸν διαλεγόμενον, ὥσπερ τοὺς ὑποκριτάς, τὴν μὲν φωνὴν καὶ τὴν δύναμιν μεγάλην ἔχειν· τὸ μέντοι στόμα μὴ διέλκειν· ὃ ποιεῖν τοὺς πολλὰ μὲν λαλοῦντας, ἀδύνατα δέ.

15. Diog. L. VII. 20, τοῖς εὖ λεγομένοις οὐκ ἔφη δεῖν καταλείπεσθαι τόπον, ὥσπερ τοῖς ἀγαθοῖς τεχνίταις εἰς τὸ θεάσασθαι· τοὐναντίον δὲ τὸν ἀκούοντα οὕτω πρὸς τοῖς λεγομένοις γίνεσθαι, ὥστε μὴ λαμβάνειν χρόνον εἰς τὴν ἐπισημείωσιν.

τόπον: perhaps we should read χρόνον, ὥσπερ τόπον.

16. Diog. L. VII. 22, μὴ τὰς φωνὰς καὶ τὰς λέξεις δεῖν ἀπομνημονεύειν, ἀλλὰ περὶ τὴν διάθεσιν τῆς χρείας τὸν νοῦν ἀσχολεῖσθαι μὴ ὥσπερ ἕψησίν τινα ἢ σκευασίαν ἀναλαμβάνοντας.

For the distinction between φωνή and λέξις cf. Diog. L. VII. 56, λέξις δ' ἔστι φωνὴ ἐγγράμματος. The meaning is:—we ought not to commit to memory the words and expressions of a maxim (χρείας as in apoph. 4), but to exercise our mind as to its arrangement, without learning it by heart like a cookery recipe. For ἀναλαμβάνειν cf. Plut. Agesil. 20, 3. Cobet, however, translates otherwise.

17. Diog. L. VII. 23, τὸ κάλλος εἶπε τῆς σωφροσύνης ἄνθος εἶναι.

So Cobet, followed by Wilamowitz, for MSS. φωνῆς... φωνήν, cf. Diog. L. VII. 130, ὥρα ἄνθος ἀρετῆς. Zeno, frag. 147, καταληπτὸν εἶναι τὸ ἦθος ἐξ εἴδους.

18. Stob. Floril. Monac. 196, Ζήνων ὁ φιλόσοφος, λεγόντων τινῶν ὅτι παράδοξα λέγει, εἶπεν, ἀλλ' οὐ παράνομα. Cf. Cleanth. frag. 107.

19. Plut. de Virt. Mor. 4, καίτοι καὶ Ζήνωνά φασιν εἰς θέατρον ἀνιόντα κιθαρῳδοῦντος Ἀμοιβέως πρὸς τοὺς μαθητάς, ἴωμεν, εἰπεῖν, ὅπως καταμάθωμεν οἵαν ἔντερα καὶ νεῦρα καὶ ξύλα καὶ ὀστᾶ λόγου καὶ ἀριθμοῦ μετασχόντα καὶ τάξεως ἐμμέλειαν καὶ φωνὴν ἀφίησιν.

Cf. Plut. Arat. c. 17, 2, ᾄδοντος Ἀμοιβέως ἐν τῷ θεάτρῳ, a passage which also fixes Amoebeus as a contemporary of Antigonus.

20. Stob. Floril. 36, 19, Ζήνων πρὸς τὸν πλείω λαλεῖν θέλοντα ἢ ἀκούειν "νεανίσκε," εἶπεν, "ἡ φύσις ἡμῖν γλῶτταν μὲν μίαν δύο δὲ ὦτα παρέσχεν, ἵνα διπλασίονα ὧν λέγομεν ἀκούωμεν." Diog. L. VII. 23, πρὸς τὸ φλυαροῦν μειράκιον, διὰ τοῦτο, εἶπε, δύο ὦτα ἔχομεν, στόμα δὲ ἕν, ἵνα πλείονα μὲν ἀκούωμεν, ἥττονα δὲ λέγωμεν, cf. Plut. de Garrul. 1, κωφότης γὰρ αὐθαίρετός ἐστιν (scil. ἡ ἀσιγησία) ἀνθρώπων, οἶμαι, μεμφομένων ὅτι μίαν μὲν γλῶτταν δύο δ' ὦτα ἔχουσιν, id. de audiendo, 3, καὶ γὰρ τὸν Ἐπαμινώνδαν ὁ Σπίνθαρος ἐπαινῶν ἔφη μήτε πλείονα γινώσκοντι μήτε ἐλάττονα φθεγγομένῳ ῥᾳδίως ἐντυχεῖν ἑτέρῳ. καὶ τὴν φύσιν ἡμῶν ἑκάστῳ λέγουσι δύο μὲν ὦτα δοῦναι μίαν δὲ γλῶτταν ὡς ἐλάττονα λέγειν ἢ ἀκούειν ὀφείλοντι.

21. Diog. L. VII. 21, νεανίσκου πολλὰ λαλοῦντος, ἔφη, τὰ ὦτά σου εἰς τὴν γλῶτταν συνερρύηκεν.

22. Diog. L. VII. 26, ἔλεγέ τε κρεῖττον εἶναι τοῖς ποσὶν ὀλισθεῖν ἢ τῇ γλώττῃ.

This is found several times in the collections of γνῶμαι, and is sometimes attributed to Socrates (cf. Stein, Psych. p. 7, n. 5): the references are given by Wachsmuth in Sauppe's Satura Philologa, p. 29.

23. Diog. L. VII. 14, πλειόνων τε περιστάντων αὐτὸν δείξας ἐν τῇ στοᾷ κατ' ἄκρου τὸ ξύλινον περιφερὲς τοῦ βωμοῦ ἔφη, τοῦτό ποτε ἐν μέσῳ ἔκειτο· διὰ δὲ τὸ ἐμποδίζειν ἰδίᾳ ἐτέθη. καὶ ὑμεῖς μὲν ἐκ τοῦ μέσου βαστάσαντες αὐτοὺς ἧττον ἡμῖν ἐνοχλήσετε.

Köhler in Rhein. Mus. XXXIX. 297 proposes βάθρου for βωμοῦ.

24. Diog. L. VII. 24, ἐρωτηθεὶς πῶς ἔχει πρὸς λοιδορίαν, καθάπερ, εἶπεν, εἰ πρεσβευτὴς ἀναπόκριτος ἀποστέλλοιτο.

The point of this bon mot appears to have been lost in the tradition: it must originally have stood:—"The man who abuses me I send away like an ambassador without an answer (καθάπερ εἰ πρεσβευτὴν ἀναπόκριτον ἀποστέλλοιμι)": so Wilamowitz.

25. Diog. L. VII. 24, ἐν συμποσίῳ κατακείμενος σιγῇ, τὴν αἰτίαν ἠρωτήθη. ἔφη οὖν τῷ ἐγκαλέσαντι ἀπαγγεῖλαι πρὸς τὸν βασιλέα, ὅτι παρῆν τις σιωπᾶν ἐπιστάμενος. ἦσαν δὲ οἱ ἐρωτήσαντες παρὰ Πτολεμαίου πρέσβεις ἀφικόμενοι, καὶ βουλόμενοι μαθεῖν τί εἴποιεν παρ' αὐτοῦ πρὸς τὸν βασιλέα. Stob. Floril. 33, 10, Ζήνων, Ἀντιγόνου πρέσβεις Ἀθήναζε πέμψαντος, κληθεὶς ὑπ' αὐτῶν σὺν ἄλλοις φιλοσόφοις ἐπὶ δεῖπνον, κἀκείνων παρὰ πότον σπευδόντων ἐπιδείκνυσθαι τὴν αὐτῶν ἕξιν, αὐτὸς ἐσίγα. τῶν δὲ πρεσβέων ζητούντων τί ἀπαγγείλωσι περὶ αὐτοῦ πρὸς Ἀντίγονον, "τοῦτ' αὐτό," ἔφη, "ὃ βλέπετε." δυσκρατέστατον γὰρ πάντων ὁ λόγος. Plut. de Garrul. IV. Ἀθήνησι δέ τις ἑστιῶν πρέσβεις βασιλικούς, ἐφιλοτιμήθη σπουδάζουσιν αὐτοῖς συναγαγεῖν εἰς ταὐτὸ τοὺς φιλοσόφους, χρωμένων δὲ τῶν ἄλλων κοινολογίᾳ καὶ τὰς συμβολὰς ἀποδιδόντων τοῦ δὲ Ζήνωνος ἡσυχίαν ἄγοντος, φιλοφρονησάμενοι καὶ προπιόντες οἱ ξένοι, περὶ σοῦ δὲ τί χρὴ λέγειν, ἔφασαν, ὦ Ζήνων, τῷ βασιλεῖ; κἀκεῖνος, ἄλλο μηδέν, εἶπεν, ἢ ὅτι πρεσβύτης ἐστὶν ἐν Ἀθήναις παρὰ πότον σιωπᾶν δυνάμενος. Also in an expanded form ap. Theodor. Metoch. p. 334, Kiessling.

The anecdote in the form related in Diog. Laert. rests on the authority of Antigonus of Carystus, and hence Wilamowitz (Antig. p. 114) concludes that the king who sent the embassy was Ptolemaeus and not Antigonus Gonatas. It was natural that in later times, when the friendly relations subsisting between Antigonus and Zeno were remembered, the country of the ambassadors should have been transferred from Egypt to Macedonia. Diogenes, however, has misconceived the object of the embassy, which appears in a less corrupted form in Plutarch. The ambassadors were sent to Athens, not to Zeno, and the assembly was not one of philosophers but of Macedonian partisans. These the ambassadors were instructed to sound, but they seem to have missed the mark in Zeno's case.

26. Aelian, Var. H. IX. 26, Ζήνωνα τὸν Κιτιέα δι' αἰδοῦς ἄγαν καὶ σπουδῆς ἦγεν Ἀντίγονος ὁ βασιλεύς. καί ποτε οὖν ὑπερπλησθεὶς οἴνου ἐπεκώμασε τῷ Ζήνωνι, καὶ φιλῶν αὐτὸν καὶ περιβάλλων ἅτε ἔξοινος ὤν, ἠξίου τί αὐτὸν προστάξαι, ὀμνὺς καὶ νεανιευόμενος σὺν ὅρκῳ μὴ ἀτυχήσειν τῆς αἰτήσεως. ὁ δὲ λέγει αὐτῷ, πορευθεὶς ἔμεσον· σεμνῶς ἅμα καὶ μεγαλοφρόνως τὴν μέθην ἐλέγξας καὶ φεισάμενος αὐτοῦ μή ποτε διαρραγῇ ὑπὸ πλησμονῆς.

27. Athen. II. 55 F, διὸ καὶ Ζήνων ὁ Κιτιεύς, σκληρὸς ὢν καὶ πάνυ θυμικὸς πρὸς τοὺς γνωρίμους, ἐπὶ πλεῖον τοῦ οἴνου σπάσας ἡδὺς ἐγίνετο καὶ μείλιχος· πρὸς τοὺς πυνθανομένους οὖν τοῦ τρόπου τὴν διαφορὰν ἔλεγε τὸ αὐτὸ τοῖς θέρμοις πάσχειν, καὶ γὰρ ἐκείνους πρὶν διαβραχῆναι πικροτάτους εἶναι, ποτισθέντας δὲ γλυκεῖς καὶ προσηνεστάτους. Galen, de Anim. Mor. 3. IV. 777 K., καὶ Ζήνων, ὥς φασιν, ἔλεγεν ὅτι, καθάπερ οἱ πικροὶ θέρμοι βρεχόμενοι τῷ ὕδατι γλυκεῖς γίνονται, οὕτω καὶ αὐτὸν ὑπ' οἴνου διατίθεσθαι. Eustath. on Hom. Od. φ, 293, p. 1910, 42, Ζήνων οὖν, φασίν, ὁ Κιτιεὺς σκληρὸς ἄλλως ὢν πρὸς τοὺς συνήθεις, ὅμως εἰ πλεῖον οἴνου πάσειε (leg. σπάσειε) ἡδὺς ἐγίνετο καὶ μείλιχος, λέγων ταὐτόν τι τοῖς θέρμοις πάσχειν, οἳ πικρότεροι ὄντες πρὶν διαβραχῆναι ποτισθέντες γλυκεῖς γίνονται καὶ προσηνέστεροι. Similarly Diog. L. VII. 26.

28. Athen. VIII. 345 c, Ζήνων δ' ὁ Κιτιεὺς ὁ τῆς Στοᾶς κτίστης, πρὸς τὸν ὀψοφάγον ᾧ συνέζη ἐπὶ πλείονα

χρόνον, καθά φησιν Ἀντίγονος ὁ Καρύστιος ἐν τῷ Ζήνωνος βίῳ (p. 119 Wil.), μεγάλου τινὸς κατὰ τύχην ἰχθύος παρατεθέντος, ἄλλου δ᾽ οὐδενὸς παρεσκευασμένου, λαβὼν ὁ Ζήνων ἀπὸ τοῦ πίνακος οἷος ἦν κατεσθίειν. τοῦ δ᾽ ἐμβλέψαντος αὐτῷ· τί οὖν, ἔφη, τοὺς συζῶντάς σοι οἴει πάσχειν, εἰ σὺ μίαν ἡμέραν μὴ δεδύνησαι ἐνεγκεῖν ὀψοφαγίαν; The same in Diog. L. VII. 19.

29. Athen. v. 186 D, ὁ δὲ Ζήνων, ἐπεί τις τῶν παρόντων ὀψοφάγων ἀπέσυρεν ἅμα τῷ παρατεθῆναι τὸ ἐπάνω τοῦ ἰχθύος, στρέψας καὶ αὐτὸς τὸν ἰχθὺν ἀπέσυρεν ἐπιλέγων· (Eur. Bacch. 1129)

Ἰνὼ δὲ τἀπὶ θάτερ᾽ ἐξειργάζετο.

The same story is told of Bion Borysthenites, id. VIII. 344 A. Schweighäuser (Ind.) thinks it is rightly attributed to Zeno.

30. Diog. L. VII. 17, δυοῖν δ᾽ ὑπανακειμένοιν ἐν πότῳ, καὶ τοῦ ὑπ᾽ αὐτὸν τὸν ὑφ᾽ ἑαυτὸν σκιμαλίζοντος τῷ ποδί αὐτὸς ἐκεῖνον τῷ γόνατι. ἐπιστραφέντος δέ, τί οὖν οἴει τὸν ὑποκάτω σου πάσχειν ὑπὸ σοῦ; see also Suidas, col. 792, s. v. σκιμαλίσω. Vulgo ὑπερανακ. and ὑπὲρ αὐτόν: corrected by Menage.

31. Stob. Floril. 57, 12, Ζήνων ὁ Στωικὸς φιλόσοφος ὁρῶν τινα τῶν γνωρίμων ὑπὸ τοῦ ἀγροῦ περισπώμενον εἶπεν· ἐὰν μὴ σὺ τοῦτον ἀπολέσῃς, οὗτος σὲ ἀπολέσει.

32. Boissonade, Anecd. Gr. vol. I. p. 450, Ζῆθι, ὦ ἄνθρωπε, μὴ μόνον ἵνα φάγῃς καὶ πίῃς ἀλλ᾽ ἵνα τὸ ζῆν πρὸς τὸ εὖ ζῆν καταχρήσῃ, attributed to Zeno in Cod. Reg. Paris, 1168, seems to be another form of the well-known saying of Socrates, ap. Stob. Floril. 17, 22, ζῶμεν οὐκ ἵνα ἐσθίωμεν ἀλλ᾽ ἐσθίωμεν ἵνα ζῶμεν. This forms frag. eth. 10 in Wachsmuth's collection (Comm. I. p. 8), who refers to other passages giving the saying to Zeno.

33. Diog. L. VII. 21, καὶ προεφέρετο τὰ τοῦ Καφησίου· ὡς, ἐπιβαλομένου τινὸς τῶν μαθητῶν μεγάλα φυσᾶν, πατάξας εἶπεν, ὡς οὐκ ἐν τῷ μεγάλῳ τὸ εὖ κείμενον εἴη, ἀλλ' ἐν τῷ εὖ τὸ μέγα.

The saying of Caphesias is recorded also by Athen. XIV. 629, A.

34. Diog. L. VII. 26, τὸ εὖ γίνεσθαι παρὰ μικρόν, οὐ μὴν μικρὸν εἶναι.

35. Plut. de vit. pud. 13, τὸ τοῦ Ζήνωνος, ὡς ἀπαντήσας τινὶ νεανίσκῳ τῶν συνηθῶν παρὰ τὸ τεῖχος ἡσυχῇ βαδίζοντι, καὶ πυθόμενος, ὅτι φεύγει φίλον ἀξιοῦντα μαρτυρεῖν αὐτῷ τὰ ψευδῆ· τί λέγεις, φησίν, ἀβέλτερε; σὲ μὲν ἐκεῖνος ἀγνωμονῶν καὶ ἀδικῶν οὐ δέδιεν οὐδ' αἰσχύνεται· σὺ δ' ἐκεῖνον ὑπὲρ τῶν δικαίων οὐ θαρρεῖς ὑποστῆναι;

36. Diog. L. VII. 16, 17, οἷον ἐπὶ τοῦ καλλωπιζομένου ποτὲ ἔφη. ὀχέτιον γάρ τι ὀκνηρῶς αὐτοῦ ὑπερβαίνοντος, δικαίως, εἶπεν, ὑφορᾷ τὸν πηλόν· οὐ γὰρ ἔστιν ἐν αὐτῷ κατοπτρίσασθαι.

37. Diog. L. VII. 19, μειρακίου δὲ περιεργότερον παρὰ τὴν ἡλικίαν ἐρωτῶντος ζήτημά τι, προσήγαγε πρὸς κάτοπτρον, καὶ ἐκέλευσεν ἐμβλέψαι. ἔπειτ' ἠρώτησεν εἰ δοκεῖ αὐτῷ ἁρμόττοντα εἶναι ὄψει τὰ τοιαῦτα ζητήματα.

38. Diog. L. VII. 21, νεανίσκου δέ τινος θρασύτερον διαλεγομένου, οὐκ ἂν εἴποιμι, ἔφη, μειράκιον, ἃ ἐπέρχεταί μοι.

39. Diog. L. VII. 21, πρὸς τὸν καλὸν εἰπόντα ὅτι οὐ δοκεῖ αὐτῷ ἐρασθήσεσθαι ὁ σοφός, οὐδέν, ἔφη, ὑμῶν ἀθλιώτερον ἔσεσθαι τῶν καλῶν (εἰ μὴ ἡμεῖς ἐρασθησόμεθα, added by Menage from Hesych. Mil.). Cf. frag. 172. Chrysipp. ap. Stob. Floril. 63. 21.

40. Diog. L. VII. 22, πάντων ἔλεγεν ἀπρεπέστερον εἶναι τὸν τῦφον, καὶ μάλιστα ἐπὶ τῶν νέων.

41. Diog. L. VII. 23, πρὸς τὸν κεχρισμένον τῷ μύρῳ, τίς ἐστιν, ἔφη, ὁ γυναικὸς ὄζων; cf. Xen. Symp. II. 3.

42. Stob. Ecl. II. 31, 81, p. 215, 13 = Exc. e MS. Flor. Ion Damasc. p. II. c. 13, 81, Ζήνων ἐρωτηθεὶς πῶς ἄν τις νέος ἐλάχιστα ἁμαρτάνοι, εἰ πρὸ ὀφθαλμῶν ἔχει, ἔφη, οὓς μάλιστα τιμᾷ καὶ αἰσχύνεται.

43. Stob. Floril. 15, 12, Ζήνων πρὸς τοὺς ἀπολογουμένους ὑπὲρ τῆς αὑτῶν ἀσωτίας καὶ λέγοντας ἐκ πολλοῦ τοῦ περιόντος ἀναλίσκειν ἔλεγεν, ἦ που καὶ τοῖς μαγείροις συγγνώσεσθε, ἐὰν ἁλμυρὰ λέγωσι πεποιηκέναι τὰ ὄψα, ὅτι πλῆθος ἁλῶν αὐτοῖς ὑπῆρχεν;

44. Diog. L. VII. 17, ἐρωτικῶς δὲ διακείμενος Χρεμωνίδου, παρακαθιζόντων αὐτοῦ τε καὶ Κλεάνθους, ἀνέστη. θαυμάζοντος δὲ τοῦ Κλεάνθους, ἔφη, καὶ τῶν ἰατρῶν ἀκούω τῶν ἀγαθῶν κράτιστον εἶναι φάρμακον πρὸς τὰ φλεγμαίνοντα ἡσυχίαν.

For Chremonides cf. Introd. p. 6.

45. Diog. L. VII. 18, πρὸς δὲ τὸν φιλόπαιδα, οὔτε τοὺς διδασκάλους ἔφη φρένας ἔχειν, ἀεὶ διατρίβοντας ἐν παιδαρίοις, οὔτε ἐκείνους.

46. Stob. Floril. 17, 43, Ζήνων δὲ ὁ Κιτιεὺς οὐδὲ νοσῶν ᾤετο δεῖν τροφὴν προσφέρεσθαι τρυφερωτέραν, ἀλλ᾽ ἐπεὶ ὁ θεραπεύων ἰατρὸς ἐκέλευεν αὐτὸν φαγεῖν νεοττὸν περιστερᾶς, οὐκ ἀνασχόμενος, "ὡς Μανῆν," ἔφη, "μὲ θεράπευε."

Manes was a common slave's name, cf. Ar. Av. 522,

οὕτως ὑμᾶς πάντες πρότερον μεγάλους ἁγίους τ' ἐνόμιζον, νῦν δ' ἀνδράποδ', ἠλιθίους, Μανᾶς. See also Sandys on Dem. Or. 45 § 86, Or. 53 § 20. There is a reference here to the Stoic cosmopolitanism (frag. 162): for their views of slavery see Zeller p. 329.

47. Diog. L. VII. 17, ὡς δὲ Κυνικός τις οὐ φήσας ἔλαιον ἔχειν ἐν τῇ ληκύθῳ προσῄτησεν αὐτὸν οὐκ ἔφη δώσειν. ἀπελθόντα μέντοι ἐκέλευε σκέψασθαι ὁπότερος εἴη ἀναιδέστερος.

48. Athen. IX. 370 C, καὶ οὐ παράδοξον εἰ κατὰ τῆς κράμβης τινὲς ὤμνυον, ὁπότε καὶ Ζήνων ὁ Κιτιεὺς ὁ τῆς Στοᾶς κτίστωρ μιμούμενος τὸν κατὰ τῆς κυνὸς ὅρκον Σωκράτους καὶ αὐτὸς ὤμνυε τὴν κάππαριν, ὡς Ἔμποδός φησιν ἐν Ἀπομνημονεύμασιν, cf. Diog. L. VII. 32.

Ἔμποδος: on this very doubtful name see Müller, Frag. Hist. Gr. IV. 403, after whom Kaibel reads Ἔμπεδος.

49. Stob. Floril. 98, 68, Ζήνων ἔλεγεν οὐδενὸς ἡμᾶς οὕτω πένεσθαι ὡς χρόνου. βραχὺς γὰρ ὄντως ὁ βίος, ἡ δὲ τέχνη μακρή, καὶ μᾶλλον ἡ τὰς τῆς ψυχῆς νόσους ἰάσασθαι δυναμένη, cf. Diog. L. VII. 23, μηδενός τε ἡμᾶς οὕτως εἶναι ἐνδεεῖς ὡς χρόνου.

So Theophrastus ap. Cic. Tusc. III. 69.

50. Stob. Floril. Monac. 197, ὁ αὐτὸς (Ζήνων) ἐρωτηθεὶς τί ἔστι φίλος, ἄλλος οἷος ἐγώ. Diog. L. VII. 23, ἐρωτηθεὶς τίς ἔστι φίλος; ἄλλος, ἔφη, ἐγώ.

So Arist. Eth. N. ix. 4, 5, ἔστι γὰρ ὁ φίλος ἄλλος αὐτός, cf. Cic. Lael. § 80 verus amicus...est tamquam alter idem, ib. § 23 and Reid's note.

51. Origen adv. Cels. VIII. 35, p. 768, Ζήνων δὲ πρὸς τὸν εἰπόντα, ἀπολοίμην ἐὰν μή σε τιμωρήσωμαι, ἐγὼ δέ, εἶπεν, ἐὰν μή σε φίλον κτήσωμαι.

52. Diog. L. VII. 23, Διονυσίου δὲ τοῦ Μεταθεμένου εἰπόντος αὐτῷ διὰ τί αὐτὸν μόνον οὐ διορθοῖ; ἔφη, οὐ γάρ σοι πιστεύω.

For Dionysius cf. Diog. L. VII. 37, 166, 167. Cic. Fin. v. 94. Athen. VII. 281 D.

53. Seneca de Benef. IV. 39. 1, Quare ergo, inquit, Zeno vester, quum quingentos denarios cuidam promisisset et illum parum idoneum comperisset, amicis suadentibus ne crederet, perseveravit credere quia promiserat? Perhaps the same circumstance is alluded to in Themist. Or. XXI. 252 B, πότε ἀφῆκας τῷ δεδανεισμένῳ, καθάπερ Ζήνων ὁ Κιτιεύς.

54. Diog. L. VII. 23, δοῦλον ἐπὶ κλοπῇ, φασίν, ἐμαστίγου· τοῦ δ' εἰπόντος, εἵμαρτό μοι κλέψαι· καὶ δαρῆναι, ἔφη.

Seneca however says:—nullum servum fuisse Zenoni satis constat (Cons. Helv. 12. 3). To have no slave was a sign of abject poverty: see the comm. on Catull. XXIII. 1.

55. Diog. L. VII. 23, τῶν γνωρίμων τινὸς παιδάριον μεμωλωπισμένον θεασάμενος, πρὸς αὐτόν, ὁρῶ σου, ἔφη, τοῦ θυμοῦ τὰ ἴχνη.

56. Diog. L. VII. 28, 29, ἐτελεύτα δὴ οὕτως. ἐκ τῆς σχολῆς ἀπιὼν προσέπταισε καὶ τὸν δάκτυλον περιέρρηξε. παίσας δὲ τὴν γῆν τῇ χειρί, φησὶ τὸ ἐκ τῆς Νιόβης,

ἔρχομαι, τί μ' αὔεις;

καὶ παραχρῆμα ἐτελεύτησεν, ἀποπνίξας ἑαυτόν. Stob. Floril. VII. 45, Ζήνων, ὡς ἤδη γέρων ὢν πταίσας κατέπεσεν, "ἔρχομαι," εἶπε, "τί με αὔεις;" καὶ εἰσελθὼν ἑαυτὸν ἐξήγαγεν. Lucian Macrob. (LXII.) 19, Ζήνων δέ...ὅν φασιν εἰσερχόμενον εἰς τὴν ἐκκλησίαν καὶ προσπταίσαντα ἀναφθέγξασθαι, τί με βοᾶς; καὶ ὑποστρέψαντα οἴκαδε καὶ ἀποσχόμενον τροφῆς τελευτῆσαι τὸν βίον.

Νιόβης: the author of the play is uncertain. Both Aeschylus and Sophocles wrote plays with this title, but Nauck thinks the words belong to the Niobe of Timotheus: cf. Soph. frag. 395 (Dind.). The situation must have been similar to the concluding scene of the Oedipus Coloneus, where Oedipus is summoned by a mysterious voice: O. C. 1626 f.

57. Theodor. Metoch. p. 812, Kiessling, καὶ ὁ μὲν Ζήνων ἔλεγεν, ἦλθε, παρῆλθεν, οὐδὲν πρὸς ἐμὲ καθόλου, περὶ τῶν ἐνταῦθα πραγμάτων καὶ τοῦ βίου φιλοσοφῶν.

This recalls Marcus Aurelius, e.g. VI. 15.

THE FRAGMENTS OF CLEANTHES.

1. Diog. L. VII. 41, ὁ δὲ Κλεάνθης ἓξ μέρη φησί· διαλεκτικόν, ῥητορικόν, ἠθικόν, πολιτικόν, φυσικόν, θεολογικόν.

ἓξ μέρη. These are only subdivisions of the triple Zenonian division: thus διαλεκτικὸν and ῥητορικὸν together occupy the same ground as λογικόν (Diog. L. VII. 41 cited in Zeno frag. 6, where Cleanthes is probably meant). For his rhetorical writings see Introd. p. 50. Hirzel II. p. 170—178 tries to establish two points in connection with this statement, (1) that Cleanthes, unlike the other Stoics, believed in the unity and indivisibility of philosophy itself, but adopted six divisions for the purpose of exposition merely, and, (2) that the sixfold division is taken from Heraclitus, cf. Diog. L. IX. 5, εἰς τρεῖς λόγους εἴς τε τὸν περὶ τοῦ παντὸς καὶ τὸν πολιτικὸν καὶ τὸν θεολογικόν. But see Stein, Psych. n. 95, Erkenntnistheorie n. 206.

πολιτικόν. Similar is Aristotle's distinction between φρόνησις (practical thought) and πολιτική (Eth. VI. 8), in which chapter φρόνησις appears both as the general term and as a special subdivision dealing with the individual. The same may be said of ἠθικόν here.

θεολογικόν. Aristotle divides Speculative (θεωρητική) Philosophy into φυσική, μαθηματική, θεολογική (Metaph. V. 1, 10). The last-named branch is identical with πρώτη φιλοσοφία and is the best of the three, because its subject-matter is the most honourable (id. x. 7. 9). In the Stoic system it would have been impossible to follow out this distinction in practice, since their materialism was destructive of metaphysic, and it may be doubted whether θεολογικὸν does not simply refer to the treatment of popular religion appearing in the book περὶ θεῶν. The hymn to Zeus belongs to θεολογικόν rather than to φυσικόν.

LOGICA.

2. Epict. Diss. I. 17. 11, τὰ λογικὰ ἄλλων ἐστὶ διακριτικὰ καὶ ἐπισκεπτικὰ καί, ὡς ἄν τις εἴποι, μετρητικὰ καὶ στατικά. τίς λέγει ταῦτα; μόνος Χρύσιππος καὶ Ζήνων καὶ Κλεάνθης; See Zeno frag. 4.

3. Sext. Emp. Math. VII. 228, (τύπωσις) περὶ ἧς εὐθὺς καὶ διέστησαν· Κλεάνθης μὲν γὰρ τὴν τύπωσιν κατὰ εἰσοχήν τε καὶ ἐξοχήν, ὥσπερ καὶ διὰ τῶν δακτυλίων γιγνομένην τοῦ κηροῦ τύπωσιν. ib. 372, εἰ γὰρ τύπωσίς ἐστιν ἐν ψυχῇ ἡ φαντασία, ἤτοι κατ' ἐξοχὴν καὶ εἰσοχὴν τύπωσίς ἐστιν, ὡς οἱ περὶ τὸν Κλεάνθην νομίζουσιν, ἢ κατὰ ψιλὴν ἑτεροίωσιν γίνεται κ.τ.λ. ib. VIII. 400, Κλεάνθους μὲν κυρίως ἀκούοντος τὴν μετὰ εἰσοχῆς καὶ ἐξοχῆς νοουμένην (τύπωσιν). id. Pyrrh. II. 70, ἐπεὶ οὖν ἡ ψυχὴ καὶ τὸ ἡγεμονικὸν πνεῦμά ἐστιν ἢ λεπτομερέστερόν τι πνεύματος, ὥς φασιν, οὐ δυνήσεταί τις τύπωσιν ἐπινοεῖν ἐν αὐτῷ οὔτε κατ' ἐξοχὴν καὶ εἰσοχήν, ὡς ἐπὶ τῶν σφραγίδων ὁρῶμεν, οὔτε κατὰ τὴν τερατολογουμένην ἑτεροιωτικήν.

Zeno's definition of φαντασία (frag. 7) became a battle ground for his successors: Cleanthes explained τύπωσις as referring to a material impression like that made upon wax by a seal, cf. Philo de mund. opif. p. 114, Pfeiff., ᾧ (scil. νῷ) τὰ φανέντα ἐκτὸς εἴσω κομίζουσαι, διαγγέλλουσι καὶ ἐπιδείκνυνται τοὺς τύπους ἑκάστων, ἐνσφραγιζόμεναι τὸ ὅμοιον πάθος. κηρῷ γὰρ ἐοικώς, δέχεται τὰς διὰ τῶν αἰσθήσεων φαντασίας, αἷς τὰ σώματα καταλαμβάνει. Chrysippus however objected that, on this view, if the soul received at the same time the impression of a triangle and a square, the same body would at the same time have different shapes attached to it, and would become at the same time square and triangular (Sext. l.c., Diog. L. VII. 45—50); and he accordingly interpreted τύπωσις by ἑτεροίωσις and ἀλλοίωσις, cf. Cic. Tusc. I. 61 an imprimi, quasi ceram, animum putamus, et esse memoriam signatarum rerum in mente vestigia? Hirzel II. pp. 160—168 finds here also the influence of Heraclitus, who, he believes, is pointed at in Plat. Theaet. p. 191 foll., θὲς δή μοι λόγου ἕνεκα ἐν ταῖς ψυχαῖς ἡμῶν ἐνὸν κήρινον ἐκμαγεῖον κ.τ.λ. He relies however entirely on the disputed frag. κακοὶ μάρτυρες ἀνθρώποις ὀφθαλμοὶ καὶ ὦτα βαρβάρους ψυχὰς ἐχόντων, which Zeller interprets in exactly the opposite sense to that of Schuster and Hirzel. The point cannot therefore be regarded as established: see Stein, Erkenntnistheorie n. 734.

εἰσοχὴν...ἐξοχήν = concavity...convexity. Cf. Sext. Pyrrh. I. 92, αἱ γοῦν γραφαὶ τῇ μὲν ὄψει δοκοῦσιν εἰσοχὰς καὶ ἐξοχὰς ἔχειν, οὐ μὴν καὶ τῇ ἁφῇ, ib. I. 120. Plat. Rep. 602 D, καὶ ταῦτα καμπύλα τε καὶ εὐθέα ἐν ὕδασί τε θεωμένοις καὶ ἔξω, καὶ κοῖλά τε δὴ καὶ ἐξέχοντα διὰ τὴν περὶ τὰ χρώματα αὖ πλάνην τῆς ὄψεως.

δακτυλίων. For ancient Greek rings see Guhl and Koner, E. T. p. 182, with the illustrations, and for κηροῦ see on Zeno frag. 50. Hirzel l.c. shows that the metaphor was common, even apart from philosophic teaching: cf. Aesch. P. V. 789, δέλτοι φρενῶν, etc.

4. Plut. Plac. IV. 11, οἱ Στωικοί φασιν· ὅταν γεννηθῇ

ὁ ἄνθρωπος ἔχει τὸ ἡγεμονικὸν μέρος τῆς ψυχῆς ὥσπερ χάρτην εὔεργον (or ἐνεργόν) εἰς ἀπογραφήν· εἰς τοῦτο μίαν ἑκάστην τῶν ἐννοιῶν ἐναπογράφεται.

The grounds upon which this is referred to Cleanthes have been stated in the Introduction, p. 38, 39. For the further illustration and exposition of the passage the reader is referred to the exhaustive and interesting note of Stein, Erkenntnistheorie, p. 112, n. 230; but it may be as well here to set out two quotations from Philo, which make strongly in favour of the hypothesis that Cleanthes was the originator of the "tabula rasa" theory: cf. Philo, quod Deus sit immut. I. 9, p. 279 Mang., φαντασία δ᾽ ἔστι τύπωσις ἐν ψυχῇ, ἃ γὰρ εἰσήγαγεν ἑκάστη τῶν αἰσθήσεων, ὥσπερ δακτύλιός τις ἢ σφραγίς, ἐναπεμάξατο τὸν οἰκεῖον χαρακτῆρα· κηρῷ δὲ ἐοικὼς ὁ νοῦς. quis rer. div. haer. c. 37, p. 498 Mang., ἡ γὰρ ψυχὴ τὸ κήρινον, ὥς εἶπέ τις τῶν ἀρχαίων.

5. Olympiodorus l. c. on Zeno frag. 12, Κλεάνθης τοίνυν λέγει ὅτι τέχνη ἐστὶν ἕξις ὁδῷ πάντα ἀνύουσα. Quintil. Inst. Or. II. 17. 41, nam sive, ut Cleanthes voluit, ars est potestas, via, id est, ordine efficiens.

Cf. also Cic. Fin. III. 18, quoted on Zeno frag. 12. Olympiodorus objects that the definition is too wide, and that it would include φύσις which is not a τέχνη (cf. Cic. N.D. II. 81), but Cleanthes might have replied that neither is φύσις an ἕξις. For ἕξις cf. on διάθεσις Zeno frag. 117, and Stob. Ecl. II. 7, 5^k p. 73, 7, ἐν ἕξει δὲ οὐ μόνας εἶναι τὰς ἀρετάς, ἀλλὰ καὶ τὰς τέχνας τὰς ἐν τῷ σπουδαίῳ ἀνδρὶ ἀλλοιωθείσας ὑπὸ τῆς ἀρετῆς καὶ γενομένας ἀμεταπτώτους, οἱονεὶ γὰρ ἀρετὰς γίνεσθαι.

6. Syrian. ad Ar. Metaph. 892 b 14—23, ὡς ἄρα τὰ εἴδη παρὰ τοῖς θείοις τούτοις ἀνδράσιν (i.e. Socrates Plato

Parmenides and the Pythagoreans) οὔτε πρὸς τὴν ῥῆσιν τῆς τῶν ὀνομάτων συνηθείας παρήγετο, ὡς Χρύσιππος καὶ Ἀρχέδημος καὶ οἱ πλείους τῶν Στωικῶν ὕστερον ᾠήθησαν... οὐ μὴν οὐδ' ἐννοήματά εἰσι παρ' αὐτοῖς αἱ ἰδέαι, ὡς Κλεάνθης ὕστερον εἴρηκεν.

This difficult fragment has been variously interpreted. Wellmann, p. 480, and Krische, p. 421, think that Cleanthes described the ideas as "subjective Gedanken," in which case the fragment is a restatement of Zeno's view: cf. Zeno frag. 23. Stein discusses the passage at length (Erkenntnistheorie, pp. 293—295): reading νοήματα, he supposes that Cleanthes' words were οὔκ εἰσιν αἱ ἰδέαι νοήματα. Zeller also p. 85 has νοήματα. However ἐννοήματα appears in the Berlin Aristotle edited by Usener, and so Wachsmuth (Comm. II. p. 3) reads. Stein explains as follows:—νοήματα represent abstract rationalised knowledge resulting from our experience by the agency of ὀρθὸς λόγος. By such νοήματα are we made aware of the existence of the gods (frag. 52), and from these we must distinguish the class conceptions (Gattungsbegriffe) which have no scientific value. Class conceptions (ἐννοήματα) can never be the criterion of knowledge, since they have no real existence. Cf. Simpl. in Cat. f. 26 C: οὔτινα τὰ κοινὰ παρ' αὐτοῖς λέγεται. But, even assuming that the distinction between νόημα and ἐννόημα is well founded, which is by no means clear, and that νοήματα is to be read here, the context in Syrian is conclusive against Stein. The meaning simply is, "nor again are the ideas in Plato etc. to be treated as ἐννοήματα": in other words, the negative οὐδὲ is no part of Cleanthes' statement, but belongs to the commentator. This is abundantly clear from the following words:—οὐδ' ὡς Ἀντωνῖνος, μιγνὺς τὴν Λογγίνου καὶ Κλεάνθους δόξαν, τῷ νῷ παρυφίσταντο κατὰ τὰς ἐννοητικὰς ἰδέας.

7. Clem. Alex. Strom. VIII. 9. 26, 930 P, 332 S, λεκτὰ γὰρ τὰ κατηγορήματα καλοῦσι Κλεάνθης καὶ Ἀρχέδημος.

λεκτά: the abstractions contained in thoughts as expressed in speech, as opposed to thoughts on the one hand and the things thought of on the other (μέσον τοῦ τε νοήματος καὶ τοῦ πράγματος). Neither again are they identical with the spoken words, which are corporeal (Sext. Math. VIII. 75). Being incorporeal they can have no real existence, and yet the Stoics seem to have hesitated to deny their existence altogether. In the ordinary terminology of the school κατηγόρημα is a subdivision of λεκτόν, and is described as λεκτὸν ἐλλιπές (Diog. VII. 64). From this passage, then, we must infer that Cleanthes was the first to restrict κατηγόρημα to its narrower sense by the introduction of the new term λεκτόν. An example of κατηγόρημα given by Sextus is ἀψίνθιον πιεῖν (Pyrrh. II. 230), but a new term was required to denote the abstraction of a complete assertion (e.g. Cato ambulat), for which κατηγόρημα was obviously insufficient. For λεκτόν generally see Stein, Erkenntnistheorie, pp. 219—222.

Ἀρχέδημος: Zeller p. 50. The most important fact recorded about him is that he placed the ἡγεμονικὸν τοῦ κόσμου in the centre of the earth (Zeller p. 147).

8. Epict. Diss. II. 19. 1—4, ὁ κυριεύων λόγος ἀπὸ τοιούτων τινῶν ἀφορμῶν ἠρωτῆσθαι φαίνεται· κοινῆς γὰρ οὔσης μάχης τοῖς τρισὶ τούτοις πρὸς ἄλληλα, τῷ πᾶν παρεληλυθὸς ἀληθὲς ἀναγκαῖον εἶναι, καὶ τῷ δυνατῷ ἀδύνατον μὴ ἀκολουθεῖν, καὶ τῷ δυνατὸν εἶναι ὃ οὔτ' ἔστιν ἀληθὲς οὔτ' ἔσται· συνιδὼν τὴν μάχην ταύτην ὁ Διόδωρος τῇ τῶν πρώτων δυοῖν πιθανότητι συνεχρήσατο πρὸς παράστασιν τοῦ μηδὲν εἶναι δυνατὸν ὃ οὔτ' ἔστιν ἀληθὲς οὔτ' ἔσται. λοιπὸν ὁ μέν τις ταῦτα τηρήσει τῶν δυοῖν, ὅτι ἔστι τέ τι δυνατόν, ὃ οὔτ' ἔστιν ἀληθὲς οὔτ' ἔσται·

καὶ δυνατῷ ἀδύνατον οὐκ ἀκολουθεῖ· οὐ πᾶν δὲ παρεληλυθὸς ἀληθὲς ἀναγκαῖόν ἐστι· καθάπερ οἱ περὶ Κλεάνθην φέρεσθαι δοκοῦσιν, οἷς ἐπὶ πολὺ συνηγόρησεν Ἀντίπατρος. οἱ δὲ τἄλλα δύο, ὅτι δυνατόν τ' ἐστὶν ὃ οὔτ' ἔστιν ἀληθὲς οὔτ' ἔσται· καὶ πᾶν παρεληλυθὸς ἀληθὲς ἀναγκαῖόν ἐστιν· δυνατῷ δ' ἀδύνατον ἀκολουθεῖ. τὰ τρία δ' ἐκεῖνα τηρῆσαι ἀμήχανον, διὰ τὸ κοινὴν εἶναι αὐτῶν μάχην. Cic. de Fato 7. 14, omnia enim vera in praeteritis necessaria sunt, ut Chrysippo placet, dissentienti a magistro Cleanthe, quia sunt immutabilia nec in falsum e vero praeterita possunt convertere.

Three propositions are here mentioned, which are inconsistent with each other in such a way that the acceptance of any two involves the rejection of the third:—
(1) Every past truth is necessary. (2) That which is possible can never become impossible. (3) A thing may be possible which does not exist and never will exist. Diodorus asserted the truth of (1) and (2) and denied (3): thus Simplicius ad Cat. 65. 6—8 describes his followers as αὐτῇ τῇ ἐκβάσει κρίνοντες τὸ δυνατόν. Cic. Fam. IX. 4 (writing to Varro) περὶ δυνατῶν me scito κατὰ Διόδωρον κρίνειν. Quapropter, si venturus es, scito necesse esse te venire: sin autem non es, τῶν ἀδυνάτων est te venire. Cleanthes asserted the truth of (2) and (3) and denied (1). Chrysippus asserted the truth of (1) and (3) and denied (2), cf. Alexander ad An. Pr. I. 15 p. 34 a 10 Χρύσιππος δὲ λέγων μηδὲν κωλύειν καὶ δυνατῷ ἀδύνατον ἕπεσθαι κ.τ.λ. Cleanthes maintained therefore that it is and was possible for past events to have happened differently. See further on this controversy Grote's Plato vol. III. p. 495 foll. On p. 499 Hobbes is quoted, who is in agreement with Diodorus. The dilemma itself was originally propounded by Diodorus the Megarian, on whom see Zeller Socratics p. 252. It went by the name of ὁ κυριεύων λόγος =

argument getting the better of others : cf. Themist. Or. II. 30 b who mentions it together with ὁ κερατίνης as the discovery of Philo or Diodorus. In Lucian Vit. Auct. c. 22 Chrysippus professes his ability to teach it as well as the θερίζων Ἠλέκτρα and ἐγκεκαλυμμένος. Aul. Gell. I. 2. 4, κυριεύοντας ἡσυχάζοντας καὶ σωρείτας. Cleanthes wrote a special treatise on the subject (Introd. p. 50).

9. Quintil. Inst. Or. II. 15. 33—35. huic eius substantiae maxime conveniet finitio, rhetoricen esse bene dicendi scientiam. nam et orationis omnes virtutes semel complectitur, et protinus etiam mores oratoris, cum bene dicere non possit nisi bonus. idem valet Chrysippi finis ille ductus a Cleanthe, scientia recte dicendi (scil. rhetorice).

Kiderlin (Jahrb. f. Class. Phil. 131, p. 123) conjectures that the word Cleanthis has fallen out after substantiae, so that, while Cleanthes defined rhetoric as ἐπιστήμη τοῦ εὖ λέγειν, the words τοῦ ὀρθῶς λέγειν would be an alteration of Chrysippus. See however Striller Rhet. Sto. pp. 7, 8. For the usual Stoic definition cf. Diog. L. VII. 42, τήν τε ῥητορικήν, ἐπιστήμην οὖσαν τοῦ εὖ λέγειν περὶ τῶν ἐν διεξόδῳ λόγων where rhetoric is contrasted with dialectic, since dialectic was also defined as ἐπιστήμη τοῦ εὖ λέγειν by the Stoics (Alex. Aphr. Top. 3. 6, quoted by Stein, Erkenntnistheorie n. 210). Sext. Emp. Math. II. 6.

10. Varro de L. L. V. 9, quod si summum gradum non attigero, tamen secundum praeteribo, quod non solum ad Aristophanis sed etiam ad Cleanthis lucubravi [secundum explained in § 7 quo grammatica escendit antiqua, quae ostendit quemadmodum quodque poeta finxerit verbum confinxerit declinarit].

11. Athen. XI. 467 d, Κλεάνθης δὲ ὁ φιλόσοφος ἐν τῷ περὶ μεταλήψεως ἀπὸ τῶν κατασκευασάντων φησὶν ὀνομασθῆναι τήν τε θηρίκλειον κύλικα καὶ τὴν δεινιάδα. ib. 471 b, Κλεάνθης δ' ἐν τῷ περὶ μεταλήψεως συγγράμματί φησι, τὰ τοίνυν εὑρήματα, καὶ ὅσα τοιαῦτα ἔτι καὶ τὰ λοιπά ἐστι, οἷον θηρίκλειος, δεινιάς, Ἰφικρατίς, ταῦτα [γὰρ] πρότερον συνιστόρει τοὺς εὑρόντας, φαίνεται δ' ἔτι καὶ νῦν· εἰ δὲ μὴ ποιεῖ τοῦτο, μεταβεβληκὸς ἂν εἴη μικρὸν τοὔνομα. ἀλλά, καθάπερ εἴρηται, οὐκ ἔστι πιστεῦσαι τῷ τυχόντι.

μεταλήψεως: the meaning of this word seems to be that explained by Quintil. VIII. 6. 37, superest ex his, quae aliter significent, μετάληψις, id est, transumtio, quae ex alio in aliud velut viam praestat: tropus et varissimus et maxime improprius, Graecis tamen frequentior, qui Centaurum Chirona, et νήσους (? ναῦς) θοὰς ὀξείας dicunt. Nos quis ferat, si Verrem suem aut Laelium doctum nominemus? cf. Arist. Top. VI. 11, p. 149 a 6.

θηρίκλειον: a kind of drinking cup, said to be named after Thericles, a Corinthian potter of some celebrity, and, according to Bentley on Phalaris § 3, a contemporary of Aristophanes. Welcker, however (Rhein. Mus. VI. 404 foll.), maintains that these cups were so called because they were decorated with the figures of animals.

δεινιάς and **Ἰφικρατὶς** are the names given to particular kinds of slippers, the latter of which was so called after the celebrated Athenian general. Cf. Poll. VII. 89, ἀπὸ δὲ τῶν χρησαμένων Ἰφικρατίδες, Δεινιάδες, Ἀλκιβιάδια, Σμινδυρίδια, Μυνάκια ἀπὸ Μυνάκου. Diod. Sic. XV. 44, τάς τε ὑποδέσεις τοῖς στρατιώταις εὐλύτους καὶ κούφας ἐποίησε, τὰς μέχρι τοῦ νῦν ἰφικρατίδας ἀπ' ἐκείνου καλουμένας. Alciphr. Ep. III. 57, ἔναγχος Κρονίων ἐνστάντων Ἰφικρατίδας μοι νεουργεῖς ἔπεμψε. Becker's Charicles E. T. p. 450, Müller Handbuch IV. 428.

γάρ is expunged by Meineke, whom Wachsm. follows.

συνιστόρει is read by Casaubon for συνιστορεῖν. It seems to mean "connoted."

εἰ δὲ μή tr. "if it does not do this, the word must have changed somewhat." For the tense cf. Dem. xxx. 10. Timocrates and Onetor were both men of substance ὥστ᾽ οὐκ ἂν διὰ τοῦτό γ᾽ εἶεν οὐκ εὐθὺς δεδωκότες.

PHYSICA.

12. Diog. L. VII. 134, δοκεῖ δ᾽ αὐτοῖς ἀρχὰς εἶναι τῶν ὅλων δύο, τὸ ποιοῦν καὶ τὸ πάσχον. τὸ μὲν οὖν πάσχον εἶναι τὴν ἄποιον οὐσίαν τὴν ὕλην, τὸ δὲ ποιοῦν τὸν ἐν αὐτῇ λόγον τὸν θεόν. τοῦτον γὰρ ἀΐδιον ὄντα διὰ πάσης αὐτῆς δημιουργεῖν ἕκαστα. τίθησι δὲ τὸ δόγμα τοῦτο... Κλεάνθης ἐν τῷ περὶ ἀτόμων. See Zeno frag. 35.

13. Tertull. Apol. 21, haec (quae Zeno dixit λόγον esse cf. Zeno frag. 44) Cleanthes in spiritum congerit quem permeatorem universitatis affirmat.

spiritum = πνεῦμα. So far as the evidence serves, Cleanthes was the first to explain the Heraclitean πῦρ as πνεῦμα. While not refusing to admit that Zeno's aether is an emanation from the Godhead (see on frag. 15), he differs from Zeno in identifying God with the sun, as the ruling part of the universe, and the ultimate source of the "Urpneuma." Stein Psych. p. 68. Hirzel's account is inconsistent: at p. 211 he attributes πνεῦμα to Chrysippus and restricts Cleanthes to πῦρ, while at p. 216 he allows that Cleanthes introduced the conception of πνεῦμα.

permeatorem. Gk. διήκειν Zeno frag. 37, probably indicates that Cl. accepted κρᾶσις δι᾽ ὅλων, cf. Alex. Aphrod. de Mixt. 142 a, ἡνῶσθαι τὴν σύμπασαν οὐσίαν, πνεύματός τινος διὰ πάσης αὐτῆς διήκοντος, ὑφ' οὗ συνάγεται καὶ συμμένει.

14. Stob. Ecl. I. 1. 29^b p. 34, 20, Διογένης καὶ Κλεάνθης καὶ Οἰνοπίδης (τὸν θεὸν) τὴν τοῦ κόσμου ψυχήν. Cic. N. D. I. 37, tum totius naturae menti atque animo tribuit hoc nomen. Minuc. Octav. XIX. 10, Theophrastus et Zeno et Chrysippus et Cleanthes sunt et ipsi multiformes, sed ad unitatem providentiae omnes revolvuntur. Cleanthes enim mentem modo animum modo aethera plerumque rationem Deum disseruit.

Cleanthes teaches the exact correspondence between the microcosm of the individual and the macrocosm of the world: there is therefore in the world a ruling principle analogous to the soul of man. Sext. Math. IX. 120, ὥστε ἐπεὶ καὶ ὁ κόσμος ὑπὸ φύσεως διοικεῖται πολυμερὴς καθεστώς, εἴη ἄν τι ἐν αὐτῷ τὸ κυριεῦον καὶ τὸ προκαταρχόμενον τῶν κινήσεων. οὐδὲν δὲ δυνατὸν εἶναι τοιοῦτον ἢ τὴν τῶν ὄντων φύσιν, ἥτις θεός ἐστιν. ἔστιν ἄρα θεός.

15. Cic. N. D. I. 37, tum ultimum et altissimum atque undique circumfusum et extremum omnia cingentem atque complexum ardorem, qui aether nominetur, certissimum deum judicat. Lactant. Inst. I. 5, Cleanthes et Anaximenes aethera dicunt esse summum Deum (quoting in support Verg. Georg. II. 325).

According to Krische, p. 428—430, Cicero has here made a blunder by importing an explanation of his own into the Greek original θεὸν εἶναι τὸν αἰθέρα, and by a confusion of the two senses in which αἰθήρ is used in the Stoic School (1) = πῦρ τεχνικόν, (2) = the fiery zone surrounding the world. Cleanthes, as will be presently seen, disagreeing with the rest of the school, regarded the sun and not the belt of aether as the ἡγεμονικόν, or, in popular language, as the abode of God (Cic. Acad. II. 126). Cleanthes therefore only meant to affirm the identity of θεός and the πῦρ τεχνικόν. This may be true, but the reasoning is not conclusive. Apart from the word certissimum, which is not important, there is no reason why Cleanthes should not have attributed divinity to the ultimus omnia cingens aether, just in the same manner as he does to the stars, where Krische feels no difficulty. Similarly Stein, Psychol. n. 99: the aether emanates from the "Urpneuma" and is a divine power, but not God himself.

ultimum i.e. farthest removed from the earth which is in the centre of the universe. Zeno, frag. 67. Cic. N. D. II. 41. 117. Diog. VII. 37.

16. Philod. περὶ εὐσεβ. c. 9, λόγον ἡγούμενον τῶν ἐν τῷ κόσμῳ. Cic. N. D. I. 37, tum nihil ratione censet esse divinius.

This, it should be remembered, is in direct opposition to the teaching of Epicurus, who speaks of the world as φύσει ἀλόγῳ ἐκ τῶν ἀτόμων συνεστῶτα (Stob. Ecl. I. 21. 3^c p. 183, 10).

17. Cic. N. D. I. 37, Cleanthes...tum ipsum mundum deum dicit esse. Cf. N. D. II. 34. 45.

See Krische p. 424—426, according to whom we are to interpret mundum here in the first of the three senses specified by Diog. L. VII. 137, 138, ἔστι κόσμος ὁ ἰδίως ποιὸς τῆς τῶν ὅλων οὐσίας. Cf. Chrysippus ap. Stob. Ecl. I. 21. 5, p. 184, 11, λέγεται δ' ἑτέρως κόσμος ὁ θεός, καθ' ὃν ἡ διακόσμησις γίνεται καὶ τελειοῦται. In any case, we have here a distinct statement that Cleanthes was a pantheist, and identified God with matter. The different meanings given to κόσμος in effect amount to this that it may be regarded either as the sum total of all existence, or as the transitory and derivative part of existence: the distinction, however, as Zeller observes, is only a relative one (see his remarks p. 159). For pantheism as advocated by Cleanthes see Hirzel II. p. 206. Stein, Psychol. p. 67 and n. 98.

18. Chalcid. in Tim. c. 144, ex quo fieri ut quae secundum fatum sunt etiam ex providentia sint. eodemque modo quae secundum providentiam ex fato, ut Chrysippus putat. alii vero quae quidem ex providentiae auctoritate, fataliter quoque provenire, nec tamen quae fataliter ex providentia, ut Cleanthes.

Zeno had affirmed the identity of εἱμαρμένη and πρόνοια (frag. 45), but omitted to discuss the difficulties involved in so broad an explanation of fatalistic doctrine. Cleanthes felt the difficulty that κακόν could not be said to exist κατὰ πρόνοιαν, even if it existed καθ' εἱμαρμένην. This point will recur in the Hymn to Zeus frag. 46, l. 17, οὐδέ τι γίνεται ἔργον ἐπὶ χθονὶ σοῦ δίχα δαῖμον...πλὴν ὁπόσα ῥέζουσι κακοὶ σφετέρῃσιν ἀνοίαις, where we shall have to discuss the nature of the solution which he offered. In support of the position here taken up by Chrysippus cf. id. ap. Plut. Sto. Rep. 34, 3, κατὰ τοῦτον δὲ τὸν λόγον τὰ παραπλήσια ἐροῦμεν καὶ περὶ τῆς ἀρετῆς ἡμῶν καὶ περὶ τῆς κακίας καὶ τὸ ὅλον τῶν τεχνῶν καὶ τῶν ἀτέχνων...οὐθὲν γάρ ἐστιν ἄλλως τῶν κατὰ μέρος γίγνεσθαι οὐδὲ τοὐλάχιστον ἀλλ' ἢ κατὰ τὴν κοινὴν φύσιν καὶ τὸν ἐκείνης λόγον. id. Comm. Not. 34, 5, εἰ δὲ οὐδὲ τοὐλάχιστον ἔστι τῶν μερῶν ἔχειν ἄλλως ἀλλ' ἢ κατὰ τὴν τοῦ Διὸς βούλησιν. Chrysippus also defined εἱμαρμένη as λόγος τῶν ἐν τῷ κόσμῳ προνοίᾳ διοικουμένων. The Sceptic objections on this head are put very clearly in Sext. Pyrrh. III. 9—12.

19. Philo de provid. II. 74 p. 94 Aucher: (astra erratica) nota sunt non solum ratione verum etiam sensu ita movente providentia, quae, ut dicit Chrysippus et Cleanthes, nihil praetermisit pertinentium ad certiorem utilioremque dispensationem. quod si aliter melius esset dispensari res mundi, eo modo sumpsisset compositionem, qua tenus nihil occurreret ad impediendum deum.

I have taken this fragment from Gercke (Chrysippea p. 708).

quae nihil praetermisit...Much of the Stoic exposition in the 2nd book of Cicero's de Natura Deorum is a commentary on this. Thus for astra erratica cf. § 103 foll. and esp. § 104, ergo, *ut oculis adsidue videmus*, sine ulla mutatione et varietate cetera labuntur...caelestia... quorum contemplatione nullius expleri potest animus naturae constantiam videre cupientis. Generally cf. M. Anton. II. 3, τὰ τῆς τύχης οὐκ ἄνευ φύσεως ἢ συγκλώσεως καὶ ἐπιπλοκῆς τῶν προνοίᾳ διοικουμένων· πάντα ἐκεῖθεν ῥεῖ· πρόσεστι δὲ τὸ ἀναγκαῖον, καὶ τὸ τῷ ὅλῳ κόσμῳ συμφέρον, οὗ μέρος εἶ.

qua tenus...At the same time we find elsewhere a chain argument of Chrysippus in Alex. de fato c. 37 p. 118 οὐ πάντα μὲν ἔστι καθ' εἱμαρμένην, οὐκ ἔστι δὲ ἀκώλυτος καὶ ἀπαρεμπόδιστος ἡ τοῦ κόσμου διοίκησις κ.τ.λ. But inconsistency was inevitable in this matter, when Chrysippus could account for the existence of evil by saying (Plut. Sto. Rep. 36. 1) κακίαν δὲ καθόλου ἆραι οὔτε δυνατόν ἐστιν οὔτ' ἔχει καλῶς ἀρθῆναι. See Zeller's lucid exposition pp. 176—193.

20. Probus ad Verg. Ecl. 6. 31, p. 10, 33, Omnem igitur hanc rerum naturae formam tenui primum et inani mole dispersam refert in quattuor elementa concretam et ex his omnia esse postea effigiata Stoici tradunt

Zenon Citiaeus et Speusippus (leg. Chrysippus) Soleus et Cleanthes Thasius (leg. Assius). See on Zeno frag. 52.

21. Hermiae Irris. Gent. Phil. 14, Diels p. 654, ἀλλ' ὁ Κλεάνθης ἀπὸ τοῦ φρέατος ἐπάρας τὴν κεφαλὴν καταγελᾷ σοῦ τοῦ δόγματος καὶ αὐτὸς ἀνιμᾷ τὰς ἀληθεῖς ἀρχὰς θεὸν καὶ ὕλην. καὶ τὴν μὲν γῆν μεταβάλλειν εἰς ὕδωρ, τὸ δὲ ὕδωρ εἰς ἀέρα τὸν δὲ ἀέρα <εἰς πῦρ> φέρεσθαι, τὸ δὲ πῦρ εἰς τὰ περίγεια χωρεῖν, τὴν δὲ ψυχὴν δι' ὅλου τοῦ κόσμου διήκειν, ἧς μέρος μετέχοντας ἡμᾶς ἐμψυχοῦσθαι.

φρέατος. This is explained by the anecdote related by Diog. VII. 168, διεβοήθη δὲ ἐπὶ φιλοπονίᾳ, ὅς γε πένης ὢν ἄγαν ὥρμησε μισθοφορεῖν· καὶ νύκτωρ μὲν ἐν τοῖς κήποις ἤντλει, μεθ' ἡμέραν δ' ἐν τοῖς λόγοις ἐγυμνάζετο· ὅθεν καὶ Φρεάντλης ἐκλήθη. The same idea is kept up by ἀνιμᾷ i.e. "hauls up."

καὶ τὴν μὲν γῆν κ.τ.λ. This constant interchange of the various elements is not so strongly brought out in the Stoic system as it was by Heraclitus with his formula πάντα ῥεῖ. Cf. Krische p. 387. It is however always implied, cf. Chrysipp. ap. Stob. Ecl. I. 10. 16^e p. 129, 18, πρώτης μὲν γιγνομένης τῆς ἐκ πυρὸς κατὰ σύστασιν εἰς ἀέρα μεταβολῆς, δευτέρας δ' ἀπὸ τούτου εἰς ὕδωρ, τρίτης δὲ ἔτι μᾶλλον κατὰ τὸ ἀνάλογον συνισταμένου τοῦ ὕδατος εἰς γῆν. πάλιν δ' ἀπὸ ταύτης διαλυομένης καὶ διαχεομένης πρώτη μὲν γίγνεται χύσις εἰς ὕδωρ, δευτέρα δ' ἐξ ὕδατος εἰς ἀέρα, τρίτη δὲ καὶ ἐσχάτη εἰς πῦρ. Cic. N. D. II. 84, et cum quattuor genera sint corporum, vicissitudine eorum mundi continuata natura est. Nam ex terra aqua, ex aqua oritur aër, ex aëre aether, deinde retrorsum vicissim ex aethere aër, inde aqua, ex aqua terra infima. Sic naturis his, ex quibus omnia constant, sursus deorsus, ultro citro commeantibus mundi partium coniunctio continetur. For Heraclitus see R. and P. § 29.

εἰς πῦρ. Some words must be supplied here: Diels inserts ἄνω.

τὸ δὲ πῦρ: the reverse process is concisely stated.

ἧς μέρος μετέχοντας: for the divine origin of the human soul see Stein Psych. p. 96, n. 169.

22. Stob. Ecl. I. 20, 1ᵉ p. 171, 2, Ζήνωνι καὶ Κλεάνθει καὶ Χρυσίππῳ ἀρέσκει τὴν οὐσίαν μεταβάλλειν οἷον εἰς σπέρμα τὸ πῦρ, καὶ πάλιν ἐκ τούτου τοιαύτην ἀποτελεῖσθαι τὴν διακόσμησιν, οἵα πρότερον ἦν. See Zeno frag. 54.

23. Philo, Incorr. Mundi p. 954, μεταβάλλειν γὰρ ἢ εἰς φλόγα ἢ εἰς αὐγὴν ἀναγκαῖον· εἰς μὲν φλόγα, ὡς ᾤετο Κλεάνθης, εἰς δ' αὐγήν, ὡς ὁ Χρύσιππος.

Philo is arguing that when everything becomes fire, it must burn itself out and cannot be created anew, but there is no importance in his objection, as he is confounding the πῦρ τεχνικὸν with πῦρ ἄτεχνον. φλόξ and αὐγὴ therefore alike express what Numenius, speaking of the school in general, calls πῦρ αἰθερῶδες i.e. πῦρ τεχνικόν (Euseb. P. E. xv. 18. 1). What then is the meaning of the divergence? Stein believes that we have here a piece of evidence showing a substantial disagreement in the views taken by Cleanthes and Chrysippus of the ἐκπύρωσις and that φλόξ is used with reference to the Sun (see on frag. 24), and αὐγὴ as a representation of the finest aether. For the connection of φλόξ with ἥλιος he quotes Diog. L. VII. 27, Aesch. Pers. 497, Soph. Trach. 693, O. T. 1425 (Stein, Psychologie pp. 70, 71 and the notes). Hirzel's explanation is similar (II. p. 211), except that he does not see any reference to the sun: according to him, Cleanthes spoke of a permeating πῦρ for which πνεῦμα was substituted by Chrysippus: but see on frag. 13. For φλόγα cf. ἐκφλογισθέντος in frag. 24.

24. Stob. Ecl. I. 17. 3, p. 153, 7, Κλεάνθης δὲ οὕτω πώς φησιν· ἐκφλογισθέντος τοῦ παντὸς συνίζειν τὸ μέσον αὐτοῦ πρῶτον, εἶτα τὰ ἐχόμενα ἀποσβέννυσθαι δι' ὅλου. τοῦ δὲ παντὸς ἐξυγρανθέντος τὸ ἔσχατον τοῦ πυρός, ἀντιτυπήσαντος αὐτῷ τοῦ μέσου, τρέπεσθαι πάλιν εἰς τοὐναντίον, εἶθ' οὕτω τρεπόμενον ἄνω φησὶν αὔξεσθαι καὶ ἄρχεσθαι διακοσμεῖν τὸ ὅλον· καὶ τοιαύτην περίοδον αἰεὶ καὶ διακόσμησιν ποιουμένου τὸν ἐν τῇ τῶν ὅλων οὐσίᾳ τόνον μὴ παύεσθαι. ὥσπερ γὰρ ἑνός τινος τὰ μέρη πάντα φύεται ἐκ σπερμάτων ἐν τοῖς καθήκουσι χρόνοις, οὕτω καὶ τοῦ ὅλου τὰ μέρη, ὧν καὶ τὰ ζῷα καὶ τὰ φυτὰ ὄντα τυγχάνει, ἐν τοῖς καθήκουσι χρόνοις φύεται. καὶ ὥσπερ τινὲς λόγοι τῶν μερῶν εἰς σπέρμα συνιόντες μίγνυνται καὶ αὖθις διακρίνονται γινομένων τῶν μερῶν, οὕτως ἐξ ἑνός τε πάντα γίνεσθαι καὶ ἐκ πάντων εἰς ἓν συγκρίνεσθαι, ὁδῷ καὶ συμφώνως διεξιούσης τῆς περιόδου.

The explanation of the first part of this difficult fragment appears to be as follows:—When everything has been set on fire and the tendency of all things to become absorbed in the πῦρ ἀειζῶον has been satisfied, the reaction commences in the centre, and spreads towards the extremities until everything except the outer rim is in a watery mass. Seneca, N. Q. III. 13. 1, nihil relinqui... aliud, igne restincto, quam humorem. In hoc futuri mundi spem latere. Then the remaining portions of the original fire, concentrated in the sun (Stein p. 71), in spite of resistance from the centre, begin to exert their creative influence, and by their ever-increasing activity, the elements and the world are formed. Phenomenal existence, then, is possible only when the tightening and slackening influences are in equilibrium or nearly so; the exclusive predominance of either destroys the balance of the universe. The centre of the σφαῖρος is always readier to admit the loosening of tension, while the bracing invigorating vivifying power, which knits together the frame of the universe as of the individual, is in fullest sway in the parts at the circumference (hence ἄνω αὔξεσθαι). This is the theory of tension as applied to the διακόσμησις, and its statement constitutes the most important contribution made by Cleanthes to Stoicism. A difficulty in the above exposition remains to be stated:—Why is there no created world in the period between ἐκπύρωσις and ἐξύγρωσις, as there must then be a time when the two influences are of equal strength? The answer, perhaps, is that during the whole of this period there is an ever-increasing slackening of tension, as the fire of the ἐκπύρωσις is gradually extinguished, and slackening of tension produces not life but death (Plut. plac. v. 24 etc.); the creation of the world only starts when τὸ ἔσχατον τοῦ πυρὸς τρέπεται εἰς τοὐναντίον. There is also a divergent view, namely, that the destruction of the world may be compassed by κατακλυσμός as well as by ἐκπύρωσις. This implies that our world can exist during the transition towards ἐξύγρωσις. Cf. Sen. N. Q. III. 29. 1 and Heraclit. Alleg. Hom. c. 25, p. 53, quoted by Zeller p. 169, 1. Schol. on Lucan VII. 813 ἐκπύρωσις, quam secuturam κατακλυσμούς adserunt Stoici, seems to have been overlooked, but is of doubtful import. Stein's account of the διακόσμησις (Psych. p. 32 foll.) is radically different, but I do not see how it can be reconciled with this passage: (1) the creation of the world is due to a slackening of tension in the original fiery substance, and (2) τὸ ἔσχατον τοῦ πυρός is what remains of the original "Urpneuma" after the four elements have been formed, whereas according to Cleanthes the creation of the world only begins when this remnant of fire begins to exert its influence. Hirzel discusses the present passage at some length (Untersuchungen II. p. 124—134). He strongly insists that τὸ ἔσχατον means extremum (das Feuer des Umkreises) and not reliquum, and that Philo περὶ ἀφθ. κόσμου 18, (μετὰ τὴν ἐκπύρωσιν ἐπειδὰν ὁ νέος κόσμος μέλλῃ δημιουργεῖσθαι σύμπαν μὲν τὸ πῦρ οὐ σβέννυται ποσὴ δέ τις αὐτοῦ μοῖρα ὑπολείπεται) follows Chrysippus and not Cleanthes. It would seem, however, that the distinction is not important, as ἔσχατον must in this case be both extremum and reliquum. Further on he suggests that Cleanthes did not maintain the doctrine of the four elements, but cf. frag. 21. Two possible anticipations of the tension theory have been noticed in Zeno's fragments, but the passage in frag. 56 is probably spurious, while in frag. 67, even if τείνεσθαι is sound, Zeno is confessedly dealing with another point, viz. the explanation of how the separate parts of the κόσμος are kept in one solid mass and why they are not scattered into the void. Ogereau p. 10 attributes the introduction of τόνος to Zeno, and depreciates the performances of Cleanthes (p. 19); but he insists throughout too strongly on the unity of the school, without considering its historical development.

τὸ μέσον, cf. Stob. Ecl. I. 21, 3^b p. 183, 3, ἀπὸ γῆς δὲ ἄρξασθαι τὴν γένεσιν τοῦ κόσμου, καθάπερ ἀπὸ κέντρου, ἀρχὴ δὲ σφαίρας τὸ κέντρον.

ἐξυγρανθέντος, cf. Diog. L. VII. 135, 136 quoted on Zeno frag. 52.

τρεπομένου. MSS. corr. Canter.

τὸν...τόνον. The MSS. have τοῦ...τόνου. The reading in the text is due to Mein., whom Wachsm. now follows, although he formerly (Comm. II. p. 11) kept the MSS. reading, removing the colon after ὅλον and inserting commas after καὶ and τόνου. There is some mistake in Stein's note on this point, Psychol. n. 41.

ἐκ σπερμάτων. Cf. Zeno frag. 54 = Cleanth. frag. 22, and see Ritter and Preller § 402.

λόγοι was unnecessarily suspected by the older edd. of Stobaeus. The conj. τόνοι is tempting, but Wachsm. quotes Marc. Aurel. IX. 1, ὥρμησεν (ἡ φύσις) ἐπὶ τήνδε τὴν διακόσμησιν συλλαβοῦσά τινας λόγους τῶν ἐσομένων κ.τ.λ. The best parallel is Zeno frag. 106, which puts the text beyond dispute. τινὲς λόγοι τῶν μερῶν = certain proportions of the constituent parts of the soul.

γινομένων P. γεινομένων F, whence γενομένων Mein. Wachsm. Diels: but the present, accepted by Hirzel II. p. 126, seems preferable.

εἰς is bracketed by Diels and Wachsm.

25. Plut. Comm. Not. 31, 10, ἔτι τοίνυν ἐπαγωνιζόμενος ὁ Κλεάνθης τῇ ἐκπυρώσει λέγει τὴν σελήνην καὶ τὰ λοιπὰ ἄστρα τὸν ἥλιον ἐξομοιώσειν πάντα ἑαυτῷ, καὶ μεταβαλεῖν εἰς ἑαυτόν.

As the sun is, according to Cleanthes, the ἡγεμονικὸν τοῦ κόσμου, the πῦρ ἀείζωον may be supposed to exist there in its purest form (cf. the authorities cited by Zeller, Stoics p. 204, 3, Krische p. 386), and to this the moon and the other stars will be assimilated at the ἐκπύρωσις.

ἐξομοιώσειν. MSS. have ἐξομοιῶσαι corr. Zeller, p. 165, n. 4.

26. Stob. Ecl. I. 15, 6ᵃ p. 146, 19, Κλεάνθης μόνος τῶν Στωικῶν τὸ πῦρ ἀπεφήνατο κωνοειδές.

Presumably this refers to the fire of the revolving aether, for the doctrine appears to be borrowed from the Pythagoreans cf. Stob. Ecl. I. 15, 6ᵃ p. 146, 14, οἱ ἀπὸ Πυθαγόρου...μόνον τὸ ἀνώτατον πῦρ κωνοειδές. This is supposed to refer to the Milky Way (Zeller, pre-Socratics, I. p. 466 n. 2), cf. infra frags. 32, 33.

27. Plut. de facie in orbe lunae c. 6, 3, ὥσπερ

Ἀρίσταρχον ᾤετο δεῖν Κλεάνθης τὸν Σάμιον ἀσεβείας προσκαλεῖσθαι τοὺς Ἕλληνας, ὡς κινοῦντα τοῦ κόσμου τὴν ἑστίαν, ὅτι <τὰ> φαινόμενα σώζειν ἀνὴρ ἐπειρᾶτο, μένειν τὸν οὐρανὸν ὑποτιθέμενος, ἐξελίττεσθαι δὲ κατὰ λοξοῦ κύκλου τὴν γῆν, ἅμα καὶ περὶ τὸν αὐτῆς ἄξονα δινουμένην.

This comes from the treatise πρὸς Ἀρίσταρχον: Introd. p. 51.

Ἀρίσταρχον: the celebrated mathematician. For the theory here attacked cf. Sext. Math. x. 174, οἵ γε μὴν τὴν τοῦ κόσμου κίνησιν ἀνελόντες τὴν δὲ γῆν κινεῖσθαι δοξάσαντες, ὡς οἱ περὶ Ἀρίσταρχον τὸν μαθηματικόν κ.τ.λ. Stob. Ecl. I. 25, 3^k p. 212, 2, Ἀρίσταρχος τὸν ἥλιον ἵστησι μετὰ τῶν ἀπλανῶν τὴν δὲ γῆν κινεῖσθαι περὶ τὸν ἡλιακὸν κύκλον. (This also illustrates κατὰ λοξοῦ κύκλου.) It appears however to be doubtful whether Aristarchus propounded this view otherwise than hypothetically: cf. Plut. quaest. Plat. VIII. 1, 2, 3.

ἀσεβείας προσκαλεῖσθαι. For the γραφὴ ἀσεβείας see Attischer Process ed. Lipsius, pp. 366—375, and cf. the case of Anaxagoras (ib. p. 370). Every γραφή, as well as an ordinary civil action, commenced with the πρόσκλησις or writ of summons (ib. p. 770 f.).

ἑστίαν: alluding to the central position of the earth. Aesch. Ag. 1056 ἑστίας μεσομφάλου, Virg. Aen. II. 512 aedibus in mediis nudoque sub aetheris axe ingens ara fuit. It is possible that Cleanthes had in his mind the Pythagorean description of the central fire as ἑστία τοῦ παντός: see Dr Thompson on Phaedr. 247 A, μένει γὰρ Ἑστία ἐν θεῶν οἴκῳ μόνη.

τὰ φαινόμενα σώζειν: "to save appearances:" for which phrase see Prof. Mayor in Journ. Phil. VI. 171.

28. Euseb. P. E. xv. 15. 7, Ar. Did. fr. 29 ap. Diels, p. 465, ἡγεμονικὸν δὲ τοῦ κόσμου Κλεάνθει μὲν ἤρεσε τὸν ἥλιον εἶναι διὰ τὸ μέγιστον τῶν ἄστρων ὑπάρχειν καὶ πλεῖστα συμβάλλεσθαι πρὸς τὴν τῶν ὅλων διοίκησιν, ἡμέραν καὶ ἐνιαυτὸν ποιοῦντα καὶ τὰς ἄλλας ὥρας. Censorin. frag. 1, 4, et constat quidem quattuor elementis terra aqua igne aere. cuius principalem solem quidam putant, ut Cleanthes. Diog. VII. 139. Stob. Ecl. I. 21. 6^e p. 187, 4, Κλεάνθης ὁ Στωικὸς ἐν ἡλίῳ ἔφησεν εἶναι τὸ ἡγεμονικὸν τοῦ κόσμου. Cic. Acad. II. 126, Cleanthes, qui quasi majorum est gentium Stoicus, Zenonis auditor, solem dominari et rerum potiri putat.

There is no warrant whatever for Krische's suggestion (p. 435), that Cleanthes probably ("wahrscheinlich") adopted the Heraclitean theory of the daily renewal of the sun: everything points the other way. At the same time, the important position assigned to the sun was probably due to his Heraclitean studies (see Introd. p. 50), for, though Heraclitus himself did not maintain this doctrine, we read of the Heraclitean school in Plat. Cratyl. 413 B, τὸν ἥλιον...διαΐοντα καὶ κάοντα ἐπιτροπεύειν τὰ ὄντα. Cf. Pliny, N. H. II. 12 (cited by Hirzel, II. p. 138).

29. Stob. Ecl. I. 25. 3ⁱ p. 211, 18, Κλεάνθης ἄναμμα νοερὸν τὸ ἐκ θαλάττης τὸν ἥλιον. περὶ δὲ τῶν τροπῶν φασι κατὰ τὸ διάστημα τῆς ὑποκειμένης τροφῆς· ὠκεανὸς δ' ἐστὶ *** ἧς τὴν ἀναθυμίασιν ἐπινέμεται. συγκαταφέρεσθαι δὲ τὸν ἥλιον κινούμενον ἕλικα ἐν τῇ σφαίρᾳ, ἀπὸ τοῦ ἰσημερινοῦ ἐπί τε ἄρκτου καὶ νότου, ἅπερ ἐστὶ πέρατα τῆς ἕλικος. Cic. N. D. III. 37, Quid enim? non eisdem vobis placet omnem ignem pastus indigere nec permanere ullo modo posse, nisi alitur: ali autem solem, lunam, reliqua astra aquis, alia dulcibus, alia marinis? eamque causam Cleanthes adfert cur se sol referat nec longius progrediatur solstitiali orbi itemque brumali, ne longius discedat a cibo. Macrob. Sat. I. 23, 2, ideo enim sicut et

Posidonius et Cleanthes affirmant, solis meatus a plaga, quae usta dicitur, non recedit, quia sub ipsa currit Oceanus, qui terram ambit et dividit.

Wachsmuth regards Cic. and Stob. ll. cc. as containing two distinct fragments (Comm. II. fr. phys. 7 and 8), but the passage in Cic. is only a verbal expansion of περὶ τροπῶν...τροφῆς. Wachsm. does not cite Macrob. l. c. This is one of the points which attest Cleanthes' study of Heraclitus, cf. Stob. Ecl. I. 25. 1^g p. 239, 5. Hirzel concludes (II. p. 122) from the evidence, that Cleanthes, like Heraclitus, spoke only of the feeding of the sun by exhalations, and not also of that of the moon and stars.

ἄναμμα κ.τ.λ. cf. Plut. plac. II. 20. 3, περὶ οὐσίας ἡλίου, οἱ Στωικοὶ ἄναμμα νοερὸν ἐκ θαλάττης. Diog. VII. 145, τρέφεσθαι δὲ τὰ ἔμπυρα ταῦτα (i.e. the sun and moon) καὶ τὰ ἄλλα ἄστρα· τὸν μὲν ἥλιον ἐκ τῆς μεγάλης θαλάττης νοερὸν ὄντα ἄναμμα, whereas the moon is fed with fresh water, and is mixed with air. Chrysippus ap. Stob. Ecl. I. 25. 5, τὸν ἥλιον εἶναι τὸ ἀθροισθὲν ἔξαμμα νοερὸν ἐκ τοῦ τῆς θαλάττης ἀναθυμιάματος. Wachsmuth adds Galen, hist. phil. c. LVIII. p. 277 K., ὠκεανὸν δὲ καὶ τὴν θάλασσαν παρέχειν τῷ ἡλίῳ τροφὴν τὴν αὐτοῦ ὑγρότητα ἔχουσαν ἐν αὐτῷ καὶ τὴν γεώδη ἀναθυμίασιν.

τροπῶν: a necessary correction by Bake for the MSS. τροφῶν.

φασι MSS. Wachsm. suggests φησι.

ἐστί: there is a lacuna after this word. Wachsmuth formerly (Comm. II. p. 10) supplied καὶ γῆ coll. Plut. plac. II. 23. 3, but he now writes: "lacuna fuit in Aetii exemplo, quod cum Ps. Plutarcho legit Stobaeus; Plut. ἡ γῆ add.; Aetius καὶ ἡ μεγάλη θάλασσα vel simile scripsit," quoting the passages cited above.

συγκαταφέρεσθαι i.e. with the aether, which is itself in motion.

ἕλικα, cf. Diog. L. VII. 144, τὸν δὲ ἥλιον λοξὴν τὴν πορείαν ποιεῖσθαι διὰ τοῦ ζωδιακοῦ κύκλου, ὁμοίως καὶ τὴν σελήνην ἑλικοειδῆ. The discovery of the inclination of the earth's orbit to that of the sun is attributed by some to Anaximander, and by others to Pythagoras (Zeller, pre-Socratics I. p. 455, 2).

30. Cic. N. D. II. 40, atque ea (sidera) quidem tota esse ignea duorum sensuum testimonio confirmari Cleanthes putat, tactus et oculorum. nam solis et candor illustrior est quam ullius ignis, quippe qui immenso mundo tam longe lateque colluceat, et is eius tactus est, non ut tepefaciat solum, sed etiam saepe comburat. quorum neutrum faceret, nisi esset igneus. "ergo," inquit, "cum sol igneus sit Oceanique alatur humoribus, quia nullus ignis sine pastu aliquo possit permanere, necesse est aut ei similis sit igni quem adhibemus ad usum atque ad victum, aut ei, qui corporibus animantium continetur. atqui hic noster ignis, quem usus vitae requirit, confector est et consumptor omnium idemque, quocumque invasit, cuncta disturbat ac dissipat. contra ille corporeus vitalis et salutaris omnia conservat, alit, auget, sustinet sensuque adficit." negat ergo esse dubium horum ignium sol utri similis sit, cum is quoque efficiat ut omnia floreant et in suo quaeque genere pubescant. quare cum solis ignis similis eorum ignium sit, qui sunt in corporibus animantium, solem quoque animantem esse oportet, et quidem reliqua astra, quae oriantur in ardore caelesti, qui aether vel caelum nominatur.

testimonio: this passage illustrates two characteristics, which are specially prominent in Cleanthes: (1) his activity in the investigation of the problems of natural science, and (2) his confidence in the results of sense observation. Stein, Psychol. p. 69, Erkenntnistheorie, p. 319.

Oceani: cf. frag. 29.

ei...igni: for the two kinds of fire cf. Zeno frag. 71.

corporeus: see on frag. 42.

aether vel caelum: hence in Zeno frag. 111 Zeus is identified with *caelum* in place of the usual gloss *aether*.

31. Clem. Alex. Strom. v. 8. 48. 674 P. 243 S., οὐκ ἀνέγνωσαν δ' οὗτοι Κλεάνθην τὸν φιλόσοφον, ὃς ἄντικρυς πλῆκτρον τὸν ἥλιον καλεῖ· ἐν γὰρ ταῖς ἀνατολαῖς ἐρείδων τὰς αὐγὰς οἷον πλήσσων τὸν κόσμον, εἰς τὴν ἐναρμόνιον πορείαν τὸ φῶς ἄγει, ἐκ δὲ τοῦ ἡλίου σημαίνει καὶ τὰ λοιπὰ ἄστρα.

πλῆκτρον: Krische p. 400 connects this with the Stoic identification of Heracles with the sun. Thus Heracles is τὸ πληκτικὸν καὶ διαιρετικόν (Plut. de Iside c. 40), and his name is derived from ἀήρ and κλάσις by Porphyrius ap. Euseb. P. E. III. p. 112 c, and Nicomachus ap. Laur. Lyd. de Mens. IV. 46. πλῆκτρον is properly "any striking instrument": hence lightning is described as πλῆκτρον διόβολον πυρὸς κεραυνόν (Eur. Alc. 128): cf. especially Plut. de Pyth. orac. c. 16 ad fin. ὕστερον μέντοι πλῆκτρον ἀνέθηκαν τῷ θεῷ χρυσοῦν ἐπιστήσαντες, ὡς ἔοικε, Σκυθίνῳ λέγοντι περὶ τῆς λύρας, ἣν ἁρμόζεται Ζηνὸς εὐειδὴς Ἀπόλλων, πᾶσαν ἀρχὴν καὶ τέλος συλλαβών· ἔχει δὲ λαμπρὸν πλῆκτρον ἡλίου φάος (quoted by Hirzel, p. 181). Eur. Suppl. 650, λαμπρὰ μὲν ἀκτίς, ἡλίου κανὼν σαφής. Sandys on Bacch. 308, and Milton's "With touch ethereal of Heaven's fiery rod."

32. Stob. Ecl. I. 26. 1[1] p. 219, 14, Κλεάνθης πυροειδῆ τὴν σελήνην, πιλοειδῆ δὲ τῷ σχήματι.

πυροειδῆ: but the fire of the moon is not so pure as that of the sun, being fed with grosser matter. Cf. Diog. L. VII. 144, εἶναι δὲ τὸν μὲν ἥλιον εἰλικρινὲς πῦρ...145, γεωδεστέραν δὲ τὴν σελήνην.

πιλοειδῆ: the MSS. have πηλοειδῆ corrected by Lipsius (Phys. Stoic II. 13), who also suggests πολυειδῆ, to πιλοειδῆ, in which correction he is followed by the editors of Stobaeus. But what is the meaning of this word as applied to shape? In this connection "like felt" (L. and S.) is nonsense. Zeller translates "ball-shaped," which is improbable because, apart from other considerations, it is almost certain that Cleanthes did not regard the moon as spherical. There remains Hirzel's suggested rendering:— "shaped like a skull-cap." The only justification for such an absurdity is to be found in the Heraclitean σκαφοειδής (Stob. Ecl. I. 26. 1ᶜ p. 218, 8), for no support can be derived from πιλήματα ἀέρος (Anaximander) or νέφος πεπιλημένον (Xenophanes), which simply refer to densely packed clouds. Krische, p. 435, boldly reads κωνοειδῆ which gives the required sense, but is not close enough to the MSS. It is suggested therefore that the true reading is ἡλιοειδῆ, the Π being due to dittography of the following H. There would be no obscurity in this, assuming Cleanthes or his epitomiser to have previously described the sun as κωνοειδής (cf. frag. 33). The other Stoics consistently describe the moon as σφαιροειδής (Stob. Ecl. I. 26. 1ᵏ 1ˡ p. 219, 20, 26).

33. Stob. Ecl. I. 24. 2ᵈ p. 205, 25, οἱ μὲν ἄλλοι <Στωικοὶ> σφαιρικοὺς αὐτούς, Κλεάνθης δὲ κωνοειδεῖς (scil. the stars). Plut. plac. II. 14. 2. Galen, hist. phil. c. 13 (XIX. 271 K.), Κλεάνθης κωνοειδεῖς τοὺς ἀστέρας. Achill. Tat. p. 133ᶜ Κλεάνθης αὐτοὺς (sc. τοὺς ἀστέρας) κωνοειδὲς ἔχειν σχῆμά φησι. Theodoret, Gr. Cur. aff. IV. 20, p. 59. 16, κωνοειδεῖς δὲ Κλεάνθης ὁ Στωικός.

Cleanthes attributed a conical shape to fire, sun, moon, and stars. There is no direct evidence as to the sun and moon, but it is a fair inference from the authorities that they also were conical. It is probable, moreover, that

Cleanthes was moved by the consideration that Heraclitus described sun, moon and stars as boat-shaped (σκαφοειδῆ), cf. Stob. Ecl. I. 25. 1ᵍ 26. 1ᶜ, Diog. L. IX. 9. Krische is apparently right in inferring that the same is true of the world, cf. Plut. plac. II. 2. 1, οἱ μὲν Στωικοὶ σφαιροειδῆ τὸν κόσμον, ἄλλοι δὲ κωνοειδῆ, οἱ δὲ ᾠοειδῆ.

34. Plut. plac. II. 16. 1, Ἀναξαγόρας καὶ Δημόκριτος καὶ Κλεάνθης ἀπὸ ἀνατολῶν ἐπὶ δυσμὰς φέρεσθαι πάντας τοὺς ἀστέρας. Galen, hist. phil. c. 13, XIX. 272 K. Ἀ. καὶ Δ. καὶ Κλ. ἀπὸ ἀνατολῶν εἰς δυσμὰς φέρεσθαι τοὺς ἀστέρας νομίζουσιν.

πάντας in Plut. apparently includes ἀπλανῆ ἄστρα as well as the πλανώμενα: the former are said συμπεριφέρεσθαι τῷ ὅλῳ οὐρανῷ, τὰ δὲ πλανώμενα κατ' ἰδίας κινεῖσθαι κινήσεις (Diog. VII. 144). Full information on the ancient theories as to the rising and setting of the stars will be found in Achill. Tat. Isag. cc. 37, 38.

35. Gemin. elem. astrom. p. 53 (in Petau's Uranologia), ὑπὸ τὴν διακεκαυμένην ζώνην τινὲς τῶν ἀρχαίων ἀπεφήναντο, ὧν ἐστι καὶ Κλεάνθης ὁ Στωικὸς φιλόσοφος, ὑποκεχύσθαι μεταξὺ τῶν τροπικῶν τὸν ὠκεανόν.

This fragment is taken from Wachsmuth's collection (fr. phys. 27, Comm. II. p. 14): cf. frag. 29 and Macrob. I. 23, 2 there cited. Krische, p. 393, refers this to the influence of Zeno's studies on Homer. "Hiernach möchte ich glauben, dass Zenon dort auch den Homerischen Ocean aufgesucht und dadurch den Kleanthes und Krates aufgefordert habe, dieselbe Betrachtung zu erneuern." Cf. Achill. Tat. Isag. c. 29, p. 89:—There are five zones: Arctic, Antarctic, two temperate (εὔκρατοι), μία δὲ διακεκαυμένη. ἡ δὲ τούτων μέση πασῶν ἔστιν ἀπὸ τοῦ θερινοῦ τροπικοῦ μέχρι τοῦ χειμερινοῦ τροπικοῦ· τοσοῦτον γὰρ πλάτος ἔχει, ὅσον καὶ ὁ ἥλιος περιέρχεται. καλεῖται δὲ διακεκαυμένη διὰ τὸ πυρώδης εἶναι, τοῦ ἡλίου δι' αὐτῆς τὴν πορείαν ἀεὶ ποιουμένου. Posidonius, as we learn from ib. 31, p. 90, made six zones, dividing the torrid zone into two.

36. Tertullian de An. c. 5, vult et Cleanthes non solum corporis lineamentis, sed et animae notis similitudinem parentibus in filios respondere, de speculo scilicet morum et ingeniorum et adfectuum: corporis autem similitudinem et dissimilitudinem capere: et animam itaque 5 corpus similitudini vel dissimilitudini obnoxiam. item corporalium et incorporalium passiones inter se non communicare. porro et animam compati corpori, cui laeso ictibus, vulneribus, ulceribus condolescit, et corpus animae, cui adflictae cura, angore, amore, coaegrescit, per detri- 10 mentum scilicet vigoris, cuius pudorem, et pavorem rubore atque pallore testetur. igitur anima corpus ex corporalium passionum commutatione. Nemesius, Nat. Hom. p. 32, ὁ Κλεάνθης τοιόνδε πλέκει συλλογισμόν· οὐ μόνον φησὶν ὅμοιοι τοῖς γονεῦσι γινόμεθα κατὰ τὸ σῶμα ἀλλὰ 15 καὶ κατὰ τὴν ψυχὴν τοῖς πάθεσι, τοῖς ἤθεσι, ταῖς διαθέσεσι. σώματος δὲ τὸ ὅμοιον καὶ τὸ ἀνόμοιον, οὐχὶ δὲ ἀσωμάτου, σῶμα ἄρα ἡ ψυχή...ἔτι δὲ ὁ Κλεάνθης φησίν· οὐδὲν ἀσώματον συμπάσχει σώματι, οὐδὲ ἀσωμάτῳ σῶμα, ἀλλὰ σῶμα σώματι· συμπάσχει δὲ ἡ ψυχὴ τῷ σώματι νοσοῦντι 20 καὶ τεμνομένῳ καὶ τὸ σῶμα τῇ ψυχῇ· αἰσχυνομένης γοῦν ἐρυθρὸν γίνεται καὶ φοβουμένης ὠχρόν· σῶμα ἄρα ἡ ψυχή. Tertullian de An. c. 25, unde oro te similitudine animae quoque parentibus de ingeniis respondemus secundum Cleanthis testimonium, si non ex animae semine 25 educimur?

The Nemesius passage is regarded as a distinct fragment from the two places in Tertullian by Wachsmuth (Comm. II. fr. phys. 20, 21), but, as Hirzel has observed, they obviously refer to the same original. Stein's observations on this passage should be consulted (Erkenntnistheorie, n. 736). The mind is a tabula rasa at birth, in the sense that it possesses no definite knowledge. But through the seed a capacity for knowledge, and ethical tendencies in particular, are transplanted from father to son: see also Introd. p. 38 f.

5. The ordinary punctuation of this passage puts a full stop at *animam*, with no stop after *capere*, but this gives no satisfactory sense. Mr Hicks would strike out the words *capere et*, remove the stop after *animam*, and alter *obnoxium* to *obnoxiam*. The latter change, which is a decided improvement, I have adopted, and, by putting the stop after *capere*, the required sense is obtained without further alteration.

15. γονεῦσι: cf. Cic. Tusc. I. 79, vult enim (Panaetius)... nasci animos, quod declaret eorum similitudo, qui procreentur, quae etiam in ingeniis, non solum in corporibus appareat. The child receives through the seed the same grade of tension in the soul as his father, and, as the activity of the soul depends on its inherent tension, the mental resemblance between children and parents is explained. Stein, Erkenntnistheorie, pp. 130, 131.

16. ἤθεσι: Wachsmuth reads ἔθεσι from the Oxf. ed. of 1671, but cf. Zeno, frag. 147, καταληπτὸν εἶναι τὸ ἦθος ἐξ εἴδους.

διαθέσεσι: cf. on Zeno, frag. 117.

17. σώματος: agreeably to Stoic tenets, for likeness and unlikeness cannot be predicated of the non-existent, cf. Zeno, frags. 34 and 91.

19. συμπάσχει: the συμπάθεια μερῶν is an indication to the Stoic of the ἕνωσις of a body: this is true of the cosmos no less than of the individual. Sext. Math. IX. 79, who continues (80), ἐπὶ δὲ τῶν ἡνωμένων συμπάθειά τις ἔστιν,

εἴ γε δακτύλου τεμνομένου τὸ ὅλον συνδιατίθεται σῶμα. ἡνωμένον τοίνυν ἐστὶ σῶμα καὶ ὁ κόσμος. id. v. 44, οὐδὲ γὰρ οὕτως ἥνωται τὸ περιέχον ὡς τὸ ἀνθρώπινον σῶμα, ἵνα, ὃν τρόπον τῇ κεφαλῇ τὰ ὑποκείμενα μέρη συμπάσχει καὶ τοῖς ὑποκειμένοις ἡ κεφαλή, οὕτω καὶ τοῖς ἐπουρανίοις τὰ ἐπίγεια. Cic. N.D. III. 28. The question as between body and soul is discussed in the pseudo-Aristotelian φυσιογνωμικά. Cf. Plat. Phaed. 83 D. M. Aurel. IX. 9.

37. Stob. Ecl. I. 48. 7, p. 317, 15, Πυθαγόρας, Ἀναξαγόρας, Πλάτων, Ξενοκράτης, Κλεάνθης θύραθεν εἰσκρίνεσθαι τὸν νοῦν.

This is an obscure statement which cannot be understood in the same manner of the various philosophers mentioned. Thus, as regards Pythagoras, it is simply a deduction from the theory of metempsychosis (Zeller, pre-Socratics I. p. 479): while for Plato and Xenocrates we may understand a reference to the previous existence of the soul before its entrance into the body (Zeller, Plato, p. 596). The terminology however is Aristotle's (de Generat. An. II. 3, p. 736 b 27, λείπεται δὲ τὸν νοῦν μόνον θύραθεν ἐπεισιέναι καὶ θεῖον εἶναι μόνον· οὐθὲν γὰρ αὐτοῦ τῇ ἐνεργείᾳ κοινωνεῖ σωματικὴ ἐνέργεια), whose doctrine is widely different from Plato's. As regards Cleanthes, the Stoics in general do not distinguish between νοῦς and ψυχή (see on Zeno, frag. 43): the latter is transmitted in the seed, developed in the womb, and brought to maturity by the action of the outer air, so that it is hard to see in what sense ψυχὴ θύραθεν εἰσκρίνεται. Perhaps the meaning is that the reasoning powers (νοῦς) are founded on external impressions, from which Knowledge is derived: cf. Zeno, frag. 82. Stein, however (Psychol. p. 163 foll.), believes that by θύραθεν is indicated the action of the outer air on the embryo at birth, whereby the ψυχὴ is developed out of a mere φύσις. In this case Cleanthes anticipated the Chrysippean doctrine of περίψυξις. Hirzel (II. p. 156 foll.) uses this passage in support of his improbable view that Cleanthes maintained a tripartite division of the soul: he sees here also the influence of Heraclitus. Cic. N.D. II. 18 might suggest a more general view, that the point referred to is the material nature of the soul as πνεῦμα, but the context in Stobaeus is against this.

38. = Zeno, frag. 83.

There is a curious contradiction in Stein's Psychologie on this point. At p. 107 and p. 155 he cites and upholds the evidence which distinctly attributes to Zeno the doctrine of the soul being fed by exhalations from the blood. Yet at p. 165 he suggests that this innovation was made by Cleanthes.

39. = Zeno, frag. 87.

40. = Zeno, frag. 88.

41. Diog. L. VII. 157, Κλεάνθης μὲν οὖν πάσας ἐπιδιαμένειν (τὰς ψυχὰς) μέχρι τῆς ἐκπυρώσεως, Χρύσιππος δὲ τὰς τῶν σοφῶν μόνον.

Cf. R. and P. § 409. Cic. Tusc. I. 77, Stoici diu mansuros aiunt animos, semper negant, cf. Zeno frag. 95. The teaching of Cleanthes is everywhere more materialistic than that of Chrysippus, who was no doubt anxious to vindicate the purity of the soul essence: see Stein Psychol. n. 279 and pp. 145—147, who compares their divergence as to the nature of τύπωσις and the "Urpneuma" (φλὸξ and αὐγή). Ar. Did. ap. Euseb. P. E. xv. 20. 3 follows the account of Chrysippus, τὴν δὲ ψυχὴν γεννητήν τε καὶ φθαρτὴν λέγουσιν· οὐκ εὐθὺς δὲ τοῦ σώματος ἀπαλλαγεῖσαν φθείρεσθαι, ἀλλ' ἐπιμένειν τινὰς χρόνους καθ' ἑαυτήν· τὴν μὲν τῶν σπουδαίων μέχρι τῆς εἰς πῦρ ἀναλύσεως τῶν πάντων, τὴν δὲ τῶν ἀφρόνων πρὸς ποσούς τινας χρόνους...τὰς δὲ τῶν ἀφρόνων καὶ ἀλόγων ζῴων ψυχὰς συναπόλλυσθαι τοῖς σώμασιν.

42. Cic. N. D. II. 24, quod quidem Cleanthes his etiam argumentis docet, quanta vis insit caloris in omni corpore: negat enim ullum esse cibum tam gravem, quin is die et nocte concoquatur, cuius etiam in reliquiis inest calor iis, quas natura respuerit.

This must be regarded as an argument in favour of the warmth of the vital principle: hence Zeno called the soul πνεῦμα ἔνθερμον (frag. 85). The excellence of the human soul consists peculiarly in a suitable mixture (εὐκρασία) of warmth and cold. Cf. Galen quod animi mores etc. IV. 783 K. (quoted at length by Stein, Psychol. p. 105). Cleanthes no doubt was influenced by Heraclitus: cf. frag. 54, Byw. αὐγὴ ξηρὴ ψυχὴ σοφωτάτη, but substituted warmth for dryness. It is highly probable that the words immediately preceding this extract, which are of great importance for the τόνος theory, are ultimately derived from Cleanthes: they are as follows: sic enim res se habet, ut omnia, quae alantur et quae crescant, contineant in se vim caloris, sine qua neque ali possent neque crescere. Nam omne, quod est calidum et igneum, cietur et agitur motu suo, quod autem alitur et crescit, motu quodam utitur certo et aequabili, qui quamdiu remanet in nobis, tam diu sensus et vita remanet, refrigerato autem et extincto calore occidimus ipsi et exstinguimur. Compare with this the remarks of Stein Psychol. p. 32, and Philo de incorr. mundi, p. 507, Mang. ἅπαν σῶμα ἀναλυόμενον εἰς πῦρ διαλύεταί τε καὶ χεῖται, σβεννυμένης δὲ τῆς ἐν αὐτῷ φλογὸς στέλλεται καὶ συνάγεται. This is one of the many points of contact between the Stoics and the medical school of Hippocrates. We are reminded of the τόνος of Cleanthes when we read that Aristoxenus, the Peripatetic and musician, described the soul as ipsius corporis intentionem quandam (Cic. Tusc. I. 20), but the doctrines were totally dissimilar: see Munro on Lucr. III. 100.

43. Seneca, Epist. 113, 18, inter Cleanthem et discipulum eius Chrysippum non convenit quid sit ambulatio: Cleanthes ait, spiritum esse a principali usque in pedes permissum; Chrysippus ipsum principale.

ambulatio: the Stoics were led to this extreme materialism by their insistence on the dogma that nothing exists but the corporeal. Cf. Plut. Comm. Not. 45, 2, ἀλλὰ πρὸς τούτοις καὶ τὰς ἐνεργείας σώματα καὶ ζῷα ποιοῦσι, τὸν περίπατον ζῷον, τὴν ὄρχησιν, τὴν ὑπόθεσιν, τὴν προσαγόρευσιν, τὴν λοιδορίαν.

spiritum: the Greek original of this would be πνεῦμα διατεῖνον ἀπὸ τοῦ ἡγεμονικοῦ μέχρι ποδῶν (cf. Plut. plac. IV. 21). The deviation of Chrysippus from the teaching of his predecessor was probably caused by a desire to insist more strongly on the essential unity of the soul. Cf. Iambl. ap. Stob. Ecl. I. 49. 33, p. 368, 12, πῶς οὖν διακρίνονται; κατὰ μὲν τοὺς Στωικοὺς ἔνιαι μὲν διαφορότητι <τῶν> ὑποκειμένων σωμάτων· πνεύματα γὰρ ἀπὸ τοῦ ἡγεμονικοῦ φασιν οὗτοι διατείνειν ἄλλα κατ' ἄλλα, τὰ μὲν εἰς ὀφθαλμούς, τὰ δὲ εἰς ὦτα, τὰ δὲ εἰς ἄλλα αἰσθητήρια· ἔνιαι δὲ ἰδιότητι ποιότητος περὶ τὸ αὐτὸ ὑποκείμενον· ὥσπερ γὰρ τὸ μῆλον ἐν τῷ αὐτῷ σώματι τὴν γλυκύτητα ἔχει καὶ τὴν εὐωδίαν, οὕτω καὶ τὸ ἡγεμονικὸν ἐν ταὐτῷ φαντασίαν, συγκατάθεσιν, ὁρμήν, λόγον συνείληφε. Sext. Math. IX. 102, πᾶσαι αἱ ἐπὶ τὰ μέρη τοῦ ὅλου ἐξαποστελλόμεναι δυνάμεις ὡς ἀπό τινος πηγῆς τοῦ ἡγεμονικοῦ ἐξαποστέλλονται, ὥστε πᾶσαν δύναμιν τὴν περὶ τὸ μέρος οὖσαν καὶ περὶ τὸ ὅλον εἶναι διὰ τὸ ἀπὸ τοῦ ἐν αὐτῷ ἡγεμονικοῦ διαδίδοσθαι. The former passage is, I find, also cited by Stein for the same purpose (Psychol. p. 168). He points out that Cleanthes explained the different soul functions by means of a πνεῦμα διατεῖνον, and Chrysippus by a πνεῦμά πως ἔχον. The former regarded only the grade, while the latter also distinguished the kind of tension. It is possible that this passage also points to the different treatment of φαντασία by Cleanthes and Chrysippus (cf. frag. 3), Cleanthes insisting more strongly on the immediate contact of the psychical aircurrent with the sense organ (Stein, Erkenntnistheorie, n. 728). Hirzel's explanation (II. p. 201) is vitiated by his fundamental error as to Cleanthes' view of the ἡγεμονικόν. See also on Zeno frag. 93. There is a certain affinity between the doctrine here mentioned and that attributed to Strato of Lampsacus by Sext. Emp. Math. VII. 350, οἱ δὲ αὐτὴν (scil. τὴν διάνοιαν) εἶναι τὰς αἰσθήσεις, καθάπερ διά τινων ὀπῶν τῶν αἰσθητηρίων προκύπτουσαν, ἧς στάσεως ἦρξε Στράτων ὁ φυσικός. Cf. Cic. Tusc. I. 46, viae quasi quaedam sunt ad oculos, ad aures, ad nares, a sede animi perforatae.

44. Clem. Alex. Strom. VII. 6. 33. 849 P. 304 S., ὅθεν καὶ ὁ Αἴσωπος οὐ κακῶς ἔφη τοὺς ὗς κεκραγέναι μέγιστον ὅταν ἕλκωνται. συνειδέναι γὰρ αὐτοῖς εἰς οὐδὲν ἄλλο χρησίμοις ἢ πλὴν εἰς τὴν θυσίαν· διὸ καὶ Κλεάνθης φησὶν ἀνθ᾽ ἁλῶν αὐτοὺς ἔχειν τὴν ψυχήν, ἵνα μὴ σαπῇ τὰ κρέα. The same saying is attributed to Chrysippus by Cic. N.D. II. 160, sus vero quid habet praeter escam? cui quidem ne putesceret animam ipsam pro sale datam dicit esse Chrysippus: to which add Porphyry de Abstin. III. 20, ἡ δὲ ὗς, ἐνταῦθα γάρ ἐστι τῶν χαρίτων τὸ ἥδιστον (scil. τοῦ Χρυσίππου), οὐ δι᾽ ἄλλο τι πλὴν θύεσθαι ἐγεγόνει, καὶ τῇ σαρκὶ τὴν ψυχὴν ὁ θεὸς οἷον ἅλας ἐνέμιξεν. Elsewhere the statement is ascribed to no definite author. Cic. Fin.

v. 38, ut non inscite illud dictum videatur in sue, animum illi pecudi datum pro sale, ne putisceret. Varro de R. R. II. 4, 10, suillum pecus donatum ab natura dicunt ad epulandum. itaque iis animam datam esse proinde ac salem quae servaret carnem. Plut. Quaest. Conv. v. 10, 3, διὸ καὶ τῶν Στωικῶν ἔνιοι τὴν ὑϊνὴν σάρκα κρέα γεγονέναι λέγουσι, τῆς ψυχῆς ὥσπερ ἁλῶν παρεσπαρμένης ὑπὲρ τοῦ διαμένειν. Lastly, we have two passages of similar import in which a suggested derivation of ὗς from θύειν is referred to: Clem. Alex. II. 20. 105, p. 174 S. p. 484 P., λέγεται γοῦν τινα τῶν φιλοσοφούντων ἐτυμολογοῦντα τὴν ὗν θῦν εἶναι φάναι, ὡς εἰς θύσιν καὶ σφαγὴν μόνον ἐτιτήδειον· δεδόσθαι γὰρ τῷδε τῷ ζώῳ ψυχὴν πρὸς οὐδὲν ἕτερον ἢ ἕνεκα τοῦ τὰς σάρκας σφριγᾶν. Varro R. R. II. 4, 9, sus Graece dicitur ὗς, olim θῦς dictus ab illo verbo, quod dicunt θύειν, quod est inmolare. ab suillo enim [genere] pecore inmolandi initium primum sumptum videtur; cuius vestigia quod initiis Cereris porci inmolantur.

Everything in the world is created for and adapted to a special end; the existence of various animals is used as an argument to prove the government of the world by πρόνοια (cf. the context in Cic. N.D. l. c.). In a similar spirit Epict. Diss. II. 8. 7 says that asses were intended to bear burdens, and that, as for this purpose they must walk, imagination has been given them to enable them to do so.

The passages here collected, as well as Zeno frag. 43, shew conclusively that Stein's theory (Psych. p. 92 f.) that the vital principle of animals is not ψυχή, but something midway between φύσις and ψυχή, ought not to be accepted. He contends that Marcus Aurelius is the first Stoic who expressly gives ψυχή to animals, but cf. Zeno frag. 50, spiritum...fore non naturam, sed animam et quidem rationabilem, which clearly points to the ἄλογος ψυχὴ of animals)(ψυχὴ λόγον ἔχουσα of men. Zeno frag. 56, l. 41, ψυχὴν ἀφῃρημένον ζῷον, Ar. Did. ap. Euseb. P.E. xv. 20. 3, τὰς δὲ τῶν ἀφρόνων καὶ ἀλόγων ζῴων ψυχάς. To the passages cited by Stein from Marcus Aurelius add v. 16, vi. 14.

45. Plut. de sollertia animalium XI. 2, 3, ὁ μὲν οὖν Κλεάνθης ἔλεγε, καίπερ οὐ φάσκων μετέχειν λόγου τὰ ζῷα, τοιαύτῃ θεωρίᾳ παρατυχεῖν· μύρμηκας ἐλθεῖν ἐπὶ μυρμηκιὰν ἑτέραν μύρμηκα νεκρὸν φέροντας· ἀνιόντας οὖν ἐκ τῆς μυρμηκιᾶς ἑτέρους οἷον ἐντυγχάνειν αὐτοῖς καὶ πάλιν κατέρχεσθαι· καὶ τοῦτο δὶς ἢ τρὶς γενέσθαι· τέλος δέ, τοὺς μὲν κάτωθεν ἀνενεγκεῖν ὥσπερ λύτρα τοῦ νεκροῦ σκώληκα, τοὺς δ' ἐκεῖνον ἀραμένους, ἀποδόντας δὲ τὸν νεκρὸν οἴχεσθαι. Aelian Nat. An. VI. 50, Κλεάνθην τὸν Ἄσσιον κατηνάγκασε καὶ ἄκοντα εἶξαι καὶ ἀποστῆναι τοῖς ζῴοις τοῦ καὶ ἐκεῖνα λογισμοῦ μὴ διαμαρτάνειν, ἀντιλέγοντα ἰσχυρῶς καὶ κατὰ κράτος, ἱστορία τοιαύτη, φασίν. ἔτυχεν ὁ Κλεάνθης καθήμενος καὶ μέντοι καὶ σχολὴν ἄγων μακροτέραν ἄλλως· οὐκοῦν μύρμηκες παρὰ τοῖς ποσὶν ἦσαν αὐτῷ πολλοί· ὁ δὲ ἄρα ὁρᾷ ἐξ ἀτραποῦ τινος ἑτέρας νεκρὸν μύρμηκα μύρμηκας ἄλλους κομίζοντας εἰς οἶκον ἑτέρων, καὶ ἑαυτοῖς οὐ συντρόφων καὶ ἐπί γε τῷ χείλει τῆς μυρμηκιᾶς ἑστῶτας αὐτῷ νεκρῷ, καὶ ἀνιόντας κάτωθεν ἑτέρους καὶ συνόντας τοῖς ξένοις ὡς ἐπί τινι, εἶτα κατιόντας τοὺς αὐτούς, καὶ πλεονάκις τοῦτο· καὶ τελευτῶντας σκώληκα, οἱονεὶ λύτρα, κομίσαι· τοὺς δὲ ἐκεῖνον μὲν λαβεῖν, προέσθαι δὲ ὅνπερ οὖν ἐπήγοντο νεκρόν· καὶ ἐκείνους ὑποδέξασθαι ἀσμένως, ὡς υἱὸν κομιζομένους ἢ ἀδελφόν.

μετέχειν λόγου τὰ ζῷα: for animals possess indeed ψυχήν, but not ψυχὴν λόγον ἔχουσαν καὶ διάνοιαν: hence the term ἄλογα ζῷα: cf. Sext. Math. XI. 99 foll:—the Stoics say that the courage of certain of the nobler (γενναῖα) animals proves that τὸ καλὸν is φύσει αἱρετόν, but only ἡ φρονίμη διάθεσις can discern τὸ καλόν: hence ὁ ἀλεκτρύων καὶ ὁ ταῦρος μὴ μετέχοντα τῆς φρονίμης διαθέσεως οὐκ ἂν βλέποι τὸ καλόν τε καὶ ἀγαθόν. Hermes ap. Stob. Ecl. I. 41. 6, p. 284, 12, πῶς οὖν ὁρῶμέν τινα τῶν ἀλόγων ἐπιστήμῃ καὶ τέχνῃ χρώμενα, οἷον τοὺς μύρμηκας τὰς τροφὰς ἀποθησαυριζομένους τοῦ χειμῶνος. It was easier, however, for the Stoics than for those who separate the soul of man from that of animals by a sharp dividing line, to make the admission which circumstances forced upon Cleanthes. For the soul of man differs from that of animals in degree only and not in kind; it is the same substance, though varying in its degrees of purity, which permeates inorganic matter as ἕξις, plants as φύσις, and men and animals as ψυχή (Diog. L. VII. 139). Chrysippus believed that dogs possessed the power of inference (Sext. Pyrrh. I. 69). Stein, Psychol. n. 165, is mistaken in quoting Ael. N.A. IV. 45 as an authority bearing on this subject. The passage, when cited in full, is seen to have an entirely different application: "Ὅμηρος μὲν οὖν φησὶν "ὡς ἀγαθὸν καὶ παῖδα καταφθιμένοιο λιπέσθαι," ἔοικε δὲ ἡ φύσις δεικνύναι, ὅτι καὶ φίλον ἑαυτῷ τιμωρὸν καταλιπεῖν, ὦ φίλε Ὅμηρε, κέρδος ἐστίν, οἷόν τι καὶ περὶ Ζήνωνος καὶ Κλεάνθους νοοῦμεν εἴ τι (or εἴτε) ἀκούομεν, i.e. it was an advantage to Zeno to leave his friend Cleanthes behind him to uphold his doctrines.

μύρμηκας: cf. Cic. N.D. III. 21, num existimas formicam anteponendam esse huic pulcherrimae urbi, quod in urbe sensus sit nullus, in formica non modo sensus sed etiam mens ratio memoria? Aristotle allowed that some animals, and especially bees, possessed νοῦς (cf. Grote's Aristotle, p. 483).

ἄλλως: "aimlessly": so Eur. Hipp. 375, ἤδη ποτ' ἄλλως νυκτὸς ἐν μακρῷ χρόνῳ θνητῶν ἐφρόντισ' ᾗ διέφθαρται βίος.

ἐξ ἀτραποῦ τινος ἑτέρας: alluding to the practice of ants to use one narrow path in passing backwards and forwards between their hole and any other place. Cf. Verg. Aen. IV. 404, praedamque per herbas convectant calle angusto. Georg. I. 379, angustum formica terens iter, where Forbiger refers to Arist. Hist. An. IX. 38, ἀεὶ μίαν ἀτραπὸν πάντες βαδίζουσιν.

46. Cic. N. D. I. 37, idemque (Cleanthes) quasi delirans in iis libris, quos scripsit contra voluptatem, tum fingit formam quandam et speciem deorum, tum divinitatem omnem tribuit astris, tum nihil ratione censet esse divinius.

quasi delirans: for the treatise περὶ ἡδονῆς see Introd. p. 53.

formam quandam: either (1) an allusion to the allegorical explanations of the popular deities, whereby they are identified with the powers of nature, or (2) referring to ἀνικήτοις ἐν χερσίν in the hymn to Zeus, as Prof. Mayor suggests.

astris: this position is proved at length in N. D. II. 40—44, cf. Chrysippus ap. Stob. Ecl. I. 21. 5. p. 185, 5, ἐν ᾧ (αἰθέρι) τὰ ἄστρα καθίδρυται...θεῖα τὴν φύσιν ὄντα καὶ ἔμψυχα καὶ διοικούμενα κατὰ τὴν πρόνοιαν.

47. Plut. Comm. Not. 31, 5, ἀλλὰ Χρύσιππος καὶ Κλεάνθης ἐμπεπληκότες, ὡς ἔπος εἰπεῖν, τῷ λόγῳ θεῶν τὸν οὐρανὸν τὴν γῆν τὸν ἀέρα τὴν θάλατταν οὐδένα τῶν τοσούτων ἄφθαρτον οὐδ᾽ ἀΐδιον ἀπολελοίπασι, πλὴν μόνου τοῦ Διός, εἰς ὃν πάντας καταναλίσκουσι τοὺς ἄλλους... ταῦτα δὲ οὐ...τοῖς δόγμασιν ἕπεται, ἀλλ᾽ αὐτοὶ μέγα βοῶντες ἐν τοῖς περὶ θεῶν καὶ προνοίας εἱμαρμένης τε καὶ φύσεως γράμμασι διαρρήδην λέγουσι τοὺς ἄλλους θεοὺς ἅπαντας εἶναι γεγονότας καὶ φθαρησομένους ὑπὸ πυρός, τηκτοὺς κατ᾽ αὐτοὺς ὥσπερ κηρίνους ἢ καττιτερίνους ὄντας.

ἐμπεπληκότες: the Stoics would readily admit this: Cicero makes his Stoic say:—quidquid enim magnam utilitatem generi adferret humano, id non sine divina bonitate erga homines fieri arbitrabantur (N.D. II. 60).

Διός: Zeus is here identified, as often, with the supreme Stoic God: see Zeller, p. 358.

ἐν τοῖς περὶ θεῶν κ.τ.λ. Chrysippus wrote περὶ θεῶν (Diog. VII. 148), περὶ προνοίας (ib. 139), περὶ εἱμαρμένης (ib. 149), and φυσικά (ib. 39). For Cleanthes περὶ θεῶν see Introd. p. 51.

φθαρησομένους: cf. Chrysipp. ap. Plut. Sto. Rep. 38, 5. Plut. de def. Or. c. 19, καίτοι τοὺς Στωικοὺς γινώσκομεν οὐ μόνον κατὰ δαιμόνων ἣν λέγω δόξαν ἔχοντας, ἀλλὰ καὶ θεῶν ὄντων τοσούτων τὸ πλῆθος ἑνὶ χρωμένους ἀϊδίῳ καὶ ἀφθάρτῳ, τοὺς δ' ἄλλους καὶ γεγονέναι καὶ φθαρήσεσθαι νομίζοντας.

48. Stob. Ecl. I. 1. 12. p. 25, 3. Κλεάνθους.

κύδιστ' ἀθανάτων, πολυώνυμε, παγκρατὲς αἰεί,
Ζεῦ, φύσεως ἀρχηγέ, νόμου μέτα πάντα κυβερνῶν,
χαῖρε· σὲ γὰρ πάντεσσι θέμις θνητοῖσι προσαυδᾶν.
ἐκ σοῦ γὰρ γένος (ἐσμέν, †ἤχου μίμημα λαχόντες
μοῦνοι, ὅσα ζώει τε καὶ ἕρπει θνήτ' ἐπὶ γαῖαν· 5
τῷ σε καθυμνήσω καὶ σὸν κράτος αἰὲν ἀείσω.
σοὶ δὴ πᾶς ὅδε κόσμος, ἑλισσόμενος περὶ γαῖαν,
πείθεται, ᾗ κεν ἄγῃς, καὶ ἑκὼν ὑπὸ σεῖο κρατεῖται·
τοῖον ἔχεις ὑποεργὸν ἀνικήτοις ἐνὶ χερσὶν
ἀμφήκη, πυρόεντ', ἀειζώοντα κεραυνόν· 10
τοῦ γὰρ ὑπὸ πληγῆς φύσεως πάντ' ἐρρίγα <σιν>·
ᾧ σὺ κατευθύνεις κοινὸν λόγον, ὃς διὰ πάντων
φοιτᾷ, μιγνύμενος μεγάλοις μικροῖς τε φάεσσι·
[ὡς τόσσος γεγαὼς ὕπατος βασιλεὺς διὰ παντός,]
οὐδέ τι γίγνεται ἔργον ἐπὶ χθονὶ σοῦ δίχα, δαῖμον, 15
οὔτε κατ' αἰθέριον θεῖον πόλον οὔτ' ἐνὶ πόντῳ,

πλὴν ὁπόσα ῥέζουσι κακοὶ σφετέρῃσιν ἀνοίαις·
ἀλλὰ σὺ καὶ τὰ περισσά<τ'>ἐπίστασαι ἄρτια θεῖναι,
καὶ κοσμεῖν τἄκοσμα καὶ οὐ φίλα σοὶ φίλα ἐστίν,
ὧδε γὰρ εἰς ἓν πάντα συνήρμοκας ἐσθλὰ κακοῖσιν,   20
ὥσθ' ἕνα γίγνεσθαι πάντων λόγον αἰὲν ἐόντα,
ὃν φεύγοντες ἐῶσιν ὅσοι θνητῶν κακοί εἰσι,
δύσμοροι, οἵ τ' ἀγαθῶν μὲν ἀεὶ κτῆσιν ποθέοντες
οὔτ' ἐσορῶσι θεοῦ κοινὸν νόμον, οὔτε κλύουσιν,
ᾧ κεν πειθόμενοι σὺν νῷ βίον ἐσθλὸν ἔχοιεν.   25
αὐτοὶ δ' αὖθ' ὁρμῶσιν ἄνοι κακὸν ἄλλος ἐπ' ἄλλο,
οἱ μὲν ὑπὲρ δόξης σπουδὴν δυσέριστον ἔχοντες,
οἱ δ' ἐπὶ κερδοσύνας τετραμμένοι οὐδενὶ κόσμῳ,
ἄλλοι δ' εἰς ἄνεσιν καὶ σώματος ἡδέα ἔργα
............ἐπ' ἄλλοτε δ' ἄλλα φέροντες,   30
σπεύδοντες μάλα πάμπαν ἐναντία τῶνδε γενέσθαι.
ἀλλὰ Ζεῦ πάνδωρε, κελαινεφές, ἀργικέραυνε,
ἀνθρώπους<μὲν>ῥύου ἀπειροσύνης ἀπὸ λυγρῆς,
ἣν σύ, πάτερ, σκέδασον ψυχῆς ἄπο, δὸς δὲ κυρῆσαι
γνώμης, ᾗ πίσυνος σὺ δίκης μέτα πάντα κυβερνᾷς,   35
ὄφρ' ἂν τιμηθέντες ἀμειβώμεσθά σε τιμῇ,
ὑμνοῦντες τὰ σὰ ἔργα διηνεκές, ὡς ἐπέοικε
θνητὸν ἐόντ', ἐπεὶ οὔτε βροτοῖς γέρας ἄλλο τι μεῖζον,
οὔτε θεοῖς, ἢ κοινὸν ἀεὶ νόμον ἐν δίκῃ ὑμνεῖν.

1. πολυώνυμε: not merely in the popular religion, but more particularly from the Stoic standpoint, cf. Diog. L. VII. 147 δημιουργὸν τῶν ὅλων, καὶ ὥσπερ πατέρα πάντων· κοινῶς τε, καὶ τὸ μέρος αὐτοῦ τὸ διῆκον διὰ πάντων, ὃ πολλαῖς προσηγορίαις προσονομάζεται κατὰ τὰς δυνάμεις. See also Krische, p. 401; Stein, Psych. n. 74.

2. νόμου: cf. Zeno, frag. 39.

4. ἐκ σοῦ γὰρ γένος ἐσμέν. Cf. Act. Apost. XVII. 28, where the words τοῦ γὰρ καὶ γένος ἐσμέν are quoted by St Paul. The divergence in reading points to the fact

that these words were taken from the Phaenomena of Aratus, 1. 5, rather than from the present passage.

ἤχου: so MS. F, an unmetrical and senseless reading, not yet satisfactorily corrected. The vulg. ἰῆς is a conjecture of Brunck, and is destitute of authority. Meineke read γενόμεσθα λόγου; Wachsm. (Comm. II. p. 18) suggested νοῦ σοῦ (or ἃ δὴ σοῦ) τμῆμα, and now proposes τίμημα for μίμημα; Usener 'cum appareat ἤχου ex glossemate natum esse' ὑδῆς (a word coined from ὑδεῖν). None of these are convincing, and all are inferior to Bergk's ὅλου, which might have been adopted, had it satisfactorily accounted for the MS. reading. Wachsmuth indeed says that it introduces "sententiam a Stoicis alienam," but he must have failed to remember frag. 24, which shows that it is a favourite thought with Cleanthes to represent the individual as a counterpart of the divine cosmos. It appears to me that an allusion to "speech" is not here appropriate, in spite of Zeller (p. 215). Meineke's λόγου, if adopted, would mean "reason" (not "speech"), cf. Euseb. P. E. XV. 15, p. 817 d (quoted by Wachsm.) κοινωνίαν δ' ὑπάρχειν πρὸς ἀλλήλους (scil. θεοῦ καὶ ἀνθρώπων) διὰ τὸ λόγου μετέχειν. If γενόμεσθα is accepted for γένος ἐσμέν, perhaps μόνου or ἐκ σοῦ.

5. ὅσα: for the omission of the antecedent cf. Soph. Ai. 1050, Trach. 350, and for the sense Hom. Il. 17. 447, Od. 18. 131. Hirzel argues (II. 201—210), mainly relying on this passage, that Cleanthes was not a pantheist in the full sense of the term, and that he allowed only a limited extension to the divine πνεῦμα: but see Introd. p. 41.

6. ἀείσω: ἀίδω F, whence ἀείδω Wachsm.; but the present is very awkward after καθυμνήσω, and it is by no means clear that Cleanthes would have preferred ἀείσομαι (see the evidence collected by Veitch s. v.).

7. κόσμος is here used, as Krische, p. 425, has observed,

in the less extended sense mentioned in Diog. VII. 138, καὶ αὐτὴν δὲ τὴν διακόσμησιν τῶν ἀστέρων κόσμον εἶναι: hence ἑλισσόμενος = κυκλοφορητικός.

9. ἐνί. So Brunck and Wachsm. ὑπό MS. F. μετά Mein. For the sense cf. Soph. O. C. 1515.

10. ἀμφήκη: alluding to forked lightning, cf. Aesch. P. V. 1040 πυρὸς ἀμφήκης βόστρυχος. Hesych. ἄμφηκες δὲ ἐξ ἑκατέρου μέρους ἠκονημένον βέλος· ἢ κεραυνός, ἢ ξίφος.

κεραυνόν: for the physical explanation cf. Zeno frag. 74. But to Cleanthes κεραυνὸς is only another name for πληγὴ πυρός, which he identifies with τόνος, cf. Heraclit. frag. 28. Byw. τὰ δὲ πάντα οἰακίζει κεραυνός.

11. ἐρρίγασιν: so Ursinus and most edd. for ἔρηγα F "in quo postea spatium 10 litt.," which might suggest ἔργα <δαμάσθη>: but there are similar spaces after vv. 12 and 13, and the text at this point is generally suspicious. Wachsm. formerly marked a lacuna after this line, but now agrees with Hirzel, II. p. 118, n. 1, in referring ᾧ in v. 12 to κεραυνόν.

13. μεγάλων μικροῖσι F, which Petersen tries to defend, was corrected by Brunck. The reference is to the sun, moon, and stars. For the general sense cf. Zeno frag. 45. A lacuna was marked after this line by Mein., who is followed by Wachsm. But it is equally possible that v. 14 is a spurious or corrupt addition, for (1) the sense is complete without it, (2) διὰ παντὸς is suspicious after διὰ πάντων in v. 12, (3) it is difficult to imagine any context which would prevent ὡς τόσσος γεγαὼς from being frigid, if not obscure, (4) the excessive sigmatism is pointless.

17—20. πλὴν ὁπόσα κ.τ.λ. The explanations given by the Stoics of this weak point in their system are hopelessly confused and contradictory, as may be seen from an examination of the passages cited in the notes to Zeller, p. 189—193. We have had occasion to refer to this subject before (frag. 18), and, putting together that passage and the present, we may perhaps suppose that Cleanthes accounted for the existence of moral evil somewhat as follows:—evil is not directly due to God, but is a necessary accompaniment of the process, whereby he created the world out of himself. At the same time, the omnipotence of God is vindicated by the consideration that evil is ultimately swallowed up in good, and that the apparent irregularity of nature is in reality only a phase in the working of a higher law. Chrysippus is inconsistent here, as elsewhere (cf. Diog. L. VII. 180), but to some extent, at least, he agreed with Cleanthes: ὡς τῶν αἰσχρῶν τὸ θεῖον παραίτιον γίνεσθαι οὐκ εὔλογόν ἐστιν (Plut. Sto. Rep. 33, 2). We may compare Plato's words Rep. II. 379 C, οὐδ' ἄρα ὁ θεός, ἐπειδὴ ἀγαθός, πάντων ἂν εἴη αἴτιος, ὡς οἱ πολλοὶ λέγουσιν, ἀλλ' ὀλίγων μὲν τοῖς ἀνθρώποις αἴτιος, πολλῶν δὲ ἀναίτιος· πολὺ γὰρ ἐλάττω τἀγαθὰ τῶν κακῶν ἡμῖν· καὶ τῶν μὲν ἀγαθῶν οὐδένα ἄλλον αἰτιατέον, τῶν δὲ κακῶν ἄλλ' ἄττα δεῖ ζητεῖν τὰ αἴτια, ἀλλ' οὐ τὸν θεόν. See further Gercke Chrysippea, p. 699.

24. κοινὸν νόμον. Cf. infra frag. 73. No doubt Cleanthes remembered Heracl. frag. 91. Byw. ξυνόν ἐστι πᾶσι τὸ φρονεῖν.

25. κεν belongs to the verb, Madv. § 137.

26. ἄνευ κακοῦ...ἄλλα F, ἄνοι Wachsm., κακόν...ἄλλο Sauppe.

28. οὐδενὶ κόσμῳ: this phrase is used by Herod. and Thuc. as an equivalent for ἀτάκτως. Here it means "inordinately, recklessly." Cleanthes was probably influenced by Homer's fondness for μὰψ ἀτὰρ οὐ κατὰ κόσμον (Il. 2. 214 etc.) and the like. al. οὐδ' ἐνὶ κόσμῳ.

30, 31. ἄλλοτεν Usener, φέρονται Meineke, while in 31 Wachsm. suggests πένεσθαι for γενέσθαι. The sense is unsatisfactory, but as the text is so mutilated conjecture seems hazardous. Mohnike (pp. 34—44) has a long discussion on these lines, which he calls the hardest in the Hymn. As the text stands, l. 31 must mean that the effect of the actions of the φαῦλοι is just the opposite to that which they intend.

32. ἀργικέραυνε. Cf. Ζεὺς ἀργής, an expression used by Empedocles to denote fire (R. and P. § 131), Zeno frag. 116, Ἄργην δὲ ἐπειδή φασι τὸν ἀργῆτα κεραυνόν.

33. μέν: add. Scaliger, but perhaps we should read ἐκρύου. ἀπειροσύνης i.e. ἄγνοια, the condition of the φαῦλοι.

36. γνώμης ᾖ πίσυνος κ.τ.λ. Another reminiscence of Heraclitus, frag. 19. Byw. ἓν τὸ σοφόν, ἐπίστασθαι γνώμην, ᾗ κυβερνᾶται πάντα διὰ πάντων.

49. Philodem. de Mus. col. 28, 1, εἰ μ<ή γε π>αρὰ Κλεάν<θ>ει λέγειν <αὐτὰ> θελήσουσ<ι>ν, ὅς φησιν ἀμείνο<νά>γε εἶναι τὰ ποιητικὰ καὶ <μουσ>ικὰ παραδεί<γμ>ατα, καὶ, τοῦ <λόγ>ου τοῦ τῆς φιλοσοφίας ἱκανῶ<ς> μὲν ἐξαγ<γ>έλλει<ν δ>υναμένου τὰ θε<ῖ>α καὶ ἀ<ν>θ<ρ>ώ<πινα, μ>ὴ ἔχον<τ>ος δὲ ψιλοῦ τῶν θείων μεγεθῶν λέξεις οἰκείας, τὰ μέτ<ρα> καὶ τὰ μέλη καὶ τοὺς ῥυθμοὺς ὡς μάλ<ι>στα προσικνεῖσθαι πρὸς τὴν ἀλήθειαν τῆς τῶν θείων θ<εω>ρίας.

For the general sense, cf. Plat. Rep. x. 607 A, εἰδέναι ὅτι ὅσον μόνον ὕμνους θεοῖς καὶ ἐγκώμια τοῖς ἀγαθοῖς ποιήσεως παραδεκτέον εἰς πόλιν. The underlying thought is that it is impossible to define the nature of God: cf. Hermes, ap. Stob. Ecl. II. 1. 26, θεὸν νοῆσαι μὲν χαλεπόν, φράσαι δὲ ἀδύνατον. Plat. Tim. 28 C, 29 C, D. The construction is not quite clear. Zeller, in citing this passage (p. 342, 1), puts a full stop after οἰκείας, but this makes τὰ μέτρα κ.τ.λ. very abrupt, and it is better to regard καὶ before τοῦ λόγου as connecting εἶναι and προσικνεῖσθαι, although this leaves ἀμείνονα without an object.

ψιλοῦ: bare prose, i.e. stripped of the advantages of metre. The history of the word is well explained in Jebb's Appendix to Oed. Col. 866. Cf. Plat. Menex. p. 239 B, C, ποιηταί...ἐν μουσικῇ ὑμνήσαντες...ἐὰν οὖν ἡμεῖς ἐπιχειρῶμεν τὰ αὐτὰ λόγῳ ψιλῷ κοσμεῖν. ψιλὸς λόγος also means "abstract reasoning" (Dr Thompson on Phaedr. 262 c), and a "bare statement" unsupported by evidence, Dem. Androt. § 22, Aphob. I. § 54.

τῶν...οἰκείας, "expressions suitable to the divine majesty."

50. Senec. Epist. 108, 10, Nam, ut dicebat Cleanthes, quemadmodum spiritus noster clariorem sonum reddit, quum illum tuba, per longi canalis angustias tractum, potentiorem novissimo exitu effudit; sic sensus nostros clariores carminis arta necessitas efficit.

tuba. Greek trumpets were long and straight, ending in a bell-shaped aperture (κώδων), cf. Aesch. Eum. 567, διάτορος Τυρσηνικὴ σάλπιγξ βροτείου πνεύματος πληρουμένη ὑπέρτονον γήρυμα φαινέτω, and Soph. Ai. 17, where Odysseus compares the voice of Athene to the sound of a trumpet.

clariorem: more distinct, cf. Cic. Div. in Q. Caecil. § 48, clarius dicere (of an actor))(multum summittere.

sensus: signification, meaning: as in Ov. Fast. V. 484, hic sensus verbi, vis ea vocis erat. Cf. Sen. Ep. 7 ad fin. 114, 1. Hence Quintilian frequently uses the word for a 'sentence' or 'period.'

arta necessitas: cf. Pind. N. IV. 33, τὰ μακρὰ δ' ἐξενέπειν ἐρύκει με τεθμός.

51. Sext. Math. IX. 88, ὁ δὲ Κλεάνθης οὕτως συνηρώτα· εἰ φύσις φύσεώς ἐστι κρείττων, εἴη ἄν τις ἀρίστη

φύσις· εἰ ψυχὴ ψυχῆς ἐστι κρείττων, εἴη ἄν τις ἀρίστη
ψυχή· καὶ εἰ ζῷον τοίνυν κρεῖττόν ἐστι ζῴου, εἴη ἄν τι
κράτιστον ζῷον. οὐ γὰρ εἰς ἄπειρον ἐκπίπτειν πέφυκε τὰ
τοιαῦτα, ὡσπεροῦν οὔτε ἡ φύσις ἐδύνατο ἐπ' ἄπειρον
αὔξεσθαι κατὰ τὸ κρεῖττον οὔθ ἡ ψυχὴ οὔτε τὸ ζῷον.
(89) ἀλλὰ μὴν ζῷον ζῴου κρεῖττόν ἐστιν, ὡς ἵππος χελώνης,
εἰ τύχοι, καὶ ταῦρος ὄνου καὶ λέων ταύρου. πάντων δὲ
σχεδὸν τῶν ἐπιγείων ζῴων καὶ σωματικῇ καὶ ψυχικῇ
διαθέσει προέχει τε καὶ κρατιστεύει ὁ ἄνθρωπος· τοίνυν
κράτιστον ἂν εἴη ζῷον καὶ ἄριστον. (90) καὶ οὐ πάνυ τι
ὁ ἄνθρωπος κράτιστον εἶναι δύναται ζῷον, οἷον εὐθέως
ὅτι διὰ κακίας πορεύεται τὸν πάντα χρόνον, εἰ δὲ μή γε,
τὸν πλεῖστον (καὶ γὰρ εἴ ποτε περιγένοιτο ἀρετῆς, ὀψὲ
καὶ πρὸς ταῖς τοῦ βίου δυσμαῖς περιγίγνεται), ἐπίκηρόν τ'
ἐστὶ καὶ ἀσθενὲς καὶ μυρίων δεόμενον βοηθημάτων,
καθάπερ τροφῆς καὶ σκεπασμάτων καὶ τῆς ἄλλης τοῦ
σώματος ἐπιμελείας, πικροῦ τινος τυράννου τρόπον ἐφεσ-
τῶτος ἡμῖν καὶ τὸν πρὸς ἡμέραν δασμὸν ἀπαιτοῦντος, καὶ
εἰ μὴ παρέχοιμεν ὥστε λούειν αὐτὸ καὶ ἀλείφειν καὶ
περιβάλλειν καὶ τρέφειν, νόσους καὶ θάνατον ἀπειλοῦντος.
ὥστε οὐ τέλειον ζῷον ὁ ἄνθρωπος, ἀτελὲς δὲ καὶ πολὺ
κεχωρισμένον τοῦ τελείου. (91) τὸ δὲ τέλειον καὶ ἄριστον
κρεῖττον μὲν ἂν ὑπάρχοι ἀνθρώπου καὶ πάσαις ταῖς
ἀρεταῖς συμπεπληρωμένον καὶ παντὸς κακοῦ ἀνεπίδεκτον,
τοῦτο δὲ οὐ διοίσει θεοῦ. ἔστιν ἄρα θεός.

This argument for the existence of God is stated in different language and a somewhat amplified form by Cic. N. D. II. 33—36: cf. especially § 35.

2. φύσις: the vital principle of plants. Zeno frag. 43.

εἰ...ἐστι...εἴη ἄν: in this form of the conditional sentence the inference is stated less bluntly than if the indicative were used: see Madv. § 135 R, 1 a. This is especially frequent with ἐθέλω or βούλομαι in the protasis: cf. Stallb. ad Plat. Symp. 208 c. Eur. Alc. 1079.

A close parallel to the use here is Dem. XXXVI. 44, εἰ δὲ τοῦτο ἀγνοεῖς, ὅτι πίστις ἀφορμὴ πασῶν ἐστι μεγίστη πρὸς χρηματισμόν, πᾶν ἂν ἀγνοήσειας.

11. διαθέσει: cf. Zeno frag. 117.

12. καί: Bekker proposed to read ἀλλά or καὶ μήν, but Wachsmuth's καίτοι is preferable.

15. περιγένοιτο: for the optative in protasis, see Jebb on Soph. Ai. 521, Ant. 666.

16. δυσμαῖς: cf. Ar. Poet. c. 21, § 13, 1457 b 22, ἢ ὃ γῆρας πρὸς βίον καὶ ἑσπέρα πρὸς ἡμέραν· ἐρεῖ τοίνυν τὴν ἑσπέραν γῆρας ἡμέρας, καὶ τὸ γῆρας ἑσπέραν βίου ἤ, ὥσπερ Ἐμπεδοκλῆς, δυσμὰς βίου. Cf. Aesch. Ag. 1123, βίου δύντος αὐγαῖς. The difficulty of attaining ἀρετή, in the Stoic sense, is illustrated by the fact that even Socrates and Antisthenes were only regarded as προκόπτοντες (Diog. VII. 91); and Alexander says that they admit the existence of a good man here and there, ὥσπερ τι παράδοξον ζῷον καὶ παρὰ φύσιν, σπανιώτερον τοῦ Φοίνικος (de Fato, c. 28). In Diog. l. c. the fact that φαῦλοι can become ἀγαθοί is given as a proof that virtue is teachable. Hirzel has traced the development of the doctrine of the wise man within the Stoa, and shews that by the earlier Stoics (Zeno and his immediate pupils) the ideal was regarded as attainable and as actually realised by themselves (pp. 274—277).

20. ἀπαιτοῦντος. The preposition conveys the idea of demanding as of right: cf. ἀποδοῦναι as used in the Halonnesus dispute (Aeschin. Ctes. § 83).

22. περιβάλλειν, "to clothe," cf. Zeno, frag. 175.

52. Cic. N. D. II. 13—15. Cleanthes quidem noster quattuor de causis dixit in animis hominum informatas deorum esse notiones. primam posuit eam, de qua modo dixi, quae orta esset ex praesensione rerum futurarum:

alteram quam ceperimus ex magnitudine commodorum, 5
quae percipiuntur caeli temperatione, fecunditate terrarum,
aliarumque commoditatum complurium copia: tertiam
quae terreret animos fulminibus, tempestatibus, nimbis,
nivibus, grandinibus, vastitate, pestilentia, terrae motibus
et saepe fremitibus, lapideisque imbribus et guttis imbrium 10
quasi cruentis, tum labibus aut repentinis terrarum
hiatibus, tum praeter naturam hominum pecudumque
portentis, tum facibus visis caelestibus, tum stellis iis,
quae Graeci cometas nostri cincinnatas vocant...tum sole
geminato...quibus exterriti homines vim quandam esse 15
caelestem et divinam suspicati sunt. quartam caussam
esse eamque vel maximam aequabilitatem motus, con-
versionem caeli, solis, lunae, siderumque omnium dis-
tinctionem, varietatem, pulcritudinem, ordinem, quarum
rerum aspectus ipse satis indicaret non esse ea fortuita. 20
Cic. N. D. III. 16, nam Cleanthes, ut dicebas, quattuor
modis formatas in animis hominum putat deorum esse
notiones. unus is modus est...qui est susceptus ex
praesensione rerum futurarum. alter ex perturbationibus
tempestatum et reliquis motibus. tertius ex commoditate 25
rerum quas perspicimus et copia. quartus ex astrorum
ordine caelique constantia.

1. *Cleanthes.* Mr Bywater concludes (Journ. Phil.
VII. 75 foll.) that Cleanthes was largely indebted to
Aristotle's dialogue περὶ φιλοσοφίας for his statement
of the four reasons given for the origin of a belief in gods,
and proves that the first and fourth in the series were
derived from that work.

2. *informatas.* It is to be observed that Cleanthes
regards the idea of God's existence as derived entirely
from our experience of external objects, and not as an
innate conception. Stein, Erkenntnistheorie, n. 737.

4. *praesensione:* this argument depends on the exis-

tence of μαντική, ἡ δι' ὀνείρων πρόρρησις etc. (Sext. Math. IX. 132), which are described as πλῆθος πραγμάτων πεπιστευμένων ἤδη παρὰ πᾶσιν ἀνθρώποις. Krische, p. 419, attributes some further arguments to Cleanthes, which the evidence does not warrant.

7. *tertiam:* there does not appear to be any extant parallel to this in the Greek texts. Although there is no reason to suppose that we have not here a reproduction of the general argument of Cleanthes, at the same time it is probable that Cicero has enlarged the list of portents from Roman sources. The prodigies mentioned are those which constantly meet us in Livy, as requiring expiation by *lustrationes, supplicationes, lectisternia* etc. Lists of prodigies illustrating those mentioned here by Cicero will be found in Liv. XXI. 62, XXII. 1, XXIV. 44, XXVI. 23, etc. Tac. H. I. 86, Juv. XIII. 65—70, and above all in the exhaustive account of Lucan, I. 525—583.

8. *quae terreret:* Prof. Mayor quotes Democritus, ap. Sext. Emp. IX. 24.

14. *cometas:* for the physical explanation, cf. on Zeno, frag. 75.

16. *quartam:* for a fuller statement of the fourth argument, cf. Sext. Math. IX. 111—118, ib. IX. 26—27: in the last passage it is simply introduced by the term ἔνιοι, but from its position between an argument of Epicurus and one belonging to some "younger Stoics," Mr Bywater (Journ. Phil. VII. 76) infers that its immediate source was one of the earlier Stoics, possibly Cleanthes.

17. *aequabilitatem.* "Cicero is probably translating some such phrase as ὁμαλότητα κινήσεως, φορὰν οὐρανοῦ," Prof. Mayor.

53. Epiphan. adv. Haeres III. 2. 9 (III. 37), Κλεάνθης τὸ ἀγαθὸν καὶ καλὸν λέγει εἶναι τὰς ἡδονάς, καὶ ἄνθρωπον ἐκάλει μόνην τὴν ψυχήν, καὶ τοὺς θεοὺς μυστικὰ σχήματα ἔλεγεν εἶναι καὶ κλήσεις ἱεράς, καὶ δᾳδοῦχον ἔφασκεν εἶναι τὸν ἥλιον, καὶ τὸν κόσμον μύστας καὶ τοὺς κατόχους τῶν θείων τελετὰς ἔλεγε.

τὸ ἀγαθόν...ἡδονάς. An obvious blunder. Krische, p. 431 n. 1, suggests that the writer of the epitome has confounded the statement by Cleanthes of his opponents' position with his own teaching.

ἄνθρωπον κ.τ.λ. Not much can be made of this mutilated statement; possibly it points to the doctrine of the soul regarded as the bond of union for the body. Stein, Psych. p. 209, finds here a trace of the correspondence between the macrocosm and the microcosm, and quotes frag. 106 τοὺς ἀπαιδεύτους μόνῃ τῇ μορφῇ τῶν θηρίων διαφέρειν.

τοὺς θεοὺς κ.τ.λ. These obscure words appear to represent an explanation of the Eleusinian mysteries from the Stoic point of view, in which the sun as the ἡγεμονικὸν is symbolised by the torchbearer who marches at the head of the procession of mystae, and (adopting Diels' corrections, v. infra) the world itself corresponds to the mystery play, while those who are inspired with divine truth are the priests. Cf. Porphyr. ap. Euseb. P. E. III. 12. p. 116, ἐν δὲ τοῖς κατ' Ἐλευσῖνα μυστηρίοις ὁ μὲν ἱεροφάντης εἰς εἰκόνα τοῦ δημιουργοῦ ἐνσκευάζεται, δᾳδοῦχος δὲ εἰς τὴν ἡλίου. For the subject in general see Prof. Mayor on Cic. N. D. I. 119. Mr Bywater however (Journ. Phil. VII. 78) believes that we have here a mutilated argument, ultimately derived from Aristotle's dialogue περὶ φιλοσοφίας, and explaining the belief in the gods as due to a feeling of awe and admiration consequent on the contemplation of the heavenly bodies. The allusion to the mysteries is brought in by way of comparison: "we seem introduced into a temple like that at Eleusis, only more august and solemn, because the figures [= the heavenly bodies] we see circling around us are not lifeless or made with hands, and the celebrants are not men, but the immortal gods." This explanation is fortified by a reference to Dio. Chrys. XII. p. 387 B, Plut. de tranq. 20, p. 477 C, D (also quoted by Diels). For μυστικὰ σχήματα see Lobeck Aglaoph. p. 130, and for κλήσεις ἱεράς ib. p. 62.

μύστας...τελετάς. Diels, p. 592, who records other suggestions, has μυστήριον...τελεστάς. Perhaps, from a comparison of Chrysipp. ap. Etym. M. 751, 16 id. Plut. Sto. Rep. 9, we ought to restore τοὺς κατόχους τῶν θείων <λόγους> τελετάς.

54. Philodem. περὶ εὐσεβ. fr. 13. ἐν δὲ τῷ δευτέ<ρῳ> (scil. περὶ θεῶν Χρύσιππος) τά τ<ε> εἰς Ὀρφέα <καὶ Μ>ουσαῖον ἀναφε<ρόμ>ε<ν>α καὶ <τ>ὰ παρ' <Ὁ>μήρῳ καὶ Ἡσιόδ<ῳ> καὶ Εὐρι<π>ίδῃ κ<αὶ> ποιηταῖς ἄλλοις <ὡ>ς κα<ὶ> Κλεάνθης <π>ειρᾶτα<ι συν>οικειοῦ<ν> ταῖς δόξαις αὐτῶ<ν>.

Cicero's paraphrase, which omits all mention of Cleanthes, is as follows (N. D. I. 41):—in secundo autem vult Orphei, Musaei, Hesiodi Homerique fabellas accomodare ad ea, quae ipse primo libro de dis immortalibus dixerat, ut etiam veterrimi poetae, qui haec ne suspicati quidem sint, Stoici fuisse videantur. As far as Cleanthes is concerned the direct evidence only applies to Homer: see Introd. p. 51, but cf. frag. 111. This passage is included by Wachsmuth (Comm. I. p. 16) under the fragments of the book περὶ θεῶν.

55. Plut. de audiendis poetis c. 11, δεῖ δὲ μηδὲ τῶν ὀνομάτων ἀμελῶς ἀκούειν, ἀλλὰ τὴν μὲν Κλεάνθους παιδιὰν παραιτεῖσθαι· κατειρωνεύεται γὰρ ἔστιν ὅτε προσποιούμενος ἐξηγεῖσθαι τὸ καὶ τὸ

Ζεῦ πάτερ Ἴδηθεν μεδέων,

Ζεῦ ἄνα Δωδωναῖε,

κελεύων ἀναγιγνώσκειν ὑφ᾽ ἕν, ὡς τὸν ἐκ τῆς γῆς ἀναθυμιώμενον ἀέρα διὰ τὴν ἀνάδοσιν Ἀναδωδωναῖον ὄντα. Wachsmuth cites Schol. B L Homer Π 233 Ζεῦ ἄνα Δωδωναῖε] τινὲς δὲ ἀναδωδωναῖε ὑφ᾽ ἓν παρὰ τὴν ἀνάδοσιν τῶν ἀγαθῶν (?)

This comes from the book περὶ τοῦ ποιητοῦ according to Krische, p. 433, and Wachsm., Comm. I. p. 17. Ζεῦ πάτερ Ἴδηθεν μεδέων, Il. III. 276, 320: Ζεῦ ἄνα Δωδωναῖε, Il. XVI. 233.

παιδιάν. It is worthy of observation that Plut. distinctly suggests that Cleanthes was not serious in his etymologies: see Introd. p. 43, 44, and cf. Plat. Cratyl. 406 B, ἀλλ᾽ ἐστὶ γὰρ καὶ σπουδαίως εἰρημένος ὁ τρόπος τῶν ὀνομάτων τούτοις τοῖς θεοῖς καὶ παιδικῶς.

ἀναθυμιώμενον: a reference to the feeding of the celestial bodies by exhalations of coarser material, cf. frag. 29 ὠκεανὸς δ᾽ ἐστι...ἧς τὴν ἀναθυμίασιν ἐπινέμεται. Cornut. c. 17, p. 84 Osann. ἀὴρ κατὰ ἀνάδοσιν. It may be observed that the attribution of this doctrine to Thales by Stob. Ecl. I. 10, 12, p. 122, 18 cannot be relied upon.

56. Plut. de Is. et Osir. 66, Φερσεφόνην δέ φησί που Κλεάνθης τὸ διὰ τῶν καρπῶν φερόμενον καὶ φονευόμενον πνεῦμα.

Dübner translates: spiritus qui per fruges dum fertur interimitur. Probably this, as well as the seven following fragments, comes from the treatise περὶ θεῶν (Wachsm. Comm. I. p. 15). Cf. Plut. de Is. c. 40, where Demeter and Persephone are explained as τὸ διὰ τῆς γῆς καὶ τῶν καρπῶν διῆκον πνεῦμα. Chrysipp. ap. Philod. περὶ εὐσεβ. col. 12, p. 79 Gomp. καὶ τὴν Δήμητρα γῆν ἢ τὸ ἐν αὐτῇ πνεῦμα. Cic. N. D. II. 66, ea (Proserpina) enim est quae Φερσεφόνη Graece nominatur, quam frugum semen esse volunt absconditamque quaeri a matre fingunt. Plato's derivations of the name will be found at Cratyl. 404 C, D. For modern views see Jebb on Soph. Ant. 894.

57. Macrob. Sat. I. 18, 14, unde Cleanthes ita cognominatum scribit (Dionysum) ἀπὸ τοῦ διανύσαι, quia cotidiano impetu ab oriente ad occasum diem noctemque faciendo caeli conficit cursum.

In the Orphic hymn, quoted just before the present passage, Dionysus is derived from δινεῖσθαι. He is elsewhere explained by the Stoics (1) as wine, Cic. N. D. II. 60, cf. Plato's derivation from δίδωμι and οἶνος, the latter being resolved into οἴεσθαι and νοῦς, (2) as τὸ γόνιμον πνεῦμα καὶ τρόφιμον, Plut. de Is. c. 40. For the identification of Dionysus with the sun see the commentators on Verg. Georg. I. 5, vos, o clarissima mundi lumina, labentem caelo quae ducitis annum, Liber et alma Ceres.

58. Macrob. Sat. I. 17, 8, Cleanthes (Apollinem) ὡς ἀπ' ἄλλων καὶ ἄλλων τόπων τὰς ἀνατολὰς ποιούμενον, quod ab aliis atque aliis locorum declinationibus faciat ortus.

Chrysippus (Macrob. l. c.) derived the word Ἀπόλλων from ἀ and πολύς, while Plato explains the various functions of the God by different etymologies of his name (Crat. p. 405 A—E), so that he is at once ἁπλοῦ, ἀεὶ βάλλοντος, ἀπολούοντος, and ὁμοπολοῦντος (ib. p. 406 A).

59. Macrob. Sat. I. 17. 36, Cleanthes Lycium Apollinem appellatum notat quod, veluti lupi pecora rapiunt, ita ipse quoque humorem eripit radiis.

Antipater in the same passage derives the name ἀπὸ τοῦ λευκαίνεσθαι πάντα φωτίζοντος ἡλίου, a guess, which, so far as the etymology of Λύκειος is concerned, has found some favour in modern times (Müller Dor. II. 6 § 8). Probably Cleanthes did not recognise a distinction between the two titles Λύκιος and Λύκειος (Soph. El. 7), and the best modern opinion seems to agree with him to this extent: see Leaf on Il. IV. 101. The connection of Apollo with wolves is indicated by the legends in Pausan. II. 9. 7, II. 19. 3. In Cornut. c. 32 the name is explained in connection with the pestilences brought by Apollo on flocks, which were therefore entrusted to him as Apollo Lycius.

humorem eripit: cf. frags. 29 and 55.

60. Macrob. Sat. 1. 17. 31, Λοξίας cognominatur, ut ait Oenopides, ὅτι ἐκπορεύεται τὸν λοξὸν κύκλον ἀπὸ δυσμῶν ἐπ᾽ ἀνατολὰς κινούμενος, id est quod obliquum circulum ab occasu ad orientem pergit: aut, ut Cleanthes scribit, ἐπειδὴ καθ᾽ ἕλικας κινεῖται, λοξαὶ γάρ εἰσι καὶ αὗται, quod flectuosum iter pergit.

Cf. Achill. Tat. Isag. 169 A, ὁ ζῳδιακὸς καὶ λοξίας ὑπό τινων καλεῖται, ἐπειδὴ ἥλιος τὰς ὁδοὺς ἐν αὐτῷ πορεύεται λοξός. ἐν δὲ τῷ ἡλίῳ ὁ Ἀπόλλων ὃς καλεῖται Λοξίας ὑπὸ τῶν ποιητῶν εἶναι πιστεύεται. Cornut. c. 32 gives two explanations: λοξῶν δὲ καὶ περισκελῶν ὄντων τῶν χρησμῶν οὓς δίδωσι Λοξίας ὠνόμασται· ἢ ἀπὸ τῆς λοξότητος τῆς πορείας ἣν ποιεῖται διὰ τοῦ ζῳδιακοῦ κύκλου. For modern derivations of the name Loxias see Jebb on Soph. O.T. 854.

ἕλικας: for the obliquity of the sun's course cf. frag. 29 and Diog. L. VII. 144 there quoted.

61. Photius s.v. λέσχαι, p. 158 ed. Herm., Κλεάνθης δέ φησιν ἀπονενεμῆσθαι τῷ Ἀπόλλωνι τὰς λέσχας, ἐξέδραις δὲ ὁμοίας γίνεσθαι, καὶ αὐτὸν δὲ τὸν Ἀπόλλω παρ᾽ ἐνίοις Λεσχηνόριον ἐπικαλεῖσθαι. So Suidas I. 541 s. v.

λέσχαι. In Harpocrat. s.v. we get the additional information that these remarks were contained in the treatise περὶ θεῶν.

Cf. Plut. de εἰ ap. Delphos c. 2: Apollo is called Λεσχηνόριος, ὅταν ἐνεργῶσι καὶ ἀπολαύωσι χρώμενοι τῷ διαλέγεσθαι καὶ φιλοσοφεῖν πρὸς ἀλλήλους. The inference drawn by Wachsmuth seems correct, viz., that Cornutus took from Cleanthes the words found in c. 32, καὶ λεσχηνόριον δ' αὐτὸν ('Ἀπόλλωνα) προσηγόρευσαν διὰ τὸ τὰς ἡμέρας ταῖς λέσχαις καὶ τῷ ὁμιλεῖν ἀλλήλοις συνέχεσθαι τοὺς ἀνθρώπους, τὰς δὲ νύκτας καθ' ἑαυτοὺς ἀναπαύεσθαι. He remarks that Cornutus appears to have devoted much attention to the study of Cleanthes. Cf. Pers. Sat. v. 63, cultor enim iuvenum purgatas inseris aures fruge Cleanthea.

ἐξέδραις. These were recesses or alcoves sometimes branching out from an open air court, and fitted with stone seats; they were especially adapted for the conversation of philosophers and rhetoricians. Cf. Cic. Fin. v. 4, ego illa moveor exedra; modo enim fuit Carneadis; quem videre videor (est enim nota imago), a sedeque ipsa, tanta ingeni magnitudine orbata, desiderari illam vocem puto. "Vitruvius in his description of the palaestra, or gymnasium, such as were attached to Roman villas of the higher class, recommends that in three of the cloisters surrounding the court there should be exedrae spatiosae in quibus philosophi, rhetores, reliquique qui studiis delectantur sedentes disputare possint v. 11." Prof. Mayor on Cic. N.D. I. 15. See also Becker, Charicles, p. 303. Guhl and Koner, p. 403.

ὁμοίας: the distinction between λέσχαι and ἐξέδραι seems to be that the former were separate buildings used entirely as lounges, whereas the latter were attached either to a private house or a public gymnasium.

THE FRAGMENTS OF CLEANTHES. 291

62. Cornut. c. 31 ad fin., τοὺς δὲ δώδεκα ἄθλους ἐνδέχεται μὲν ἀναγαγεῖν οὐκ ἀλλοτρίως ἐπὶ τὸν θεόν, ὡς καὶ Κλεάνθης ἐποίησεν· οὐ δεῖν δὲ δοκεῖ πανταχοῦ εὑρεσίλογον πρεσβεύειν.

It seems clear from the account of Cornutus that there were two current modes of allegorical interpretation of the myths which centre round Heracles. By one set of interpreters Heracles was regarded as an ordinary mortal and by others as a god. Cleanthes apparently explained the twelve labours from the latter point of view. An illustration of this line of interpretation may be seen in the explanation given by Cornutus of Heracles as an archer: καὶ τοξότης δ' ἂν ὁ θεὸς παρεισάγοιτο, κατά τε τὸ πανταχοῦ διϊκνεῖσθαι κ.τ.λ. But in the account of the twelve labours in Heraclitus, All. Hom. c. 33, Heracles is represented simply as a wise man who brought to light the hidden truths of philosophy: Ἡρακλέα δὲ νομιστέον οὐκ ἀπὸ σωματικῆς δυνάμεως ἀναχθέντα τοσοῦτον ἰσχῦσαι τοῖς τότε χρόνοις. ἀλλ' ἀνὴρ ἔμφρων καὶ σοφίας οὐρανίου μύστης γεγονώς, ὡσπερεὶ κατὰ βαθείας ἀχλύος ὑποδεδυκυῖαν ἐφώτισε τὴν φιλοσοφίαν, καθάπερ ὁμολογοῦσι καὶ Στωικῶν οἱ δοκιμώτατοι. Zeller, pp. 368, 369, relying on the concluding words of the passage cited, thinks that the account is derived from Cleanthes, but, if so, there is a discrepancy with Cornutus. Krische (p. 400) on the other hand says:—"irre ich nicht, so führte Kleanthes, gleichwie später Porphyrius (bei Euseb. P.E. III. 112 c), die zwölf Arbeiten des Herakles auf die Bahn der Sonne durch die zwölf Zeichen des Zodiakus zurück (Cornut. de N. D. p. 91 G)."

εὑρεσίλογον: "expectes τόν," Lang. Osann interprets this to mean that Cornutus apologises for referring to the authority of Cleanthes by saying that such a trifler ought not to be respected in all cases. This derives a certain amount of support from Plutarch de aud. poet. p. 31 where

Chrysippus is spoken of as εὑρεσιλογῶν ἀπιθάνως. But it seems strange that Cornutus should have alluded to Cleanthes in this manner. Why cannot the word be used in a good sense as in Diog. L. IV. 37? Mr Hicks suggests εὑρεσιλογίαν.

63. Schol. in Hom. Il. III. 64, ap. Bekker, p. 99 b. 23, Κλεάνθης δὲ ἐν Λέσβῳ οὕτω τιμᾶσθαι χρυσῆν Ἀφροδίτην.

Wachsmuth (Comm. I. p. 15) classes this among the fragments of the work περὶ θεῶν, but there is more likelihood in Krische's view (p. 433) that it belongs to the περὶ τοῦ ποιητοῦ, for there is no reason to separate it from frags. 55 and 65. Perhaps Cleanthes tried to explain the currency of the epithet χρυσέη by the existence of a gilded statue of Aphrodite at Lesbos. For the figurative meaning of χρυσοῦς = precious, which is perhaps all that is implied in the epithet, see Jebb on Soph. Ant. 699.

64. Athen. XIII. 572 f., πόρνης δὲ Ἀφροδίτης ἱερόν ἐστι παρὰ Ἀβυδηνοῖς, ὥς φησι Πάμφιλος· κατεχομένης γὰρ τῆς πόλεως δουλείᾳ τοὺς φρουροὺς τοὺς ἐν αὐτῇ ποτε θύσαντας, ὡς ἱστορεῖ Κλεάνθης ἐν τοῖς Μυθικοῖς, καὶ μεθυσθέντας ἑταίρας πλείονας προσλαβεῖν· ὧν μίαν, κατακοιμηθέντας αὐτοὺς ἰδοῦσαν, ἀνελομένην τὰς κλεῖς καὶ τὸ τεῖχος ὑπερβᾶσαν, ἀπαγγεῖλαι τοῖς Ἀβυδηνοῖς. τοὺς δ' αὐτίκα μεθ' ὅπλων ἀφικομένους, ἀνελεῖν μὲν τοὺς φύλακας, κρατήσαντας δὲ τῶν τειχῶν καὶ γενομένους ἐγκρατεῖς τῆς ἐλευθερίας χαριστήρια τῇ πόρνῃ ἀποδίδοντας Ἀφροδίτης Πόρνης ναὸν ἱδρύσασθαι.

Πόρνης: cf. Aphrodite Pandemos, and the worship of Aphrodite Ourania at Corinth (Becker's Charicles, p. 246). The object of Cleanthes was doubtless to explain away the discreditable legends attaching themselves to the gods, and thus in the present instance the debased worship at

Abydos is shown to be due to the accident of a historical circumstance, and not to the essential characteristics of the goddess. There is however considerable doubt as to the genuineness of this fragment, see Introd. p. 51.

65. Schol. in Hom. Od. I. 52, ap. Cramer, Anecd. Oxon. III. 416, ὀλοόφρονος] Κλεάνθης δασύνει· τοῦ περὶ τῶν ὅλων φρονοῦντος.

Wachsmuth also quotes Eustath. in Hom. p. 1389, 55, τὸν Ἄτλαντα...οἱ μὲν ἀλληγοροῦσιν εἰς τὴν ἀκάματον καὶ ἀκοπίατον πρόνοιαν τὴν πάντων αἰτίαν καὶ ὀλοόφρονα τὸν τοιοῦτον Ἄτλαντα νοοῦσιν, ὡς τὸν ὑπὲρ ὅλων φρονοῦντα ἤγουν τῶν ὅλων φροντιστικόν. διὸ καὶ ὁ Κλεάνθης, ὥς φασιν, ἐδάσυνε τὸ ὅ τῆς ἀρχούσης. Cf. Cornut. de nat. d. c. 26, ὀλοόφρονα δ' αὐτὸν (Ἄτλαντα) εἰρῆσθαι διὰ τὸ περὶ τῶν ὅλων φροντίζειν καὶ προνοεῖσθαι τῆς πάντων αὐτοῦ τῶν μερῶν σωτηρίας. See also Flach Glossen u. Scholien zur Hes. Th. p. 76. Cleanthes identified Atlas with πρόνοια, as holding together the framework of the world (cf. ἕξις).

66. Apollon. soph. lex. Homer, p. 114 ed. Bekk. v. μῶλυ (κ. 305), Κλεάνθης δὲ ὁ φιλόσοφος ἀλληγορικῶς φησι δηλοῦσθαι τὸν λόγον, δι' οὗ μωλύνονται αἱ ὁρμαὶ καὶ τὰ πάθη.

This frag. is taken from Wachsmuth (Comm. I. p. 18): cf. Zeno, frag. 160, διαλάμπει τῆς ψυχῆς τὸ φανταστικὸν καὶ παθητικὸν ὑπὸ τοῦ λόγου διακεχυμένον. Stob. Ecl. II. 7. 10[a] p. 89, 16, πάντες δ' οἱ ἐν τοῖς πάθεσιν ὄντες ἀποστρέφονται τὸν λόγον. In this connection we may observe that Odysseus was taken by the Stoic school as one of the few typical wise men (Sen. de Const. 2. 1, de Benef. 13. 3). This is the earliest known instance of the word ἀλληγορία.

67. Certamen Homer. et Hesiod., p. 4, 18, ed. Nietzsch (in act. societ. philol. Lips. tom. I. fasc. 1), Ἑλλάνικος μὲν γὰρ καὶ Κλεάνθης Μαίονα (sic coni. Sturz, Hellanic. frg. p. 171 et Welcker ep. cycl. p. 149 pro βίονα) λέγουσι (πατέρα Ὁμήρου).

This frag. is taken from Wachsm. Comm. I. p. 17. Cf. Procl. vit. Hom. ap. Gaisford Hephaestion, p. 516, οἱ μὲν οὖν Σμυρναῖον αὐτὸν ἀποφαινόμενοι Μαίονος μὲν πατρὸς λέγουσιν εἶναι. ib. p. 517, Μαίονα γάρ φασι (scil. Ἑλλάνικος καὶ Δαμαστὴς καὶ Φερεκύδης) τὸν Ὁμήρου πατέρα.

68. Porphyr. vit. Pythag. 1, 2, Κλεάνθης ἐν τῷ πέμπτῳ τῶν μυθικῶν Σύρον, ἐκ Τύρου τῆς Συρίας (scil. Mnesarchus, the father of Pythagoras). σιτοδείας δὲ καταλαβούσης τοὺς Σαμίους προσπλεύσαντα τὸν Μνήσαρχον κατ' ἐμπορίαν μετὰ σίτου τῇ νήσῳ καὶ ἀποδόμενον
5 τιμηθῆναι πολιτείᾳ. Πυθαγόρου δ' ἐκ παίδων εἰς πᾶσαν μάθησιν ὄντος εὐφυοῦς, τὸν Μνήσαρχον ἀπαγαγεῖν αὐτὸν εἰς Τύρον, ἐκεῖ δὲ τοῖς Χαλδαίοις συστάντα μετασχεῖν τούτων ἐπὶ πλεῖον ποιῆσαι, ἐπανελθόντα δ' εἰς τὴν Ἰωνίαν ἐντεῦθεν τὸν Πυθαγόραν πρῶτον μὲν Φερεκύδῃ τῷ Συρίῳ
10 ὁμιλῆσαι δεύτερον δ' Ἑρμοδάμαντι τῷ Κρεωφυλίῳ ἐν Σάμῳ ἤδη γηράσκοντι. λέγει δ' ὁ Κλεάνθης ἄλλους εἶναι οἳ τὸν πατέρα αὐτοῦ Τυρηνὸν ἀποφαίνονται τῶν τὴν Λῆμνον ἀποικησάντων ἐντεῦθεν δὲ κατὰ πρᾶξιν εἰς Σάμον ἐλθόντα καταμεῖναι καὶ ἀστὸν γενέσθαι. πλέοντος δὲ τοῦ
15 Μνησάρχου εἰς τὴν Ἰταλίαν συμπλεύσαντα τὸν Πυθαγόραν νέον ὄντα κομιδῇ σφόδρα οὖσαν εὐδαίμονα καὶ τόθ' ὕστερον εἰς αὐτὴν ἀποπλεῦσαι. καταλέγει δ' αὐτοῦ καὶ ἀδελφοὺς δύο Εὔνουστον καὶ Τυρρηνὸν πρεσβυτέρους. Wachsmuth also quotes Clem. Alex. Strom. I. p. 129 S. ὡς δὲ Κλεάνθης (MSS. Νεάνθης) Σύριος ἢ Τύριος (fuit Pythagoras). Theodoret, Graec. aff. cur. p. 8, 43, ὁ δὲ Κλεάνθης (MSS. Νεάνθης) Τύριον (Πυθαγόραν) ὀνομάζει.

This frag. must stand or fall with frag. 64. The facts

in the life of Pythagoras with which these statements are concerned will be found fully discussed by Zeller, pre-Socratics, I. p. 324 foll. After εὐδαίμονα in l. 16 some such word as αἰσθέσθαι seems wanted.

69. Pseudo-Plut. de Fluviorum nominibus, v. 3, παράκειται δ' [αὐτῷ] τὸ Καυκάσιον ὄρος· ἐκαλεῖτο δὲ τὸ πρότερον Βορέου κοίτη δι' αἰτίαν τοιαύτην. Βορέας δι' ἐρωτικὴν ἐπιθυμίαν Χιόνην ἁρπάσας, τὴν Ἀρκτούρου θυγατέρα, κατήνεγκεν εἴς τινα λόφον Νιφάντην καλούμενον, καὶ ἐγέννησεν ἐκ τῆς προειρημένης υἱὸν Ὕρπακα, 5 τὸν διαδεξάμενον Ἡνιόχου τὴν βασίλειαν. μετωνομάσθη δὲ τὸ ὄρος κοίτη Βορέου. προσηγορεύθη δὲ Καύκασος διὰ περίστασιν τοιαύτην. μετὰ τὴν γιγαντομαχίαν Κρόνος ἐκκλίνων τὰς Διὸς ἀπειλάς, ἔφυγεν εἰς τὴν ἀκρώρειαν Βορέου κοίτης, καὶ εἰς κροκόδειλον μεταμορφωθεὶς <ἔλαθεν· 10 ὁ δὲ Προμηθεὺς> ἕνα τῶν ἐγχωρίων ποιμένα, Καύκασον, ἀνατάμων, καὶ κατανοήσας αὐτοῦ τὴν διάθεσιν τῶν σπλάγχνων, εἶπεν οὐ μακρὰν εἶναι τοὺς πολεμίους. ὁ δὲ Ζεὺς ἐπιφανεὶς τὸν μὲν πατέρα δήσας πλεκτῷ ἐρίῳ, κατεταρτάρωσε· τὸ δ' ὄρος εἰς τιμὴν τοῦ ποιμένος Καύ- 15 κασον μετονομάσας, προσέδησεν αὐτῷ τὸν Προμηθέα καὶ ἠνάγκασεν αὐτὸν ὑπὸ σπλαγχνοφάγου ἀετοῦ βασανίζεσθαι, ὅτι παρηνόμησεν εἰς τὰ σπλάγχνα, ὡς ἱστορεῖ Κλεάνθης ἐν γ' θεομαχίας.

The treatise *de Fluviis* was composed perhaps in the reign of Hadrian or Trajan, but all or nearly all the authorities which the author cites are impudent fictions. For further information see the Preface to Hercher's edition of the tract (Lips. 1851) and especially § 3.

2. **Βορέου κοίτη**: cf. Pind. Nem. I. 3, Ὀρτυγία δέμνιον Ἀρτέμιδος. Hom. Il. XXIV. 615, ἐν Σιπύλῳ ὅθι φασὶ θεάων ἔμμεναι εὐνὰς νυμφάων.

10. **μεταμορφωθείς**. Wyttenbach saw that some words

had fallen out here, since a reference to Prometheus is required. He supplied therefore the words within brackets and substituted ἀναταμὼν for ἀναπαύων. For ἀναπαύων ἀναρπάζων (Reinesius) and ἀνασπῶν (Dodwell) have also been suggested.

70. Pseudo-Plut. de Fluv. v. 4, γεννᾶται δ' ἐν αὐτῷ (Caucasus) βοτάνη Προμήθειος καλουμένη, ἣν Μήδεια συλλέγουσα καὶ λειοτριβοῦσα, πρὸς ἀντιπαθείας τοῦ πατρὸς ἐχρήσατο, καθὼς ἱστορεῖ ὁ αὐτός (scil. Cleanthes).

Προμήθειος, cf. Ap. Rhod. III. 843,

ἡ δὲ τέως γλαφυρῆς ἐξείλετο φωριαμοῖο
φάρμακον, ὅ ῥρά τε φασὶ Προμήθειον καλέεσθαι,

where a lengthy description of the plant and its virtues is given. Prop. I. 12. 9, num me deus obruit, an quae lecta Prometheis dividit herba iugis.

71. Pseudo-Plut. de Fluv. XVII. 4, γεννᾶται δ' ἐν αὐτῷ (Taygetus) βοτάνη καλουμένη Χαρισία ἣν <αἱ> γυναῖκες ἔαρος ἀρχομένου τοῖς τραχήλοις περιάπτουσι καὶ ὑπὸ τῶν ἀνδρῶν συμπαθέστερον ἀγαπῶνται· καθὼς ἱστορεῖ Κλεάνθης ἐν α΄ περὶ ὀρῶν.

Χαρισία: Hercher thinks this word is invented from the name of a city in Arcadia.

ETHICA.

72. Stob. Ecl. II. 7. 6ᵃ, p. 76, 3, Κλεάνθης...οὕτως ἀπέδωκε· τέλος ἐστὶ τὸ ὁμολογουμένως τῇ φύσει ζῆν. Cf. Diog. L. VII. 87, Clem. Alex. Strom. II. 21. 129, p. 497 P., 179 S., Κλεάνθης δὲ (scil. τέλος ἡγεῖται) τὸ ὁμολογουμένως τῇ φύσει ζῆν ἐν τῷ εὐλογιστεῖν, ὃ ἐν τῇ τῶν κατὰ φύσιν ἐκλογῇ κεῖσθαι διελάμβανεν.

In the extract from Clement, Krische, p. 423 n., proposes to insert the words Διογένης δὲ between ζῆν and ἐν τῷ εὐλογιστεῖν on the evidence afforded by Diog. L. VII. 88, Stob. Ecl. II. 7. 6ᵃ, p. 76, 9, who both expressly attribute the definition εὐλογιστεῖν ἐν τῇ τῶν κατὰ φύσιν ἐκλογῇ to Diogenes Babylonius. His suggestion is approved by Wachsmuth (Comm. II. p. 4) and Heinze, Stoic. Eth. p. 11 n. For the question as to whether Cleanthes first introduced the words τῇ φύσει into the definition, see on Zeno, frag. 120.

73. Diog. L. VII. 89, φύσιν δὲ Χρύσιππος μὲν ἐξακούει, ᾗ ἀκολούθως δεῖ ζῆν, τήν τε κοινὴν καὶ ἰδίως ἀνθρωπίνην· ὁ δὲ Κλεάνθης τὴν κοινὴν μόνην ἐκδέχεται φύσιν, ᾗ ἀκολουθεῖν δεῖ, οὐκέτι δὲ καὶ τὴν ἐπὶ μέρους· τήν τε ἀρετὴν διάθεσιν εἶναι ὁμολογουμένην καὶ αὐτὴν δι' αὐτὴν εἶναι αἱρετήν, οὐ διά τινα φόβον ἢ ἐλπίδα ἤ τι τῶν ἔξωθεν· ἐν αὐτῇ τε εἶναι τὴν εὐδαιμονίαν, ἅτε οὔσῃ ψυχῇ πεποιημένῃ πρὸς τὴν ὁμολογίαν παντὸς τοῦ βίου· διαστρέφεσθαι δὲ τὸ λογικὸν ζῷον ποτὲ μὲν διὰ τὰς τῶν ἔξωθεν πραγματειῶν πιθανότητας, ποτὲ δὲ διὰ τὴν κατήχησιν τῶν συνόντων, ἐπεὶ ἡ φύσις ἀφορμὰς δίδωσιν ἀδιαστρόφους.

Diogenes leads us to suppose that Cleanthes and Chrysippus dissented as to the interpretation of φύσις, and that Cleanthes refused to allow that human nature is included. This however is scarcely credible (cf. the next frag.), although it is quite possible that Cleanthes laid special stress on κοινὴ φύσις and κοινὸς νόμος, cf. frag. 48, l. 24, Cic. Fin. III. 73, utrum conveniat necne natura hominis cum universa. So Zeller, p. 229, who is followed by Wellmann, p. 448. To attain this conformity an acquaintance with physics is necessary (Cic. l. c., Chrysipp. ap. Plut. Sto. Rep. 9). Hirzel II. pp. 112—118, thinks that Diogenes' account is substantially right. He regards Zeno as the upholder of Cynicism in preference to which Cleanthes devoted himself to the study of Heraclitus, cf. Heracl. fr. 7, Sch., διὸ δεῖ ἕπεσθαι τῷ ξυνῷ, τοῦ λόγου δὲ ἐόντος ξυνοῦ ζώουσιν οἱ πολλοὶ ὡς ἰδίαν ἔχοντες φρόνησιν. To the objection that Zeno had already recognised the Heraclitean λόγος as a leading physical principle, Hirzel answers that it does not follow that he also transferred it to the region of ethics, and that Cleanthes must be credited with this innovation. The latter part of the fragment has been included in deference to the judgment of Wachsmuth, but it appears extremely doubtful whether we are justified in tracing the epitomised views back to Cleanthes, because his name appears in the context.

διάθεσιν ὁμολογουμένην: for διάθεσιν see on Zeno, frag. 117, and for the general sense cf. Chrysipp. ap. Stob. Ecl. II. 7. 5^(b1), p. 60, 7, κοινότερον δὲ τὴν ἀρετὴν διάθεσιν εἶναί φασι ψυχῆς σύμφωνον αὐτῇ περὶ ὅλον τὸν βίον.

ἅτ' οὔσῃ: Zeller (p. 238, 3) corrects οὔσης ψυχῆς πεποιημένης.

ἀφορμάς, cf. frag. 82.

74. Stob. Ecl. II. 7. 6^e, p. 77, 21, εὐδαιμονία δ' ἐστὶν εὔροια βίου. κέχρηται δὲ καὶ Κλεάνθης τῷ ὅρῳ τούτῳ ἐν τοῖς ἑαυτοῦ συγγράμμασι καὶ ὁ Χρύσιππος καὶ οἱ ἀπὸ τούτων πάντες τὴν εὐδαιμονίαν εἶναι λέγοντες οὐχ ἑτέραν τοῦ εὐδαίμονος βίου, καίτοι γε λέγοντες τὴν μὲν εὐδαιμονίαν σκοπὸν ἐκκεῖσθαι τέλος δ' εἶναι τὸ τυχεῖν τῆς εὐδαιμονίας, ὅπερ ταὐτὸν εἶναι τῷ εὐδαιμονεῖν. Sext. Emp. Math. XI. 30, εὐδαιμονία δέ ἐστιν, ὡς οἱ περὶ τὸν Κλεάνθην, εὔροια βίου.

σκοπόν. For the distinction between σκοπὸς and τέλος, cf. Stob. Ecl. II. 7. 3^c, p. 47, 8, καὶ ἔστι σκοπὸς μὲν τὸ προκείμενον εἰς τὸ τυχεῖν, οἷον ἀσπὶς τοξόταις· τέλος δ' ἡ τοῦ προκειμένου τεῦξις. βούλονται γὰρ ἐνέργημα ἡμέτερον εἶναι πρὸς τὸ τέλος, ib. II. 7. 6ᶜ, p. 77, 1—5. Wachsmuth believes the distinction to be due to Chrysippus. The difficult passage in Cic. Fin. III. 22 is not really parallel to this: see Madv. in loc. On the whole matter see Hirzel, p. 550 foll.: he argues that the distinction between σκοπὸς and τέλος was foreign to the earlier Stoa, and was introduced by Panaetius.

75. Clem. Alex. Protrept. VI. 72, p. 21 S., 61 P., Κλεάνθης δὲ ὁ Ἀσσεύς, ὁ ἀπὸ τῆς Στοᾶς φιλόσοφος ὃς οὐ θεογονίαν ποιητικὴν θεολογίαν δὲ ἀληθινὴν ἐνδείκνυται, οὐκ ἀπεκρύψατο τοῦ θεοῦ πέρι ὅτι περ εἶχεν φρονῶν·

> τἀγαθὸν ἐρωτᾷς μ᾽ οἷον ἔστ᾽; ἄκουε δή·
> τεταγμένον, δίκαιον, ὅσιον, εὐσεβές,
> κρατοῦν ἑαυτοῦ, χρήσιμον, καλόν, δέον,
> αὐστηρόν, αὐθέκαστον, αἰεὶ συμφέρον,
> ἄφοβον, ἄλυπον, λυσιτελές, ἀνώδυνον,   5
> ὠφέλιμον, εὐάρεστον, ἀσφαλές, φίλον,
> ἔντιμον   *   *   *   ὁμολογούμενον,
> εὐκλεές, ἄτυφον, ἐπιμελές, πρᾷον, σφοδρόν,
> χρονιζόμενον, ἄμεμπτον, αἰεὶ διαμένον.

The same occurs in Strom. V. 14, 110, p. 715 P., 257 S., introduced by the words ἔν τινι ποιήματι περὶ τοῦ θεοῦ and also in Euseb. P. E. XIII. 13, p. 679.

Clement's mistake in referring these lines to Cleanthes' conception of the deity, when they really refer to the ethical *summum bonum*, is obvious, and has been pointed out by Krische, p. 420 f. Krische thinks that they may have formed a poetical appendix to the prose work, which is either the περὶ τέλους or the περὶ καλῶν.

Seven of these epithets, viz. δίκαιον, χρήσιμον, καλόν, δέον, συμφέρον, λυσιτελές, ὠφέλιμον are predicated of ἀγαθόν in Diog. L. VII. 98, 99, with the addition of αἱρετόν and εὔχρηστον: cf. Stob. Ecl. II. 7. 5ᵈ, p. 69, 11, πάντα δὲ τἀγαθὰ ὠφέλιμα εἶναι καὶ εὔχρηστα καὶ συμφέροντα καὶ λυσιτελῆ καὶ σπουδαῖα καὶ πρέποντα καὶ καλὰ καὶ οἰκεῖα, ib. 5¹, p. 72, 19, ib. 11ʰ, p. 100, 15 foll. Chrysippus proved similar statements by his favourite chain arguments, Plut. Sto. Rep. c. 13, Cic. Fin. III. 27, Tusc. V. 45.

3. κρατοῦν ἑαυτοῦ: pointing to the virtue ἐγκράτεια (frag. 76): reliquum est, ut tute tibi imperes, Cic. Tusc. II. 47.

4. αὐστηρόν: cf. Diog. L. VII. 117, καὶ αὐστηροὺς δέ φασιν εἶναι πάντας τοὺς σπουδαίους, Stob. Ecl. II. 7. 11ᵍ, p. 114, 22.

αὐθέκαστον: in Ar. Eth. IV. 7. 4 the αὐθέκαστος is the mean between the ἀλαζὼν and the εἴρων, and is described as ἀληθευτικὸς καὶ τῷ βίῳ καὶ τῷ λόγῳ. We may compare then Stob. Ecl. II. 7, 11ᵐ, p. 108, 11, where the wise man is said to be ἁπλοῦς καὶ ἄπλαστος while τὸ εἰρωνεύεσθαι belongs alone to the φαῦλος, ib. p. 111, 11, ἐν πᾶσιν ἀληθεύειν τὸν σοφόν.

5. ἄφοβον, ἄλυπον, ἀνώδυνον: because the wise man is ἀπαθής.

7. Some word has dropped out here. In Clem. Alex. Strom. V. 1. c. the words ἀσφαλὲς φίλον ἔντιμον are omitted and ὁμολογούμενον is placed at the end of l. 6. In Euseb. l. c. we have two complete lines but εὐάρεστον is repeated from l. 6, thus:—ἔντιμον εὐάρεστον ὁμολογούμενον: this is perhaps the original reading, where the error is due to εὐάρεστον having been copied from the previous line in place of the genuine word. The reading in book V. is due to the scribe's eye wandering from the first εὐάρεστον to the second. Mohnike however thinks (p. 51) that Eusebius had the work of Clement

before him while writing, and that the second εὐάρεστον is mere patchwork to mend the metre.

8. ἄτυφον, cf. Diog. L. VII. 117, ἄτυφον τε εἶναι τὸν σοφόν.

πρᾷον, cf. Stob. Ecl. II. 7. 11⁸, p. 115, 10—12.

76. Plut. Sto. Rep. VII. 4, ὁ δὲ Κλεάνθης ἐν ὑπομνήμασι φυσικοῖς εἰπὼν ὅτι "πληγὴ πυρὸς ὁ τόνος ἐστί, κἂν ἱκανὸς ἐν τῇ ψυχῇ γένηται πρὸς τὸ ἐπιτελεῖν τὰ ἐπιβάλλοντα ἰσχὺς καλεῖται καὶ κράτος," ἐπιφέρει κατὰ λέξιν, "ἡ δ' ἰσχὺς αὕτη καὶ τὸ κράτος ὅταν μὲν ἐπὶ τοῖς φανεῖσιν ἐμμενετέοις ἐγγένηται, ἐγκράτειά ἐστιν· ὅταν δ' ἐν τοῖς ὑπομενετέοις, ἀνδρεία· περὶ τὰς ἀξίας δὲ δικαιοσύνη· περὶ τὰς αἱρέσεις καὶ ἐκκλίσεις σωφροσύνη."

Cf. Stob. Ecl. II. 7. 5ᵇ⁴, p. 62, 24, καὶ ὁμοίως ὥσπερ ἰσχὺς τοῦ σώματος τόνος ἐστὶν ἱκανὸς ἐν νεύροις οὕτω καὶ ἡ τῆς ψυχῆς ἰσχὺς τόνος ἐστὶν ἱκανὸς ἐν τῷ κρίνειν καὶ πράττειν ἢ μή. See also Zeller, p. 128, 2, 256, 2.

πληγὴ πυρός. This is the material air-current which forms the ἡγεμονικόν of the individual, being an efflux of the divine πνεῦμα. Cleanthes here brings his ethical teaching into close dependence on his physical researches: of the physical aspect of τόνος we have spoken at frag. 24. Zeno's φρόνησις is explained as ἱκανὸς τόνος ψυχῆς, i.e. as ἰσχὺς καὶ κράτος. Possibly Cleanthes was influenced by the Cynic use of τόνος: see the passage quoted by Stein, Psych. p. 30 n. 37. Not that Cleanthes intended to deny the fundamental position of Zeno that virtue is wisdom, for we shall find that he expressly declared it to be teachable (frag. 79): and cf. frag. 89. Still, he expanded and developed his master's teaching in two ways, (1) by showing that the doctrine of virtue rests on a psychological basis, and (2) by clearing up an ambiguity in Zeno's statement with regard to the four cardinal virtues.

Zeno held, or appeared to hold, that φρόνησις is found in a double sense, (1) as the essential groundwork of all virtue, and (2) as the first of its four main divisions. This inconsistency is therefore removed by retaining φρόνησις in the wider, but substituting ἐγκράτεια in the narrower meaning: see Hirzel II. p. 97 foll. Chrysippus on the other hand restored φρόνησις as the cardinal virtue, but represented by ἐπιστήμη that notion of φρόνησις which was common to Zeno and Cleanthes.

φανεῖσιν: so Hirzel, p. 97, 2, for ἐπιφάνεσιν, coll. Stob. Ecl. II. 7. 5^{b2}, p. 61, 11, ἐγκράτειαν δὲ ἐπιστήμην ἀνυπέρβατον τῶν κατὰ τὸν ὀρθὸν λόγον φανέντων. We find also definitions of ἐγκράτεια in Diog. L. VII. 93, Sext. Math. IX. 153, which are substantially identical with that cited from Stobaeus: in Stob. it appears as a subdivision of σωφροσύνη, while both in Diog. and Stob. the word ἐμμενετέον is found in connection with καρτερία, a subdivision of ἀνδρεία. No doubt their account is derived from Chrysippus: it is noteworthy, however, that ὀρθὸς λόγος appears in these definitions: see Hirzel, l.c., Stein, Erkenntnistheorie, p. 262. In giving this prominent position to ἐγκράτεια Cleanthes was following in the steps of Socrates (Xen. Mem. I. 5. 4, ἆρά γε οὐ χρὴ πάντα ἄνδρα ἡγησάμενον τὴν ἐγκράτειαν ἀρετῆς εἶναι κρηπῖδα), and the Cynics (Diog. L. VI. 15).

ἀξίας: the full definition, probably that of Chrysippus, appears in Stob. Ecl. II. 7. 5^{b1}, p. 59, 11, δικαιοσύνην δὲ ἐπιστήμην ἀπονεμητικὴν τῆς ἀξίας ἑκάστῳ, ib. 7^f, p. 84, 15.

αἱρέσεις καὶ ἐκκλίσεις: σωφροσύνη is concerned with the regulation of the ὁρμαί (Stob. Ecl. II. 7. 5^{b2}, p. 60, 13, ib. 5^{b5}, p. 63, 16), and is therefore directed to the avoidance of πάθη, among which φόβος is defined as ἔκκλισις ἀπειθὴς λόγῳ (Stob. Ecl. II. 7. 10^b, p. 90, 11).

77. Clem. Alex. Strom. II. 22, 131, p. 499 P., 179 S., διὸ καὶ Κλεάνθης ἐν τῷ δευτέρῳ περὶ ἡδονῆς τὸν Σωκράτην φησὶ παρ' ἕκαστα διδάσκειν ὡς ὁ αὐτὸς δίκαιός τε καὶ εὐδαίμων ἀνὴρ καὶ τῷ πρώτῳ διελόντι τὸ δίκαιον ἀπὸ τοῦ συμφέροντος καταρᾶσθαι ὡς ἀσεβές τι πρᾶγμα δεδρακότι· ἀσεβεῖς γὰρ τῷ ὄντι οἱ τὸ συμφέρον ἀπὸ τοῦ δικαίου τοῦ κατὰ νόμον χωρίζοντες.

Cf. Cic. Off. III. 11, itaque accepimus Socratem exsecrari solitum eos qui primum haec natura cohaerentia opinione distraxissent. cui quidem ita sunt Stoici assensi ut et quidquid honestum esset id utile esse censerent nec utile quicquam quod non honestum. id. Leg. I. 33, recte Socrates exsecrari eum solebat qui primus utilitatem a iure seiunxisset: id enim querebatur caput esse exitiorum omnium.

For Socrates, who identified τὸ ὠφέλιμον with τὸ ἀγαθόν, cf. Zeller, Socrates, p. 150 foll. Cleanthes, as we have seen (frag. 75), asserted that the good was also συμφέρον and ὠφέλιμον: for the school in general see Zeller, Stoics, p. 229, 2.

78. Diog. L. VII. 92, πλείονας (εἶναι ἀρετὰς ἢ τέτταρας) οἱ περὶ Κλεάνθην καὶ Χρύσιππον καὶ Ἀντίπατρον.

Zeller, p. 258, thinks that this simply means that Cleanthes enumerated the various subdivisions of the four cardinal virtues. Hirzel, p. 97, 2, prefers to suppose that it is due to the mistake of placing φρόνησις, which is the source of the several virtues, on the same level as the four main divisions of virtue.

79. Diog. L. VII. 91, διδακτήν τε εἶναι αὐτὴν (λέγω δὲ τὴν ἀρετὴν) καὶ Χρύσιππος ἐν τῷ πρώτῳ περὶ τέλους φησὶ καὶ Κλεάνθης.

This is, of course, ultimately traceable to Socrates, but

was also enforced by the Cynics: cf. Diog. VI. 10 (Antisthenes) διδακτὴν ἀπεδείκνυε τὴν ἀρετήν, ib. 105, ἀρέσκει δ' αὐτοῖς καὶ τὴν ἀρετὴν διδακτὴν εἶναι, καθά φησιν Ἀντισθένης ἐν τῷ Ἡρακλεῖ.

80. Diog. L. VII. 127, καὶ μὴν τὴν ἀρετὴν Χρύσιππος μὲν ἀποβλητήν, Κλεάνθης δὲ ἀναπόβλητον, ὁ μὲν ἀποβλητὴν διὰ μέθην καὶ μελαγχολίαν, ὁ δὲ ἀναπόβλητον διὰ βεβαίους καταλήψεις.

On this point Cleanthes is in agreement with the Cynics (Diog. L. VI. 105), whence Wellmann, p. 462, infers that Zeno's teaching must have been in agreement with Cleanthes rather than with Chrysippus. See also the authorities cited by Zeller, p. 295, 3, and add Cic. Tusc. II. 32, amitti non potest virtus.

μέθην: but Zeno held that the wise man οὐ μεθυσθήσεσθαι (frag. 159).

μελαγχολίαν: Cic. Tusc. III. 11, quod (furor) cum maius esse videatur quam insania, tamen eiusmodi est, ut furor (μελαγχολία) in sapientem cadere possit, non possit insania.

βεβαίους καταλήψεις: although κατάληψις is shared by the wise man with the fool (see on Zeno, frag. 16), its especial cultivation and possession belongs to the wise man only: cf. Stein, Erkenntnistheorie, p. 184, 185. Cf. also Sext. Math. II. 6 (quoted on frag. 9). According to Hirzel, p. 68, 3, the meaning is not that Cleanthes denied that the wise man would get drunk and so lose his virtue, but that the strength of his καταλήψεις is so great, that even melancholy and drunkenness fail to shake him. In support of this he quotes Epict. diss. I. 18. 21—23, τίς οὖν ὁ ἀήττητος; ὃν οὐκ ἐξίστησιν οὐδὲν τῶν ἀποπροαιρέτων. τί οὖν ἂν καῦμα ᾖ τούτῳ; τί ἂν οἰνώμενος ᾖ; τί ἂν μελαγχολῶν; τί ἐν ὕπνοις; οὗτός μοι ἐστὶν ὁ ἀνίκητος ἀθλητής. II. 17. 33, ἤθελον δ᾽ ἀσφαλῶς ἔχειν καὶ ἀσείστως, καὶ οὐ μόνον ἐγρηγορὼς ἀλλὰ καὶ καθεύδων καὶ οἰνώμενος καὶ ἐν μελαγχολίᾳ. He thinks that the later Stoics invented the distinction between οἰνοῦσθαι and μεθύειν to explain the divergence between Cleanthes and Chrysippus on so important a point as the loss of virtue. So substantially Von Arnim, Quellen Studien zu Philo, p. 106.

81. Diog. L. VII. 128, ἀρέσκει δὲ αὐτοῖς καὶ διὰ παντὸς χρῆσθαι τῇ ἀρετῇ, ὡς οἱ περὶ Κλεάνθην φασίν. ἀναπόβλητος γάρ ἐστι· καὶ πάντοτε τῇ ψυχῇ χρῆται οὔσῃ τελείᾳ ὁ σπουδαῖος.

82. Stob. Ecl. II. 7. 5[b8], p. 65, 8, πάντας γὰρ ἀνθρώπους ἀφορμὰς ἔχειν ἐκ φύσεως πρὸς ἀρετήν, καὶ οἱονεὶ τὸν τῶν ἡμιαμβείων λόγον ἔχειν κατὰ Κλεάνθην· ὅθεν ἀτελεῖς μὲν ὄντας εἶναι φαύλους τελειωθέντας δὲ σπουδαίους.

ἀφορμάς. For this sense of the word cf. frag. 73 ἀφορμὰς ἀδιαστρόφους "uncorrupted impulses." Stob. Ecl. II. 7. 5[b8], p. 62, 9 ἔχειν γὰρ (τὸν ἄνθρωπον) ἀφορμὰς παρὰ τῆς φύσεως καὶ πρὸς τὴν τοῦ καθήκοντος εὕρεσιν καὶ πρὸς τὴν τῶν ὁρμῶν εὐστάθειαν καὶ πρὸς τὰς ὑπομονὰς καὶ πρὸς τὰς ἀπονεμήσεις. As a general rule, however, it is contrasted with ὁρμή as "aversion")("impulse towards," Stob. Ecl. II, 7. 9, p. 87, 5, Sext. Pyrrh. III. 273, ἐγκράτειαν...ἐν ταῖς πρὸς τὸ καλὸν ὁρμαῖς καὶ ἐν ταῖς ἀπὸ τοῦ κακοῦ ἀφορμαῖς, ib. Math. XI. 210. Cleanthes regarded our capacity for virtue as innate, but whether at the same time he denied an innate intellectual capacity is open to question, cf. Stein, Erkenntnistheorie, n. 735.

Cf. M. Aurel. ix. 1, ἀφορμὰς γὰρ προειλήφει παρὰ τῆς φύσεως, ὧν ἀμελήσας οὐχ οἷός τέ ἐστι νῦν διακρίνειν τὰ ψευδῆ ἀπὸ τῶν ἀληθῶν.

τόν: so Zeller, (p. 243, 1), for τό.

ἡμιαμβείων: so Wachsm. for MSS. ἡμιαμβειαίων. Meineke reads μιμιαμβείων. The meaning is that men possess latent capacities which must be brought into play by their own exertions, if they would attain to perfection, cf. Cic. Tusc. III. 2, sunt enim ingeniis nostris semina innata virtutum, quae si adolescere liceret, ipsa nos ad beatam vitam natura perduceret.

83. Themist. Or. II. 27 c, εἰ δὲ αὖ φήσειέ τις κολακείαν εἶναι τῷ Πυθίῳ παραβάλλειν τὸν βασιλέα, Χρύσιππος μὲν ὑμῖν καὶ Κλεάνθης οὐ συγχωρήσει καὶ ὅλον ἔθνος φιλοσοφίας ἢ ὁ ἐκ τῆς ποικίλης χορὸς οἱ φάσκοντες εἶναι τὴν αὐτὴν ἀρετὴν καὶ ἀλήθειαν ἀνδρὸς καὶ θεοῦ.

This doctrine depends on the divine origin of the human soul. Hence the Stoics could say that good men were friends of the gods, and Chrysippus declared that the happiness of the wise man was as great as that of Zeus, since they only differ in point of time, which is immaterial for happiness. Cf. Procl. in Tim. Plat. II. 106 f, οἱ δὲ ἀπὸ τῆς Στοᾶς καὶ τὴν αὐτὴν ἀρετὴν εἶναι θεῶν καὶ ἀνθρώπων εἰρήκασιν. Cic. Leg. I. 25, iam vero virtus eadem in homine ac deo est neque alio ullo ingenio praeterea.

84. Galen. Hipp. et Plat. plac. v. 6, v. p. 476 K., τὴν μὲν τοῦ Κλεάνθους γνώμην ὑπὲρ τοῦ παθητικοῦ τῆς ψυχῆς ἐκ τῶνδε φαίνεσθαί φησι τῶν ἐπῶν.

Λογισμός. τί ποτ' ἐσθ' ὅτι βούλει, θυμέ; τοῦτό μοι φράσον.

Θυμός. ἔχειν, λογισμέ, πᾶν ὃ βούλομαι ποιεῖν.

Λ. ναὶ βασιλικόν γε· πλὴν ὅμως εἰπὸν πάλιν.

Θ. ὧν ἂν ἐπιθυμῶ ταῦθ' ὅπως γενήσεται.

ταυτὶ τὰ ἀμοιβαῖα Κλεάνθους φησὶν εἶναι Ποσειδώνιος ἐναργῶς ἐκδεικνύμενα τὴν περὶ τοῦ παθητικοῦ τῆς ψυχῆς γνώμην αὐτοῦ, εἴ γε δὴ πεποίηκε τὸν Λογισμὸν τῷ Θυμῷ διαλεγόμενον ὡς ἑταῖρον ἑταίρῳ.

2, 3. ἐγὼ λογισμόν...βασιλικόν γε MSS. ἔχειν, λογισμέ, Wyttenbach βασιλικόν ἐστι Mullach, βασιλικόν· εὖ γε Scaliger, ναὶ β. γ. Mein. Perhaps we should read ποιεῖν λογισμόν...ἐγὼ βασιλικός.

4. ὧν Meineke, Mullach, ὡς MSS., ὅσ' Wyttenbach.

Mohnike, p. 52, thinks that this fragment comes either from περὶ ὁρμῆς or περὶ λόγου.

Posidonius uses the verses to prove that Cleanthes was in substantial agreement with himself in supposing that the various functions of the ἡγεμονικὸν are radically distinct. Zeller, p. 215, 3, says that this is to confound a rhetorical flourish with a philosophical view, and it may be added that Posidonius must have been hard pressed for an argument to rely on this passage at all. Hirzel, however, pp. 147—160, labours to prove that Posidonius is right, but he mainly relies on frag. 37, θύραθεν εἰσκρίνεσθαι τὸν νοῦν, where see note, and is well refuted by Stein, Psych. pp. 163—167.

85. Galen, Hipp. et Plat. IX. 1, V. p. 653 K., Ποσειδώνιος...δείκνυσιν ἐν τῇ περὶ παθῶν πραγματείᾳ διοικουμένους ἡμᾶς ὑπὸ τριῶν δυνάμεων, ἐπιθυμητικῆς τε καὶ θυμοειδοῦς καὶ λογιστικῆς· τῆς δ' αὐτῆς ὁ Ποσειδώνιος ἔλεξεν εἶναι καὶ τὸν Κλεάνθην.

Though there is no direct proof that Cleanthes adhered to the eightfold division of the soul, yet everything points that way, and Hirzel's opinion (p. 138) that he only recognised three divisions is unfounded: see on frag. 84. The present passage of Galen ought perhaps rather to be added as a testimonium to frag. 84 than cited as a distinct fragment, since the whole argument of Posidonius, so far as we know, was founded on the dialogue between λογισμός and θυμός. For δυνάμεις see Hirzel, II. p. 486, 1.

86. Stob. Floril. 108, 59, ὁ δὲ Κλεάνθης ἔλεγε τὴν λύπην ψυχῆς παράλυσιν.

This appears to be the only remaining indication of the position of Cleanthes as regards the definition of the πάθη, but it is not without significance. Zeno had probably defined λύπη as ἄλογος συστολὴ ψυχῆς (see on Zeno frag. 143), but Cleanthes saw his way to a better explanation from the standpoint of τόνος: the soul of the wise man, informed by right reason, is characterised by ἰσχύς, ἱκανὸς τόνος, εὐτονία, but if the emotions overpower the natural reason of a man, there supervenes a resolution of tension, ἀτονία or ἀσθένεια. This view of the emotions was adopted by Chrysippus, cf. Galen, Hipp. et Plat. v. 387 K. ἡ ὀρθὴ κρίσις ἐξηγεῖται μετὰ τῆς κατὰ τὴν ψυχὴν εὐτονίας: see especially the long passage beginning ib. p. 404 K. where the view of πάθος as ἀτονία or ἀσθένεια is explained at length by Chrysippus. With regard to λύπη cf. Tusc. III. 61, omnibus enim modis fulciendi sunt, qui ruunt nec cohaerere possunt, propter magnitudinem aegritudinis. Ex quo ipsam aegritudinem λύπην Chrysippus quasi solutionem totius hominis appellatam putat. ib. II. 54, animus intentione sua depellit pressum omnem ponderum, remissione autem sic urgetur, ut se nequeat extollere. No doubt Cleanthes, like Plato, derived λύπη from λύω: Plat. Crat. p. 419 c. See also Stein, Erkenntnistheorie, p. 130.

87. Galen, Hipp. et Plat. III. 5, v. 332 K., οὐ μόνον Χρύσιππος ἀλλὰ καὶ Κλεάνθης καὶ Ζήνων ἑτοίμως αὐτὰ τιθέασιν (scil. τοὺς φόβους καὶ τὰς λύπας καὶ πάνθ' ὅσα τοιαῦτα πάθη κατὰ τὴν καρδίαν συνίστασθαι) = Zeno, frag. 141.

Hirzel's contention (p. 152 f.) that Cleanthes placed the ἡγεμονικόν in the brain, and that hence we are to explain Plut. plac. IV. 21. 5, is controverted by Stein, Psych. p. 170, from this passage, for we have seen that the πάθη are affections of the ἡγεμονικόν. Hirzel replies (p. 154) that ὁρμαί and πάθη, though dependent on the ἡγεμονικόν, are yet distinct from it. The improbability of Hirzel's whole theory lies in the fact that, if it is correct, Cleanthes was in vital opposition to the whole Stoa down to Posidonius on the most important doctrines of psychology. Such an inference ought not to be accepted, unless the evidence conclusively points to it, and no one will affirm that such is the case here.

88. Sext. Emp. Math. XI. 74, ἀλλὰ Κλεάνθης μὲν μήτε κατὰ φύσιν αὐτὴν (ἡδονὴν) εἶναι μήτ' ἀξίαν ἔχειν [αὐτὴν] ἐν τῷ βίῳ, καθάπερ δὲ τὸ κάλλυντρον κατὰ φύσιν μὴ εἶναι.

ἡδονή is, according to Cleanthes, not merely an ἀδιάφορον but also παρὰ φύσιν, being entirely devoid of ἀξία, cf. Diog. L. VII. 105, and see on Zeno, frag. 192.

κάλλυντρον cannot here mean "a broom," but must be "an ornament": see Suidas s.v. All kinds of personal adornment appeared to the Stoics, as to the Cynics, to be contrary to nature: Zeno wore the τρίβων (Diog. L. VII. 26), recommended the same dress for males and females (frag. 177), and forbade young men to be ἑταιρικῶς κεκοσμημένοι (frag. 174).

αὐτήν is bracketed by Bekker. Hirzel discusses this passage at length (pp. 89—96). He thinks that the first part (μήτε...βίῳ) contains a climax: ἡδονή has no connection with virtue and therefore is not ἀγαθόν (κατὰ φύσιν); further, it has no ἀξία and is not even προηγμένον. Hence Zeno and Cleanthes did not identify τὰ κατὰ φύσιν with προηγμένα: for in that case they could not have treated προηγμένα as ἀδιάφορα. Zeller and Wellmann are, therefore, wrong in regarding Cleanthes' attitude towards pleasure as cynical; rather, his position is that pleasure *in itself* (for this is the force of the second αὐτὴν which should be retained) is ἀδιάφορον in the narrower sense. Cf. Stob. Ecl. II. 7. 7ᵇ, p. 81, 14 οὔτε δὲ προηγμένα οὔτ' ἀποπροηγμένα...ἡδονὴν πᾶσαν καὶ πόνον καὶ εἴ τι ἄλλο τοιοῦτο. Next, κατὰ φύσιν μὴ εἶναι is a gloss, and when this is struck out we should supply ἀξίαν ἔχειν with καθάπερ δὲ κάλλυντρον. In short, Cleanthes treats pleasure as an ἐπιγέννημα (Diog. L. VII. 86): cf. Seneca Ep. 116, 3, voluptatem natura necessariis rebus admiscuit, non ut illam peteremus, sed ut ea, sine quibus non possumus vivere, gratiora nobis faceret illius accessio. But it does not follow that, because virtue consists in τὸ ὁμολογουμένως τῇ φύσει ζῆν, therefore everything, which is κατὰ φύσιν, is ἀρετὴ or μετέχον ἀρετῆς. Cf. Stob. Ecl. 7. 7ᵃ, p. 80, 9 διότι κἂν, φασί, λέγωμεν ἀδιάφορα τὰ σωματικὰ καὶ τὰ ἐκτός, πρὸς τὸ εὐσχημόνως ζῆν (ἐν ᾧπέρ ἐστι τὸ εὐδαιμόνως) ἀδιάφορά φαμεν αὐτὰ εἶναι, οὐ μὰ Δία πρὸς τὸ κατὰ φύσιν ἔχειν οὐδὲ πρὸς ὁρμὴν καὶ ἀφορμήν. Rather, we have seen reason to hold that the class of τὰ κατὰ φύσιν is wider, or, at any rate, certainly not narrower than that of τὰ προηγμένα. Indeed, this is apparent from the present passage:—ὁ δὲ Ἀρχέδημος κατὰ φύσιν μὲν εἶναι ὡς τὰς ἐν μασχάλῃ τρίχας, οὐχὶ δὲ καὶ ἀξίαν ἔχειν, i.e. there are some things which may be κατὰ φύσιν and yet devoid of ἀξία. Again, Sextus obviously treats Cleanthes as more hostile to pleasure than Archedemus, but the view which Hirzel would attribute to Cleanthes is scarcely to be distinguished from that of Archedemus. Certainly, the passage from Seneca ought not to be quoted as an illustration of Cleanthes' meaning: contrast μήτε κατὰ φύσιν εἶναι with natura—admiscuit. The inelegant repetition of μή...εἶναι has an object, namely, to contrast τὸ κάλλυντρον with τὰς ἐν μασχάλῃ τρίχας, whereas, on the other hand, if the second αὐτὴν is retained, it cannot be interpreted differently to the first αὐτὴν, and to press the latter would make nonsense.

89. Stob. Floril. 6. 37, Κλεάνθης ἔλεγεν, εἰ τέλος ἐστὶν ἡδονή, πρὸς κακοῦ τοῖς ἀνθρώποις τὴν φρόνησιν δεδόσθαι.

This is no doubt directed against the Epicureans. Diog. L. x. 128, τὴν ἡδονὴν ἀρχὴν καὶ τέλος λέγομεν εἶναι τοῦ μακαρίως ζῆν. Chrysippus also wrote a treatise described as ἀπόδειξις πρὸς τὸ μὴ εἶναι τὴν ἡδονὴν τέλος (Diog. L. VII. 202). τὴν φρόνησιν furnishes a proof that Cleanthes upheld Zeno's view of virtue as φρόνησις: see on frag. 76.

δεδόσθαι: so Meineke for δίδοσθαι. Cf. Cic. de Senec. § 40, cumque homini sive natura sive quis deus nihil mente praestabilius dedisset, huic divino muneri ac dono nihil tam esse inimicum quam voluptatem.

90. Cic. Fin. II. 69, pudebit te illius tabulae quam Cleanthes sane commode verbis depingere solebat. iubebat eos qui audiebant secum ipsos cogitare pictam in tabula Voluptatem, pulcherrimo vestitu et ornatu regali in solio sedentem: praesto esse Virtutes ut ancillulas, quae nihil aliud agerent, nullum suum officium ducerent, nisi ut Voluptati ministrarent et eam tantum ad aurem admonerent, si modo id pictura intellegi posset, ut caveret ne quid faceret imprudens quod offenderet animos hominum aut quicquam e quo oriretur aliquis dolor. "nos quidem Virtutes sic natae sumus, ut tibi serviremus; aliud negotii nihil habemus." Cf. Aug. de civit. dei v. 20, solent

philosophi, qui finem boni humani in ipsa virtute constituunt, ad ingerendum pudorem quibusdam philosophis, qui virtutes quidem probant, sed eas voluptatis corporalis fine metiuntur et illam per se ipsam putant adpetendam, istas propter ipsam, tabulam quandam verbis pingere, ubi voluptas in sella regali quasi delicata quaedam regina considat, eique virtutes famulae subiciantur, observantes eius nutum ut faciant quod illa imperaverit, quae prudentiae iubeat ut vigilanter inquirat quo modo voluptas regnet et salva sit; iustitiae iubeat ut praestet beneficia quae potest ad comparandas amicitias corporalibus commodis necessarias, nulli faciat iniuriam, ne offensis legibus voluptas vivere secura non possit; fortitudini iubeat, ut si dolor corpori acciderit qui non compellat in mortem, teneat dominam suam, id est, voluptatem, fortiter in animi cogitatione ut per pristinarum deliciarum suarum recordationem mitiget praesentis doloris aculeos; temperantiae iubeat, ut tantum capiat alimentorum et si qua delectant ne per immoderationem noxium aliquid valetudinem turbet et voluptas, quam etiam in corporis sanitate Epicurei maximam ponunt, graviter offendatur. ita virtutes cum tota suae gloria dignitatis tanquam imperiosae cuidam et inhonestae mulierculae servient voluptati; nihil hac pictura dicunt esse ignominiosius et deformius et quod minus ferre bonorum possit aspectus; et verum dicunt.

Further references ap. Zeller, p. 235—239. Epiphan. Hæres. III. 2. p. 1090 C Κλεάνθης τὸ ἀγαθὸν καὶ καλὸν λέγει εἶναι τὰς ἡδονὰς is a stupid blunder of the epitomator: cf. Krische, p. 431. Hirzel, p. 96, 1, holds that it is merely an exaggeration of Cleanthes' position: see on frag. 88.

pulcherrimo vestitu: this illustrates κάλλυντρον in frag. 88.

si modo...possent: Madvig points out that these words belong to Cleanthes' statement, and are not a part of Cicero's comment.

Virtutes ut ancillulas: on the controversial character of the work περὶ ἡδονῆς see Krische, pp. 430—432. In the Epicurean system virtue has only a conditional value, as furnishing a means to pleasure. Diog. L. x. 138 διὰ δὲ τὴν ἡδονὴν καὶ τὰς ἀρετὰς δεῖν αἱρεῖσθαι, οὐ δι᾽ αὐτάς· ὥσπερ καὶ τὴν ἰατρικὴν διὰ τὴν ὑγίειαν, καθά φησι Διογένης.

91. Epict. Man. c. 53.

ἄγου δέ μ᾽, ὦ Ζεῦ, καὶ σύγ᾽ ἡ πεπρωμένη,
ὅποι ποθ᾽ ὑμῖν εἰμὶ διατεταγμένος,
ὡς ἕψομαί γ᾽ ἄοκνος· ἢν δὲ μὴ θέλω
κακὸς γενόμενος, οὐδὲν ἧττον ἕψομαι.

The first line is quoted by Epict. diss. II. 23. 42, and two lines by id. ib. III. 22. 95, IV. 1. 131, and IV. 4. 34. Senec. Epist. 107, 10, et sic adloquamur Iovem cuius gubernaculo moles ista dirigitur, quemadmodum Cleanthes noster versibus disertissimis adloquitur; quos mihi in nostrum sermonem mutare permittitur Ciceronis disertissimi viri exemplo. si placuerint boni consules; si displicuerint, scies me in hoc secutum Ciceronis exemplum.

> duc, o parens celsique dominator poli,
> quocumque placuit; nulla parendi mora est.
> adsum impiger. fac nolle, comitabor gemens,
> malusque patiar, quod pati licuit bono.
> ducunt volentem fata, nolentem trahunt.

See also the commentary of Simplicius on Epict. l. c. p. 329. These celebrated lines constitute the true answer of the Stoa to the objection that the doctrine of πρόνοια is incompatible with the assertion of free-

will. Zeller p. 182. The matter is put very plainly in the passage of Hippolyt. Philosoph. 21, 2, Diels p. 571, quoted at length in the note on Zeno frag. 79. The spirit of Stoicism survives in the words of a modern writer:—
"It has ever been held the highest wisdom for a man not merely to submit to Necessity,—Necessity will make him submit,—but to know and believe well that the stern thing which Necessity had ordered was the wisest, the best, the thing wanted there. To cease his frantic pretension of scanning this great God's world in his small fraction of a brain; to know that it had verily, though deep beyond his soundings, a just law, that the soul of it was Good;—that his part in it was to conform to the Law of the Whole, and in devout silence follow that; not questioning it, obeying it as unquestionable." (Carlyle, Hero-Worship, chap. II.) Marcus Aurelius often dwells on the contrast between τὰ ἐφ' ἡμῖν and τὰ οὐκ ἐφ' ἡμῖν. Cf. especially x. 28, καὶ ὅτι μόνῳ τῷ λογικῷ ζώῳ δέδοται, τὸ ἑκουσίως ἕπεσθαι τοῖς γινομένοις· τὸ δὲ ἕπεσθαι ψιλόν, πᾶσιν ἀναγκαῖον. So ib. VI. 41, 42; VII. 54, 55; VIII. 7; XII. 32.

92. Seneca Epist. 94, 4, Cleanthes utilem quidem iudicat et hanc partem (philosophiae quae dat cuique personae praecepta, nec in universum componit hominem, sed marito suadet quomodo se gerat adversus uxorem, patri quomodo educat liberos, domino quomodo servos regat), sed imbecillam nisi ab universo fluit, nisi decreta ipsa philosophiae et capita cognovit.

The branch of philosophy here referred to is known as the παραινετικὸς or ὑποθετικὸς τόπος. Aristo regarded it as useless, and it is very possible that his "letters to Cleanthes" (πρὸς Κλεάνθην ἐπιστολῶν δ' Diog. L. VII. 163) dealt with this controversy. Cf. Sext. Math. VII. 12, καὶ Ἀρίστων ὁ Χῖος οὐ μόνον, ὥς φασί, παρῃτεῖτο τήν τε φυσικὴν καὶ λογικὴν θεωρίαν διὰ τὸ ἀνωφελὲς καὶ πρὸς κακοῦ τοῖς φιλοσοφοῦσιν ὑπάρχειν ἀλλὰ καὶ τοῦ ἠθικοῦ τόπους τινὰς συμπεριέγραφεν, καθάπερ τόν τε παραινετικὸν καὶ τὸν ὑποθετικὸν τόπον· τούτους γὰρ εἰς τίτθας καὶ παιδαγωγοὺς πίπτειν. The words in which Philo of Larissa described the τόπος ὑποθετικὸς illustrate Seneca's statement: Stob. Ecl. II. 7. 2, p. 42, 18, ἐπεὶ δὲ καὶ τῶν μέσως διακειμένων ἀνθρώπων πρόνοιαν ποιητέον, οὕστινας ἐκ τῶν παραινετικῶν λόγων ὠφελεῖσθαι συμβαίνει, μὴ δυναμένους προσευκαιρεῖν τοῖς διεξοδικοῖς πλάτεσιν ἢ διὰ χρόνου στενοχωρίας ἢ διά τινας ἀναγκαίας ἀσχολίας, ἐπεισενεκτέον τὸν ὑποθετικὸν λόγον, δι' οὗ τὰς πρὸς τὴν ἀσφάλειαν καὶ τὴν ὀρθότητα τῆς ἑκάστου χρήσεως ὑποθήκας ἐν ἐπιτομαῖς ἕξουσιν. The importance attached by Cleanthes to παραινετικὴ illustrates the practical spirit of Stoicism: see also Hirzel, II. p. 104.

93. Cic. Tusc. III. 76, sunt qui unum officium consolantis putent malum illud omnino non esse, ut Cleanthi placet.

Consolatio (παραμυθητικὴ) is a branch of παραινετικὴ and is concerned with removing the πάθη, cf. Eudorus ap. Stob. Ecl. II. 7. 2. p. 44, 15 ὁ δὲ περὶ τῶν ἀποτρεπόντων καλεῖται παραμυθητικός, ὃς καλούμενός ἐστι πρὸς ἐνίων παθολογικός. Cf. Sen. Epist. 95, 65. As emotion is founded on false opinion (see on Zeno, frag. 138), the duty of him who offers consolation to another is to explain that what appears to the other to be an evil is not really so.

malum illud: the context in Cicero shows that the reference is particularly to death, for which cf. Zeno, frag. 129. The construction is not to be explained by an ellipse of docere or the like, but rather *esse* is nominalised so that *malum...esse* = τὸ κακόν...εἶναι. This is common in Lucr., see Munro on I. 331, 418 and cf. Verr. v. 170, quid dicam in crucem tollere ? Cicero even writes: inter optime valere et gravissime aegrotare (Fin. II. 43). Draeger, § 429.

94. Cic. Tusc. III. 77, nam Cleanthes quidem sapientem consolatur, qui consolatione non eget. nihil enim esse malum, quod turpe non sit, si lugenti persuaseris, non tu illi luctum, sed stultitiam detraxeris; alienum autem tempus docendi. et tamen non satis mihi videtur vidisse hoc Cleanthes, suscipi aliquando aegritudinem posse ex eo ipso, quod esse summum malum Cleanthes ipse fateatur.

Cicero's criticism here is twofold: (1) that what is called consolation is really only instruction, which is ineffective to assuage grief, because it is inopportune, and as regards the wise man, who is ἀπαθής, is unnecessary; (2) that grief may be caused by baseness, which is an evil. Cf. Tusc. II. 30.

This cannot be treated as merely containing Cicero's comment on frag. 93, for we have the additional statement *sapientem consolatur*, which is surely not an inference from Cleanthes' definition. The statement is strange and perhaps not to be entirely explained in the fragmentary state of our knowledge, but it is not inconceivable that Cleanthes held that the wise man ought to be reminded of Stoic principles when attacked by μελαγχολία or when in severe pain, in spite of his βεβαίας καταλήψεις (see on frag. 80 and cf. Stob. Floril. 7. 21 ἀλγεῖν μὲν τὸν σοφόν, μὴ βασανίζεσθαι δέ. Cic. Fin. v. 94, quasi vero hoc didicisset a Zenone, non dolere, quum doleret! Zeno, frag. 158): cf. generally Sext. Math. XI. 130—140 and esp. 139 εἰ δ᾽ ἁπλῶς διδάσκει ὅτι τουτὶ μὲν ὀλιγωφελές ἐστι, πλείονας δ᾽ ἔχει τὰς ὀχλήσεις, σύγκρισιν ἔσται ποιῶν αἱρέσεως καὶ φυγῆς πρὸς ἑτέραν αἵρεσιν καὶ φυγήν, καὶ οὐκ ἀναίρεσιν τῆς ταραχῆς. ὅπερ ἄτοπον· ὁ γὰρ ὀχλούμενος οὐ βούλεται μαθεῖν τί μᾶλλον ὀχλεῖ καὶ τί ἧττον, ἀλλ' ἀπαλλαγῆναι τῆς ὀχλήσεως πεπόθηκεν.

95. Stob. Floril. 6. 19.

ὅστις ἐπιθυμῶν ἀνέχετ' αἰσχροῦ πράγματος οὗτος ποιήσει τοῦτ' ἐὰν καιρὸν λάβῃ.

For the doctrine that virtuous action depends on the intention and not on the deed itself, see Zeller, p. 264 and cf. Zeno frags. 146 and 181.

96. Stob. Floril. 28, 14, Κλεάνθης ἔφη τὸν ὀμνύοντα ἤτοι εὐορκεῖν ἢ ἐπιορκεῖν καθ' ὃν ὄμνυσι χρόνον. ἐὰν μὲν γὰρ οὕτως ὀμνύῃ ὡς ἐπιτελέσων τὰ κατὰ τὸν ὅρκον εὐορκεῖν, ἐὰν δὲ πρόθεσιν ἔχων μὴ ἐπιτελεῖν, ἐπιορκεῖν.

See on frag. 95, and cf. Chrysipp. ap. Stob. Floril. 28, 15.

97. Seneca de Benef. v. 14. 1, Cleanthes vehementius agit: "licet," inquit, "beneficium non sit quod accipit, ipse tamen ingratus est: quia non fuit redditurus, etiam si accepisset. sic latro est, etiam antequam manus inquinet: quia ad occidendum iam armatus est, et habet spoliandi atque interficiendi voluntatem. exercetur et aperitur opere nequitia, non incipit. ipsum quod accepit, beneficium non erat, sed vocabatur. sacrilegi dant poenas, quamvis nemo usque ad deos manus porrigat."

This and the two next following fragments probably come from the book περὶ χάριτος. Introd. p. 52. Eudorus the Academic ap. Stob. Ecl. II. 7. 2, p. 44, 20 speaks in Stoic terminology of ὁ περὶ τῶν χαρίτων τόπος as arising ἐκ τοῦ λόγου τοῦ κατὰ τὴν πρὸς τοὺς πλησίον σχέσιν ὑπάρχειν.

beneficium non sit: because the question is concerning an act of kindness to a bad man, on whom, according to

Stoic principles, it was impossible to confer a favour (Senec. Benef. v. 12. 3), cf. Stob. Ecl. II. 7. 11^d p. 95, 5, μηδένα δὲ φαῦλον μήτε ὠφελεῖσθαι μήτε ὠφελεῖν, Plut. Comm. Not. 21.

sacrilegi: the edd. quote Phædr. IV. 11. Senec. de Benef. VII. 7. 3, iniuriam sacrilegus Deo quidem non potest facere: quem extra ictum sua divinitas posuit: sed punitur quia tanquam Deo fecit. De Const. Sap. 4, 2.

98. Seneca de Benef. VI. 11. 1, beneficium voluntas nuda non efficit: sed quod beneficium non esset, si optimae ac plenissimae voluntati fortuna deesset, id aeque beneficium non est, nisi fortunam voluntas antecessit; non enim profuisse te mihi oportet, ut ob hoc tibi obliger, sed ex destinato profuisse. Cleanthes exemplo eiusmodi utitur: " ad quaerendum," inquit, " et arcessendum ex Academia Platonem, duos pueros misi; alter totum porticum perscrutatus est, alia quoque loca in quibus illum inveniri posse sperabat, percucurrit, et domum non minus lassus quam irritus rediit: alter apud proximum circulatorem resedit, et, dum vagus atque erro vernaculis congregatur et ludit, transeuntem Platonem, quem non quaesierat, invenit. illum, inquit, laudabimus puerum qui quantum in se erat quod iussus est fecit: hunc feliciter inertem castigabimus."

Another illustration of the value of the virtuous intention apart from the results attained by it. Cf. Cic. Parad. III. 20 nec enim peccata rerum eventu, sed vitiis hominum metienda sunt.

Academia: see the description of this place in Diog. L. III. 7: there was doubtless a στοά attached to it, whence *totum porticum* infra.

circulatorem: a quack, mountebank: cf. Apul. Met. 1. c. 4, Athenis proximo ante Poecilen porticum circulatorem adspexi equestrem spatham praeacutam mucrone infesto devorare. Probably a translation of θαυματοποιός: with respect to these men see the passages collected by Becker, Charicles. E. T. pp. 185—189, Jebb's Theophrastus, p. 227, and add Ar. Met. i. 2. 15, Isocr. Or. 15 § 213, where tame lions and trained bears are spoken of.

99. Seneca de Benef. VI. 12. 2, multum, ut ait Cleanthes, a beneficio distat negotiatio, cf. ib. II. 31. 12, a benefit expects no return: non enim sibi aliquid reddi voluit (qui beneficium dat), aut non fuit beneficium sed negotiatio.

negotiatio: probably a translation of χρηματισμός, for the Stoic wise man is described as the only true man of business: Stob. Ecl. II. 7. 11^d, p. 95, 21, μόνον δὲ τὸν σπουδαῖον ἄνδρα χρηματιστικὸν εἶναι, γινώσκοντα ἀφ' ὧν χρηματιστέον καὶ πότε καὶ πῶς καὶ μέχρι πότε.

100. Clem. Alex. Strom. v. 3. 17, p. 655 P. 237 S., καὶ ἡ Κλεάνθους δὲ τοῦ Στωικοῦ φιλοσόφου ποιητικὴ ὧδέ πως τὰ ὅμοια γράφει

μὴ πρὸς δόξαν ὅρα, ἐθέλων σοφὸς αἶψα γενέσθαι,
μηδὲ φοβοῦ πολλῶν ἄκριτον καὶ ἀναιδέα δόξαν·
οὐ γὰρ πλῆθος ἔχει συνετὴν κρίσιν οὔτε δικαίαν
οὔτε καλήν, ὀλίγοις δὲ παρ' ἀνδράσι τοῦτό κεν εὕροις.

Clement also quotes an anonymous comic fragment to the same effect:—αἰσχρὸν δὲ κρίνειν τὰ καλὰ τῷ πολλῷ ψόφῳ. Stein, Erkenntnistheorie, p. 326 says:—"hätte auch er (Kleanthes) den sensus communis, die κοιναὶ ἔννοιαι oder προλήψεις gebilligt, wie konnte er dann so wegwerfend und verächtlich über das allgemeine Laienurteil aburteilen?" He concludes therefore that Cleanthes threw over altogether the Stoic concession to rationalism implied in the doctrine of ὀρθὸς λόγος and προλήψεις, but see Introd. pp. 39, 40. Cf. generally Cic. Tusc. III. 3, 4.

δόξαν: this is changed to βάξιν by Meineke, who is followed by Wachsmuth, and Cludius is reported as suggesting ἄλογον for ἄκριτον. The reason given for the change by Wachsmuth is that δόξαν "male coniungitur cum ἄκριτον," presumably because δόξα implies κρίσις, but surely the words may mean " undiscriminating opinion " as explained by the next line. The text is confirmed by M. Aurel. IV. 3, τὸ εὐμετάβολον καὶ ἄκριτον τῶν εὐφημεῖν δοκούντων. Cf. ib. II. 17.

οὐ...οὔτε...οὔτε, is justified by Homer, Il. VI. 450, ἀλλ' οὔ μοι Τρώων τόσσον μέλει ἄλγος ὀπίσσω οὔτ' αὐτῆς Ἑκάβης οὔτε Πριάμοιο ἄνακτος, κ.τ.λ. Cf. Soph. Ant. 952.

101. Clem. Alex. Strom. v. 14. 110, p. 715 P. 257 S., ὁ δὲ αὐτὸς (Κλεάνθης) κατὰ τὸ σιωπώμενον τὴν τῶν πολλῶν διαβάλλων εἰδωλολατρίαν ἐπιφέρει

ἀνελεύθερος πᾶς ὅστις εἰς δόξαν βλέπει
ὡς δὴ παρ' ἐκείνης τευξόμενος καλοῦ τινος.

In Clem. Alex. Protrept. VI. 72, p. 21 S. 61 P., the same two lines are cited as the conclusion of frag. 75, but they are obviously distinct.

δόξαν: for Zeno's definition, cf. Zeno, frag. 15. Cleanthes wrote a separate treatise περὶ δόξης, from which we may conjecture that the present and the preceding fragments are derived. Introd. p. 52. The Cynics described εὐγενείας τε καὶ δόξας as προκοσμήματα κακίας (Diog. L. VI. 72). The Stoics regarded them as προηγμένα (Diog. L. VII. 106).

102. Mantiss. proverb. (in paroemiogr. Gr. vol. II. p. 757) cent. I. 85.

κακῶς ἀκούειν κρεῖσσον ἢ λέγειν κακῶς.

Κλεάνθους. This is taken from Wachsmuth (Comm. II. p. 8), whose note is as follows:—"Inter ecclesiasticorum scriptorum sententias hic trimeter laudatur ab Antonio Meliss. I. 53 et a Maximo 10, vid. Gregor. Nazianz. carm. p. 157[d]."

103. Stob. Floril. 42. 2.

κακουργότερον οὐδὲν διαβολῆς ἔστι πω·
λάθρα γὰρ ἀπατήσασα τὸν πεπεισμένον
μῖσος ἀναπλάττει πρὸς τὸν οὐδὲν αἴτιον.

διαβολῆς: defined, ap. Stob. Ecl. II. 7. 11[s], p. 115, 21, εἶναι δὲ τὴν διαβολὴν διάστασιν φαινομένων φίλων ψευδεῖ λόγῳ, and hence, reasoning on the basis that slander is only connected with apparent and not with true friendship, the Stoics declare that the wise man is ἀδιάβολος both in the active and the passive sense (i.e. μήτε διαβάλλειν μήτε διαβάλλεσθαι), but their utterances are not consistent on this point: see Zeller, p. 253 n. 6, who in citing passages to the contrary effect fails to notice this discrepancy.

104. Stob. Ecl. II. 7. 11[l], p. 103, 12, ἱκανῶς δὲ καὶ Κλεάνθης περὶ τὸ σπουδαῖον εἶναι τὴν πόλιν λόγον ἠρώτησε τοιοῦτον· πόλις μὲν <εἰ> ἔστιν οἰκητήριον κατασκεύασμα, εἰς ὃ καταφεύγοντας ἔστι δίκην δοῦναι καὶ λαβεῖν, οὐκ ἀστεῖον δὴ πόλις ἐστίν; ἀλλὰ μὴν τοιοῦτόν ἐστιν ἡ πόλις οἰκητήριον· ἀστεῖον ἄρ' ἔστιν ἡ πόλις.

Possibly this belongs to the πολιτικός: Introd. p. 52. Cleanthes has here adopted the syllogistic form of argument, which occurs so frequently in Zeno's fragments: see Introd. p. 33. The Cynics' line of argument is somewhat similar. Diog. L. VI. 72 οὐ γάρ, φησίν (Diogenes), ἄνευ πόλεως ὄφελός τι εἶναι ἀστείου· ἀστεῖον δὲ ἡ πόλις· νόμου δὲ ἄνευ, πόλεως οὐδὲν ὄφελος· ἀστεῖον ἄρα ὁ νόμος. Cicero's definition is as follows, Rep. I. 39, res publica est res populi, populus autem...coetus multitudinis iuris consensu et utilitatis communione sociatus. Cf. Ar. Pol. I. 2. 1253 a 37.

εἰ, inserted by Heeren, who is followed by Wachsm. Meineke omits it and changes δή before πόλις into δ' ἡ.

105. Seneca Tranq. An. I. 7, promptus compositusque sequor Zenonem, Cleanthem, Chrysippum: quorum tamen nemo ad rem publicam accessit, nemo non misit.

See on Zeno, frag. 170.

106. Stob. Floril. 4, 90, Κλεάνθης ἔφη τοὺς ἀπαιδεύτους μόνῃ τῇ μορφῇ τῶν θηρίων διαφέρειν.

The same occurs in Stob. Ecl. II. 31. 64, p. 212, 22, where Wachsmuth cites other authorities. Stein, Erkenntnistheorie, p. 326, quotes this frag. in support of his theory that Cleanthes refused to admit any inborn intellectual capacity. Zeno declared τὴν ἐγκύκλιον παιδείαν ἄχρηστον (frag. 167 and note), with which opinion this passage is not necessarily inconsistent, though it probably implies an advance in teaching. See also on frag. 53.

107. Epict. diss. IV. 1. 173, παράδοξα μὲν ἴσως φασὶν οἱ φιλόσοφοι, καθάπερ καὶ ὁ Κλεάνθης ἔλεγεν, οὐ μὴν παράλογα.

παράδοξα: the Stoics themselves accepted and defended this description of their doctrines. Cic. Paradox. Prooem. 4 quia sunt admirabilia contraque opinionem omnium ab ipsis etiam παράδοξα appellantur. Plut. Comm. Not. 3

τὰ κοινὰ καὶ περιβόητα, ἃ δὴ παράδοξα καὶ αὐτοί, μετ' εὐκολίας δεχόμενοι τὴν ἀτοπίαν.

108. Plut. vit. Alc. VI. 2, ὁ μὲν οὖν Κλεάνθης ἔλεγε τὸν ἐρώμενον ὑφ' ἑαυτοῦ μὲν ἐκ τῶν ὤτων κρατεῖσθαι, τοῖς δ' ἀντερασταῖς πολλὰς λαβὰς παρέχειν ἀθίκτους ἑαυτῷ, τὴν γαστέρα λέγων καὶ τὰ αἰδοῖα καὶ τὸν λαιμόν.

This may be referred to the ἐρωτικὴ τέχνη or περὶ ἔρωτος, Introd. p. 52. See on Zeno, frags. 172 and 173, and cf. Diog. L. VII. 24 (Zeno apoph. 7) λαβὴ φιλοσόφων ἐστὶν ἐπιδέξιος ἡ διὰ τῶν ὤτων.

109. Sext. Emp. Pyrrh. III. 200, οἱ περὶ τὸν Κλεάνθην ἀδιάφορον τοῦτο (τὸ τῆς ἀρρενομιξίας) εἶναί φασιν = Zeno frag. 182.

110. Stob. Floril. 6, 20.

πόθεν ποτ' ἄρα γίνεται μοιχῶν γένος;
ἐκ κριθιῶντος ἀνδρὸς ἐν ἀφροδισίοις.

μοιχῶν: for Stoic views on μοιχεία, see Zeno, frag. 178.

κριθιῶντος: for this word cf. Buttmann's Lexilogus, s. v. ἀκοστήσας, E. T. p. 78.

111. Plut. de Aud. Poet. c. 12, p. 33, ὅθεν οὐδ' αἱ παραδιορθώσεις φαύλως ἔχουσιν, αἷς καὶ Κλεάνθης ἐχρήσατο καὶ Ἀντισθένης· ὁ μέν κ.τ.λ....ὁ δὲ Κλεάνθης περὶ τοῦ πλούτου,

φίλοις τε δοῦναι σῶμά τ' εἰς νόσους πεσὸν
δαπαναῖσι σῶσαι,
μεταγράφων οὕτω·
πόρναις τε δοῦναι σῶμά τ' εἰς νόσους πεσὸν
δαπαναῖς ἐπιτρῖψαι.

The lines in question are from Eur. El. 428, 9, where

ξένοις is read in place of φίλοις. Stob. Floril. 91, 6 quoting the passage has φίλοις.

The ordinary view of the school regarded πλοῦτος as a προηγμένον, and we have seen that Zeno concurred in this (frag. 128). It would be hazardous to infer from evidence of this kind that Cleanthes dissented from his master's opinion on this point: a similar question arises with regard to δόξα (frag. 101), but that word is ambiguous.

112. Diog. L. VII. 14, ἐνίους δὲ καὶ χαλκὸν εἰσέπραττε τοὺς περιϊσταμένους (ὁ Ζήνων) ὥστε δεδιότας τὸ διδόναι μὴ ἐνοχλεῖν, καθά φησι Κλεάνθης ἐν τῷ περὶ χαλκοῦ.

For the title of the book see Introd. p. 53. The above is Cobet's text; omitting ὥστε δεδιότας, Wachsmuth reads χαλκοῦ for χαλκὸν MSS., and also suggests ἐνίοτε for ἐνίους, but ἐνίους implies that the payment was not always exacted, while the article shows that, when made, it was made by all. Similarly Soph. O. T. 107 τοὺς αὐτοέντας χειρὶ τιμωρεῖν τινας and Ar. Pac. 832.

113. Philodem. περὶ φιλοσόφων ap. Vol. Hercul. VIII. col. 13, v. 18, κ<αὶ Κλ>εάνθης ἐν <τῷ>ι περὶ στ<ήλη>ς <τῆ>ς Διογένους αὐτῆ<ς> μνη<μονεύ>ει καὶ ἐπαιν<εῖ> καὶ <μικρὸν> ὕστε<ρ>ον ἐν αὐτ<ῶι τού>τ<ωι καθά>π<ερ ἐτ>έρ<ω>θ᾽ ἐνίων <ἔ>χθεσι<ν> [l. ἔκθεσιν] <ποι>ε<ῖτ>αι.

Such is the restoration of Gomperz in Zeitschrift für die Oesterr. Gymn. Jahrg. 29 (1878) p. 252 foll., who, in justification of this somewhat strange title, refers to a book by Aristocreon, the nephew of Chrysippus, entitled αἱ Χρυσίππου ταφαί (Comparetti, Papiro Ercolanense col. 46). For the circumstances of the burial of Diogenes cf. Diog. L. VI. 78. αὐτῆς refers to the πολιτεία of Diogenes.

114. Schol. ad Nic. Ther. 447, p. 36, 12 Keil, κραντῆρες λέγονται οἱ ὕστερον ἀναβαίνοντες ὀδόντες παρὰ τὸ κραίνειν καὶ ἀποπληροῦν τὴν ἡλικίαν. νεωτέρων γὰρ ἤδη ἡμῶν γενομένων φύονται οἱ ὀδόντες οὗτοι. Κλεάνθης δὲ σωφρονιστῆρας αὐτοὺς καλεῖ. νῦν ἁπλῶς τοὺς ὀδόντας. σωφρονιστῆρες δὲ διὰ τὸ ἅμα τῷ ἀνιέναι αὐτοὺς καὶ τὸ σῶφρον τοῦ νοῦ λαμβάνειν ἡμᾶς.

For κραντῆρες cf. Arist. Hist. An. II. 4. φύονται δὲ οἱ τελευταῖοι τοῖς ἀνθρώποις γόμφιοι, οὓς καλοῦσι κραντῆρας, περὶ τὰ εἴκοσιν ἔτη καὶ ἀνδράσι καὶ γυναιξί. It seems fairly safe to infer that Cleanthes the Stoic is meant, and the account given above is probably more correct than that appearing in Etym. M. p. 742, 35 κατὰ τὴν τοῦ φρονεῖν ὥραν περὶ τὸ εἰκοστὸν ἔτος, and Melet. ap. Cramer Anecd. Ox. III. 82, 26 τοὺς δὲ μυλίτας τῶν ὀδόντων τινὲς σωφρονιστῆρας ἐκάλεσαν διὰ τὸ φύεσθαι περὶ τὴν τοῦ ἄρχεσθαι φρονεῖν τοὺς παῖδας ὥραν. Thus, while the growth of the reasoning powers is complete in the fourteenth year (Zeno, frag. 82), the attainment of σωφροσύνη may well have been assigned to the conclusion of the third ἑβδομάς.

115. = Zeno frag. 184.

APOPHTHEGMATA OF CLEANTHES.

1. Diog. L. VII. 169, φασὶ δὲ καὶ Ἀντίγονον αὐτοῦ πυθέσθαι ὄντα ἀκροατήν, διὰ τί ἀντλεῖ; τὸν δ' εἰπεῖν, ἀντλῶ γὰρ μόνον; τί δ' οὐχὶ σκάπτω; τί δ' οὐκ ἄρδω, καὶ πάντα ποιῶ φιλοσοφίας ἕνεκα; καὶ γὰρ ὁ Ζήνων αὐτὸν συνεγύμναζεν εἰς τοῦτο, καὶ ἐκέλευεν ὀβολὸν φέρειν ἀποφορᾶς. Plut. de vitand. aere alieno 7, 5, Κλεάνθη δὲ ὁ βασιλεὺς Ἀντίγονος ἠρώτα διὰ χρόνου θεασάμενος ἐν ταῖς Ἀθήναις, ἀλεῖς ἔτι, Κλεάνθες; ἀλῶ, φησίν, ὦ βασιλεῦ, ὃ ποιῶ ἕνεκα τοῦ ζῆν· μόνος δὲ ἀποστῆναι μηδὲ φιλοσοφίας. Cf. Stob. Floril. 17, 28, Χρύσιππος ὁ Σολεὺς ἐποιεῖτο τὸν βίον ἐκ πάνυ ὀλίγων, Κλεάνθης δὲ καὶ ἀπὸ ἐλαττόνων. Epict. diss. III. 26. 23, πῶς Κλεάνθης ἔζησεν ἅμα σχολάζων καὶ ἀντλῶν. Senec. Ep. 44, 2, Cleanthes aquam traxit et rigando hortulo locavit manus.

2. Diog. L. VII. 170, καί ποτε ἀθροισθὲν τὸ κέρμα ἐκόμισεν εἰς μέσον τῶν γνωρίμων, καί φησι, Κλεάνθης μὲν καὶ ἄλλον Κλεάνθην δύναιτ' ἂν τρέφειν, εἰ βούλοιτο. οἱ δ' ἔχοντες ὅθεν τραφήσονται, παρ' ἑτέρων ἐπιζητοῦσι τὰ ἐπιτήδεια, καίπερ ἀνειμένως φιλοσοφοῦντες. ὅθεν δὴ καὶ δεύτερος Ἡρακλῆς ὁ Κλεάνθης ἐκαλεῖτο.

3. Diog. L. VII. 171, προκρίνων δὲ τὸν ἑαυτοῦ βίον τοῦ τῶν πλουσίων, ἔλεγεν, ἐν ᾧ σφαιρίζουσιν ἐκεῖνοι αὐτὸς γῆν σκληρὰν καὶ ἄκαρπον ἐργάζεσθαι, σκάπτων.

4. Diog. L. VII. 170, καὶ σκωπτόμενος δὲ ὑπὸ τῶν συμμαθητῶν ἠνείχετο, καὶ ὄνος ἀκούων προσεδέχετο· λέγων αὐτὸς μόνος δύνασθαι βαστάζειν τὸ Ζήνωνος φορτίον.

5. Diog. L. VII. 171, καί ποτε ὀνειδιζόμενος ὡς δειλός, διὰ τοῦτο, εἶπεν, ὀλίγα ἁμαρτάνω.

6. Diog. L. VII. 174, ὀνειδίσαντος αὐτῷ τινος εἰς τὸ γῆρας, κἀγώ, ἔφη, ἀπιέναι βούλομαι· ὅταν δὲ πανταχόθεν ἐμαυτὸν ὑγιαίνοντα περινοῶ καὶ γράφοντα καὶ ἀναγινώσκοντα, πάλιν μένω.

7. Diog. L. VII. 171, πολλάκις δὲ καὶ ἑαυτῷ ἐπέπληττεν· ὧν ἀκούσας Ἀρίστων, τίνι, ἔφη, ἐπιπλήττεις; καὶ ὃς γελάσας, πρεσβύτῃ, φησί, πολιὰς μὲν ἔχοντι, νοῦν δὲ μή.

8. Diog. L. VII. 173, Σωσιθέου τοῦ ποιητοῦ ἐν θεάτρῳ εἰπόντος πρὸς αὐτὸν παρόντα,

οὓς ἡ Κλεάνθους μωρία βοηλατεῖ,

ἔμεινεν ἐπὶ ταὐτοῦ σχήματος. ἐφ' ᾧ ἀγασθέντες οἱ ἀκροαταί, τὸν μὲν ἐκρότησαν, τὸν δὲ Σωσίθεον ἐξέβαλον. μεταγινώσκοντα δὲ αὐτὸν ἐπὶ τῇ λοιδορίᾳ προσήκατο, εἰπὼν ἄτοπον εἶναι, τὸν μὲν Διόνυσον καὶ τὸν Ἡρακλέα φλυαρουμένους ὑπὸ τῶν ποιητῶν μὴ ὀργίζεσθαι, αὐτὸν δὲ ἐπὶ τῇ τυχούσῃ βλασφημίᾳ δυσχεραίνειν. Cf. Plut. de Adulat. 11.

9. Diog. L. VII. 171, εἰπόντος δέ τινος Ἀρκεσίλαον μὴ ποιεῖν τὰ δέοντα, παῦσαι, ἔφη, καὶ μὴ ψέγε. εἰ γὰρ καὶ λόγῳ τὸ καθῆκον ἀναιρεῖ, τοῖς γοῦν ἔργοις αὐτὸ τιθεῖ. καὶ ὁ Ἀρκεσίλαος, οὐ κολακεύομαι, φησί. πρὸς ὃν ὁ Κλεάνθης, ναί, ἔφη, σὲ κολακεύω, φάμενος ἄλλα μὲν λέγειν, ἕτερα δὲ ποιεῖν.

10. Diog. L. VII. 173, ἔλεγε δὲ καὶ τοὺς ἐκ τοῦ περιπάτου ὅμοιόν τι πάσχειν ταῖς λύραις αἳ καλῶς φθεγξάμεναι αὐτῶν οὐκ ἀκούουσι.

11. Cic. Tusc. II. 60, e quibus (philosophis) homo sane levis Heracleotes Dionysius, cum a Zenone fortis esse didicisset, a dolore dedoctus est. nam cum ex renibus laboraret, ipso in eiulatu clamitabat falsa esse illa, quae antea de dolore ipse sensisset. quem cum Cleanthes condiscipulus rogaret quaenam ratio eum de sententia deduxisset, respondit: quia si, cum tantum operae philosophiae dedissem, dolorem tamen ferre non possem, satis esset argumenti malum esse dolorem. plurimos autem annos in philosophia consumpsi nec ferre possum: malum est igitur dolor. tum Cleanthem, cum pede terram percussisset, versum ex Epigonis ferunt dixisse:

Audisne haec, Amphiarae, sub terram abdite?
Zenonem significabat a quo illum degenerare dolebat.

Dionysius ὁ μεταθέμενος is mentioned also in Zeno apoph. 52, where see note. For the quotation from the Epigoni, cf. Soph. fr. 194, 195. (Dind.)

3. *renibus:* but according to Diog. L. VII. 37, 166 and Cic. Fin. V. 94 the disease was ophthalmia.

7. *si:* inserted by Madv. (on Fin. V. 94), who is followed by the later editors.

12. Stob. Floril. 82, 9 = Ecl. II. 2. 16, Κλεάνθης ἐρωτώμενος διὰ τί παρὰ τοῖς ἀρχαίοις οὐ πολλῶν φιλοσοφησάντων ὅμως πλείους διέλαμψαν ἢ νῦν, ὅτι, εἶπε, τότε μὲν ἔργον ἠσκεῖτο, νῦν δὲ λόγος.

13. Diog. L. VII. 172, μειρακίῳ ποτὲ διαλεγόμενος ἐπύθετο εἰ αἰσθάνεται· τοῦ δ' ἐπινεύσαντος, διὰ τί οὖν, εἶπεν, ἐγὼ οὐκ αἰσθάνομαι ὅτι αἰσθάνει;

14. Diog. L. VII. 172, ἐρομένου τινὸς τί ὑποτίθεσθαι δεῖ τῷ υἱῷ, τὸ τῆς Ἠλέκτρας, ἔφη, σῖγα σῖγα λεπτὸν ἴχνος.
The quotation is from Eurip. Orest. 140.

15. Stob. Floril. 33, 8, σιωπῶντος τοῦ Κλεάνθους, ἐπεί τις ἔφη, τί σιγᾷς; καὶ μὴν ἡδὺ τοῖς φίλοις ὁμιλεῖν. ἡδύ, ἔφη, ἀλλ᾽ ὅσῳπερ ἥδιον τοσῷδε μᾶλλον αὐτοῦ τοῖς φίλοις παραχωρητέον.

16. Diog. L. VII. 174, πρὸς δὲ τὸν μονήρη καὶ ἑαυτῷ λαλοῦντα, οὐ φαύλῳ, ἔφη, ἀνθρώπῳ λαλεῖς.

17. Exc. e MS. Ioan. Flor. Damasc. II. c. 13. 125 = Stob. Ecl. II. 31. 125 Wachsm., ἦ οὐ τοιοῦτος παῖς ἐκεῖνος ὁ Λάκων, ὃς Κλεάνθην τὸν φιλόσοφον ἠρώτησεν εἰ ἀγαθὸν ὁ πόνος ἐστίν; οὕτω γὰρ ἐκεῖνος φαίνεται φύσει πεφυκὼς καλῶς καὶ τεθραμμένος εὖ πρὸς ἀρετὴν ὥστε ἔγγιον εἶναι νομίζειν τὸν πόνον τῆς τἀγαθοῦ φύσεως ἢ τῆς τοῦ κακοῦ· ὅς γε ὡς ὁμολογουμένου τοῦ μὴ κακὸν ὑπάρχειν αὐτὸν εἰ ἀγαθὸν τυγχάνει ὢν ἐπυνθάνετο. ὅθεν καὶ ὁ Κλεάνθης ἀγασθεὶς τοῦ παιδὸς εἶπεν ἄρα πρὸς αὐτόν, αἵματος εἰς ἀγαθοῖο, φίλον τέκος, οἷ᾽ ἀγορεύεις (Hom. Od. IV. 611). Diog. L. VII. 172. Λάκωνός τινος εἰπόντος, ὅτι ὁ πόνος ἀγαθόν, διαχυθεὶς φησιν, αἵματος εἰς ἀγαθοῖο, φίλον τέκος.

πόνος is an ἀδιάφορον (Stob. Ecl. II. 7. 5ᵃ p. 58, 3. Diog. L. VII. 102), but it may perhaps be inferred from this passage that Cleanthes classed it among the προηγμένα. See on Zeno frag. 128. Antisthenes regarded it as ἀγαθόν (Diog. L. VI. 2).

18. Stob. Floril. 95, 28, Κλεάνθης, ἐρωτώμενος πῶς ἄν τις εἴη πλούσιος, εἶπεν, εἰ τῶν ἐπιθυμιῶν εἴη πένης.

19. Exc. e MS. Ioan. Flor. Damasc. II. 13. 63 = Stob. Ecl. II. 31. 63 Wachsm., Κλεάνθης, ἑταίρου ἀπιέναι μέλλοντος καὶ ἐρωτῶντος πῶς ἂν ἥκιστα ἁμαρτάνοι, εἶπεν, εἰ παρ' ἕκαστα ὧν πράττεις δοκοίης ἐμὲ παρεῖναι. Cf. Zeno, apoph. 42, and Maxim. Serm. 5.

20. Diog. L. VII. 173, λέγεται δέ, φάσκοντος αὐτοῦ κατὰ Ζήνωνα καταληπτὸν εἶναι τὸ ἦθος ἐξ εἴδους, νεανίσκους τινὰς εὐτραπέλους ἀγαγεῖν πρὸς αὐτὸν κίναιδον ἐσκληραγωγημένον ἐν ἀγρῷ, καὶ ἀξιοῦν ἀποφαίνεσθαι περὶ τοῦ ἤθους· τὸν δὲ διαπορούμενον κελεῦσαι ἀπιέναι τὸν ἄνθρωπον, ὡς δὲ ἀπιὼν ἐκεῖνος ἔπταρεν, ἔχω, εἶπεν, αὐτόν, ὁ Κλεάνθης, μαλακός ἐστιν. Cf. Zeno, frag. 147.

21. Diog. L. VII. 172, φησὶ δὲ ὁ Ἑκάτων ἐν ταῖς χρείαις, εὐμόρφου μειρακίου εἰπόντος εἰ ὁ εἰς τὴν γαστέρα τύπτων γαστρίζει, καὶ ὁ εἰς τοὺς μηροὺς τύπτων μηρίζει, ἔφη, σὺ μὲν τοὺς διαμηρισμοὺς ἔχε, μειράκιον. [αἱ δ' ἀνάλογοι φωναὶ τὰ ἀνάλογα οὐ πάντως σημαίνουσι πράγματα.] Cobet brackets the concluding words.

22. Diog. L. VII. 176, καὶ τελευτᾷ τόνδε τὸν τρόπον· διῴδησεν αὐτῷ τὸ οὖλον· ἀπαγορευσάντων δὲ τῶν ἰατρῶν δύο ἡμέρας ἀπέσχετο τροφῆς. καί πως ἔσχε καλῶς ὥστε τοὺς ἰατροὺς αὐτῷ πάντα τὰ συνήθη συγχωρεῖν. τὸν δὲ μὴ ἀνασχέσθαι ἀλλ' εἰπόντα ἤδη αὐτῷ προωδοιπορῆσθαι καὶ τὰς λοιπὰς ἀποσχόμενον τελευτῆσαι. Lucian, Macrob. 19, Κλεάνθης δὲ ὁ Ζήνωνος μαθητὴς καὶ διάδοχος ἐννέα καὶ ἐνενήκοντα οὗτος γεγονὼς ἔτη φῦμα ἔσχεν ἐπὶ τοῦ χείλους καὶ ἀποκαρτερῶν ἐπελθόντων αὐτῷ παρ' ἑταίρων τινῶν γραμμάτων προσενεγκάμενος τροφὴν καὶ πράξας περὶ ὧν ἠξίουν οἱ φίλοι, ἀποσχόμενος αὖθις τροφῆς ἐξέλιπε τὸν βίον. Stob. Floril. 7, 54, Κλεάνθης ὑπὸ γλώττης ἕλκους αὐτῷ γενομένου τὴν τροφὴν οὐκ ἐδύνατο παραπέμπειν· ὡς δὲ ῥᾷον ἔσχε καὶ ὁ ἰατρὸς αὐτῷ τροφὴν προσήγαγεν, σὺ δέ με, ἔφη, βούλει ἤδη τὸ πλέον τῆς ὁδοῦ κατανύσαντα ἀναστρέφειν, εἶτα πάλιν ἐξ ὑπαρχῆς τὴν αὐτὴν ἔρχεσθαι; καὶ ἐξῆλθεν τοῦ βίου.

INDICES.

[The references are to the numbers of the fragments, except where p. is prefixed.]

I. INDEX FONTIUM.

A

Achill. Tat. Isag. 124 E .... Z 35
—— —— 129 E .... Z 65
—— —— 133 c .... C 33
Aelian. Nat. An. vi. 50 .... C 45
Ambros. de Abraham, ii. 7 ... Z 148
Anon. τέχνη ap. Spengel Rhet.
 Gr. i. 434. 23 .... Z 25
Anon. τέχνη ap. Spengel Rhet.
 Gr. i. 447. 11 .... Z 26
Anon. variae coll. math. in
 Hulstchiana Heronis geom.
 et stereom. edit. p. 275 ...... Z 28
Anton. Meliss. i. 52 .... Z 189
Apollon. soph. lex. Hom. p.
 114 Bekk. .... C 66
Arnob. ad Nat. ii. 9 .... Z 54
Arrian. Epict. diss. i. 17. 10,
 11 .... Z 4, C 2
Arrian. Epict. diss. i. 20. 14 ... Z 123
—— —— ii. 19. 1—4 ... C 8
—— —— ii. 23. 42 ... C 91
—— —— iii. 22. 95 ... C 91
—— —— iv. 1. 131 ... C 91
—— —— iv. 1. 173 ... C 107
—— —— iv. 4. 34 ...... C 91
—— —— iv. 8. 12 ...... Z 3
Athenaeus iv. 158 b .... Z 156
—— vi. 233 b, c .... Z 169
—— xi. 467 d .... C 11
—— xi. 471 b .... C 11
—— xiii. 561 c .... Z 163

Athenaeus xiii. 563 e .... Z 173
—— xiii. 565 d .... Z 191
—— xiii. 572 f .... C 64
Augustin. c. Acad. ii. 11 ...... Z 153
—— —— iii. 7. 16 ... Z 125
—— —— iii. 9. 18 ... Z 11
—— —— iii. 17. 38 ... Z 42, 95
—— de Civ. Dei v. 20 ... C 90
—— de Trinit. xiii. 5. 8 ... Z 125
Aul. Gell. ix. 5. 5 .... Z 128

C

Censorin. de die nat. iv. 10 ... Z 80
—— xvii. 2 ... Z 77
—— frag. i. 4 .... C 28
Certamen Hom. et Hes. p. 4.
 18 Nietzsch .... C 67
Chalcid. in Tim. c. 144 ...... C 18
—— —— c. 220 ...... Z 90
—— —— c. 290 ...... Z 49
—— —— c. 292 ...... Z 50
Chrysost. Hom. i. in Matt. 4 ... Z 162
Cicero Acad. i. 36 .... Z 130
—— —— i. 38 .... Z 134, 138
—— —— i. 39 ...... Z 34, 46, 86
—— —— i. 41 ...... Z 8, 9, 11, 15,
 17, 19, 20
—— —— i. 42 ... Z 10, 18, 21, 22
—— —— ii. 18 .... Z 11
—— —— ii. 77 .... Z 11
—— —— ii. 113 ...... Z 11, 153
—— —— ii. 126 ...... Z 41, C 28

332 INDEX FONTIUM.

Cicero Acad. II. 145 .... Z 33
—— de Div. II. 119 ....Z 103
—— Fam. IX. 22. 1 ....Z 186
—— Fin. II. 17 .... Z 32
—— —— II. 69 .... C 90
—— —— III. 52 ....Z 131
—— —— IV. 12 .... Z 86
—— —— IV. 14 ....Z 120
—— —— IV. 47 ....Z 126
—— —— IV. 60 ....Z 126
—— —— IV. 72 ....Z 120
—— —— V. 38 .... C 44
—— —— V. 79 ....Z 125
—— —— V. 84 ....Z 151
—— —— V. 88 ....Z 120
—— Muren. 61...Z 132, 133, 148,
150, 151, 152, 153, 155
—— Nat. De. I. 36 ...Z 37, 39, 41,
72, 110
—— —— I. 37 ...C 14, 15, 16, 17,
46
Cicero Nat. De. I. 70 .... Z 8
—— —— II. 13—15 ... C 52
—— —— II. 21 .... Z 61
—— —— II. 22...Z 59, 60, 63
—— —— II. 24 .... C 42
—— —— II. 40 .... C 30
—— —— II. 57 .... Z 46
—— —— II. 58 .... Z 48
—— —— II. 160 ...... C 44
—— —— III. 16 .... C 52
—— —— III. 27 .... Z 46
—— —— III. 37 .... C 29
—— Orat. 32. 113 .... Z 32
—— Tusc. I. 19 .... Z 86
—— —— II. 29 ....Z 127
—— —— III. 74. 75 ......Z 143
—— —— III. 76 .... C 93
—— —— III. 77 .... C 94
—— —— IV. 11 ....Z 136
—— —— IV. 47 ....Z 136
—— —— V. 27 ....Z 127
Clem. Alex. Paedag. III. 11. 74.. Z 174
—— Protrept. VI. 72...C 75, 101
—— Strom. II. 20. 105... C 44
—— —— II. 20. 125...Z 187
—— —— II. 21. 129...Z 120,
C 72
—— —— II. 22. 131.. C 77
—— —— V. 3. 17 ...C 100
—— —— V. 8. 48 ... C 31
—— —— V. 12. 76...Z 164
—— —— V. 14. 95...Z 149
—— —— V. 14. 110...C 75, 101

Clem. Alex. Strom. VII. 6. 33... C 44
—— —— VIII. 9. 26... C 7
Cornut. de Nat. De. c. 31 ...... C 62
Cyrill. Lex. Bodl. II. 11. ap.
Cramer Anecd. Par. IV. 190...Z 31

D

Dio Chrysost. LIII. 4 ....Z 195
Diog. Laert. VI. 91 ....Z 194
—— VII. 14 ....C 112
—— 18 .... Z 30
—— 22 ....Z 175
—— 23 .... Z 16
—— 25 ......Z 145, 196
—— 32 ......Z 154, 167
—— 33 ... Z 149, 166,
168, 177
—— 39 .... Z 1
—— 40 .... Z 2
—— 41 .... C 1
—— 84 ....Z 119
—— 87 ... Z 120, C 72
—— 89 .... C 73
—— 91 .... C 79
—— 92 .... C 78
—— 107 ....Z 145
—— 108 ....Z 145
—— 110 ....Z 136
—— 120 ....Z 132
—— 121 ....Z 171
—— 122 ....Z 148
—— 127 ... Z 125, C 80
—— 128 .... C 81
—— 129 ....Z 172
—— 131 ....Z 176
—— 134 ......Z 35, C 12
—— 135 .... Z 52
—— 136 .... Z 52
—— 139 .... C 28
—— 140 ....Z 142
—— 142 .... Z 52
—— 143 .... Z 58
—— 145 .... Z 73
—— 146 .... Z 73
—— 148 .... Z 66
—— 149 ... Z 45 A, 118
—— 150 .... Z 51
—— 153 .... Z 74
—— 154 .... Z 74
—— 157 ......Z 85, C 41
—— 161 ....Z 134
—— 173 ....Z 147
—— VIII. 48 ....Z 193

INDEX FONTIUM.

E

Epict. Man. 53 .... C 91
Epiphan. Haeres. I. 5 .... Z 51
——— III. 2. 9 (III. 36) .... Z 37, 79, 95, 164, 185
Epiphan. Haeres. III. 2. 9 (III. 37) .... C 53
Euseb. P. E. XIII. 13, p. 671...Z 149
——— ——— p. 679... C 75
——— XV. 15. 7 .... C 28
——— 18. 3 .... Z 54
——— 20. 1 .... Z 106
——— 20. 2...Z 83, C 38
——— 45 .... Z 23
Eustath. in Il. Σ. 506, p. 1158. 37 .... Z 99

G

Galen de cogn. anim. morb. v. 13. Kühn .... Z 188
Galen in Hippocr. de humor. I. 1 (XVI. 32 K.) .... Z 53
Galen Hipp. et Plat. plac. II. 5 (v. 241 K.) .... Z 100
Galen Hipp. et Plat. plac. II. 5 (v. 247 K.) .... Z 101
Galen Hipp. et Plat. plac. II. 8 (v. 283 K.) .... Z 87, C 39
Galen Hipp. et Plat. plac. III. 5 (v. 322 K.) .... Z 102
Galen Hipp. et Plat. plac. III. 5 (v. 332 K.) .... Z 141, C 87
Galen Hipp. et Plat. plac. IV. 2 (v. 367 K.) .. .. Z 139
Galen Hipp. et Plat. plac. IV. 3 (v. 377 K.) .... Z 139
Galen Hipp. et Plat. plac. IV. 7 (v. 416 K.) .... Z 143
Galen Hipp. et Plat. plac. V. 1 (v. 429 K.) .... Z 139
Galen Hipp. et Plat. plac. V. 6 (v. 476 K.) .... C 84
Galen Hipp. et Plat. plac. IX. 1 (v. 653 K.) .... C 85
Galen Hist. Phil. 5 (XIX. 241 K.) Z 36
——— ——— 9 (XIX. 254 K.) Z 91
——— ——— 10 (XIX. 258 K.) Z 78
——— ——— 13 (XIX. 271 K.) C 33
——— ——— 13 (XIX. 272 K.) C 34
——— ——— 31 (XIX. 322 K.) ...Z 106, 107
Galen. nat. facult. I. 2 (II. 5 K.) Z 53
Gemin. Elem. Astron. p. 53 (in Petau's Uranol.) .... C 35

H

Harpocration s. v. λέσχαι...... C 61
Hermias Irris. Gent. Phil. 14. p. 654 Diels .... C 21
Hippolyt. philosoph. 21. 1 ... Z 36

L

Lactant. Epit. ad Pentad. 38...Z 144
——— Inst. I. 5 .... Z 39, C 15
——— ——— III. 4 .... Z 153
——— ——— III. 7 .... Z 120
——— ——— III. 8 .... Z 120
——— ——— III. 23 ...... Z 132, 144
——— ——— IV. 9 .... Z 44
——— ——— VII. 7 .... Z 97
——— de Ira dei 11 .... Z 109
——— de Ver. Sap. 9......... Z 44
Longinus ap. Euseb. P. E. XV. 21. 3 .... Z 88, C 40

M

Macrob. Sat. I. 17. 8 .... C 58
——— ——— I. 17. 31 .... C 60
——— ——— I. 17. 36 .... C 59
——— ——— I. 18. 14 .... C 57
——— ——— I. 23. 2 .... C 29
——— Somn. Scip. I. 14. 19... Z 89
Mantiss. Proverb. (in paroem. Gr. II. p. 757) cent. I. 85...C 102
Maxim. Floril. c. 6 .... Z 190
Minuc. Fel. Octav. XIX. 10... Z 39, 41, 44, 111, C 14

N

Nemes. Nat. Hom. p. 32...... C 36
——— ——— p. 96...... Z 93
Numenius ap. Euseb. P. E. XIV. 6. p. 733................. Z 11

O

Olympiodorus in Plat. Gorg. p. 53 f. .... Z 12, C 5
Origen c. Cels. I. 5. p. 324 ...Z 164
——— ——— VII. 63. p. 739...Z 178

P

Philargyrius ad Verg. G. II.336. Z 57
Philo liber quis virt. stud. p.
880 ....Z 157
Philo mund. incorr. p. 505. 27. C 23
— — p. 510. 11. Z 56
Philo de Provid. I. 22 .... Z 35
— — II. 74 .... C 19
Philodemus περὶ εὐσεβ. c. 8 Z 40,117
— — c. 9 ... C 16
— — c. 13... C 54
— — p. 84 G....Z 109
— περὶ μουσικῆς c. 28. C 49
— περὶ φιλοσόφων c. 13. C 113
Philoponus on Ar. Phys. IV. 6.
p. 213 a. 31 .... Z 70
Photius s. v. λέσχαι .... C 61
Plutarch Alc. 6. 2..............C 108
— Alex. virt. 6 ....Z 162
— Arat. 23. 3 ....Z 148
— Aud. Poet. 11......... C 55
— — 12...... Z 197
— — 12...... C 111
— Cohib. Ir. 15........Z 106
— Comm. Hesiod 9 ...Z 196
— — Not. 23. 1...Z 120
— — — 31. 5... C 47
— — — 31. 10. C 25
— de facie in orbe lunae
6. 3 .... C 27
Plutarch de fluv. 5. 3............ C 69
— — 5. 4............ C 70
— — 17. 4............ C 71
— frag. de an. Wytt. V².
p. 899 ....Z 121
Plutarch Is. et Osir. 66 ...... C 56
— Lycurg. 31 ....Z 163
— plac. I. 3. 39 .... Z 35
— — I. 10. 4 .... Z 23
— — I. 15. 5 .... Z 78
— — II. 14. 2......... C 33
— — II. 16. 1......... C 34
— — II. 20. 3 .... C 29
— — IV. 11. 1......... C 4
— — IV. 21. 4......... Z 98
— — V. 4. 1 ....Z 106
— — V. 5. 2 ....Z 107
— prof. in virt. 12......Z 160
— quaest. Conv. III. 6. 1.. Z 180
— — V. 10. 3 C 44
— Soll. an. 11. 2, 3 ... C 45
— Sto. Rep. 2. 1.. ......Z 162
— — 6. 1.........Z 164

Plutarch Sto. Rep. 7. 1, 2 ...Z 134
— — 7. 4......... C 76
— — 8. 1......... Z 29
— — 8. 2......... Z 6
— — 30. 1 ......Z 131
— Virt. Mor. 2 ....Z 134
— — 3 ......Z 135
Porphyr. de Abstin. III. 19 ...Z 122
— III. 20 ... C 44
— vit. Pythag. 1. 2...... C 68
Probus ad Virg. Ed. VI. 31. p.
10. 33 Keil...............Z 52, C 20
Probus ad Virg. Ed. VI. 31. p.
21. 14 Keil ....Z 112
Proclus ad Hes. Op. 291 ......Z 196

Q

Quintil. Inst. Or. II. 15. 33—35 C 9
— — II. 17. 41... C 5
— — II. 20. 7 . Z 32
— — IV. 2. 117... Z 27

R

Rufus Ephes. de part. hom.
p. 44 .... Z 84

S

Schol. ad Apoll. Rhod. I. 498...Z 113
— Arist. 22 b. 29 Brandis Z 6
— Dionys. Thrac. ap.
Bekk. Anecd. p. 663. 16 ... Z 13
Schol. ad Hes. Theog. 117 ...Z 114
— — 134 ...Z 115
— — 139 ...Z 116
— Hom. Il. III. 64 ... C 63
— — XVI. 233... C 55
— Hom. Od. I. 52 (Cramer A. O. III. 416)............ C 65
Schol. ad Lucian. Cal. 8 ...... Z 29
— Nic. Ther. 447......C 114
— Plat. Alc. I. 121 E... Z 82
Seneca de Benef. II. 31. 12 ... C 99
— — V. 14. 1...... C 97
— — VI. 11. 1 ... C 98
— — VI. 12. 2 ... C 99
— Epist. 82. 7 ....Z 129
— — 83. 8 ....Z 159
— — 94. 4 .... C 92
— — 104. 21 ....Z 161
— — 107. 10 .... C 91
— — 108. 10 .... C 50
— — 113. 18 .... C 43

INDEX FONTIUM.

Seneca de Ira I. 16. 7 ....Z 158
—— Nat. Quaest. VII. 19. 1 .. Z 75
—— de Otio Sap. 30. 2 ...Z 170
—— Tranq. An. I. 7...Z 170, C 105
Sext. Emp. Math. II. 7......... Z 32
—— —— VII. 151 ... Z 15
—— —— VII. 227 ... Z 10
—— —— VII. 228...Z 7, C 3
—— —— VII. 236 ... Z 7
—— —— VII. 248 ... Z 11
—— —— VII. 253 ... Z 10
—— —— VII. 372...Z 14, C 3
—— —— VII. 422 ...Z 132
—— —— VII. 426 ... Z 11
—— —— VIII. 355... Z 8
—— —— VIII. 400... C 3
—— —— IX. 88...... C 51
—— —— IX. 101 ... Z 59
—— —— IX. 104 ... Z 61
—— —— IX. 107 ... Z 62
—— —— IX. 133 ...Z 108
—— —— XI. 30...Z 124, C 74
—— —— XI. 74 ...... C 88
—— —— XI. 77 ......Z 128
—— —— XI. 190...Z 179, 181
—— —— XI. 191 ...Z 180
—— Pyrrh. II. 4 .... Z 11
—— —— II. 70......... C 3
—— —— III. 200 ......Z 182
—— —— III. 205 ......Z 180
—— —— III. 206 ......Z 183
—— —— III. 245 ......Z 179
—— —— III. 246 ......Z 180
Simplic. ad Cat. 80 a. 4......... Z 76
—— in Epict. Man. 53 ... C 91
Stob. Ecl. I. 1. 12. p. 25. 3 ... C 48
—— 1. 29^b. p. 34. 20... C 14
—— —— p. 35. 9... Z 42
—— 5. 15. p. 78. 18... Z 45
—— 8. 40^e. p. 104. 7. Z 76
—— 10. 14. p. 126. 17. Z 35
—— 11. 5^a. p. 132. 26. Z 51
—— 12. 3. p. 136. 21. Z 23
—— 13. 1^c. p. 138. 14. Z 24
—— 15. 6^a. p. 146. 19. C 26
—— —— p. 146. 21. Z 68
—— 16. 1. p. 149. 8... Z 78
—— 17. 3. p. 152. 19. Z 52
—— —— p. 153. 7... C 24
—— 18. 1^d. p. 156. 27. Z 69
—— 19. 4. p. 166. 4... Z 67
—— 20. 1^e. p. 171. 2
    ...Z 54, C 22
—— 21. 6^e. p. 187. 4... C 28

Stob. Ecl. I. 22. 3^b. p. 199. 10. Z 58
—— 23. 1. p. 200. 21. Z 64
—— 24. 2^d. p. 205. 25. C 33
—— 25. 3^i. p. 211. 18. C 29
—— 25. 5. p. 213. 15. Z 71
—— 26. 1^i. p. 219. 12. Z 71
—— —— p. 219. 14. C 32
—— 48. 7. p. 317. 15. C 37
—— 49. 33. p. 367. 18. Z 92
—— 49. 34. p. 369. 6. Z 93
—— II. 2. 12. p. 22. 12... Z 5
—— 7. 1. p. 38. 15 ...Z 146
—— —— p. 39. 5 ...Z 137
—— —5^a. p. 57. 18...Z 128
—— —5^{b8}. p. 65. 8... C 82
—— —6^a. p. 75. 11...Z 120
—— —6^a. p. 76. 3 ... C 72
—— —6^e. p. 77. 20...Z 124
—— —6^e. p. 77. 21... C 74
—— —7^g. p. 84. 21...Z 131
—— —11^g. 99. 3 ....Z 148
—— —11^i. p. 103. 12..C 104
—— 31. 64. p. 212. 22. C 106
Stob. Floril. 4. 90 ....C 106
—— 4. 107 ....Z 202
—— 6. 19 ....C 95
—— 6. 20 ....C 110
—— 6. 34 ....Z 201
—— 6. 37 ....C 89
—— 6. 62 .... Z 192
—— 14. 4.................Z 189
—— 28. 14 .... C 96
—— 36. 26 ... .Z 200
—— 42. 2 ....C 103
—— 43. 88 ....Z 165
—— 95. 21 ....Z 199
—— 108. 59 .... C 86
Strabo VII. 3. 6 ....Z 198
Suidas s. v. λέσχαι .... C 61
Syrian. ad Metaph. 892 b. 14... C 6

T

Tatian ad Graec. c. 3 .... Z 47
—— —— c. 5 .... Z 55
Tertullian de Anim. c. 5 ..Z 89, C 36
—— —— c. 14...... Z 94
—— —— c. 25...... C 36
—— Apol. 21.........Z 44, C 13
—— Marc. I. 13 .... Z 41
—— Nat. II. 2 .... Z 46
—— —— 4 .... Z 38
—— Praes. Cup. 7 ...... Z 51

Themist. de An. 68 a .... Z 96
—— —— 72 b .... Z 43
—— —— 90 b ....Z 140
—— Or. II. 27 c............ C 83
—— Or. VIII. 108 c.........Z 196
—— Or. XIII. 171 D ......Z 196
—— Phys. 40 b .... Z 70
Theodoret Gr. Cur. Aff. III.
　p. 780 ....Z 164
Theodoret Gr. Cur. Aff. IV. 12. Z 35
　—— —— IV. 20. C 33
　—— —— v. 25. Z 106
Theodoret Gr. Cur. Aff. v. 25
　p. 934 ....Z 88, C 40

Theodoret Gr. Cur. Aff. VI. 14. Z 45
Theon progymn. 12. p. 251...Z 108
Theoph. ad Autol. III. 5. p.
　119 c ....Z 184, C 115

V

Varro Ling. Lat. v. 9 .... C 10
　—— —— v. 59 ....Z 105
　—— R. R. II. 1. 3 .... Z 81
　—— —— II. 4. 9 .... C 44

Z

Zonaras s. v. σολοικίζειν ...... Z 31

II. INDEX NOMINUM.

A

Academics, Z 169.
Alcmaeon, Z 82.
Alexander, Z 30.
Alexandria, Z 30.
Alexinus, Z 5, 61.
Amoebeus, p. 226.
Anaxagoras, Z 81, 113, C 27.
Anaximander, Z 81, C 29.
Anaximenes, Z 52.
Antigonus Carystius, p. 228.
—— Gonatas, p. 2, 5, 6, 228.
Antiochus, p. 17, 25, Z 126.
Antipater, p. 114, C 59.
Antisthenes, p. 19, 20, 22, 53, Z 3, 23, 109, 162, 163, 171, 187, 195, C 79.
Apollodorus, p. 19.
Apollonius, p. 2, 4, 26.
Arcesilas, Z 11, 145.
Archedemus, C 7.
Archelaus, Z 81.
Aristarchus, p. 42, 51, C 27.
Aristippus, Z 197.
Aristo, p. 36, Z 5, 131, 191, C 92.
Aristotle, p. 24, 25, Z 12, 26, 35, 49, 50, 53, p. 110, Z 65, 67, 68, 69, 81, 99, 104, 112, 116, 117, 128, 134, 135, 136, 163, 167, 168, 169, 195, C 1, 37, 52, 53.
Aristoxenus, C 42.

B

Bion Borysthenes, p. 230.
Boethus, Z 54.

C

Caphesias, p. 231.
Carneades, Z 11.
Chremonides, p. 6, 232.

Chrysippus, p. 7, 20, 27, 28, 34, 36, 38, 40, 43, 45, 48, 49, 50, Z 2, 7, 11, 14, 21, 23, 24, 49, 52, 66, 72, 74, 76, 79, 100, 102, 136, 139, 143, 144, 160, 167, 185, C 3, 8, 9, 13, 18, 19, 23, 24, 37, 41, 43, 44, 48 (17), 76.
Cicero, p. 34, Z 126.
Cleanthes, p. 1, 23, 35, 36—53, Z 3, 7, 13, 14, 35, 45 A, 52, 56 (54), 58, 79, 93, 120, 128.
Crates, p. 3, 31, Z 165.
—— of Mallus, Z 198.
Critolaus, p. 111.
Cynics, p. 18—21, 30, Z 9, 125, 149, 162, 164, 167, 171, 172, 176, 177, 184, 186, 194, C 76, 79, 80, 88, 101, 104.

D

Demetrius, p. 27.
Diodorus, p. 40, C 8.
Diogenes, p. 18, 19, 20, 21, Z 9, 168, 171, 185, p. 225, C 113.
—— of Apollonia, Z 42, 81.
—— of Babylon, Z 100, 108, C 72.
Dionysius (ὁ μεταθέμενος), p. 234, 328.

E

Empedocles, p. 114, Z 73, 81, 110.
Empedus, p. 233.
Epicurus and Epicureans, Z 8, 9, 21, 50, 55, 58, 69, 72, 73, 74, 85, 102, 112, 167, C 16, 89, 90.

H

Heraclitus, p. 21—23, 50, Z 52, 54, p. 114, Z 64, 65, 77, 83, 85, 87, C 1, 3, 21, 28, 29, 33, 48 (10, 24, 36).

INDEX NOMINUM.

Herillus, p. 52, Z 17.
Herodicus, Z 77.
Hesiod, p. 31, 32, Z 29, (*Theog.* 118, 119) Z 113, (*Theog.* 126—128) Z 193, (*Op.* 291), Z 196.
Hippocrates, Z 106, C 42.
Homer, p. 31, 43, 51, Z 174, 195, 198.

I

Indians, Z 187.

M

Marcus Aurelius, Z 52, 162, C 44.
Megarians, Z 5.

N

Neanthes, p. 51.

P

Panaetius, Z 54.
Parmenides, Z 64, 81.
Peripatetics, p. 110 f., Z 159, 169.
Persaeus, p. 31, 53.
Phocylides, Z 29.
Plato, p. 25, 26, 30, Z 1, 16, 21, 23, 34, 35, 62, 65, 91, 99, 103, 110, 112, 134, 135, 136, 142, 149, 162, 163, 166, 167, 168, 169, 172, 177, 197, C 37, 57, 58.
—— Cratylus, p. 44.

Polemo, p. 3, 25.
Posidonius, p. 49, Z 24, 49, 52, 66, 76, 80, 131, 143, 198, C 35, 84.
Ptolemy, Philadelphus, p. 5, 6, 228.
Pythagoras and Pythagoreans, Z 50, 55, 65, 70, 73, 81, C 26, 27, 29, 37, 68.

S

Seneca, Z 162.
Socrates, p. 45, 53, Z 59, 123, 134, 158, 159, 162, 194, p. 227, 230, C 76, 77, 79.
Sophocles (frag. 711), Z 197.
Stilpo, p. 3, 28.
Strato, Z 64, C 43.

T

Thales, Z 73.
Theophrastus, p. 110 f., 233.

V

Virgil, Z 97.

X

Xenocrates, p. 3, Z 1, 128, C 37.
Xenophanes, Z 56 (33), 81, 113, 117.

Z

Zeno, p. 1—35, 46, C 13, 18, 24, 76.
—— of Tarsus, Z 57, 87.

III. INDEX VERBORUM.

ἀγαθά, p. 14, 15, Z 127, 128, C 75.
ἀγέλη σύννομος, Z 162.
ἄγνοια, Z 18.
ἀδεής, Z 169.
ἀδιάφορα, p. 14, 15, 17, 46, Z 127, 128, 129, 145, 154, 161, 171, 172, 178.
ἀήττητος, Z 148, 157.
ἀθάνατος (νοῦς), Z 95.
ἀθαύμαστος, Z 169.
αἰθέρος τὸ ἔσχατον, Z 65.
αἰθήρ, Z 41, C 15.
αἷμα, Z 87, 88.
αἰσθήσεως (περί), p. 50, 51.
αἴσθησις, Z 8, 20, 121.
αἰσθητόν, Z 20.
αἴτιον, Z 24.
ἀκολασία, Z 138.
ἀλλαγή, Z 168.
ἀλλοίωσις, Z 52.
ἄλλως, C 45.
ἄλογα ζῷα, C 44, 45.
ἁμάρτημα, p. 15, Z 132, 133.
ἀμετάπτωτον, Z 135.
ἀμφήκης, C 48 (10).
ἄν, Z 190.
ἀναδωδωναῖε, C 55.
ἀναθυμίασις, p. 23, Z 83, C 55.
ἀναλαμβάνειν, p. 226.
ἄναμμα νοερόν, C 29.
ἀναπεπταμένον, Z 174.
ἀνδρεία, Z 134, C 76.
ἀνεπιτρεπτεῖν, Z 194.
ἀνθρωποβορίας, Z 184, C 115.
ἄνω κάτω ὁδός, Z 52.
ἀξία, p. 14, Z 130, 131.
ἀξιωματικός, Z 148 (16).
ἀπάθεια, Z 158.
ἀπαιδεύτους, C 106.
ἀπαξία, p. 14, Z 130, 131.
ἀπέριττος, Z 169.
ἀπέριττος, Z 169.
ἁπλῶς γένεσις, Z 50.

ἀποκρίνεσθαι, Z 56 (45).
Ἀπόλλων, C 58.
ἀπομνημονεύματα Κράτητος, p. 31, Z 199.
ἀπονεμητέοις, Z 134.
ἀποπροηγμένον, v. προηγμένον.
ἀπόρων (περί), p. 49.
Ἄραβες, Z. 198.
ἀργικέραυνε, C 48 (32).
ἀρετή, Z 125, 128, 134, 135, C 78, 79, 80, 83.
ἀρετῶν (περί), p. 52.
Ἀρίσταρχον (πρός), p. 51.
ἀρρωστήματα, Z 144.
ἀρχαί, Z 35.
ἀρχαιολογία, p. 51.
ἀρχαιότεροι, p. 40, Z 10.
ἀρωγῆς (περί), p. 47, 52.
ἀσεβείας γραφή, C 27.
ἀσόλοικος, Z 30.
ἀστέρες, C 33, 34.
ἀστραπή, Z 74.
ἀτόμων (περί), p. 47.
ἀτραπός, C 45.
αὐγή, C 23.
αὐθέκαστος, C 75.
αὐλή, Z 131.
ἀφορμαί, C 82.
Ἀφροδίτη, C 63, 64.

βάρος, Z 67.
βασιλείας (περί), p. 52.
βασιλικός, Z 148 (16).
βιάζεται, Z 148 (12).
βίος, Z 145.
βουλῆς (περί), p. 52.
βροντή, Z 74.

γάμος, Z 171.
γάμου (περί), p. 51.
γενεά, Z 77.
γεωμετρία, Z 28.

γιγάντων (περί), p. 51.
Γοργίππου (περί), p. 52.
γυμνάσια, Z 166.
γυναῖκες, Z 176.

δακτυλίων, C 3.
Δεινιάς, C 11.
δεσπόζει, Z 148 (12).
δημιουργεῖν, Z 35.
δημιουργός, Z 48.
Δημόκριτον (πρός), p. 51.
δῆξις, Z 139, 158.
διαβολή, C 103.
διαθέσεις, Z 117, 135, C 36, 51.
διαίρεσις, Z 51.
διαιρετέοις, Z 134.
διακεκλασμένον, Z 174.
διακόσμησις, Z 52.
διαλεκτική, Z 6, 32, C 1.
διαλεκτικῆς (περί), p. 49.
διαλεκτικοί, p. 33, Z 5.
διάνοια, Z 100, 135.
διατριβαί, p. 30, Z 179.
διατριβῶν β', p. 53.
διαχύσεις, Z 139.
διαψεύδεται, Z 148 (14).
διήγησις, Z 25.
διήκειν, C 13.
δικάζειν (περὶ τοῦ), p. 52.
δίκαιον, C 77.
δικαιοσύνη, Z 122, 134.
δικαστήρια, Z 166.
Διόνυσος, C 57.
Διοσκούρους, Z 117.
δόξα, Z 15, 143, 153.
δόξης (περί), p. 47, 48, 50, 52, C 100, 101.
δυνάμεις ψυχῆς, Z 93, C 85.
δυνατόν, C 8.
δυνατῶν (περί), p. 50.
δυσμαὶ βίου, C 51.

ἐγκράτεια, p. 45, C 76.
ἐγκύκλιος παιδεία, Z 167.
εἱμαρμένη, Z 19, 45, 45 A, C 18.
εἰσοχή, C 3.
ἔκκλισις, Z 143, C 76.
ἐκλείψεις, Z 71, 73.
ἐκπύρωσις, Z 52, 54, 55, C 22, 24.
ἔλεγχε σαυτόν, Z 189.
ἔλεος, Z 144, 152.
ἐλευθερίας (περί), p. 52.
ἐλευθέρους, Z 149.
ἕλιξ, C 29, 60.

Ἑλληνικῆς παιδείας (περί), p. 30.
ἐναπομεμαγμένος, Z 11.
ἐνάργεια, p. 34, Z 9.
ἐνδυμάτων, Z 31.
ἐνεργητέοις, Z 134.
ἐννοήματα, Z 23, C 6.
ἔννοια, p. 10, 34, Z 21.
ἐξαγωγή, Z 161.
ἐξέδραι, C 61.
ἕξις, Z 43, p. 110, Z 56 (53), 117, 134, 135, C 5.
ἐξοχή, C 3.
ἐξύγρωσις, Z 52, C 24.
ἔπαρσις, Z 139, 143.
ἕπεσθαι θεοῖς, Z 123.
ἐπιγεννήματα, p. 46.
ἐπιγιγνόμενα κρίσεσιν, Z 138, 139.
ἐπιθυμία, Z 142, 172.
ἐπιστήμη, Z 16, 17, 18, 33, 134.
ἐπιστήμης (περί), p. 50.
ἐπιστολαί, p. 31.
ἔρως, Z 113, 163, 172.
ἐρωτικὴ τέχνη, p. 30, 52, Z 174, C 108.
ἔρωτος (περί), p. 52.
ἐσθής, Z 177.
ἐσθίειν ἀτάκτως, Z 31.
Ἑστία, Z 110, C 27.
ἔσχατον τοῦ πυρός, C 24.
εὐβουλίας (περί), p. 47, 52.
εὐδαιμονία, Z 124, C 74.
εὐκρασία, p. 23, C 42.
εὔλογον, Z 145.
εὐπρέπεια, Z 56 (63).
εὑρεσίλογος, C 62.
εὔροια, Z 124, C 74.
εὐφυΐα, Z 172.
εὐφυΐας (περί), p. 52.
ἐφ' ἡμῖν, Z 79, C 91.

Ζεύς, Z 111.
Ζήνωνος (περὶ τῆς Ζ. φυσιολογίας β'), p. 50.
ζῴδιον, Z 71.
ζώνη διακεκαυμένη, C 35.
ζῷον (ὁ κόσμος), Z 62.

ἡγεμονικόν, p. 13, 42, Z 24, 33, 67, 93, 101, 135, 141, C 15, 25, 28, 84.
ἡδονή, p. 46, Z 127, 128, 139, 142, 143, C 88, 89, 90.
ἡδονῆς (περί), p. 47, 53.
ἠθικά, p. 31.

INDEX VERBORUM. 341

ἠθικόν, Z 2, 119.
ἦθος, Z 146, 147, C 36.
ἥλιος, C 25, 28, 29, 30, 31.
Ἡρακλείτου ἐξηγήσεων δ΄, p. 50.
Ἡρακλῆς, C 62.
Ἥρη, Z 110.
Ἥριλλον (πρός), p. 52.
Ἥφαιστος, Z 111.

θάνατος, Z 129.
θαυματοποιός, C 98.
θεολογικόν, C 1.
θεομαχία, p. 51.
θεός, Z 35, 108, 109.
θεὸς κακῶν ποιητής, Z 47, C 48 (17).
θεὸς φθαρησόμενος, C 47.
θεῶν (περί), p. 49, 51, C 47.
θερίζων, p. 224.
θερμασία, Z 84.
θέσει, Z 39.
Θηρίκλειον, C 11.
θύραθεν, C 37.

Ἰαπετός, Z 115.
ἰδέαι, Z 23, C 6.
ἴδιον, p. 49.
ἰδίων (περί), p. 49.
ἰδίως ποιόν, Z 49.
ἱερά, Z 164.
ἰλύς, Z 113.
ἴσος, v. ἁμάρτημα.
Ἰφικρατίς, C 11.

καθάπαξ ἀδιάφορα, Z 130.
καθαρός, Z 36, 174.
καθέλκειν, Z 30.
καθῆκον, p. 15, 34, Z 145, 161, 169, 170, 171, 172, 177, 178, 192.
καθήκοντος (περί), p. 29, 52.
καθολικά, p. 27, Z 23.
κακά, p. 14, Z 127, 128.
κακία, p. 46.
κάλλυντρον, C 88.
καλῶν (περί), p. 52.
καρδία, Z 141, C 87.
κατά, Z 145.
κατὰ φύσιν, p. 14, 15, Z 130, 169, 192, C 88.
— — (περὶ τοῦ κ. φ. βίου), p. 29.
καταληπτική, v. φαντασία.
καταληπτόν, Z 147.
κατάληψις, p. 34, Z 10, 16, 18, 33, C 80.

καταπίνεται, Z 102.
κατηγόρημα, Z 23, 24, C 7.
κατηγορημάτων (περί), p. 50.
κατόρθωμα, p. 15, 34, Z 145.
κεκοσμημένος, Z 174.
κενόν, Z 69, 70.
κεραυνός, Z 74, C 48 (10).
κηρία, Z 38.
κηρός, Z 50.
κίνησις, Z 91.
κληθείς, Z 29.
κλήσεις ἱεραί, C 53.
κοινῶς ποιόν, Z 49.
Κοῖος, Z 115.
κομῆται, Z 75.
κόσμος, Z 57, 66, 71, 162, 193, C 17, 48 (7).
κραντῆρες, C 114.
κρᾶσις δι' ὅλου, p. 11, 23, Z 51, 52, 53, 96, C 13.
Κρεῖος, Z 115.
κρίσεις, Z 136, 139, 143.
Κρόνος, Z 113.
Κύκλωπες, Z 116.
κυριεύων, C 8.
κυριεύοντος (περί), p. 50.
κωνοειδής, C 26, 33.

λεκτόν, p. 40, Z 24, C 7.
λέσχαι, C 61.
Λεσχηνόριον, C 61.
λέξεων (περί), p. 27, Z 30, 31.
λέξις, p. 27, 226.
ληπτά, Z 130, 131.
λιτός, Z 169.
λογικά, Z 4, C 2.
λογική, Z 1.
λογικόν, Z 2.
λόγος, p. 22, Z 3, 37, 44, C 16.
— σπερματικός, Z 46, C 24.
λόγου (περί), p. 27
— (περὶ τοῦ), p. 50.
— στοιχεῖα, Z 3.
λογόφιλος, Z 200.
Λοξίας, C 60.
λοξός, Z 73.
Λύκειος, C 59.
Λύκιος, C 59.
λύπη, p. 46, Z 127, 128, 139, 142, 143, 144, C 86.
λύσεις καὶ ἔλεγχοι, p. 28.
λύσις, Z 139.

Μαίονα, C 67.

Μανῆς, p. 232.
μαντική, p. 29, Z 118.
Μαργίτης, Z 195.
μέγας, Z 148.
μέθη, C 80.
μεθύειν, Z 159.
μείωσις, Z 139.
μελαγχολία, C 80
μέρη (ψυχῆς), Z 93, 94.
μέσον, C 24.
μέσα, Z 145.
μεταβάλλεσθαι, Z 153.
μεταβολή, p. 23.
μεταλήψεως (περί), p. 50, C 11.
μετανοεῖν, Z 153.
μετέχοντα, p. 46, Z 128.
μῖξις, Z 51, 52.
μνήμη, Z 14.
μοιχεύειν, Z 178, C 110.
μυθικά, p. 51.
μύρμηκες, C 45.
μυροπώλια, Z 174.
μυστικὰ σχήματα, C 53.
μῶλυ, C 66.

ναοί, Z 164.
νοήματα, C 6.
νόμισμα, Z 168.
νόμος, Z 39.
νόμου (περί), p. 30.
νόμων (περί), p. 52.
νοσήματα, Z 144.
νόσοι, Z 144.
νοῦς, Z 43, C 37.
νοῦς (κόσμου), Z 42.

ὁδοποιητική, Z 13.
οἴησις, Z 15, 16.
οἰκείωσις, Z 121, 122, 126.
ὁλοόφρονος, C 65.
ὅλου (περί), p. 28.
ὁμολογία φύσει, Z 120, 123, C 72.
ὁμόνοια, Z 163.
ὀνείρων, Z 160.
ὅρασις, Z 104.
ὄρεξις, Z 143.
ὄρη, Z 56 (8).
ὀρθὸς λόγος, pp. 8—10, 40, Z 3, 117, 123, 157.
ὀρθῶς λέγειν, C 9.
ὁρμαί, Z 123, 138.
ὁρμῆς (περί), p. 29, 52.
ὁρῶν (περί), p. 52.
οὐρανός, Z 66.

οὐσία, p. 41, Z 49, 50, 51, 53, p. 110.
οὐσίας (περί), p. 29.
ὄψεως (περί), p. 29.

πάθη, p. 45, Z 135—144, 172, C 86.
παθῶν (περί), p. 29, 184.
παιδαγωγοί, Z 188.
παιδεία, v. ἐγκύκλιος.
πανσέληνος, Z 73.
παραβάλλειν, Z 185.
παράδειγμα, Z 26.
παράδοξα, C 107.
παράθεσις, Z 51.
παραινετική, p. 47, C 92.
παράλογα, C 107.
παραμυθητική, C 93, 94.
παρὰ φύσιν, p. 14, 15, Z 130, 169.
πάσχον, Z 34, 35.
περιβολή, Z 175.
περιέχω, C 65.
περίοδος, Z 52, 56 (43).
περιπατεῖν ἀκόσμως, Z 31.
περίστασις, p. 15, Z 169, 170, 184.
πηγή, Z 146.
πιλοειδής, C 32.
πληγὴ πυρός, C 76.
πλῆκτρον, C 31.
πλοῦτος, Z 169, C 111.
πνεῦμα, p. 11, 40, 42, Z 41, 48, p. 110, Z 84, 85, C 13.
——— διατεῖνον, C 43.
πνευματικὴ δύναμις, p. 110.
πνευματικὸς τόνος, Z 56 (54).
ποιητικῆς ἀκροάσεως (περί), p. 31.
ποιητοῦ (περί), p. 51.
ποιά, Z 23, 49.
ποιότης, Z 53, 92.
ποιοῦν, Z 34, 35.
πόλις, C 104.
πολῖται, Z 149.
Πολιτεία, p. 20, 29, Z 23, 97, 149, 162.
πολιτεύεσθαι, Z 170.
πολιτικόν, C 1.
πολιτικός, p. 52.
πολυχρόνιος, Z 95.
πολυώνυμος, C 48 (1).
πόνος, Z 128, 187, 201.
πορεία, Z 175.
Ποσειδῶν, Z 111.
πράξεων (περί), p. 52.
προβλημάτων Ὁμηρικῶν, p. 31.
προηγμένον, p. 15, 34, Z 127, 128, 131, 145, 169.

INDEX VERBORUM. 343

προηγούμενος, p. 15, Z 123, 131, 169, 170.
προκοπή, p. 34.
προκόπτοντες, Z 160.
πρόληψις, p. 10, 34, 40, Z 21.
πρόνοια, Z 36, 45 A, C 18, 19, 44.
προπέτεια, Z 22.
προσδοκία, Z 143.
προσηγορία, Z 23.
προσίεσθαι, Z 160.
προσκαλεῖσθαι, C 27.
πρὸς χάριν, Z 189.
πρόσωπον, Z 25.
προτρεπτικός, p. 52.
πρῶτα κατὰ φύσιν, Z 122, 126.
πτοία, Z 137.
πτῶσις, Z 23, 139.
Πυθαγορικά, p. 29.
πῦρ τεχνικόν, p. 23, Z 41, 42, 46, 68, 71, C 13, 15, 23, 26, 30.
πυροειδής, C 32.

ῥέω, Z 25, 56 (56), C 21.
ῥητορική, Z 32, C 9.

σελήνη, Z 73, C 32.
σημείων (περί), p. 29.
σκοπός, p. 45, C 74.
σολοικίζειν, Z 31.
σοφίσματα, Z 6.
σοφόν (περὶ τοῦ τὸν σ. σοφιστεύειν), p. 53.
σπέρμα, Z 106, 107, C 24.
σπουδαῖος, Z 148—159.
στατικά, Z 4.
στήλης (περί), C 113.
στίχοι, Z 166.
στοᾶς (περί), p. 53.
στοιχεῖα, Z 3, 35.
στρατηγικός, Z 148.
στρογγύλος, Z 32.
συγκατάθεσις, p. 34, Z 15, 19, 33, 123, 139, 158.
σύγχυσις, Z 51.
συλληφθείς, Z 106.
συμβεβηκός, Z 24.
συμπάθεια μερῶν, Z 58.
συμποσίου (περί), p. 47, 53.
συμφέρον, p. 45, C 77.
συναπτική, Z 40.
συνεκτική, Z 40.
συνεστώτων, Z 67.
συνέχον, Z 96.
συνιστορεῖν, C 11.

σύνοδος, Z 73.
συστολή, Z 139, 143.
σφαῖρα, Z 67.
σφάλλεσθαι, Z 153.
σχέσις, Z 134.
σῶμα, Z 24, 34, 36, 91.
σωφρονιστῆρες, C 114.
σωφροσύνη, Z 134, 138, C 76.

ταπεινώσεις, Z 139.
τείνεσθαι, Z 67.
τέλειος λόγος, Z 82.
τελετάς, C 53.
τέλος, p. 45, Z 120, 124, C 74.
τέλους (περί), p. 52.
τέχνη, p. 27, Z 5, 12, 13, 118, C 5.
τέχνης (περί), p. 50.
τεχνίτης, Z 48.
τίθεσθαι (ὄνομα), Z 116.
τιμῆς (περί), p. 47, 52.
τινά, Z 23.
Τιτᾶνας, Z 115.
τόνος, p. 8, 22, 23, 42, 45, 51, Z 33, 35, p. 110, Z 91, 103, C 24, 42, 76.
τόπος, Z 69.
τρίβων, Z 194.
τριμερής, Z 1.
Τριτογένεια, Z 1.
τρόπων (περί), p. 50.
τυγχάνοντα, Z 23.
τύπωσις, p. 34, Z 7.

ὕλη, Z 35, 49, 50, 51.
ὑμεναίου (περί), p. 51
ὑπακούειν, Z 29.
Ὑπερίων, Z 115.
ὑπόθεσις, Z.25.
ὑποθετικὸς τόπος, p. 47, C 92.
ὑπομενετέοις, Z 134.
ὑποπίπτειν, Z 23.
ὑποστάθμη, Z 114.
ὗς, C 44.

φαινόμενα σώζειν, C 27.
φακῆ, Z 156.
φαντασία, p. 24, 38, Z 7, 8, 33, 123, 158, C 3.
—— καταληπτική, p. 8, 9, 24, Z 10, 11.
φάντασμα, Z 23.
φανταστικόν, Z 160.
φαῦλος, Z 148, 154.
Φερσεφόνη, C 56.
φθονερίας (περί), p. 47, 52.

φθορὰ τοῦ κόσμου, Z 56.
φιλία, Z 163.
φιλίας (περί), p. 47, 53.
φιλόλογος, Z 200.
φίλους, Z 149.
φλόξ, C 23.
φόβος, p. 46, Z 128, 142, 143.
φορά (ἐγκύκλιος), Z 71, 116.
Φρεάντλης, p. 35, C 21.
φρόνησις, p. 15, 16, 45, Z 134, 156.
φυγάς, Z 155.
φύσει, Z 39, p. 110.
φύσεως (περί), p. 28.
φυσικόν, Z 2.
φύσις, p. 14, Z 43, 45, 46, C 51, v. ὁμολογία and κατά.
―― (κοινή), C 73.
φύω, Z 106.
φωνᾶεν, Z 98.
φωνή, Z 99, 100, p. 226.

χαλκοῦ (περί), p. 53, C 112.
χάος, Z 112, 113.
χάριτος (περί), p. 47, 52, C 97—99.
χάρτην εὔεργον, C 4.
χρεῖαι, p. 31, Z 194.
χρειῶν (περί), p. 53.
χρηματισμός, C 99.
χρόνου (περί), p. 50.
χρόνος, Z 76.
χρώματα, Z 78.
χώρα, Z 69.

ψιλός, C 49.
ψυχή, Z 43, 56(60), 83—96, C 36—45.
―― τοῦ κόσμου, C 14, 21.

ὡς ἄν, Z 56(99).
ὠφέλιμος, Z 190, C 75, 77.

CAMBRIDGE: PRINTED BY C. J. CLAY, M.A. & SONS, AT THE UNIVERSITY PRESS.

PUBLICATIONS OF

The Cambridge University Press.

THE HOLY SCRIPTURES, &c.

The Cambridge Paragraph Bible of the Authorized English Version, with the Text revised by a Collation of its Early and other Principal Editions, the Use of the Italic Type made uniform, the Marginal References remodelled, and a Critical Introduction, by F. H. A. SCRIVENER, M.A., LL.D. Crown 4to., cloth gilt, 21s.

THE STUDENT'S EDITION of the above, on *good writing paper*, with one column of print and wide margin to each page for MS. notes. Two Vols. Crown 4to., cloth, gilt, 31s. 6d.

The Lectionary Bible, with Apocrypha, divided into Sections adapted to the Calendar and Tables of Lessons of 1871. Cr. 8vo. 3s. 6d.

The Old Testament in Greek according to the Septuagint. Edited by the Rev. Professor H. B. SWETE, D.D. Vol. I. Genesis—IV Kings. Crown 8vo. 7s. 6d. Vol. II. I Chronicles—Tobit. [*Nearly ready.*

The Book of Psalms in Greek according to the Septuagint. Being a portion of Vol. II. of above. Crown 8vo. 2s. 6d.

The Book of Ecclesiastes. Large Paper Edition. By the Very Rev. E. H. PLUMPTRE, Dean of Wells. Demy 8vo. 7s. 6d.

Breviarium ad usum insignis Ecclesiae Sarum. Juxta Editionem maximam pro CLAUDIO CHEVALLON et FRANCISCO REGNAULT A.D. MDXXXI. in Alma Parisiorum Academia impressam: labore ac studio FRANCISCI PROCTER, A.M., et CHRISTOPHORI WORDSWORTH, A.M.

FASCICULUS I. In quo continentur KALENDARIUM, et ORDO TEMPORALIS sive PROPRIUM DE TEMPORE TOTIUS ANNI, una cum ordinali suo quod usitato vocabulo dicitur PICA SIVE DIRECTORIUM SACERDOTUM. Demy 8vo. 18s.

FASCICULUS II. In quo continentur PSALTERIUM, cum ordinario Officii totius hebdomadae juxta Horas Canonicas, et proprio Completorii, LITANIA, COMMUNE SANCTORUM, ORDINARIUM MISSAE CUM CANONE ET XIII MISSIS, &c. &c. Demy 8vo. 12s.

FASCICULUS III. In quo continetur PROPRIUM SANCTORUM quod et Sanctorale dicitur, una cum Accentuario. Demy 8vo. 15s.

FASCICULI I. II. III. complete £2. 2s.

Breviarium Romanum a FRANCISCO CARDINALI QUIGNONIO editum et recognitum iuxta editionem Venetiis A.D. 1535 impressam curante JOHANNE WICKHAM LEGG. Demy 8vo. 12s.

The Pointed Prayer Book, being the Book of Common Prayer with the Psalter or Psalms of David, pointed as they are to be sung or said in Churches. Royal 24mo, cloth, 1s. 6d.

The same in square 32mo. cloth, 6d.

The Cambridge Psalter, for the use of Choirs and Organists. Specially adapted for Congregations in which the "Cambridge Pointed Prayer Book" is used. Demy 8vo. cloth, 3s. 6d. Cloth limp cut flush, 2s. 6d.

London: Cambridge Warehouse, Ave Maria Lane.

PUBLICATIONS OF

The Paragraph Psalter, arranged for the use of Choirs by the Right Rev. B. F. WESTCOTT, D.D., Lord Bp. of Durham. Fcp. 4to. 5*s.*
The same in royal 32mo. Cloth, 1*s.* Leather, 1*s.* 6*d.*

Psalms of the Pharisees, commonly known as the Psalms of Solomon, by H. E. RYLE, M.A. and M. R. JAMES, M.A. Demy 8vo. 15*s.*

The Authorised Edition of the English Bible (1611), its Subsequent Reprints and Modern Representatives. By F. H. A. SCRIVENER, M.A., D.C.L., LL.D. Crown 8vo. 7*s.* 6*d.*

The New Testament in the Original Greek, according to the Text followed in the Authorised Version, together with the Variations adopted in the Revised Version. Edited by F. H. A. SCRIVENER, M.A., D.C.L., LL.D. Small Crown 8vo. 6*s.*

The Parallel New Testament Greek and English. The New Testament, being the Authorised Version set forth in 1611 Arranged in Parallel Columns with the Revised Version of 1881, and with the original Greek, as edited by F. H. A. SCRIVENER, M.A., D.C.L., LL.D. Crown 8vo. 12*s.* 6*d.* (*The Revised Version is the joint Property of the Universities of Cambridge and Oxford.*)

Greek and English Testament, in parallel columns on the same page. Edited by J. SCHOLEFIELD, M.A. *New Edition, with the marginal references as arranged and revised by* DR SCRIVENER. 7*s.* 6*d.*

Greek and English Testament. THE STUDENT'S EDITION of the above on *large writing paper.* 4to. 12*s.*

Greek Testament, ex editione Stephani tertia, 1550. Sm. 8vo. 3*s.* 6*d.*

The Four Gospels in Anglo-Saxon and Northumbrian Versions. By Rev. Prof. SKEAT, Litt.D. One Volume. Demy Quarto. 30*s.* Each Gospel separately. 10*s.*

The Missing Fragment of the Latin Translation of the Fourth Book of Ezra, discovered and edited with Introduction, Notes, and facsimile of the MS., by Prof. BENSLY, M.A. Demy 4to. 10*s.*

The Harklean Version of the Epistle to the Hebrews, Chap. XI. 28—XIII. 25. Now edited for the first time with Introduction and Notes on this version of the Epistle. By ROBERT L. BENSLY. Demy 8vo. 5*s.*

Codex S. Ceaddae Latinus. Evangelia SSS. Matthaei, Marci, Lucae ad cap. III. 9 complectens, circa septimum vel octavum saeculum scriptvs, in Ecclesia Cathedrali Lichfeldiensi servatus. Cum codice versionis Vulgatae Amiatino contulit, prolegomena conscripsit, F. H. A. SCRIVENER, A.M., LL.D. Imp. 4to. £1. 1*s.*

The Origin of the Leicester Codex of the New Testament. By J. R. HARRIS, M.A. With 3 plates. Demy 4to. 10*s.* 6*d.*

Notitia Codicis Quattuor Evangeliorum Graeci membranacei viris doctis hucusque incogniti quem in museo suo asservat Eduardus Reuss Argentoratensis. 2*s.*

London: Cambridge Warehouse, Ave Maria Lane.

THEOLOGY—(ANCIENT).

**Theodore of Mopsuestia's Commentary on the Minor Epistles of
S. Paul.** The Latin Version with the Greek Fragments, edited from the
MSS. with Notes and an Introduction, by H. B. SWETE, D.D. Vol. I.,
containing the Introduction, and the Commentary upon Galatians—Colossians. Demy Octavo. 12s.

Volume II., containing the Commentary on 1 Thessalonians—Philemon,
Appendices and Indices. 12s.

Chagigah from the Babylonian Talmud. A Translation of the
Treatise with Notes, etc. by A. W. STREANE, M.A. Demy 8vo. 10s.

The Greek Liturgies. Chiefly from original Authorities. By C. A.
SWAINSON, D.D., late Master of Christ's College. Cr. 4to. 15s.

Sayings of the Jewish Fathers, comprising Pirqe Aboth and
Pereq R. Meir in Hebrew and English, with Critical Notes. By C.
TAYLOR, D.D., Master of St John's College. 10s.

**Sancti Irenæi Episcopi Lugdunensis libros quinque adversus
Hæreses,** edidit W. WIGAN HARVEY, S.T.B. Collegii Regalis olim
Socius. 2 Vols. Demy Octavo. 18s.

The Palestinian Mishna. By W. H. LOWE, M.A. Royal 8vo. 21s.

M. Minucii Felicis Octavius. The text newly revised from the
original MS. with an English Commentary, Analysis, Introduction, and
Copious Indices. By H. A. HOLDEN, LL.D. Cr. 8vo. 7s. 6d.

Theophili Episcopi Antiochensis Libri Tres ad Autolycum. Edidit
Prolegomenis Versione Notulis Indicibus instruxit GULIELMUS GILSON
HUMPHRY, S.T.B. Post Octavo. 5s.

Theophylacti in Evangelium S. Matthæi Commentarius. Edited
by W. G. HUMPHRY, B.D. Demy Octavo. 7s. 6d.

Tertullianus de Corona Militis, de Spectaculis, de Idololatria
with Analysis and English Notes, by G. CURREY, D.D. Crown 8vo. 5s.

Fragments of Philo and Josephus. Newly edited by J. RENDEL
HARRIS, M.A. With two Facsimiles. Demy 4to. 12s. 6d.

The Teaching of the Apostles. Newly edited, with Facsimile Text
and Commentary, by J. R. HARRIS, M.A. Demy 4to. 21s.

The Rest of the Words of Baruch: A Christian Apocalypse of
the year 136 A.D. The Text revised with an Introduction by J. RENDEL
HARRIS, M.A. Royal 8vo. 5s.

The Acts of the Martyrdom of Perpetua and Felicitas; the original Greek Text now first edited from a MS. in the Library of the
Convent of the Holy Sepulchre at Jerusalem, by J. RENDEL HARRIS and
SETH K. GIFFORD. Royal 8vo. 5s.

Biblical Fragments from Mount Sinai, edited by J. RENDEL
HARRIS, M.A. Demy 4to. 10s. 6d.

The Diatessaron of Tatian. By J. RENDEL HARRIS, M.A. Royal
8vo. 5s.

London: Cambridge Warehouse, Ave Maria Lane.

THEOLOGY—(ENGLISH).

Works of Isaac Barrow, compared with the original MSS. A new Edition, by A. NAPIER, M.A. 9 Vols. Demy 8vo. £3. 3s.

Treatise of the Pope's Supremacy, and a Discourse concerning the Unity of the Church, by I. BARROW. Demy 8vo. 7s. 6d.

Pearson's Exposition of the Creed, edited by TEMPLE CHEVALLIER, B.D. 3rd Edition revised by R. SINKER, D.D. Demy 8vo. 12s.

An Analysis of the Exposition of the Creed, written by the Right Rev. Father in God, JOHN PEARSON, D.D. Compiled by W. H. MILL, D.D. Demy Octavo. 5s.

Wheatly on the Common Prayer, edited by G. E. CORRIE, D.D. late Master of Jesus College. Demy Octavo. 7s. 6d.

The Homilies, with Various Readings, and the Quotations from the Fathers given at length in the Original Languages. Edited by G. E. CORRIE, D.D. late Master of Jesus College. Demy 8vo. 7s. 6d.

Two Forms of Prayer of the time of Queen Elizabeth. Now First Reprinted. Demy Octavo. 6d.

Select Discourses, by JOHN SMITH, late Fellow of Queens' College, Cambridge. Edited by H. G. WILLIAMS, B.D. late Professor of Arabic. Royal Octavo. 7s. 6d.

De Obligatione Conscientiæ Prælectiones decem Oxonii in Schola Theologica habitæ a ROBERTO SANDERSON, SS. Theologiæ ibidem Professore Regio. With English Notes, including an abridged Translation, by W. WHEWELL, D.D. Demy 8vo. 7s. 6d.

Cæsar Morgan's Investigation of the Trinity of Plato, and of Philo Judæus. 2nd Ed., revised by H. A. HOLDEN, LL.D. Cr. 8vo. 4s.

Archbishop Usher's Answer to a Jesuit, with other Tracts on Popery. Edited by J. SCHOLEFIELD, M.A. Demy 8vo. 7s. 6d.

Wilson's Illustration of the Method of explaining the New Testament, by the early opinions of Jews and Christians concerning Christ. Edited by T. TURTON, D.D. Demy 8vo. 5s.

Lectures on Divinity delivered in the University of Cambridge. By JOHN HEY, D.D. Third Edition, by T. TURTON, D.D. late Lord Bishop of Ely. 2 vols. Demy Octavo. 15s.

S. Austin and his place in the History of Christian Thought. Being the Hulsean Lectures for 1885. By W. CUNNINGHAM, D.D. Demy 8vo. Buckram, 12s. 6d.

Christ the Life of Men. Being the Hulsean Lectures for 1888. By Rev. H. M. STEPHENSON, M.A. Crown 8vo. 2s. 6d.

The Gospel History of our Lord Jesus Christ in the Language of the Revised Version, arranged in a Connected Narrative, especially for the use of Teachers and Preachers. By Rev. C. C. JAMES, M.A. Crown 8vo. 3s. 6d.

London: Cambridge Warehouse, Ave Maria Lane.

GREEK AND LATIN CLASSICS, &c.
(See also pp. 16, 17.)

Sophocles: the Plays and Fragments. With Critical Notes, Commentary, and Translation in English Prose, by R. C. JEBB, Litt. D., LL.D., Regius Professor of Greek in the University of Cambridge.
- Part I. Oedipus Tyrannus. Demy 8vo. *Second Edit.* 12s. 6d.
- Part II. Oedipus Coloneus. Demy 8vo. *Second Edit.* 12s. 6d.
- Part III. Antigone. Demy 8vo. *Second Edit.* 12s. 6d.
- Part IV. Philoctetes. Demy 8vo. 12s. 6d.

Select Private Orations of Demosthenes with Introductions and English Notes, by F. A. PALEY, M.A., & J. E. SANDYS, Litt.D.
- Part I. Contra Phormionem, Lacritum, Pantaenetum, Boeotum de Nomine, de Dote, Dionysodorum. Cr. 8vo. *New Edition.* 6s.
- Part II. Pro Phormione, Contra Stephanum I. II.; Nicostratum, Cononem, Calliclem. Crown 8vo. *New Edition.* 7s. 6d.

Demosthenes, Speech of, against the Law of Leptines. With Introduction and Critical and Explanatory Notes, by J. E. SANDYS, Litt.D. Demy 8vo. 9s.

Demosthenes against Androtion and against Timocrates, with Introductions and English Commentary by WILLIAM WAYTE, M.A. Crown 8vo. 7s. 6d.

Euripides. Bacchae, with Introduction, Critical Notes, and Archæological Illustrations, by J. E. SANDYS, Litt.D. New Edition, with additional Illustrations. Crown 8vo. 12s. 6d.

Euripides. Ion. The Greek Text with a Translation into English Verse, Introduction and Notes by A. W. VERRALL, Litt.D. Demy 8vo. 7s. 6d.

An Introduction to Greek Epigraphy. Part I. The Archaic Inscriptions and the Greek Alphabet. By E. S. ROBERTS, M.A., Fellow and Tutor of Gonville and Caius College. Demy 8vo. 18s.

Aeschyli Fabulae.—ΙΚΕΤΙΔΕΣ ΧΟΗΦΟΡΟΙ in libro Mediceo mendose scriptae ex vv. dd. coniecturis emendatius editae cum Scholiis Graecis et brevi adnotatione critica, curante F. A. PALEY, M.A., LL.D. Demy 8vo. 7s. 6d.

The Agamemnon of Aeschylus. With a translation in English Rhythm, and Notes Critical and Explanatory. **New Edition, Revised.** By the late B. H. KENNEDY, D.D. Crown 8vo. 6s.

The Theætetus of Plato, with a Translation and Notes by the same Editor. Crown 8vo. 7s. 6d.

P. Vergili Maronis Opera, cum Prolegomenis et Commentario Critico pro Syndicis Preli Academici edidit BENJAMIN HALL KENNEDY, S.T.P. Extra fcp. 8vo. 3s. 6d.

Essays on the Art of Pheidias. By C. WALDSTEIN, Litt.D., Phil.D. Royal 8vo. With Illustrations. Buckram, 30s.

M. Tulli Ciceronis ad M. Brutum Orator. A Revised Text. Edited with Introductory Essays and Critical and Explanatory Notes, by J. E. SANDYS, Litt.D. Demy 8vo. 16s.

London: Cambridge Warehouse, Ave Maria Lane.

M. Tulli Ciceronis pro C. Rabirio [Perduellionis Reo] Oratio ad Quirites. With Notes, Introduction and Appendices. By W. E. HEITLAND, M.A. Demy 8vo. 7s. 6d.

M. T. Ciceronis de Natura Deorum Libri Tres, with Introduction and Commentary by JOSEPH B. MAYOR, M.A. Demy 8vo. Vol. I. 10s. 6d. Vol. II. 12s. 6d. Vol. III. 10s.

M. T. Ciceronis de Officiis' Libri Tres with Marginal Analysis, an English Commentary, and Indices. New Edition, revised, by H. A. HOLDEN, LL.D., Crown 8vo. 9s.

M. T. Ciceronis de Officiis Libri Tertius, with Introduction, Analysis and Commentary by H. A. HOLDEN, LL.D. Cr. 8vo. 2s.

M. T. Ciceronis de Finibus Bonorum libri Quinque. The Text revised and explained by J. S. REID, Litt.D. [*In the Press.*
Vol. III., containing the Translation. Demy 8vo. 8s.

Plato's Phædo, literally translated, by the late E. M. COPE, Fellow of Trinity College, Cambridge. Demy Octavo. 5s.

Aristotle. The Rhetoric. With a Commentary by the late E. M. COPE, Fellow of Trinity College, Cambridge, revised and edited by J. E. SANDYS, Litt.D. 3 Vols. Demy 8vo. 21s.

Aristotle.—ΠΕΡΙ ΨΥΧΗΣ. Aristotle's Psychology, in Greek and English, with Introduction and Notes, by E. WALLACE, M.A. Demy 8vo. 18s.

ΠΕΡΙ ΔΙΚΑΙΟΣΥΝΗΣ. The Fifth Book of the Nicomachean Ethics of Aristotle. Edited by H. JACKSON, Litt.D. Demy 8vo. 6s.

Pronunciation of Ancient Greek translated from the Third German edition of Dr BLASS by W. J. PURTON, B.A. Demy 8vo. 6s.

Pindar. Olympian and Pythian Odes. With Notes Explanatory and Critical, Introductions and Introductory Essays. Edited by C. A. M. FENNELL, Litt.D. Crown 8vo. 9s.

— The Isthmian and Nemean Odes by the same Editor. 9s.

The Types of Greek Coins. By PERCY GARDNER, Litt.D., F.S.A. With 16 plates. Impl. 4to. Cloth £1. 11s. 6d. Roxburgh (Morocco back) £2. 2s.

SANSKRIT, ARABIC AND SYRIAC.

Lectures on the Comparative Grammar of the Semitic Languages from the Papers of the late WILLIAM WRIGHT, LL.D. Demy 8vo. 14s.

The Divyâvadâna, a Collection of Early Buddhist Legends, now first edited from the Nepalese Sanskrit MSS. in Cambridge and Paris. By E. B. COWELL, M.A. and R. A. NEIL, M.A. Demy 8vo. 18s.

Nalopakhyânam, or, The Tale of Nala; containing the Sanskrit Text in Roman Characters, with Vocabulary. By the late Rev. T. JARRETT, M.A. Demy 8vo. 10s.

Notes on the Tale of Nala, for the use of Classical Students, by J. PEILE, Litt.D., Master of Christ's College. Demy 8vo. 12s.

London: Cambridge Warehouse, Ave Maria Lane.

The History of Alexander the Great, being the Syriac version of the Pseudo-Callisthenes. Edited from Five Manuscripts, with an English Translation and Notes, by E. A. BUDGE, M.A. Demy 8vo. 25s.

The Poems of Beha ed dín Zoheir of Egypt. With a Metrical Translation, Notes and Introduction, by the late E. H. PALMER, M.A. 2 vols. Crown Quarto.
    Vol. I. The ARABIC TEXT. Paper covers. 10s. 6d.
    Vol. II. ENGLISH TRANSLATION. Paper covers. 10s. 6d.

The Chronicle of Joshua the Stylite edited in Syriac, with an English translation and notes, by W. WRIGHT, LL.D. Demy 8vo. 10s. 6d.

Kalīlah and Dimnah, or, the Fables of Bidpai; with an English Translation of the later Syriac version, with Notes, by the late I. G. N. KEITH-FALCONER, M.A. Demy 8vo. 7s. 6d.

Maḳála-i-Shakhsí Sayyáḥ ki dar Ḳaẓiyya-i-Báb Navishta-Ast (a Traveller's Narrative written to illustrate the Episode of the Báb). Persian text, edited, translated and annotated, in two volumes, by E. G. BROWNE, M.A., M.B. [*Nearly ready.*

MATHEMATICS, PHYSICAL SCIENCE, &c.

Mathematical and Physical Papers. By Sir G. G. STOKES, Sc.D., LL.D. Reprinted from the Original Journals and Transactions, with additional Notes by the Author. Vol. I. Demy 8vo. 15s. Vol. II. 15s.
    [Vol. III. *In the Press.*

Mathematical and Physical Papers. By Sir W. THOMSON, LL.D., F.R.S. Collected from different Scientific Periodicals from May, 1841, to the present time. Vol. I. Demy 8vo. 18s. Vol. II. 15s. Vol. III. 18s.

The Collected Mathematical Papers of ARTHUR CAYLEY, Sc.D., F.R.S. Demy 4to. 10 vols.
    Vols. I., II. and III. 25s. each. [Vol. IV. *In the Press.*

A History of the Study of Mathematics at Cambridge. By W. W. ROUSE BALL, M.A. Crown 8vo. 6s.

A History of the Theory of Elasticity and of the Strength of Materials, from Galilei to the present time. Vol. I. GALILEI TO SAINT-VENANT, 1639–1850. By the late I. TODHUNTER, Sc.D., edited and completed by Prof. KARL PEARSON, M.A. Demy 8vo. 25s.
    Vol. II. By the same Editor. [*In the Press.*

The Elastical Researches of Barre de Saint-Venant (extract from Vol. II. of TODHUNTER'S History of the Theory of Elasticity), edited by Professor KARL PEARSON, M.A. Demy 8vo. 9s.

Theory of Differential Equations. Part I. Exact Equations and Pfaff's Problem. By A. R. FORSYTH, Sc.D., F.R.S. Demy 8vo. 12s.

A Treatise on the General Principles of Chemistry, by M. M. PATTISON MUIR, M.A. Second Edition. Demy 8vo. 15s.

Elementary Chemistry. By M. M. PATTISON MUIR, M.A., and CHARLES SLATER, M.A., M.B. Crown 8vo. 4s. 6d.

Practical Chemistry. A Course of Laboratory Work. By M. M. PATTISON MUIR, M.A., and D. J. CARNEGIE, M.A. Cr. 8vo. 3s.

A Treatise on Geometrical Optics. By R. S. HEATH, M.A. Demy 8vo. 12s. 6d.

An Elementary Treatise on Geometrical Optics. By R. S. HEATH, M.A. Crown 8vo. 5s.

A Treatise on Dynamics. By S. L. LONEY, M.A. Cr. 8vo. 7s. 6d.

A Treatise on Analytical Statics. By E. J. ROUTH, Sc.D., F.R.S.
[*Nearly ready.*

A Treatise on Plane Trigonometry. By E. W. HOBSON, M.A. Demy 8vo. [*Nearly ready.*

Lectures on the Physiology of Plants, by S. H. VINES, Sc.D., Professor of Botany in the University of Oxford. Demy 8vo. 21s.

A Short History of Greek Mathematics. By J. GOW, Litt. D., Fellow of Trinity College. Demy 8vo. 10s. 6d.

Notes on Qualitative Analysis. Concise and Explanatory. By H. J. H. FENTON, M.A., F.C.S. New Edit. Crown 4to. 6s.

Diophantos of Alexandria; a Study in the History of Greek Algebra. By T. L. HEATH, M.A. Demy 8vo. 7s. 6d.

A Catalogue of the Portsmouth Collection of Books and Papers written by or belonging to SIR ISAAC NEWTON. Demy 8vo. 5s.

A Treatise on Natural Philosophy. By Prof. Sir W. THOMSON, LL.D., and P. G. TAIT, M.A. Part I. Demy 8vo. 16s. Part II. 18s.

Elements of Natural Philosophy. By Professors Sir W. THOMSON, and P. G. TAIT. *Second Edition.* Demy 8vo. 9s.

An Elementary Treatise on Quaternions. By P. G. TAIT, M.A. *Second Edition.* Demy 8vo. 14s.

A Treatise on the Theory of Determinants and their Applications in Analysis and Geometry. By R. F. SCOTT, M.A. Demy 8vo. 12s.

Counterpoint. A practical course of study. By the late Prof. Sir G. A. MACFARREN, Mus. D. 5th Edition, revised. Cr. 4to. 7s. 6d.

The Analytical Theory of Heat. By JOSEPH FOURIER. Translated with Notes, by A. FREEMAN, M.A. Demy 8vo. 12s.

The Scientific Papers of the late Prof. J. Clerk Maxwell. Edited by W. D. NIVEN, M.A. 2 vols. Royal 4to. £3. 3s. (net.)

The Electrical Researches of the Honourable Henry Cavendish, F.R.S. Written between 1771 and 1781. Edited by J. CLERK MAXWELL, F.R.S. Demy 8vo. 18s.

Practical Work at the Cavendish Laboratory. Heat. Edited by W. N. SHAW, M.A. Demy 8vo. 3s.

Hydrodynamics, a Treatise on the Mathematical Theory of Fluid Motion, by HORACE LAMB, M.A. Demy 8vo. 12s.

The Mathematical Works of Isaac Barrow, D.D. Edited by W. WHEWELL, D.D. Demy Octavo. 7s. 6d.

Illustrations of Comparative Anatomy, Vertebrate and Invertebrate. Second Edition. Demy 8vo. 2s. 6d.

London: Cambridge Warehouse, Ave Maria Lane.

THE CAMBRIDGE UNIVERSITY PRESS.

A Catalogue of Australian Fossils. By R. ETHERIDGE, Jun., F.G.S. Demy 8vo. 10s. 6d.

The Fossils and Palæontological Affinities of the Neocomian Deposits of Upware and Brickhill, being the Sedgwick Prize Essay for 1879. By W. KEEPING, M.A. Demy 8vo. 10s. 6d.

The Bala Volcanic Series of Caernarvonshire and Associated Rocks, being the Sedgwick Prize Essay for 1888, by A. HARKER, M.A., F.R.S. Demy 8vo. 7s. 6d.

A Catalogue of Books and Papers on Protozoa, Coelenterates, Worms, etc. published during the years 1861–1883, by D'ARCY W. THOMPSON, M.A. Demy 8vo. 12s. 6d.

A Revised Account of the Experiments made with the Bashforth Chronograph, to find the resistance of the air to the motion of projectiles. By FRANCIS BASHFORTH, B.D. Demy 8vo. 12s.

An attempt to test the Theories of Capillary Action, by F. BASHFORTH, B.D., and J. C. ADAMS, M.A. Demy 4to. £1. 1s.

A Catalogue of the Collection of Cambrian and Silurian Fossils contained in the Geological Museum of the University of Cambridge, by J. W. SALTER, F.G.S. Royal Quarto. 7s. 6d.

Catalogue of Osteological Specimens contained in the Anatomical Museum of the University of Cambridge. Demy 8vo. 2s. 6d.

Astronomical Observations made at the Observatory of Cambridge from 1846 to 1860, by the late Rev. J. CHALLIS, M.A.

Astronomical Observations from 1861 to 1865. Vol. XXI Royal 4to., 15s. From 1866 to 1869. Vol. XXII. 15s.

LAW.

Elements of the Law of Torts. A Text-book for Students. By MELVILLE M. BIGELOW, Ph.D. Crown 8vo. 10s. 6d.

A Selection of Cases on the English Law of Contract. By GERARD BROWN FINCH, M.A. Royal 8vo. 28s.

Bracton's Note Book. A Collection of Cases decided in the King's Courts during the Reign of Henry the Third, annotated by a Lawyer of that time, seemingly by Henry of Bratton. Edited by F. W. MAITLAND. 3 vols. Demy 8vo. £3. 3s. (net.)

Tables shewing the Differences between English and Indian Law. By Sir ROLAND KNYVET WILSON, Bart., M.A., LL.M. Demy 4to. 1s.

The Influence of the Roman Law on the Law of England. Being the Yorke Prize Essay for the year 1884. By T. E. SCRUTTON, M.A. Demy 8vo. 10s. 6d.

Land in Fetters. Being the Yorke Prize Essay for 1885. By T. E. SCRUTTON, M.A. Demy 8vo. 7s. 6d.

Commons and Common Fields, or the History and Policy of the Laws of Commons and Enclosures in England. Being the Yorke Prize Essay for 1886. By T. E. SCRUTTON, M.A. Demy 8vo. 10s. 6d.

History of the Law of Tithes in England. Being the Yorke Prize Essay for 1887. By W. EASTERBY, B.A., LL.B. Demy 8vo. 7s. 6d.

London: Cambridge Warehouse, Ave Maria Lane.

History of Land Tenure in Ireland. Being the Yorke Prize Essay for 1888. By W. E. MONTGOMERY, M.A., LL.M. Demy 8vo. 10s. 6d.

History of Equity as administered in the Court of Chancery. Being the Yorke Prize Essay for 1889. By D. M^cKENZIE KERLY, M.A., St John's College. Demy 8vo. 12s. 6d.

An Introduction to the Study of Justinian's Digest. By HENRY JOHN ROBY. Demy 8vo. 9s.

Justinian's Digest. Lib. VII., Tit. I. De Usufructu, with a Legal and Philological Commentary by H. J. ROBY. Demy 8vo. 9s.
The Two Parts complete in One Volume. Demy 8vo. 18s.

A Selection of the State Trials. By J. W. WILLIS-BUND, M.A., LL.B. Crown 8vo. Vols. I. and II. In 3 parts. 30s.

The Institutes of Justinian, translated with Notes by J. T. ABDY, LL.D., and BRYAN WALKER, M.A., LL.D. Cr. 8vo. 16s.

Practical Jurisprudence. A comment on AUSTIN. By E. C. CLARK, LL.D., Regius Professor of Civil Law. Crown 8vo. 9s.

An Analysis of Criminal Liability. By the same. Cr. 8vo. 7s. 6d.

The Fragments of the Perpetual Edict of Salvius Julianus, Arranged, and Annotated by the late BRYAN WALKER, LL.D. Cr. 8vo. 6s.

The Commentaries of Gaius and Rules of Ulpian. Translated and Annotated, by J. T. ABDY, LL.D., and BRYAN WALKER, M.A., LL.D. New Edition by Bryan Walker. Crown 8vo. 16s.

Grotius de Jure Belli et Pacis, with the Notes of Barbeyrac and others; an abridged Translation of the Text, by W. WHEWELL, D.D. Demy 8vo. 12s. The translation separate, 6s.

Selected Titles from the Digest, by BRYAN WALKER, M.A., LL.D. Part I. Mandati vel Contra. Digest XVII. 1. Cr. 8vo. 5s.

Part II. **De Adquirendo rerum dominio, and De Adquirenda vel amittenda Possessione**, Digest XLI. 1 and 2. Crown 8vo. 6s.

Part III. **De Condictionibus**, Digest XII. 1 and 4—7 and Digest XIII. 1—3. Crown 8vo. 6s.

HISTORICAL WORKS.

The Life and Letters of the Reverend Adam Sedgwick, LL.D., F.R.S. (Dedicated, by special permission, to Her Majesty the Queen.) By JOHN WILLIS CLARK, M.A., F.S.A., and THOMAS M^cKENNY HUGHES, M.A. 2 vols. Demy 8vo. 36s.

The Growth of English Industry and Commerce during the Early and Middle Ages. By W. CUNNINGHAM, D.D. Demy 8vo. 16s.

The Architectural History of the University of Cambridge and of the Colleges of Cambridge and Eton, by the late Professor WILLIS, M.A., F.R.S. Edited with large Additions and a Continuation to the present time by J. W. CLARK, M.A. 4 Vols. Super Royal 8vo. £6. 6s.
Also a limited Edition of the same, consisting of 120 numbered Copies only, large paper Quarto; the woodcuts and steel engravings mounted on India paper; of which 100 copies are now offered for sale, at Twenty-five Guineas **net** each set.

London: Cambridge Warehouse, Ave Maria Lane.

The University of Cambridge from the Earliest Times to the Royal Injunctions of 1535. By J. B. MULLINGER, M.A. Demy 8vo. 12s.
—— Part II. From the Royal Injunctions of 1535 to the Accession of Charles the First. Demy 8vo. 18s.
History of the College of St John the Evangelist, by THOMAS BAKER, B.D., Ejected Fellow. Edited by JOHN E. B. MAYOR, M.A., Fellow of St John's. Two Vols. Demy 8vo. 24s.
Scholae Academicae: some Account of the Studies at the English Universities in the Eighteenth Century. By CHRISTOPHER WORDSWORTH, M.A. Demy 8vo. 10s. 6d.
Life and Times of Stein, or Germany and Prussia in the Napoleonic Age, by J. R. SEELEY, M.A. Portraits and Maps. 3 vols. Demy 8vo. 30s.
The Constitution of Canada. By J. E. C. MUNRO, LL.M. Demy 8vo. 10s.
Studies in the Literary Relations of England with Germany in the Sixteenth Century. By C. H. HERFORD, M.A. Crown 8vo. 9s.
Chronological Tables of Greek History. By CARL PETER. Translated from the German by G. CHAWNER, M.A. Demy 4to. 10s.
Travels in Arabia Deserta in 1876 and 1877. By CHARLES M. DOUGHTY. With Illustrations. Demy 8vo. 2 vols. £3. 3s.
History of Nepāl, edited with an introductory sketch of the Country and People by Dr D. WRIGHT. Super-royal 8vo. 10s. 6d.
A Journey of Literary and Archæological Research in Nepal and Northern India, 1884—5. By C. BENDALL, M.A. Demy 8vo. 10s.

Cambridge Historical Essays.

Political Parties in Athens during the Peloponnesian War, by L. WHIBLEY, M.A. (Prince Consort Dissertation, 1888.) Second Edition. Crown 8vo. 2s. 6d.
Pope Gregory the Great and his relations with Gaul, by F. W. KELLETT, M.A. (Prince Consort Dissertation, 1888.) Crown 8vo. 2s. 6d.
The Constitutional Experiments of the Commonwealth, being the Thirlwall Prize Essay for 1889, by E. JENKS, B.A., LL.B. Cr. 8vo. 2s. 6d.
On Election by Lot at Athens, by J. W. HEADLAM, B.A. (Prince Consort Dissertation, 1890.) Crown 8vo. [In the Press.
The Destruction of the Somerset Religious Houses and its Effects. By W. A. J. ARCHBOLD, B.A., LL.B. (Prince Consort Dissertation, 1890.) Crown 8vo. [In the Press.

MISCELLANEOUS.

The Engraved Gems of Classical Times with a Catalogue of the Gems in the Fitzwilliam Museum by J. H. MIDDLETON, M.A. Royal 8vo. 12s. 6d.
Erasmus. The Rede Lecture, delivered in the Senate-House, Cambridge, June 11, 1890, by R. C. JEBB, Litt.D. Cloth, 2s. Paper Covers, 1s.
The Literary remains of Albrecht Dürer, by W. M. CONWAY. With Transcripts from the British Museum Manuscripts, and Notes upon them by LINA ECKENSTEIN. Royal 8vo. 21s.
The Collected Papers of Henry Bradshaw, including his Memoranda and Communications read before the Cambridge Antiquarian Society. With 13 facsimiles. Edited by F. J. H. JENKINSON, M.A. Demy 8vo. 16s.

London: Cambridge Warehouse, Ave Maria Lane.

Memorials of the Life of George Elwes Corrie, D.D. formerly Master of Jesus College. By M. HOLROYD. Demy 8vo. 12s.

The Latin Heptateuch. Published piecemeal by the French printer WILLIAM MOREL (1560) and the French Benedictines E. MARTÈNE (1733) and J. B. PITRA (1852—88). Critically reviewed by JOHN E. B. MAYOR, M.A. Demy 8vo. 10s. 6d.

Kinship and Marriage in early Arabia, by W. ROBERTSON SMITH, M.A., LL.D. Crown 8vo. 7s. 6d.

Chapters on English Metre. By Rev. JOSEPH B. MAYOR, M.A. Demy 8vo. 7s. 6d.

A Catalogue of Ancient Marbles in Great Britain, by Prof. ADOLF MICHAELIS. Translated by C. A. M. FENNELL, Litt.D. Royal 8vo. Roxburgh (Morocco back). £2. 2s.

From Shakespeare to Pope. An Inquiry into the causes and phenomena of the Rise of Classical Poetry in England. By E. GOSSE, M.A. Crown 8vo. 6s.

The Literature of the French Renaissance. An Introductory Essay. By A. A. TILLEY, M.A. Crown 8vo. 6s.

A Latin-English Dictionary. Printed from the (Incomplete) MS. of the late T. H. KEY, M.A., F.R.S. Demy 4to. £1. 11s. 6d.

Ecclesiae Londino-Batavae archivum. TOMVS PRIMVS. ABRAHAMI ORTELII et virorum eruditorum ad eundem et ad JACOBVM COLIVM ORTELIANVM Epistulae, (1524—1628). TOMVS SECVNDVS. EPISTVLAE ET TRACTATVS cum Reformationis tum Ecclesiae Londino-Batavae Historiam Illustrantes 1544—1622. Ex autographis mandante Ecclesia Londino-Batava edidit JOANNES HENRICVS HESSELS. Demy 4to. Each vol., separately, £3. 10s. Taken together £5. 5s. Net.

An Eighth Century Latin-Anglo-Saxon Glossary preserved in the Library of Corpus Christi College, Cambridge, edited by J. H. HESSELS. Demy 8vo. 10s.

Contributions to the Textual Criticism of the Divina Commedia. Including the complete collation throughout the *Inferno* of all the MSS. at Oxford and Cambridge. By the Rev. E. MOORE, D.D. Demy 8vo. 21s.

The Despatches of Earl Gower, English Ambassador at the court of Versailles, June 1790 to August 1792, and the Despatches of Mr Lindsay and Mr Monro. By O. BROWNING, M.A. Demy 8vo. 15s.

Rhodes in Ancient Times. By CECIL TORR, M.A. With six plates. 10s. 6d.

Rhodes in Modern Times. By the same Author. With three plates. Demy 8vo. 8s.

The Woodcutters of the Netherlands during the last quarter of the Fifteenth Century. By W. M. CONWAY. Demy 8vo. 10s. 6d.

Lectures on the Growth and Training of the Mental Faculty, delivered in the University of Cambridge. By FRANCIS WARNER, M.D., F.R.C.P. Crown 8vo. 4s. 6d.

Lectures on Teaching, delivered in the University of Cambridge. By J. G. FITCH, M.A., LL.D. Cr. 8vo. 5s.

Lectures on Language and Linguistic Method in the School. By S. S. LAURIE, M.A., LL.D. Crown 8vo. 4s.

Occasional Addresses on Educational Subjects. By S. S. LAURIE, M.A., F.R.S.E. Crown 8vo. 5s.

London: Cambridge Warehouse, Ave Maria Lane.

A Manual of Cursive Shorthand, by H. L. CALLENDAR, M.A. Extra Fcap. 8vo. 2s.

A System of Phonetic Spelling, adapted to English by H. L. CALLENDAR, M.A. Extra Fcap. 8vo. 6d.

A Primer of Cursive Shorthand. By H. L. CALLENDAR, M.A. 6d.

Reading Practice in Cursive Shorthand. Easy extracts for Beginners. St Mark, Pt. I. Vicar of Wakefield, Chaps. I.—IV. Alice in Wonderland, Chap. VII. Price 3d. each.

Essays from the Spectator in Cursive Shorthand, by H. L. CALLENDAR, M.A. 6d.

Gray and his Friends. Letters and Relics in great part hitherto unpublished. Edited by the Rev. D. C. TOVEY, M.A. Crown 8vo. 6s.

A Grammar of the Irish Language. By Prof. WINDISCH. Translated by Dr NORMAN MOORE. Crown 8vo. 7s. 6d.

A Catalogue of the Collection of Birds formed by the late Hugh EDWIN STRICKLAND, now in the possession of the University of Cambridge. By O. SALVIN, M.A., F.R.S. £1. 1s.

Admissions to Gonville and Caius College in the University of Cambridge March 1558—9 to Jan. 1678—9. Edited by J. VENN, Sc.D., and S. C. VENN. Demy 8vo. 10s.

A Catalogue of the Hebrew Manuscripts preserved in the University Library, Cambridge. By the late Dr SCHILLER-SZINESSY. 9s.

Catalogue of the Buddhist Sanskrit Manuscripts in the University Library, Cambridge. Edited by C. BENDALL, M.A. 12s.

A Catalogue of the Manuscripts preserved in the Library of the University of Cambridge. Demy 8vo. 5 Vols. 10s. each.

Index to the Catalogue. Demy 8vo. 10s.

A Catalogue of Adversaria and printed books containing MS. notes, in the Library of the University of Cambridge. 3s. 6d.

The Illuminated Manuscripts in the Library of the Fitzwilliam Museum, Cambridge, by W. G. SEARLE, M.A. 7s. 6d.

A Chronological List of the Graces, etc. in the University Registry which concern the University Library. 2s. 6d.

Catalogus Bibliothecæ Burckhardtianæ. Demy Quarto. 5s.

Graduati Cantabrigienses: sive catalogus exhibens nomina eorum quos gradu quocunque ornavit Academia Cantabrigiensis (1800—1884). Cura H. R. LUARD, S. T. P. Demy 8vo. 12s. 6d.

Statutes for the University of Cambridge and for the Colleges therein, made, published and approved (1878—1882) under the Universities of Oxford and Cambridge Act, 1877. Demy 8vo. 16s.

Statutes of the University of Cambridge. 3s. 6d.

Ordinances of the University of Cambridge. 7s. 6d. Supplement to ditto. 1s.

Trusts, Statutes and Directions affecting (1) The Professorships of the University. (2) The Scholarships and Prizes. (3) Other Gifts and Endowments. Demy 8vo. 5s.

A Compendium of University Regulations. Demy 8vo. 6d.

London: Cambridge Warehouse, Ave Maria Lane.

The Cambridge Bible for Schools and Colleges.

GENERAL EDITOR: J. J. S. PEROWNE, D.D., BISHOP OF WORCESTER.

"It is difficult to commend too highly this excellent series."—*Guardian.*

Now Ready. Cloth, Extra Fcap. 8vo. With Maps.

Book of Joshua. By Rev. G. F. MACLEAR, D.D. 2s. 6d.
Book of Judges. By Rev. J. J. LIAS, M.A. 3s. 6d.
First Book of Samuel. By Rev. Prof. KIRKPATRICK, B.D. 3s. 6d.
Second Book of Samuel. By Rev. Prof. KIRKPATRICK, B.D. 3s. 6d.
First Book of Kings. By Rev. Prof. LUMBY, D.D. 3s. 6d.
Second Book of Kings. By Rev. Prof. LUMBY, D.D. 3s. 6d.
Book of Job. By Rev. A. B. DAVIDSON, D.D. 5s.
Book of Ecclesiastes. By Very Rev. E. H. PLUMPTRE, D.D. 5s.
Book of Jeremiah. By Rev. A. W. STREANE, M.A. 4s. 6d.
Book of Hosea. By Rev. T. K. CHEYNE, M.A., D.D. 3s.
Books of Obadiah and Jonah. By Arch. PEROWNE. 2s. 6d.
Book of Micah. By Rev. T. K. CHEYNE, M.A., D.D. 1s. 6d.
Books of Haggai, Zechariah & Malachi. By Arch. PEROWNE. 3s. 6d.
Book of Malachi. By Archdeacon PEROWNE. 1s.
Gospel according to St Matthew. By Rev. A. CARR, M.A. 2s. 6d.
Gospel according to St Mark. By Rev. G. F. MACLEAR, D.D. 2s. 6d.
Gospel according to St Luke. By Archdeacon FARRAR. 4s. 6d.
Gospel according to St John. By Rev. A. PLUMMER, D.D. 4s. 6d.
Acts of the Apostles. By Prof. LUMBY, D.D. 4s. 6d.
Epistle to the Romans. Rev. H. C. G. MOULE, M.A. 3s. 6d.
First Corinthians. By Rev. J. J. LIAS, M.A. 2s.
Second Corinthians. By Rev. J. J. LIAS, M.A. 2s.
Epistle to the Galatians. By Rev. E. H. PEROWNE, D.D. 1s. 6d.
Epistle to the Ephesians. Rev. H. C. G. MOULE, M.A. 2s. 6d.
Epistle to the Hebrews. By Archdeacon FARRAR, D.D. 3s. 6d.
Epistle to the Philippians. By Rev. H. C. G. MOULE, M.A. 2s. 6d.
Epistles to the Thessalonians. By Rev. G. G. FINDLAY, B.A. 2s.
General Epistle of St James. By Very Rev. E. H. PLUMPTRE. 1s. 6d.
Epistles of St Peter and St Jude. By the same Editor. 2s. 6d.
Epistles of St John. By Rev. A. PLUMMER, M.A., D.D. 3s. 6d.
Book of Revelation. By Rev. W. H. SIMCOX, M.A. 3s.

Preparing.

Book of Genesis. By the BISHOP OF WORCESTER.
Books of Exodus, Numbers and Deuteronomy. By Rev. C. D. GINSBURG, LL.D.

London: *Cambridge Warehouse, Ave Maria Lane.*

Books of Ezra and Nehemiah. By Rev. Prof. RYLE, M.A.
Book of Psalms. Part I. By Rev. Prof. KIRKPATRICK, B.D.
Book of Isaiah. By Prof. W. ROBERTSON SMITH, M.A.
Book of Ezekiel. By Rev. A. B. DAVIDSON, D.D.
Epistles to Colossians & Philemon. By Rev. H. C. G. MOULE, M.A.
Epistles to Timothy and Titus. By Rev. A. E. HUMPHREYS, M.A.

The Smaller Cambridge Bible for Schools.

The Smaller Cambridge Bible for Schools *will form an entirely new series of commentaries on some selected books of the Bible. It is expected that they will be prepared for the most part by the Editors of the larger series (the Cambridge Bible for Schools and Colleges). The volumes will be issued at a low price, and will be suitable to the requirements of preparatory and elementary schools.*

Now ready. Price 1s. each.

First and Second Books of Samuel. By Prof. KIRKPATRICK, B.D.
First and Second Books of Kings. By Rev. Prof. LUMBY, D.D.
Gospel according to St Matthew. By Rev. A. CARR, M.A.
Gospel according to St Mark. By Rev. G. F. MACLEAR, D.D.
Gospel according to St Luke. By Archdeacon FARRAR, D.D.
Gospel according to St John. By Rev. A. PLUMMER, D.D.
Acts of the Apostles. By Professor LUMBY, D.D.

THE CAMBRIDGE GREEK TESTAMENT
FOR SCHOOLS AND COLLEGES

with a Revised Text, based on the most recent critical authorities, and English Notes, prepared under the direction of the General Editor,

J. J. S. PEROWNE, D.D., BISHOP OF WORCESTER.

Gospel according to St Matthew. By Rev. A. CARR, M.A. 4s. 6d.
Gospel according to St Mark. By Rev. G. F. MACLEAR, D.D. 4s. 6d.
Gospel according to St Luke. By Archdeacon FARRAR. 6s.
Gospel according to St John. By Rev. A. PLUMMER, D.D. 6s.
Acts of the Apostles. By Prof. LUMBY, D.D. 4 Maps. 6s.
First Epistle to the Corinthians. By Rev. J. J. LIAS, M.A. 3s.
Second Epistle to the Corinthians. By Rev. J. J. LIAS, M.A.
[*Preparing.*
Epistle to the Hebrews. By Archdeacon FARRAR, D.D. 3s. 6d.
Epistles of St John. By Rev. A. PLUMMER, M.A., D.D. 4s.

London: Cambridge Warehouse, Ave Maria Lane.

THE PITT PRESS SERIES.

⁎ *Copies of the Pitt Press Series may generally be obtained in two volumes, Text and Notes separately.*

I. GREEK.

Aristophanes. Aves—Plutus—Ranae. By W. C. Green, M.A., late Assistant Master at Rugby School. 3s. 6d. each.
Euripides. Heracleidae. By E. A. Beck, M.A. 3s. 6d.
Euripides. Hercules Furens. By A. Gray, M.A., and J. T. Hutchinson, M.A. 2s.
Euripides. Hippolytus. By W. S. Hadley, M.A. 2s.
Euripides. Iphigeneia in Aulis. By C. E. S. Headlam, B.A. 2s. 6d.
Herodotus. Book V. By E. S. Shuckburgh, M.A. 3s.
Herodotus. Book VI. By the same Editor. 4s.
Herodotus. Books VIII., IX. By the same Editor. 4s. each.
Herodotus. Book VIII., Ch. 1—90. Book IX., Ch. 1—89. By the same Editor. 3s. 6d. each.
Homer. Odyssey, Book IX. Book X. By G. M. Edwards, M.A. 2s. 6d. each.
Homer. Odyssey, Book XXI. By the same Editor. 2s.
Homer. Iliad. Book XXII. By the same Editor. 2s.
Homer. Iliad. Book XXIII. By the same Editor. [*Nearly ready.*]
Luciani Somnium Charon Piscator et De Luctu. By W. E. Heitland, M.A., Fellow of St John's College, Cambridge. 3s. 6d.
Lucian. Menippus and Timon. By E. C. Mackie, M.A.
[*Nearly ready.*]
Platonis Apologia Socratis. By J. Adam, M.A. 3s. 6d.
—— **Crito.** By the same Editor. 2s. 6d.
—— **Euthyphro.** By the same Editor. 2s. 6d.
Plutarch's Lives of the Gracchi.—Sulla—Timoleon. By H. A. Holden, M.A., LL.D. 6s. each.
Plutarch's Life of Nicias. By the same Editor. 5s.
Sophocles.—Oedipus Tyrannus. School Edition. By R. C. Jebb, Litt.D., LL.D. 4s. 6d.
Thucydides. Book VII. By Rev. H. A. Holden, M.A., LL.D.
[*Nearly ready.*]
Xenophon—Agesilaus. By H. Hailstone, M.A. 2s. 6d.
Xenophon—Anabasis. By A. Pretor, M.A. Two vols. 7s. 6d.
—— —— **Books I. III. IV. and V.** By the same Editor. Price 2s. each. **Books II. VI. and VII.** 2s. 6d. each.
Xenophon—Cyropaedeia. Books I. II. By Rev. H. A. Holden, M.A., LL.D. 2 vols. 6s.
—— —— **Books III. IV. and V.** By the same Editor. 5s.
—— —— **Books VI. VII. and VIII.** By the same Editor. 5s.

London: Cambridge Warehouse, Ave Maria Lane.

II. LATIN.

Beda's Ecclesiastical History, Books III., IV. Edited by J. E. B. MAYOR, M.A., and J. R. LUMBY, D.D. Revised Edit. 7s. 6d.

Caesar. De Bello Gallico Comment. I. By A. G. PESKETT, M.A. 1s. 6d. Com. II. III. 2s.
—— Comment. I. II. III. 3s. Com. IV. V. 1s. 6d. Com. VI. and Com. VIII. 1s. 6d. each. Com. VII. 2s.
—— De Bello Civili. Comment. I. By the same Editor. 3s.

M. T. Ciceronis de Amicitia.—de Senectute.—pro Sulla Oratio. By J. S. REID, Litt.D., Fellow of Gonville and Caius College. 3s. 6d. each.

M. T. Ciceronis Oratio pro Archia Poeta. By the same. 2s.

M. T. Ciceronis pro Balbo Oratio. By the same. 1s. 6d.

M. T. Ciceronis in Gaium Verrem Actio Prima. By H. COWIE, M.A., Fellow of St John's Coll. 1s. 6d.

M. T. Ciceronis in Q. Caecilium Divinatio et in C. Verrem Actio. By W. E. HEITLAND, M.A., and H. COWIE, M.A. 3s.

M. T. Ciceronis Oratio pro Tito Annio Milone. By JOHN SMYTH PURTON, B.D. 2s. 6d.

M. T. Ciceronis Oratio pro L. Murena. By W. E. HEITLAND, M.A. 3s.

M. T. Ciceronis pro Cn. Plancio Oratio, by H. A. HOLDEN, LL.D. Second Edition. 4s. 6d.

M. Tulli Ciceronis Oratio Philippica Secunda. By A. G. PESKETT, M.A. 3s. 6d.

M. T. Ciceronis Somnium Scipionis. By W. D. PEARMAN, M.A. 2s.

Horace. Epistles, Book I. By E. S. SHUCKBURGH, M.A. 2s. 6d.

Livy. Books IV., XXVII. By H. M. STEPHENSON, M.A. 2s. 6d. each.
—— Book V. By L. WHIBLEY, M.A. 2s. 6d.
—— Book XXI. Book XXII. By M. S. DIMSDALE, M.A. 2s. 6d. each.

M. Annaei Lucani Pharsaliae Liber Primus. By W. E. HEITLAND, M.A., and C. E. HASKINS, M.A. 1s. 6d.

Lucretius, Book V. By J. D. DUFF, M.A., Fellow of Trinity College. *Price* 2s.

P. Ovidii Nasonis Fastorum Liber VI. By A. SIDGWICK, M.A. 1s. 6d.

Quintus Curtius. A Portion of the History (Alexander in India). By W. E. HEITLAND, M.A. and T. E. RAVEN, B.A. 3s. 6d.

P. Vergili Maronis Aeneidos Libri I.—XII. By A. SIDGWICK, M.A. 1s. 6d. each.

P. Vergili Maronis Bucolica. By the same Editor. 1s. 6d.

P. Vergili Maronis Georgicon Libri I. II. By the same Editor. 2s. **Libri III. IV.** By the same Editor. 2s.

Vergil. The Complete Works. By the same Editor. Two Vols. Vol. I. Introduction and Text. 3s. 6d. Vol. II. Notes. 4s. 6d.

III. FRENCH.

Bataille de Dames. By SCRIBE and LEGOUVÉ. By Rev. H. A. BULL, M.A. 2s.

Dix Années d'Exil. Livre II. Chapitres 1—8. Par MADAME LA BARONNE DE STAËL-HOLSTEIN. By the late G. MASSON, B.A. and G. W. PROTHERO, M.A. New Edition, enlarged. 2s.

London: Cambridge Warehouse, Ave Maria Lane.

Histoire du Siècle de Louis XIV. par Voltaire. **Chaps. I.—XIII.** By GUSTAVE MASSON, B.A. and G. W. PROTHERO, M.A. 2s. 6d. Chaps. XIV.—XXIV. 2s. 6d. Chap. XXV. to end. 2s. 6d.

Fredégonde et Brunehaut. A Tragedy in Five Acts, by N. LEMERCIER. By GUSTAVE MASSON, B.A. 2s.

Jeanne D'Arc. By A. DE LAMARTINE. By Rev. A. C. CLAPIN, M.A. Revised Edition by A. R. ROPES, M.A. 1s. 6d.

La Canne de Jonc. By A. DE VIGNY. By Rev. H. A. BULL, M.A. 2s.

La Jeune Sibérienne. Le Lépreux de la Cité D'Aoste. Tales by COUNT XAVIER DE MAISTRE. By GUSTAVE MASSON, B.A. 1s. 6d.

La Picciola. By X. B. SAINTINE. By Rev. A. C. CLAPIN, M.A. 2s.

La Guerre. By MM. ERCKMANN-CHATRIAN. By the same Editor. 3s.

La Métromanie. A Comedy, by PIRON. By G. MASSON, B.A. 2s.

Lascaris ou Les Grecs du XVE Siècle, Nouvelle Historique, par A. F. VILLEMAIN. By the same. 2s.

La Suite du Menteur. A Comedy by P. CORNEILLE. By the same. 2s.

Lazare Hoche—Par EMILE DE BONNECHOSE. With Four Maps. By C. COLBECK, M.A. 2s.

Le Bourgeois Gentilhomme, Comédie-Ballet en Cinq Actes. Par J.-B. Poquelin de Molière (1670). By Rev. A. C. CLAPIN, M.A. 1s. 6d.

Le Directoire. (Considérations sur la Révolution Française. Troisième et quatrième parties.) Revised and enlarged. By G. MASSON, B.A. and G. W. PROTHERO, M.A. 2s.

Les Plaideurs. RACINE. By E. G. W. BRAUNHOLTZ, M.A., Ph.D. 2s.

———— ———— (Abridged Edition.) 1s.

Les Précieuses Ridicules. MOLIÈRE. By E. G. W. BRAUNHOLTZ, M.A., Ph.D. 2s.

———— ———— (Abridged Edition.) 1s.

L'École des Femmes. MOLIÈRE. By GEORGE SAINTSBURY, M.A. 2s. 6d.

Le Philosophe sans le savoir. Sedaine. By Rev. H. A. BULL, late Master at Wellington College. 2s.

Lettres sur l'histoire de France (XIII—XXIV). Par AUGUSTIN THIERRY. By G. MASSON, B.A. and G. W. PROTHERO. 2s. 6d.

Le Verre D'Eau. A Comedy, by SCRIBE. Edited by C. COLBECK, M.A. 2s.

Le Vieux Célibataire. A Comedy, by COLLIN D'HARLEVILLE. With Notes, by G. MASSON, B.A. 2s.

M. Daru, par M. C. A. SAINTE-BEUVE (Causeries du Lundi, Vol. IX.). By G. MASSON, B.A. Univ. Gallic. 2s.

Recits des Temps Merovingiens I—III. THIERRY. By the late G. MASSON, B.A. and A. R. ROPES, M.A. Map. 3s.

London: Cambridge Warehouse, Ave Maria Lane.

IV. GERMAN.

A Book of Ballads on German History. By WILHELM WAGNER, PH.D. 2s.
A Book of German Dactylic Poetry. By WILHELM WAGNER, Ph.D. 3s.
Benedix. Doctor Wespe. Lustspiel in fünf Aufzügen. By KARL HERMANN BREUL, M.A., Ph.D. 3s.
Culturgeschichtliche Novellen, von W. H. RIEHL. By H. J. WOLSTENHOLME, B.A. (Lond.). 3s. 6d.
Das Jahr 1813 (THE YEAR 1813), by F. KOHLRAUSCH. By WILHELM WAGNER, Ph.D. 2s.
Der erste Kreuzzug (1095—1099) nach FRIEDRICH VON RAUMER. THE FIRST CRUSADE. By W. WAGNER, Ph.D. 2s.
Der Oberhof. A Tale of Westphalian Life, by KARL IMMERMANN. By WILHELM WAGNER, Ph.D. 3s.
Der Staat Friedrichs des Grossen. By G. FREYTAG. By WILHELM WAGNER, PH.D. 2s.
Die Karavane, von WILHELM HAUFF. By A. SCHLOTTMANN, Ph.D. 3s. 6d.
Goethe's Hermann and Dorothea. By W. WAGNER, Ph.D. Revised edition by J. W. CARTMELL. 3s. 6d.
Goethe's Knabenjahre. (1749—1761.) **Goethe's Boyhood.** By W. WAGNER, Ph.D. Revised edition by J. W. CARTMELL, M.A. 2s.
Hauff, Das Bild des Kaisers. By KARL HERMANN BREUL, M.A., Ph.D. 3s.
Hauff, Das Wirthshaus im Spessart. By A. SCHLOTTMANN, Ph.D., late Assistant Master at Uppingham School. 3s. 6d.
Mendelssohn's Letters. Selections from. By JAMES SIME, M.A. 3s.
Schiller. Wilhelm Tell. By KARL HERMANN BREUL, M.A., Ph.D. 2s. 6d.
—— —— (Abridged Edition.) 1s. 6d.
Selected Fables. Lessing and Gellert. By KARL HERMANN BREUL, M.A., Ph.D. 3s.
Uhland. Ernst, Herzog von Schwaben. By H. J. WOLSTENHOLME, B.A. (Lond.). 3s. 6d.
Zopf und Schwert. Lustspiel in fünf Aufzügen von KARL GUTZKOW. By H. J. WOLSTENHOLME, B.A. (Lond.). 3s. 6d.

V. ENGLISH.

An Apologie for Poetrie by Sir PHILIP SIDNEY. By E. S. SHUCKBURGH, M.A. The text is a revision of that of the first edition of 1595. 3s.
An Elementary Commercial Geography. A Sketch of the Commodities and Countries of the World. By H. R. MILL, Sc.D., F.R.S.E. 1s.
An Atlas of Commercial Geography. (Companion to the above.) By J. G. BARTHOLOMEW, F.R.G.S. With an Introduction by Dr H. R. MILL. 3s.

London: Cambridge Warehouse, Ave Maria Lane.

Ancient Philosophy from Thales to Cicero, A Sketch of, by JOSEPH B. MAYOR, M.A. 3s. 6d.
Bacon's History of the Reign of King Henry VII. By the Rev. Professor LUMBY, D.D. 3s.
British India, a Short History of. By Rev. E. S. CARLOS, M.A. 1s.
Cowley's Essays. By Prof. LUMBY, D.D. 4s.
General Aims of the Teacher, and Form Management. Two Lectures by F. W. FARRAR, D.D. and R. B. POOLE, B.D. 1s. 6d.
John Amos Comenius, Bishop of the Moravians. His Life and Educational Works, by S. S. LAURIE, A.M., F.R.S.E. 3s. 6d.
Locke on Education. By the Rev. R. H. QUICK, M.A. 3s. 6d.
Milton's Arcades and Comus. By A. W. VERITY, M.A. 3s.
Milton's Tractate on Education. A facsimile reprint from the Edition of 1673. Edited by O. BROWNING, M.A. 2s.
More's History of King Richard III. By J. RAWSON LUMBY, D.D. 3s. 6d.
On Stimulus. A Lecture delivered for the Teachers' Training Syndicate at Cambridge, May 1882, by A. SIDGWICK, M.A. New Ed. 1s.
Outlines of the Philosophy of Aristotle. Compiled by EDWIN WALLACE, M.A., LL.D. Third Edition, Enlarged. 4s. 6d.
Sir Thomas More's Utopia. By Prof. LUMBY, D.D. 3s. 6d.
Theory and Practice of Teaching. By E. THRING, M.A. 4s. 6d.
The Teaching of Modern Languages in Theory and Practice. By C. COLBECK, M.A. 2s.
The Two Noble Kinsmen. By Professor SKEAT, Litt.D. 3s. 6d.
Three Lectures on the Practice of Education. I. On Marking by H. W. EVE, M.A. II. On Stimulus, by A. SIDGWICK, M.A. III. On the Teaching of Latin Verse Composition, by E. A. ABBOTT, D.D. 2s.

VI. MATHEMATICS.

Euclid's Elements of Geometry, Books I. and II. By H. M. TAYLOR, M.A. 1s. 6d. **Books III. and IV.** By the same Editor. 1s. 6d.
——— ——— **Books I.—IV. in one volume.** 3s.
Elementary Algebra (with Answers to the Examples). By W. W. ROUSE BALL, M.A. 4s. 6d.
Elements of Statics and Dynamics. By S. L. LONEY, M.A. Part I. Elements of Statics. 4s. 6d. Part II. Elements of Dynamics.
[*Nearly ready.*]

London: C. J. CLAY AND SONS,
CAMBRIDGE WAREHOUSE, AVE MARIA LANE.
Glasgow: 263, ARGYLE STREET.
Cambridge: DEIGHTON, BELL AND CO. **Leipzig:** F. A. BROCKHAUS.
New York: MACMILLAN AND CO.

www.ingramcontent.com/pod-product-compliance
Ingram Content Group UK Ltd.
Pitfield, Milton Keynes, MK11 3LW, UK
UKHW022327200125
4189UKWH00014BA/83